THE WAIT

HTML 3
HOW-TO

THE DEFINITIVE HTML 3
PROBLEM-SOLVER

David Kerven, Jeff Foust, John Zakour

WAITE GROUP PRESS™
A Division of Sams Publishing
Corte Madera, CA

Publisher Mitchell Waite
Editor-in-Chief Charles Drucker

Acquisitions Editor Jill Pisoni

Editorial Director John Crudo
Managing Editor Dan Scherf
Content Editor Scott Rhoades
Copy Editor Merrilee Eggleston
Technical Reviewer David S. Fox

Production Director Julianne Ososke
Production Manager Cecile Kaufman
Design Sestina Quarequio
Production Tom Debolski
Illustrations Tom Debolski, Larry Wilson
Cover Design Karen Johnston
Cover Illustration © David Tillinghast

© 1996 by The Waite Group, Inc.®
Published by Waite Group Press™, 200 Tamal Plaza, Corte Madera, CA 94925.

Waite Group Press™ is a division of Sams Publishing.

Waite Group Press™ is distributed to bookstores and book wholesalers by Publishers Group West,
Box 8843, Emeryville, CA 94662, 1-800-788-3123 (in California 1-510-658-3453).

All rights reserved. No part of this manual shall be reproduced, stored in a retrieval system, or transmitted by any means, electronic, mechanical, photocopying, desktop publishing, recording, or otherwise, without permission from the publisher. No patent liability is assumed with respect to the use of the information contained herein. While every precaution has been taken in the preparation of this book, the publisher and author assume no responsibility for errors or omissions. Neither is any liability assumed for damages resulting from the use of the information contained herein.

All terms mentioned in this book that are known to be registered trademarks, trademarks, or service marks are listed below. In addition, terms suspected of being trademarks, registered trademarks, or service marks have been appropriately capitalized. Waite Group Press cannot attest to the accuracy of this information. Use of a term in this book should not be regarded as affecting the validity of any registered trademark, trademark, or service mark.

The Waite Group is a registered trademark of the The Waite Group, Inc.
Waite Group Press and The Waite Group logo are trademarks of The Waite Group, Inc.

All other product names are trademarks, registered trademarks, or service marks of their respective owners.

Printed in the United States of America
96 97 98 99 • 10 9 8 7 6 5 4 3 2 1

Library of Congress Cataloging-in-Publication Data

Kerven, David.
    HTML 3 how-to / David Kerven, Jeff Foust, John Zakour.
       p. cm.
    Includes index.
    ISBN 1-57169-050-6
     1. Hypertext systems   2. HTML (Document markup language)
    I. Foust, Jeff. II. Zakour, John. III. Title.
    QA76.76.H94K47 1995
    005.7'2--dc20
                                                                                     95-45364
                                                                                      CIP

DEDICATION

I would like to dedicate this book to the loving memory of my father, Arnold Hilton Kerven, who continues to be an inspiration to me in everything I do.
> **—David Kerven**

To Mom
> **—Jeff Foust**

To my parents, as after all, if it wasn't for them, I wouldn't be here.
> **—John Zakour**

Message from the
Publisher

WELCOME TO OUR NERVOUS SYSTEM

Some people say that the World Wide Web is a graphical extension of the information superhighway, just a network of humans and machines sending each other long lists of the equivalent of digital junk mail.

I think it is much more than that. To me the Web is nothing less than the nervous system of the entire planet—not just a collection of computer brains connected together, but more like a billion silicon neurons entangled and recirculating electro-chemical signals of information and data, each contributing to the birth of another CPU and another Web site.

Think of each person's hard disk connected at once to every other hard disk on earth, driven by human navigators searching like Columbus for the New World. Seen this way, the Web is more of a super entity, a growing, living thing, controlled by the universal human will to expand, to be more. Yet, unlike a purposeful business plan with rigid rules, the Web expands in a nonlinear, unpredictable, creative way that echoes natural evolution.

We created our Web site not just to extend the reach of our computer book products but to be part of this synaptic neural network, to experience, like a nerve in the body, the flow of ideas and then to pass those ideas up the food chain of the mind. Your mind. Even more, we wanted to pump some of our own creative juices into this rich wine of technology.

TASTE OUR DIGITAL WINE

And so we ask you to taste our wine by visiting the body of our business. Begin by understanding the metaphor we have created for our Web site—a universal learning center, situated in outer space in the form of a space station. A place where you can journey to study any topic from the convenience of your own screen. Right now we are focusing on computer topics, but the stars are the limit on the Web.

If you are interested in discussing this Web site or finding out more about the Waite Group, please send me email with your comments and I will be happy to respond. Being a programmer myself, I love to talk about technology and find out what our readers are looking for.

Sincerely,

Mitchell Waite

Mitchell Waite, C.E.O. and Publisher

200 Tamal Plaza
Corte Madera CA 94925
415 924 2575
415 924 2576 fax

Internet email:
support@waite.com

Website:
http://www.waite.com/waite

CREATING THE HIGHEST QUALITY COMPUTER BOOKS IN THE INDUSTRY

Waite Group Press
Waite Group New Media

Come Visit
WAITE.COM
Waite Group Press World Wide Web Site

Now find all the latest information on Waite Group books at our new Web site, **http://www.waite.com/waite**. You'll find an online catalog where you can examine and order any title, review upcoming books, and send email to our authors and editors. Our FTP site has all you need to update your book: the latest program listings, errata sheets, most recent versions of Fractint, POV Ray, Polyray, DMorph, and all the programs featured in our books. So download, talk to us, ask questions, on **http://www.waite.com/waite**.

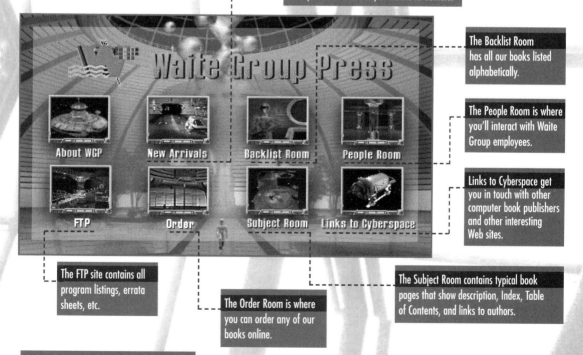

The New Arrivals Room has all our new books listed by month. Just click for a description, Index, Table of Contents, and links to authors.

The Backlist Room has all our books listed alphabetically.

The People Room is where you'll interact with Waite Group employees.

Links to Cyberspace get you in touch with other computer book publishers and other interesting Web sites.

The FTP site contains all program listings, errata sheets, etc.

The Order Room is where you can order any of our books online.

The Subject Room contains typical book pages that show description, Index, Table of Contents, and links to authors.

World Wide Web:

COME SURF OUR TURF—THE WAITE GROUP WEB

http://www.waite.com/waite
Gopher: gopher.waite.com
FTP: ftp.waite.com

ACKNOWLEDGMENTS

I would first like to thank my wife Jenny for her loving forbearance and support through the entire writing process. I would also like to acknowledge the inspiration and impetus provided by Dr. Wayne Dominick and Dr. Dennis Moreau, who started me on my adventures in hypermedia. In addition, I would like to thank the editors at Waite Group Press for their diligence and uncommon perseverance in wading through my unpolished drafts. Special thanks go to Troy Downing, who contributed How-To 12.5 on how to set up the MacHTTP server. Finally, I would like to acknowledge the support of G-d, my family, and my department at Clark Atlanta University.

—David Kerven

Chris Lewicki and others at the University of Arizona chapter of Students for the Exploration and Development of Space (SEDS), who have created a first-class Web site (http://www.seds.org/) and provided me with space to experiment with Web designs for some time.

—Jeff Foust

To my wife Olga and my son Jay, who put up with me during those "one or two days" I was running behind schedule. To Ron, who was always there with computer advice. To Tom, who's always there with grammatical advice. To my ex-boss Linda, who would always let me take an hour or two off when I needed it.

—John Zakour

ABOUT THE AUTHORS

David Kerven

was born in Newark, New Jersey, in 1967. He was raised in Livingston, New Jersey. He received his B.S. in Electrical Engineering from The Johns Hopkins University and his Ph.D. in Computer Science from the University of Southwestern Louisiana. Dr. Kerven is currently living in Atlanta with his wife Jenny where he is an Assistant Professor of Computer Science at Clark Atlanta University. He currently conducts research in hypermedia environments and the application of hypermedia technology to education.

Jeff Foust

is a graduate student in planetary astronomy at MIT. A native of Council Bluffs, Iowa, he holds a B.S. in planetary science from Caltech. He has been exploring the Web and creating pages for it since the fall of 1993. His Shoemaker-Levy 9 impact page, with information and images of the impact of the comet with Jupiter, received national attention in *Astronomy, Macworld,* and *Wired* magazines. When not working on his thesis or using the Web, he has been active in a number of space-related ventures, including serving as editor of *SpaceViews,* a monthly space journal, and is a former co-chair of Students for the Exploration and Development of Space (SEDS). Jeff is also a (frustrated) Boston Red Sox fan.

John Zakour

is currently an HTML consultant and a freelance writer. Some of his writing—daily computer cartoons, the novel *The Doomsday Brunette,* and a new novel *Plutonium Blond*—can be found on Prodigy On-Line Service's World Wide Web pages. John majored in Computer Science at Potsdam State University. Upon completion of his studies at Postdam, he worked as a database programmer for Cornell University. Upon his return to New York, he was a Web page designer for Cornell University's New York State Agriculture Experiment Station. As an HTML consultant, John also has a Web page. You can see it at http://www.valleynet.com/~jmz5/.

CONTENTS

Preface xvi
Installation xix
The Chameleon Sampler xxiii

PART 1: INTRODUCTION 1
Chapter 1: Web Basics 3

PART 2: AUTHORING 25
Chapter 2: HTML Basics 27
Chapter 3: Adding HTML Character Effects 91
Chapter 4: Managing Document Spacing 119
Chapter 5: HTML Math and Tables 133
Chapter 6: HTML Lists 161
Chapter 7: Establishing Links 195
Chapter 8: Using Images in Your Documents 237
Chapter 9: Adding Multimedia Objects 269
Chapter 10: HTML Interactive Forms 305

PART 3: SERVING 337
Chapter 11: Server Basics 339
Chapter 12: Handling Server Security 379
Chapter 13: The Common Gateway Interface (CGI) 439
Chapter 14: Beyond HTML 495
Chapter 15: Some of the Best Sites on the Web 563

Appendix A: HTML Quick Reference 577
Appendix B: WWW Resources 587
Appendix C: Multipurpose Internet Mail Extensions (MIME) 601
Appendix D: UNIX Quick Reference 607
Appendix E: HTML Style Guide 611
Appendix F: Summary of Selected Server Software 615
Appendix G: The HyperText Transfer Protocol (HTTP) 621

Index 627

TABLE OF CONTENTS

Preface xvi
Installation xix
The Chameleon Sampler xxiii

PART 1: INTRODUCTION 1
Chapter 1: Web Basics 3
    1.1   Get on the Web from America Online 7
    1.2   Establish a connection to the Internet 8
    1.3   Find a Web browser 11
    1.4   Navigate via browser features 14
    1.5   Follow a link 15
    1.6   Open a location 16
    1.7   Find a Web authoring tool 17
    1.8   Find a home for my Web pages 19
    1.9   Get information about the evolution of HTML 20
    1.10 Design effective Web pages 22

PART 2: AUTHORING 25
Chapter 2: HTML Basics 27
    2.1   Recognize an HTML document 32
    2.2   Build a simple HTML document 36
    2.3   Create HTML documents without manually inserting tags 42
    2.4   Convert word processed documents to HTML 48
    2.5   Convert other types of files to HTML 51
    2.6   Insert an HTML element 54
    2.7   Include a comment 58
    2.8   Add body text 62
    2.9   Insert special characters into a document 67
    2.10 Align text 73
    2.11 Change font size 78
    2.12 Create a home page 82
    2.13 View my home page 87

Chapter 3: Adding HTML Character Effects 91
    3.1   Use heading styles 97
    3.2   Force bold character style 99
    3.3   Force italic character style 100
    3.4   Underline text 101
    3.5   Use a fixed-width font 102
    3.6   Use strikethrough formatting 103
    3.7   Include superscripts and subscripts 104
    3.8   Place emphasis and strong emphasis 105
    3.9   Specify a citation 107
    3.10 Place an embedded quotation 108
    3.11 Include small segments of code and variables 109
    3.12 Emphasize a defined term 110
    3.13 Provide a sample of literal characters 111
    3.14 Tag computer commands, arguments, and keyboard input 112
    3.15 Mark an abbreviation or acronym 113
    3.16 Identify a proper name 114
    3.17 Denote inserted or deleted text 115
    3.18 Spruce up my home page 116

Chapter 4: Managing Document Spacing 119
    4.1   Add a horizontal line to an HTML document 122
    4.2   Manage vertical spacing: paragraphs vs. line breaks 124
    4.3   Manage space with the <PRE> tag 127
    4.4   Space my home page 130

Chapter 5: HTML Math and Tables 133
    5.1   Add mathematical symbols 136
    5.2   Include a table 140
    5.3   Place a caption in a table 143
    5.4   Insert a table heading 145
    5.5   Define data for a cell or table element 148
    5.6   Create a new row of data 150
    5.7   Put a table in my home page 152

Chapter 6: HTML Lists 161
    6.1   Create a numbered list 165
    6.2   Create a bulleted list 170

6.3	Create an unmarked list	173
6.4	Create a multicolumn list	175
6.5	Create a menu list	178
6.6	Create a directory list	179
6.7	Create a glossary list	181
6.8	Nest lists together	184
6.9	Use lists to jazz up my home page	192

Chapter 7: Establishing Links 195

7.1	Interpret a URL	200
7.2	Understand a relative URL	202
7.3	Add a base for relative URLs within the body of a document	205
7.4	Specify a relationship between this document and other resources	206
7.5	Create a link to a local page	209
7.6	Create a link to other pages	211
7.7	Send data to an HTTP server via a URL	213
7.8	Create a link to a specific part of a page	214
7.9	Create a link to an FTP site	216
7.10	Create a link to a Gopher site	218
7.11	Create a link to a Telnet site	220
7.12	Create a link to a WAIS site	221
7.13	Create a link to a Usenet newsgroup	223
7.14	Create a link to electronic mail	224
7.15	Create links to pages in other users' home directories	225
7.16	Add links to lists and tables	227
7.17	Change the shape of a link	229
7.18	Add links to my home page	231

Chapter 8: Using Images in Your Documents 237

8.1	Build an icon to use in an HTML document	241
8.2	Add an inline image	244
8.3	Align images and text on a page	246
8.4	Use the <ALT> tag for nongraphical browsers	249
8.5	Include an image with a transparent background	251
8.6	Create an interlaced inline image on my page	254
8.7	Create a thumbnail version of an image	256
8.8	Use an image as a link	258

8.9   Create a clickable imagemap 260
8.10 Create a background pattern for my page 263
8.11 Align images and text using the advanced HTML 3 tags ...265

Chapter 9: Adding Multimedia Objects 269
9.1   Build my multimedia home page 274
9.2   Add an external image 278
9.3   Convert between image formats 282
9.4   Insert a video 285
9.5   Convert between video file formats 289
9.6   Insert a sound file 291
9.7   Convert between audio file formats 294
9.8   Include a PostScript document 297
9.9   Include a device independent (DVI) file 300

Chapter 10: HTML Interactive Forms 305
10.1 Create a basic form 309
10.2 Add a text box to a form 313
10.3 Add check boxes to a form 316
10.4 Add radio buttons to a form 319
10.5 Add password fields to a form 321
10.6 Add pulldown menus to a form 323
10.7 Pass information between forms 326
10.8 Choose a request method to send data to the HTTP server 327
10.9 Process a form 329

PART 3: SERVING 337
Chapter 11: Server Basics 339
11.1 Choose server software 343
11.2 Install server software 348
11.3 Configure the server 353
11.4 Register additional MIME types 360
11.5 Install documents 363
11.6 Start or stop the server 367
11.7 Register my server 371
11.8 Use Netscape's Client Pull 373

Chapter 12: Handling Server Security 379
   12.1   Specify allowable features on an HTTPD server 384
   12.2   Establish domain and address security on an HTTPD server 391
   12.3   Set up user and password security on an HTTPD server 395
   12.4   Use HTTPD server side includes 402
   12.5   Establish directory-level security on a CERN HTTP server 407
   12.6   Set up file-level security on a CERN HTTP server 418
   12.7   Install a CERN proxy server 420
   12.8   Establish domain and address security and password
            authentication on a MacHTTP server 427
   12.9   Use public key encryption 432

Chapter 13: The Common Gateway Interface (CGI). 439
   13.1   Pass data to a CGI application 443
   13.2   Send information to a browser from CGI applications 454
   13.3   Create a simple CGI application 459
   13.4   Install a CGI application 463
   13.5   Create a query document using the <ISINDEX> element 468
   13.6   Access client data in sh CGI scripts 474
   13.7   Parse client data in CGI programs and scripts 477
   13.8   Specify Netscape Server Push 485
   13.9   Write a CGI application to send me e-mail 489

Chapter 14: Beyond HTML 495
   14.1   Add sound tracks to my Web page 500
   14.2   Add marquees of scrolling text 502
   14.3   Include an AVI video in my Web page .506
   14.4   Change the font size and color 508
   14.5   Include frames in my Web page 510
   14.6   Include client side imagemaps 517
   14.7   Create new windows for linked documents 520
   14.8   Create an HTML style sheet 522
   14.9   Cascade HTML style sheets 529
   14.10 Write a basic Java applet 533
   14.11 Include a Java applet in an HTML document 537
   14.12 Include a JavaScript script in an HTML document 542

    14.13 Write a basic JavaScript script 545
    14.14 Find a VRML browser 553
    14.15 Create a VRML document 555

Chapter 15: Some of the Best Sites on the Web 563

Appendix A: HTML Quick Reference 577
    Document Basics 577
    Physical Text Styles 577
    Content Text Styles 578
    Document Spacing 579
    Mathematical Formatting 580
    Tables 581
    Lists 582
    Links 583
    Images 583
    Forms 584

Appendix B: WWW Resources 587
    Basic Information on WWW and HTML 587
    Indexes 588
    Browsers 589
    Servers 592
    HTML Editors 594
    HTML Document Development 597
    Common Gateway Interface (CGI) 597
    Forms and Imagemaps 598
    WWW Usenet Newsgroups 598
    WWW Mailing Lists 600

Appendix C: Multipurpose Internet Mail Extensions (MIME) 601

Appendix D: UNIX Quick Reference 607
    Changing Directories 607
    Listing the Contents of a Directory 608
    Moving and Deleting Files and Changing Filenames 608
    Creating and Removing Directories 609
    Setting File and Directory Permissions 609

Appendix E: HTML Style Guide 611
    Suggestions for Do's and Don'ts 611

Appendix F: Summary of Selected Server Software 615
    UNIX 615
    VMS 617
    Windows NT 617
    OS/2 618
    OS2HTTPD 619
    Macintosh 619
    Windows 3.1 619

Appendix G: The HyperText Transfer Protocol (HTTP) 621

Index 627

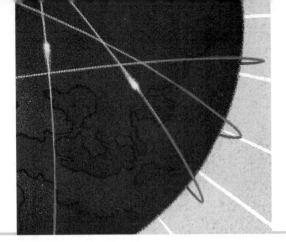

PREFACE

Welcome to World Wide Web authoring. Surfing the Internet through the World Wide Web has escaped the confines of academia and is quickly becoming a common sport in board rooms and family rooms. *HTML 3 How-To* will provide you with a road map to enter the dynamic environment of Internet publishing on the World Wide Web. Unlike existing HyperText Markup Language (HTML) documentation, *HTML 3 How-To* presents many real world document development problems along with specific step-by-step solutions, explanations, and examples. With *HTML 3 How-To* as your guide, you can concentrate on developing your information rather than your implementation. To give you a jump start on the information superhighway, all example documents, program code, and multimedia objects presented in the book are included on the CD-ROM.

The World Wide Web is expanding at an incredible pace. Approximately ten new Web servers are coming online everyday with no end in sight. The basic building blocks of the World Wide Web are documents developed using HTML. The Internet traffic devoted to the retrieval of HTML documents is increasing likewise. Both small and large scale HTML projects are being initiated daily by both individuals and large commercial entities. With this kind of volume usage, HTML has become the de facto development language for network-based hypermedia information.

From purchasing flowers in Maine to a pizza in California, commercial ventures are beginning to enter this arena. Financial institutions, retailers, publishers, and other corporate entities are only beginning to explore the potential of the worldwide electronic community. *HTML 3 How-To* is not another manual nor is it a technical specification; it is a guide that will provide direction for entering this rapidly growing environment and enhancing existing documents.

PREFACE

Each How-To in the book states a problem; describes the circumstances leading to the problem; develops a step-by-step solution; delineates relevant tips, comments, warnings, and, occasionally, alternative solutions. Each How-To will walk you step-by-step through the solution to a common development problem. *HTML 3 How-To* is not another style manual; rather, it is a user-oriented, goal-driven guide that will change the way you develop HTML documents. *HTML 3 How-To* provides everything you need to know to begin developing world-class HTML documents. So, jump into *HTML 3 How-To* and share your vision with the world.

Chapter 1 introduces several key concepts about the World Wide Web. Most of this information should be familiar ground to prospective authors. The information serves as a review and a reminder while potentially filling gaps. Finally, the How-To's set the stage for the HTML 3 details to come.

Chapter 2 introduces you to the basic concepts of authoring documents in HTML 3. You will learn how to identify and construct simple HTML documents. The How-To's tell you how to begin developing HTML documents. They will also introduce you to several of the key HTML elements.

Chapter 3 continues by describing the various character effects possible with HTML 3. Each How-To walks you through the use of these character effects. Documented examples demonstrate the proper use of these elements while also addressing relevant stylistic issues.

Chapter 4 examines the management of space in HTML 3 documents. How you space the information in your Web page substantially affects the impact of the page upon a viewer. HTML 3 provides several elements to control spacing. The How-To's in this chapter provide clear instructions on the use of these spacing elements.

Chapter 5 looks at the management of data and mathematical formulae under HTML 3. HTML 3 provides a significant improvement in these areas over earlier versions of HTML. HTML 3 supports both mathematical symbols as well as table representations of data. Tables also support strict formatting of desired elements, such as images and text, by providing row/column alignment. The How-To's in this chapter instruct you in the use of mathematical elements and tables.

Chapter 6 walks you through the myriad of list types supported by HTML 3. Lists serve an essential function in the organization of many HTML documents. The How-To's explain the different types of lists available and provide step-by-step instructions on inserting each type of list into your pages.

Chapter 7 covers the creation of links in HTML 3 documents. Links are the glue that connect HTML documents around the world. Links potentially connect your Web page to both other Web pages and a variety of other Internet-based information. The How-To's in this chapter examine the creation of links to other Web pages and other network-based information.

Chapter 8 jumps into the topic of images. HTML 3 allows the incorporation of images directly into your Web pages. This chapter also introduces the creation and use of imagemaps. Imagemaps allow you to click upon a particular location within the image and trigger a link associated with the location. The How-To's in this chapter step you through the process of image inclusion and imagemap construction.

Chapter 9 steps further into the multimedia arena. This chapter examines how HTML 3 supports the inclusion of a variety of multimedia data types. The How-To's provide stylistic and technical information on the inclusion of these data types.

Chapter 10 begins the examination of HTML forms. Authors use HTML forms to request data from viewers of pages. HTML provides a variety of input styles, such as text entry windows and lists of selections. The How-To's in this chapter explain the use of those HTML elements used in form creation.

Chapter 11 examines how to make HTML 3 documents available on the World Wide Web by establishing your own Web site. The How-To's in this chapter examine the various tasks required to accomplish this goal.

Chapter 12 addresses the issue of providing security for your HTML 3 documents. If you wish to restrict access to a selection of your Web pages, you will likely find your answer in this chapter. Several of the procedures discussed may require the actions of your Web site administrator; however, many of the How-To's in this chapter provide instructions that you may use to restrict access to your Web pages.

Chapter 13 provides information on gateway applications. Gateway applications process the data gathered by HTML forms, as described in Chapter 10. These applications generally author dynamic documents based upon the information available both on the server and through forms. The How-To's in this chapter examine the issues involved in creating gateway applications and provide instructions on and examples of how you can develop such applications.

Chapter 14 touches on subjects that are going beyond HTML 3. New buzzwords have hit the Internet arena: Java, Virtual Reality Modeling Language (VRML), and LiveObjects. While not a comprehensive examination of each of these topics, we introduce them to you for experimentation. Also covered are some Netscape Navigator and Microsoft Explorer extensions and how you can design your Web pages to take advantage of these cutting-edge browsers.

Chapter 15 brings you on a brief tour of Web pages where the author has taken advantage of the cooler aspects of HTML. There is a surfeit of pages on the Web that are cool; this chapter touches on the cream of the crop.

Where just a year ago few had heard of the World Wide Web and even fewer still knew of HTML, now these terms have become almost commonplace, appearing in advertising and even nationally syndicated comic strips. Commensurate with this exposure, the Web has experienced and is still experiencing a rapid growth in size and usage.

With this exposure, individuals and businesses who wish to keep pace with technology must learn the valuable skills necessary not only to passively use this medium but also to actively participate in the evolution of this medium through authoring. This book provides the weapons to enter this arena in a clearly defined and explicit how-to format.

INSTALLATION

The companion CD-ROM contains all of the code for the How-To's in the book, as well as shareware and freeware programs to view and edit graphics, HTML, audio, and video.

What follows is the top-level directory structure of the CD.

```
\
+-ARCHIVES
+-CH01
+-CH02
+-CH03
+-CH04
+-CH05
+-CH06
+-CH07
+-CH08
+-CH09
+-CH10
+-CH11
+-CH12
+-CH13
+-CH14
+-PROGRAMS
```

All of the utilities, viewers, and browsers can be found in their own subdirectories under PROGRAMS. It is best to copy the programs from the CD-ROM to your hard drive before using them. See the Installing to Your Hard Drive section for how to do this.

Since all of the software in this book is shareware or freeware, we have included a compressed file that contains each program (except the NetManage Chameleon) for distributing to your friends in ARCHIVES.

> Note: The companion CD-ROM to this book contains freeware and unregistered shareware programs. If you use a shareware product for the amount of time specified in the program's documentation, you should register the program according to its documentation.

The CH01, CH02, etc. directories contain the source code used in the chapter broken down by How-To directories, such as HT01, HT02, etc. Contained within these subdirectories are all of the files that make up the How-To.

If you don't already have a World Wide Web browser, we have included NetManage's Chameleon. Please refer to The Chameleon Sampler section for installation instructions.

Installing to Your Hard Drive

Since all of the code for the How-To's in this book are on the companion CD-ROM, there is no need to type the code if you want to use it for your own projects. We will illustrate how to copy the files from the companion CD-ROM to your hard drive for the code and the utilities that are supplied on this disc.

PC

There are two different ways to copy files on the PC platform: DOS and Windows. Pick the environment you are most comfortable in, and follow the steps below.

DOS

If you are in DOS or using Windows' DOS Prompt, follow these steps:

1. Move to the drive that you want to copy the files to. If you want to copy the files onto the C: drive, type

```
C:
CD\
```

and press [ENTER] after each line.

2. Create the directory you would like to store your files into. If you want to store the files into the HTML3HT directory, type

```
MD HTML3HT
```

and press [ENTER].

3. Move to that directory. If you created a directory called HTML3HT, move to that directory by typing

```
CD HTML3HT
```

and press [ENTER].

4. If you want to copy individual subdirectories from the CD-ROM to your hard drive, skip to step 5. If you want to copy the entire CD-ROM to your hard drive in this directory, type

```
XCOPY D:\*.* /V /S
```

assuming that D: is the drive letter of your CD-ROM drive. Notice there are some switches after the xcopy command. These switches are required to successfully copy the contents of the CD-ROM to your hard drive; /V tells xcopy to verify the files, and /S tells xcopy to copy the subdirectories.

5. To copy individual subdirectories from the CD-ROM to your hard drive, you must create the chapter directories before you copy the contents. For example, if you wanted to copy the code for Chapters 2, 5, and 7, you would type

```
MD CH02
MD CH05
MD CH07
```

and press ENTER after each line. Then you would type

```
CD \HTML3HT\CH02
XCOPY D:\CH02 /V /S

CD \HTML3HT\CH05
XCOPY D:\CH05 /V /S

CD \HTML3HT\CH07
XCOPY D:\CH07 /V /S
```

and press ENTER after each line. We are assuming that D: is the drive letter of your CD-ROM drive.

Windows

If you are using Windows 3.x or Windows 95, please follow these steps:

1. Open the File Manager in Windows 3.x or the Explorer in Windows 95.

2. In both File Manager or Explorer, locate the drive you want to copy to and click on it.

3. Select the location to copy the files to or create a new directory. In File Manager, select File, Create Directory; in Explorer, select File, New, Folder. Type in the directory name you want to copy your files to and select OK.

4. In both File Manager and Explorer, select the directory you want to copy files to.

5. In the File Manager, select the drive letter of your CD-ROM drive. In Explorer, open up a new copy of Explorer with the drive letter of your CD-ROM drive.

6. If you are copying individual directories from the CD-ROM to the hard drive, skip to step 7. Using both programs, drag the contents of the CD-ROM to the destination drive. Depending on the speed of your computer and the options set for it, the copying process may take a few moments or a few minutes.

7. Select each directory you want to copy to the destination drive by holding down CTRL and clicking on the directory with the mouse. When you are finished selecting directories, drag your selection over to the destination.

> Note: When Windows (any version) copies a CD-ROM, it does not change the Read Only attribute for the files it copies. You can view the files, but you cannot edit them until you remove this attribute. To change it on all of the files, select the top-most directory with the files in it. In both File Manager and Explorer, select File, Properties, click on the Read Only checkbox, and click on OK.

Macintosh

Copy the files from the CD-ROM to your hard drive in the same way that you normally copy files on your computer.

1. Double-click on the CD-ROM icon.
2. If you want to copy only certain folders to your hard drive, skip to step 3. Select all of the folders on the CD-ROM and drag the files to your hard drive.
3. Select the individual folders you want to copy by holding down the SHIFT key and clicking on each directory. Drag the selection onto your hard drive.

UNIX

Since you must log onto root or have superuser access from your account, you already know everything about your particular UNIX workstation that you need to know to access and copy the files from the CD-ROM.

THE CHAMELEON SAMPLER

The NetManage Internet Chameleon is one of the most versatile and easy-to-use set of Internet tools in the world. Chameleon helps you sign up with an Internet provider, connect cleanly to the Internet, and access a variety of resources—including a pretty cool Web browser. The Chameleon package includes

- *Custom,* for connecting to the Internet
- *WebSurfer,* a full-featured World Wide Web browser
- *Gopher,* which lets you access any Gopher menu worldwide
- *NEWTNews,* a Usenet newsreader
- *Mail,* a convenient way to send and receive e-mail
- *Archie,* which lets you search for a file over the Internet
- *Telnet,* for connecting to a remote computer
- *FTP,* for transferring files over the Internet
- *FTP Server,* which lets you allow others to download or upload files to your PC
- *Mail Utilities,* programs that help you compact or organize your mailbox files to save space
- *Ping,* to test if you're connected to a remote computer

- **HTML** *Finger,* to check if a friend is connected to the Internet
- **HTML** *Whois,* to get information about people registered in the NIC (Network Information Center) database

You can sample the Chameleon tools for 30 days at no charge. If you like what you see, you can register everything for 50 bucks.

Installing the Chameleon

> NOTE: In the installation directions here, we assume that your hard disk is the C: drive and your CD-ROM is the D: drive. If this doesn't match your computer, substitute C: or D: with the correct drive designation.

To copy the sampler software onto your hard disk, run the Setup program. While under Windows, select File, Run in the Program Manager. In the Run dialog box, type

```
d:\programs\ntmanage\disk_1\setup.exe
```

and then press the OK button.

The Setup program will ask you where to install the NetManage program. The default suggested is fine for most people. If you want it installed elsewhere, type in the drive and directory of your choosing and select Continue.

After a few moments, the Setup program will ask you to type in the path of the second batch of files. Select the *1* in *DISK_1* and change it to *2,* and select Continue.

After another few moments, the Setup program will ask you to type in the path of the third batch of files. Select the *2* in *DISK_2* and change it to *3,* and select Continue.

Click OK when Setup tells you that installation is complete. You are now ready to set up your Internet account!

Signing Up for an Internet Provider Account

If you don't already have one, the Chameleon package makes it easy to sign up with one of several popular Internet providers. Read Chapter 1 for more information about what services are offered by Internet providers.

If you'd like to sign up using the Chameleon software, run the Automatic Internet-Click to Start icon.

To learn about a particular Internet provider, click one of the tabs (other than NetManage) in the Select Internet Provider window. Most providers give you several hours (or even a month) of free trial time. To read about the locations an Internet provider can cover, the monthly price, and other important information, click the More Info button at the bottom of the screen. If you have specific questions, contact the provider directly.

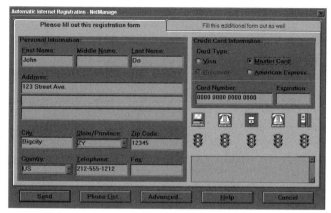

Figure I-1 The easiest way to sign up for an Internet provider

When you're ready to begin the sign-up procedure, click the Signup button. You'll see a registration screen similar to the one in Figure I-1. Fill in your name (as it appears on your credit card), address, phone number, and credit card information.

> NOTE: You will not actually be charged any provider fees until you officially register with the service. You can cancel the registration transaction at any time during the sign-on process. If you do decide to register, your credit card number will be sent over a secure phone line.

As you work through the sign-up process, there may be other tabs asking for additional information. If so, click these tabs and fill in the forms.

Select the Phone List button at the bottom of the screen. The Phone List dialog appears, listing possible phone numbers you can use to register. If one of the numbers is in your area code, select it. Otherwise, select the toll-free 800 number.

> NOTE: If necessary, you can edit the registration phone number. Some systems, for example, require you to dial a 9 to reach an outside line. Just type in this 9.

When you've typed in all your vital stats, return to the first registration tab. Click Send to dial the toll-free number and begin the registration process. The icons to the right will light up as each stage of the dialing process is completed. The set of traffic lights tells you if each stage—initializing the modem, dialing, connecting, and communicating—has worked.

> NOTE: You may need to click the Advanced button to specify special modem ports or commands.

Follow the instructions that appear as the registration proceeds. You will be given the option to select from various service and pricing plans. Your account information (username, e-mail address, password, dial-up number, and IP address) will automatically be configured into the Chameleon package. An interface will be created for the Custom program, which quickly and flawlessly connects you to the Internet.

That's it! You can now reboot your system to kick-start everything.

Registering the Chameleon Software

If you already have an Internet account, you can set up the Internet Chameleon software (shown in Figure I-2) and start using it within minutes. Run the Automatic Internet-Click to Start program.

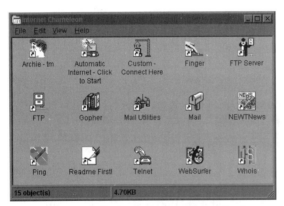

Figure I-2 The full Chameleon package in the Internet Chameleon program group

Make sure the NetManage tab is selected, and then click the Signup button. You can now activate the software for a free 30-day demonstration period. After this period, the Chameleon software will no longer work. If you decide to register the Chameleon package (for $50), your credit card will be charged and your software will be activated permanently.

Fill in all the information on both forms, as shown in Figure I-1, including your credit card number (which won't be charged unless you complete the registration). You may need to contact your Internet provider for the Internet information on the second form.

Select the Phone button, and choose a local or toll-free phone number. Then click the Send button to dial in to NetManage and get your software activated.

Once you connect, you are given the following choices:

- **HTML** Activate your software for a free 30-day demonstration.
- **HTML** Purchase your software to activate it permanently.
- **HTML** Configure your connection (if your Chameleon software has already been activated).

Connecting to the Internet

Now that you have selected a provider and registered your software, you can actually get hooked into the Internet. To do this, you need to run the Custom program (Figure I-3) from Windows File Manager.

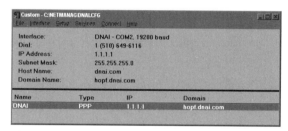

Figure I-3 Your customized on-ramp onto the Information Superhighway

If you used the Chameleon package to sign up with your Internet provider, an automatic configuration file should have been already written for you. Otherwise, Chameleon comes with the configurations for most popular Internet providers. Select File, Open and look for the configuration file for your provider. If your provider is not listed, you'll need to contact them and ask what the proper settings are. They may even be able to send you a prewritten Chameleon configuration file.

If you do need to enter the connection settings yourself, use the appropriate values you have obtained from your Internet provider. You can verify or edit the following information under the Setup menu:

- **HTML** IP Address
- **HTML** Subnet Mask
- **HTML** Host Name
- **HTML** Domain Name
- **HTML** Port
- **HTML** Modem
- **HTML** Dial

- Login
- Interface Name
- BOOTP

You may also need to fill in the following under the Services menu:

- Default Gateway
- Domain Servers

Read Chapter 1 for more information about these terms.

Logging In

Once your configuration settings are in place, simply click the Connect menu to dial up your Internet provider and get connected. If all goes well, you should hear a small beep, and a program known as Newt will run. This program lets Windows communicate with the Internet. You can then minimize the Custom program and run the Internet application of your choice.

Logging Out

When you're done using the Internet, call up the Custom program and click the Disconnect menu.

Web Browsing with WebSurfer

WebSurfer is a full-featured World Wide Web browser similar to Mosaic. You can read all about browsers in Chapter 2 and about Mosaic in Chapter 5. To start exploring the Web, first use the Chameleon Custom program to connect to the Internet. Then run the WebSurfer program.

Like Mosaic, WebSurfer has a toolbar (see the top of Figure I-4) that acts as a shortcut for most commands. The toolbar contains

- Show Connection Status: Shows you which links are currently being loaded.
- Go to URL: Opens a specific Web URL (defined in Chapter 1).
- Get URL: Reloads the current document.
- Hotlist: Shows the list of your favorite Web pages for you to choose from. To go to a page, just double-click on it. You can also delete pages from the list by selecting the page and clicking Remove.
- Make Hot: Adds the current Web page to your hotlist.
- Back: Revisits the Web page you just came from.
- Forward: Goes to the next Web page in the series, if applicable.

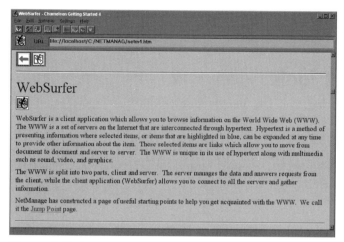

Figure I-4 The WebSurfer browser in all its glory

- **HTML** Home: Returns to the Web page you started from.
- **HTML** Cancel All: Stops the loading of the current Web page.

> NOTE: If you have any problems loading WebSurfer under Windows 95, try connecting with Windows' built-in TCP/IP stack. See your Windows' documentation for details.

Loading a Web Page from the Internet

Like Mosaic, WebSurfer combines text and graphics on the same page. Any text in blue or graphics with a blue border are hypertext links to other Web pages, multimedia files, or Internet areas. To load a link, just click on it.

You can also load up a document directly. Just select Retrieve, Go To URL and type in the document's exact URL. Alternatively, you can type a document's URL in the Dialog bar's URL box and press [ENTER] to load it.

If the document is a Web page, it will be displayed. If the document is a graphic, sound, or movie, the WebSurfer program will attempt to call up a viewer program to display/play it. If the document is any other type of multimedia file, WebSurfer allows you to save the document directly to your hard disk.

To find out more about the current Web document, select Retrieve, Properties.

Loading a Web Page from Your Hard Disk

If you have any Web pages on your hard disk (perhaps ones that you've created yourself), you can easily use WebSurfer to view them. Select Retrieve, Open Local File. Choose the file you want to view and click OK.

You can even edit the current Web document—a very handy capability for Web developers. Select Retrieve, Edit HTML. Then access the Retrieve, Refresh From Disk menu item to reload the page in a flash and see what your edits look like.

Other Internet Tools

The Chameleon package contains software for every Internet resource you could possibly want. To use FTP, e-mail, Telnet , Gopher , or any other Internet program, first connect to the Internet using the Custom application. Then you can communicate with friends across the world using Mail, read or post messages to thousands of newsgroups using NEWTNews, browse menus of data using Gopher , download tons of cool software using FTP, and much more.

CHAPTER 1
WEB BASICS

WEB BASICS

How do I...

1.1 **Get on the Web from America Online?**
1.2 **Establish a connection to the Internet?**
1.3 **Find a Web browser?**
1.4 **Navigate via browser features?**
1.5 **Follow a link?**
1.6 **Open a location?**
1.7 **Find a Web authoring tool?**
1.8 **Find a home for my Web pages?**
1.9 **Get information on the evolution of HTML?**
1.10 **Design effective Web pages?**

The World Wide Web, or simply, the Web, has been called the "killer app" of the Internet. Certainly its ability to display text and graphics and provide access to other pages and information resources has made it the fastest-growing component of the Internet. You may already know how to explore the universe of information on the Web. But you may not know how to take advantage of the Web to provide your own information to the world, information about you, your personal interests, or your business.

This chapter is intended as an introduction to the World Wide Web and a guide to get you on the Web and ready to create HTML documents. This chapter is not intended to be a thorough introduction to the Web; there are other resources, both on the Web and in books, that can provide a more detailed explanation of the Web

CHAPTER 1
WEB BASICS

and how to use it. This chapter simply explains the basics of the Web, including how to find an access provider, how to use a browser, and how to find space for the Web pages you create. Once this groundwork is in place, you can learn in future chapters how to create your own Web pages using HTML.

1.1 Get on the Web from America Online

Major online services—America Online, CompuServe, and Prodigy—now provide access to the World Wide Web. This How-To discusses how America Online's Internet service works and how you can use it to access the Web.

1.2 Establish a Connection to the Internet

Another option for Web access is to get an account with an Internet service provider, or ISP. These accounts usually include access to Internet resources, including the World Wide Web, and often include space to store Web pages you create. This How-To explains how to find a local provider and get the kind of Internet access you need to explore the Web.

1.3 Find a Web Browser

As the Web has exploded, the number of browser programs—the programs you use to explore the Web—has increased. There are browsers now for nearly every conceivable type of computer. The sophistication of these programs has also increased to support advanced HTML features and extensions. This How-To explains how to find a Web browser for your computer.

1.4 Navigate via Browser Features

Once you have Web access and a working browser, you need to be able to move around on the Web. The easiest way to navigate on the Web is to use the features incorporated into your browser to move between pages. This How-To shows how to use these basic features to start moving around the Web.

1.5 Follow a Link

One of the key features the World Wide Web offers the user is the ability to move from page to page by selecting specific highlighted words, phrases, or images. These are called links. This How-To explains what links are and how you can use them to explore the Web.

1.6 Open a Location

Another way to move around the Web is to go directly to a specific page, provided you have the address, or URL, of the page. This How-To explains how to go directly to a specific location on the Web using basic features found on Web browsers.

1.7 Find a Web Authoring Tool

Seeing the variety of pages on the Web may inspire you to create your own. One of the easiest ways to do this is to find an authoring tool, or HTML editor, that will allow you to create your pages much as you would using a word processor, without worrying about the right HTML tags to use. This How-To explains how authoring tools work and how to find them on the Internet.

1.8   Find a Home for My Web Pages

Once you've created your pages, you need a place to store them so they can be accessed by other people on the Web. This usually involves finding an ISP that provides Web space for its customers. This How-To discusses how to look for a home for your Web pages.

1.9   Get Information on the Evolution of HTML

Your initial forays into the World Wide Web and page creation may pique your interest in the language of the Web, HTML, and its evolution. There are resources on HTML and its development (in addition to what's in this book) available on the Web. This How-To shows you how to find information on the evolution and future directions of HTML.

1.10   Design Effective Web Pages

Even if you don't know anything about HTML yet, you can still learn how to design effective pages. Many of the attributes of an effective page—its layout, design, and ease of use—transcend HTML. This How-To discusses the basics of an effective Web page.

1.1   How do I... Get on the Web from America Online?

COMPLEXITY
EASY

COMPATIBILITY: NOT APPLICABLE

Problem

I plan to be a member of America Online. How can I get on the World Wide Web using this service?

Technique

To use the World Wide Web from America Online you need version 2.61 of the America Online software and a modem.

Steps

The following steps show how to get on the World Wide Web from America Online.

CHAPTER 1
WEB BASICS

1. If you don't have version 2.61 of the America Online software on your hard disk, install it. The installation process is very easy and straightforward. Just follow the onscreen prompts. The one thing to watch out for is that the AOL modem setting defaults to a Hayes modem configuration. If you do not have a Hayes modem, make sure you change this setting to match your modem.
2. Once America Online 2.61 is installed, start it up by double-clicking on the America Online icon. Sign on to America Online. This brings you to the Main Menu.
3. Select Internet Connection from the Main Menu. This brings you to the Internet Connection Menu that contains a series of Internet-related topics. Figure 1-1 shows this menu.
4. Select the World Wide Web icon.
5. The America Online browser will load. Your screen will then resemble Figure 1-2.

How It Works

America Online makes getting on the World Wide Web surprisingly easy. Loading the 2.61 software and browser gives you all the tools you need.

Comments

If you have an older version of the America Online software, you will find the upgrade software in the Internet Connection section.

The faster the modem you have, the better.

COMPLEXITY
EASY

1.2 How do I... Establish a connection to the Internet?

COMPATIBILITY: ALL

Problem

Instead of using one of the online service providers, I'd like to get an account with a company that will provide me with direct Internet access. How can I get an Internet account, and what kind of connection do I need to be able to access the Web from it?

1.2
ESTABLISH A CONNECTION TO THE INTERNET

Figure 1-1 The America Online Internet connection menu

Figure 1-2 The America Online browser

Technique

The number of companies that provide direct Internet access is rapidly increasing. These companies are usually called Internet service providers, or ISPs; they offer an account on their systems and access to the Internet. To take advantage of the graphical nature of the Web, though, you will likely need to look into special connections, such as SLIP and PPP (see below), that can turn your computer into a temporary site on the Internet.

A shell account is the most basic type of Internet access. You dial into the Internet provider's computer and use a command-line interface (like UNIX or DOS) or a text-based menu. The provider's computer has all the software for e-mail, news, and other utilities. Your computer serves as a "dumb" terminal for the connection.

A Serial Line Interface Protocol (SLIP) or Point to Point Protocol (PPP) connection turns your computer into a temporary site on the Internet. You dial into the provider's computer as you would if you had a shell account, but instead of using that computer's software, you use programs on your own computer for e-mail, news, and other applications. The provider simply provides Internet access for your computer.

The Integrated Services Digital Network (ISDN) line is a new technology becoming available in many urban areas. These special phone lines provide connections that are faster than those possible over ordinary phone lines. ISDN lines also feature two channels, so you can send a fax or talk on the phone while using your modem on the other channel. The speed can be expensive, though; it may cost several hundred dollars to install an ISDN line in your home or office.

Steps

The key to establishing an Internet connection is determining the level of access to require. This is addressed in the first steps below, followed by tips for finding providers in your area and determining which one best suits your needs.

CHAPTER 1
WEB BASICS

1. First, determine the level of Internet access you need. Since with a shell account you are limited to the provider's text-based applications, you can only use a text-based browser like Lynx. You can install software like The Internet Adaptor (TIA) in your shell account that allows it to mimic a SLIP/PPP connection, but this is not as efficient as using a real SLIP or PPP connection.

    If you plan on using a browser that displays graphics, like Netscape or Mosaic (see How-To 1.3), your best choice is a SLIP/PPP account so you can use the browser software on your machine to explore the Web. You should get at least a 14.4K (14,400 baud) modem, and preferably a 28.8K modem, so that large files will transfer quickly to and from your computer.

    If you plan on doing some heavy-duty Web surfing and need more speed than a SLIP/PPP connection, you should consider an ISDN line. The setup cost can be steep; however, you will save that money, and then some, by being able to transfer large files very quickly, saving on access charges.

2. Next, you need to identify the ISPs in your area. You can do this in any number of ways. You can ask friends or colleagues who have Internet access about the providers they use or know about. If you have access to Usenet through another account (or know someone who does), the newsgroup alt.internet.access.wanted is a good source of information on Internet providers. There are also resources on the Web, if you or someone you know can gain access to it. The site http://thelist.com/ provides a detailed list of hundreds of ISPs, broken down by area code (in the U.S. and Canada) and country code (outside North America).

3. Once you're armed with a list of local ISPs, contact them and ask for information about the services they provide. Be sure to get information on:

    - **HTML** The type of Internet services they provide (shell accounts, SLIP/PPP, ISDN)
    - **HTML** The monthly fee for their services
    - **HTML** Whether they have an access number (or POP, Point of Presence) in your local calling area
    - **HTML** Any per-hour charges they may include, especially for premium services or types of connection
    - **HTML** The highest modem speed they support (it should be at least 14.4K bps, and preferably 28.8K)
    - **HTML** The amount of disk space provided for each user, and any surcharges for additional space

    Costs will vary from provider to provider, and may differ from area to area, depending on the local competition. As a rule of thumb, though, for a standard shell or SLIP/PPP connection, you will pay approximately as much per month as you will for a month of cable TV. Of course, the Internet will likely be a lot more informative and educational than cable TV.

How It Works

Internet service providers usually buy access from larger network providers, in the form of access to fast 57.6K, T1, and T3 lines. ISPs then combine this network access with computers and banks of modems (to handle incoming calls from customers), and sell packages of Internet access based on this system to the public.

Comments

If you live in a small city or rural area, there may not be any local ISPs in your area. If that is the case, you may want to investigate using one of the major online services or look into services that provide long-distance Internet access (often through 800 numbers) for $5-10 an hour.

1.3 How do I... Find a Web browser?

COMPLEXITY: INTERMEDIATE

COMPATIBILITY: ALL

Problem

I now have access to the Internet and the World Wide Web. Before I can start exploring the Web, though, I need some kind of browser program to access the Web. How can I find a browser program that best fits my needs?

Technique

There are many Web browsers now available, covering nearly all computer systems. Your system may already have a browser set up for your use; if not, there are plenty of options from which to choose. Here are some of the more popular browsers:

- **HTML** Netscape Naviagtor (see Figure 1-3) is far and away the most popular browser. Up to 75 percent of all Web browsers in use are Windows, Macintosh, and UNIX versions of Netscape. Netscape has taken the lead by providing its browser software at little or no cost and by developing extensions to HTML to improve the graphics quality of Web pages.

- **HTML** Mosaic, the browser that started the Web explosion, is still around, although no longer as popular due to the development of Netscape

CHAPTER 1
WEB BASICS

(see Figure 1-4). New versions of Mosaic are still being developed at the National Center for Supercomputer Applications at the University of Illinois, where Macintosh, UNIX, and Windows versions of the browser are available at no cost. Mosaic has also been licensed to a number of companies that are creating their own enhanced versions of the browser.

Figure 1-3 The Netscape home page

Figure 1-4 The Mosaic home page

HTML EINet has developed MacWeb and WinWeb, for Macintosh and Windows computers respectively, which have gained a degree of popularity for their speed and ease of use.

HTML Those with an interest in HTML 3, the new version of HTML currently in development, and access to UNIX accounts should consider Arena (see Figure 1-5). Arena is designed as a "testbed" browser for the development of HTML 3.

HTML For people limited to text-only access, either through a shell account or with DOS, the best option for Web access is Lynx, a text-based browser. While you cannot see the graphics used in Web pages with this browser, you can download the images for later viewing offline.

1.3
FIND A WEB BROWSER

Figure 1-5 The Arena home page

Steps

The type of browser you should use depends on the type of Internet access you have and what software (if any) is already configured on your system. Although Netscape is the most popular browser currently, there are a number of browsers out there that may better suit your needs, so it doesn't hurt to look around.

1. If you already have an account through your school or employer, there's a very good chance that you already have one or more Web browsers available. Check with your local system administrator, or ask fellow users what browsers they use.

2. If you're using a dialup shell account without any adapter software, you'll be limited to using a text-based browser like Lynx. Your ISP may already have Lynx installed; check with the provider's support staff to see if this is the case.

3. If you're accessing the Internet from a SLIP/PPP or ISDN connection, you'll need to get your own browser software. Fortunately, there are many browsers to choose from. In addition to the popular browsers listed above, you can find a detailed list of browsers for most computer systems in Appendix B. Once you've installed the software, you're ready to explore the Web.

How It Works

Web browsers serve as the interface with the World Wide Web. They send out requests for particular Web pages and documents over the Internet. When they receive the files, they turn the HTML files into the formatted versions displayed on the screen. Web browsers are also equipped to handle requests for information by FTP and Gopher, among other methods.

CHAPTER 1
WEB BASICS

Comments

The availability of Web browsers changes frequently as new browsers are released and current ones are upgraded. While Netscape is the current king of the browsers, a new browser may take its place at any time. This is an important point to keep in mind when you begin to design Web pages: Netscape uses a number of extensions to HTML that are not part of the standard HTML specification and are not supported by other browsers. If people stop using Netscape (or any other browser with its own extensions to HTML), the extensions in your page will no longer be used.

1.4 How do I...
Navigate via browser features?

COMPLEXITY
EASY

COMPATIBILITY: ALL

Problem

I've got my browser program running and I'm starting to explore the Web. I want to be able to easily move around from page to page and return to my home page. How can I navigate on the Web using my browser's features?

Technique

Nearly all browsers feature a set of basic navigational features that allow you to go from page to page at a single mouse-click or keypress. Browsers also allow you to go to a "home page," that can be predefined by the user.

Steps

Start up your browser. You will notice, either in the browser window or in one of the browser's menus, a number of commands like Home, Forward, and Back. These commands allow you to move back and forth among the Web sites you've visited.

1. Most browsers feature a Home button or menu option. When this option is selected, the browser returns the user to its home page, or the page that was automatically loaded when the browser started up. This is usually the home page of your Internet service provider or the home page of the company that created the browser. However, many browsers allow you to change the default home page, usually by entering the appropriate address, or URL, of the page you desire in the appropriate field of the Preferences dialog box (or other similar option).

2. To go from the current page to the previous page you viewed, use the Back button or menu option on most browsers. You can use the Back option to go all the way back to the home page of the browser.

3. Similarly, you can use the Forward option to go forward in the history of Web pages, all the way to the most recent page you loaded. You can only use the Forward option if you've previously used the Back option to back up from the last page loaded.

4. While not strictly a navigational feature, browsers usually offer a Reload option to reload a Web page from a server you previously viewed. This is important if you've used the Back and Forward commands to go through some of the pages you've loaded and want to make sure a page you loaded some time ago is the current version of your history. Reload is also useful if the page updates itself periodically or the page did not load properly the first time you accessed it.

How It Works

Web browsers store pages in memory. When a Forward or Back button is selected, the required page loads from memory. Since the page contents may have changed since you last loaded it, the Reload command allows you to reload the page from the server and get any additions or corrections to the page.

Comments

If you back up several pages in your Web browser, then select a different link to follow, any pages that are listed forward of the new page you are viewing will be removed from your history of pages. That is, you can only keep going backward and forward through your history of pages until you choose a new page somewhere in the list. When you choose a new page, all the pages forward of the current page are removed from memory.

COMPLEXITY
EASY

1.5 How do I... Follow a link?

COMPATIBILITY: ALL

Problem

I've noticed that there are a number of words and phrases, and even some pictures, that are highlighted on Web pages. I understand that these are called "links" and will take me to other places on the Web. How do I use a link to go from page to page?

Technique

Links use selected words or graphics, called anchors, to provide a gateway to another Web page, ftp site, Gopher menu, or other Internet resource. When you select the link, you are automatically taken to the new location.

Steps

1. If you're using a graphical browser like Mosaic or Netscape, links appear as words that are highlighted and/or underlined. Graphics that serve as links have highlighted borders of the same color as the highlighted text. To select a link, move the mouse cursor over the highlighted text or graphic and press the mouse button. The browser will automatically follow the link.

2. If you're using a text-based browser, links usually appear as either bold or underlined text, or with numbers beside them. To select a link, either enter the number of the link or use the arrow keys to move the cursor to the link and press the appropriate key.

How It Works

The document stores the location of the link along with the text or graphic that serves as the anchor for the link. When a user selects a particular link, the browser loads the Web page or other file associated with the link.

Comments

Many browsers let the user display the destination of the link at the bottom of the screen when the cursor passes over the link. This is a useful feature that lets you know exactly where the link goes and helps you decide whether to choose the link.

COMPLEXITY
EASY

1.6 How do I... Open a location?

COMPATIBILITY: ALL

Problem

A friend has told me about a great page on the Web. I don't know how I would find it using links, but my friend gave me something called a "URL." How can I use this URL to open the page?

Technique

Another method of locating pages is by going directly to them, using the page's Universal Resource Locator (URL), which gives the location of the page. The URL is nothing more than the address of the page. You can enter this URL in your browser to go directly to the page.

Steps

Before you can open a location, you need to have the URL of the location. A typical Web URL looks something like this:

```
http://www.fake.com/homepage.html
```

The URL consists of the protocol (HTTP for Web pages), the computer on which the file is located, and the name of the file. Chapter 7 discusses URLs in greater detail.

Once you have the URL for the page, choose the Open or Open Location command on most browsers, then enter the URL in the appropriate dialog box. The browser goes directly to that page and loads the contents into the browser for you to view.

How It Works

When a user enters a URL into the Open Location command of a browser, the browser loads the page associated with the URL. This works just as if a link to that page had been selected, since links use URLs to define their destinations.

Comments

URLs can be used to describe more than just Web pages. They can be used for ftp sites, Gopher menus, Usenet newsgroups, electronic mail, and Telnet as well. The use of all types of URLs is discussed in greater detail in Chapter 7.

COMPLEXITY
EASY

1.7 How do I... Find a Web authoring tool?

COMPATIBILITY: ALL

Problem

I'd like to get started creating Web pages, but for now I'd like to avoid learning all the markup tags I need to create an HTML document. I understand that a way around this is to use an HTML editor or authoring tool that will allow me to create HTML documents in much the same way I would using a word processor. How do I find one of these programs?

Technique

HTML editors, or authoring tools, are programs that allow people to create HTML documents for their Web pages without getting into the nuts and bolts of HTML. These programs use a format similar to a word processor or page layout program to allow people to place text and graphics on a page. In addition, a number of new word processors, including WordPerfect and Microsoft Word, include HTML editing features. While you still need to know some basic HTML to use these programs, they do make it easier for beginners to create Web pages.

Steps

Before starting to look for a Web authoring tool, make sure you know how much memory and hard disk space you have available on your system; this will let you know what software will work on it.

1. Just as you did in your search for Web browsers, you may find that your Internet provider already has programs available for you to use. Check with your provider's support staff to see if they have any HTML authoring tools available.

2. If your provider has no authoring tools, you can search the Web for any number of authoring tools for Macintosh, UNIX, Windows, and other systems. A good place to start is http://www.w3.org/hypertext/WWW/Tools/. This page, provided by the World Wide Web Consortium, lists a number of editors, converters, and other tools to help create HTML documents, with links to more information and the locations from which you can download the software.

How It Works

A converter is a program that reads in a file in one format (such as a standard word processor format) and converts it into an HTML document, with all the tags already added. An HTML editor is a program that works like a word processor and allows you to create HTML files by inserting HTML tags from menu items rather than typing in the tags.

Comments

Some editors claim to be WYSIWYG (What You See Is What You Get). But remember that not all browsers display documents in the same way, and some browsers support HTML extensions that others do not. Thus, some browsers may

1.8 How do I... Find a home for my Web pages?

display the documents the way they look in the editor, but others may not. This is important to keep in mind when creating Web pages.

COMPLEXITY: EASY

COMPATIBILITY: ALL

Problem

I've created some pages that I'd like to place on the Web for everyone to see. However, I need to put the pages somewhere so that they're accessible to anyone on the Web. How do I find a home for these pages?

Technique

Most Internet service providers give users space to place their Web pages, sometimes at an additional charge. If your provider doesn't offer Web space, there are some other options.

Steps

When you look for a place to store your Web pages, decide beforehand how much space you need for your pages and what other special options, such as CGI scripts, you'll need to have. You can then more intelligently choose a home for your pages.

1. The first place to check for Web storage space is with your Internet service provider. ISPs often give a certain amount of Web space to their customers for little or no additional charge. Special services, such as scripts for forms in Web pages, may also be provided at an additional charge.

2. If you already have an account with your school or employer but don't have Web space, or are a subscriber to an online service that doesn't offer Web space to its customers, many ISPs will offer Web-only accounts at a special rate. Although you won't have a full account with the provider, you will have space for your Web pages and a method (often e-mail or FTP) to send new and updated versions of Web pages. The provider may also include other services, such as scripts, for an additional charge.

3. When looking for Web space with a provider, be sure to ask:

HTML How much space is available per user, and how much is charged for extra space.

CHAPTER 1
WEB BASICS

- **HTML** How easy it is to edit current pages and include new pages (whether this can be done online or via FTP or e-mail).

- **HTML** How much "traffic" is available for free, and what the charges are for extra traffic. Traffic here refers to the number of times your pages are accessed and is usually measured in megabytes. If you have a 10 kilobyte page that is accessed 5,000 times in a month, you would have 50 megabytes of traffic that month.

- **HTML** Which special services, like script creation, graphic design, etc., are available, and how much they charge for these services.

How It Works

ISPs usually provide some space for users to place Web pages. This space might be in a special directory, or it might be linked to the home directory of the user. Providers may also allow users to include special scripts, or programs, in specific directories on the server for interactive Web pages.

Comments

While many providers offer special assistance in creating Web pages, this usually comes at a steep cost: often upwards of $25 an hour. A small investment of time learning HTML can save you a lot of money in the long run when you create your pages.

COMPLEXITY
EASY

1.9 How do I... Get information about the evolution of HTML?

COMPATIBILITY: ALL

Problem

Now that I'm starting to use HTML, I'd like to learn more about how HTML has developed and what its future directions are. Where can I find this information on the Web?

Technique

Information on the current state of HTML and future plans for it is available on the Web, particularly from the World Wide Web Consortium (W3C).

1.9
GET INFORMATION ABOUT THE EVOLUTION OF HTML

Steps

1. To get information on the current level of standard HTML, known as HTML 2.0, check the URL http://www.w3.org/hypertext/WWW/MarkUp/html-spec/index.html. This document provides links to other documents describing the features of HTML 2.0, which is in final draft stage before being officially submitted as an Internet standard, although all browsers currently support HTML 2.0.

2. The next level of HTML, known as HTML 3.0, is currently under development, although some browsers have already implemented a number of new features proposed for HTML 3. A draft description of the features of HTML 3.0 is available on the Web at http://www.hpl.hp.co.uk/people/dsr/html/CoverPage.html. This version of HTML is still in flux, and most of its features are not yet supported by most browsers, but it does give a good picture of how HTML is evolving.

3. For a detailed description of Universal Resource Locators, check the URL http://www.w3.org/hypertext/WWW/Addressing/Addressing.html. It explains all the various types of URLs and how they can be used in Web documents.

4. If you are interested in including some of the HTML extensions developed by Netscape, check the Netscape Extensions page at http://home.mcom.com/assist/net_sites/html_extensions.html. This page describes in detail the extensions Netscape has provided for HTML, and includes examples of advanced features, such as tables, backgrounds, and dynamic documents.

How It Works

These links provide access to updated documents on the status of the current HTML draft (HTML 2.0), future HTML development (HTML 3.0), and how URLs work.

Comments

While it is safe to use the features in HTML 2.0, many features in HTML 3.0 are still under review and development. Thus, few browsers support more than a handful of HTML 3.0 tags (the exception being Arena, a UNIX browser designed specifically as an HTML 3.0 testbed). Since the HTML 3.0 design is still in flux, don't expect more features to be supported in the near future. The Netscape extensions to HTML are not currently part of either version of HTML, although some of the tags may be included in a later draft of HTML 3. Although a page that contains Netscape extensions can be read by other browsers, it will not be formatted in the same way as it is in Netscape.

CHAPTER 1
WEB BASICS

1.10 How do I... Design effective Web pages?

COMPLEXITY
EASY

COMPATIBILITY: ALL

Problem

I want to make sure that the pages I create stand out (in a good way, of course), even though I'm just beginning to learn HTML. What are some of the basic techniques I need to know in order to create effective Web pages?

Technique

There are several fundamental considerations in designing a home page that transcend HTML. These concerns include layout, design, and ease of use. There are some basic tips that can be used to help create any kind of Web page, from the simplest page to advanced pages with forms and graphics.

Steps

Before you begin to design your Web pages, review the tips below. These steps will help you sharpen the design of your pages and avoid embarrassing mistakes.

1. First, decide what you're going to say. It sounds obvious, but there are many Web pages (not to mention other types of publications) that fail because they lack focus. The key points you want to present to the readers need to be clear. If people become confused trying to figure out what you're trying to say, they probably won't come back to other pages you create, and will steer others clear of them as well. (Word-of-mouth is especially powerful on the Internet.)

2. Once you've decided on the goals of your Web page, you need to decide what you want to include on the page. This is a good time to start subdividing material by content. The material can either be put on separate pages or combined on one page, depending on your mode of presentation.

3. Unless your page is going to be very short, it helps to have a short introductory page describing the purpose of your pages, what information is available, and how to get to it. This serves as both an introduction and a table of contents, allowing the reader to quickly decide if the contents of the page are interesting enough to continue reading. Other pages, with more information about your topic, can be included as links on the introductory page. (See Chapter 7 for more information on links.)

4. If possible, make each page you design relatively short. There should be no more than one or two screens of text and graphics per page. If the page is longer, readers will have to scroll repeatedly to read the whole page, which can disrupt the flow of the document. If you have to make longer pages, make it easier for people to find information by including a table of contents and links to specific places within the document.

5. Don't overload a page with graphics. Graphics files can be very large, which means it takes much longer for a browser to load a page that includes them. The neat graphics you included on your page may take minutes for others to load. While you may have a fast network connection, other people may have relatively slow access over a modem.

6. When creating your pages, keep in mind that they will be viewed by people using a wide variety of browsers, from text-only browsers though the latest versions of Mosaic and Netscape. Thus, be sure to conform to the HTML standards when composing your document so that it is usable by the largest possible number of readers. Also, do not make your page overly reliant on graphics. Some people use text-only browsers or turn off image loading (an option provided by many browsers to enable documents to load faster). This doesn't mean you shouldn't take advantage of graphics and HTML extensions, but be careful that you don't make the document unusable to many readers in the process.

7. Before you announce your pages to the world, carefully check them over to make sure they are free of errors and bad HTML. Look at the pages with different browsers (or ask friends who use different browsers to look at the pages) and make sure everything looks right. Putting an error-laden, poorly designed set of pages on the Web can be very embarrassing.

How It Works

The proper design of Web pages is not much different from the proper design of printed materials. The key is to put your point across to your readers as succinctly as you can with as few errors as possible.

Comments

Good style is largely in the eye of the beholder. What may appear stylish and hip to one person may appear ugly and boring to another. However, the steps listed above should be useful for any Web pages you design because they transcend the content of the pages and focus on the basics of presentation.

PART 2
AUTHORING

HOW TO
CREATE AND MODIFY
HTML DOCUMENTS

CHAPTER 2
HTML BASICS

HTML BASICS

How do I...

- 2.1 Recognize an HTML document?
- 2.2 Build a simple HTML document?
- 2.3 Create HTML documents without manually inserting tags?
- 2.4 Convert word processed documents to HTML?
- 2.5 Convert other types of files to HTML?
- 2.6 Insert an HTML element?
- 2.7 Include a comment?
- 2.8 Add body text?
- 2.9 Insert special characters into a document?
- 2.10 Align text?
- 2.11 Change font size?
- 2.12 Create a home page?
- 2.13 View my home page?

The World Wide Web is an ever growing online information space filled with a myriad of commercial, educational, and entertaining materials. These materials, in the form of hypermedia documents accessed through the Internet, can be located anywhere in the world. No matter where it originates, every Web document is created using HyperText Markup Language (HTML).

CHAPTER 2
HTML BASICS

HTML authoring is the process of creating and defining such documents. HTML version 3 is the most recent incarnation of this powerful authoring language; unless otherwise indicated, the term HTML refers to the language as a general entity, while HTML 3 and HTML 2 refer to the specific version of the language. This chapter begins to explore how you can use HTML to publish hypermedia documents on the World Wide Web.

HTML elements are used to define document structure and format. An HTML element is the inclusive region defined by either a single tag or a pair of tags. (Tags are described more completely in How-To 2.6.) A tag is a string in the language surrounded by a less than (<) and a greater than (>) sign. An opening tag is any tag in which the string does not begin with a slash (/); in addition, you may see associated a list of allowable attribute/value pairs within an opening tag. An ending or closing tag is a string that does begin with a slash (/). Appendix A provides a quick reference to those elements supported by HTML 3.

The material in this chapter covers the recognition and creation of simple HTML documents. The detailed usage of individual editors and converters is beyond the scope of this book, although several How-To's provide a brief introduction to them. You are also led through the processes for developing and viewing a simple home page.

The topics covered in this chapter introduce the essential basics of HTML authoring. Later chapters will provide you with insights and examples. The information in this chapter will jump-start you into the publication of your own HTML documents.

2.1 Recognize an HTML Document

You can present information in a variety of forms: GIF images, WAV sound, PostScript text. HTML documents format textual information with embedded markup tags that provide style and structure information. In this How-To, you will learn the structure of HTML documents and how to identify a document as an HTML document.

2.2 Build a Simple HTML Document

HTML documents are the basis upon which the World Wide Web is built. Any attempt to author hypermedia objects for the World Wide Web will require the development of a suitable HTML document. This How-To provides step-by-step instructions for developing a simple HTML document. This simple example can serve not only as your first HTML document but also as your guide for developing well-structured HTML documents. In this How-To, you will learn how to build your first HTML page.

CHAPTER 2
HTML BASICS

2.3 Create HTML Documents without Manually Inserting Tags

If you want to jump straight into authoring but have no wish to become enmeshed in the details of HTML formatting, then this How-To may be your answer. It answers the question, "Is there a way to generate an HTML document without having to manually insert the formatting tags?" In this How-To, you will learn how to find and use HTML authorware.

2.4 Convert Word Processed Documents to HTML

You have been developing documents using word processors for a long time. Some of these documents are exactly the ones that you wish to publish on the World Wide Web. Is there any easy way to transform these documents into HTML? In this How-To, you will learn how to automatically convert word processed documents to HTML pages.

2.5 Convert Other Types of Files to HTML

You have been developing documents using a variety of text formatting languages. You have documents that you have developed in TeX and Scribe. You need to alter the markup tags to conform to HTML rather than the native formatting commands. Are there automatic tools to help with this task? In this How-To, you will learn how to convert text formatted documents to HTML pages.

2.6 Insert an HTML Element

Markup tags are the glue holding HTML documents together. These tags determine the various elements that are contained within your document. To a large extent, these elements define how the information in your document is treated and rendered. In this How-To, you will learn the process for placing this structural and formatting information into your HTML document.

2.7 Include a Comment

Comments provide a mechanism for documenting the reasons you have developed a document in the way that you have. You don't want this information presented to the viewer, but it should be available to those interested in the design and development process. In this How-To, you will learn how to format comments in HTML.

2.8 Add Body Text

The body is the meat of an HTML document. The body element represents the information content of a document. In this How-To, you will learn how to author the body of HTML pages.

CHAPTER 2
HTML BASICS

2.9 Insert Special Characters into a Document

A variety of symbols beyond the standard alphanumeric characters may be required in your HTML documents. In this How-To, you will learn how to include such characters so that they appear correctly in a viewing environment such as Mosaic or Netscape.

2.10 Align Text

HTML 3 provides elements to support the alignment of the textual content of your HTML documents. This How-To describes these elements, explains their usage, and provides concrete examples. In this How-To, you will learn how to add horizontal alignment elements to your HTML pages.

2.11 Change Font Size

HTML 3 supports elements that allow textual information to be presented in a variety of font sizes. Some browsers such as Mosaic or Netscape automatically increase the font size for a variety of HTML elements; however, if you wish to explicitly change font size, you will make use of the information in this How-To. In this How-To, you will learn how to explicitly change font sizes in your HTML pages.

2.12 Create a Home Page

You have created a few simple pages; now you are ready to create a page of your own where people can find information about you. This How-To walks you through the creation of a simple home page that may be expanded as your skill in HTML increases. In this How-To, you will learn how to create a basic home page.

2.13 View My Home Page

You have created an HTML document, but you have no idea what it will look like in Netscape or some other browser application. You need to view the documents that you create to determine how they will appear when viewed not only in your current browser but also in other browsers. In this How-To, you will learn how to view and test an HTML page.

COMPLEXITY
EASY

2.1 How do I... Recognize an HTML document?

COMPATIBILITY: HTML

Problem

What is an HTML document? How do I create one? How can I tell that a document has been formatted using HTML? What are the telltale signs?

2.1
RECOGNIZE AN HTML DOCUMENT

Technique

Formatted textual information can be stored in a variety of ways:

- **HTML** Word processed documents
- **HTML** PostScript documents
- **HTML** HTML documents
- **HTML** DVI documents

HTML documents serve as the basis for information published on the World Wide Web.

To determine whether a text file is an HTML document, you can check its document structure and look for the presence of HTML elements. These are the characteristics to identify an HTML document.

First attempt to display the document using an HTML browser. If the text file is displayed properly within a browser's viewing window, then most likely the file is an HTML document.

Follow this by looking at the document with a text editor. Examine the file for HTML tags. A tag is a string in the language surrounded by a less than (<) and a greater than (>) sign. An opening tag is any tag in which the string does not begin with a slash (/). An ending or closing tag is a string that does begin with a slash (/). The inclusive region between an opening tag and a closing tag with the same string is referred to as an element.

Steps

The procedure below determines whether a document is an HTML document. If at any particular step you determine that the file in question is or is not an HTML document, you are done and need not continue with the remainder of the steps.

1. Use your favorite browser to attempt to view the document in question. You can do this with most browsers either via a menu option or a command line argument. For example, with Mosaic you execute an Open Local from the File menu. To open a local file /amihtm.htm using Lynx, issue the following command. Be sure that you have named the local file with the .html (or .htm for PC) filename extension. This indicates to most browsers that the local file is to be accessed as an HTML document.

```
lynx /amihtm.htm
```

If the document does not appear in the browser's display, then more than likely the file is not an HTML document. This is not a definitive test, however, since there are several possible conditions that could potentially cause an HTML document not to appear.

2. Open the file in question using your favorite text editor. If the document fails to open due to an error indicating that the document is a binary document of unknown format, then you can conclude that the file is not an HTML document. All HTML documents are ASCII text documents. If you receive an error message indicating that the file contains lines that are too long, you should attempt to open the file using another editor with a greater line length limit.

3. Examine the text file in the editor window. HTML documents should begin with an <HTML> tag. Tags are used to delimit structural or formatting elements in HTML. An opening and a closing <HTML> tag should surround the entire document. You should also find opening and closing tags for <HEAD> and <BODY> elements. An HTML document should appear as shown in the code below:

```
<HTML>
<HEAD>
......
</HEAD>
<BODY>
......
</BODY>
</HTML>
```

If you find these statements in your document, you are looking at an HTML document. However, older HTML documents may not have these structural elements.

4. At this point, you are looking at either an old-style HTML document or some other ASCII text-based document, PostScript for instance. You should scan through the document looking for any of the HTML elements specified in Appendix A. If no tags can be found, the file is not an HTML document. If tags are present, then the file is likely an HTML document that was developed using a loose HTML specification. For example, the following code might represent an old-style HTML document.

```
<TITLE>Old Style Document</TITLE>
....
```

How It Works

As you begin authoring HTML documents, you may wish to examine other authors' HTML documents and styles. Having a knowledge of the common architecture of HTML documents will allow you to analyze and adapt existing documents to suit your goals.

The first step in the identification process is to examine the document in question with an HTML browser such as Chameleon's WebSurfer. If the document fails to display, then it is likely that the document is not HTML. However, this is not certain. A few possible explanations for such a failure are

2.1
RECOGNIZE AN HTML DOCUMENT

HTML The filename extension used for the file you are viewing is not appropriate for an HTML document.

HTML The remapping of the .html (.htm) filename extension to indicate a type other than HTML.

HTML An error in the HTML code of the document.

Most browsers will not render a file as an HTML document, even though it is, unless the file is appropriately named. Without the suitable filename extension (usually .html or .htm), the browser may treat the document as simple plain text (or as whatever the configured default type is). If the document fails to display for this reason, make sure you add the appropriate extension to your file before trying to view it with your browser.

To correct the second situation, either remap the .html (.htm) extension to indicate an HTML document or rename the file with the appropriate extension. If you plan to examine a number of local files, you may wish to perform the latter operation through your browser's menus or through its configuration files.

Next, all HTML documents are text based. In other words, you should be able to examine them with a standard text editor such as EDIT on a PC or SimpleText on a Mac. If the document is a binary file, then, by default, it is not an HTML document.

In addition, all well-constructed HTML 3 documents conform to a common document structure. By examining the text of the file for architectural features, you should be able to make an initial judgment concerning a document. Figure 2-1 illustrates this common architecture.

In some cases this architectural information may not be sufficient to make an absolute determination, particularly for documents built upon an earlier HTML standard. (See the Comments section below.) In this case, you need to examine the document for HTML elements. These elements may be of any type specified in Appendix A.

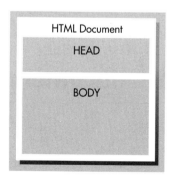

Figure 2-1 Structure of an HTML document

CHAPTER 2
HTML BASICS

Comments

The procedure outlined above will work for any HTML document. Certain caveats should be kept in mind, however.

PC, UNIX, and Mac platforms use slightly different combinations of carriage returns and line feeds to designate the end of a line; therefore, if the text file you are attempting to view was developed on a platform different from the one you are currently using, strange characters may appear at the end of text lines or the file may appear as a single long string of text. This latter situation may cause difficulties with text editors that have fixed line length limits.

With respect to structural features, certain browsers such as Mosaic can scan and display less well constructed HTML documents. These capabilities permit the display of HTML documents that conform to a looser standard.

Browser applications perform a two-step procedure for determining whether a file is an HTML document or some other data object. First, the browser examines the server response header sent with the data object. If a *Content-type: text/html* line is present, then the browser assumes that the document is HTML. If the browser cannot determine the object type from the server, either because the object did not come from a server (a local file) or a server did not supply a complete response header, it examines the file's filename extension. By default, if the extension is .html (.htm for PC), the browser attempts to display the object as an HTML document. You can often configure the specific filename extensions used by a particular browser through menu options or configuration files.

Servers determine that a file is an HTML document based solely on the filename extension. For HTML, the usual filename extension is .html (.htm for PC-based servers). As is true with browsers, you can usually configure the filename extensions for a server. (See Chapters 11 and 12.)

COMPLEXITY
EASY, ADVANCED
(<META>, <STYLE> ELEMENTS)

2.2 How do I... Build a simple HTML document?

COMPATIBILITY: HTML, HTML 3 (<HEAD> ELEMENTS)

Problem

I know how to browse the World Wide Web to find information. Now I want to take the next step and add information of my own. Where do I start?

2.2
BUILD A SIMPLE HTML DOCUMENT

Technique

Use the procedure outlined below to create a simple HTML document. This document delineates the components you need to include in your own documents to create meaningful, well-structured HTML 3 documents.

The procedure defined below leads you through the definition of the overall HTML document and the construction of the head and body components. Several HTML elements and their use are introduced in the document development process.

Steps

The following steps lead you through the creation of a single HTML document titled "My First Page". This document contains the single statement "Hello World!"

You can follow these steps and alter the aforementioned strings to begin generating documents of your own.

1. Change directories to the location where you wish to develop your HTML documents. Create a new file in your favorite text editor. Be sure to choose a filename with an extension that indicates an HTML document to your browser.

```
edit first.htm
```

2. Begin with an <HTML> opening tag. Enter the following line in your document.

```
<HTML>
```

3. Indicate that you are beginning the <HEAD> element of the document by issuing a <HEAD> opening tag. The following line should appear next in your document. If a <HEAD> element is included, it must appear within the scope of an <HTML> element.

```
<HEAD>
```

A complete list of elements that you may include within your <HEAD> element is provided in the How It Works section below.

4. The <TITLE> element is used to indicate the title of an HTML document. <TITLE> tags are placed within the head component of a document. The title of the document is placed between the opening and closing <TITLE> tags. Add this <TITLE> element to your document.

```
<TITLE>My First Page</TITLE>
```

Use of this element is required in all HTML 3 documents. This element usually will not have any visible effect within a browser's viewing window;

however, the enclosed title may be used in the window title and/or the history list for the browser.

5. To end the head area, issue a <HEAD> closing tag.

```
</HEAD>
```

Thus, the <HEAD> element is nested within the <HTML> element.

6. At this point, the body of the document needs to be developed. A <BODY> opening tag indicates that this point has been reached. Enter the following line:

```
<BODY>
```

7. In this case, the body of the document is simply a text statement. More complex elements that can appear within the body component will be covered in other How-Tos. For now, add the following statement to your file.

```
Hello World!
```

8. A </BODY> closing tag marks the end of the <BODY> element. Similar to the <HEAD> element, the <BODY> element is also completely nested within the <HTML> element. To end the <BODY> element, issue the closing tag in your document.

```
</BODY>
```

9. Finally, terminate the <HTML> element with an </HTML> closing tag. Add this to your document to complete your first HTML document.

```
</HTML>
```

10. Save the file. Remember to use the .html or .htm filename extension to indicate an HTML document.

How It Works

An HTML document consists of nested elements. An element is a document component enclosed between opening and closing tags. (Closing tags are not required for all elements.) The outermost element is an <HTML> element, beginning with an <HTML> opening tag, and ending with an </HTML> closing tag. The remainder of the document is nested within this element.

The two primary subcomponents nested within the <HTML> element are a <HEAD> and a <BODY> element. Both of these elements appear within an <HTML> element, but neither appears nested within the other.

The <HEAD> element of a document contains metainformation about the information contained in the <BODY> element. This metainformation usually does not

2.2
BUILD A SIMPLE HTML DOCUMENT

have a direct visible effect within a browser's viewing window; however, the browser does have access to this metainformation. The following elements may appear within the scope of a <HEAD> element:

(HTML) <BASE>
How-To 7.3 describes the usage of this element in detail.

(HTML) <ISINDEX>
How-To 13.6 details the use of this element.

(HTML) <LINK>
How-To 7.4 fully describes the usage of this element.

(HTML) <META...>
This element is used to specify additional metainformation not supported by another <HEAD> element or to specify additional information that should be sent by a server as part of a response header (see How-To 11.8) when the document is generated. Netscape's client pull (How-To 11.9) is one example using this element.

ATTRIBUTE	VALUE
CONTENT	Data associated with the name or http-equiv
HTTP-EQUIV	HTTP response header field to generate with the value specified in the content
NAME	Name of the metainformation in content

(HTML) <NEXTID...>
This element contains a single attribute /value pair within the tag. The N attribute takes a value of the form z123 where z indicates an alphabetic character and 123 represents a three-digit number. Several HTML editing environments use this element to generate unique identifiers. You should not use this element when manually creating HTML documents.

(HTML) <RANGE...>
This element allows you to define and name regions within the body of the document. This element uses several attribute /value pairs. These pairs are specified in the following table:

ATTRIBUTE	VALUE
CLASS	Specify the class of region being defined
FROM	Name of the location within the body marking the beginning of the region
ID	Name that you wish associated with the defined region
UNTIL	Name of the location within the body marking the end of the region

CHAPTER 2
HTML BASICS

HTML `<STYLE...>...</STYLE>`

This element allows you to specify additional style and format information associated with both particular elements in the document and the document as a whole. The desired style information is enclosed between the tags. In addition, this element supports a single attribute/value pair within the opening tag. The allowable attribute is NOTATION; the value of this attribute indicates the notation used to specify the style information. The actual specification of style elements is still under development. For example, the style element below specifies in css notation that the left margin for the <BODY> element is 1 inch.

```
<STYLE NOTATION="css">
      BODY: margin.left = 1in
   </STYLE>
```

HTML `<TITLE>...</TITLE>`

This is a required element in HTML 3. You should use this element to specify the title of the document defined in the <BODY> element. How-To 2.8 describes the creation of the <BODY> element in greater detail.

Creating an HTML document is, thus, a process of nesting appropriate elements. The architecture of the sample HTML document whose code appears below is seen in Figure 2-2. Extending this, it can be seen that complex documents require deep levels of nesting.

```
<HTML>
<HEAD>
<TITLE>My First Page</TITLE>
</HEAD>
<BODY>
Hello World!
</BODY>
</HTML>
```

The resultant rendering of this document appears in Figure 2-3. For the Mosaic browser, the <TITLE> element generates a document title appearing in the Title area of the user interface. The body appears as normal text in the display area.

Comments

A reference to the tags specified in the HTML 3 standard appears in Appendix A. The table below shows the elements discussed in this How-To.

2.2
BUILD A SIMPLE HTML DOCUMENT

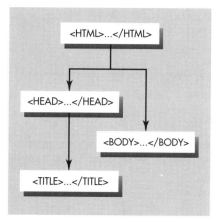

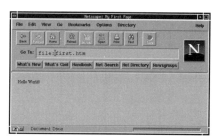

Figure 2-3 Rendering of example HTML document (Netscape)

Figure 2-2 Architecture of a simple HTML document

ELEMENT	LOCATION	PURPOSE
<HTML>...</HTML>	file	Defines scope of an HTML document. How-To 2.1
<HEAD>...</HEAD>	HTML	Defines head of an HTML document. How-To 2.1
<META...>	HEAD	Includes other metainformation about the document
<NEXTID...>	HEAD	Used by HTML editors to generate unique ids
<RANGE...>	HEAD	Names a region within the document body
<STYLE...>...</STYLE>	HEAD	Specifies style information for use in the document
<TITLE>...</TITLE>	HEAD	Defines the title of an HTML document
<BODY>...</BODY>	HTML	Defines body of an HTML document. How-To 2.8

When authoring HTML documents, remember that the way the final document looks depends on the browser application. Each application may process HTML elements in its own way. For example, the Lynx browser renders the sample document in a slightly different manner than Mosaic. Figure 2-4 shows the Lynx rendering of the sample document.

Notice that even for this very simple document, significant differences exist in the rendering. You need to keep this fact in mind while authoring, since your documents could potentially be viewed by any browser application. Thus, authoring to maximize appearance in a particular browser may result in poor appearance in other applications. With this in mind, you may wish to select a set of common browser applications such as Mosaic and Netscape and attempt to maximize appearance in the common browsers while providing at least a minimal usability with other browsers.

Figure 2-4 Rendering of example HTML document (Lynx)

COMPLEXITY
EASY

2.3 How do I... Create HTML documents without manually inserting tags?

COMPATIBILITY: HTML 2

Problem

I want to start creating HTML documents, but I do not feel the need to learn every little HTML element. Some tools must exist that allow me to create a document without having to manually insert each and every tag. I see the relationship between text formatting languages such as PostScript and word processors. Why not a similar editor for HTML?

Technique

The editors used to create HTML documents tend to fall into three categories:

- **HTML** Text editors—Manual insertion of HTML tags
- **HTML** Text editors with macros/pull-down menu tag selection—Creation of HTML elements through application of macros/menu items on selected areas of text
- **HTML** WYSIWYG (What You See Is What You Get) style—Tags inserted as with macro/menu based approach; however, formatting displays as it will ultimately be rendered. (See the Comments section below concerning HTML "WYSIWYG" limitation.)

This How-To examines these three classes of applications and gives a general means of acquiring them so you can use them to develop your documents.

2.3 CREATE HTML DOCUMENTS WITHOUT MANUALLY INSERTING TAGS

Steps

The procedures below are broken down by the categories listed above. Each category provides the steps necessary to acquire an editor of this type for your platform, followed by a generic walk-through of the creation of a simple document.

The acquisition phase of each process is broken down by development platform. Further, the use of anonymous ftp or ftp URLs is required to retrieve most of the HTML editors described.

Text Editors

1. Determine the development platform you wish to use.

2. Find a text editor that you wish to use. The following table gives examples of typical text editors by platform.

EDITOR/ENVIRONMENT	PLATFORM(S)	AVAILABILITY
BBEdit-Lite	MAC	ftp://ftp.std.com/pub/bbedit/freeware/bbedit-lite-30.hqx
TeachText	MAC	standard
EDIT	PC	standard
Notepad	PC (Windows)	standard
emacs	PC, UNIX	GNU archive sites
vi	PC, UNIX	PC archive sites, standard

3. Manually enter tags. Follow the procedure developed for creation of simple HTML documents defined in How-To 2.2.

Macro Packages and Editors with Pull-down Menu Tag Selection

1. Determine the development platform you wish to use.

2. Find an editor that you wish to use. The following table lists examples of some of these editors by platform and provides pointers to information concerning them.

EDITOR/ENVIRONMENT	PLATFORM(S)	AVAILABILITY
Alpha	MAC	ftp://cs.rice.edu/pub/Alpha
BBEdit Ext. 1	MAC	http://www.york.ac.uk/~ld11/BBEditTools.html
BBEdit Ext. 2	MAC	http://www.uji.es/bbedit-html-extensions.html
HoTMetaL	PC (Windows), UNIX	ftp://ftp.icm.edu.pl/pub/unix/www/contrib/SoftQuad/hotmetal

continued on next page

continued from previous page

EDITOR/ENVIRONMENT	PLATFORM(S)	AVAILABILITY
HTMLed	PC (Windows)	ftp://ftp.std.com/src/pc/www/htmled12.zip
emacs HTML helper	PC, UNIX	http://www.santafe.edu/~nelson/tools/
tkHTML	UNIX	http://www.infosystems.com/tkHTML/tkHTML.html

Review the materials suggested in the above table before making your final decision.

3. Retrieve the desired editor from the location(s) suggested above.

4. Uncompress, unarchive, and install the software as and where necessary.

> **HTML** On a UNIX platform, use the uncompress and tar commands to uncompress and unarchive the desired editor.

> **HTML** On a PC platform, the most common compression/archival program is ZIP. Use the unzip application to uncompress and unarchive the desired editor.

> **HTML** On a Mac platform, the common compression/archival program is StuffIt. Use the StuffIt program to uncompress and unarchive the desired editor.

You are now ready to begin.

5. Open the editor to start creating the document.

6. Type the text of what is to appear in your document. Add all information content at this time.

7. Use the pull-down menus or the macros to insert appropriate HTML tags to create the desired document elements.

8. Save the document in a file with the filename extension indicating that the file content is an HTML document. This extension is usually .html (or .htm).

WYSIWYG Style

1. Determine the development platform you wish to use.

2. Find an HTML editor that you wish to use. The following table gives examples of some of these environments by platform and pointers to information concerning them.

EDITOR/ENVIRONMENT	PLATFORM(S)	AVAILABILITY
HTML Editor	MAC	http://dragon.acadian.ca:1667/~giles/HTML_Editor/Documentation.html
GT_HTML.DOT	PC (Word for Windows)	http://www.gatech.edu/word_html/release.htm

2.3 CREATE HTML DOCUMENTS WITHOUT MANUALLY INSERTING TAGS

EDITOR/ENVIRONMENT	PLATFORM(S)	AVAILABILITY
Internet Assistant	PC (Word for Windows)	http://www.microsoft.com/pages/deskapps/word/ia/support.htm
tkWWW	UNIX	http://tk-www.mit.edu:8001/tk-www/help/

Review the materials suggested in the above table before making your final decision.

3. Retrieve the desired HTML editor from the location(s) suggested above.

4. Uncompress, unarchive, and install the software as and where necessary.

> **HTML** On a UNIX platform, use the uncompress and tar commands to respectively uncompress and unarchive the converter. These applications are provided with the operating system.

> **HTML** On a PC platform, the most common compression/archival program is ZIP. Use the unzip application to uncompress and unarchive the acquired converter. Several ZIP applications are available through PC ftp sites, BBSs, and users' groups.

> **HTML** On a Mac platform, the common compression/archival program is StuffIt. Use the StuffIt program to uncompress and unarchive the converter. The StuffIt program is available through a variety of Mac ftp sites, BBSs, and users' groups.

You are now ready to begin.

5. Open the HTML editor to start creating the document.

6. Use the menus and macros to format your document. Commands have an immediate impact upon the way the information looks. Insert the desired information. Select formatting and linking tags from the available pull-down menus, hotkeys, and macros.

7. Save the file with an appropriate filename extension indicating that the file is an HTML document.

How It Works

The above procedures explain the three types of editing environments used in developing HTML documents. Deciding which type to use is a question of weighing priorities.

Due to availability and familiarity, a text editor may be the easiest and quickest to use in developing documents; however, most text editors do not provide suitable support for HTML authors. This type of authoring requires the author to have a good working knowledge of HTML tags and syntax. The other two types of editing environments will require some HTML knowledge for fine tuning, but the

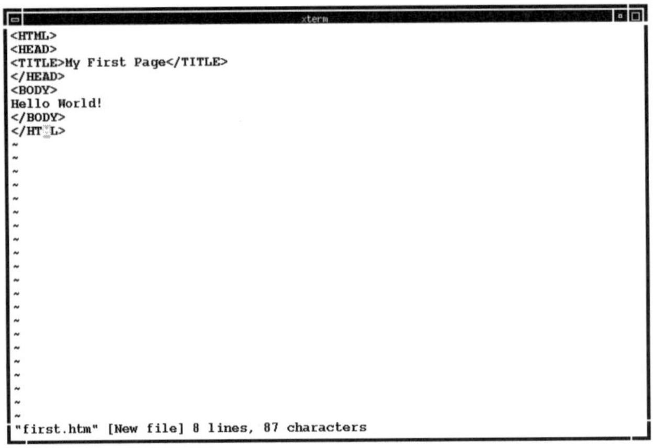

CHAPTER 2
HTML BASICS

```
<HTML>
<HEAD>
<TITLE>My First Page</TITLE>
</HEAD>
<BODY>
Hello World!
</BODY>
</HTML>
```

"first.htm" [New file] 8 lines, 87 characters

Figure 2-5 HTML document creation with a text editor

bulk of development and tag insertion can be handled by the environment; on the other hand, these tools are more difficult or more expensive to obtain. Figure 2-5 displays an example of a text editor editing environment.

With a pull-down menu/macro type environment, you mark blocks of text and provide formatting information. The way you format each block of text varies by editor. On the surface, this type of environment might seem ideal, since it requires minimal knowledge of HTML syntax while making it easy to insert appropriate formatting tags and rendering information. However, knowledge gained in this type of environment may not be portable. If you learn the macros and menu systems of a particular editor, that information may not apply in another authoring environment. Figure 2-6 shows an example of an environment of this type.

Finally, a WYSIWYG editor is useful because the document looks the same in development as it will when you are finished. However, unless the users accessing your documents are restricted to a particular browser application, the visible aspects of a document under development will not be as significant. Figure 2-7 shows such an environment.

For additional information about a particular editor or editing environment, refer to the documentation for the package in question. Table 2-1 lists the various applications and the location of available documentation.

EDITING PACKAGE	PLATFORM(S)	DOCUMENTATION
Alpha	MAC	http://ww.cs.umd.edu/~keleher/alpha.html
BBEdit-Lite	MAC	ftp://ftp.std.com/pub/bbedit/freeware/
		bbedit-lite-30.hqx
BBEdit Ext. 1	MAC	http://www.york.ac.uk/~ld11/BBEditTools.html

2.3 CREATE HTML DOCUMENTS WITHOUT MANUALLY INSERTING TAGS

EDITING PACKAGE	PLATFORM(S)	DOCUMENTATION
BBEdit Ext. 2	MAC	http://www.uji.es/bbedit-html-extensions.html
HTML Editor	MAC	http://dragon.acadian.ca:1667/~giles/HTML_Editor/Documentation.html
GT_HTML.DOT	PC (Word for Windows)	http://www.gatech.edu/word_html/release.htm
HTMLed	PC (Windows)	http://info.cern.ch/hypertext/WWW/Tools/HTMLed.html
Internet Assistant	PC (Word for Windows)	http://www.microsoft.com/pages/deskapps/word/ia/support.htm
emacs	UNIX, PC	within emacs, GNU archive sites
emacs HTML helper	UNIX, PC	http://www.santafe.edu/~nelson/tools/
vi	UNIX, PC	UNIX man pages and external references
tkHTML	UNIX	http://www.infosystems.com/tkHTML/tkHTML.html
tkWWW	UNIX	http://tk-www.mit.edu:8001/tk-www/help/

Table 2-1 Editor documentation

Comments

The term WYSIWYG (What You See Is What You Get) is definitely a misnomer when applied to any particular HTML editor. What you see as an author may be significantly different from what a user gets when he or she accesses your

Figure 2-6 HTML document creation with a macro/menu editor

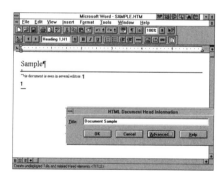

Figure 2-7 HTML document creation with a WYSIWYG editor

document. So any claim that an HTML editor is WYSIWYG should be viewed with caution. WYSIWYG features should not be discounted; however, you should still actively test your documents in a variety of browsers to guarantee that your document design carries through to most, if not all, viewing environments.

Furthermore, even though you use a "higher level" editor to abstract the lower level HTML syntax, a general knowledge of HTML is still useful for fine tuning documents. Many editor-generated documents could be improved through the judicious use of manual alterations made in a text editor.

Finally, many HTML 3 features have not been incorporated in any of the editors currently available. To include these features at this time, you must use a text editor. You can create a document in any of the environments; however, placement of level 3 elements is only possible if you manually insert them.

2.4 How do I... Convert word processed documents to HTML?

COMPLEXITY
EASY

COMPATIBILITY: HTML 2

Problem

I don't want to start authoring documents from scratch. I have already developed a whole bank of documents suitable for use on the World Wide Web using my word processor. Is there any way I can use these preexisting documents without having to recreate them using HTML?

Technique

Converters exist for a number of popular word processing packages. These converters accept word processor documents and generate appropriate HTML documents as output. This How-To provides step-by-step instructions for acquiring and applying an appropriate converter.

The process requires a familiarity with the use of anonymous ftp or ftp URLs. Your first task is the identification of an appropriate converter. Next, acquire the converter. Then apply the converter to your existing documents. Finally, fine tune your document in an HTML editing environment.

Steps

This procedure provides the necessary steps to acquire and use word processor document converters.

2.4
CONVERT WORD PROCESSED DOCUMENTS TO HTML

1. Determine the word processing application you used to develop your documents.

2. Find the converter you will need to use. The following table gives examples of some of these environments by software package and provides pointers to information concerning them. If you cannot find your particular word processor in the table below, you may wish to use a Web search application to find an applicable converter.

WORD PROCESSOR	CONVERTERS	AVAILABILITY
Word for Windows	rtftohtml	ftp://ftp.cray.com/src/WWWstuff/RTF
	rtftohtm	ftp://oak.oakland.edu/SimTel/msdos/windows3/html1060.zip
	Internet Assistant	http://www.microsoft.com/pages/deskapps/word/ia/support.htm
WordPerfect	WPTOHTML	ftp://oak.oakland.edu/SimTel/msdos/wordperf/wpt60d10.zip
	Wp2x	http://journal.biology.carleton.ca/pub/software/
FrameMaker	WebMaker	http://www.cern.ch/WebMaker/
	miftrans	ftp://ftp.alumni.caltech.edu/pub/mcbeath/web/miftran/
	frame2html	ftp://bang.nta.no/pub/

Table 2-2 Common word processor conversion applications

3. Use anonymous ftp or an ftp URL to acquire an appropriate converter package. Uncompress, unarchive, and install the converter application as appropriate for your platform.

 On a UNIX platform, use the uncompress and tar commands to uncompress and unarchive the converter.

 On a PC platform, the most common compression/archival program is ZIP. Use the unzip application to uncompress and unarchive the acquired converter.

 On a Mac platform, the common compression/archival program is StuffIt. Use the StuffIt program to uncompress and unarchive the converter.

4. Apply the converter to your word processed documents.

5. Use the process described in How-To 2.3 to fine tune the converted documents.

CHAPTER 2
HTML BASICS

How It Works

Many preexisting word processor documents may be suitable for use in the World Wide Web environment. Therefore, converter applications have been developed to take word processed documents and generate equivalent HTML documents from them. The first step in converting these documents is acquiring a suitable converter.

Several converters have been developed for this purpose. The table provided in step 2 provides references to several of them. Many commercial applications are also available.

Once the converter is installed, converting existing documents into HTML is just a matter of judiciously applying the converter application. This will lead to HTML documents that look the way they did within the word processing environment.

The final step of this procedure is to use an editing environment to fine tune the converted document. This fine tuning includes two parts: corrections and additions.

Corrections are sometimes necessary when the converter does not know how to deal with a particular type of formatting in the word processed file. These corrections may be performed using any of the authoring environment methods discussed in How-To 2.3.

Additions are also likely, since most word processors do not support hypertext linking. Links provide associative connections between HTML documents. These connections link a location in one document to a location within another document; HTML designates these locations using the anchor tags <A...>...</A>. Therefore, the addition of anchors to word processed documents is a common one. (See Chapter 7 for detailed information on the use of the anchor element.)

Further, you may also add logical elements, in contrast to purely physical elements, at your discretion. Word processors usually support the conversion of physical elements such as bold and italics (How-Tos 3.2 and 3.3); however, they do not support logical HTML elements such as strong and emphasis (How-To 3.8). Hence, desired logical elements need to be added after document conversion.

Finally, converters currently available do not support HTML level 3 elements. Inclusion of such elements involves editing the converted document using the methods described in How-To 2.3.

Converters are by no means perfect; therefore, remembering to perform this final step in the procedure is important. Simply taking the results of a conversion and asking your Web site administrator to install the documents may lead to disappointing results. Check your documents thoroughly in both Web browsers such as Mosaic and Netscape and HTML editing environments (as described in How-To 2.3).

2.5 CONVERT OTHER TYPES OF FILES TO HTML

Comments

The converters mentioned in this How-To are not necessarily a comprehensive list. They do represent a sampling of converters for many popular word processors. For converting documents developed in a word processor not mentioned in Table 2-2, you may wish to use any of the available Web search pages such as Lycos (http://lycos.cs.cmu.edu) or infoseek (http://www.infoseek.com).

Finally, not all converters are equal. Some commercially available products and contact information is provided in the following table.

PRODUCT	FORMATS	CONTACT
Cyberleaf	FrameMaker, Interleaf, Word, WordPerfect	Interleaf, Inc.
FasTag	FrameMaker, Interleaf, Word, WordPerfect	Avalanche Development
TagWrite	FrameMaker, Interleaf, Word, Ventura Publisher,	Zandar Corp
	WordPerfect	

2.5 How do I... Convert other types of files to HTML?

COMPLEXITY
EASY

COMPATIBILITY: HTML 2

Problem

I have developed my documents using a document formatting language. I want to use these documents on my Web site. How can I use these documents with minimal additional effort? I've already inserted my formatting information through my development language. All that I need is a way to transform that information into HTML.

Technique

Many documents have been developed through such formatting languages as PostScript, TeX, and troff. This How-To provides step-by-step instructions for acquiring and applying converters to such documents. These packages will accept documents developed in common formatting languages and generate appropriate HTML documents as output.

The process requires a familiarity with the use of anonymous ftp or ftp URLs. First, identify an appropriate converter. Next, acquire the converter. Then apply the converter to your existing documents. Finally, fine tune your document in an HTML editing environment.

Steps

The following steps are necessary to acquire and use document converters.

1. Determine the formatting language you used to develop your documents.
2. The following table shows examples of some of the available converters by document formatting language and provides pointers to information concerning them. Find the converter that you will need to use. You may wish to use a Web search page such as Lycos (http://lycos.cs.cmu.edu) to find an applicable converter if you need one for a document processing language not listed below.

FORMATTING LANGUAGE	CONVERTERS	AVAILABILITY
TeX/LaTeX/Texinfo	latex2html	http://cbl.leeds.ac.uk/nikos/tex2html/doc/latex2html/latext2html.html
	tex2rtf	ftp://skye.aiai.ed.ac.uk/pub/tex2rtf
	texi2html	ftp://src.doc.ic.ac.uk/computing/information-systems/www/tools/translator
troff	ms2html	http://cui_www.unige.ch/ftp/PUBLIC/oscar/scripts/
	mm2html	ftp://bells.s.ucl.ac.uk/darpa/
PostScript	ps2html	http://stasi.bradley.edu/ftp/pub/ps2html/ps2html-v2.html
Scribe	Scribe2html	ftp://gatekeeper.dec.com/pub/DEC/NSL/www/

Table 2-3 Common formatting language conversion applications

3. Use anonymous ftp or an ftp URL to acquire an appropriate converter package. Uncompress, unarchive, and install the converter application as appropriate for your platform.

    HTML On a UNIX platform, use the uncompress and tar commands to uncompress and unarchive the desired converter.

    HTML On a PC platform, the most common compression/archival program is ZIP. Use the unzip application to uncompress and unarchive the acquired converter.

    HTML On a Mac platform, the common compression/archival program is StuffIt. Use the StuffIt program to uncompress and unarchive the converter.

2.5 CONVERT OTHER TYPES OF FILES TO HTML

4. Apply the converter to your formatted documents.

5. Use the process described in How-To 2.3 to fine tune the converted documents.

How It Works

Many preexisting documents may be suitable for use in the World Wide Web environment. Therefore, applications have been developed to convert such formatted documents to equivalent HTML documents. The first step in this process is acquiring a suitable converter. Table 2-3 names and references several of them.

Most document formatting languages support a similar suite of formatting commands. The primary difference is the syntax of the language. Once the converter has been installed, it will map documents in the source formatting language to HTML documents.

The final step of this procedure is to fine tune the converted document using the editing facilities described in How-To 2.3. This fine tuning includes both additions and corrections.

Most converters will not add hypermedia links into your document. Since most document formatting languages such as PostScript and troff do not support hypertext links, links do not appear in documents of this type; consequently, direct translation of such documents will not include links. Any desired hypertext links need to be added by the author after conversion. Chapter 7 provides comprehensive information on link creation.

Despite their similarities, not all document formatting languages provide the same structuring and formatting elements. You may wish to add HTML elements to enhance the converted documents. For example, HTML supports logical elements as well as purely physical ones. The mark up for a bolded statement (How-To 3.2) might carry over with no problem; however, if you wish to specify emphasis elements (How-To 3.8) that will connote semantic as well as physical characteristics, you will have to add these by hand.

Corrections will sometimes be necessary when the converter does not know how to deal with a particular type of formatting element in the source document. The converter may generate either no element or an erroneous element in the HTML document. In either case, the document needs correction to maintain the desired formatting.

Comments

The list of converters mentioned in this How-To is not necessarily comprehensive. It does contain a sampling of converters for many popular document formatting languages. For converting documents developed with a formatting language not mentioned in Table 2-3, you may wish to use any of the available Web search engines.

As with word processor conversion programs, different converters support different inputs and outputs. Further, converters have varying degrees of success in

CHAPTER 2
HTML BASICS

maintaining formatting integrity. Prior to installing a converter on your server, you should view a document converted by it using several browsing packages to guarantee that your document looks the way you want it to look. For consistency, you may wish to compare this view to the appearance of the document in its original form.

Finally, basic elements can be automatically added to standard ASCII text files. One such program is asc2html. This application (reference ftp://src.doc.ic.ac.uk/computing/information-systems/www/tools/translators) will take a plain text file and generate an HTML document with a simple body containing the file's data within a <PRE> element. (See How-To 4.4 for information on the <PRE> element.) A title is inserted based upon the filename, and URLs in the data are converted into hypertext links.

2.6 How do I... Insert an HTML element?

COMPLEXITY
EASY

COMPATIBILITY: HTML

Problem

I want to build documents that will be used and usable. How do I structure my documents? How do I specify logical grouping within the information? How can I get browsers to render my documents with the appropriate formatting?

Technique

HTML uses elements to define document formatting and structuring. Document elements are created via tags. Elements are defined by an opening tag and, if necessary, a closing tag.

An opening tag is composed of an element name followed by an appropriate series of attribute/value pairs enclosed by a less than sign (<) and a greater than sign (>). Closing tags are similar to opening tags in that they mark one end of an element; however, they differ in terms of syntax. A closing tag will consist of an element name preceded by a slash (/). In addition, closing tags will not contain attribute/value lists.

Tagged elements follow four basic patterns:

HTML Empty element

```
<TAG>
```

HTML Empty element with attributes

54

2.6
INSERT AN HTML ELEMENT

```
<TAG ATTRIBUTE1="VALUE" ATTRIBUTE2="VALUE">
```

HTML Element with content

```
<TAG>
Enclosed Text
</TAG>
```

HTML Element with content and attributes

```
<TAG ATTRIBUTE1="VALUE" ATTRIBUTE2="VALUE">
Enclosed Text
</TAG>
```

Use an editing environment to add tags. The types of editing environments and the ways to acquire them for your development platform are described in How-To 2.3. The steps below indicate procedures for inserting tagged elements into your HTML documents through your editing environment. The insertion procedure is the same for all HTML elements.

Steps

Inserting tagged elements into HTML documents depends significantly upon the editing environment used to create the document. In a strictly text-based development environment, you insert all tags manually. With other editing environments, you add the tags through macros and/or menu usage provided by the software.

Either way, the resultant HTML document will have the appropriate elements included demarked by the appropriate tags.

1. Open the HTML document that you wish to edit in your favorite editing environment. (See How-To 2.3 on editing environments.)

2. Locate the position where you wish to add the desired element. If the element that you wish to add does not require any enclosed information (such as a horizontal rule described in How-To 4.1), go to step 3. Insert the text that will be enclosed between the opening and closing tags. An example of such a textual message is included in the code below.

```
This text should appear in bold.
```

3. If the desired tags cannot be inserted with macro or menu options, skip to step 5. To insert an empty element, proceed to step 4. Select the body text you wish to include in the element.

4. If the macros work through inserting opening and closing tags, follow the instructions in steps 5 and 6; however, when you are instructed to insert a tag manually, you should use the appropriate macro. Otherwise, use the appropriate macro or menu option to format the selected text as desired. So for the example text, the sentence would be highlighted, and the macro or menu option for bold would be selected. You are now ready to proceed to step 7.

5. Move your insertion point to where you wish the element to begin. Insert an opening tag at this location. The following code illustrates the insertion of an opening bold tag. (How-To 3.2 provides detailed information on the use of the bold tag.)

```
<B>This text should appear in bold.
```

To insert an empty element, just insert the opening tag and proceed to step 7.

6. Move your insertion point to the end of the enclosed text and insert a closing tag at this location. The following code illustrates the insertion of a closing bold tag.

```
<B>This text should appear in bold.</B>
```

7. Save your document and continue adding elements by returning to step 2.

How It Works

The final product of this process is an HTML document with appropriate elements added. HTML documents are based on ASCII text; therefore, you should be able to view them as simple text, independent of how they appear in your editing environment. Each element should appear as an opening and a closing tag surrounding appropriate content information.

The following examples show a variety of possible opening tags.

```
<B>
```

This tag simply indicates the beginning of a bold element. The content information appearing between the opening and closing tags appears as bold text when displayed by a browsing package such as Mosaic. (See How-To 3.2 for information on bold elements.)

```
<HR>
```

This tag indicates the placement of a horizontal rule (line). Elements such as this one that do not require a closing tag are often referred to as empty elements, since no content information is necessary. (See How-To 4.1 for information on the horizontal rule element.)

```
<META NAME="GENERATOR" CONTENT="Internet Assistant for Word ">
```

Finally, the above HTML code represents another type of empty element: the metainformation element. This element provides supportive information about the

2.6
INSERT AN HTML ELEMENT

document rather than a specific indication of how the document is presented. This element does not have content information in between opening and closing tags; however, information content is represented as attribute/value pairs contained within the opening tag itself. (See How-To 2.2 for information on the <META> element.)

Elements that are not empty are concluded with a closing tag. So for example, to close the bolding element <B>, the closing tag would appear as </B>.

In a text-based editing environment, all HTML tags must be inserted manually. When you want to include a particular element, you enclose the desired text with appropriate opening and closing tags.

In a macro/menu-based editing environment, tags, and consequently elements, are added to HTML documents through available macros and menu options. If elements are not supported by a particular editing environment, they may be added manually as described for purely text-based editors.

WYSIWYG editors handle tag insertion in a manner similar to the one used in a macro/menu-based environment; however, the tags for the elements may not be visible. Most character level elements will be rendered as appropriate for the element. Bold elements appear in bold rather than as <B>...</B> tags.

The addition of various elements may also be performed automatically by your editing environment. For example, a sample document developed using Microsoft's Internet Assistant will automatically have the <HTML>, <HEAD>, <BODY>, and several <META> elements included automatically. The code for the HTML document seen in Figure 2-8 was developed in this editing environment and appears below.

```
<HTML>
<HEAD>
<META NAME="GENERATOR" CONTENT="Internet Assistant for Word ">
<META NAME="BUILD" CONTENT="Feb 10 1995">
<META NAME="AUTHOR" CONTENT="">
<META NAME="CREATIM" CONTENT="1995:5:12:22:22:">
<META NAME="VERSION" CONTENT="1">
</HEAD>
<BODY>
<B>This text should appear as bold.</B>
</BODY>
</HTML>
```

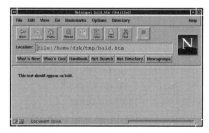

Figure 2-8 Document with bold tags inserted

CHAPTER 2
HTML BASICS

Comments

Most WYSIWYG and macro/menu editing environments currently support HTML level 2 elements. Level 3 elements and extensions require the use of a text editor and manual insertion. This situation will change as additional HTML editors are developed.

A reference to HTML 3 standard elements appears in Appendix A. The elements discussed in this How-To are delineated in the table below. The location field indicates the scope in which the element may appear.

ELEMENT	LOCATION	PURPOSE
<HTML>...</HTML>	file	Defines scope of an HTML document. How-To 2.1
<HEAD>...</HEAD>	HTML	Defines head of an HTML document. How-To 2.1
<META...>	HEAD	Supplies metainformation. How-To 2.2
<TITLE>...</TITLE>	HEAD	Defines the title of an HTML document. How-To 2.2
<BODY>...</BODY>	HTML	Defines body of an HTML document. How-To 2.8
<B>...</B>	BODY	This represents a bolded element. How-To 3.2
<HR>	BODY	Places a horizontal rule when displayed. How-To 4.1

2.7 How do I... Include a comment?

COMPLEXITY: EASY

COMPATIBILITY: HTML

Problem

I want information about my documents to be available to me or to future authors. I wish this information to be included in my HTML document; however, I don't want it displayed to every casual viewer of the document.

Technique

HTML allows authors to include comments that reside in the document yet do not appear when the document is rendered. The process involves the use of a construct similar to an opening tag. A comment can be viewed as a very specific type of logical element that has no visual representation to the common user.

The following procedure takes you through the process of creating comments within your HTML documents. Comments have two primary uses. First, they serve

2.7
INCLUDE A COMMENT

as a means for documenting design decisions you make while creating a document. Comments of this type become quite useful in the future for maintenance and modification. Second, certain applications will use "comments" to include additional application-specific information within an HTML document.

Steps

Comment element insertion is similar in many respects to the insertion of other logical elements. The following process steps through the insertion of comment elements using a typical editing environment that does not support comment inclusion via a macro or menu mechanism. If yours does, you should refer to the documentation for your particular editing environment.

1. Open the HTML document you wish to edit in your favorite editing environment (see How-To 2.3 on editing environments).

2. Locate the position where you wish to add your comment element.

3. Move your insertion point to this location.

4. Begin the comment tag by typing <.

```
<
```

5. The code for a comment continues with an exclamation point immediately following the < sign. The code for your comment should now appear as follows:

```
<!
```

6. The exclamation point is followed by two dashes. Insert these two dashes into your HTML document. No spaces should be placed between any of these characters.

```
<!--
```

7. Type the remainder of your comment. Do not include a > sign within the body of your comment, since this would be interpreted as the termination of your comment.

```
<!-- THIS IS A SAMPLE COMMENT
```

8. Your comment will be ended by a greater than sign preceded by two dashes. Spaces may appear between these two dashes and the closing >.

```
<!-- THIS IS A SAMPLE COMMENT -->
```

9. The comment has now been added to your document. You are now ready to save your HTML document and/or continue developing the document. If you wish to add further comments to this document, return to step 2 and proceed as before.

> Note: Comments cannot be nested. Also, comments can span multiple lines; however, this usage is not recommended in practice due to lack of support in many browsers. Below is an example of a multiline comment.
>
> ```
> <!--
>     This is a multiline comment. By definition it is valid
>     HTML 3; however, in practice, many viewers will
>     misinterpret it.
> -->
> ```

How It Works

The addition of comments to documents that you are developing is generally considered a good practice. For simple, self-explanatory documents, comments may not be necessary, but for more complex documents, comments are not only desirable but necessary.

HTML provides for comments by specifying an appropriate construct for their inclusion. Comments appear as similar to standard HTML tags. In this way, applications scanning HTML documents can easily identify comments and treat them appropriately.

Comments are similar in structure to HTML opening tags. (For additional information on opening tags, see How-To 2.6.) The comment is enclosed in < and > signs. The first character after the less than sign is an exclamation point (!). Two dashes immediately follow the exclamation point. This string indicates the beginning of a comment.

A comment is terminated by two dashes followed by the greater than sign. Spaces may appear between the dashes and the terminating >. You may place the text of your comment within these stated bounds. Some example comments and explanations are provided below.

```
<!-- This is a sample of a valid comment. -- >
```

This is a standard comment style. You should note that the space after the final pair of dashes does not alter the comment status.

```
<!--
    This is a multiline comment. By definition it is valid
    HTML 3; however, in practice, many viewers will misinterpret
    it.
-->
```

2.7
INCLUDE A COMMENT

The example HTML segment above represents a multiline comment. Many viewers do not handle this type of comment appropriately. A better practice would be to use the following HTML segment.

```
<!-- This is a multiline comment. By definition it is valid -->
<!-- HTML 3; however, in practice, many viewers will misinterpret -->
<!-- it. -->
```

This version will work with any viewer that supports comments, whereas the first may fail with some browsing programs.

```
<!-- Commented HTML tags are often <B>misinterpreted</B> -->
```

Finally, you should not attempt use comment syntax to surround existing HTML elements. The example code above will be misinterpreted by most browser applications and yield undesirable effects. A better approach to making the desired text a comment appears in the following HTML segment.

```
<!-- Commented HTML tags are often --><!-- B --><!-- misinterpreted --><!--
/B-->
```

This comment will be handled appropriately. To comment existing HTML tags, you must carefully examine the code being commented in each case.

Figure 2-9 shows how the comments that appear in the following HTML code might be rendered. Note that this browsing and editing environment handles the multiline comment; however, it interprets that "commented" tag for a bold element as the termination of the comment.

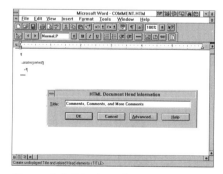

Figure 2-9 Display of comments document

```
<HTML>
<HEAD>
<TITLE>Comments, Comments, and More Comments</TITLE>
</HEAD>
<BODY>
<!-- This is a sample of a valid comment. -- >
```

continued on next page

CHAPTER 2
HTML BASICS

continued from previous page

```
<!--
    This is a multiline comment. By definition it is valid
    HTML 3; however, in practice, many viewers will misinterpret
    it.
-->
<!-- Commented HTML tags are often <B>misinterpreted</B> -->
</BODY>
</HTML>
```

Comments

Comments are not treated equally by various application programs. Some browsers ignore comments completely. Others treat them as potential directives or even as document content, depending on how the comment was entered. Some browsers may have a particularly difficult time with multiline comments.

Several applications use specially tailored comments for application-specific tasks. NCSA server side includes discussed in How-To 12.2 are an example of one such usage. Another example is the internal tracking of documents by Microsoft's Internet Assistant. This application automatically inserts specially tailored comments to track documents created within its environment.

A reference to HTML 3 standard elements appears in Appendix A. The elements discussed in this How-To are delineated in the table below. The location field indicates the scope in which the element may appear.

ELEMENT	LOCATION	PURPOSE
<HTML>...</HTML>	file	Defines scope of an HTML document. How-To 2.1
<!--...-->	HTML	An HTML comment element. How-To 2.7
<HEAD>...</HEAD>	HTML	Defines head of an HTML document. How-To 2.1
<TITLE>...</TITLE>	HEAD	Defines the title of an HTML document. How-To 2.2
<BODY>...</BODY>	HTML	Defines body of an HTML document. How-To 2.8
<B>...</B>	BODY	This represents a bolded element. How-To 3.2

COMPLEXITY
EASY

2.8 How do I... Add body text?

COMPATIBILITY: HTML, HTML 3 (BODY ATTRIBUTES)

Problem

I want to add content to my HTML document. Where do I put this information? And what limitations are there on this information?

2.8
ADD BODY TEXT

Technique

The <BODY> element represents the information content of an HTML document. This element defines the portion of your document that includes all information that will be rendered in a browser's display area.

Such content can be composed of any valid nested elements plus any pure text you wish to include. This following procedure provides a step-by-step description for creating the meat of your HTML document.

Steps

The basic tasks involved in beginning development of HTML document information content are given below. The procedure as outlined assumes that you are using a simple text-based editor to author your HTML document.

If this is not the case, you can tailor the procedure by ignoring steps that are handled implicitly by your environment. For example, if your environment automatically creates the <BODY> element, you can skip the step involving insertion of the <BODY> tag. You will need to reference the documentation for your particular editing environment to make such judgments.

1. Open the HTML document you wish to edit in your favorite editing environment. (See How-To 2.3 on editing environments.)

2. Locate the position where you wish to begin adding content. This location will vary depending upon your editing environment. In a text editor, this location is inside the scope of the <HTML> element and after the <HEAD> element.

3. Move your insertion point to this location.

4. If your document already contains a <BODY> element, proceed to step 5. Begin the content portion by inserting a <BODY> opening tag. You will begin your comment with the code below.

```
<BODY>
```

This opening tag may have several attribute/value pairs associated with it; the How It Works section below describes these pairs.

5. You are now ready to write the body of your HTML document. Enter any desired text and legal elements in the locations desired within the <BODY> element. Make any necessary corrections or additions. In Figure 2-10, the highlighted information represents the content added at this step in a text editor (Notepad). If you are creating this <BODY> element for the first time in this document, proceed with step 6; otherwise, continue with step 7.

6. End the body components of your HTML document with a <BODY> closing tag. This will end your <BODY> element.

```
</BODY>
```

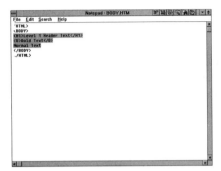

Figure 2-10 Content information example

> Note: Keep in mind while editing that carriage returns in an HTML document do not necessarily imply a carriage return in the rendered document. Spaces and carriage returns in the text of the BODY element are largely ignored when displayed by browsers; therefore, if spaces or carriage returns are desired, you will need to use appropriate HTML elements to force them. (See Chapter 3.)

7. You have now successfully added the <BODY> element of your HTML document. Save your document.

How It Works

The HTML <BODY> element represents the information content of your document. When you add or modify content, you alter this element.

A <BODY> opening tag may contain a list of attribute/value pairs associated with the <BODY> element. The following list describes the valid attributes and their potential values.

HTML ID="string"

The ID attribute associates an identifier with the <BODY> element. Style effects and hypertext links may use this value for addressing purposes. The value must be unique within the scope of the HTML document.

HTML LANG="aa.bb"

The LANG attribute defines the language standard used within the context of the <BODY> element. The value is composed of two period-separated components: the two-letter abbreviation for the language and the two-letter abbreviation for the country variation. For example, LANG="en.uk" would indicate that the <BODY> element content should use the conventions associated with the English language as used in the United Kingdom.

2.8
ADD BODY TEXT

HTML **CLASS="string"**
This attribute associates a class name with the <BODY> element. Searches and styles may make use of this class information.

HTML **BACKGROUND="image"**
This attribute associates an image that serves as the background for the information in the <BODY> element. The value is the location of the image.

A <BODY> element can contain any desired textual information as well as any element allowed within the scope of a <BODY> element. When you add text and elements to HTML documents, you are assumed to be in fill mode. The effect of this is that all text and many elements you enter will appear contiguously in the rendered document. Some nested elements cause a carriage return in the rendered document while others do not. Issues of spacing in document presentation are covered more deeply in Chapter 4.

Each HTML document can have at most one <BODY> element. If all information can be contained within a document's <HEAD> element, then the <BODY> component is not required.

For example, Figure 2-11 shows a document containing several nested elements as well as a single line of straight text. (See How-To's 3.1 and 3.2 for information on the heading <H1> and bold <B> elements, respectively.)

The full HTML code for this document appears below.

```
<HTML>
<HEAD>
<TITLE>Figure 2-11: Document with Content Information</TITLE>
</HEAD>
<BODY>
<H1>Level 1 Header Text</H1>
<B>Bold Text</B>
Normal Text
</BODY>
</HTML>
```

Compare the above code with Figure 2-11. Note that the carriage returns in the HTML code and the rendered document do not match. This is due to the way the browser interprets the level 1 heading element and the bold element. According to the viewer in Figure 2-11, a heading 1 element implies a carriage return in the rendered output while a bold element does not.

Comments

This section introduces the basics of creating information content. Methods of including links, images, tables, lists, and other elements are clearly described in other portions of this book. The following table provides a quick reference to these locations.

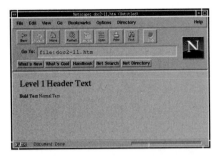

Figure 2-11 Document with content information

INFORMATION TYPE	REFERENCE
Aligned text	How-To 2.10
Character effects	Chapter 3
Comments	How-To 2.7
Images	Chapter 8
Links	Chapter 7
Lists	Chapter 6
Math symbols and effects	How-To 5.1
Multimedia objects	Chapter 9
Special characters	How-To 2.9
Tables	Chapter 5

A reference to the tags specified in the HTML 3 standard appears in Appendix A. The elements discussed in this How-To are delineated in the table below. The location field indicates the scope in which the element may appear.

ELEMENT	LOCATION	PURPOSE
<HTML>...</HTML>	file	Defines scope of an HTML document. How-To 2.1
<!--...-->	HTML	An HTML comment element. How-To 2.7
<HEAD>...</HEAD>	HTML	Defines head of an HTML document. How-To 2.1
<TITLE>...</TITLE>	HEAD	Defines the title of an HTML document. How-To 2.2
<BODY>...</BODY>	HTML	Defines body of an HTML document. How-To 2.1
<B>...</B>	BODY	This represents a bolded element. How-To 3.2.
<H1>...</H1>	BODY	Level 1 heading element. How-To 3.1

2.9 How do I... Insert special characters into a document?

COMPLEXITY: INTERMEDIATE

COMPATIBILITY: HTML, NETSCAPE

Problem

I would like to use characters in my documents that are interpreted as HTML code. Not only that, I would like to include some words from a variety of languages. HTML supports the ISO Latin 1 character set, but my editing environment does not. How do I include these characters?

Technique

Any ISO Latin 1 character can be specified in an HTML document. HTML provides two reference types for including characters.

- **HTML** Character references—Any character can be included through the use of its ISO Latin 1 character code.

- **HTML** Entity references—Some frequently used characters have been assigned mnemonics. These characters can be included by specifying the appropriate mnemonic.

Steps

The following steps will allow you to insert special characters into your HTML documents. For character codes and entity references of specific special characters, refer to Table 2-4.

1. Open the HTML document you wish to edit in your favorite text editor. (See How-To 2.3 on HTML editing environments.)

2. Locate the position where you wish to insert a special character in the text. This location varies depending upon your editor. In a text editor, this location is usually within the document's BODY element.

3. Move your insertion point to this location.

4. Enter an ampersand (&) at this point in the code.

&

5. Follow the ampersand with either a character reference or an entity reference. (Refer to Table 2-4.) If you use a character reference, the ampersand is

followed by a pound symbol (#), followed by the decimal code for the desired character. If you use an entity reference, the ampersand is followed by the mnemonic for the character that you wish to insert.

```
&#38
&amp
```

6. Finally, end the reference with a semicolon. The following sample code indicates the inclusion of two ampersands in the rendered HTML document.

```
&#38;
&amp;
```

7. Save your document or continue editing.

How It Works

By using either a character or entity reference, you can enter any ISO Latin 1 character into an HTML document. Many platforms do not support the full ISO Latin character set; therefore, HTML provides these two methods for including unsupported characters. Table 2-4 provides a list of ISO Latin characters beyond U.S. ASCII as well as those characters that hold particular significance in HTML.

CHARACTER	CODE	ENTITY REFERENCE	COMMENT
"	34	&quot;	HTML code
&	38	&amp;	HTML code
<	60		HTML code
>	62	&gt;	HTML code
¡	161		
¢	161		
£	163		
¤	164		
¥	165		
¦	166		
§	167		
¨	168		
©	169	&copy;	Netscape support
ª	170		
«	171		
¬	172		
	173		
®	174	&reg;	Netscape support

2.9
INSERT SPECIAL CHARACTERS INTO A DOCUMENT

CHARACTER	CODE	ENTITY REFERENCE	COMMENT
¯	175		
°	176		
±	177		
²	178		
³	179		
´	180		
µ	181		
¶	182		
·	183		
¸	184		
¹	185		
º	186		
»	187		
¼	188		
½	189		
¾	190		
¿	191		
À	192	&Agrave;	
Á	193	&Aacute;	
Â	194	&Acirc;	
Ã	195	&Atilde;	
Ä	196	&Auml;	
Å	197	&Aring;	
Æ	198	&AElig;	
Ç	199	&Ccedil;	
È	200	&Egrave;	
É	201	&Eacute;	
Ê	202	&Ecirc;	
Ë	203	&Euml;	
Ì	204	&Igrave;	
Í	205	&Iacute;	
Î	206	&Icirc;	
Ï	207	&Iuml;	
Ð	208		
Ñ	209	&Ntilde;	
Ò	210	&Ograve;	

continued on next page

continued from previous page

CHARACTER	CODE	ENTITY REFERENCE	COMMENT
Ó	211	&Oacute;	
Ô	212	&Ocirc;	
Õ	213	&Otilde;	
Ö	214	&Ouml;	
×	215		
Ø	216	&Oslash;	
Ù	217	&Ugrave;	
Ú	218	&Uacute;	
Û	219	&Ucirc;	
Ü	220	&Uuml;	
Ý	221	&Yacute;	
Þ	222	&THORN;	
ß	223	&szlig;	
à	224	&agrave;	
á	225	&aacute;	
â	226	&acirc;	
ã	227	&atilde;	
ä	228	&auml;	
å	229	&aring;	
æ	230	&aelig;	
ç	231	&ccedil;	
è	232	&egrave;	
é	233	&eacute;	
ê	234	&ecirc;	
ë	235	&euml;	
ì	236	&igrave;	
í	237	&iacute;	
î	238	&icirc;	
ï	239	&iuml;	
ð	240	&eth;	
ñ	241	&ntilde;	
ò	242	&ograve;	
ó	243	&oacute;	
ô	244	&ocirc;	
õ	245	&otilde;	
ö	246	&ouml;	

2.9
INSERT SPECIAL CHARACTERS INTO A DOCUMENT

CHARACTER	CODE	ENTITY REFERENCE	COMMENT
÷	247		
ø	248	&oslash;	
ù	249	&ugrave;	
ú	250	&uacute;	
û	251	&ucirc;	
ü	252	&uuml;	
ý	253	&yacute;	
þ	254	&thorn;	
ÿ	255	&yuml;	

Table 2-4 ISO Latin 1 character set—special characters and beyond ASCII

Figure 2-12 shows these special ASCII characters—quotes, ampersand, greater than, and less than. These characters hold a particular significance in HTML. The quotes symbol is used to delimit attribute values. The ampersand is used to indicate a character or entity reference, and the greater than and less than signs are used to delimit HTML tags. A special entity is required for a nonbreaking space to differentiate it from a normal space. Both types of space are character code 32; however, a nonbreaking space implies that the text around the space should not be broken between lines.

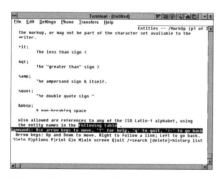

Figure 2-12 Special ASCII characters

HTML 3 also provides entity references for several non–ISO Latin 1 characters, such as the nonbreaking space. Table 2-5 outlines these entities.

CHARACTER	ENTITY REFERENCE	COMMENTS
Baseline dots	&ldots;	Three dots on the baseline
Center dots	&cdots;	Three dots on same level as a minus sign

continued on next page

continued from previous page

CHARACTER	ENTITY REFERENCE	COMMENTS
Diagonal dots	&ddots;	Diagonal dots (top left to bottom right)
Dot fill	&dotfill;	Center dots filling column in an array
Em dash	&emdash;	Dash length of an em space
Em space		Space size of point size of current spot
En dash	&endash;	Dash the length of an en space
En space		Space size of half the point size
Large space	&quad;	Huge space
Medium space	&sp;	Medium space
Nonbreaking space		ASCII 32, but with nonbreaking caveat
Thin space		Thin space
Vertical dots	&vdots;	Three vertical dots
Alpha	&alpha;	alpha
Beta	&beta;	beta
Gamma	&gamma;	gamma
Delta	&delta;	delta
Epsilon	&epsilon;	epsilon
Var Epsilon	&vepsilon;	var epsilon
Zeta	&zeta;	zeta
Eta	&eta;	eta
Theta	&theta;	theta
Iota	&iota;	iota
Kappa	&kappa;	kappa
Lambda	&lambda;	lambda
Mu	&mu;	mu
Nu	&nu;	nu
Xi	&xi;	xi
Omicron	&omicron;	omicron
Pi	&pi;	pi
Var Pi	&varpi;	var pi
Rho	&rho;	rho
Var Rho	&varrho;	var rho
Sigma	&sigma;	sigma
Var Sigma	&vsigma;	var sigma
Tau	&tau;	tau
Upsilon	&upsilon;	upsilon
Phi	&phi;	phi

CHARACTER	ENTITY REFERENCE	COMMENTS
Var Phi	&varphi;	var phi
Chi	&chi;	chi
Psi	&psi;	psi
Omega	&omega;	omega

 Table 2-5 Entity references for non–ISO Latin 1 Characters

In either situation, special characters and non-ASCII characters can be included in HTML documents through the use of character or entity references. When a browser detects an ampersand in your HTML code, it interprets the semicolon-terminated value that follows as a reference. If the first character beyond the ampersand is a pound symbol, the value is taken as a character reference; therefore, when the document is rendered, the character indicated by the code is drawn. Otherwise, the value is taken to be an entity reference. The browser maps this reference to the appropriate character.

Comments

Some browsers may understand different entity references than others. Further, browsers may also limit which references are supported. For example, certain text-based browsers may not support non-ASCII characters of any kind.

2.10 How do I... Align text?

COMPATIBILITY: HTML 3, NETSCAPE

Problem

I would like to control the horizontal spacing in my document. I want to be able to specify where I want items to appear, and whether the items are centered, left justified, or right justified. With HTML 3, how can I specify this type of formatting information?

Technique

There are two ways to specify horizontal alignment of text.

> **HTML** Center element—This element is an HTML extension understood by the Netscape Navigator browser application. A center element

is added like any other element. Use the procedure defined in How-To 2.6.

HTML Tab elements—Tab elements are used to establish horizontal tabs in your HTML document. Since tabs are part of the HTML 3 specification, they are more likely to be understood and rendered than a center element.

Steps

Use the following steps to set and use tabs within an HTML document. These tabs enable you to align text within the body of your HTML documents.

1. Open the HTML document you wish to edit in your favorite text editor. (See How-To 2.3 on editing environments.) If your HTML editor allows you to create <TAB> elements with macro or menu options, follow the instructions for the editor.

> Note: Even if your editor supports tabs in documents, it may not support HTML <TAB> elements. Do not assume that the tabs in your editing environment equate to <TAB> elements in your saved HTML document. Check your editor's documentation, or test your editor by examining a saved HTML document.

2. Place the insertion point where you wish to place the <TAB> element within your document.

3. Insert the appropriate <TAB> element in your document. <TAB> elements are empty and therefore do not require a closing tag. Use the following table to select the proper <TAB> element for your use.

TAB ELEMENT FORMAT	PURPOSE
<TAB ID="name">	Sets a tab at the current location default aligned left
<TAB ID="name" ALIGN="alignment">	Sets a tab with a particular alignment
<TAB TO="name">	Jumps to the specified tab location
<TAB INDENT=x>	Indents x en spaces
<TAB ALIGN="right">	Places remainder of the line flush right
<TAB ALIGN="center">	Centers text between margins
<TAB ALIGN="left">	Places text flush to the left

4. Save your document or continue editing. If you wish to add additional <TAB> elements, return to step 2.

2.10
ALIGN TEXT

How It Works

You can align text horizontally with tabs. The <TAB> element supports the followng attributes:

- **HTML** ALIGN="alignment"
  This specifies the alignment of the tab. This attribute has one of four values: "left", "right", "center", and "decimal". These values determine how text is situated with respect to the tab.

- **HTML** DP="c"
  This attribute specifies the character to be used by a decimal tab to align text. The default value is the period. However, if you wished to align a tab with another character, you would include this attribute with the desired tab character as a value. For example, if you included DP="$" in the <TAB> opening tag, the tab would align along the dollar sign.

- **HTML** ID="name"
  This associates a name with a specific horizontal tab location. You can use the value associated with ID as the value of a TO attribute. In effect, using the ID attribute sets a tab at the named location. See the examples provided below.

- **HTML** INDENT="x"
  This allows the specification of a leading indent. The integer value associated with this attribute specifies the number of en spaces to indent a particular line. This attribute should not be used in conjunction with a TO attribute.

- **HTML** TO="name"
  Like ID, this takes a name as a value. The value indicates the horizontal position for the browser to tab forward to before rendering the text.

To indent several lines of text, use a <TAB> element with the INDENT attribute set. For example, the following code indents the specified line 5 en spaces. The <BR> element is used to force a line break at the location where the element appears. (See How-To 4.3 for further information on the line break element.)

```
This line has no indentation.<BR>
<TAB INDENT=5>This line is indented 5 en spaces.
```

The resulting text looks like this:

```
This line has no indentation.
     This line is indented 5 en spaces.
```

CHAPTER 2
HTML BASICS

Use a <TAB> element with an ID attribute to set tab locations. If you want a tab stop with other than left alignment, use the ALIGN attribute to specify the alignment. For example, use the following code to specify a left-aligned tab after the word "bear." The second line represents a line indented right below the first.

```
We will watch the bear <TAB ID="bear"> walk through<BR>
<TAB TO="bear> the woods and take joy in this delight.
```

This would be rendered by browsers as follows:

```
We will watch the bear walk through
                      the woods and take joy in this delight.
```

If you use the ALIGN attribute without a TO attribute, the tab overrides the default alignment with respect to the margins of the page. If no paragraph elements are used, then this default alignment is left. If paragraph elements are used, you can set a default alignment for a particular paragraph using the same ALIGN attribute values as specified for a tab. (See How-To 4.3 for further information on the paragraph element.)

```
<P ALIGN="center">
This line is centered.<BR>
So is this one.<BR>
<TAB ALIGN="left">This one is left justified.<BR>
Back to center.
```

This would appear in a browser as shown below.

```
                    This line is centered.
                       So is this one.
This one is left justified.
                        Back to center.
```

If you use a <TAB> element with both an ALIGN attribute and a TO attribute, the text following the tab is placed at the tab stop identified as the TO value and aligned as specified in the ALIGN value. The DP attribute allows you to define the character to align around. The default is the decimal point.

```
I will set my <TAB ID="here"> at this point.<BR>
<TAB ALIGN="decimal" TO="here">$500.00<BR>
<TAB ALIGN="decimal" TO="here">$1000.00<BR>
<TAB ALIGN="decimal" TO="here">approx $50.00
```

These lines appear as shown below.

```
I will set my at this point.
              $500.00
             $1000.00
         approx $50.00
```

The tab in this case is aligned around the decimal point.

2.10
ALIGN TEXT

Figure 2-13 HTML 3 centered paragraph

The Netscape <CENTER> element works in a manner similar to the paragraph alignment in HTML 3. The primary difference between the two uses is that the Netscape <CENTER> element can be used within the scope of a paragraph element to override the default paragraph alignment. The HTML code for the document shown in Figure 2-13 is as follows:

HTML HTML 3

```
<HTML>
<HEAD>
<TITLE>Centered Text</TITLE>
</HEAD>
<BODY>
<P ALIGN="center">
This line is centered.<BR>
So is this one.<BR>
</BODY>
</HTML>
```

HTML Netscape

```
<HTML>
<HEAD>
<TITLE>Centered Text</TITLE>
</HEAD>
<BODY>
<CENTER>
This line is centered.<BR>
So is this one.
</CENTER>
</BODY>
</HTML>
```

Comments

A more complete discussion of the paragraph element is provided in How-To 4.3. This element can be used to establish the default horizontal alignment for a block of lines.

CHAPTER 2
HTML BASICS

A reference of HTML 3 standard elements appears in Appendix A. The elements discussed in this How-To are listed in the table below. The location field indicates the scope in which the element may appear.

ELEMENT	LOCATION	PURPOSE
<HTML>...</HTML>	file	Defines scope of an HTML document. How-To 2.1
<HEAD>...</HEAD>	HTML	Defines head of an HTML document. How-To 2.1
<TITLE>...</TITLE>	HEAD	Defines the title. How-To 2.2
<BODY>...</BODY>	HTML	Defines body of document. How-To 2.8
<B>...</B>	BODY	Bolding. How-To 3.2
 	BODY	Line break. How-To 4.3
<CENTER>...</CENTER>	BODY	Netscape Center Text
<P...>	BODY	Paragraph. How-To 4.3
<TAB...>	BODY	Establish horizontal tabs

COMPLEXITY
EASY

2.11 How do I... Change font size?

COMPATIBILITY: HTML 3, NETSCAPE

Problem

I know alternate font sizes are not supported by all browser applications; however, I think that I need to include different-sized fonts in my documents. Most of the users accessing my documents will have browsers capable of rendering these fonts.

Technique

Font changes are accomplished with elements that specify that the enclosed text should be rendered using a different font size.

Two procedures for accomplishing this task are provided below. The first method describes the use of the elements proposed in the HTML 3 standard. The second process describes the use of the font change elements supported by the Netscape viewer.

Steps

The procedures below provide step-by-step instructions for changing the font size used to render portions of HTML documents. The first process uses HTML 3, and the second uses Netscape's HTML extensions.

2.11
CHANGE FONT SIZE

The process assumes that you are using a text editor to perform your modification tasks. If you are not, you should check the documentation for your particular editing environment.

HTML 3

1. Open the HTML document you wish to edit in your favorite text editor.
2. Locate the position where you want to change the font size in your document. Move your insertion point to this location.
3. Insert the appropriate opening tag for the desired font change element in your document. If you wish to use a larger font, insert a <BIG> tag; if you wish to use a smaller font, insert a <SMALL> tag. The example below starts an element for including text in a larger font.

```
<BIG>
```

4. Insert the text that you wish to appear in this font size.

```
This text will appear in a larger font.
```

5. End the font change element with the appropriate closing tag.

```
</BIG>
```

6. Save your document or continue editing. If you wish to add additional font change elements return to step 2.

Netscape HTML Extension

1. Open the HTML document you wish to edit in your favorite text editor.
2. The Netscape HTML extensions provide an element for establishing the default font for a document. If this element is not included, the default size of three is used. If you do not wish to change this, proceed with step 3. To change the base font size of your document, include a <BASEFONT> element. This element changes the default font for the remainder of the <BODY> element. The <BASEFONT> element uses a SIZE attribute to designate the default font size. This size can range from values of 1 to 7, where 1 represents the smallest font and 7 the largest. So to set a base font size of 5 throughout the document, include the element appearing in the following code.

```
<BASEFONT SIZE="5">
```

3. Move your insertion point to the position in your document where you want to change the font size.

4. Insert the appropriate opening tag for the desired font change. Insert a <FONT...> tag with the SIZE attribute set to either the absolute size you desire the font to be or a relative size indicated with a plus or minus sign as the first character followed by an increment or decrement value respectively. A relative value is taken as a modification of the base font size of the document. The example below starts a tag for including text in a font two sizes larger than the base font.

```
<FONT SIZE="+2">
```

5. Insert the text that you wish to appear in this font size.

```
This text will appear in a larger font.
```

6. End the font change element with the appropriate closing tag.

```
</FONT>
```

7. Save your document or continue editing. If you wish to add additional font change elements return to step 3.

How It Works

Both the HTML 3 standards committee and the developers of Netscape have defined HTML elements to allow the specification of font size information. The general approach is similar: both use new elements that will indicate that the enclosed text should be rendered using a font size other than the standard.

Currently, only the Netscape Navigator browser supports the use of their extension; the HTML 3 elements are supported by HTML 3 compliant browsers. The support for font size modifications varies in different HTML editors, so you should check the relevant documentation for your particular editor to determine which type of font change elements are supported, if any.

When a browser encounters a font size element, the text enclosed within the element is rendered using the font size specified by the tag. The text surrounding the element is displayed using the font size established for the document as a whole.

Figures 2-14 and 2-15 show the use of several different font sizes. The HTML code for the document appearing in Figure 2-14 appears below.

```
<HTML>
<HEAD>
<TITLE>Figure 2-14 HTML 3 font size elements</TITLE>
</HEAD>
<BODY>
<BIG>
This is big.<BR>
</BIG>
```

2.11
CHANGE FONT SIZE

```
This is regular.<BR>
<SMALL>
This is small.
</SMALL>
</BODY>
</HTML>
```

Figure 2-14 HTML 3 font size elements

Figure 2-15 Netscape viewer font size support

The following code generates the document rendered with the Netscape viewer seen in Figure 2-15.

```
<HTML>
<HEAD>
<TITLE>Figure 2-15 Netscape viewer font size support</TITLE>
</HEAD>
<BODY>
<FONT SIZE=7>
This is big.<BR>
</FONT>
This is regular.<BR>
<FONT SIZE=1>
This is small.
</FONT>
</BODY>
</HTML>
```

The actual fonts associated with <BIG>/<SMALL> elements and Netscape sizes is left to the discretion of the particular browsing environment.

Comments

Many HTML editors do not as yet support HTML 3 standards. Therefore, most font size changes will not be visible in some WYSIWYG type editors. For more information on editing environments see How-To 2.3.

A reference to the tags specified in the HTML 3 standard appears in Appendix A. The elements discussed in this How-To are listed in the table below. The location field indicates the scope in which the element may appear.

ELEMENT	LOCATION	PURPOSE
<HTML>...</HTML>	file	Defines scope of an HTML document. How-To 2.1
<HEAD>...</HEAD>	HTML	Defines head of an HTML document. How-To 2.1
<TITLE>...</TITLE>	HEAD	Defines the title of an HTML document. How-To 2.2
<BODY>...</BODY>	HTML	Defines body of an HTML document. How-To 2.1
<BASEFONT...>	BODY	Netscape specification of document font size
<BIG>...</BIG>	BODY	Renders enclosed text in big relative font size
 	BODY	Line break. How-To 4.3.
<FONT...>...</FONT>	BODY	Netscape renders enclosed text in font size specified
<SMALL>...</SMALL>	BODY	Renders enclosed text in small relative font size

2.12 How do I... Create a home page?

COMPLEXITY
EASY

COMPATIBILITY: HTML

Problem

I know some of the HTML basics, and I want to create a home page to provide information about myself to the World Wide Web community. I don't need anything very fancy just yet, but I would like to create and install a functional home page.

Technique

The home page creation process is very similar to the creation process defined in How-To 2.2. Use the same document structure as that developed for any other HTML 3 document, with a few additional elements included to mark the various sections.

Create the document with several sections. Create a contact information area, a bio area, and a modification date area. These areas will be separated by horizontal rules.

Steps

The following leads you through the creation of a single HTML document titled "Home Page of John Q. Public." This document will serve as your business card in the World Wide Web community.

2.12
CREATE A HOME PAGE

This process assumes that you are using a normal text editor to create your document. If you use a different editor, some of the steps outlined may not be necessary; be sure to check the documentation for your particular editor to determine which steps apply.

1. Change directories to the location where you wish to develop your HTML document. Open a file in your editor. (See How-To 2.3 on editing environments.) Be sure to choose a filename with the extension indicating an HTML document to your browser.

```
edit homepage.htm
```

2. Begin with an <HTML> opening tag. Enter the following line in your document.

```
<HTML>
```

3. Indicate that you are beginning the header area of the document by issuing a <HEAD> opening tag. The following line should appear next in your document. The <HEAD> element must appear within the scope of an <HTML> tag.

```
<HEAD>
```

4. The <TITLE> element indicates the title of an HTML document. Place <TITLE> tags in the header component of a document. Place the document title between the opening and closing <TITLE> tags. Add this title element to your document. Substitute your name for John's below.

```
<TITLE>Home Page of John Q. Public</TITLE>
```

This element is required. Many browsers use this information to generate and display the title of the document. If you omit this element, browsers that require strict HTML adherence may not display your document.

5. To end the head area, issue a <HEAD> closing tag.

```
</HEAD>
```

6. At this point, the body of the document needs to be developed. A <BODY> opening tag is used to indicate that this point has been reached. Enter the following line of code.

```
<BODY>
```

7. The body of your document consists of three components. The first part includes your contact information. You may wish to provide less or more information than the sample code below as determined by your needs.

CHAPTER 2
HTML BASICS

```
<!-- Mark the beginning of this portion with a horizontal rule. -->
<HR>
<!-- Center your name as a level 1 header. -->
<H1 ALIGN="center">John Q. Public</H1>
<!-- Provide any desirable contact information. -->
999 Peachtree St.<BR>
Atlanta, GA 30314<BR>
USA<BR>
E-Mail: my_id@mysite.edu
```

8. The second portion of your document content includes your biographical statement.

```
<!-- Mark the beginning of this portion with a horizontal rule. -->
<HR>
<!-- Choose the heading text that you feel appropriate. -->
<H1>About Me</H1>
<!-- The formatting & information should be developed to suit your needs. -->
<TAB INDENT=5>This is the first paragraph in this section about myself.
I have been at MY BUSINESS for the past X years.
<P>
<TAB INDENT=5>I am currently working on several projects.
These projects include...
```

As you learn more about HTML, you will likely enhance this portion with other HTML 3 elements such as links, externally viewable objects, and inline images.

9. Finally, end your document by specifying the date and identifying the individual who last modified this document.

```
<!-- Mark the beginning of this portion with a horizontal rule. -->
<HR>
<!-- Substitute the appropriate information in your document. The date should -->
<!-- appear in a long format with the month name written out since the order -->
<!-- conventions for date abbreviations vary. -->
Last modified on CURRENT_DATE by YOUR_NAME (YOUR_E-MAIL)
```

10. Use a <BODY> closing tag to mark the end of the <BODY> element. Similar to the <HEAD> element, the <BODY> element is also completely nested within the <HTML> element. To end the <BODY> element, issue the closing tag in your document.

```
</BODY>
```

11. End the <HTML> element with an <HTML> closing tag. Add this to your document to complete your first HTML document.

```
</HTML>
```

12. Save the file. Remember to use the filename extension to indicate an HTML document.

13. Attempt to view your home page using as many different browsing applications as you can.
14. If there are problems with the way items display, modify the document as appropriate.
15. When you feel that your home page is ready for the rest of the world, ask your site administrator to install your document on your Web site; follow his or her instructions to install the document in your home directory.

How It Works

Use the above procedure to develop an initial home page that will serve as your introduction to the World Wide Web community. This first attempt at a home page provides information about you and your interests to network browsers around the world.

The procedure described above steps through the development of a basic HTML document composed of an <HTML> element and the two nested <HEAD> and <BODY> elements. The <BODY> element described contains three discrete components:

- **HTML** Contact information—This section provides information on how people viewing the page can get in touch with you.

- **HTML** Biographical information—This section gives you the opportunity to tell people about yourself. You can include information on what you have done, what you are doing, and what you are interested in doing.

- **HTML** Creation/modification information—This final component should be included as a general practice in most HTML documents. Considering the fluidity of electronic information, the area provides your viewer with an idea of how current your information content is.

Figure 2-16 displays how the home page developed in the procedure above would appear in a browser. The complete HTML definition of this document appears below.

```
<HTML>
<HEAD>
<TITLE>Home Page of John Q. Public</TITLE>
</HEAD>
<BODY>

<!-- Mark the beginning of this portion with a horizontal rule. -->
<HR>
<!-- Center your name as a level 1 header. -->
<H1 ALIGN="center">John Q. Public</H1>
<!-- Provide any desirable contact information. -->
```

continued on next page

CHAPTER 2
HTML BASICS

continued from previous page

```
999 Peachtree St.<BR>
Atlanta, GA 30314<BR>
USA<BR>
E-Mail: my_id@mysite.edu

<!-- Mark the beginning of this portion with a horizontal rule. -->
<HR>
<!-- Choose the heading text that you feel appropriate. -->
<H1>About Me</H1>
<!-- The formatting and information should be developed to suit your needs.
-->
<TAB INDENT=5>This is the first paragraph in this section about myself.
I have been at MY BUSINESS for the past X years.
<P>
<TAB INDENT=5>I am currently working on several projects.
These projects include...

<!-- Mark the beginning of this portion with a horizontal rule. -->
<HR>
<!-- Substitute the appropriate information in your document. The date should -->
<!-- appear in a long format with the month name written out since the order -->
<!-- conventions for date abbreviations vary. -->
Last modified on CURRENT_DATE by YOUR_NAME (YOUR_E-MAIL)

</BODY>
</HTML>
```

The example shown in Figure 2-16 was done using an HTML 2 compliant viewer. Consequently, the effects of the <TAB> elements do not appear.

As you become more experienced with HTML, you can enhance this basic home page with a large assortment of elements. You will be able to include lists (Chapter 6), multimedia objects (Chapter 9), links to other pages (Chapter 7), and a variety of other advanced features.

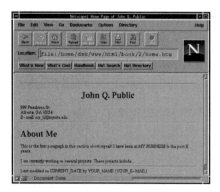

Figure 2-16 Home page example

Comments

Remember when adding elements of your own that the document you are creating may be viewed by thousands if not millions of people. You should take into consideration the variety of browsing environments with differing presentation capabilities during your document development.

A reference to the HTML 3 standard elements appears in Appendix A. The elements discussed in this How-To are listed in the table below.

ELEMENT	LOCATION	PURPOSE
<HTML>…</HTML>	file	Defines scope of an HTML document. How-To 2.1
<!--…-->	HTML	An HTML comment element. How-To 2.7
<HEAD>…</HEAD>	HTML	Defines head of an HTML document. How-To 2.1
<TITLE>…</TITLE>	HEAD	Defines the title of an HTML document. How-To 2.2
<BODY>…</BODY>	HTML	Defines body of an HTML document. How-To 2.1
<B>…</B>	BODY	This represents a bolded element. How-To 3.2
 	BODY	Line break. How-To 4.3
<H1>…</H1>	BODY	Level 1 heading element. How-To 3.1
<HR>	BODY	Places a horizontal rule when displayed. How-To 4.1
<P…>	BODY	Paragraph. How-To 4.3
<TAB…>	BODY	Establishes horizontal tabs. How-To 2.10

2.13 How do I… View my home page?

COMPLEXITY: EASY

COMPATIBILITY: BROWSER SPECIFIC

Problem

I have created my home page using an editor. I don't know how the document will appear in a browser until I actually view it. I'd like to take a look at the page in a few different editors so that I get a feel for what other people will see when they view my page.

Technique

Use a browser to view the home page, or any other page that you create. Browsers typically provide mechanisms for examining local HTML documents. There are three common interfaces used to perform this task.

HTML Command line—The path to the file that you wish to open is passed to the browser application as a command line argument.

HTML Open file—The browser application offers a menu option that accesses a local file.

HTML Open URL—The browser application has a menu option that allows you to open a URL. The protocol for a local file is simply *file*.

Procedures for opening local documents through these three interface types are provided below.

Steps

The following methods open locally created documents for viewing within browser applications. Step-by-step instructions are provided for the three common interface types for specifying local files.

Consult the documentation for your particular browser application to determine which interfaces are appropriate. In all cases, your browser is assumed to be able to interpret the document that you are opening as HTML rather than plain text.

Command Line

1. Be sure that you name the local file with the .html (or .htm for PC) filename extension. This indicates to most browsers that the local file is to be accessed as an HTML document, whether it truly is or not.

2. Invoke your browser application with the file you wish to open as a command line argument. For example, to attempt to open the file myhome.htm in the current directory using the Lynx browser, you would issue the following command:

```
lynx myhome.htm
```

Open File

1. Name the local file with the .html (or .htm for PC) filename extension. This indicates to most browsers that the local file is to be accessed as an HTML document, whether the document truly is HTML or not.

2. Load your browser applicaton.

3. Select the menu option or hotkey for opening a local file.

4. The interface for entering the file information varies among browsers. Consult the browser documentation to determine how to complete this operation successfully. In Netscape, a File Selection Dialog is presented; you can browse the local directory hierarchy until you find the desired file.

Open URL

1. Be sure that you named the local file with the .html (or .htm for PC) filename extension. This indicates to most browsers that the local file is to be accessed as an HTML document, whether the document truly is or not.

2. Load your browser application from the command line or an appropriate icon.

3. Select the menu option or hotkey for opening a URL.

4. The interface for entering the file information will vary depending upon your particular browser. You should consult the browser documentation to determine how to successfully complete this operation. In Lynx, you press [G], and the system prompts you to enter the URL you wish to open. If you want to open the local file myhome.htm in the path_info directory, you enter the URL that appears below.

```
file://localhost/path_info/myhome.htm
```

How It Works

When opening a local file, your browser application determines how to treat the contents of a file based upon the extension on the filename. The browser maps filename extensions to particular content types and will render the file as it deems appropriate. Your HTML files should have the .html extension (.htm on PC platforms).

The three methods examined for opening a local file accomplish the same task. The goal of the interface is to provide the browser with a path to the file that you wish to open. The command line interface method takes this information directly when the application is started.

Many browsers support an open local file function. Since most HTML documents require viewing prior to installation on a Web site, the ability to view a local file is extremely useful in the authoring process. Many individuals track private information through personal webs stored locally rather than accessible to the world. Figure 2-17 exhibits this interface method. The desired file can be selected from a File Selection Dialog window.

Local files can also be accessed via a standard Open URL facility. Specifying a *file* protocol type clues the browser that the desired files can be found in the local file system. The Go feature of the Lynx browser is displayed in Figure 2-18.

Once the browser receives sufficient information to find the requested file, it attempts to open it according to provided information. The browser determines the display type of this file by mapping the filename extension to a suitable content type. The browser reads the content and displays it according to the type determined. HTML 3 files display as HTML documents.

Figure 2-17 Netscape's open local facility

Figure 2-18 Lynx Go interface

Comments

Different browser applications support different subsets of these interfaces for opening local documents. The documentation for your particular browser contains the information on how this task is performed.

If your HTML documents are being opened as plain text documents, the most likely reason is that your browser is not properly configured to treat these files as HTML documents. The browser determines that a file contains an HTML document based upon the filename extension of the file being accessed. The most commonly used extension to indicate an HTML file is .html (.htm on PC platform). If your files have this extension and are still not opening properly, check the configuration of your browser application. You may need to configure this extension to indicate an HTML document. For more information on this process, consult the documentation for your browser application.

CHAPTER 3
ADDING HTML CHARACTER EFFECTS

ADDING HTML CHARACTER EFFECTS

How do I...

- 3.1 Use heading styles?
- 3.2 Force bold character style?
- 3.3 Force italic character style?
- 3.4 Underline text?
- 3.5 Use a fixed-width font?
- 3.6 Use strikethrough formatting?
- 3.7 Include superscripts and subscripts?
- 3.8 Place emphasis and strong emphasis?
- 3.9 Specify a citation?
- 3.10 Place an embedded quotation?
- 3.11 Include small segments of code and variables?
- 3.12 Emphasize a defined term?
- 3.13 Provide a sample of literal characters?
- 3.14 Tag computer commands, arguments, and keyboard input?
- 3.15 Mark an abbreviation or acronym?

CHAPTER 3
ADDING HTML CHARACTER EFFECTS

3.16 Identify a proper name?
3.17 Denote inserted or deleted text?
3.18 Spruce up my home page?

When creating an HTML page, there will be times when you want to emphasize or otherwise set apart a word or phrase from the rest of the text. Just as word processors provide a number of styles, such as bold and italic, that can be used to alter the appearance of text, HTML offers a similar set of styles. These styles can be divided into two groups: physical styles, such as bold and italic, which are used to physically alter the look of the text; and content styles, which identify words and phrases as citations, quotations, or other text elements, and which may also alter the look of text. This chapter examines physical styles in How-To's 3.2–3.7 and content styles in How-To's 3.8–3.17. How-To 3.1 looks specifically at headings, and how to use style features to make them effective.

3.1 Use Heading Styles

You often want to give your page a bold, distinct title to help readers identify it. Also, it's useful to add subheadings to a document to identify different areas of interest to readers. This simple How-To explains how to add headings of various styles to your page.

3.2 Force Bold Character Style

When you create a document on a word processor, there are often specific words and phrases you want to emphasize to bring them to the attention of the reader. This is frequently done by making the characters bold. HTML lets you do the same thing. This simple How-To explains how to add bold text to your page.

3.3 Force Italic Character Style

Certain names and other text elements—names of books, movies, etc.—require formatting in italics for proper style. You may also want to emphasize certain words in the text this way. This simple How-To explains how to place words and phrases in your page in italics.

3.4 Underline Text

Another way to emphasize text is to underline it. This is often done when italics and bold aren't available or would not fit the style of the document. This simple How-To explains how to underline words and phrases in your page.

3.5 Use a Fixed-Width Font

Samples of computer input and output, as well as other text items that require precise alignment, are often displayed in a fixed-width (or typewriter-style) font. This simple How-To explains how to add fixed-width text to your page.

CHAPTER 3
ADDING HTML CHARACTER EFFECTS

3.6 Use Strikethrough Formatting

Strikethrough formatting is often used to show examples of incorrect text, such as the incorrect input for a computer program. This How-To explains how to include strikethrough formatting in your pages.

3.7 Include Superscripts and Subscripts

Superscripts and subscripts are used to move text elements above or below the rest of the line. These are often used in footnotes and mathematical and scientific formulas. This How-To explains how to add superscripts and subscripts to your page using the new features of HTML 3.

3.8 Place Emphasis and Strong Emphasis

There may be words or phrases in your pages that you want to emphasize or strongly emphasize, but it doesn't matter whether the text is bold, italicized, or underlined. This simple How-To explains how to emphasize and strongly emphasize key words and phrases in your pages, allowing different browsers to render them differently.

3.9 Specify a Citation

If you are placing an essay or journal paper on the Web, you will want to include citations to other papers and documents. Rather than developing your own style for including citations, it is useful to mark a section of text as a citation and let the reader's browser do all the work. This How-To explains how to mark text as a citation for this purpose.

3.10 Place an Embedded Quotation

Often you have a quotation you would like to insert into a document. This is very simple to do manually, but HTML 3 provides more sophisticated ways of inserting quotations in pages, including using different quotation marks for different languages. This simple How-To explains how to add an embedded quotation to your page.

3.11 Include Small Segments of Code and Variables

Often Web pages include references to computer code, and specifically the names of variables used in programs. These text elements are often best rendered in a format different from the rest of the text. This How-To explains how to use HTML tags to easily format sections of computer code and variables.

3.12 Emphasize a Defined Term

Your page may include a number of terms that are defined in the text. This simple How-To explains how to use the new <DFN> feature in HTML 3 to emphasize these words and phrases in your page.

CHAPTER 3
ADDING HTML CHARACTER EFFECTS

3.13 Provide a Sample of Literal Characters

There are cases when you want to include literal, otherwise unformatted characters in your page. This How-To explains how to include a sample of literal characters in your page.

3.14 Tag Computer Commands, Arguments, and Keyboard Input

In the course of writing your page, you may want to insert brief sections of keyboard input, computer commands, or arguments. This How-To explains how you can format these text elements in HTML.

3.15 Mark an Abbreviation or Acronym

In your document, you may refer to a number of abbreviations or acronyms, which may require special formatting. This simple How-To explains how to use the new tags in HTML 3 to mark these items.

3.16 Identify a Proper Name

You may wish to identify proper names in your document, either for formatting purposes or to make the names easily extractable by indexing programs. This simple How-To explains how to use the new tags in HTML 3 to identify proper names.

3.17 Denote Inserted or Deleted Text

Bills, contracts, and other legal documents often include sections that have been inserted or deleted since they were originally drawn up. This How-To explains how to use the new tags in HTML 3 to easily include references to inserted or deleted sections of text.

3.18 Spruce Up My Home Page

The character effects described in this chapter can be used to make a more impressive, interesting, and effective document. They can also be used to make a document ugly and difficult to read. This How-To explains how to best use these character effects to improve the look of your pages.

3.1 USE HEADING STYLES

COMPLEXITY
EASY

3.1 How do I... Use heading styles?

COMPATIBILITY: HTML 2 OR ABOVE

Problem

I would like to include a title on my page. I would also like to include headings for specific parts of my page, but I don't want these headings to be as large as the title. How do I include titles and headings of various sizes in my page?

Technique

HTML allows users to identify titles and subtitles in a document through the <H*n*> tag, where *n* is a number from 1 to 6. The largest title is <H1> and the smallest is <H6>. You can also use attributes with these tags to align the headings to various parts of the page, or to include images within the heading.

Steps

Go to your document and identify the words and phrases that will serve as titles and headings in the document.

1. To identify a section of text as a title, place <H*n*> at the beginning of the text and </H*n*> at the end of the text, where *n* is replaced by an integer between 1 and 6:

```
<H1>This is an example of a level 1 heading</H1>
<H6>This is an example of a level 6 heading</H6>
```

2. In HTML 3, to align a title to the left, center, or right of the window, or to justify the header, include the ALIGN attribute at the beginning of the title. The default alignment is to the left.

```
<H1 ALIGN=LEFT>This is a level 1 heading aligned to the left of the window</H1>
<H1 ALIGN=CENTER>This is a level 1 heading aligned to the center of the window</H1>
<H1 ALIGN=RIGHT>This is a level 1 heading aligned to the right of the window</H1>
<H1 ALIGN=JUSTIFY>This is a level 1 heading that has been justified</H1>
```

3. In HTML 3, to include an image such as a bullet at the beginning of the header, use the SRC attribute at the beginning of the title, along with the name of the image. For example, if you wanted a graphic called mybullet.gif to serve as the bullet, you would type:

```
<H1 SRC=MYBULLET.GIF>This is a level 1 heading with a bullet</H1>
```

4. In HTML 3, you can include the NOWRAP attribute at the beginning of the title to tell the browser not to automatically wrap the text contained in the title. You can then use the line break tag
 (see Chapter 4) to specify the exact location of the line break. This is very useful if you have a long title but want to make sure that the line break is included in the right place:

```
<H1 NOWRAP>I have now turned off the automatic line wrap<br>
Thus, this part of the title is on the next line</H1>
```

An example of how headings appear in Arena, an HTML 3 browser, is shown in Figure 3-1. An example of how headings appear in Netscape, which includes some HTML 3 elements, is shown in Figure 3-2. The code for both examples is available on the CD-ROM as file 3-1.html.

How It Works

When a browser encounters a heading tag, it automatically formats the text contained in the title according to its programming. This often includes changing the size of the text, making the text bold, and including carriage returns and line spacing. The exact way headings are formatted differs from browser to browser.

Comments

Since headings are rendered differently from browser to browser, take care when referring to them by their appearance within a document. Also, as a rule, headings below level 3 are the same size as normal text, if not smaller, so their use as titles

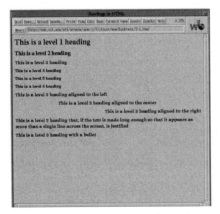

Figure 3-1 Various styles of headings (Arena)

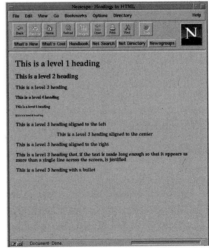

Figure 3-2 Various styles of headings (Netscape)

may not be as effective as you'd like. Finally, while HTML 3 requires the use of the NOWRAP attribute before you can include line breaks in headings, you can usually include line breaks without the NOWRAP attribute in older versions of HTML. Bullets in headings are not currently supported as of this writing, but that should change soon.

COMPLEXITY
EASY

3.2 How do I... Force bold character style?

COMPATIBILITY: HTML 2 OR ABOVE

Problem

I have some text I would like to emphasize by making it bold. How do I make text bold in HTML?

Technique

It is very easy to make text bold in HTML. Simply by using the <B> tag, you can make any amount of text, from one letter to entire paragraphs, appear bold.

Steps

To make text bold, place the <B> tag at the beginning of the text and the </B> tag at the end of the text:

```
This is normal text and <B>this is bold text.</B>
I only want to make the first letter of this <B>w</B>ord bold.
```

An example of bold and other physical styles as displayed in Arena is shown in Figure 3-3. The same example as displayed in Netscape is shown in Figure 3-4. The code is also available on the CD-ROM as file 3-2.html

How It Works

When a browser encounters a <B> tag, it displays the text contained between the <B> and the </B> tags as bold text. The browser does no other processing on the text.

Comments

Some browsers do not permit you to mix <B> with other tags, such as italics (<I>, see How-To 3.3). The <STRONG> tag (see How-To 3.8) often formats text in the

CHAPTER 3
ADDING HTML CHARACTER EFFECTS

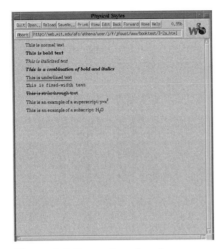

Figure 3-3 Examples of various physical styles (Arena)

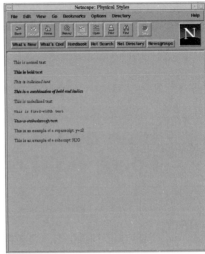

Figure 3-4 Examples of various physical styles (Netscape)

same manner as <B>. Which one to use is up to you. See How-To 3.18 for a discussion of using styles effectively.

COMPLEXITY
EASY

3.3 How do I... Force italic character style?

COMPATIBILITY: HTML 2 OR ABOVE

Problem

I have some text, including the titles of some books, that I need to show in italics. How do I display text in italics in HTML?

Technique

It is very easy to italicize text in HTML. The <I> and </I> tags will italicize any amount of text contained between them.

Steps

To italicize text, place the <I> tag at the beginning of the text, and the </I> tag at the end of the text:

```
This is normal text and <I>this is italicized text.</I>

I only want to put the first letter of this <I>w</I>ord in italics.
```

Examples of italics and other physical styles are shown in Figures 3-3 and 3-4. This code is also available on the CD-ROM as file 3-2.html.

How It Works

When a browser encounters an <I> tag, it displays the text contained between the <I> and the </I> tags in italics. The browser does no other processing on the text.

Comments

Some browsers do not permit you to mix <I> with other text style tags, such as <B>. The <EM> tag (see How-To 3.8) often formats text in the same manner as <I>. Which one you use is up to you.

COMPLEXITY
EASY

3.4 How do I... Underline text?

COMPATIBILITY: HTML 2 OR ABOVE

Problem

I have some text in my document that I would like to underline. How can I underline text in HTML?

Technique

Underlining text is a simple process in HTML. The <U> and </U> tags will underline any amount of text contained between them.

Steps

To underline text, place the <U> tag at the beginning of the text, and the </U> tag at the end of the text:

```
This is normal text and <U>this is underlined text.</U>

I only want to underline the first letter of this <U>w</U>ord.
```

Examples of underlines and other physical styles are shown in Figures 3-3 and 3-4. This code is also available on the CD-ROM as file 3-2.html.

How It Works

When a browser encounters a <U> tag, it underlines the text contained between the <U> and the </U> tags. The browser does no other formatting on the text.

Comments

Some browsers do not permit you to mix <U> tags with other tags, such as bold and italic, when trying to format the same word or phrase. Some browsers, such as Netscape, do not support underlined text.

COMPLEXITY
EASY

3.5 How do I... Use a fixed-width font?

COMPATIBILITY: HTML 2 OR ABOVE

Problem

I have some text that I would like to place in a fixed-width font to maintain the exact alignment of the words. How do I put words in a fixed-width font in HTML?

Technique

It is very simple to put text into a fixed-width font. Any text placed between the <TT> and </TT> (for TeleType or Typewritten text) tags will be rendered in a fixed-width font.

Steps

To place text in a fixed-width font, put <TT> at the beginning of the text and </TT> at the end of the text:

```
This is normal text and <TT>this is text in fixed-width font.</TT>

I only want to put the first letter of this <TT>w</TT>ord in fixed-width font.
```

Examples of fixed-width font and other physical styles are shown in Figures 3-3 and 3-4. The code is also available on the CD-ROM in file 3-2.html.

How It Works

When a browser encounters a <TT> tag, it renders the text between the <TT> and the </TT> tags in a fixed-width font. The actual fixed width font used (i.e., Courier,

Monaco, etc.) depends on the browser and can often be modified by the user. No other formatting of the text is done by the <TT> tag.

Comments

Some browsers don't allow you to combine <TT> with other text style tags, such as <B> and <I>, to format the same text. Since many browsers allow users to choose which fixed-width font to display text marked by <TT>, the displayed text may not appear to any given user as it appears in your original.

COMPLEXITY
EASY

3.6 How do I... Use strikethrough formatting?

COMPATIBILITY: HTML 3

Problem

As an example of what text should not be entered into a program, I would like to show the text in a strikethrough style, that is, with a horizontal line running through it. How can I use strikethrough style in HTML?

Technique

HTML 3 supports the use of the <S> tag, which converts any text placed between it and the corresponding </S> tag into strikethrough style, that is, text with a horizontal line running though it.

Steps

To place text in strikethrough style, put the <S> tag at the beginning of the text and the </S> tag at the end of the text:

```
This is normal text and <S>this is strikethrough style text.</S>

I only want to strikethrough the first letter of this <S>w</S>ord.
```

Examples of strikethrough style are shown in Figures 3-3 and 3-4. The code is also available on the CD-ROM as file 3-2.html.

How It Works

When a browser encounters an <S> tag, it places the text between the <S> and </S> tags in strikethrough style by replacing the text with an identical font that has a horizontal line running through it.

CHAPTER 3
ADDING HTML CHARACTER EFFECTS

Comments

Some browsers do not have access to a strikethrough font. If it doesn't, the browser may choose to use an alternative method for displaying the text. Also, some browsers, such as Netscape, support the <STRIKE> and </STRIKE> tags instead of <S> and </S>. To permit your text to be correctly displayed by the most browsers, you should use both <S> and <STRIKE> around the text you want to place in strikethrough style:

```
Most browsers should display <STRIKE><S>this text</S></STRIKE> in strikethrough style.
```

COMPLEXITY
EASY

3.7 How do I... Include superscripts and subscripts?

COMPATIBILITY: HTML 3

Problem

I have a paper I want to convert to HTML that includes mathematical equations, chemical formulas, and numbered footnotes. These all require numbers to be placed in superscripts and subscripts. How do I create superscripted and subscripted text in HTML?

Technique

HTML 3 provides support for superscripts (text shifted above the normal level of the line) and subscripts (text shifted below the normal level of the line). The _{and} tags place any text between them below the level of the line, in a smaller font when possible. The ^{and} tags place any text between them above the level of the line, also in a smaller font when possible.

Steps

1. To create a subscript, place the _{tag at the beginning of the text to be subscripted and the} tag at the end of the text to be subscripted:

```
The chemical formula of water is H<SUB>2</SUB>O.
```

2. To create a superscript, place the ^{tag at the beginning of the text to be superscripted and the} tag at the end of the text to be superscripted:

```
A simple formula for a parabola is y = x<SUP>2</SUP>.
```

Examples of subscripts and superscripts are shown in Figures 3-3 and 3-4. The code is also available on the CD-ROM as file 3-2.html.

How It Works

When a browser encounters a <SUB> tag, it shifts all the text between the _{and} tags below the level of the rest of the line, and, depending on the browser, renders the text in a smaller size. When a browser encounters a <SUP> tag, it shifts all the text between the ^{and} tags above the level of the rest of the line, and, again depending on the browser, renders the text in a smaller size.

Comments

Since <SUB> and <SUP> have only been introduced in HTML 3, people using older, pre-HTML 3 browsers will not be able to see the subscripts or superscripts. To accommodate these users, an alternative for creating subscripts and superscripts in chemical formulas and mathematical equations is to create a graphic of the formula or equation in another program and include the graphic in the page as an inline graphic (see How-To 8.1).

COMPLEXITY
EASY

3.8 How do I... Place emphasis and strong emphasis?

COMPATIBILITY: HTML 2 OR ABOVE

Problem

I would like to emphasize certain words and phrases on my page. However, I don't need a specific style, like bold or italics, applied to them. How can I generically emphasize and strongly emphasize text in HTML?

Technique

HTML supports the content-style tags <EM> and <STRONG> for emphasis and strong emphasis, respectively. These tags highlight specific areas of text without requiring the browser to use a specific physical style for them.

Steps

Open your document and locate the text you wish to emphasize.

1. To emphasize a word or phrase, place <EM> at the beginning of the text and </EM> at the end of the text:

```
This is normal text and <EM>this is emphasized text.</EM>

I only want to emphasize the first letter of this <EM>w</EM>ord.
```

2. To strongly emphasize a word or phrase, place <STRONG> at the beginning of the text and </STRONG> at the end of the text:

```
This is normal text and <STRONG>this is strongly emphasized text.</STRONG>

I only want to strongly emphasize the first letter of this <STRONG>w</STRONG>ord.
```

An example of <EM>, <STRONG>, and other content styles, as displayed in Arena, is given in Figure 3-5. The same example, as displayed in Netscape, is shown in Figure 3-6. The code is also available on the CD-ROM as file 3-3.html.

How It Works

When a browser encounters an <EM> tag, it emphasizes the text contained between the <EM> and </EM> tags using the browser's specific instructions for emphasized text. When a browser encounters a <STRONG> tag, it emphasizes the

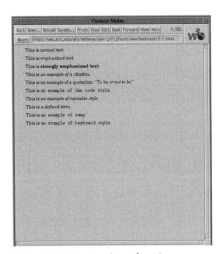

Figure 3-5 Examples of various content styles (Arena)

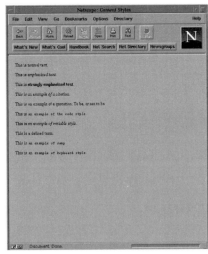

Figure 3-6 Examples of various content styles (Netscape)

text contained between the <STRONG> and </STRONG> tags, once again using its specific instructions for strongly emphasized text.

Comments

Most browsers interpret <EM> the same as <I> (that is, they use italics), and <STRONG> the same as <B> (that is, they use bold). However, some browsers interpret these tags in different ways or allow the user to define the interpretation of <EM> and <STRONG>. How and where to use <EM>, <STRONG>, <B>, and <I> is discussed in How-To 3.18.

3.9 How do I... Specify a citation?

COMPLEXITY
EASY

COMPATIBILITY: HTML 2 OR ABOVE

Problem

I am putting an essay on the Web, and I would like a simple way to format the references to other papers on the page. How can I format citations in HTML?

Technique

HTML makes it easy to format citations. The <CITE> tag will format a citation using the style built into the browser.

Steps

To format a citation, place the <CITE> tag at the beginning of the citation and </CITE> at the end of the citation:

```
Jane Doe's work showed how this could be accomplished <CITE>(Doe, 1998).</CITE>
```

Examples of citations and other content styles are shown in Figure 3-5 and 3-6. The code is also available on the CD-ROM as file 3-3.html.

Technique

When a browser encounters the <CITE> tag, it formats the text between the <CITE> and </CITE> tags according to the style built into the browser.

Comments

Most browsers render the text marked by <CITE> in italics. However, since <CITE> is a content and not a physical style, some browsers may choose to render the text differently. Thus, take care when referencing a citation or some part of a citation by style.

COMPLEXITY
INTERMEDIATE

3.10 How do I... Place an embedded quotation?

COMPATIBILITY: HTML 3

Problem

I want to include a quotation in my page. However, I would like the browser to do the work of including the appropriate quotation marks for a given language. How can I embed this quotation using HTML?

Technique

HTML 3 introduces the <Q> tag, which places quotation marks around the tagged text. By adding the LANG attribute, it is possible to tell the browser to use the quotation marks specific to a certain language.

Steps

1. To insert an embedded quotation, place the <Q> tag at the beginning of the text and </Q> at the end of the text:

```
Hamlet said, <Q>To be, or not to be, that is the question.</Q>
```

2. To use the quotation marks from a specific language, insert the LANG attribute in the <Q> tag and set it equal to a language. Languages are usually referred to by a two-letter abbreviation, such as EN for English, FR for French, DE for German, etc. The following line of code calls for the use of English (specifically, American English, which is represented by EN.US) quotation marks:

```
Hamlet said, <Q LANG="EN.US">To be, or not to be, that is the question.</Q>
```

To render the quotes as used in German, the code would look like this:

```
Hamlet said, <Q LANG="DE">To be, or not to be, that is the question.</Q>
```

Examples of embedded quotations and other content styles are shown in Figures 3-5 and 3-6. The code is also available on the CD-ROM as file 3-3.html.

How It Works

When a browser encounters a <Q> tag, it replaces the <Q> and </Q> tags with opening and closing quotes, respectively. The text and the quotes are also rendered in italics. It uses the quotes for the language specified by the LANG attribute, or the default quotes if none is given.

Comments

The <Q> tag has only been introduced in HTML 3, so it is not supported by older browsers. And while the <Q> tag may be useful for rendering quotation symbols, especially for other languages, it may be simpler just to add the quote symbols manually, if they are available. As of this writing, no browser supports quotation symbols used in non-English languages.

COMPLEXITY
EASY

3.11 How do I... Include small segments of code and variables?

COMPATIBILITY: HTML 2 OR ABOVE

Problem

I have some samples of code from a program, and some variables, that I want to include in my page. I would like to format these to set them off from the rest of the text, but don't want to go though a lot of work choosing a physical style. Is there an easy way to format code examples and variables in HTML?

Technique

HTML offers the <CODE> tag, which can be used to display sections of code from a program, usually in a fixed-width font, and <VAR>, which can be used to show variables from programs or other applications, often in italics.

Steps

Go to your document and locate the text you want to display as a variable or in code format.

1. To place a section of text in code format, place the <CODE> tag at the beginning of the text and the </CODE> tag at the end of the text:

CHAPTER 3
ADDING HTML CHARACTER EFFECTS

```
The <CODE>goto 20</CODE> statement in the program should be replaced to
improve the programming style.
```

2. To display a word as a variable, place the <VAR> tag at the beginning of the text and the </VAR> tag at the end of the text:

```
The <VAR>count</VAR> variable keeps track of the number of iterations of the loop.
```

Examples of the code and variable styles as well as other content styles are shown in Figures 3-5 and 3-6. The code is also available on the CD-ROM as file 3-3.html.

How It Works

When a browser encounters a <CODE> tag, it places the text contained between the <CODE> and </CODE> tags in a style used by the browser for rendering code. This is usually a fixed-width font. When a browser encounters a <VAR> tag, it places the text contained between the <VAR> and </VAR> tags in the style used by the browser for variables. This is often italics.

Comments

Since <CODE> and <VAR> are not physical styles, the way they are presented depends on the browser. Thus, as with other content styles, take care when referring to specific items based on their style.

COMPLEXITY
EASY

3.12 How do I... Emphasize a defined term?

COMPATIBILITY: HTML 2 OR ABOVE

Problem

I have a number of words and phrases that are defined in my pages. I would like to call attention to those words, but I don't specifically want to use bold, italics, or another style. How can I emphasize these words in HTML?

Technique

HTML supports the <DFN> tag, which is designed specifically for words and phrases that are defined in the text. The physical method of emphasizing the words is left to the browser.

Steps

To mark a word or phrase that has been defined, place the <DFN> tag at the beginning of the text and </DFN> at the end of the text.

```
A batter has a <DFN>full count</DFN> when he has three balls and two strikes.
```

Examples of definitions and other content styles are shown in Figures 3-5 and 3-6. The code is also available on the CD-ROM as file 3-3.html.

How It Works

When a browser encounters a <DFN> tag, it changes the style of the text contained between the <DFN> and </DFN> tags. The style used is dependent on the browser, but is usually either bold or italics.

Comments

Since the style is chosen by the browser and not by you, the defined terms may appear in a different style than you might anticipate. Thus, be careful when referring to defined words based on their style.

COMPLEXITY
EASY

3.13 How do I... Provide a sample of literal characters?

COMPATIBILITY: HTML 2 OR ABOVE

Problem

I have some characters that I would like to show as a sample of literal, unformatted characters. How can I do this in HTML?

Technique

HTML offers the <SAMP> tag, which will display any text contained within the <SAMP> and </SAMP> tags as a sample of literal characters. This tag works in much the same way as <CODE> and <TT> discussed above.

Steps

To display text as a sample of literal characters, place the <SAMP> tag at the beginning of the text and </SAMP> at the end of the text:

```
This is an example of <SAMP>a sample of literal characters</SAMP>

In this case I only want to place <SAMP>o</SAMP>ne character in the sample.
```

Examples of sample text and other content styles are shown in Figures 3-5 and 3-6. The code is also available on the CD-ROM as file 3-3.html.

How It Works

When a browser encounters the <SAMP> tag, it formats the text contained between the <SAMP> and </SAMP> tags according to the rules built into the browser. Usually this means rendering the text in a fixed-width font, identical to the fonts used for <CODE> and <TT>, explained above, and <KBD>, explained in How-To 3.14.

Comments

Although text tagged with <SAMP> usually looks the same when rendered as text tagged with a number of other styles, it is still best to use <SAMP> when referring to a specific sample, if for no other reason than to allow an indexing program to properly identify the tagged item.

COMPLEXITY
EASY

3.14 How do I... Tag computer commands, arguments, and keyboard input?

COMPATIBILITY: HTML 2 OR ABOVE

Problem

On my page I would like to include some samples of input to a computer program. I would like to format these samples differently than the standard text is formatted. How can I do this in HTML?

Technique

The HTML keyboard style tag <KBD> allows you to mark text to be typed by the user. Use it also to display computer commands and arguments, especially those entered by the user. The text tagged by <KBD> is usually shown in a fixed-width font.

Steps

To specify text that is to be keyboarded by the user, place the <KBD> tag at the beginning of the text and the </KBD> tag at the end of the text:

```
At the prompt enter the command <KBD>lpr output.txt</KBD>

Using the <KBD>-l</KBD> flag causes a long form of the directory to be listed.
```

Examples of keyboard style and other content styles are shown in Figures 3-5 and 3-6. The code is also available on the CD-ROM as file 3-3.html.

How It Works

When a browser encounters a <KBD> tag, it places everything between the <KBD> and </KBD> tags in keyboard style. Such text is usually rendered in a fixed-width font, but font style can vary among browsers.

Comments

Since <KBD> is a content style, its appearance may vary among browsers. The <KBD> style is also very similar to other styles, such as <CODE> and <SAMP>, so it can be used interchangeably with those styles. This is discussed in more detail in How-To 3.18.

COMPLEXITY
EASY

3.15 How do I... Mark an abbreviation or acronym?

COMPATIBILITY: HTML 3

Problem

I have a page that includes a number of abbreviations and acronyms. I would like to call attention to them, but I don't require a specific physical style. Is there a generic way to call attention to these items in HTML?

Technique

HTML 3 supports two new tags, <ABBREV> and <ACRONYM>, that can be used to mark abbreviations and acronyms, respectively. The physical style used for these items varies from browser to browser.

Steps

Open your document and locate the text you want to identify as an abbreviation or an acronym.

1. To identify an abbreviation, place the <ABBREV> tag at the beginning of the abbreviation and </ABBREV> at the end of the abbreviation:

```
The paper by Smith <ABBREV>et al.</ABBREV> shows how this can be done.
```

2. To identify an acronym, place the <ACRONYM> tag at the beginning of the abbreviation and </ACRONYM> at the end of the acronym:

```
The National Aeronautics and Space Administration, or <ACRONYM>NASA</ACRONYM>,
was founded in 1958.
```

How It Works

When a browser encounters either an <ABBREV> or an <ACRONYM> tag, it formats the text contained between the <ABBREV> and </ABBREV> tags or the <ACRONYM> and </ACRONYM> tags accordingly. The actual physical style applied to the text contained within these tags will be controlled by the browser viewing the document.

Comments

Since formatting applied to the <ABBREV> and <ACRONYM> tags will vary from browser to browser, it may be bold, italics, or something else entirely. As of this writing, the Arena browser made no visible style changes with either tag. Thus, it's better to refer to acronyms or abbreviations by content rather than by style. Because they are additions to HTML 3, neither <ABBREV> nor <ACRONYM> is supported by older browsers.

COMPLEXITY
EASY

3.16 How do I... Identify a proper name?

COMPATIBILITY: HTML 3

Problem

I would like to call attention to the names of people and to other proper names in my pages. The names do not necessarily have to be highlighted, but someone running an indexing program through my pages should be able to pull out the names easily. How can I do this in HTML?

Technique

HTML 3 provides two new tags, <AU> and <PERSON>, that can be used to identify the names of people as well as other proper names. <AU> identifies an author, while <PERSON> identifies any person (or other proper name).

Steps

Open your document and locate the text you want to identify as a proper name.

1. To identify the name of an author, place <AU> at the beginning of the name and </AU> at the end of the name:

```
<AU>William Faulkner</AU> wrote many novels set in Mississippi.
```

2. To identify the name of a person, place <PERSON> at the beginning of the name and </PERSON> at the end of the name:

```
<PERSON>Ronald Reagan</PERSON> was the 40th president of the United States.
```

How It Works

When a browser encounters either an <AU> or a <PERSON> tag, it does nothing to alter the style of the text; these tags simply identify names for outside indexing programs.

Comments

The <AU> and <PERSON> tags are only supported by HTML 3, so older, pre-HTML 3 browsers cannot take advantage of them. These tags are primarily used by programs that scan HTML files and index their contents.

COMPLEXITY
EASY

3.17 How do I... Denote inserted or deleted text?

COMPATIBILITY: HTML 3

Problem

I'm putting some legal documents on my Web page, and I would like to point out where sections of the text have been amended either by additions of new sections or deletions of old sections. Is there a way I can easily mark this in HTML?

Technique

HTML 3 provides two new tags, <INS> and <DEL>, that allow you to mark sections of text that have been inserted or deleted from the original version of a document. As with other content styles, the physical rendering of the text depends on the browser.

Steps

Open your document and locate the text you would like to display as inserted or deleted text.

1. To mark text that has been inserted, place <INS> at the beginning of the inserted text and </INS> at the end of the inserted text:

```
His latest contract called for $3.5 million a year <INS>and a beachfront condo</INS>.
```

2. To mark text that has been deleted, place <DEL> at the beginning of the section that has been deleted and </DEL> at the end of the text:

```
The people on the team now include John, Jane, <DEL>Bob,</DEL> and Arnold.
```

How It Works

When a browser encounters an <INS> or a <DEL> tag, it formats the text contained within the tags according to the style programmed into the browser. This style may vary from browser to browser.

Comments

The <INS> and <DEL> tags don't actually insert or delete text; rather, they point out where text has been added to or removed from a document. These features were added to HTML 3, so pre-HTML 3 browsers do not support these tags. As of this writing, the Arena browser did not make any style changes to text within these tags, which could cause confusion when they are used in a document.

COMPLEXITY
INTERMEDIATE

3.18 How do I... Spruce up my home page?

COMPATIBILITY: HTML 2/3

Problem

Now that I've learned about all these different styles, how can I use them most effectively to make my page more readable?

Technique

This problem is similar to that encountered using fonts and type styles in word processors and page layout programs. With all the different styles available, there is the strong temptation to try them all. (After all, that's why they exist, right?) However, this can lead to pages that are aesthetically unpleasing and difficult to read. This How-To contains some tips to help you use these styles effectively to spruce up your home page.

Steps

The following points will help you make the best use of physical or content styles in your Web pages.

1. Styles most effectively emphasize a point when used sparingly. If you make every other word bold or place large sections of text in italics, it becomes much harder to bring an important point to the attention of the reader.

2. In addition to diluting emphasis, changing styles often, from normal to bold to italics and so on, makes it harder to read a document, since your eyes have to stop and adjust to the new type style before you can continue to read. Keep style changes to a minimum to avoid this problem.

3. There has been considerable discussion among WWW users and document creators about the appropriate use of <B> versus <STRONG> and <I> versus <EM>. On most (but not necessarily all!) browsers, the tags do the same thing and are interchangeable. There is no single right way to use these tags. As a general rule, though, consider the following: whenever you want to emphasize a word or phrase, use <EM> or <STRONG>. When the particular word or phrase, like the title of a book or a specific name, requires a specific formatting, use <I> or <B> instead. When in doubt, say the sentence that contains the word or phrase in question out loud. If you want to format the document to bring out the emphasis on the word or phrase as you would say it, use <EM> or <STRONG>.

4. HTML features another set of tags that are indistinguishable from one another when rendered on most browsers: <TT>, <CODE>, <SAMP>, and <KBD> all place text in a fixed-width format. Unlike the case described in step 3, things here are a bit more clear-cut. When you want to insert some code from a program, use the <CODE> tag. When you want to display the user input into a program, use the <KBD> tag. Use the <SAMP> tag when you want to display a sample of literal characters. Any other cases where you need to display text in a fixed-width font can be handled by the <TT> tag. This division not only allows individual browsers to choose the best method for displaying information, but it allows indexing programs that scan web pages to identify any examples of code, input, and so on, through the tags used. If nothing but <TT> were used for all fixed-width type purposes, the output would probably look the same on most browsers, but the indexing program would have a much harder time finding code and input examples on Web pages.

Comments

With the judicious use of styles, you can easily spruce up your new home page and make it more interesting to read. Physical styles can improve the appearance of a page, if care is taken with their use and it is understood that not all browsers will render physical styles in precisely the same way. The proper use of content styles will enable users to find the information of interest to them, and will allow indexing programs to better catalog the contents of your pages.

CHAPTER 4
MANAGING DOCUMENT SPACING

4. MANAGING DOCUMENT SPACING

How do I...

4.1   **Add a horizontal line to an HTML document?**

4.2   **Manage vertical spacing: paragraphs vs. line breaks?**

4.3   **Manage space with the <PRE> tag?**

4.4   **Space my home page?**

How you lay out or space your page is important in making a home page that is tight and readable. Spacing is often initially overlooked when planning a home page, which can be a mistake. A page that is properly spaced is easier to read and, therefore, visited more often by readers. A poorly spaced page might cause readers to miss information that is either too far off a page or too clumped together with other information to be noticed. This chapter will help you create an easy-to-read home page.

4.1 Add a Horizontal Line to an HTML Document

Horizontal lines separate distinct sections of documents. This How-To shows you how to add horizontal lines to your documents.

4.2 Manage Vertical Spacing: Paragraphs vs. Line Breaks

Two of the simplest tags in HTML are the paragraph <P> and line break <BR> tags. This How-To shows you the difference between the two tags and when you might want to use each one.

CHAPTER 4
MANAGING DOCUMENT SPACING

4.3 Manage Space with the <PRE> Tag

All text delimited by <PRE> tags is displayed by a browser in a fixed-width font, including any white space within that text. This simple How-To shows you how to make the best use of the <PRE> tag.

4.4 Space My Home Page

At first, spacing of a page might seem trivial. However, proper spacing can lead to a page that is easier to read and, therefore, read more often. Improper spacing can cause a reader to either intentionally or unintentionally skip over important information. This How-To helps you space your page in a user-friendly manner.

COMPLEXITY
EASY

4.1 How do I... Add a horizontal line to an HTML document?

COMPATIBILITY: HTML

Problem

I want to separate the credits for my page from the other information on my page. I see other pages that use horizontal lines to do this. How can I add a horizontal rule or line to my document?

Technique

Add horizontal lines to documents by using the <HR> tag.

Steps

The following four steps show how to add a horizontal rule to a document.

1. Create an HTML document with any editor or word processor that can save files as text or ASCII.

2. Decide where you want to add a horizontal rule. In the example shown below there is a horizontal rule separating the page's body from its footer. This is a common use for horizontal rules.

3. Enter an <HR> tag wherever you want to place a horizontal rule. For example:

```
<HTML>
<HEAD><TITLE>My <HR> Example</TITLE></HEAD>
<BODY>
<H2>How to add a horizontal rule to a document</H2>
```

4.1
ADD A HORIZONTAL LINE TO AN HTML DOCUMENT

```
Horizontal lines or rules are added to documents through the use of the
HR tag. They are very easy to use and can make a document look quite
professional. Horizontal Rules are so easy to add that some people may
get carried away with their use. This is something you should be careful
with. Still, <b>experiment</b>! Have fun!
<P>
<P>
<HR>
This page was created by John Smith on 1/1/95. It was last modified on 6/1/95.
</BODY>
</HTML>
```

4. View your document with the browser of your choice to make sure it looks the way you think it will. The horizontal line should make it clear that the author information is related to but separate from the text. It should look very much like Figure 4-1.

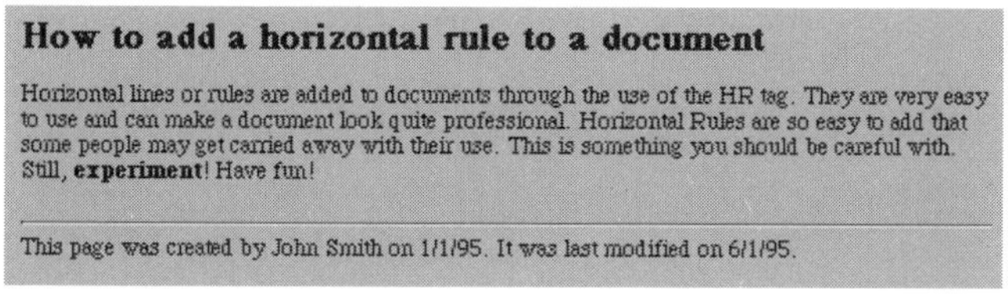

Figure 4-1 The sample document with a horizontal line acting as a separator

5. Make any edits or changes needed. Feel free to experiment.
6. If necessary, transfer the document to your server machine, and inform your system administrator about the presence of the new document.

How It Works

Adding the line isn't very complicated at all. The browser sees the <HR> tag and displays a horizontal line.

Comments

The real trick here is not adding the line, but deciding where the line should go, and for that matter how many lines you should have on a page. The latter is largely a matter of taste. Some people believe you should use no more than two horizontal lines per page. Others believe the more the merrier. There are a few "standard" places where horizontal lines are often used in documents:

- **HTML** Around forms to separate the form from the rest of document
- **HTML** At the end of a document to separate information about the document (date created, author, etc.) from actual information contained in the document

It is possible to get carried away with horizontal lines, making your document harder to read and bigger than it should be. Be yourself, but use caution.

COMPLEXITY
EASY

4.2 How do I... Manage vertical spacing: paragraphs vs. line breaks?

COMPATIBILITY: HTML

Problem

How can I tell when I should use a new paragraph tag <P> and when I should use a line break tag
?

Technique

Normally, a browser displays text across the available area of your text window. Text starts on a new line only when a complete word cannot be displayed on the current line. You have two methods of controlling where text breaks: the paragraph <P> and the line break <BR> tags. The one you use is sometimes a matter of personal taste and sometimes a matter of the situation you are in. Use a <P> tag to start a new paragraph, to which you may assign new attributes if you wish. Most browsers also place extra space after a <P>. A <BR> causes the browser to maintain the current paragraph attributes but to start placing text on a new line. The <BR> element is useful for such things as separating items in a list and breaking up lines of a song or a poem.

Steps

1. Create an HTML document with the text editor of your choice.

2. In the document, decide where you wish to use new paragraphs and where you wish to use simple line breaks. Usually it is pretty clear where to use each. A <P> tag is used wherever you would start a new paragraph if you were using a word processor. Use a line break <BR> if you wish to keep information grouped together within the same paragraph, but on separate lines. For instance, you would not want a name and address to be in separate paragraphs, but you would want them to be on separate lines.

The format of the new paragraph tag can be as simple as

```
<P>text
```

since this tag does not need to be closed.

4.2
MANAGE VERTICAL SPACING: PARAGRAPHS VS. LINE BREAKS

While the simple tag is fine in most cases, the new paragraph tag has been expanded in HTML 3 to include alignment of the paragraph. This format is

```
<P ALIGN=RIGHT | LEFT | CENTER> text </P>
```

The text and images between the <P> ... </P> tags are aligned to either the right, left, or center of the window depending on the option you select. Which format you choose is a matter of personal taste and the browser you are using.

The format of the break tag is also simple:

```
<BR>
```

However, this tag has been expanded on when working with images and text that are aligned. See Chapter 8 for more details.

The following code was used to create the sample document in Figure 4-2, which illustrates some of the differences between <BR> and <P>.

```
<HTML>
<HEAD>
<TITLE>Demo of Paragraph <P> vs. Line
Breaks<BR></TITLE>
</HEAD>
<BODY>
This is the first line. A simple paragraph tag.&lt;P&gt;<P>
Second line. Line break &lt;BR&gt;<BR>
This is the third line.
<P ALIGN=CENTER>
Remember a browser normally does not break a sentence until it no longer has
room to display the current word in the window. A new paragraph tag causes a new
paragraph to begin, to which new attributes can be assigned. A line break tag
causes a line break, giving you a little more control of things.</P>
<P ALIGN=left>
Here is a paragraph aligned to the left. The text flows until it comes to the
end of the window, or a new paragraph tag or line break. This line is followed
by a line break.&lt;BR&gt;<BR>
Notice the difference between that line and this one ended by a new paragraph
&lt;P&gt;.<P>
This is the next line.
Unordered list with paragraphs between items:
<UL>
<LI>One&lt;P&gt;<p>
<LI>Two&lt;P&gt;<p>
</UL>
<P>
Unordered list with line breaks:
<UL>
<LI>One&lt;BR&gt;<br>
<LI>Two&lt;BR&gt;<br>
</UL>
</BODY>
</HTML>
```

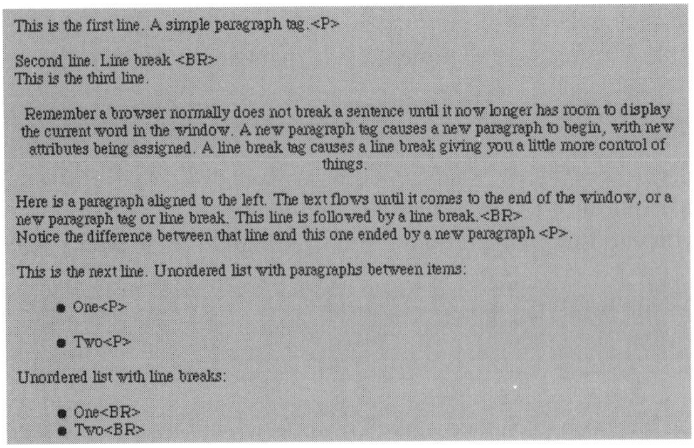

Figure 4-2 The <P> vs.
 demo

3. View your document to make sure it looks the way you think it should.
4. Make any changes that might be needed.
5. If necessary, transfer the document to your server and inform your system administrator about the presence of the new document.

How It Works

A browser displays text across the current line of the window until one of following things happens:

- **HTML** There isn't enough room on the current line to display the current word.
- **HTML** A <BR> tag is encountered, in which case the browser starts a new line in the same paragraph.
- **HTML** A <P> tag is encountered, in which case the browser not only begins a new paragraph but also allows the document creator to assign new paragraph attributes to the text that follows.

Comments

With the new structure of the <P> tag, some people think it is a nice touch to close paragraphs with a </P>. While this may be a good practice, it is not needed, because the browser assumes a </P> tag precedes a <P> tag.

Also, remember that the exact way a paragraph is displayed is governed by a combination of factors, such as the browser used, style sheet setup, and various other tags.

4.3 How do I... Manage space with the <PRE> tag?

COMPLEXITY: EASY

COMPATABILITY: HTML 3

Problem

I see a lot of pages in which the author includes rows of text evenly displayed in a monospace font, in which all the letters are the same size. How do I do this?

Technique

You can use the <PRE> ... </PRE> tags to display preformatted blocks of text with a fixed-space font. When they appear inside <PRE> tags, white space, line breaks, and tabs are also displayed. The format for this tag is

`<PRE>text</PRE>`

Placing text between the <PRE> tags allows you set up a sort of poor man's table and is also good for simulating program listings.

Steps

Follow these steps to add preformatted text to your documents.

1. Create a basic HTML document using any text editor.

2. Enter your <PRE> and </PRE> tags in the body of the document. For example:

```
<HTML>
<HEAD>
<TITLE>Preformatted text example</TITLE>
<BODY>
</HEAD>
<H2>Gross Sales By Sales People</H2>
<HR>
<PRE>
            <B>Gross sales</B>
Salesman                Sales Ranking
Tim                     $10,000     2
Tom                     $5,000      3
Tammy                   $20,000     1
<P><P><P>
These figures reflect the last quarter of 95. The first column of numbers was
created with spaces, the second with tabs. There are also carriage returns in
this paragraph within the sentences that would continue past the screen.
```

continued on next page

continued from previous page
```
</PRE>

<HR>
Compiled by Jz: 12/31/95
</BODY>
</HTML>
```

In the chart the first set of numbers is separated by spaces, the second set by tabs, since tabs are not ignored in text that appears between the preformatted text tags.

3. View your document to make sure it looks the way you think it should. The example document looks like Figure 4-3 when displayed.

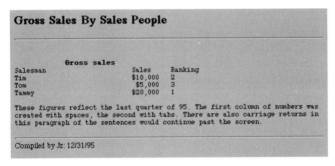

Figure 4-3 Preformatted text

Notice how the carriage returns after each salesman's sale figures work. Also notice how the bold <B> tags still work inside the <PRE> tags but the new paragraph tags <P> are ignored.

4. Make any edits or changes needed. Feel free to experiment.

5. If necessary, transfer the document to your server and inform your system administrator about the presence of the new document.

How It Works

The browser displays all text between the <PRE> ... </PRE> tags in a fixed-width font without ignoring carriage returns and tabs. The following example shows the difference between how the same information is displayed when it appears between <PRE> ... </PRE> tags and when it does not appear between <PRE> ... </PRE> tags. The results can be seen in Figure 4-4.

```
<HTML>
<HEAD>
<TITLE>Preformatted text example</TITLE>
```

4.3
MANAGE SPACE WITH THE <PRE> TAG

```
<BODY>
</HEAD>
<H2>Gross Sales By Sales People</H2>
<HR>
<PRE>
              Gross sales                      <CR>
Salesman                         Sales<CR>
Tim                              $10,000<CR>
Tom                              $5,000<CR>
Tammy                            $20,000<CR>
Each line has a carriage return after it. Also notice what happens to this line.
</PRE>
<HR>
<H2>Gross Sales without Pre Tags</H2>
<HR>
              Gross sales                      <P>
Salesman                         Sales<P>
Tim                              $10,000<P>
Tom                              $5,000<P>
Tammy                            $20,000<P>
</HR>
Carriage returns are replaced by new paragraph tags or everything would run together.
</BODY>
</HTML>
```

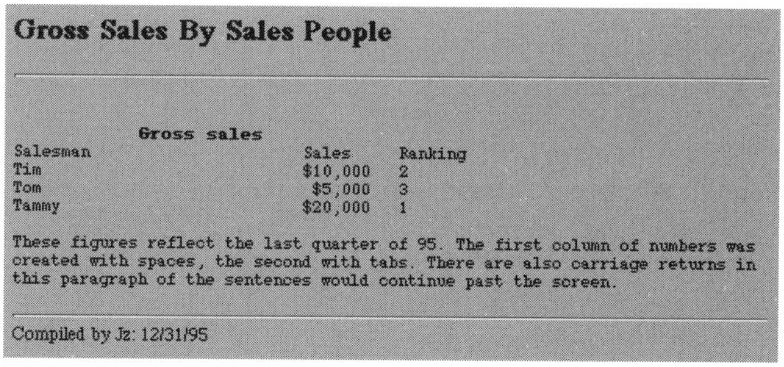

Figure 4-4 The difference between using and not using the <PRE> tags

Comments

While the <PRE> ... </PRE> tags may be useful for quick and dirty tables, the advent of <TABLE> tags in HTML 3 has made doing tables with <PRE> somewhat less desirable. Probably the biggest use for <PRE> now is displaying program listings in documents. <PRE> can also be useful in forms if you wish to have fields line up underneath one another.

CHAPTER 4
MANAGING DOCUMENT SPACING

4.4 How do I... Space my home page?

COMPLEXITY
EASY

Problem

How can I make a home page so that it is easily readable, yet still compact enough that readers don't have to scroll a lot?

Technique

The technique used here is a mixture of good judgment, common sense, and personal taste. Spacing is often a matter of personal taste. Bad spacing is easy to identify: if you can't read your page, nobody else can, either. Good spacing is a bit harder to identify. You wrote your page, so you can tell where everything is, but that doesn't mean that another reader will be able to. Have a few people read your page and give you feedback on it. There are also a few pointers to follow that will help make your page flow smoothly and be easy to read.

- **HTML** Be consistent with your spacing.
- **HTML** Be consistent with how you use horizontal lines.
- **HTML** Remember a home page is a starting point, so it doesn't need to be very big.
- **HTML** Feel free to ignore points 1, 2, and 3. After all, it is your page. Just remember, though, that if things are run together or spaced too far apart, readers may miss something you want them to read.

Steps

The following steps give general instructions on how to space your page. Feel free to follow or ignore any suggestions given.

1. Decide which type of spacing and horizontal line rules you wish to use, if any.

2. Incorporate these rules into your pages. The following document is a very simple home page about poetry. It uses an <HR> to separate the two poems and another <HR> to separate the footer from the main text body of the page. It also uses <BR> tags to cause each verse of the poem to appear on a separate line.

```
<HTML>
<HEAD>
<TITLE>My Page of Poems</TITLE>
<BODY>
```

4.4
SPACE MY HOME PAGE

```
</HEAD>
<H2>My Poetry Page</H2>
Here are a couple of my favorite poems:<P>
This one from my childhood:
<P ALIGN=CENTER>
Mary had a little lamb<BR>
Its fleece was white as snow<BR>
Everywhere that Mary went the lamb was sure to go!<BR>
</P>
<HR>
This one from my adulthood:
<P ALIGN=CENTER>
Roses are Red<BR>
Violets are Blue<BR>
I love you<BR>
<HR>
<CITE>
This page is maintained by: J. Smith.
</CITE>
</BODY>
</HTML>
```

3. Experiment to see what you think works best. The example document will look like Figure 4-5 when viewed.

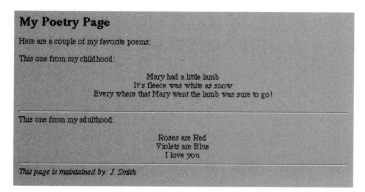

Figure 4-5 A demo using horizontal rules and line breaks

How It Works

You blend elements and tags such as <P>, <BR>, <HR>, and different levels of headers to create a page that is pleasing to the eye, informative, and yet not too long. It is helpful to have a set of rules that governs the use of certain tags. For example:

> **HTML** Use an <HR> after a level heading.

> **HTML** Use an <HR> before any footer or trailer information.

- **HTML** Use an <HR> to separate distinct items.
- **HTML** Use two <P> elements to separate new sections.
- **HTML** Use <BR> between lines of addresses.
- **HTML** Always start a page with a title displayed as a level 2 header.

Comments

For the most part, pages can be broken down into three sections:

- **HTML** Heading information that could include a snappy logo, who you are, where you are
- **HTML** Body content that includes information or links to information you find important
- **HTML** Footer information such as where to reach you, when the document was last updated, links to sites that are directly related to your page, and e-mail address

CHAPTER 5
HTML MATH AND TABLES

HTML MATH AND TABLES

How do I...

5.1 Add mathematical symbols?
5.2 Include a table?
5.3 Place a caption in a table?
5.4 Insert a table heading?
5.5 Define data for a cell or table element?
5.6 Create a new row of data?
5.7 Put a table in my home page?

There are some powerful new techniques in HTML 3 that improve your ability to display the information on your page. Among them are the new mathematical symbols that allow you to display simple and complex mathematical and scientific equations. There are also new table formatting commands in HTML 3 that let you create tables and give you control over the size and alignment of the table contents. The How-To's in this chapter will show you how to effectively include math and tables in your Web pages.

5.1 Add Mathematical Symbols

If your page covers topics in math, science, or engineering, you may run across the need to display special mathematical symbols not available in normal ASCII text. This How-To explains how to insert various types of mathematical symbols, including characters, vectors, and matrices, in your page, and how to properly format complex mathematical equations.

5.2   Include a Table

The <TABLE> element in HTML 3 gives you the power to control the format and alignment of your information. You can place information into tables and be sure it will be properly aligned with the other information in the table, a great advantage when you're trying to display related information on a topic. This How-To gives the basics on including a table in your page.

5.3   Place a Caption in a Table

Captions are titles of tables, usually centered above the top of the table. This simple How-To explains how to add a caption to your table.

5.4   Insert a Table Heading

Table headings are the top row of the table and usually define what is in each column of the table. This How-To explains how to set up a table heading so you can easily identify the data in your table.

5.5   Define Data for a Cell or Table Element

Once you've set up a table, you need to be able to put data into it. In a table, data is stored in table elements, or cells. This How-To explains how to create cells and put your information into them.

5.6   Create a New Row of Data

Once you've started creating table elements, you will want to put different items in different rows of the table. This How-To explains how to end one row of data and start a new row.

5.7   Put a Table in My Home Page

When you've mastered the basics of creating tables, you'll no doubt be eager to include them in your pages. This How-To covers some tips and tricks for effective use of tables, including some things you may not have thought of as tables.

COMPLEXITY
INTERMEDIATE

5.1   How do I...
Add mathematical symbols?

COMPATIBILITY: HTML 3

Problem

The material I want to include on my page contains a number of mathematical formulas that are difficult to show using normal text characters. I would like to

5.1 ADD MATHEMATICAL SYMBOLS

show these equations as text, without having to resort to graphics. How can I format mathematical equations in HTML?

Technique

HTML 3 includes a number of elements that can be used to format mathematical equations in the text of a page. The <MATH> element is used to identify equations, and tags contained within the <MATH> tag are used to format the equation. With these tags, it is possible to display complicated equations with subscripts and superscripts, square roots, vectors and other special symbols, and arrays. Other tags can be used do display integrals, summation symbols, and other mathematical symbols. Unfortunately, these commands do not exist in HTML 2, so older browsers can't recognize them, and thus can't format the text correctly.

Steps

Open your document and locate the areas in the document where you would like to place mathematical formulas. Type plain-text versions of the formulas now to guide you later, when you add the HTML <MATH> tags.

1. To identify any equation, place the $tag at the beginning of the function and the$ tag at the end of the function:

```
The equation for kinetic energy is <MATH>E = 1/2mv2</MATH>

The function of the curve is <MATH>y = (3 + x)/(5 - 2x)</MATH>
```

2. As discussed in Chapter 3, you can use the <SUP> and <SUB> tags for superscripts and subscripts, respectively. However, within the and tags, you can use shortcuts for those tags: ^ for ^{and}, and _ for _{and}:

```
The equation for kinetic energy is <MATH>E = 1/2mv^2^</MATH>

The line can be represented by the equation <MATH>y = c_0_ + c_1_*x</MATH>
```

3. To express fractions, you can use the <BOX> and <OVER> tags. Place <BOX> at the beginning of the fraction, </BOX> at the end of the fraction, and <OVER> where the division between the numerator and denominator occurs. Within the <MATH> tag, you can substitute { (the left brace) for <BOX> and } (the right brace) for </BOX>:

```
The equation for kinetic energy is <MATH>E =
<BOX>1<OVER>2</BOX>mv^2^</MATH>

The equation for kinetic energy is <MATH>E = {1<OVER>2}mv^2^</MATH>
```

4. To place fractions and other mathematical equations in parentheses, brackets, braces, or horizontal lines, use the <BOX> tag and the desired symbol. Use the <LEFT> tag at the beginning of the expression, just after the symbol, and the <RIGHT> tag at the end of the expression, just before the closing symbol:

```
<MATH>{(<LEFT>3+x<OVER>5-2x<RIGHT>)}</MATH>

<MATH>{[<LEFT>3+2x<OVER>5-2x<RIGHT>]}</MATH>

<MATH>{|<LEFT>3+2x<OVER>5-2x<RIGHT>|}</MATH>

<MATH>{&ltbrace;<LEFT>3+2x<OVER>5-2x<RIGHT>&rtbrace;}</MATH>
```

Note that in order to display something within braces, you must use the special characters `&ltbrace;` and `&rtbrace;` for the left brace and right brace symbols respectively.

5. HTML 3 also provides a number of tags you can use within the <MATH> element to display special modified characters such as vectors, dots, and bars:

TAG	DEFINITION
<VEC>	Displays a vector over a character
<BAR>	Displays a horizontal bar over a character
<DOT>	Displays a single dot over a character
<DDOT>	Displays a double dot over a character
<HAT>	Displays a hat (^) over a character
<TILDE>	Displays a tilde (~) over a character

Special Mathematical Symbols in HTML

For example:

```
The equation for kinetic energy is <MATH><VEC>E</VEC> =
1/2m<VEC>v</VEC>^2^</MATH>

The average value of x, <MATH><BAR>x</BAR></MATH>, was 42.
```

6. The <SQRT> tag places the text found between it and the </SQRT> tag inside the square root symbol. A more general form is the <ROOT> tag, which, along with the <OF> tag, places the text between the <OF> and </ROOT> tags inside the root symbol and places the text located between the <ROOT> and <OF> in the area of the root symbol used to designate the power of the root (2 for square root, 3 for cube root, etc.):

```
The Pythagorean theorem states that <MATH>c = <SQRT>a^2^ +
b^2^</SQRT></MATH>

The radius of a sphere with volume V is
<MATH><ROOT>3<OF>{3V<OVER>4pi}</ROOT></MATH>
```

5.1
ADD MATHEMATICAL SYMBOLS

7. To create an array, use the <ARRAY> tag to define the beginning of an array, and </ARRAY> to mark the end of the array. Within these tags, the <ROW> tag marks the beginning of a new row in the array, and <ITEM> marks a new entry in the array:

```
<ARRAY>
    <ROW><ITEM>a<ITEM>b
    <ROW><ITEM>c<ITEM>d
</ARRAY>

<ARRAY>
    <ROW><ITEM>a<ITEM>b<ITEM>c
    <ROW><ITEM>d<ITEM>e<ITEM>f
</ARRAY>
```

8. To align the array within the window, use the ALIGN attribute within the ARRAY tag:

```
<ARRAY ALIGN=CENTER>
    <ROW><ITEM>a<ITEM>b
    <ROW><ITEM>c<ITEM>d
</ARRAY>
```

9. To align columns in the array, use the COLDEF attribute within the ARRAY tag. This attribute uses a capital letter to signify the alignment for each column in the array: L for left, C for center, R for right. For example, to align the first two columns in the center but align the third column on the right, enter

```
<ARRAY COLDEF="CCR">
    <ROW><ITEM>a<ITEM>b
    <ROW><ITEM>c<ITEM>d
</ARRAY>
```

Examples of the various mathematical styles are shown in Figure 5-1. The code is also available on the CD-ROM as file 5-1.html.

How It Works

The <MATH> tag alerts the browser that the text contained within the and tags requires special formatting, including symbols that have different meanings within the <MATH> tags than they have in normal text. The special tags encountered within the <MATH> tags are then converted into appropriate graphics and spacing according to the specifications of the browser.

Comments

Because this mathematical notation is only available in HTML 3, people using pre-HTML 3 browsers will not be able to see the appropriate graphics and spacing,

CHAPTER 5
HTML MATH AND TABLES

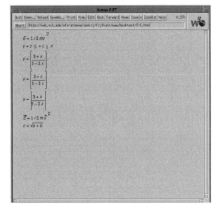

Figure 5-1 Mathematical symbols and styles in HTML

which may render some equations more confusing than if they had been left as plain text. Keep this in mind when creating your documents. Also, as of this writing, not all of the mathematical elements had been incorporated into Arena, the HTML 3 testbed browser; the browser did not yet support arrays, roots, and some special characters. Netscape does not support mathematical symbols of any kind, including subscript and superscript, at this time.

COMPLEXITY
EASY

5.2 How do I... Include a table?

COMPATIBILITY: HTML 3

Problem

I have a collection of data that I would like to display as a table in my page. How do I define a table in HTML?

Technique

HTML 3 supports tables, which allow you to control the row and column placement of information on your page. This How-To explains how to define a table in HTML, by using the <TABLE> and </TABLE> tags. How to format the data to include in the table will be covered later in the chapter.

5.2
INCLUDE A TABLE

Steps

Open your document. Identify where in the document you want to include a table. You may want to enter the table data into your document now, to serve as a guide when you add HTML <TABLE> tags later.

1. To specify data presented as a table, place the <TABLE> tag at the beginning of the data and </TABLE> at the end of the data:

```
<TABLE>
    <!-- Here's where the table information goes... -->
</TABLE>
```

2. HTML does not include, as a default, borders around the cells of the table. If you want to display the borders using the lines programmed into the browser, add the BORDER attribute to the <TABLE> tag:

```
<TABLE BORDER>
    <!-- Here's where the table information goes... -->
</TABLE>
```

3. As with other HTML elements, such as headings, you can use the ALIGN attribute to control the horizontal location of the table on the page. The ALIGN attribute can take on the following values:

OPTION	DESCRIPTION
"bleedleft"	Flush with the left edge of the browser window
"left"	Flush with the left margin of the text
"center"	Centered between the left and right text margins
"right"	Flush with the right margin of the text
"bleedright"	Flush with the right edge of the browser window
"justify"	Fits the space between the left and right margins

 Alignment Options for Tables

For example, to center a table with a border, enter

```
<TABLE BORDER ALIGN=CENTER>
    <!-- Here's the data for the table... -->
</TABLE>
```

Or to place a borderless table flush against the left edge of the window, enter

```
<TABLE ALIGN=BLEEDLEFT>
    <!-- Here's the data for the table... -->
</TABLE>
```

4. When formatting a table, the browser automatically chooses a size for each column based on the text contained in each column. However, if you want to set a fixed size for each column, you can do so with the COLSPEC attribute in the <TABLE> tag. The COLSPEC attribute is followed by a series of letters and numbers; for example, "L50 R30 C10". The letter stands for alignment of the text in the column: L for left, C for center, and R for right. The number is the width of the column. The units are set by the UNITS attribute, with the following choices:

OPTION	DESCRIPTION
"en"	en units (1 en = 1/2 point = 1/144 inch). This is the default
"relative"	relative units: the browser sums the units to determine the relative width of each column
"pixels"	pixels on the browser display

 Options for the UNITS Attribute

For example, to define three columns, each left aligned and each a ½ inch wide, enter

```
<TABLE COLSPEC="L72 L72 L72">
    <!-- Table data goes here... -->
</TABLE>
```

To create a four-column table with the first three columns left-aligned and the fourth right-aligned and half as wide as the others, enter

```
<TABLE UNITS=RELATIVE COLSPEC="L2 L2 L2 R1">
    <!-- Table data goes here... -->
</TABLE>
```

To create a table that has three columns, one left-aligned, one centered, and one right-aligned, each with a width of 100 pixels, enter

```
<TABLE UNITS=PIXELS COLSPEC="L100 C100 R100">
    <!-- Table data goes here... -->
</TABLE>
```

5. Similarly, you can control the width of the entire table by using the WIDTH attribute in the <TABLE> tag. Using the units defined by the UNITS attribute, it fixes the width of the table. If the UNITS attribute is set to "relative", WIDTH interprets the number as the fraction of the distance between the left and right margins. For example, to set the width of a table to 4 inches (= 4*144 = 576 en), enter

```
<TABLE WIDTH=576>
    <!-- Table data goes here... -->
</TABLE>
```

To create a table that is centered on the screen and covers three-fourths of the distance between the left and right margins, enter

```
<TABLE ALIGN=CENTER UNITS=RELATIVE WIDTH=0.75>
    <!-- Table data goes here... -->
</TABLE>
```

How It Works

When a browser encounters a <TABLE> tag, it sets up the formatting to handle the data contained between the <TABLE> and </TABLE> tags. By reading the attributes contained between them, it knows where to override its default settings for creating tables, including the size and placement of the table.

Comments

The BORDER attribute tells the browser to use the lines defined within the browser; it is not currently possible to tell a browser to use a certain style of line, or to use lines only on specific cells. If you use the "pixel" unit for COLSPEC and WIDTH, note that not all pixels are the same size, so something that formats one way on your browser may look different on another browser. It's probably better to stick to "en" and "relative" units to ensure that formatting works the way you want it to.

COMPLEXITY
EASY

5.3 How do I... Place a caption in a table?

COMPATIBILITY: HTML 3

Problem

I would like to add a title to the table in my page. I can do this with a heading, but is there a way to include a title as part of the table itself?

Technique

You can add a title, or caption, to the top or bottom of your table by using the <CAPTION> tag. Any text contained between the <CAPTION> and </CAPTION> tags is aligned with the table and, depending on the browser, may also be specially formatted in bold or italic.

Steps

Open your document. Decide on an appropriate caption for your table. It can be a title or a brief description of the table.

1. Enter the text for your caption in the table between the <TABLE> and </TABLE> tags.
2. To add a caption to a table, place the <CAPTION> tag at the beginning of the caption text and a </CAPTION> tag at the end of the text. If you want the caption to appear above the table, place the caption above the data in the table:

```
<TABLE>
    <CAPTION>This is the table caption</CAPTION>
    <!-- Here's the table data... -->
</TABLE>
```

To place a caption below the table, put the caption text and tags below the table data but before the </TABLE> tag:

```
<TABLE>
    <!-- Here's the table data... -->
    <CAPTION>This is the table caption</CAPTION>
</TABLE>
```

3. You can format the text within the <CAPTION> tags just as you would any other text, using the markup tags described in Chapter 3. For example, to emphasize the caption of a table, enter

```
<TABLE>
    <CAPTION><EM>This is an emphasized caption!</EM></CAPTION>
    <!-- Here's the table data... -->
</TABLE>
```

You can also insert line breaks (as explained in Chapter 4) to control the layout of the caption:

```
<TABLE>
    <CAPTION>This is the top line of the caption<BR>
    and this is the bottom line of the caption</CAPTION>
    <!-- Here's the table data... -->
</TABLE>
```

How It Works

When a browser encounters the <CAPTION> tag inside a table, it places the text contained between the <CAPTION> and </CAPTION> tags either above or below the table, depending on where it encounters the caption. The caption is usually aligned with the table. Some browsers may also format the caption with bold or italics.

Comments

Because some browsers may format the caption, be careful when using text formatting tags like <B> and <I> in the caption. These tags may be ignored by the browser, override the default setting, or be combined with the browser's format for the caption. For example, if a browser is programmed to render captions in bold text, placing <I> and </I> around your caption text might mean the caption appears in italics, remains in bold, or appears as bold italics.

COMPLEXITY
INTERMEDIATE

5.4 How do I... Insert a table heading?

COMPATIBILITY: HTML 3

Problem

In my table, I would like to have the top row consist of headings describing the contents of each column. I would like to easily set these headings off from the rest of the text. How can I accomplish this in HTML?

Technique

You can specify special heading cells in the table by using the <TH> tag. The text listed after the <TH> tag is considered to be part of the heading cell. You can use this tag anywhere in the table; headings do not necessarily have to be at the top of a column. HTML also includes a number of sophisticated attributes that allow you to precisely format your table headings.

Steps

Open your document. Choose names for the heading cells. Heading cells can go across the columns or down the rows of your table, although for the example below we will consider heading cells across the columns of a table.

1. Enter the word or phrase for each column heading in the table, between the <TABLE> and </TABLE> tags.

2. For each column in your table, place a <TH> tag followed by the text for that column. For example, for a three-column table, enter

```
<TABLE>
    <CAPTION>Here's my table</CAPTION>
    <TH>Column 1<TH>Column 2<TH>Column 3
    <!-- Here's the data for the rest of the table... -->
</TABLE>
```

3. Although most browsers format the contents of heading cells differently from the rest of the text, you can still use normal text markup tags to alter the style of the heading. For example, to place the heading for the second column of the above example in italics, enter

CHAPTER 5
HTML MATH AND TABLES

```
<TABLE>
    <CAPTION>Here's my table</CAPTION>
    <TH>Column 1<TH><I>Column 2</I><TH>Column 3
    <!-- Here's the data for the rest of the table... -->
</TABLE>
```

4. You can make a heading extend across more than one row or more than one column by using the ROWSPAN and COLSPAN attributes, respectively, in the <TH> tag. For these attributes, you state how many rows down or columns across you would like the heading cell to extend. For example, to make the heading for the second column extend over to the third column as well, enter

```
<TABLE>
    <CAPTION>Here's my table</CAPTION>
    <TH>Column 1<TH COLSPAN=2>Column 2
    <!-- Here's the data for the rest of the table... -->
</TABLE>
```

Similarly, to make the heading for column 1 extend down two rows, enter

```
<TABLE>
    <CAPTION>Here's my table</CAPTION>
    <TH ROWSPAN=2>Column 1<TH>Column 2<TH>Column 3
    <!-- Here's the data for the rest of the table... -->
</TABLE>
```

The uses of the ROWSPAN and COLSPAN attributes will be discussed in greater detail in How-To 5.7.

5. You can use the ALIGN attribute inside the <TH> tag to define the alignment of the text within the header cell. The standard options of "left", "center", "right", and "justify" are available. To center the heading for the second column in the above example, enter

```
<TABLE>
    <CAPTION>Here's my table</CAPTION>
    <TH ROWSPAN=2>Column 1<TH ALIGN=CENTER>Column 2<TH>Column 3
    <!-- Here's the data for the rest of the table... -->
</TABLE>
```

In addition to the standard alignment options, a fifth option, "decimal", is also available. This is used to align the decimal points on each line of the cell if, for example, your cell has several lines of numbers (such as dollar amounts). If a line doesn't have a decimal point, the line is centered. You can use the DP attribute in the <TH> tag to define a decimal point if you want to use a character other than the default decimal point (.) symbol. An example of this would be to use a colon as the decimal point to align a table of times, such as 1:15, 2:45, 3:30, etc.

5.4 INSERT A TABLE HEADING

6. In addition to the horizontal alignment described above, you can align text vertically within a cell by using the VALIGN attribute. There are four options for VALIGN:

OPTION	DESCRIPTION
"top"	Aligns text at the top of the cell
"middle"	Aligns text in the middle of the cell
"bottom"	Aligns text at the bottom of the cell
"baseline"	Aligns all the text in a row with this alignment attribute set on a common baseline

 Vertical Alignment Options for Table Cells

For example, to have the heading for the third column align along the top of the cell, enter

```
<TABLE>
    <CAPTION>Here's my table</CAPTION>
    <TH>Column 1<TH>Column 2<TH VALIGN=TOP>Column 3
    <!-- Here's the data for the rest of the table... -->
</TABLE>
```

To have the first and third columns aligned on the same baseline while the second column is aligned in the middle of its cell, enter

```
<TABLE>
    <CAPTION>Here's my table</CAPTION>
    <TH VALIGN=BASELINE>Column 1<TH VALIGN=MIDDLE>Column 2<TH VALIGN=BASELINE>Column 3
    <!-- Here's the data for the rest of the table... -->
</TABLE>
```

How It Works

The <TH> tag tells the browser that the text after that tag and before the next <TH> tag (or <TD> or <TR> tag, discussed below) is part of a cell that has been designated as a heading cell. Most browsers will format the text in a bold or emphasized style, although some will treat a heading cell the same as a data cell (see How-To 5.5 below).

Comments

When using the ROWSPAN and COLSPAN attributes to specify the size of rows, be careful you don't end up with overlapping cells. This could cause a table to render in a way you didn't plan, or it may not even display at all, depending on the browser.

CHAPTER 5
HTML MATH AND TABLES

COMPLEXITY
INTERMEDIATE

5.5 How do I... Define data for a cell or table element?

COMPATIBILITY: HTML 3

Problem

Now that I've defined a table, added a caption, and set up headings for each column, I want to add my data to the table. How do I place data into table cells in HTML?

Technique

The process of adding data cells, or table elements, to your table is very similar to the technique used for adding table headings described in How-To 5.4. The <TD> tag indicates that the text after it and before the next table-related tag is to be placed into a cell. As with <TH>, there are a number of sophisticated attributes that can be used to control the placement and appearance of table cells.

Steps

Open your document. If you haven't done so already, enter the data you want to display in the table.

1. To place text in a data cell, put the <TD> tag in front of the text. The cell includes all the text that follows the data tag until it reaches another table-specific tag, such as <TD>, <TH>, <TR>, etc. Here is an example for the first row of a three-column table:

```
<TABLE>
    <CAPTION>The table caption</CAPTION>
    <TH>Column 1<TH>Column 2<TH>Column 3
    <TR><TD>Data 1<TD>Data 2<TD>Data 3
</TABLE>
```

(Don't worry about the <TR> tag right now; it is explained in detail in How-To 5.6. Basically, it creates a new row in the table.)

2. As with heading cells in a table, you can use formatting tags like <B>, <I>, <EM>, etc., to format the contents of a cell. Since data cells usually do not receive special formatting, unlike heading cells, this is a useful way to draw attention to a specific cell. For example, to highlight the data in the second column of the above table, enter

5.5
DEFINE DATA FOR A CELL OR TABLE ELEMENT

```
<TABLE>
    <CAPTION>The table caption</CAPTION>
    <TH>Column 1<TH>Column 2<TH>Column 3
    <TR><TD>Data 1<TD><B>Data 2<B><TD>Data 3
</TABLE>
```

3. As described in How-To 5.4, you can use the ROWSPAN and COLSPAN attributes to identify data cells that have extended rows and columns. For example, to make the first data cell in the above table extend an extra column to the right, enter

```
<TABLE>
    <CAPTION>The table caption</CAPTION>
    <TH>Column 1<TH>Column 2<TH>Column 3
    <TR><TD COLSPAN=2>Data 1<TD>Data 3
</TABLE>
```

4. You can use the ALIGN attribute in <TD> to horizontally align the contents of the cell. As with <TH>, you can set ALIGN to "left", "center", "right", "justify", and "decimal", the last one being used to align the contents of the cell by using the decimal point (or another character specified using the DP attribute discussed in How-To 5.4). For example, to center the contents of the third data cell in the above table, enter

```
<TABLE>
    <CAPTION>The table caption</CAPTION>
    <TH>Column 1<TH>Column 2<TH>Column 3
    <TR><TD>Data 1<TD>Data 2<TD ALIGN=CENTER>Data 3
</TABLE>
```

5. You can also use the VALIGN attribute to vertically align the contents of a cell. As with heading cells, the options for VALIGN are "top", "middle", "bottom", and "baseline". To set the contents of the first data cell along the top of the cell, enter

```
<TABLE>
    <CAPTION>The table caption</CAPTION>
    <TH>Column 1<TH>Column 2<TH>Column 3
    <TR><TD VALIGN=TOP>Data 1<TD>Data 2<TD>Data 3
</TABLE>
```

How It Works

When a browser encounters a <TD> tag in a table, it creates a new data cell in the table, placing all the text from the <TD> tag to the next table-related tag (<TH>, <TR>, <CAPTION>, </TABLE>) in the cell. Any formatting for the contents of the cell depends on the attributes set for the cell, as well as on any formatting tags contained within the cell.

CHAPTER 5
HTML MATH AND TABLES

Comments

As with the <TH> tag, you should take care when using ROWSPAN and COLSPAN with <TD> in your table. If you create overlapping cells by misusing the tags, your table will not be rendered correctly, and it may not even display at all, depending on the browser's settings.

COMPLEXITY
INTERMEDIATE

5.6 How do I... Create a new row of data?

COMPATIBILITY: HTML 3

Problem

Now that I can add data cells to my table, I would like to split the cells up into rows. How can I divide the cells of my table into rows in HTML?

Technique

The <TR> tag creates a new row of cells in a table. You can use attributes with this tag to define the horizontal and vertical alignment of the contents of the row as well.

Steps

Open your document. If you have not already done so, enter the rest of the data for your table, using the <TH> and <TD> tags described in How-To's 5.4 and 5.5

1. To help you decide the number and length of your rows (and to make it easier to correct errors in code later), enter carriage returns at the end of each row of data.

```
<TABLE>
    <CAPTION>The table caption</CAPTION>
    <TH>Column 1<TH>Column 2<TH>Column 3
    <TD>Data 1<TD>Data 2<TD>Data 3
    <TD>Data 4<TD>Data 5<TD>Data 6
</TABLE>
```

2. To specify the end of one row and the beginning of another, add the <TR> tag at the beginning of the new row:

```
<TABLE>
    <CAPTION>The table caption</CAPTION>
    <TR><TH>Column 1<TH>Column 2<TH>Column 3
    <TR><TD>Data 1<TD>Data 2<TD>Data 3
```

5.6
CREATE A NEW ROW OF DATA

```
    <TR><TD>Data 4<TD>Data 5<TD>Data 6
</TABLE>
```

The <TR> tag at the beginning of the first row of the table is optional, but it helps provide parallelism to the HTML code describing the table and does not upset the formatting of the table.

3. To set the horizontal alignment of all the cells of the row to the same value, use the ALIGN attribute in the <TR> tag. ALIGN in this context takes on the same values it has with the <TD> and <TH> tags: "left", "center", "right", "justify", and "decimal". To center the cells in the second row of data in the above example, you can do the following:

```
<TABLE>
    <CAPTION>The table caption</CAPTION>
    <TR><TH>Column 1<TH>Column 2<TH>Column 3
    <TR><TD>Data 1<TD>Data 2<TD>Data 3
    <TR ALIGN=CENTER><TD>Data 4<TD>Data 5<TD>Data 6
</TABLE>
```

You can override the formatting for a cell in that row by setting the ALIGN attribute within the particular cell. For example, if you wanted the cell in the second column of the second data row shown above aligned to the right side of the cell, and not centered like the rest of the text, you could do the following:

```
<TABLE>
    <CAPTION>The table caption</CAPTION>
    <TR><TH>Column 1<TH>Column 2<TH>Column 3
    <TR><TD>Data 1<TD>Data 2<TD>Data 3
    <TR ALIGN=CENTER><TD>Data 4<TD ALIGN=RIGHT>Data 5<TD>Data 6
</TABLE>
```

The alignment specified in the COLSPEC attribute in the table overrides any formatting you set with the <TR> tag, although you can override the COLSPEC alignment in individual cells.

4. You can set the vertical alignment of all cells in the row by using the VALIGN attribute in the <TR> tag. In heading and data cells, VALIGN takes on the values "top", "middle", "bottom", and "baseline". For example, to set the vertical alignment of the second data row in the above example to the middle of the cell, enter

```
<TABLE>
    <CAPTION>The table caption</CAPTION>
    <TR><TH>Column 1<TH>Column 2<TH>Column 3
    <TR><TD>Data 1<TD>Data 2<TD>Data 3
    <TR VALIGN=MIDDLE><TD>Data 4<TD>Data 5<TD>Data 6
</TABLE>
```

To override the vertical alignment for a row in a given cell, set the alignment within that particular cell. To set the middle cell of the second data row above to a bottom alignment, you can use the following code.

```
<TABLE>
    <CAPTION>The table caption</CAPTION>
    <TR><TH>Column 1<TH>Column 2<TH>Column 3
    <TR><TD>Data 1<TD>Data 2<TD>Data 3
    <TR VALIGN=MIDDLE><TD>Data 4<TD VALIGN=BOTTOM>Data 5<TD>Data 6
</TABLE>
```

How It Works

When a browser encounters the <TR> tag, it creates a new row in the table and places the cells located between the <TR> and the next <TR> or the end of the table in that row. If alignment attributes are specified, they are applied to all the cells in that row, unless individual cells (or the COLSPEC attribute in <TABLE>) contain information that overrides the alignment specified in <TR>.

Comments

If you set the column alignments using the COLSPEC attribute in the <TABLE> tag, then any horizontal alignment placed in the <TR> tags will be ignored. The order of precedence for defining cell alignments is

<TH> and <TD>
COLSPEC in <TABLE>
<TR>

COMPLEXITY
INTERMEDIATE

5.7 How do I... Put a table in my home page?

COMPATIBILITY: HTML 3

Problem

Now that I know all the elements of a table in HTML, I would like to start adding tables to my pages. How can I use these tables to effectively display my information? What sort of tips and tricks can I use to make my tables look better?

Technique

Tables are a good way to control the layout and format of information on a Web page. A good way to learn how to create effective tables is to go through a few examples of them step by step to see how they are constructed.

5.7
PUT A TABLE IN MY HOME PAGE

Steps

These examples will give you an idea of how to create tables and use them to display different types of information.

1. First, look at a simple table that might be used by someone listing a number of products for sale and their prices. It might look like this:

Widget Price List (September 1997)

ITEM	COST
Mini Widget	$19.95
Widget	$29.95
Super Widget	$39.95
Widget Royale *(with cheese)*	$79.95

HTML To produce this table, begin by setting up the <TABLE> tags at the beginning and end of the list. Let the browser choose the size of the cells, but put a border around the table:

```
<TABLE BORDER>

</TABLE>
```

HTML Now add a title as a caption at the top of the list. Again, let the browser choose the style for the caption; don't include any style tags here. For the sake of clarity, indent the contents of the <CAPTION> tag, as well as anything else contained between the <TABLE> tags, to help set it off from the rest of the code for the page:

```
<TABLE BORDER>
    <CAPTION>Widget Price List (September 1997)</CAPTION>

</TABLE>
```

HTML Now add the heading cells for the table. There are two columns in this table, so create two heading cells using the <TH> tag. You can start off the row with the <TR> tag, although it is not explicitly required.

```
<TABLE BORDER>
    <CAPTION>Widget Price List (September 1997)</CAPTION>
    <TR><TH>Item<TH>Cost

</TABLE>
```

CHAPTER 5
HTML MATH AND TABLES

HTML Now add the rows of items and their prices. Start each row with the <TR> tag and put the <TD> tag in front of each item. Use italics (<I>) here to emphasize the phrase "(with cheese)" as shown above.

```
<TABLE BORDER>
    <CAPTION>Widget Price List (September 1997)</CAPTION>
    <TR><TH>Item<TH>Cost
    <TR><TD>Mini Widget<TD>$19.95
    <TR><TD>Widget<TD>$29.95
    <TR><TD>Super Widget<TD>$39.95
    <TR><TD>Widget Royale <I>(with cheese)</I><TD>$79.95
</TABLE>
```

HTML You've now made a full-fledged, complete table, although you can still tweak it a little bit to improve its appearance if need be. For example, if you included another item in the table with a price of more than $100.00, the formatting of the price column (which defaults to flush left) would become less than attractive. To improve this, you can set the alignment for the price cells to be flush right:

```
<TABLE BORDER>
    <CAPTION>Widget Price List (September 1997)</CAPTION>
    <TR><TH>Item<TH>Cost
    <TR><TD>Mini Widget<TD ALIGN=RIGHT>$19.95
    <TR><TD>Widget<TD ALIGN=RIGHT>$29.95
    <TR><TD>Super Widget<TD ALIGN=RIGHT>$39.95
    <TR><TD>Widget Royale <I>(with cheese)</I><TD ALIGN=RIGHT>$79.95
    <TR><TD>Mega Deluxe Widget<TD ALIGN=RIGHT>$109.95
</TABLE>
```

HTML You could also use the COLSPEC attribute in the heading if you also wanted to specify the size of the columns. Try this, using relative units and making the left column three times as wide as the right column:

```
<TABLE BORDER UNITS=RELATIVE COLSPEC="L3 R1">
    <CAPTION>Widget Price List (September 1997)</CAPTION>
    <TR><TH>Item<TH>Cost
    <TR><TD>Mini Widget<TD>$19.95
    <TR><TD>Widget<TD>$29.95
    <TR><TD>Super Widget<TD>$39.95
    <TR><TD>Widget Royale <I>(with cheese)</I><TD>$79.95
    <TR><TD>Mega Deluxe Widget<TD>$109.95
</TABLE>
```

The output of the table is shown in Figure 5-2. The code is also available on the CD-ROM as file 5-2.html.

2. Now try another type of table, which will show an effective way of using COLSPAN and ROWSPAN. Say you want to include the score from a baseball game in a Web page as a table. An example of a score is shown below.

5.7
PUT A TABLE IN MY HOME PAGE

Today's Game

TEAM	SCORE		
	R	H	E
Red Sox	8	11	0
Yankees	0	3	1

HTML As you did in the first example, start with the <TABLE> tags and include the title of the table as the caption. For this example exclude a border; all you want to do here is format the text the right way.

```
<TABLE>
    <CAPTION>Today's Game</CAPTION>
</TITLE>
```

HTML Before you proceed any further, sketch out how the rows and columns will be set up. It's clear that this table will have four columns: one for the name of the team and three for the various score categories (R, H, and E, which stand for Runs, Hits, and Errors). In this table, unlike the one in the previous example, there won't be an item for every cell. One way to deal with this would be to just skip cells by including cell tags in the table but not putting any text in them. To do that, you immediately follow one table-

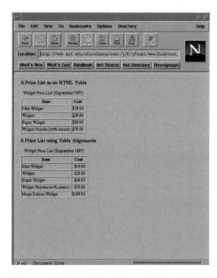

Figure 5-2 A price list table in HTML

CHAPTER 5
HTML MATH AND TABLES

related tag with another. Apply this to the first row of the table, where only two of the four columns contain any text:

```
<TABLE>
    <CAPTION>Today's Game</CAPTION>
    <TR><TH>Team<TH><TH>Score<TH>

</TABLE>
```

The second row is similar, but only missing one cell:

```
<TABLE>
    <CAPTION>Today's Game</CAPTION>
    <TR><TH>Team<TH><TH>Score<TH>
    <TR><TH><TH>R<TH>H<TH>E

</TABLE>
```

Finish the rest of the table using data cells for the team names and scores:

```
<TABLE>
    <CAPTION>Today's Game</CAPTION>
    <TR><TH>Team<TH><TH>Score<TH>
    <TR><TH><TH>R<TH>H<TH>E
    <TR><TD>Red Sox<TD>8<TD>11<TD>0
    <TR><TD>Yankees<TD>0<TD>3<TD>1
</TABLE>
```

The output of this table is shown in Figure 5-3. The code is also available on the CD-ROM as file 5-3.html.

HTML This layout succeeds in skipping cells, but the result is less than aesthetically pleasing. The third column, which contains the number of hits, also includes the word "Score." Since this word is much larger than the numbers or the letter H, the column is automatically sized wide enough to fit "Score," which ends up disrupting the flow of the layout for the scores below. A solution to this problem is to use COLSPAN: you can define the top row to have only two columns but have the second column of the row be three columns wide:

```
<TABLE>
    <CAPTION>Today's Game</CAPTION>
    <TR><TH>Team<TH COLSPAN=3>Score
    <TR><TH><TH>R<TH>H<TH>E
    <TR><TD>Red Sox<TD>8<TD>11<TD>0
    <TR><TD>Yankees<TD>0<TD>3<TD>1
</TABLE>
```

5.7
PUT A TABLE IN MY HOME PAGE

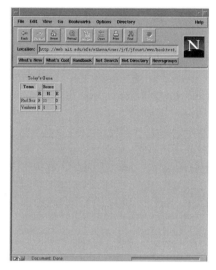

Figure 5-3 A box score table made by skipping cells

> **HTML** Note that when you added the COLSPAN attribute, you must delete the extra <TH> tags; if you don't, the table will include the extra columns and its flow will be disrupted. While you're at it, use the ROWSPAN attribute on the first cell in the first row ("Team") to make it two rows deep:

```
<TABLE>
    <CAPTION>Today's Game</CAPTION>
    <TR><TH ROWSPAN=2>Team<TH COLSPAN=3>Score
    <TR><TH>R<TH>H<TH>E
    <TR><TD>Red Sox<TD>8<TD>11<TD>0
    <TR><TD>Yankees<TD>0<TD>3<TD>1
</TABLE>
```

> **HTML** Note that when you add the ROWSPAN attribute, you must delete the extra <TH> tag in the second row, which is no longer needed and would otherwise disrupt the layout of the table. While this doesn't affect the layout as much as the COLSPAN attribute did, it makes it easier to change the alignment of the text in the cell. For example, if you wanted the word "Team" in that cell placed on the bottom of the cell instead of the top, you could write

```
<TABLE>
    <CAPTION>Today's Game</CAPTION>
    <TR><TH ROWSPAN=2 VALIGN=BOTTOM>Team<TH COLSPAN=3>Score
```

continued on next page

CHAPTER 5
HTML MATH AND TABLES

continued from previous page

```
    <TR><TH>R<TH>H<TH>E
    <TR><TD>Red Sox<TD>8<TD>11<TD>0
    <TR><TD>Yankees<TD>0<TD>3<TD>1
</TABLE>
```

This is easier, and is also better style, than making empty cells and moving text among the cells when you want to change the layout. The output of this table is shown as Figure 5-4 and is also available on the CD-ROM as file 5-4.html.

3. The examples shown above and elsewhere in the chapter have assumed you have short, one-line entries for the tables. However, there is no reason the tables need to have only short entries for each cell. You can use tables to format larger pieces of text, and control their layout better than if you used line breaks, paragraphs, or other HTML features discussed in Chapter 4. For example, you want to format a troubleshooting guide for a product that will consist of a series of stated problems and a set of solutions for them. Here's how you can format this using a table:

HTML First, create the <TABLE> tags and include the title of the table:

```
<TABLE BORDER>
    <CAPTION>Widget Troubleshooting Guide</CAPTION>

</TABLE>
```

HTML The best way to format this would be to use two columns: one column with problems and the other with the corresponding solutions. Place heading cells into the table based on this:

```
<TABLE BORDER>
    <CAPTION>Widget Troubleshooting Guide</CAPTION>
    <TR><TH>Problem<TH>Solution

</TABLE>
```

HTML Now add the problems and the solutions. Add the text just as you would for any other table. Since HTML considers all text placed between the <TD> tag and the next table-specific tag as part of a single cell, you can easily put multiple lines of text into a single cell. For example:

```
<TABLE BORDER>
    <CAPTION>Widget Troubleshooting Guide</CAPTION>
    <TR><TH>Problem<TH>Solution
    <TR>
        <TD>Widget won't turn on
        <TD>Make sure the widget is plugged in. Also make sure the power
switch is in the on position. If the widget still will not turn on, take
your widget to the nearest repair shop for servicing.
```

```
<TR>
    <TD>Widget behaving erratically
    <TD>Press the reset button on the underside of the widget. If the
widget still behaves erratically, turn the power off and then back on. If
this does not work, take your widget to the nearest repair shop for
servicing.
</TABLE>
```

You can continue to do this, making table cells many lines long if necessary. The only limit is the amount of your data (although style may play a part, too).

The output of this code is shown in Figure 5-5. The code is also available on the CD-ROM as file 5-5.html.

How It Works

Browsers format based on their own predefined settings, plus any specific commands contained in the table. These commands give you considerable power to control the layout of the table.

Comments

As you have seen, tables are a powerful way to format text in your pages. Tables are versatile: not only can they be shaped to best display your information, they are not just limited to plain text. Tables can be used to display graphics (Chapter 8), forms (Chapter 9), or format lists of links to other documents (Chapter 7). Tables can

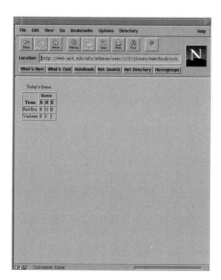

Figure 5-4 A box score table made with ROWSPAN and COLSPAN

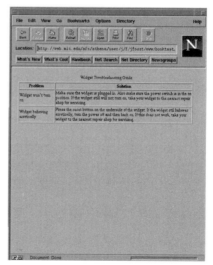

Figure 5-5 A troubleshooting list as a table in HTML

include essentially any HTML element, including line breaks and paragraphs, and even lists (Chapter 6). Tables take a little time to completely understand, but that effort will result in the ability to better control the layout and presentation of your information.

CHAPTER 6
HTML LISTS

HTML LISTS

How do I...

6.1 Create a numbered list?

6.2 Create a bulleted list?

6.3 Create an unmarked list?

6.4 Create a multicolumn list?

6.5 Create a menu list?

6.6 Create a directory list?

6.7 Create a glossary list?

6.8 Nest lists together?

6.9 Use lists to jazz up my home page?

A lot of information is best displayed in lists: ingredients for a recipe, your top ten favorite albums, the outline for a presentation, or the definitions for a set of terms. You can use tags like <P> and
 (see Chapter 4) to manage the placement of items in a document and create lists, but these tags are cumbersome and provide you with little flexibility to create the types of lists that best fit your information. Fortunately, HTML has other tags that permit you to create lists that include numbers, bullets, indentations, and other features. Moreover, HTML 3 includes new attributes that give you even greater ability to create the best lists for your data. This chapter covers the various types of lists that can be generated in HTML and shows you how they can be used to create a more effective home page.

CHAPTER 6
HTML LISTS

6.1 Create a Numbered List

Some information is ideally suited to be displayed in a numbered list: rankings, "top ten" lists, step-by-step procedures, etc. This simple How-To shows how you can create a numbered, or ordered, list that appears in a document with the ranking automatically included.

6.2 Create a Bulleted List

Some information is better suited to a point-by-point list: outlines, menus, etc. Each item on such a list is usually marked with a point, or bullet, to set it apart from other elements of the list. This simple How-To shows you how to create a bulleted list.

6.3 Create an Unmarked List

In some cases, neither a numbered list nor a bulleted list is appropriate to the information you want to include in a document. Sometimes the best type of list is one without any sort of numbers or marks in front of each item. This How-To explains how to create an unmarked list.

6.4 Create a Multicolumn List

You may have information you would like to display in a series of lists, side by side, such as a comparison of the characteristics of different items. This How-To will explain how to use the WRAP attribute for bulleted lists in HTML 3 to create multicolumn lists.

6.5 Create a Menu List

Lists, when combined with links to other documents or other locations in the same document, are often the best way to present the reader of a document with a menu of choices. The How-To explains how to use the menu feature in versions of HTML predating HTML 3.0 to create menus.

6.6 Create a Directory List

Some information takes the form of a list of entries from a directory: a list of files, a list of people, etc. This How-To explains how to use the directory feature in versions of HTML predating HTML 3.0 to create a directory of that information.

6.7 Create a Glossary List

Creating a glossary—a list of words and their definitions—requires special formatting to achieve the best results. This How-To explains how to use features in HTML to easily create a glossary.

6.8 Nest Lists Together

Some elements of a list may in fact be lists themselves, such as entries in an outline. This How-To shows how to nest lists within lists, as well as mix different types of lists together.

6.9 Use Lists to Jazz Up My Home Page

With the knowledge of how to use lists, it is now possible to create a better-structured home page that gives readers easier access to the information they need. This How-To provides some tips on style and explains how to effectively add lists to a page.

COMPLEXITY
EASY

6.1 How do I... Create a numbered list?

COMPATIBILITY: HTML 2 OR ABOVE

Problem

I have a set of data I would like to display as a list. I want each item in the list to be preceded by a number. However, since the order of the list items may change from time to time, I would like to have the numbers generated automatically, so I don't have to spend time manually editing the number for each item. How can I create a numbered list in HTML?

Technique

HTML allows you to create a numbered, or ordered, list that will automatically generate numbers in front of each item in the list. The number placed in front of an item depends on the location of the item in the list: the first item gets the numeral 1, the second 2, and so on. You can do this by using the <OL> and <LI> tags described below.

Steps

Open your document. Identify the locations in your document where you want to include a list.

1. First, place the items to be included in the list in your document. For clarity, separate each item with a carriage return. For example:

```
<H2>My Five Favorite Baseball Teams</H2>
Red Sox
Cubs
Royals
Dodgers
Indians
```

2. At the beginning of the list, place the <OL> (for ordered list) tag. At the end of the list, place the </OL> tag:

CHAPTER 6
HTML LISTS

```
<H2>My Five Favorite Baseball Teams</H2>
<OL>
Red Sox
Cubs
Royals
Dodgers
Indians
</OL>
```

3. In front of each item in the list, place the <LI> (list item) tag:

```
<H2>My Five Favorite Baseball Teams</H2>
<OL>
<LI>Red Sox
<LI>Cubs
<LI>Royals
<LI>Dodgers
<LI>Indians
</OL>
```

4. Some browsers permit you to conserve space in a document by making a list more compact. A compacted list usually has less space between list entries and may use a smaller, more compressed font. To specify a compacted list, replace the <OL> at the beginning of the list with <OL COMPACT>:

```
<H2>My Five Favorite Baseball Teams (compact form)</H2>
<OL COMPACT>
<LI>Red Sox
<LI>Cubs
<LI>Royals
<LI>Dodgers
<LI>Indians
</OL>
```

5. In HTML 3, you can create a list caption that will be placed at the beginning of the list, like a header. To add a list caption, place the caption text between <LH> and </LH> tags just after the <OL>:

```
<H2>My Five Favorite Baseball Teams</H2>
<OL>
<LH>Here's the list caption</LH>
<LI>Red Sox
<LI>Cubs
<LI>Royals
<LI>Dodgers
<LI>Indians
</OL>
```

6. In HTML 3, it is possible to create a second list that begins where the first one left off by using the <OL CONTINUE> tag at the beginning of the second list:

6.1
CREATE A NUMBERED LIST

```
<H2>My Five Favorite Baseball Teams</H2>
<OL>
<LI>Red Sox
<LI>Cubs
<LI>Royals
<LI>Dodgers
<LI>Indians
</OL>

<OL CONTINUE>
<LI>Angels
<LI>White Sox
</OL>
```

7. In HTML 3, you can create a list that starts with a specific number other than one. This is accomplished by replacing <OL> with <OL SEQNUM=N>, and replacing N with the desired number. For example, to create a list that begins with item 10, enter

```
<H2>My Five Favorite Baseball Teams</H2>
<OL SEQNUM=10>
<LI>Red Sox
<LI>Cubs
<LI>Royals
<LI>Dodgers
<LI>Indians
</OL>
```

8. In Netscape, the SEQNUM attribute is replaced with the START attribute, which works the same way. To create the example from the previous step in Netscape, enter

```
<H2>My Five Favorite Baseball Teams</H2>
<OL START=10>
<LI>Red Sox
<LI>Cubs
<LI>Royals
<LI>Dodgers
<LI>Indians
</OL>
```

You can also use the VALUE attribute within the <LI> tag to change the numbering sequence within a list. For example, to start numbering a list at 1 but change to a higher value later in the list, enter

```
<H2>My Five Favorite Baseball Teams</H2>
<OL>
<LI>Red Sox
<LI>Cubs
<LI>Royals
<LI VALUE=10>Dodgers
<LI>Indians
</OL>
```

9. In Netscape, you can select the type of numbering system to be used with the TYPE attribute. The table below lists the possible values of the TYPE attribute.

ATTRIBUTE VALUE	DEFINITION
"A"	Use uppercase letters (A, B, C, etc.)
"a"	Use lowercase letters (a, b, c, etc.)
"I"	Use uppercase Roman numerals (I, II, III, etc.)
"i"	Use lowercase Roman numerals (i, ii, iii, etc.)
"1"	Use standard numbers, the default (1, 2, 3, etc.)

 Values for the TYPE attribute

For example, to use uppercase letters in a list, enter

```
<H2>My Five Favorite Baseball Teams</H2>
<OL TYPE=A>
<LI>Red Sox
<LI>Cubs
<LI>Royals
<LI>Dodgers
<LI>Indians
</OL>
```

You can also use the TYPE attribute within the <LI> tag to change the numbering scheme within a list. For example, to change from standard numerals to uppercase Roman numerals, enter

```
<H2>My Five Favorite Baseball Teams</H2>
<OL>
<LI>Red Sox
<LI>Cubs
<LI TYPE=I>Royals
<LI>Dodgers
<LI>Indians
</OL>
```

Examples of numbered lists are shown in Figure 6-1. The code is also available on the CD-ROM as file 6-1.html. Examples of Netscape's START, VALUE, and TYPE attributes are shown in Figure 6-2. The code is also availble on the CD-ROM as file 6-2.html.

How It Works

When an HTML browser, such as Mosaic or Netscape, loads a numbered list such as the one shown above, it converts each <LI> it finds between the <OL> and the

6.1 CREATE A NUMBERED LIST

</OL> into a number; the first <LI> becomes the number 1, the second becomes 2, and so on. The browser also puts a carriage return just before the number to better format the text.

Comments

With the exception of numbers specified by the SEQNUM attribute in HTML 3 and the START and VALUE attributes in Netscape, the only type of numbering that HTML currently supports is sequential numbering by whole number starting with the number 1. In other words, you can't have HTML create a numbered list that counts down instead of up, skips numbers, or (for versions of HTML before HTML 3), starts at a number other than 1. If you want to generate lists that use numbers in this way, you will have to add the numbers manually to the document and then format the list in another way, such as making it an unmarked list (see How-To 6.3).

Some attributes of <OL> are not currently supported by most browsers. The COMPACT attribute is not used by most major browsers, and the CONTINUE, SEQNUM, and SRC attributes have not yet been implemented in Arena (the testbed HTML 3 browser) or Netscape.

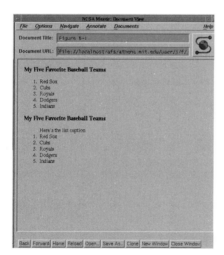

Figure 6-1 Examples of numbered lists

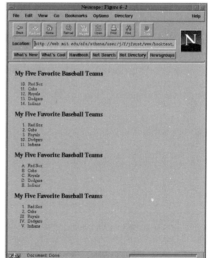

Figure 6-2 Examples of Netscape's attributes for numbered lists

CHAPTER 6
HTML LISTS

6.2 How do I... Create a bulleted list?

COMPLEXITY
EASY

COMPATIBILITY: HTML 2 OR ABOVE

Problem

I have a set of data that I would like to display as a list. I want to call attention to each item on the list by placing a bullet in front of it, and I would like to have the bullet created automatically so I don't have to design a special graphic. How can I create a bulleted list in HTML?

Technique

HTML allows you to create a bulleted, or unordered, list with the bullets automatically created and placed in front of each list item. The technique is very similar to the numbered list technique; the only difference is in the tags that are used at the beginning and the end of the list.

Steps

Open your document. Identify the locations in your document where you want to include a list.

1. First, place the items to be included in the list in your document. For clarity, separate each item with a carriage return. For example:

```
<H2>My Five Favorite Baseball Teams</H2>
Red Sox
Cubs
Royals
Dodgers
Indians
```

2. At the beginning of the list, place the <UL> (for unordered list) tag. At the end of the list, place the </UL> tag:

```
<H2>My Five Favorite Baseball Teams</H2>
<UL>
Red Sox
Cubs
Royals
Dodgers
Indians
</UL>
```

3. In front of each item in the list, place the <LI> tag:

6.2
CREATE A BULLETED LIST

```
<H2>My Five Favorite Baseball Teams</H2>
<UL>
<LI>Red Sox
<LI>Cubs
<LI>Royals
<LI>Dodgers
<LI>Indians
</UL>
```

4. Some browsers permit you to conserve space in your document by making your list more compact. A compacted list usually has less space between list entries and may use a smaller, more compressed font. To create a compacted list, replace the <UL> tag at the beginning of the list with <UL COMPACT>:

```
<H2>My Five Favorite Baseball Teams (compact form)</H2>
<UL COMPACT>
<LI>Red Sox
<LI>Cubs
<LI>Royals
<LI>Dodgers
<LI>Indians
</UL>
```

5. In HTML 3, you can add a list caption that appears at the beginning of the list, like a heading. To create the caption, place the text of the caption between <LH> and </LH> tags at the beginning of the list:

```
<H2>My Five Favorite Baseball Teams</H2>
<UL>
<LH>Here's the list caption</LH>
<LI>Red Sox
<LI>Cubs
<LI>Royals
<LI>Dodgers
<LI>Indians
</UL>
```

6. In HTML 3, you can replace the default bullet with a special graphic. To do so, include the SRC attribute in the <UL> tag and include the filename of the graphic. For example, to replace the bullet with a graphic called mybullet.gif, enter

```
<H2>My Five Favorite Baseball Teams</H2>
<UL SRC="MYBULLET.GIF">
<LI>Red Sox
<LI>Cubs
<LI>Royals
<LI>Dodgers
<LI>Indians
</UL>
```

CHAPTER 6
HTML LISTS

Examples of bulleted lists are shown in Figure 6-3. The code is also available on the CD-ROM as file 6-3.html.

How It Works

Just as it does for a numbered list, a browser converts each <LI> it finds between the <UL> and </UL> tags, in this case into a bullet. It also inserts a carriage return immediately before the bullet to format the text.

Comments

The actual shape and size of the bullet is determined by the browser; different browsers use different shapes for bullets. When bullets are used in nested lists (see How-To 6.8), different bullet shapes may be used at different levels of nesting; again, this depends on the browser. If you want to use a bullet with a specific shape, or another special graphic, you should consider creating an inline image of the desired bullet (see How-To 8.1) and placing this in front of each item using an unmarked list, as described in How-To 6.3.

Some attributes of <UL> are not currently supported by most browsers. The COMPACT attribute is not used by most major browsers, and the SRC attribute has not yet been implemented in Arena (the testbed HTML 3 browser) or Netscape.

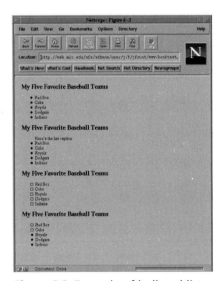

Figure 6-3 Example of bulleted lists

6.3 How do I... Create an unmarked list?

COMPLEXITY: EASY

COMPATIBILITY: HTML 2 OR ABOVE

Problem

I have a set of data that I would like to display as a list. I want to display this simply as a list of items, separated by carriage returns, without numbers or bullets. How can I do this in HTML?

Technique

There are several ways to do this in HTML. Perhaps the simplest way is to insert line breaks, <BR>, after each list element. There are other techniques, though, that allow you to create unmarked lists and even set them off from the rest of the text. These methods are described below.

Steps

Open your document. Identify the locations in your document where you want to include a list.

1. To separate list items using line breaks, place <BR> tags after each list element:

```
<H2>My Five Favorite Baseball Teams, using &lt;BR &rt;</H2>
Red Sox<BR>
Cubs<BR>
Royals<BR>
Dodgers<BR>
Indians<BR>
```

(The **<** and **&rt;** are special key sequences which will print the "<" and ">" characters respectively. They are used here since < and > are reserved for HTML commands.)

2. In HTML 2.0, you can create an identical list using the <DL> and <DT> tags:

Place a <DL> (for descriptive list) at the beginning of the list and a </DL> at the end of the list:

```
<H2>My Five Favorite Baseball Teams</H2>
<DL>
Red Sox
Cubs
Royals
```

continued on next page

continued from previous page

```
Dodgers
Indians
</DL>
```

HTML Place the <DT> tag in front of each item of the list:

```
<H2>My Five Favorite Baseball Teams, using &lt;DT &rt;</H2>
<DL>
<DT>Red Sox
<DT>Cubs
<DT>Royals
<DT>Dodgers
<DT>Indians
</DL>
```

3. To create a list that is indented from normal text, use the <DL> and </DL> tags at the beginning and end of the list, but use <DD> instead of <DT> in front of each list item:

```
<H2>My Five Favorite Baseball Teams, using &lt;DT &rt;</H2>
<DL>
<DD>Red Sox
<DD>Cubs
<DD>Royals
<DD>Dodgers
<DD>Indians
</DL>
```

4. In HTML 3, you can create an unmarked list by using the <UL> tag and adding the attribute BLANK, which suppresses the printing of bullets:

```
<H2>My Five Favorite Baseball Teams, using &lt;UL BLANK &rt;</H2>
<UL BLANK>
<LI>Red Sox
<LI>Cubs
<LI>Royals
<LI>Dodgers
<LI>Indians
</UL>
```

The output generated by these different kinds of unmarked lists is shown in Figure 6-4. The code is also available on the CD-ROM as 6-4.html.

How It Works

For the first kind of unmarked list, your browser simply replaces all the <BR> tags it finds with carriage returns. For the second kind of unmarked list, the browser replaces all the <DT> tags between the <DL> and </DL> tags with carriage returns. The browser does the same with the <DD> tags in the third kind of list, only it also includes a tab before the list item. The length of the indentation is set by the

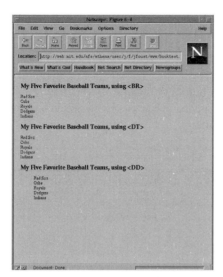

Figure 6-4 Several types of unmarked lists

browser and can't be controlled within the document. For the final kind of unmarked list, the BLANK attribute simply tells the browser to suppress printing bullets for that list.

Comments

The current HTML 3 specification states that the <DT> or <DD> tags will only continue to be supported in glossary lists (see How-To 6.7). Note that the BLANK attribute in <UL> will suppress all bullets in a list; it's not possible to selectively include or remove bullets using <UL BLANK>. Keep in mind that the <UL BLANK> tag is not supported by pre-HTML 3.

COMPLEXITY
INTERMEDIATE

6.4 How do I... Create a multicolumn list?

COMPATIBILITY: HTML 3

Problem

I have a set of data I would like to display as a list. The data includes a number of different quantities, and I would like to display them side by side to make it easier for the reader to compare them. I don't want this to look like a table, though. How do I do this in HTML?

Technique

In HTML 3, the WRAP attribute added to a bulleted list will wrap list items across the screen into a set of columns. You can combine this with other attributes, such as BLANK, to create unmarked multicolumn lists.

Steps

Open your document. Identify the locations in your document where you want to include a list.

1. First, place the items you want to include in the list in your document, using carriage returns to separate the items for clarity:

```
Red Sox
Cubs
Royals
Dodgers
Indians
Angels
White Sox
```

2. Place an <LI> tag in front of each list item:

```
<LI>Red Sox
<LI>Cubs
<LI>Royals
<LI>Dodgers
<LI>Indians
<LI>Angels
<LI>White Sox
```

3. To create a list in which the items go across the screen and then down, use the <UL> and </UL> tags with the attribute WRAP="horiz":

```
<UL WRAP=HORIZ>
<LI>Red Sox
<LI>Cubs
<LI>Royals
<LI>Dodgers
<LI>Indians
<LI>Angels
<LI>White Sox
</UL>
```

4. To create a list in which the items go down the page before starting a new column, use the attribute WRAP="vert":

6.4
CREATE A MULTICOLUMN LIST

```
<UL WRAP=VERT>
<LI>Red Sox
<LI>Cubs
<LI>Royals
<LI>Dodgers
<LI>Indians
<LI>Angels
<LI>White Sox
</UL>
```

Examples of these lists are shown in Figure 6-5 using Netscape Navigator 2.0. The code is also available on the CD-ROM as file 6-5.html.

How It Works

When an HTML 3-compliant browser reads the WRAP attribute, it formats the list items that follow it according to the attribute's value. If the WRAP attribute is set to "horiz", it places the list items across the screen in a row until the end of the window is reached, then it starts a new row. When the WRAP attribute is set to "vert", it places list items down the screen until it reaches the bottom of the window, then it starts a new column.

Comments

In a multicolumn list, the number of columns and the contents of each is controlled solely by the browser, not by the text. If you want explicit control over the layout of a multicolumn list, it would be better to set it up as a table, which provides explicit control over layout. Chapter 5 discusses tables in detail.

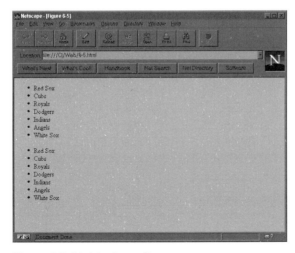

Figure 6-5 Multicolumn lists

177

CHAPTER 6
HTML LISTS

6.5 How do I... Create a menu list?

COMPLEXITY
EASY

COMPATIBILITY: HTML 2

Problem

I have a set of data that I wish to display as a list. I want to show the items specifically as a menu of options for users to choose from. How do I do this in HTML?

Technique

HTML versions 2.0 and earlier support a tag called <MENU>, which allows list items to be displayed as a menu. It is not likely that <MENU> will be supported in HTML 3; however, if you are working in an environment that uses older browsers, the <MENU> tag may still be useful.

Steps

Open your document. Identify the locations in your document where you want to include a list. If you haven't done so already, enter the list items in the document, separated by carriage returns.

1. Place the <MENU> tag at the beginning of the list and the </MENU> tag at the end of the list:

```
<H2>My Five Favorite Baseball Teams</H2>
<MENU>
Red Sox
Cubs
Royals
Dodgers
Indians
</MENU>
```

2. In front of each item of the list, place an <LI> tag:

```
<H2>My Five Favorite Baseball Teams</H2>
<MENU>
<LI>Red Sox
<LI>Cubs
<LI>Royals
<LI>Dodgers
<LI>Indians
</MENU>
```

Figure 6-6 shows the output of this list. The code is also available on the CD-ROM in file 6-6.html.

6.6 CREATE A DIRECTORY LIST

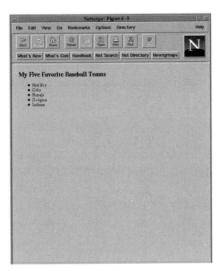

Figure 6-6 A menu list

How It Works

As with other lists, a browser replaces all the <LI> tags between <MENU> and </MENU> with its predefined symbol or spacing. Often this is a bullet, so a list using the <MENU> tag frequently looks the same as the bulleted list described in How-To 6.2.

Comments

<MENU> may not be supported in HTML 3; thus, any documents that include a <MENU> list may not format correctly when displayed on an HTML 3-compliant browser. However, if you are designing pages for a closed environment using older browsers, the <MENU> tag will continue to work, and may be the best way to format your information.

COMPLEXITY
EASY

6.6 How do I... Create a directory list?

COMPATIBILITY: HTML 2

Problem

I have a set of data that I want to display as a directory of related items. How can I create a directory list in HTML?

CHAPTER 6
HTML LISTS

Technique

HTML versions 2.0 and earlier support a tag called <DIRECTORY>, which lists the items as if they were filenames in a computer directory. HTML 3 does not support the <DIRECTORY> tag; however, if you are working in a specific environment that uses older browsers, the <DIRECTORY> tag may still be useful.

Steps

Open your document. Identify the locations in your document where you want to include a list. If you haven't done so already, enter the list items in the document, separated by carriage returns.

1. Place the <DIRECTORY> tag at the beginning of the list and the </DIRECTORY> tag at the end of the list:

```
<H2>My Five Favorite Baseball Teams</H2>
<DIRECTORY>
Red Sox
Cubs
Royals
Dodgers
Indians
</DIRECTORY>
```

2. In front of each item, place an <LI> tag:

```
<H2>My Five Favorite Baseball Teams</H2>
<DIRECTORY>
<LI>Red Sox
<LI>Cubs
<LI>Royals
<LI>Dodgers
<LI>Indians
</DIRECTORY>
```

Figure 6-7 shows the output of this list. The code is also available on the CD-ROM in file 6-7.html.

How It Works

As with other lists, a browser turns each <LI> tag into a predefined symbol or spacing. Most browsers interpret <DIRECTORY> lists by turning <LI> tags into carriage returns, making the lists another form of unmarked list (see How-To 6.3). Some browsers, such as Netscape, add a bullet in front of each item, turning directory lists into bulleted lists.

Comments

Since HTML 3 does not support the <DIRECTORY> tag, any use of these tags in a document read by an HTML 3-compliant browser means the document may not

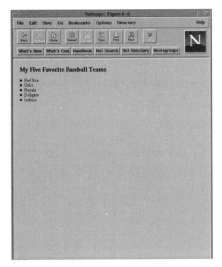

Figure 6-7 A directory list

format properly. Older browsers can still read and interpret these lists, though, so if you are designing pages for a closed environment using older browsers, this may still be a useful way to display information.

6.7 How do I... Create a glossary list?

COMPLEXITY
EASY

COMPATIBILITY: HTML 2 OR ABOVE

Problem

I have a set of data that I would like to display as a list of terms and their definitions. I would like to emphasize the terms and set them apart from their definitions. How can I create such a glossary in HTML?

Technique

How-to 6.3 discusses the use of the <DL>, <DT>, and <DD> tags in HTML 2.0 as a way to format an unmarked list. For the unmarked list, the <DT> and <DD> are used separately; however, they can be combined to create a glossary that emphasizes words and their definitions.

HTML LISTS

Steps

Open your document. Decide what information you would like to present as a glossary list.

1. Compile a list of terms and their definitions, separating them by carriage returns and tabs for clarity:

```
<H2>Some terms and definitions</H2>
Term 1
     This is the definition for term 1
Term 2
     This is the definition for term 2
```

2. Place the <DL> tag at the beginning of the list and the </DL> tag at the end of the list:

```
<H2>Some terms and definitions</H2>
<DL>
Term 1
     This is the definition for term 1
Term 2
     This is the definition for term 2
</DL>
```

3. Place the <DT> tag in front of each word to be defined:

```
<H2>Some terms and definitions</H2>
<DL>
<DT>Term 1
     This is the definition for term 1
<DT>Term 2
     This is the definition for term 2
</DL>
```

4. Place the <DD> tag in front of each definition:

```
<H2>Some terms and definitions</H2>
<DL>
<DT>Term 1
     <DD>This is the definition for term 1
<DT>Term 2
     <DD>This is the definition for term 2
</DL>
```

5. Some browsers permit you to conserve space in your document by making your list more compact. A compacted list usually has less space between list entries and may use a smaller, more compressed font. To create a compacted list, replace the <DL> tag with the <DL COMPACT> tag:

6.7
CREATE A GLOSSARY LIST

```
<H2>Some terms and definitions (compact form)</H2>
<DL COMPACT>
<DT>Term 1
    <DD>This is the definition for term 1
<DT>Term 2
    <DD>This is the definition for term 2
</DL>
```

6. In HTML 3, you can include a list caption at the beginning of the list, like a heading. Place the text of the list caption between the <LH> and </LH> tags immediately after the <DL> tag:

```
<H2>Some terms and definitions</H2>
<DL>
<LH>The list caption</LH>
<DT>Term 1
    <DD>This is the definition for term 1
<DT>Term 2
    <DD>This is the definition for term 2
</DL>
```

Figure 6-8 shows the output of these lists. The code is also available on the CD-ROM as file 6-8.html.

How It Works

The browser software converts each <DT> found between the <DL> and </DL> tags into a carriage return. The browser converts the <DD> tags into a carriage return and an indentation.

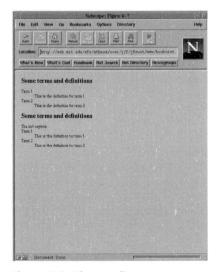

Figure 6-8 Glossary lists

Comments

HTML 3 requires that whenever you use the <DL> and </DL> tags, you also use both the <DD> and <DT> tags in the list. While this makes it more difficult to create unmarked lists (see How-To 6.3), it has no impact here, since glossary lists need both types of tags to provide the best formatting.

6.8 How do I... Nest lists together?

COMPLEXITY
EASY

COMPATIBILITY: HTML 2 OR ABOVE

Problem

I have a set of data that I would like to display as an outline, so that each main heading has subheadings, etc. Can I use nested lists to create a formatted outline in HTML?

Technique

HTML makes it easy to nest lists. Lists can be inserted within lists and be interpreted by a browser as sublists. These lists will then be set off from the main list. Examples of different kinds of nested lists are provided below.

Steps

Open your document. Identify the lists in your document you would like to nest, decide what type of list you would like to create, and follow the steps below for the given type of list.

Numbered List

1. For a numbered list, enter the items for each list level, using carriage returns to set them apart and tabs to better show the level of nesting of each item in the outline:

```
<H2>An Example of Nested Lists</H2>
Point 1
    Subpoint 1
        Subsubpoint 1
        Subsubpoint 2
        Subsubpoint 3
```

6.8
NEST LISTS TOGETHER

```
    Subpoint 2
    Subpoint 3
Point 2
    Subpoint 1
    Subpoint 2
Point 3
```

2. For the top-level list, place an <OL> at the beginning of the list, an </OL> at the end of the list, and an <LI> in front of only the top-level points:

```
<H2>An Example of Nested Lists</H2>
<OL>
<LI>Point 1
    Subpoint 1
        Subsubpoint 1
        Subsubpoint 2
        Subsubpoint 3
    Subpoint 2
    Subpoint 3
<LI>Point 2
    Subpoint 1
    Subpoint 2
<LI>Point 3
</OL>
```

3. For each sublist, place an <OL> at the beginning of the sublist, an </OL> at the end of the sublist, and an <LI> in front of each list item for that particular sublist. Continue this process for all the sublists:

```
<H2>An Example of Nested Numbered Lists</H2>
<OL>
<LI>Point 1
    <OL>
    <LI>Subpoint 1
        <OL>
        <LI>Subsubpoint 1
        <LI>Subsubpoint 2
        <LI>Subsubpoint 3
        </OL>
    <LI>Subpoint 2
    <LI>Subpoint 3
    </OL>
<LI>Point 2
    <OL>
    <LI>Subpoint 1
    <LI>Subpoint 2
    </OL>
<LI>Point 3
</OL>
```

The output of this list is shown in Figure 6-9. The code is available on the CD-ROM in file 6-9.html.

Bulleted List

For bulleted lists, the technique is exactly the same as that for a numbered list, except that the <OL> and </OL> tags are replaced with <UL> and </UL>:

```
<H2>An Example of Nested Bulleted Lists</H2>
<UL>
<LI>Point 1
    <UL>
    <LI>Subpoint 1
        <UL>
        <LI>Subsubpoint 1
        <LI>Subsubpoint 2
        <LI>Subsubpoint 3
        </UL>
    <LI>Subpoint 2
    <LI>Subpoint 3
    </UL>
<LI>Point 2
    <UL>
    <LI>Subpoint 1
    <LI>Subpoint 2
    </UL>
<LI>Point 3
</UL>
```

Figure 6-10 shows the output of a nested bulleted list. The code is available on the CD-ROM in file 6-10.html.

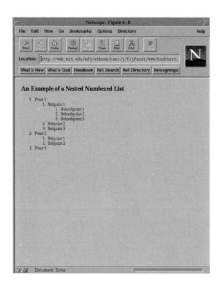

Figure 6-9 A nested numbered list

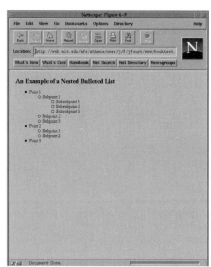

Figure 6-10 A nested bulleted list

Menu List

For menu lists, follow the steps as shown for a nested bulleted list, and use <MENU> and </MENU>:

```
<H2>An Example of Nested Menu Lists</H2>
<MENU>
<LI>Point 1
    <MENU>
    <LI>Subpoint 1
        <MENU>
        <LI>Subsubpoint 1
        <LI>Subsubpoint 2
        <LI>Subsubpoint 3
        </MENU>
    <LI>Subpoint 2
    <LI>Subpoint 3
    </MENU>
<LI>Point 2
    <MENU>
    <LI>Subpoint 1
    <LI>Subpoint 2
    </MENU>
<LI>Point 3
</MENU>
```

Figure 6-11 shows the output of this list, which usually appears just the same as a nested bulleted list. The code is available on the CD-ROM in file 6-11.html.

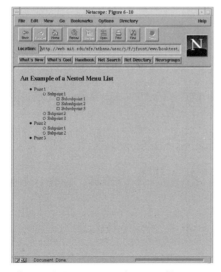

Figure 6-11 A nested menu list

Directory List

Most browsers, such as Netscape, do not support nested directory lists. Each item in a directory list is shown together with the other items, regardless of the level of nesting indicated for that item.

For a directory list, follow the steps as shown for nested menu lists, and use <DIRECTORY> and </DIRECTORY>:

```
<H2>An Example of Nested Directory Lists</H2>
<DIRECTORY>
<LI>Point 1
    <DIRECTORY>
    <LI>Subpoint 1
        <DIRECTORY>
        <LI>Subsubpoint 1
        <LI>Subsubpoint 2
        <LI>Subsubpoint 3
        </DIRECTORY>
    <LI>Subpoint 2
    <LI>Subpoint 3
    </DIRECTORY>
<LI>Point 2
    <DIRECTORY>
    <LI>Subpoint 1
    <LI>Subpoint 2
    </DIRECTORY>
<LI>Point 3
</DIRECTORY>
```

The output of this list is shown in Figure 6-12. The code is available on the CD-ROM in file 6-12.html.

Unmarked List

You cannot create nested unmarked lists using the <BR> tag, since there is no way for the browser to know to what list level each item belongs. However, by using the <DL> and </DL> list tags, and either the <DT> or <DD> tags for each list item, you can create a nested unmarked list.

For a simple nested unmarked list, use <DL> and </DL> at the beginning and end of each list and sublist, and <DT> in front of each list item:

```
<H2>A Nested Unmarked List Using &lt; DT &rt;</H2>
<DL>
<DT>Point 1
    <DL>
    <DT>Subpoint 1
        <DL>
        <DT>Subsubpoint 1
        <DT>Subsubpoint 2
        <DT>Subsubpoint 3
        </DL>
```

6.8
NEST LISTS TOGETHER

```
        <DT>Subpoint 2
        <DT>Subpoint 3
        </DL>
<DT>Point 2
    <DL>
        <DT>Subpoint 1
        <DT>Subpoint 2
        </DL>
<DT>Point 3
</DL>
```

Figure 6-13 shows the output of this nested unmarked list. The code is available on the CD-ROM in file 6-13.html.

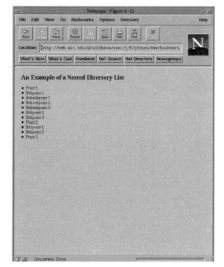

Figure 6-12 An attempted nested directory list

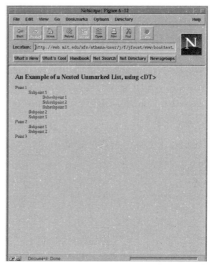

Figure 6-13 A nested unmarked list, using <DT>

For a nested unmarked list that is indented from the rest of the text, use <DD> in place of <DT> in the above example:

```
<H2>A Nested Unmarked List Using &lt; DD &rt;</H2>
<DL>
<DD>Point 1
    <DL>
    <DD>Subpoint 1
        <DL>
        <DD>Subsubpoint 1
        <DD>Subsubpoint 2
        <DD>Subsubpoint 3
        </DL>
```

continued on next page

189

continued from previous page

```
    <DD>Subpoint 2
    <DD>Subpoint 3
    </DL>
<DD>Point 2
    <DL>
    <DD>Subpoint 1
    <DD>Subpoint 2
    </DL>
<DD>Point 3
</DL>
```

Figure 6-14 shows the output of this unmarked nested list. The code is available on the CD-ROM in file 6-14.html. You can also mix the <DT> and <DD> tags to create nested glossary lists.

In HTML 3, nested unmarked lists can be created by using the BLANK attribute in <UL>, so the creation of nested unmarked lists is similar to the creation of nested bulleted lists.

Combining Lists

You can combine and nest different kinds of lists. The example below shows how to nest a bulleted list within a numbered list, which in turn is nested within an unmarked list:

```
<H2>A Nested List Using Unmarked, Numbered, and Bulleted Elements</H2>
<DL>
<DT>Point 1
    <OL>
    <LI>Subpoint 1
        <UL>
        <LI>Subsubpoint 1
        <LI>Subsubpoint 2
        <LI>Subsubpoint 3
        </UL>
    <LI>Subpoint 2
    <LI>Subpoint 3
    </OL>
<DT>Point 2
    <OL>
    <LI>Subpoint 1
    <LI>Subpoint 2
    </OL>
<DT>Point 3
</DL>
```

Figure 6-15 shows the output of this combined nested list. The code is available on the CD-ROM in file 6-15.html.

Take care when mixing nested unmarked lists inside other types of lists. In some browsers, if you use the <DT> tag to mark list items in the unmarked list, the items may appear on the next higher list level. If you were to replace the bulleted sublist

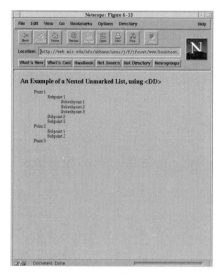

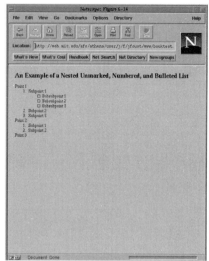

Figure 6-14 A nested unmarked list using <DD>

Figure 6-15 A nested list using three different list types

in the above example with an unmarked list using <DT> in front of each list item, you might get an aesthetically unpleasing result. By using <DD> in place of <DT>, you get a better result. However, for other browsers, such as Mosaic, this is not a problem; either <DD> or <DT> will work for unmarked nested lists, and in some cases <DT> works better than <DD>. Figures 6-16 and 6-17 show how <DD> and <DT> work in nested unmarked lists in Netscape.

The code used to create these examples is available on the CD-ROM in files 6-16.html and 6-17.html.

How It Works

When a browser encounters a tag that marks the start of a new list before it encounters a tag that marks the end of the current list, it considers the contents of the new list to be a sublist nested inside the current list. The browser then formats the sublist accordingly. The format of the sublist may vary from browser to browser.

Comments

Different browsers use different styles to format nested lists. Some browsers may mix letters and numbers in different levels of nested numbered lists, and some browsers may use bullets of different shapes and sizes for different levels of nested bulleted lists. Thus, when designing your pages, be careful when referring to specific list items by number or bullet, as the reader may not see the same number

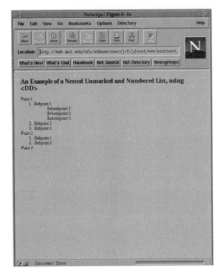 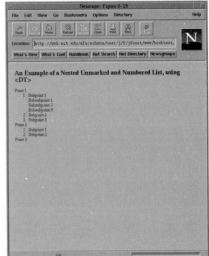

Figure 6-16 A nested list using <DD> in an unmarked sublist

Figure 6-17 A nested list using <DT> in an unmarked sublist

or bullet that you do. Also note that when mixing lists, some browsers will use the bullet or number style appropriate to that level, even if this is the first list of that type being used. In other cases, bullets may be selected seemingly at random: in the example displayed in Figure 6-15, the bullets used are the second-level bullets, even though it is a third-level list. In short, be cautious about making references to specific numbers or bullets.

COMPLEXITY
EASY, INTERMEDIATE

6.9 How do I... Use lists to jazz up my home page?

COMPATIBILITY: HTML 2 OR ABOVE

Problem

I would like to add lists to my home page so that I can better present my information. How can I effectively use lists to jazz up my home page?

Technique

Like any aspect of HTML, lists can be used—and abused. The right way to use lists varies depending on what information you want to put into a list.

Steps

1. Avoid very long lists. Long lists are boring and difficult to read, and it's hard for the user to find a particular piece of information in them. Instead, break up any long lists into smaller lists, subdivided by topic. This is where nested lists can be useful.
2. Maintain parallelism in your lists. Don't change verb tenses or make other style changes in the middle of a list.
3. Along those lines, keep each list item about the same length. Lists can be made of short, one-word elements or long, paragraph-length statements, but the two shouldn't be combined.

How It Works

These tips help make your lists more effective by allowing a user to quickly find the information of interest to him or her. By grouping list items into related groups and by using parallel structure, it becomes easy for a user to sort through the information provided.

Comments

Proper use of lists and good list style help set the good Web pages apart from the rest. With a little practice, you'll soon be able to create all sorts of useful lists for your pages.

CHAPTER 7
ESTABLISHING LINKS

ESTABLISHING LINKS

How do I...

7.1   Interpret a URL?

7.2   Understand a relative URL?

7.3   Add a base for relative URLs within the body of a document?

7.4   Specify a relationship between this document and other resources?

7.5   Create a link to a local page?

7.6   Create a link to other pages?

7.7   Send data to an HTTP server via a URL?

7.8   Create a link to a specific part of a page?

7.9   Create a link to an FTP site?

7.10   Create a link to a Gopher site?

7.11   Create a link to a Telnet site?

7.12   Create a link to a WAIS site?

7.13   Create a link to a Usenet newsgroup?

7.14   Create a link to electronic mail?

7.15   Create links to pages in other users' home directories?

7.16   Add links to lists and tables?

CHAPTER 7
ESTABLISHING LINKS

7.17 Change the shape of a link?

7.18 Add links to my home page?

With only a small amount of markup, you can format text files for effective presentation on the World Wide Web. This alone makes HTML and WWW a good way to publish documents over the Internet. But it only captures a small fraction of the potential of the World Wide Web. Imagine being able to give the reader of your document the ability, with a single keypress or mouse click, to move to another part of your document, another document on your computer, or Internet resources around the world. HTML provides the ability to add links to other documents and resources. You'll learn about links in this chapter, starting with some background about how links work and progressing through a series of methods to connect other documents to your own.

7.1 Interpret a URL

Universal Resource Locators, or URLs, are what World Wide Web browsers use to locate files on the Internet. This How-To explains the various parts of a URL and shows how to construct URLs to point to various kinds of documents.

7.2 Understand a Relative URL

If you have a number of pages located on your computer but placed in various directories, relative URLs let you identify their location without typing the entire pathname of the file. This How-To explains how relative URLs work and how you can create relative URLs for your own needs.

7.3 Add a Base for Relative URLs within the Body of a Document

If a page contains relative URLs and is transferred from one location to another, the relative URLs will no longer work in the new location. This How-To explains how to get around this problem by specifying a base for the URLs within the body of your page.

7.4 Specify a Relationship between This Document and Other Resources

A page you're developing may be one of a set of related pages, and you would like to be able to show how a particular page fits in with the other pages. This How-To explains how to specify relationships between a page and other pages and resources.

7.5 Create a Link to a Local Page

The simplest type of link is linking a page you've created with other pages and files on your computer. This simple How-To shows how to link together the pages you've created on your computer.

CHAPTER 7
ESTABLISHING LINKS

7.6 Create a Link to Other Pages
The World Wide Web connects thousands of pages around the world. This How-To shows how to connect your page to any number of pages around the world.

7.7 Send Data to an HTTP Server via a URL
When using forms or key word searches, there are instances when you want to pass some information on to an application on a specific computer. This How-To explains how to attach key word information to a URL to be passed on to an application.

7.8 Create a Link to a Specific Part of a Page
When creating a page, especially a very long page, it may be useful to provide links to other parts of the page to make it easy for readers to move around the document. This How-To explains how to create links to a specific part of a page.

7.9 Create a Link to an FTP Site
File Transfer Protocol (FTP) is a popular method of transferring files across the Internet. There are FTP servers located around the world with information on a wide range of topics, including, no doubt, useful information for your pages. This How-To explains how to link an FTP site to your page.

7.10 Create a Link to a Gopher Site
Gopher provides an easy-to-use, menu-based interface to information resources on the Internet. This How-To explains how to link a Gopher site, and specific items at the site, to your page.

7.11 Create a Link to a Telnet Site
Some sites on the Internet provide information by Telnet, requiring a user to log on to the computer to access information. This How-To explains how to link a Telnet site to your page.

7.12 Create a Link to a WAIS Site
The Wide Area Information Servers (WAIS) technology is a method of providing searchable databases on the Internet, making them useful for finding specific items of information. This How-To explains how to link a WAIS site to your page.

7.13 Create a Link to a Usenet Newsgroup
There are thousands of Usenet newsgroups that cover seemingly every conceivable topic under the sun, as well as a number of inconceivable topics. This How-To explains how to link a Usenet newsgroup to your page.

7.14 Create a Link to Electronic Mail
It's often useful for people to easily contact you or other people concerning the contents of your page. One way to do this is to make it possible for readers to

automatically e-mail people. This How-To explains how to link electronic mail to your page.

7.15 Create Links to Pages in Other Users' Home Directories

You may want to include links to pages located in the directories of other users on a multiuser machine. Rather than specifying the full pathname for the page, you can use a shortcut to create a link to that page. This How-To explains how to create a simple link to a page in another user's directories.

7.16 Add Links to Lists and Tables

Lists and tables provide ways to efficiently organize information. They can be combined with links to create easy-to-use menus of options. This How-To explains how to add links to the lists and tables in your page.

7.17 Change the Shape of a Link

Links have been limited to text and other objects, but HTML 3 provides a way to create a link within a part of an image by specifying the location and shape of the area in an image to serve as a link. This How-To shows how to create links of different shapes and embed them in images using HTML 3.

7.18 Add Links to My Home Page

Links can be simple and fun to add to your pages, but if done incorrectly can make your page difficult to understand or use. This How-To explains how to add links to your page that will increase the information content of your page and make it fun to read.

COMPLEXITY
INTERMEDIATE

7.1 How do I... Interpret a URL?

COMPATIBILITY: HTML 2 OR ABOVE

Problem

I want to include links in my page, so I understand that I'll need to use URLs. However, I'm unfamiliar with the structure and composition of URLs: what goes into them, and where. How do I interpret a URL?

Technique

HTML uses Universal Resource Locators, or URLs, to provide a simple, consistent way of accessing information using a wide variety of protocols. A URL consists of three main items: a protocol code, the address of the computer with the desired

7.1
INTERPRET A URL

file (or an e-mail address or newsgroup name), and the location and filename of the file.

Steps

The following steps illustrate how to interpret a URL.

1. The first part of a URL is the protocol. The protocol indicates what method should be used to obtain the requested information. There are seven main protocols, listed in Table 7-1, which will be discussed in greater detail later in the chapter.

PROTOCOL	DESCRIPTION
ftp	File Transfer Protocol (FTP)
gopher	Gopher
http	HyperText Transfer Protocol (HTTP)
mailto	Electronic Mail
news	Usenet News
telnet	Telnet
wais	Wide Area Information Servers (WAIS)

Table 7-1 URL Protocols

2. For five of the seven protocols (ftp, gopher, http, telnet, and wais), the protocol is followed by a colon and two forward slashes (//). Immediately following the slashes is the address of the computer that is host to the relevant information. Some examples are

```
http://www.stateu.edu
ftp://ftp.widgets.com
gopher://info.stateu.edu
```

For the mailto protocol, the protocol is followed by a single colon and an e-mail address.

```
mailto:john@stateu.edu
mailto:help@widgets.com
```

For the news protocol, the protocol is followed by a single colon and the name of a Usenet newsgroup.

```
news:alt.widgets
news:comp.infosystems.www.users
```

3. For protocols other than mailto and news, the address of the computer is followed by the path to the desired file or directory. Some examples are

```
http://www.stateu.edu/pub/teams/yankees.html
ftp://ftp.widgets.com/etc/images/widget1.gif
gopher://info.stateu.edu/00/pubinfo/good%20restaurants
```

How It Works

When a browser encounters a URL, it first checks the protocol to determine what method the program must use to get the information. The browser then gets the address of the computer (or newsgroup name or e-mail address), accesses the site, and uses the path information in the URL to find the file and bring a copy back to the browser's computer.

Comments

Some browsers don't support some URL protocols, like news and mailto; such browsers require additional software or connections to work properly. A browser must be configured to use a communications program in order to use any telnet URLs, and it must have access to a WAIS server or be able to use a WAIS server elsewhere as a proxy in order to use any WAIS URLs.

To better understand the structure of URLs, you may want to look at the URLs contained in a variety of Web pages. Those URLs will provide additional examples on how URLs are constructed.

7.2 How do I... Understand a relative URL?

COMPLEXITY: INTERMEDIATE

COMPATIBILITY: HTML 2 OR ABOVE

Problem

When I've looked at some World Wide Web pages, I've seen URLs that don't have a protocol of any kind. Instead, it's just a filename or some kind of path. How do these kinds of URLs work?

Technique

When a URL does not begin with a protocol, that means it is referencing a file local to that computer (or possibly a file based on another computer; see How-To 7.3). Pathnames can be used to find files in directories other than the base directory.

Steps

To better understand the examples below, refer to Figure 7-1. This figure is a graphical representation of the directory structure used in the examples.

7.2
UNDERSTAND A RELATIVE URL

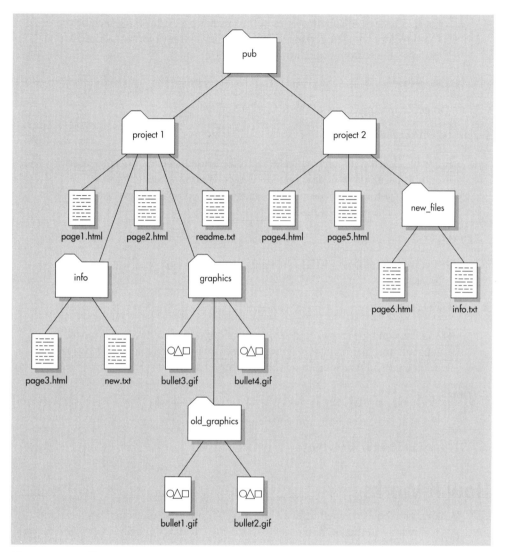

Figure 7-1 A directory structure

1. To access a file located in the same directory the current page is in, use only the name of the file as the URL. For example, if you are in page1.html and you want to go to page2.html, simply enter

`page2.html`

If you are in project1.txt and you want to access info.txt, enter

`info.txt`

2. For files located in subdirectories of the current page's directory, include the sub-directory name(s), separated from the filename by a forward slash (/). For example, to get from page1.html to page4.html, enter

`xpages/page4.html`

To get from project1.txt to the file bullet2.gif, enter

`graphics/bullet2.gif`

3. For files located in parent directories (directories above the directory of the current page), use a double period (..) separated from the filename by a forward slash for each level up. For example, if you want to get back to page2.html from page 4.html, enter

`../page2.html`

If you are in bullet2.gif and you want to access file2.txt, you will need to enter

`../../file2.txt`

4. You can combine steps 2 and 3 to access files located in directory branches separate from the branch the current directory is in. For example, if you are in file2.txt and you want to go to page2.html, enter

`../pages/page2.html`

If you are in page4.html and you want to open info.txt, enter

`../../files/projects/info.txt`

How It Works

When a protocol is omitted from a URL, a Web browser assumes that the location given is relative to the location of the current page. It uses the path information to move up or down directories to locate and retrieve the file.

Comments

Relative URLs are a great way to specify the location of pages and other files without having to write out a full pathname. However, if the page with the relative URLs is moved to another directory, then the URLs will no longer work, since they will point the way to files and directories that are not in the same relative location they originally were. (Unless, of course, all the files and directories are moved along with the page.) You can solve this problem by using the <BASE> element described in How-To 7.3.

7.3 How do I... Add a base for relative URLs within the body of a document?

COMPLEXITY: INTERMEDIATE

COMPATIBILITY: HTML 2 OR ABOVE

Problem

I need to move a page with a number of relative URLs in it. However, I can't move the files along with the page, and I don't want to spend the time editing the page to insert the new, longer pathnames for these files. How can I define a base for URLs in my document?

Technique

HTML has an element called <BASE> that can be included in the heading of a document to specify the base for all the relative URLs in the document. This allows you to move your page around without breaking the relative URLs, or permits you to use shortcuts in your URLs if you need to reference a number of files from the same location.

Steps

Open your document and go to the heading section (between the <HEAD> and </HEAD> tags; see Chapter 2 for background information about headings in HTML documents).

1. Inside your page heading, insert the <BASE> tag. Inside the <BASE> tag, include the attribute HREF and set it equal to the full path for the desired directory, assuming that directory is located on the same computer as the page. For example, if you want to set the base for relative URLs to the directory /pub/projects/data/, enter

```
<HEAD>
<TITLE>My Page</TITLE>
<BASE HREF="/pub/projects/data/">
</HEAD>
```

2. If the desired base for your URLs is located on another computer, include the full-fledged URL, including the protocol and name of the computer. If, for example, the base is on a Web server at www.stateu.edu in the directory pub/images, you would enter

```
<HEAD>
<TITLE>My Page</TITLE>
```

continued on next page

continued from previous page

```
<BASE HREF="http://www.stateu.edu/pub/images/">
</HEAD>
```

Or if the base is located on the FTP server ftp.stateu.edu in the directory /pub/images, the code would be

```
<HEAD>
<TITLE>My Page</TITLE>
<BASE HREF="ftp://ftp.stateu.edu/pub/images/">
</HEAD>
```

How It Works

The <BASE> element tells the browser to append the URL contained in it to any relative URLs located in the document. The contents of the <BASE> element are ignored for any URLs in the document that are fully formed, that is, that have protocols.

Comments

You can set the <BASE> element only once in a document, in the header. The <BASE> element does not work outside of the header. Thus, if you have two sets of relative URLs for which you want to specify separate bases, you can use the <BASE> element for only one set. You must edit the other set to include the full pathnames and protocols.

COMPLEXITY
INTERMEDIATE

7.4 How do I... Specify a relationship between this document and other resources?

COMPATIBILITY: HTML 2 OR ABOVE

Problem

I'm creating a number of Web pages that are all related to one another. I would like to be able to specify the relationship of each page to other pages for possible use by Web browsers. How can I specify a relationship between pages in HTML?

Technique

Use the <LINK> element in the header of an HTML document to identify relationships between documents and other resources. These relationships include

7.4 SPECIFY A RELATIONSHIP BETWEEN THIS DOCUMENT AND OTHER RESOURCES

preceding and following documents, tables of contents, indexes, and other document parts. The <LINK> element can also identify the author of a document.

Steps

Open your document and go to the heading section (between the <HEAD> and </HEAD> tags).

1. Place the <LINK> element in the header of a page.

```
<HEAD>
<TITLE>My Page</TITLE>
<LINK>
</HEAD>
```

2. The <LINK> element supports two kinds of attributes, REL and REV. REL indicates a relationship between the current document and a document listed in the element using the HREF attribute (as in How-To 7.3). The REL attribute can take on a number of different values. The most common ones, which have been reserved in HTML, are listed in Table 7-2.

VALUE	DESCRIPTION
"bookmark"	A specific section of a document
"copyright"	A document with copyright information
"glossary"	A glossary document
"help"	A help document
"home"	The home page or top of a hierarchy
"index"	An index document
"next"	The next document in a series
"previous"	The previous document in a series
"toc"	A table of contents document
"up"	The parent document to the current one

 Table 7-2 Values for the REL attribute in LINK

A common use for these attributes is to identify the previous and next pages in a sequence of documents. For example, if your current page is the document page4.html, and you want to identify the previous document (page3.html) and the next document (page5.html) you could use

```
<HEAD>
<TITLE>Page 4</TITLE>
<LINK REL=Previous HREF="page3.html">
<LINK REL=Next HREF="page5.html">
</HEAD>
```

207

Note that each reference is contained in a separate <LINK> element in the header.

3. The REV attribute is the opposite of REL. Instead of specifying another document's relationship to the current page, it specifies the current page's relationships to other pages. Applying this to the above example results in the following:

```
<HEAD>
<TITLE>Page 4</TITLE>
<LINK REV=Next HREF="page3.html">
<LINK REV=Previous HREF="page5.html">
</HEAD>
```

You are now saying that this document (page4.html) is page3.html's next document and page5.html's previous document, instead of saying that page4.html's previous document was page3.html and page4.html's next document was page5.html. Confusing? This kind of confusion can be avoided by using only one of the two attributes to specify relationships. REL is the attribute of choice for most people.

4. REV has found another use as a way to identify the author of the page. This can be done by placing the e-mail address of the author in a mailto URL (see How-Tos 7.1 and 7.14 for more information about mailto URLs) and setting it equal to REV.

```
<HEAD>
<TITLE>Page 4</TITLE>
<LINK REV="mailto:jfoust@mit.edu">
</HEAD>
```

How It Works

The browser reads and stores the information contained in the <LINK> elements regarding the location of related files. Some browsers provide users with the ability to select those documents, using a toolbar or other techniques.

Comments

<LINK> elements are a good way to indicate relationships among documents, but many Web browsers ignore the information contained in them. If you want to be sure that all readers have the ability to go to the files you've referenced in the <LINK> elements, you should include the links in the body of your page. Techniques for including these links are discussed starting in the next How-To.

7.5 How do I... Create a link to a local page?

COMPLEXITY: EASY

COMPATIBILITY: HTML 2 OR ABOVE

Problem

I would like to link one page I've created with another page, which is also located on my computer. How can I create a link in one of my pages that references a local page in HTML?

Technique

HTML uses the <A> and </A> tags to identify areas of the text that serve as anchors for links to other files. The HREF attribute in the <A> tag lists the location of the page or other resource.

Steps

Open your document. Decide what documents you would like to link to the current document.

1. Identify the word or phrase in your page that you want to use as an anchor for the link. Place the <A> tag at the beginning of the anchor and the </A> tag at the end of the anchor.

```
I enjoy watching <A>baseball</A>, but I'm not a good player.

I've visited <A>New York</A> a few times.
```

2. Inside the <A> tag, place the HREF attribute, and set it equal to the filename of the other page, provided the destination page is located in the same directory as the page you're working on. The filename should be enclosed in double quotation marks.

```
I enjoy watching <A HREF="baseball.html">baseball</A>, but I'm not a good player.

I've visited <A HREF="newyork.html">New York</A> a few times.
```

3. If the destination page is located in a subdirectory of the directory that contains your current page, you can indicate the path by including the subdirectory name(s) in the HREF attribute, separating the subdirectory names from each other and the filename with a forward slash (/), as shown in How-To 7.2:

CHAPTER 7
ESTABLISHING LINKS

```
I enjoy watching <A HREF="sports/baseball.html">baseball</A>, but I'm not a good player.

I've visited <A HREF="usa/cities/east-coast/newyork.html">New York</A> a few times.
```

4. If the destination page is located in a directory above the directory of your current page, you can go up the directory structure by using (..), two periods without any spacing between them, as shown in How-To 7.2.

```
I enjoy watching <A HREF="../baseball.html">baseball</A>, but I'm not a good player.

I've visited <A HREF="../../newyork.html">New York</A> a few times.
```

5. Links can retrieve more than just other pages. You can include sounds, graphics, text files, even compressed binary files in a link. For example, to include a link to a text file, enter

```
I have some <A HREF="info.txt">older information</A> about this subject.
```

Or to include a link to an image, enter

```
I took a <A HREF="gcanyon.gif">picture</A> of the Grand Canyon from the South Rim.
```

Figure 7-2 shows some examples of links. The code is included on the CD-ROM as file 7-2.html.

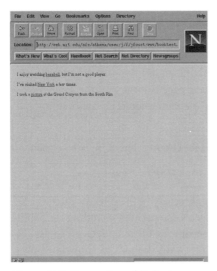

Figure 7-2 Examples of links in an HTML document

How It Works

The <A> and </A> tags tell the browser to identify the text contained between them as a link, which is usually done by highlighting or underlining the text. The HREF attribute provides the location of the file the browser should load if the link is selected. If the location of the file includes directory information, the browser assumes the location is given relative to the location of the current page. The <BASE> element (How-To 7.3) can be used to set that location to another path, or even to another computer.

Comments

When a browser encounters a link to a file other than another WWW page, the browser decides how to deal with the file. Most browsers display a text file the same as an HTML file (although with no formatting), and launch an external application for other files: a graphics program for an image, an audio program for a sound file, and so on. This depends on the availability of a compatible external application. If no application exists on the reader's computer to handle a file, the file cannot be viewed or heard. Thus, when including links to images, sounds, and animations, try to use common formats for these files whenever possible.

COMPLEXITY
EASY

7.6 How do I... Create a link to other pages?

COMPATIBILITY: HTML 2 OR ABOVE

Problem

I would like to include a link to a great page that has a lot of information relevant to my page. However, the page is located on another computer, so I can't use a link to a local page. How can I create a link to a page on another computer?

Technique

Using the HyperText Transfer Protocol (HTTP), you can connect to one computer and transfer a copy of a document on that computer to a browser running on another computer by placing the URL of the document in the anchor of a link, using the HREF attribute.

Steps

Open your document. Locate the words or phrases to be used for the links.

1. Identify the text you want to use as a link by placing the <A> tag at the beginning of the anchor text and the </A> tag at the end of the anchor text.

```
I enjoy watching <A>baseball</A>, but I'm not a good player.

I've visited <A>New York</A> a few times.
```

2. Place the HREF attribute in the <A> tag and set it equal to the URL of the page. (See How-To 7.1 for more information about URLs.) Enclose the URL in double quotation marks.

```
I enjoy watching <A HREF="http://www.stateu.edu/sports/baseball.html">baseball</A>, but I'm not a good player.

I've visited <A HREF="http://www.stateu.edu/cities/newyork.html">New York</A> a few times.
```

3. This technique can transfer other types of files, such as text files and images. For example, to transfer a text file, simply use that file's pathname in the URL.

```
I have some <A HREF="http://www.stateu.edu/info/info.txt">older information</A> about this subject.
```

Or to transfer an image, use the image file's pathname.

```
I took a <A HREF="http://www.stateu.edu/images/scenic/gcanyon.gif">picture</A> of the Grand Canyon from the South Rim.
```

4. You can use an http URL without a filename on the end for some special cases. This displays the default page in the directory (usually named index.html or default.html, depending on how the HTTP server on that computer is configured), if it exists. Otherwise it displays the contents of the directory, with the filenames linked to the files. For example, to load the default file on a subdirectory of www.stateu.edu, enter

```
I've created a new <A HREF="http://www.stateu.edu/pub/users/john/">home page</A> in my user's directory.
```

How It Works

The "http" in the URL tells a browser to use the HyperText Transfer Protocol to locate and transfer the file listed in the URL. The browser displays the page just like a local file. For text files, images, and other files, the browser uses the URL to locate the file and then transfers a copy using HTTP. The browser then displays the contents of the file or transfers the file to the appropriate external application.

Comments

Web servers often use different filenames for the default file. For example, CERN HTTPD uses default.html while NCSA HTTPD uses index.html. Some browsers may be configured to use a specific name instead of either of these two; check the server documentation or ask the Webmaster of the site for specific information.

COMPLEXITY
INTERMEDIATE

7.7 How do I... Send data to an HTTP server via a URL?

COMPATIBILITY: HTML 2 OR ABOVE

Problem

I'm developing a form to include in a page using a search key word, and I want to be able to send the results to a server to be processed by a program there. Is there a way to include that response or other information in a URL to send to a server?

Technique

It is possible to include key words or other basic pieces of information in a URL. A question mark is placed at the end of the URL for an application, followed by the data. Browsers usually do this automatically when they submit data.

Steps

Open your document. Locate the words or phrases for the links to the HTTP server.

1. If you want to include a key word or other data in a link, first create an anchor in the text appropriate to the data you want to send. For example, to create a pair of links that will send the answers "yes" or "no" to a question, enter

```
<H3>Do you want to subscribe to our magazine?</H3>?
<UL>
<LI><A>Yes!</A>
<LI><A>No thanks</A>
</UL>
```

2. Now, use the HREF attribute to add a link to a program on an HTTP server that will receive the data. (For now, don't worry about the specifics of the program. Forms and CGI applications are covered in Chapters 10 and 13,

CHAPTER 7
ESTABLISHING LINKS

respectively.) If, for example, the program is called "response" and is located on the http server at www.stateu.edu, your code would look like this:

```
<H3>Do you want to subscribe to our magazine?</H3>?
<UL>
<LI><A HREF="http://www.stateu.edu/applications/response">Yes!</A>
<LI><A HREF="http://www.stateu.edu/applications/response">No thanks</A>
</UL>
```

3. Now add to end of the URL a question mark and the key word you desire to be sent to the application. For this example, let the responses be "yes" and "no".

```
<H3>Do you want to subscribe to our magazine?</H3>?
<UL>
<LI><A HREF="http://www.stateu.edu/applications/response?yes">Yes!</A>
<LI><A HREF="http://www.stateu.edu/applications/response?no">No thanks</A>
</UL>
```

How It Works

The browser interprets anything in a URL after a question mark to be data that is sent to a URL. The application referenced in the URL then receives the key word as input and processes it accordingly.

Comments

The example shown above can actually be done better with forms. See Chapter 10 to find out how to create forms for your pages, and Chapter 13 to see how to write applications to process the data. When key word searching is enabled (using the <ISINDEX> tag in the header, as shown in Chapter 13), the question mark and key word are added automatically and don't need to be manually included in the URL.

COMPLEXITY
INTERMEDIATE

7.8 How do I... Create a link to a specific part of a page?

COMPATIBILITY: HTML 2 OR ABOVE

Problem

I have a long document I am converting into a WWW page using HTML. I want to use a table of contents to refer to the various sections of a document so the reader

7.8
CREATE A LINK TO A SPECIFIC PART OF A PAGE

can quickly refer to those sections. I would also like to be able to refer to different sections of the document from other pages. How can I create a link to a specific part of a page in HTML?

Technique

The NAME attribute used in the anchor tag identifies a section of a page. Users can then access this section via a link from within the document or from other documents.

Steps

Open your document. Identify the words or phrases that will serve as links. Also, decide what sections of the document you want links to lead to.

1. To identify a section of a document, place the <A> and </A> tags at the beginning of the section. Include the NAME attribute in the <A> tag and set it to the name you wish to give the section. Enclose the name in double quotation marks. Unlike the <LINK> tags, there is no need to include any text between the <A> and </A> tags.

```
<A NAME="section1"></A>
<H1>Section 1</H1>
<!-- text of section 1 -->
```

2. To include a link to the named section elsewhere in your page, create a link as described in How-To 7.5 and set HREF equal to the name of the section as defined by the NAME attribute. Enclose the name in double quotation marks and precede it with a pound symbol (#) to differentiate it from the name of another document.

```
You will find the relevant background information in <A HREF="#section1">section 1</A>.
```

3. To include a link to the named section from another local document, create a local link as described in How-To 7.5 and include the name of the section, preceded by the pound symbol (#), in the location of the link defined by the HREF attribute.

```
You will find the relevant background information in <A HREF="report.html#section1">section 1</A>.
```

4. For documents located on other computers, the process is similar. Attach the name of the section, preceded by the pound symbol (#), to the end of the URL for the document.

```
You will find the relevant background information in <A HREF="http://www.stateu.edu/documents/report.html#section1">section 1</A>.
```

How It Works

When a browser loads a URL with a # symbol, it looks for the section of the document with an anchor tag matching the name after the # symbol. The browser then displays the loaded page, with the beginning of the named section at the top of the screen.

Comments

When used to create links, the <A> tag must include text. When <A> tags are used merely to identify a section of a document, text is not necessary. This is because the tag is being used only to mark a section of a document for later use in a link, not to function itself as a link to another document. There is no need to include text between the tags, since this text is not highlighted and cannot be used to jump to another document or section of a document.

7.9 How do I... Create a link to an FTP site?

COMPLEXITY: EASY

COMPATIBILITY: HTML 2 OR ABOVE

Problem

I've found a file that I would like to include as a link in my page. However, the file is not accessible on the World Wide Web, only by anonymous FTP. How can I add a link to a file on an FTP site?

Technique

You can construct a URL for the file located on the FTP site and include that in a standard HTML link. The link will function like a link to a page or other document accessible via HTTP.

Steps

Open the document and find the words or phrases you want to use as links.

1. To construct the URL, you need to know the name of the site where the file is located, and the path for the file (that is, the directory where the file is located). For example, to access a file named contents.txt located on the server ftp.stateu.edu in the directory pub/info, you would use this URL:

```
ftp://ftp.stateu.edu/pub/info/contents.txt
```

7.9
CREATE A LINK TO AN FTP SITE

To access the image file gcanyon.gif from ftp.stateu.edu in the directory pub/photos/arizona, you would use this URL:

```
ftp://ftp.stateu.edu/pub/photos/arizona/gcanyon.gif
```

2. You can now include either of these URLs in a link by setting the HREF attribute of the link equal to the URL.

```
The <A HREF="ftp://ftp.stateu.edu/pub/info/contents.txt">contents</A> of the
directory can be easily viewed.

I took an incredible <A
HREF="ftp://ftp.stateu.edu/pub/photos/arizona/gcanyon.gif">photo</A> of the
Grand Canyon during my last trip there!
```

3. You can use FTP URLs to access entire directories and display their contents in the browser window. To do this, include the pathname to the directory in the URL, but do not add a filename to the end of the URL.

```
My <a HREF="ftp://ftp.stateu.edu/pub/photos/">photos directory</A> contains
a lot of pictures I took while on vacation in Arizona.
```

Figure 7-3 shows an example of an FTP directory accessed in HTML.

4. By default, the FTP URL uses anonymous FTP. However, you can create an FTP URL that uses nonanonymous FTP. To do so, include the username and

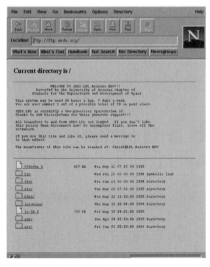

Figure 7-3 An FTP directory accessed by a World Wide Web browser

password, separated by a colon, in front of address of the FTP site. Include the @ symbol between the password and the computer address. To access the FTP server at ftp.stateu.edu as user "weather", using the password "stormy", you would use the following code.

```
There is an archive of <A
HREF="ftp://weather:stormy@ftp.stateu.edu/pub/weather/">weather data</A> that
includes satellite photos and updated forecasts.
```

How It Works

When a link with an FTP URL is selected, the browser opens an FTP connection with the specified computer. It goes to the appropriate directory and copies the file. The file then appears in the browser window or in an external application, depending on the type of file retrieved.

Comments

Unlike manually FTPing files, there is no need to specify whether to transfer a file as a binary, or ASCII, file. The browser checks the suffix of the file. If it matches with a suffix associated with binary files, the file is transferred as a binary file. Otherwise, it is transferred as a text file. Also, unless a username and password are specified, most browsers automatically log in to the FTP site as anonymous and transfer a string, usually your e-mail address, as the password. If you do include a nonanonymous FTP URL in your page, remember that the password is available for anyone to view, so don't put the password to your account there. This should only be used for special, limited-use accounts whose passwords can be distributed freely.

COMPLEXITY
INTERMEDIATE

7.10 How do I... Create a link to a Gopher site?

COMPATIBILITY: HTML 2 OR ABOVE

Problem

I would like to reference a file stored on a Gopher server for my page. How can I add a link to a Gopher server? Can I go directly to the file or do I have to go through the directory structure of the Gopher server?

Technique

A few years ago, Gopher servers were a popular method of making information easily available to Internet users. Even with the rapid growth of the World Wide

7.10
CREATE A LINK TO A GOPHER SITE

Web, many Gopher servers are still in use and contain information you may wish to reference on your page. This can be done with a Gopher URL, either to the top-level directory or directly to the file.

Steps

Open the document and find the words or phrases you want to use as links.

1. First, define the anchor text in your page using the <A> tag.

```
There is a <A>Gopher site</A> with more information on baseball.
```

2. To construct a URL for the top-level directory of a Gopher server, take the address of the Gopher site and attach "gopher://" to the front of it, such as gopher://gopher.stateu.edu. You can then set the HREF attribute in the link tag equal to this URL.

```
There is a <A HREF="gopher://gopher.stateu.edu">Gopher site</A> with more information on baseball.
```

3. To construct a URL for a specific file or directory on a Gopher server, you need to know the full path to it. To get this information, you will need to check the Gopher server and find the URL for it (usually available by selecting the "Display technical information about this item" option in most Gopher programs). As a rule, files have a /00/ in their URL after the name of the server, directories have a /11/ after the name of the server, and spaces in file or directory names are represented in the URL by the code %20. For example, to reference a file on a Gopher server, enter

```
There is a <A HREF="gopher://gopher.stateu.edu/00/teams/yankees.txt">file</A> with more information on the New York Yankees.
```

To reference a directory on a Gopher server, enter

```
There is a <A HREF="gopher://gopher.stateu.edu/11/teams">directory</A> with information on all the major league baseball teams.
```

To reference a file with a space in its name, enter

```
There is a <A HREF="gopher://gopher.stateu.edu/00/teams/the%20yankees">file</A> with information on the New York Yankees.
```

How It Works

When a Gopher link is selected, the browser contacts the site given in the URL using the Gopher protocol and returns the information requested, either a file or a directory. The browser displays the file based on its rules for file types; text files usually display in the window, but image and sound files retrieved by Gopher are sent to the appropriate external application. If a directory is retrieved, it appears in the window, with each directory item serving as a link to another Gopher item.

Comments

Before including a link to a specific directory or file on a Gopher server, be sure to check the exact URL for the file. Different servers use different methods of defining paths to files and directories, and the name of the file or directory given in the Gopher menu may be entirely different from the real name and location of the resource.

COMPLEXITY
INTERMEDIATE

7.11 How do I... Create a link to a Telnet site?

COMPATIBILITY: HTML 2 OR ABOVE

Problem

I would like to include a link to an Internet resource accessible only by Telnet. I don't know how to include all the information, including the username and port number, in the URL. How do I create a link to a Telnet site in HTML?

Technique

A Telnet URL is similar to those used for FTP and Gopher sites. You can specify the port number, the username, and the password for logging in to the site.

Steps

Open the document and find the words or phrases you want to use as links.

1. As with other links, first specify the anchor text for the link in your document. Place the <A> tag at the beginning of the anchor and the </A> tag at the end of the anchor.

```
The State University<A>weather server </A> provides updated forecasts and weather conditions.
```

2. To create a standard Telnet log-in, using the standard port and not specifying the username or password, place "telnet://" in front of the address of the site, such as telnet://suvax.stateu.edu. You can now set the HREF attribute in the anchor tag equal to this URL.

```
The State University<A HREF="telnet://suvax.stateu.edu">weather server </A> provides updated forecasts and weather conditions.
```

3 Many special services offered by Telnet operate from a nonstandard port. To specify the port to Telnet to, place a colon after the address of the site and add the port number after the colon.

```
The State University<A HREF="telnet://suvax.stateu.edu:3000">weather server </A> provides updated forecasts and weather conditions.
```

4. To specify the username to be used when logging in to the Telnet site, place the username in front of the site address and separate the two with the @ symbol.

```
The State University<A HREF="telnet://weather@suvax.stateu.edu">weather server </A> provides updated forecasts and weather conditions.
```

5. To provide a password as well as a username, place a colon after the username and insert the password between the colon and @ symbol.

```
The State University<A HREF="telnet://weather:stormy@suvax.stateu.edu">weather server </A> provides updated forecasts and weather conditions.
```

How It Works

When a Telnet link is selected, the browser starts up a Telnet session using the Telnet program set by the browser. The port number, username, and password, if provided, are used to establish the connection.

Comments

To be able to use a Telnet link, a browser must be able to access a Telnet program on the browser's computer, otherwise the link cannot be used. The Telnet program that the browser uses is defined by the browser and can usually be changed by the reader. Since URLs are freely available and not encrypted, placing the password for an account in a URL creates a serious security hazard to that computer, unless the account is especially designed to be used solely for special applications. When in doubt, do not place the password to a computer account in a URL.

COMPLEXITY
INTERMEDIATE

7.12 How do I... Create a link to a WAIS site?

COMPATIBILITY: HTML 2 OR ABOVE

Problem

I would like to access a WAIS database of information relevant to a topic on my page. How can I include a link to a WAIS server on my page?

Technique

WAIS provides the ability to conduct key word searches on a variety of databases. You can include a link to a WAIS URL in your document that allows users to search a specific database on a topic or topics.

Steps

Open the document and find the words or phrases you want to use as links.

1. First, identify the anchor for the link. Place the <A> tag at the beginning of the link and </A> at the end of the link.

```
You can also search a <A>database</A> of reports and other information on this topic.
```

2. Create the URL for the WAIS database by adding the protocol tag "wais://" in front of the name of the server. Include information on the location of the database after the name of the server. If the WAIS server is running on a port other than the standard port (210), include the port number after the address of the computer and separate the two items with a colon. Set the HREF attribute in the anchor tag equal to this URL.

```
You can also search a <A HREF="wais://server.stateu.edu/report-database.src">database</A> of reports and other information on this topic.

You can also search a <A HREF="wais://server.stateu.edu:8001/report-database.src">database</A> of reports and other information on this topic.
```

3. To specify a key word for a WAIS search, include the key word at the end of the URL and separate it from the name of the database with the question mark symbol. To search for all documents that contain the key word "baseball", enter

```
You can also search a <A HREF="wais://server.stateu.edu/report-database.src?baseball">database</A> of reports and other information on this topic.
```

How It Works

The WAIS protocol tag in a URL informs the browser to start a WAIS search on the given database, using the key word if provided. The browser then returns the results of the search in the window, often listing the filenames of the documents that have the given key word and providing links to the files.

Comments

Many browsers either do not support WAIS searches, or require special software be installed to run the searches. Fortunately, there are not many WAIS databases available, and few people include links to WAIS databases in their pages. There has been some development of software that allows users to conduct WAIS searches using forms. (See Chapter 10 for more information on how forms work.) This method will probably supersede the WAIS protocol tag in HTML.

7.13 How do I... Create a link to a Usenet newsgroup?

COMPLEXITY: EASY

COMPATIBILITY: HTML 2 OR ABOVE

Problem

I want to reference a Usenet newsgroup that is relevant to the subject of my page. How do I create a link to a Usenet newsgroup in HTML? Does the reader need special newsreading software to access the newsgroup?

Technique

Usenet newsgroups, forums for discussion on a wide range of topics, can be accessed from a page. No special software is needed; the titles of the articles usually appear as a list of links to the articles themselves within the Web browser once the user specifies the address of a news server.

Steps

Open the document and find the words or phrases you want to use as links.

1. As with other links, mark the anchor text for the link. Place the <A> tag at the beginning of the anchor text and the </A> tag at the end of the text.

```
A number of <A>discussions</A> about the Big Bang are in progress.
```

2. You can create the URL for the newsgroup by appending the name of the newsgroup to the protocol tag "news:". You can then set the HREF attribute equal to this URL.

```
A number of <A HREF="news:sci.astro">discussions</A> about the Big Bang are in progress.
```

How It Works

When a news URL is selected, the browser accesses the newsgroup from its newsfeed. The titles of the unread articles (articles you have not yet read) appear in the window, serving as links to the full text of the articles.

Comments

To successfully use a news link, the reader's browser must have access to a newsfeed, and the newsgroup in question must be carried by the browser's newsfeed. Keep this in mind when creating links to local, limited-distribution newsgroups; if you include links to Seattle-area newsgroups, for example, it's unlikely that a reader in Boston has a newsfeed that carries these newsgroups, and hence won't be able to access them.

COMPLEXITY
EASY

7.14 How do I... Create a link to electronic mail?

COMPATIBILITY: HTML 2 OR ABOVE

Problem

I would like to include a link that will allow readers to send e-mail to me with their comments about my page. I want to keep this simple, and not go to the time and trouble of creating a form and software to parse the form. How can I include a link to electronic mail in HTML?

Technique

HTML includes a URL tag called mailto, which identifies the address to which e-mail should be sent. If the link is selected, the browser will start a mail program to send a message to the recipient listed in the URL.

Steps

Open the document and find the words or phrases you want to use as links.

1. Identify the anchor text to be used for the link by placing the <A> tag at the beginning of the anchor and the </A> tag at the end of the anchor.

```
Send me <A>e-mail</A> with your comments about my page.
```

2. Create the URL for the link by placing the protocol tag "mailto:" in front of the e-mail address to which mail should be sent. Set the HREF attribute in <A> equal to this URL.

```
Send me <A HREF="mailto:nobody@stateu.edu">e-mail</A> with your comments about my page.
```

How It Works

When a mailto link is selected, the browser starts up its electronic mail program (as defined by the browser), setting the *To:* line in the message to the address given in the URL.

Comments

The mailto URL works successfully only if the browser has access to an electronic mail program. The program used can usually be set by the user. Using forms (Chapter 10) is often a better way to get feedback on a page, since it doesn't require the use of an external program.

COMPLEXITY
EASY

7.15 How do I... Create links to pages in other users' home directories?

COMPATIBILITY: HTML 2 OR ABOVE

Problem

I'd like to access some pages located in another user's directory. However, I would like to be able to shorten the length of the URL and not type the full path to the page. Is there a way I can easily create links to pages in other users' home directories?

Technique

On UNIX filesystems, it is possible to abbreviate the path to a user's home directory by using the username preceded by the tilde (~) symbol. This can be used on local and remote systems to shorten the length of the URL of a page.

Steps

Open the document and find the words or phrases you want to use as links.

1. Specify the anchored text in your document. Place the <A> tag at the beginning of the anchor and </A> at the end of the anchor.

```
There's more information on the topic on <A>John's page</A>.
```

2. If the page is located in another user's directory on the same computer as your page, you can reach that user's home directory by using the username, preceded by a tilde. For example, to access a page in user John's home directory, enter

```
There's more information on the topic on <A HREF=""~john/info.html>John's page</A>.
```

You can also access another user's subdirectories by including them in the URL. For example, if the page listed above was located in the subdirectory pub; you would enter

```
There's more information on the topic on <A HREF=""~john/pub/info.html>John's page</A>.
```

3. This technique also works for pages in users' directories on other computers. If John's page was located on the computer www.stateu.edu, in his home directory, you could create the following link to it.

```
There's more information on the topic on <A HREF="http://www.stateu.edu/~john/info.html>John's page</A>.
```

If the page was located in a subdirectory, it could be accessed by including the directory path in the URL.

```
There's more information on the topic on <A HREF="http://www.stateu.edu/~john/pub/info.html>John's page</A>.
```

How It Works

The ~ symbol in the URL tells the browser to go to the home directory or to the listed subdirectory of the specified user and retrieve the document.

Comments

The ~ notation only works for those computer systems that support multiple users and use UNIX or a variation of UNIX. Also, for a document to be retrievable in this way, its author must have given permission by making the contents of the directory readable by all users.

7.16 How do I... Add links to lists and tables?

COMPLEXITY
EASY

COMPATIBILITY: HTML 2 OR ABOVE (LISTS), HTML 3 (TABLES)

Problem

I would like to create a menu for the reader by organizing a set of links to different pages. It seems that the best way to do this is with a list or a table. How can I add links to lists and tables in HTML?

Technique

You can add links to lists and tables just as you would to ordinary text on a page. Each list item or table entry can serve as a link to a different page, FTP site, etc.

Steps

Open the document and decide what information you would like to display in lists or tables, and what resources you would like to link to a different page, FTP site, etc.

1. First, create the list or table, including all the list items and table entries, just as you would with an ordinary list or table. For example, a list might look like this:

```
<UL>
    <LI>Boston Red Sox
    <LI>New York Yankees
    <LI>Toronto Blue Jays
</UL>
```

A similar table might be formatted as follows:

```
<TABLE BORDER>
    <CAPTION>Three American League Teams</CAPTION>
    <TR><TH>Team<TH>Wins<TH>Losses
    <TR><TD>Boston Red Sox<TD>90<TD>72
    <TR><TD>New York Yankees<TD>88<TD>74
    <TR><TD>Toronto Blue Jays<TD>77<TD>85
</TABLE>
```

2. Now add the links where appropriate in the list or table, just as you would in the text of a document.

```
<UL>
    <LI><A HREF="redsox.html">Boston Red Sox</A>
    <LI><A HREF="yankees.html">New York Yankees</A>
```

continued on next page

continued from previous page

```
    <LI><A HREF="bluejays.html">Toronto Blue Jays</A>
</UL>

<TABLE BORDER>
    <CAPTION>Three American League Teams</CAPTION>
    <TR><TH>Team<TH>Wins<TH>Losses
    <TR><TD><A HREF="redsox.html">Boston Red Sox</A><TD>90<TD>72
    <TR><TD><A HREF="yankees.html">New York Yankees</A><TD>88<TD>74
    <TR><TD><A HREF="bluejays.html">Toronto Blue Jays</A><TD>77<TD>85
</TABLE>
```

Figure 7-4 shows the output of this list and table. The code is also available on the CD-ROM as file 7-4.html.

How It Works

Links in lists and tables are treated the same as links elsewhere in a document. You can add links of all types that function exactly the same as links in other parts of a document.

Comments

A good way to use links in lists and tables is to create a table of contents or a menu of choices for the reader. This works best if each link is given one line of the list or one entry in the table. Links can extend over multiple list or table entries, but they become less useful that way.

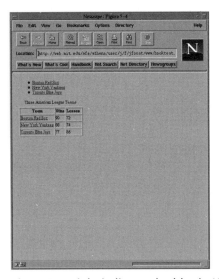

Figure 7-4 Links in lists and tables in HTML

7.17 How do I... Change the shape of a link?

COMPLEXITY: INTERMEDIATE

COMPATIBILITY: HTML 3

Problem

I would like to define a certain area of a figure on my page as a link to a specific document. I don't want to go though the hassle of creating an imagemap, though. Is there a way to accomplish this using HTML 3?

Technique

The HTML 3 SHAPE attribute permits links of different shapes and sizes to be included in figures (using the new HTML 3 <FIGURE> tag). SHAPE lets you do many of the same things an imagemap (Chapter 8) does, but without the need to create a separate map file or deal with CGI scripts.

Steps

Open your document. Also, load an image with a viewer that allows you to get the pixel locations on the image, so you can specify image locations in the links.

1. First, decide what areas on the image will serve as links. These areas can be circles, rectangles, or even complex polygons. Note the pixel locations of the areas: the x coordinate increases to the right, and the y coordinate increases downwards.

2. Create a list of links, as described in How-To 7.16. For each link, include the SHAPE attribute. The SHAPE attribute can take on the forms shown in Table 7-3.

ATTRIBUTE	DESCRIPTION
circle x,y,r	A circle centered at the point (x,y) with radius r.
rect x,y,w,h	A rectangle of width w and height h with its upper left corner at (x,y).
polygon x1,y1,x2,y2,...	A polygon that consists of lines linking the points (x1,y1), (x2,y2), etc. The polygon is closed by a line linking the last set of points to the first set.
default	The background of the figure, which includes those points not inside a circle, rectangle, or polygon.

Table 7-3 SHAPE attribute types

For example, a simple list consisting of a circle, rectangle, and triangle (three-point polygon), as well as a default link for the rest of the figure, might look like this:

```
<UL>
    <LI><A SHAPE="circle 10,10,5" HREF="page1.html">Page 1</A>
    <LI><A SHAPE="rect 30,20,10,5" HREF="page2.html">Page 2</A>
    <LI><A SHAPE="polygon 50,40,40,40,40,30" HREF="page3.html">Page 3</A>
</UL>
```

See Figure 7-5 for an example of how this would look.

3. This list of shaped links is then incorporated into a figure, using the HTML 3 <FIGURE> tag. An example using the above list might look like this:

```
<FIG SRC="book.gif">
    <UL>
        <LI><A SHAPE="circle 10,10,5" HREF="page1.html">Page 1</A>
        <LI><A SHAPE="rect 30,20,10,5" HREF="page2.html">Page 2</A>
        <LI><A SHAPE="polygon 50,40,40,40,40,30" HREF="page3.html">Page 3</A>
    </UL>
</FIG>
```

How It Works

The SHAPE attribute defines an area on the image as a link. If a reader selects that part of the image, the link is activated the way any other link would be. This works just as an imagemap would, but without the need to create a separate map file of the image or write a script to interpret the imagemap.

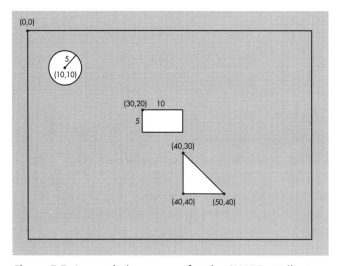

Figure 7-5 A sample imagemap for the SHAPE attribute

Comments

If a person selects an area of an image where two or more links overlap, the browser finds the link whose center is closest to the selected point and chooses it. If the default link is not created in the figure, any part of the figure outside the linked areas is not active and is not linked to other documents.

COMPLEXITY
EASY, INTERMEDIATE

7.18 How do I... Add links to my home page?

COMPATIBILITY: HTML2/HTML 3

Problem

I now know all about creating links in a page. However, I'm not sure how to put them into my document; that is, where they should go, how they should relate to the text of my document, and so on. How can I effectively add links to my home page?

Technique

There are many ways links can be used in a page. Consequently, there are many ways links can be misused, as well. Some common problems with the use of links are described below, with solutions to those problems.

Steps

These steps assume you know the basics of constructing links. These tips will help you use that knowledge to create effective ones.

1. First and foremost, a link must have some text or graphics (see How-To 8.8) that a reader can select. The following link might be to the best resource on the World Wide Web

```
<A HREF="http://www.stateu.edu/cool.html"></A>
```

but it will be useless for the reader of the document, since, with no text between the anchor elements, there is no way to select the link. Always make sure there is some relevant text between the anchor elements to permit readers to select the link.

An exception to this is when the NAME attribute is used in the anchor. Since the NAME attribute only identifies a specific location in a document, and is itself not a link to another resource, the following usage is valid.

```
<A NAME="section1"></A>
```

In fact, this is often the best way to identify sections of a page without including additional text.

2. One of the most common problems with links, and one of the most annoying, is what is often called the "click here" syndrome. An example of code with this problem might look like this:

```
<A HREF="coolpic.gif">Click here</A> for a cool picture I took!
```

There are several problems with this statement. First, it disrupts the flow of a document. To understand this better, look at the following example.

```
The St. Louis Browns were one of baseball's most infamous teams. <A
HREF="badteams.html">Click here</A> for information on other bad teams in baseball
history. They appeared in only one World Series, in 1944, when most of baseball's
stars were in the armed forces during World War II. For more information on the
World Series, click <A HREF="series.html">here</A>. Their Series opponents were
their hometown rivals, the St. Louis Cardinals. All the games in that series were
played in one stadium, Sportsman's Park, the home stadium for both teams. <A
HREF="sportsman.gif">Click here</A> for a picture of Sportsman's Park.
```

(This paragraph is shown in Figure 7-6. The code is available on the CD-ROM as file 7-6.html.)

Imagine reading this without being able to access the links. All the "click here" statements disrupt the flow of the paragraph. While it's thoughtful of the writer to explain what all the links are, the extra sentences make it harder to understand the main points of the paragraph. A solution to this problem is to use relevant words and phrases in the paragraph as anchors for the links. This will be discussed in more detail below.

Another problem with the "click here" statement is that it assumes that all readers of the page are using a graphical Web browser. Many people access the Web using a text-based browser such as Lynx. For these users, links are usually selected by a number, not by using a mouse, so the "click here" terminology is not useful for them and can even be confusing.

3. Another problem with links, at an extreme from the "click here" problem, are poorly labeled links. Ideally, the anchor phrase, and the context of that phrase within the document, should indicate where, in general, the link will lead. However, it's not uncommon for links to refer to resources that don't clearly follow from the anchor text. For example:

```
The St. Louis Browns were one of baseball's most infamous <A
HREF="badteams.html">teams</A>. They <A HREF="series.html">appeared</A> in only
```

7.18
ADD LINKS TO MY HOME PAGE

```
one World Series, in 1944, when most of baseball's stars were in the armed
forces during World War II. Their Series opponents were their hometown rivals,
the St. Louis Cardinals. All the games in that series were played in one <A
HREF="sportsman.gif">stadium</A>, Sportsman's Park, the home stadium for both
teams.
```

(This paragraph is shown in Figure 7-7. The code is available on the CD-ROM as file 7-7.html.)

The problem here is not a profusion of "click here" statements but of vague links. If a user reads this and sees the word "teams" in the top line linked, he or she may not know where that link leads: a list of bad teams, or a list of all the teams in baseball, or general information about teams.

There is a middle ground between these two problems, a way to smoothly incorporate links into a document and still make it clear from the context of the document what the function of each link is. The sample paragraph, reworked, illustrates the solution.

```
The St. Louis Browns were one of baseball's most <A HREF="badteams.html">infamous
teams</A>. They appeared in only one <A HREF="series.html">World Series</A>, in
1944, when most of baseball's stars were in the armed forces during World War II.
Their Series opponents were their hometown rivals, the St. Louis Cardinals. All
the games in that series were played in one stadium, <A
HREF="sportsman.gif">Sportsman's Park</A>, the home stadium for both teams.
```

(This paragraph is shown in Figure 7-8. The code is available on the CD-ROM as file 7-8.html.)

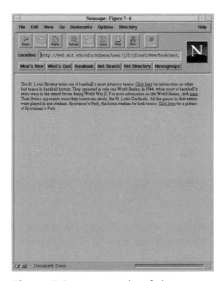

Figure 7-6 An example of the "click here" syndrome

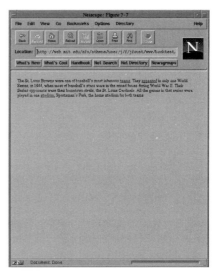

Figure 7-7 An example of vague links

The "click here" statements have been eliminated and the function of the links is clearer. Seeing "infamous teams" linked, for example, suggests to the reader that the link probably leads to some specific information on bad teams. In some cases you may need to rewrite the text slightly to use this technique, but it is best if links can derive their meaning from the context of the document.

4. Similarly, it is often useful to add explanatory information when using links in lists. Using short link names in a list of links may make it easy to create the list, but it may make it harder for a reader to decipher what each option specifically offers. For example, consider this list of links:

```
<H3>Menu of Options</H3>
<UL>
<LI><A HREF="intro.html">Introduction</A>
<LI><A HREF="techdata.html">Technical Data</A>
<LI><A HREF="prices.html">Price List</A>
<LI><A HREF="comments.html">Comments</A>
</UL>
```

Reading this, you can get some idea of what each link leads to, but it's hard to tell what information each option has short of selecting it. Adding a bit of description can help a user better understand the contents of each list option. A good way to do this is with a glossary list (see Chapter 6). Applying a glossary list to the above example would create the following:

```
<H3>Menu of Options</H3>
<DL>
<DT><A HREF="intro.html">Introduction</A>
<DD>A welcome message from the President and some background material about widgets.
<DT><A HREF="techdata.html">Technical Data</A>
<DD>Technical specifications for all 13 types of widgets we sell
<DT><A HREF="prices.html">Price List</A>
<DD>A complete list of prices for all widgets and information on special sales
<DT><A HREF="comments.html">Comments</A>
<DD>How to send us your comments and suggestions
</DL>
```

This list gives the reader a much clearer idea of the functionality of each link. These two lists are shown in Figure 7-9. This code is available on the CD-ROM as file 7-9.html.

How It Works

The key to using links is to incorporate them into the text of your document as smoothly as possible, but also without obscuring their meaning. The above examples show that with some practice, this can be done.

7.18
ADD LINKS TO MY HOME PAGE

Comments

Links make the World Wide Web just that: a web of information spanning the globe. By incorporating links to other documents in your pages (and, invariably, having your pages included as links in other people's documents), you can spin your own little section of the World Wide Web.

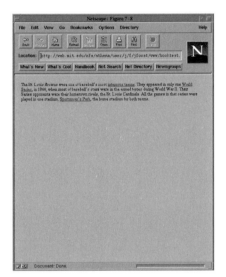

Figure 7-8 An example of good use of links

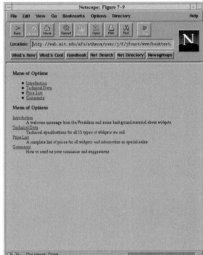

Figure 7-9 Examples of vague and well-defined lists with links in HTML

CHAPTER 8
USING IMAGES IN YOUR DOCUMENTS

USING IMAGES IN YOUR DOCUMENTS

How do I...

- **8.1** Build an icon to use in an HTML document?
- **8.2** Add an inline image?
- **8.3** Align images and text on a page?
- **8.4** Use the <ALT> tag for nongraphical browsers?
- **8.5** Include an image with a transparent background?
- **8.6** Create an interlaced inline image on my page?
- **8.7** Create a thumbnail version of an image?
- **8.8** Use an image as a link?
- **8.9** Create a clickable imagemap?
- **8.10** Create a background pattern for my page?
- **8.11** Align images and text using the advanced HTML 3 tags?

One of the key features that distinguishes the World Wide Web from other parts of the Internet is images. Images, when used correctly, can liven up a Web page. This chapter shows numerous ways in which you can add images to make your HTML documents more interesting to read and to look at.

CHAPTER 8
USING IMAGES IN YOUR DOCUMENTS

8.1 Build an Icon to Use in an HTML Document
Icons liven up an HTML document and help make a page more concise and compact by replacing a lot of words with one picture. This How-To shows how you can create icons for your documents.

8.2 Add an Inline Image
Now that you know how to create an icon, you need to include it in your HTML documents. This How-To shows how easy it is to add images to your documents.

8.3 Align Images and Text on a Page
This How-To shows you the number of options you may use when aligning text and images in your documents.

8.4 Use the <ALT> Tag for Nongraphical Browsers
Sometimes a reader looking at your document is either using a browser that can't view images or that has image loading turned off. This How-To shows how to use the <ALT> tag to put up a text description in place of an image.

8.5 Include an Image with a Transparent Background
Standard inline images display on a browser with white space around the edges. While this is sometimes acceptable, it can at times look unprofessional. This How-To shows how to make an image's background transparent so it will blend in with the document.

8.6 Create an Interlaced Inline Image on My Page
Standard GIF images load from top to bottom. This is fine, but somewhat bland. Interlacing allows an entire image to load in a complete but low-resolution form, then build up to higher and higher resolution. This How-To shows how to make GIF images into interlaced images.

8.7 Create a Thumbnail Version of an Image
Thumbnail versions of images are not as large and as time-consuming to load as full-fledged versions of images. Therefore, there are times when it is beneficial to display a thumbnail copy of an image on a page. This How-To shows a number of ways to create thumbnail images.

8.8 Use an Image as a Link
It can be a nice touch to either replace or augment a text link with an image that links to another document. This How-To shows how to use images as links.

8.9 Create a Clickable Imagemap
Clickable imagemaps are often used in place of text menus or as interactive maps. They are images that link a user to certain spots, depending on where the user

clicks on that image. They add a nice graphical touch to your user interface. This How-To shows how to add imagemaps to documents.

8.10   Create a Background Pattern for My Page

Netscape 1.1 has the added HTML 3 feature of being able to change your background color. This How-To demonstrates how to change the background on your pages to be virtually anything you find pleasing.

8.11   Align Images and Text Using the Advanced HTML 3 Tags

Netscape has added the HTML 3 features that allow you to extend the ALIGN attribute in the <IMG SRC> tag. These new extensions include the ability to align text and images left and right, thus adding the ability to wrap text around a graphic. This How-To explains these Netscape extensions.

COMPLEXITY
EASY

8.1 How do I... Build an icon to use in an HTML document?

COMPATIBILITY: HTML

Problem

My documents work fine, but I would like to make them look snappier by adding icons. How can I create one or more icons that I can use later in my documents?

Technique

Icons are small graphical images saved in GIF format. Icons are usually small—either 64 by 64 or 32 by 32 pixels—but there is no set rule on this. They are created much as you would any other image for your computer, with a graphics program. You create the image, save the image in GIF format or in another format, and then convert that image to GIF format. Finally, you transfer the GIF image to your server.

Steps

The following procedure shows you how to create icons. The actual process will vary depending on the software you use and the machine you are on, but the concepts remain the same.

1. Lay out your image on paper. Decide what you want to show and how you want it to look. Unless you are a talented artist, it is best to start simply.

CHAPTER 8
USING IMAGES IN YOUR DOCUMENTS

Figure 8-1 A simple image to use for an icon

Something like the little balloon (a circle with a line) shown in Figure 8-1 is good for learning purposes.

2. Decide which graphics program you would like to use. Practically any graphics package available can be made to work. There are also a number of programs whose sole purpose is to facilitate the creation of images on the Web. The decision on which to use is usually a matter of availability and personal preference. There are a number of features, though, that do come in handy when creating images for the Web: being able to easily control the pixel size of an image, a simple way to control the number of colors the image may have, and the ability to save in GIF format. You may want to take these into account before choosing your program. One popular program available for the Macintosh that meets all these standards is GraphicConverter. One popular program for the UNIX and PC worlds is GIFTOOL.

3. Open a new image. It is best to set the pixel size and the number of colors at the beginning. Pixel size is the number of horizontal and vertical squares that you use to create the image. The unwritten standard seems to be either 64 by 64 or 32 by 32, but, like most other things on the Web, there are no set rules, only conventions or suggestions. If your image fits in a 1 inch by 1 inch square, you should be in pretty good shape. When choosing colors, keep the number as low as possible, because the more colors you use, the bigger the image will be and the longer it will take to load. Use four or five colors to create an image that looks nice and is fairly colorful, but is not very large.

4. Use whatever tools your application has to draw your image. This is where no book in the world can help you. If you have artistic ability, go crazy! Still, even if you have no artistic ability, creating something like the balloon used in this example should be fairly simple.

5. Once you are satisfied with your icon, save the image. If your program allows you to pick the format to save in, choose GIF. If GIF is not available, then TIFF and PICT make good alternatives to this as they easily convert to GIF. It is best to save the image with a short, descriptive name. For our example, something like balloon.gif works well.

8.1
BUILD AN ICON TO USE IN AN HTML DOCUMENT

6. If your graphics program does not have a GIF option to save in, find one of the many available GIF converter programs and convert the image to GIF. Some possible choices for converting images to GIF are GifConverter for the Macintosh, GIFTOOL for UNIX and PC machines, or the PBMPLUS library available for a number of UNIX environments. All these programs work in the same way: you open up balloon.tiff (for example) then save it in GIF format as balloon.gif.

7. If your finished GIF icon is on a different machine than your server, transfer the icon to the appropriate machine. You will then be ready to go.

How It Works

There is no trick at all to this. Icons are just like any other graphic you create with your computer. The only difference between an icon you create for your Web pages and an icon you see on your computer's windows is that your icon is saved in GIF format.

Comments

Even if you have absolutely no artistic ability at all you can still create nice-looking images for icons by using graphical text. Figure 8-2 shows an example of using graphical text as an icon.

Figure 8-2 Graphical text icon

GIF stands for Graphic Interchange Format, which loosely translates to: "this format is readable by a wide number of different machines." That is what makes GIF so convenient to use on the Web. Currently, GIF is the only graphical format that most browsers can show without the aid of a helper application, but it should be noted that JPEG format is also easily displayed by a wide number of browsers.

It should also be pointed out there is no one right way to convert an image to GIF format. While all the tools mentioned in steps 2 and 6 may work a little differently, they all do work. The PBMPLUS library may not be as easy to use as the other choices, but it offers great control and large number of options. The downside to the PBMPLUS library is that you must write scripts in order to perform conversions. The following Perl script is included as an example of how the PBMPLUS library is used. This program not only converts a TIFF to a GIF but it also rotates the GIF 90 degrees. This example illustrates both the power and "complexity" of the library.

```perl
#!/usr/bin/perl

$netpbm = '/home/netpbm.bin';

# Get a list of all .tif files in the current directory.

opendir(DIR, ".");
@TIFFS = grep(/\.TIF$/, readdir(DIR));
closedir(DIR);

# Add the NetPBM tool directory to our path.

$ENV{'PATH'} = "$netpbm:$ENV{'PATH'}";

# Convert all the files

foreach $TIFF (@TIFFS) {
  $GIF = $TIFF; $GIF =~ s/\.TIF$/\.GIF/;
  print "Translating $TIFF to $GIF\n";
#   system("tifftopnm $TIFF | pnmflip -rotate90 | ppmtogif >$GIF");
  system("tifftopnm $TIFF | ppmtogif >$GIF");
  unlink $TIFF || print "Couldn't delete $TIFF: $!\n";
  print "\n";
}

exit 0;
```

8.2 How do I... Add an inline image?

COMPLEXITY: EASY

COMPATIBILITY: HTML

Problem

I have an HTML document and I have an image that's saved as a GIF. Now how do I include this image in my document?

Technique

Adding an image to an HTML document is surprisingly easy. You must either create the image with a graphics program or by scanning an existing image. Once you have the image, save it in GIF format. Then use the <IMG SRC> tag to include the image in your document.

Steps

The following procedure shows you how to add images to your documents.

8.2
ADD AN INLINE IMAGE

1. Create the GIF image you wish to include in your document. For learning purposes, it is best to keep the image simple, such as the balloon.gif used in the previous How-To. If you are unsure how to create this image, refer to How-To 8-1.

2. Create the HTML document that will eventually hold the image. Again, for learning purposes, it is best to keep this document simple. For instance:

```
<HTML>
<HEAD><TITLE>My First Image</TITLE></HEAD>
<BODY>
<H1>My First Image</H1>
This is a picture of a balloon:
</BODY>
</HTML>
```

3. Add the image to your document with the <IMG SRC> tag. This tag is an empty tag with the basic format:

```
<IMG SRC="URL">
```

Other optional attributes that can be added to this tag will be discussed later in this chapter.

After adding the tag, the document will resemble the following:

```
<HTML>
<HEAD><TITLE>My First Image</TITLE></HEAD>
<BODY>
<H1>My First Image</H1>
This is a picture of a balloon:
<IMG SRC ="BALLOON.GIF">
</BODY>
</HTML>
```

4. Save your HTML document as a text document, giving it a meaningful name such as balloon.html.

5. Make sure everything looks the way you think it should by viewing the document with either the Open Local or Open File command in your browser. If all went well, your document should resemble Figure 8-3.

Figure 8-3 The balloon now in a document

6. Transfer the completed HTML document and the GIF file to the server where they will reside and inform your system administrator about the presence of the new document.

How It Works

Whenever a browser encounters an <IMG SRC ="URL"> tag, it attempts to display the image addressed by the URL. If the image is in GIF format, the browser displays it on the screen without using a helper application. This creates the effect of the image being "inline" in your document.

Comments

For this example, the URL of the image was a very simple relative address, since the image resides in the same directory as the document. This is not always the case. You may use any image at any URL, even if it doesn't reside on your server.

8.3 How do I... Align images and text on a page?

COMPLEXITY
EASY

COMPATIBILITY: HTML

Problem

I have an HTML document with an inline image. What options do I have for aligning this image with some text?

Technique

Aligning an inline image with text is easy. First, create an HTML document and the GIF image you wish to include. After you have the document and the image, add the ALIGN attribute to the <IMG SRC> tag. With standard HTML, you have three options you may use with the ALIGN attribute: "top", "middle", and "bottom". HTML 3 also adds "left", "right", and "center" to these.

Steps

The following procedure shows different ways to align images and text in your documents, and how these different alignments are displayed.

1. Create a GIF image you wish to include in your document. For now it is best to use a simple image, such as the balloon.gif shown in Figure 8-1.

8.3
ALIGN IMAGES AND TEXT ON A PAGE

2. Create the HTML document that will eventually hold the image. Once again, it is best to keep this document simple. For example:

```
<HTML>
<HEAD><TITLE>My First Image</TITLE>
<BODY>
<H1>My First Image</H1>
This is a picture of a balloon:
</BODY>
</HTML>
```

3. Add the image to your document using an <IMG SRC> tag with the SRC pointing to the document's URL. The basic tag will look like this:

```
<IMG SRC = "BALLOON.GIF">
```

4. Add the ALIGN attribute to the <IMG SRC> tag. The basic format of this tag using ALIGN is

```
<IMG ALIGN=TOP|MIDDLE|BOTTOM SRC ="URL">
```

For example, if ALIGN = "top", the document code would be as follows:

```
<HTML>
<HEAD><TITLE>Image Alignment Top</TITLE>
<BODY>
<H1>Image Alignment Top</H1>
This is a picture of a balloon aligned top:
<IMG ALIGN=TOP SRC ="BALLOON.GIF">
</BODY>
</HTML>
```

This will cause the text next to the image to display on the top of the image. This is shown in Figure 8-4.

The image would look like Figure 8-5 if the <IMG SRC> tag was changed to

```
<IMG ALIGN=BOTTOM SRC ="BALLOON.GIF">
```

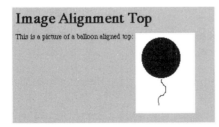

Figure 8-4 The balloon when ALIGN="top"

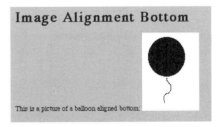

Figure 8-5 The balloon when ALIGN="bottom"

The image would look like Figure 8-6 if the <IMG SRC> tag was changed to

```
<IMG ALIGN=MIDDLE SRC ="BALLOON.GIF">
```

5. After you decide which ALIGN option you prefer, save your HTML document as a text document, giving it a meaningful name such as balloon.html.

6. Make sure everything looks the way you think it should by viewing the document with either the Open Local or Open File command in your browser.

7. If necessary, transfer the completed HTML document and the GIF file to the server where they will reside and inform your system administrator about the presence of the new document and file.

How It Works

Whenever a browser comes across an <IMG SRC> tag, the browser displays the image on the screen without the aid of a helper application if that image is in GIF format. If there is no ALIGN option included in the tag, the image is not associated with any text. If there is an ALIGN option, any text in same paragraph as the <IMG SRC> tag is associated with that image and placed in a position adjacent to the image. If the text appears before the image in the document, the text appears before the image on the browser. For example, your browser's image looks very much like Figure 8-7 if you use the following tags:

```
This is a picture of a balloon:
<IMG SRC ="BALLOON.GIF">
That was a balloon.
```

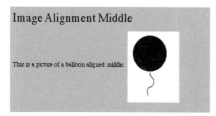

Figure 8-6 The balloon when ALIGN="middle"

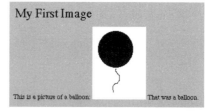

Figure 8-7 Balloon image with text on each side

Comments

While the standard ALIGN options come in handy, if the text you are trying to align to the image is longer than the screen width, this text gets broken up and placed after the end of the image. The following HTML document results in something that looks very much like Figure 8-8.

USE THE <ALT> TAG FOR NONGRAPHICAL BROWSERS

```
<HTML>
<HEAD><TITLE>Too Much Text</TITLE></HEAD>
<BODY>
<H1>Too Much text</H1>
<IMG ALIGN=TOP SRC ="BALLOON.GIF">
The following is a picture of a balloon aligned top, but it is also an
example that shows what happens when you get too much text next to an
image. The text drops down past the end of the image.
</BODY>
</HTML>
```

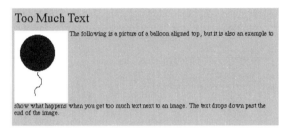

Figure 8-8 Balloon with too much text to handle

HTML 3 has extensions to the ALIGN attribute that allow text to wrap left or right around an image without breaking the text apart. These extensions are discussed in How-To 8.11.

COMPLEXITY
EASY

8.4 How do I... Use the <ALT> tag for nongraphical browsers?

COMPATIBILITY: HTML

Problem

I have an HTML document with an image in it. How can I show people with nongraphical browsers that there is an image in my document?

Technique

Images are added to documents with the <IMG SRC> tag. To inform nongraphical browsers or a browser with image loading turned off that there is an image in your document, include the ALT option in the tag, setting the ALT attribute to a text message that tells users what they are missing.

Steps

The following procedure shows you how to use the ALT attribute in your documents.

1. Create a GIF image you wish to include in your document. For now, let's stick with the balloon, balloon.gif.
2. Create the HTML document that will eventually hold the image. At first, keep this document simple, like the document used in the previous section.
3. Add the image to your document with the <IMG SRC> tag. The document should resemble the following:

```
<HTML>
<HEAD><TITLE>An Alt Example</TITLE></HEAD>
<BODY>
<H1>An Alt Example</H1>
This is a picture of a balloon:
<IMG SRC ="BALLOON.GIF">
</BODY>
</HTML>
```

4. Add the ALT option to the <IMG SRC> tag. The format of the <IMG> tag with the ALT option is:

```
<IMG ALT="some text" SRC = "URL">
```

Which in the sample document becomes:

```
<IMG ALT="a picture of a balloon goes here" SRC ="BALLOON.GIF">
```

The result is something like Figure 8-9 when viewed through a nongraphical browser.

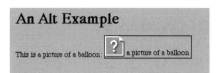

Figure 8-9 Use of the ALT attribute

5. Save your HTML document as a text document.
6. Make sure everything looks the way you think it should by viewing the document with either the Open Local or Open File command in your browser.
7. If necessary, transfer the completed HTML document and the GIF file to the server where they will reside and inform your system administrator about the presence of the new document.

How It Works

Whenever a browser comes across an <IMG SRC> tag, the browser attempts to display the image if it is in GIF format. If the browser is unable to display the image, it replaces it with any text found in the ALT="text" attribute.

Comments

It is considered good net manners to use the ALT attribute whenever possible. This way, people using nongraphical browsers, such as Lynx, will still get the general idea of how a page is meant to be laid out. It is also a good idea to test how your <IMG ALT SRC> tags work by turning off automatic image loading in your browser, then checking out your documents.

COMPLEXITY
EASY

8.5 How do I... Include an image with a transparent background?

COMPATIBILITY: HTML

Problem

Now I have an inline image in my HTML document, but there is a lot of white space around it. How do I remove this white space so my image will have a transparent background that blends in better with my page?

Technique

With the right tools, creating an image with a transparent background is only slightly more complicated than creating an image without one. You still follow the same process to create the image, but you need to add an extra step or two. Once you create the image, you must fill in the areas that you want to be transparent with a color that is not used anywhere else in the image. Then set that fill color to be the transparent GIF color, and save the image in GIF89a format.

Steps

The following procedure gives you a general overview of what you must do to create a transparent image. How you create the image depends on the machine you are working on and the tools you are using, but the basic procedure remains the same.

CHAPTER 8
USING IMAGES IN YOUR DOCUMENTS

1. Lay out your image on paper. Decide what you want to show and how you want it to look. For learning purposes it is best to start with something simple like the balloon (balloon.gif) used throughout this chapter.

2. Decide which graphics program to use. Your choice is almost endless, because almost any available graphics program will work. There are also a number of utility programs around whose sole purpose is the creation of transparent images on the Web. The decision on which to use is usually a matter of availability and personal preference.

There are a number of features that come in handy when creating images for the Web. Some of these are listed below.

- **HTML** The ability to easily control the pixel size of an image
- **HTML** The number of colors the image may have
- **HTML** The ability to select a transparent color
- **HTML** The ability to save in GIF89a format

You may want to take these into account before deciding on the package you want to use. Programs such as GraphicConverter for the Macintosh and GIFTOOL for UNIX and PCs are good choices.

3. Open up a new image. It is best to set the pixel size and the number of colors at the outset. Pixel size is the number of horizontal and vertical squares that you use to create the image. When choosing colors, keep the number as low as possible. The more colors you use, the bigger the image will be and the longer it will take to load. Use four or five colors to create an image that looks nice and is fairly colorful, but is not very large.

4. Draw your image. The file balloon.gif should be very simple to create. It is simply a circle with a line attached.

5. Fill in the area you wish make transparent with a color not used in the image. It does not matter what the color is as long as it not used elsewhere in the image.

6. Set the transparent GIF color to the color you filled with. This is done slightly differently depending on the application you are using. For example, with GraphicConverter for the Macintosh, this setting can be found at the bottom of the Colors item found in the Picture menu.

7. Save your image in the GIF89a format. For this example, the new image is named balloont.gif. In practice you do not need to use an altered name to differentiate between transparent and nontransparent images.

8. If your finished image is on a different machine than your server, transfer the icon to the appropriate machine.

8.5 INCLUDE AN IMAGE WITH A TRANSPARENT BACKGROUND

How It Works

The color you use as the transparent color is automatically set to whatever a browser looking at that image happens to have as its background, the effect being that your image blends in perfectly with the background.

Comments

The only difference between a transparent GIF and a nontransparent GIF is the format the two are saved in. The HTML tags are identical. For example:

```
<HTML>
<HEAD><TITLE>Transparent Demo</TITLE>
<BODY>
<H1>Transparent Demo</H1>
This is a balloon:
<IMG SRC="BALLOON.GIF">
This is a transparent balloon:
<IMG SRC="BALLOONT.GIF">
</BODY>
</HTML>
```

The tags are identical except for the URL, but the results are quite different, as shown by Figure 8-10.

Figure 8-10 A comparison between a transparent GIF and a nontransparent GIF

It is easy to turn an existing image into a transparent GIF. Open the image, then perform steps 5 and 6.

People often use transparent GIFs to add unique horizontal rules in a document. For example, if you wish to have a red, white, and blue horizontal rule in one of your pages instead of using the <HR> command (which doesn't allow for color) you can use the following procedure:

1. Use a graphics program to create a red, white, and blue line.

2. Save the line as a transparent GIF, naming it something like cline.gif.

253

3. Insert the following <IMG SRC> tag into the document where you want to place the line.

```
<IMG SRC="CLINE.GIF">
```

This causes the browser to insert the red, white, and blue line wherever it finds this tag. It should be noted, though, that some people consider using images for horizontal lines to be a waste of server time, since it takes longer to load a graphical image than a line drawn with the horizontal rule tag <HR>. Still, this is a personal call. If you want a colorful line on your page, go ahead and make one. It is, after all, your page.

Finally, due to the number of choices you have when converting an image to a transparent GIF, this chapter only touched the surface. The following are other options you might want to consider:

- **HTML** GIFTOOL: available for UNIX and DOS machines
- **HTML** The PBMPLUS library: available for UNIX machines
- **HTML** GraphicConverter or Transparency: available for the Macintosh

8.6 How do I... Create an interlaced inline image on my page?

COMPLEXITY: EASY

COMPATIBILITY: NETSCAPE

Problem

I have a document with an inline image that works fine, but my image loads from top to bottom. I see other people's images occasionally load progressively; first a complete rough image appears and then this image becomes finer and finer. How can I get my images to appear like this?

Technique

The technique used to cause an image to appear gradually is called *interlacing*. With the right tools, it is a simple step to convert a normal image to an interlaced GIF image. GifConverter on the Macintosh and GIFTOOL for UNIX and PC machines convert a graphic from any number of formats to an interlaced GIF.

8.6 CREATE AN INTERLACED INLINE IMAGE ON MY PAGE

Steps

The following procedure gives you a general overview of what you must do to create an interlaced image. Some details of how you do it depend on the machine and the tools you are using. Still, the basic procedure remains the same.

1. Find or create an image you wish to turn into an interlaced GIF. The balloon.gif file from the previous section would work well as an example.
2. Decide which program you would like to use to convert the image to an interlaced GIF. There are many available options across the three major platforms. Some of the major choices are GifConverter for the Macintosh, GIFTOOL for UNIX machines and PCs, and the PBMPLUS tools for UNIX machines.
3. Open the image.
4. Save the image as an interlaced GIF. This procedure differs depending on the application you are using but is usually very easy to figure out. In GifConverter, for example, you click the interlaced box that appears in the Save As dialog box.
5. View the image locally with your browser to make sure it looks the way you think it should.
6. If necessary, transport the image to your server.

How It Works

There really isn't much work for you to do here. The tool performs the conversion. Now when a browser loads the new interlaced image, the entire image appears gradually, going from a low resolution outline to the finished image. You really don't need to know more than that.

Comments

The steps shown in this How-To vary depending on what graphics program you use and what system you are on; still, the technique is the same. Interlacing is so easy to accomplish it is possible to get carried away and have too many interlaced images on a page. So feel free to experiment, just try not to go overboard.

CHAPTER 8
USING IMAGES IN YOUR DOCUMENTS

COMPLEXITY
EASY

8.7 How do I... Create a thumbnail version of an image?

COMPATIBILITY: HTML

Problem

I have a large image that some people may be interested in seeing and others may not be. How can I make a thumbnail version of this image?

Technique

Thumbnail images are no different from any other images you see on the Web. They just happen to be smaller. You can make one by using any graphics program that has scaling ability to shrink the image to thumbnail size. You can then make the thumbnail image work like a button by clicking on it to load the original image. This technique is shown in How-To 8.9.

Steps

The following procedure gives you a general overview of what you must do to create a thumbnail image. How you create the image depends on the machine and the tools you are using. Still, the basic procedure remains the same.

1. Find or create an image you wish to turn into a thumbnail. For this example, use balloon.gif from the previous section.

2. Decide which program you would like to use to scale the image to thumbnail size. Almost any graphics program has the ability to scale (or resize) images. Choose a graphics program that both scales and saves images in GIF format.

3. Open the image with the graphics program of your choice.

4. Find and select the scale option.

5. Set the new, smaller size of your image. How this works may differ slightly from application to application, but it always involves changing the percentage of the object's size. In this case the object is being shrunk to 30 percent of its original size.

6. Save the smaller image as a GIF, or in some format that you can easily translate to GIF. Make sure you give the new image a distinct but related name such as ballon_s.gif. The name ballon_s.gif is less likely to be confused with the original than balloons.gif, but readers using Macintoshes, Windows 95, or UNIX should feel free to use a longer, more distinctive name.

The following document will resemble Figure 8-11 when viewed through a browser:

```
<HTML>
<HEAD><TITLE>Thumbnails</TITLE></HEAD>
<BODY>
<H1>Thumbnails</H1>
This is the original: <IMG SRC="BALLOON.GIF">
This is the resized thumbnail: <IMG SRC="BALLON_S.GIF">
</BODY>
</HTML>
```

7. If necessary, transfer the finished image to your server machine.

How It Works

There isn't anything tricky at all here. The thumbnail version of the image is nothing more than a scaled-down version of the original. The most difficult task in this How-To is choosing which software package to do the work in.

Comments

One of the best uses for thumbnails is as clickable images that lead to the full-sized image. How-To 8.9 shows how to make them work that way.

Many programs, such as Adobe Photoshop and GraphicConverter, automatically create thumbnails of images when you save them. You can copy these thumbnails and paste them into your own documents. Consult your system's documentation for instructions on how to do this.

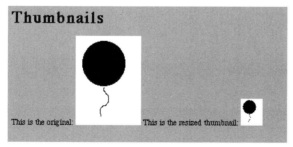

Figure 8-11 The thumbnail of balloon.gif

8.8 How do I... Use an image as a link?

COMPLEXITY
EASY

COMPATIBILITY: HTML

Problem

I have noticed Web authors often use images for links, either in place of text or along with text. How can I do this?

Technique

Using an image as a link to another image or document is very simple. Image links are no different from regular hypertext links. To create an image link, place the <IMG SRC> tag with the URL of the image between <A HREF = "URL">...</A> tags.

Steps

The following procedure shows you step by step how to use an image as a link.

1. Find or create the image you wish to use. For this example, the ballon_s.gif image from the previous section is a good choice.

2. Decide what you want the image to link to. In this case, the small balloon image links to an HTML document with the full-sized balloon image and a description of balloons.

3. Create the base HTML document that will contain the link. The document, kept small, would look something like this:

```
<HTML>
<HEAD><TITLE>My First Image Link</TITLE>
<BODY>
<H1>My first image Link</H1>
This is a small balloon:
<IMG SRC="BALLON_S.GIF"> click on it to go to a page with a larger balloon.<p>
</BODY>
</HTML>
```

4. Add the link. If the document you want to link to is called bal_info.html, then the link would be

```
<A HREF="BAL_INFO.HTML"><IMG SRC="BALLON_S.GIF"></A>
```

This is fairly straightforward. If you understand hypertext links, you should have no trouble at all with this structure. The hypertext that is normally placed between the <A HREF>...</A> tags is in this case replaced by an <IMG SRC> tag. The document now looks like this:

8.8
USE AN IMAGE AS A LINK

```
<HTML>
<HEAD><TITLE>My First Image Link</TITLE>
<BODY>
<H1>My first image link</H1>
This is a small balloon:
<A HREF="BAL_INFO.HTML><IMG SRC="BALLON_S.GIF"></A>click on it to go to a
page with a larger balloon<p>
</BODY>
</HTML>
```

When viewed through a browser, the page looks much like Figure 8-12. As you can see, the small balloon image is highlighted, which means it is a link. Selecting that image sends the browser off to whatever URL is specified in the <A HREF="URL"> tag.

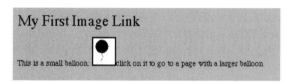

Figure 8-12 A small image being used as a link

5. Save your document as a text file. Give it any name that is simple yet descriptive and unique. In this case ball_lnk.html seems acceptable.

6. View the document locally with your browser.

7. Make any fine tuning changes that may be needed, then save the document.

8. If necessary, transfer the finished document and image to your server and inform your system administrator about the presence of the new document and image.

How It Works

When a browser comes across the <A HREF="URL"> ... </A> tags, it uses any text or valid URL of an image as the anchor for that tag, thus making text and images interchangeable for links. When a reader selects the hyperimage, he or she will be brought to the URL set with the <A HREF="URL"> tag.

Comments

It is also possible to combine text and images between the <A HREF="URL"> ... </A> tags.

Note: People using Macintoshes, Windows 95, and UNIX systems should feel free to use variable and document names that contain more than eight characters and a three-letter tag.

8.9 How do I... Create a clickable imagemap?

COMPLEXITY
INTERMEDIATE

COMPATIBILITY: HTML 2

Problem

There are places on the Web that use clickable pictures for menu bars and navigational tools. How can I add such clickable images to my own documents?

Technique

Clickable images or imagemaps are not really all that much different from regular inline GIF images. The only real difference is that imagemaps have had hot spots assigned to them. Hot spots are areas of the image that link to certain URLs when you click in them. The hot spots are often assigned through a utility imagemap program whose sole function is to assist you in setting the coordinates for hot spots. You inform a browser that an image is a clickable imagemap by appending the ISMAP attribute to an <IMG SRC> tag. This tag appears between <A HREF="URL"> ... </A> tags that contain the URL of the text file that contains the imagemap coordinates. The browser then uses a Common Gateway Interface to parse the results and figure out where to establish the link.

Steps

The following procedure gives you a general overview of what you must do to create an imagemap. How you create it depends on the machine you are using, the tools you have available, and the type of server your system is on. Still, the basic procedure remains the same.

1. Find or create a suitable image for your imagemap. This image can be as big and as complicated as you would like it to be. However, the less complicated it is, the easier it will be for the user to figure out what he or she can or can't click on, and the less time-consuming it will be to load. Imagemaps place a significant burden on the server and do have a delay time while the server processes your click, so frequent mis-clicks can be frustrating. For this example, the simple word W E B ! is a good choice. It should be easy to create with any graphics program, plus it has four distinct parts (each character) that are easily differentiated from one another. Call this image web.gif.

2. Now that you have the image, you need to map out the location of the hot spots. You need some way of telling the server that the pixels of the image between these points lead to this URL. The area of the hot spot may be square, round, or a polygon. You need to compute the boundaries of each

8.9
CREATE A CLICKABLE IMAGEMAP

hot spot. For each area you wish to make a hot spot, you must find the coordinates and then define the URL these coordinates will link to. Figure 8-13 depicts some sample coordinates for the web.gif image.

While you can do all this by hand, it is usually preferable to use a utility program to map out areas for you. There are many tools to choose from depending on what platform you are using. On the Macintosh, WebMap is a good public domain choice. On Windows and X Windows systems, MapEdit is a popular choice. All these utilities work in the same way: they present you with a series of familiar tools that let you capture the coordinates of the parts of the image you wish to use as hot spots. Figure 8-14 shows WebMap in action.

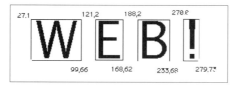

Figure 8-13 web.gif's coordinates

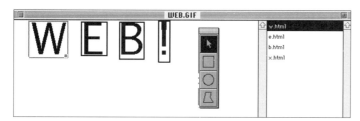

Figure 8-14 WebMap capturing the W's coordinates

3. After you have mapped out the boundaries of your imagemap, save these boundaries as a text file, naming it web.map. The web.map file for the above example, making each letter selectable, will look like this:

```
default DEFALT.HTM
rect W.HTML 27,1 99,66
rect E.HTML 121,2 168,62
rect B.HTML 188,2 233,68
rect X.HTML 257,0 279,73
```

4. Transfer the web.map text file to the server.
5. Create the HTML base document that will contain the imagemap.
6. Now that you have the document, enter the <IMG SRC> tag inside of an <A HREF> tag:

CHAPTER 8
USING IMAGES IN YOUR DOCUMENTS

```
<A HREF="/cgi-bin/imagemap/WEB.MAP"><IMG SRC="WEB.GIF" ISMAP></A>
```

The ISMAP attribute at the end of the <IMG SRC> tag is the key here. That tells the browser that this GIF file is a clickable imagemap and that the text file named at the end of the <A HREF> tag should be the file fed to the imagemap CGI gateway to interrupt clicks. The complete document would look like this:

```
<HTML>
<HEAD>
<TITLE>Sample Image Map</TITLE>
<BODY>
<H1>This is a sample imagemap!</H1>
Clicking on any letter will bring you to a description of that letter:
<A HREF="/cgi-bin/imagemap/WEB.MAP"><IMG SRC="WEB.GIF" ISMAP></A>
</BODY>
</HTML>
```

7. Create any of the linked to documents that you might need. This example would need five more documents: one for each letter, one for the exclamation point, and one default document that gets returned when the user clicks on a spot that is not a hot spot. The document names should match the ones used in the map file. A sample document might look like this:

```
<HTML>
<HEAD>
<TITLE> W!!</TILE>
</HEAD>
<BODY>
<-- This document is W.HTML -->
You selected the W -- the 23rd letter of the alphabet.<P>
</BODY>
</HTML>
```

8. If necessary, transfer the HTML document(s) to your server.

9. Ask your system administrator to activate your new imagemap document. You should soon have a working imagemap just like (if not much cooler than) the one shown in Figure 8-15.

How It Works

An imagemap is really nothing more than a GIF file that is related to a text file through your server's CGI imagemap interface. The CGI interface can be a bit tricky if you had to write it—luckily all the major servers come with this interface already written for you, you just have to access it. When the browser encounters the <ISMAP> tag, it relates the GIF file in the tag to the text document pointed to by the URL in the <A HREF="URL"> tag.

8.10 CREATE A BACKGROUND PATTERN FOR MY PAGE

Figure 8-15 A complete working imagemap

Comments

Because of the overhead involved, some systems don't allow their users to have imagemaps in their documents. It is a good idea to check with your system administrator before starting an imagemap.

Imagemaps vary slightly from server to server. NCSA deals with the coordinates of hot spots a little differently than CERN. If you use the proper tools, these differences will be largely handled for you. Still, it is always a good idea to consult with your server system's documentation or with your system's Webmaster before starting an imagemap.

COMPLEXITY
EASY

8.10 How do I... Create a background pattern for my page?

COMPATIBILITY: NETSCAPE

Problem

I see a lot of pages on the Web that appear in Netscape with different backgrounds than the standard Netscape gray. How can I change the background on my page?

Technique

Change backgrounds by using the BACKGROUND attribute. The BACKGROUND attribute is an HTML 3 extension to the <BODY> tag. You can use the BACKGROUND attribute to set the URL of a GIF that will be used as the document's background.

Steps

The following eight steps show you how you can add a unique background to your documents.

1. Decide what kind of background you would like to use. Remember, you will place text on top of this background, so it is best to keep it light and simple.

2. Select the graphics program of your choice. You can use any graphics program, but it saves a conversion step if you use a program that can save images in GIF format.

3. Open a new image.

4. Set the document size to something relatively small. A 1-inch by 1-inch square works well.

5. Select a small color palette. It is best to stick with 4 or 16 colors.

6. Create a new image. Here artistic skill helps, but it is possible to do a fairly nice job with very little ability. Remember, keep the colors light. Also, remember that this color box is repeatedly juxtaposed on the background, so strive for something that will flow smoothly. Experiment until you come up with something you like.

7. Once you have something you like, save it as GIF. For example, backgr.gif.

8. Add the BACKGROUND attribute to any <BODY> tag in any document in which you wish to have backgr.gif as the background color. The format of this is

```
<BODY BACKGROUND="BACKGR.GIF"> Document here!</BODY>
```

How It Works

When Netscape 1.1 or higher encounters a BACKGROUND attribute, it sets the screen's background to the GIF file specified by that background.

Comments

Backgrounds look nice but do have a cost—speed. Loading a background image increases the amount of time your page takes to load. The speed factor is the reason it is best to keep the background simple.

To check out possible background colors go to the following URL: http://www.infi.net/wwwimages/colorindex.html.

8.11 How do I...
Align images and text using the advanced HTML 3 tags?

COMPLEXITY
EASY

COMPATIBILITY: HTML 3 (NETSCAPE)

Problem

I have an HTML document with an inline image. I would like to wrap some text to the left of one image and to the right of another. How do I accomplish this?

Technique

HTML 2 allows for simple aligning of text and images by adding the ALIGN attribute to the <IMG SRC> tag. HTML 3 expands this attribute by adding "left" and "right" options. When you use these options, text flows down the right or left side of an image aligned to them. The text flow continues until either the text passes the image, the text ends, or the browser encounters a <BR CLEAR="left|right|all"> tag.

Steps

The following steps show you how to use the advanced text and picture alignment capabilities in your documents and the effect each of the alignment options has on images and text.

1. Create a GIF image you wish to include in your document. The balloon.gif image used earlier in this chapter can serve as an example.

2. Create the HTML document that will eventually hold the image. To help illustrate the point, this example contains two versions of the image:

```
<HTML>
<HEAD><TITLE>Practicing with Align</TITLE>
<BODY>
<H1>My First Image</H1>
Here is a picture:
<! picture goes here ->
Here is another picture:
<! another goes here ->
</BODY>
</HTML>
```

3. Replace the comments with <IMG SRC> tags.

```
<IMG SRC ="BALLOON.GIF">
```

CHAPTER 8
USING IMAGES IN YOUR DOCUMENTS

4. Add the ALIGN option to the <IMG SRC> tag. The basic format of this tag with the ALIGN option is

```
<IMG ALIGN=TOP|MIDDLE|BOTTOM SRC"URL">
```

Netscape and HTML 3 add "left" and "right" to these. The "left" option puts the image on the left side of the browser and then aligns any adjacent text to this image. The "right" option does the opposite. The two image tags look like this:

```
<IMG ALIGN=LEFT   SRC="BALLOON.GIF">
<IMG ALIGN=RIGHT  SRC="BALLOON.GIF">
```

5. Place any descriptive text around the first image.

6. Insert the <BR CLEAR="left"> command at the spot in the descriptive text where you want the text to stop flowing around the image.

7. Place any descriptive text around the second image.

8. Insert the <BR CLEAR="right"> command at the spot in the text where you wish the text to stop flowing around the second image. When you are done, the document should resemble the following:

```
<HTML>
<HEAD><TITLE>Practicing with Align</TITLE>
<BODY>
<H1>Netscape align</H1>
Here is a picture aligned left:<P>
<IMG ALIGN=LEFT SRC="BALLOON.GIF">
This is a balloon. Balloons float in the air. Balloons come in many colors and
sizes. Balloons can now even be given as gifts for birthdays and such. Balloons are
cool.
<P>
Just put in a new paragraph so you could see the results.
<BR CLEAR=LEFT>
Here is the same picture aligned right:
<!-- No new paragraph marker so you can see the difference -- if any -->
<IMG ALIGN=RIGHT SRC="BALLOON.GIF">
This is a second balloon. It is identical to the first except for its
position on the screen. Text flow can look very good, especially when using
better images than smiley faces.
<BR CLEAR=RIGHT>
This text should no longer flow around the image.
</BODY>
</HTML>
```

9. Make sure everything looks the way you think it should by viewing the document locally with your browser. If all went well, your document should resemble Figure 8-16.

10. After you decide which ALIGN option you prefer, save your HTML document as a text document.

8.11
ALIGN IMAGES AND TEXT USING THE ADVANCED HTML 3 TAGS

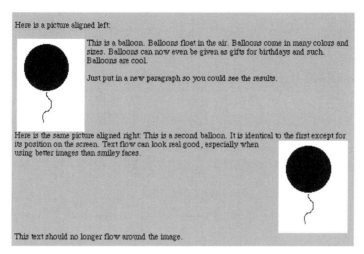

Figure 8-16 An example of ALIGN "left" and "right"

11. If necessary, transfer the completed HTML document and the GIF file to the server where they will reside and inform your system administrator or Webmaster about the presence of the new document and file.

How It Works

Wherever a browser comes across an <IMG SRC> tag, the browser displays that image on the screen without a helper application if the image is in GIF format. If there is no ALIGN option included in the tag, the image is not associated with any text. If there is an ALIGN "left" or "right" option, any text in the same paragraph as the <IMG SRC> tag will flow into that image until either the text surpasses the image, the text runs out, or the browser encounters a corresponding <BR CLEAR = "left|right|all"> tag.

Comments

These extensions to this attribute add a great deal of power to the <IMG SRC> tag. When combined with the new <TABLE> tags, these expressions can even make an HTML 3 document appear much like a multiple column document you might create with a desktop publishing package.

It is also possible to get the same effects as these extensions provide by adding the ALIGN attribute to the <P> tag in HTML 3. See Chapter 4 for more information on this.

CHAPTER 9
ADDING MULTIMEDIA OBJECTS

ADDING MULTIMEDIA OBJECTS

How do I...

9.1   Build my multimedia home page?
9.2   Add an external image?
9.3   Convert between image formats?
9.4   Insert a video?
9.5   Convert between video file formats?
9.6   Insert a sound file?
9.7   Convert between audio file formats?
9.8   Include a PostScript document?
9.9   Include a device independent (DVI) file?

Multimedia information is generally more intuitive and more informative than plain textual information. However, HTML 3 does not provide a means for directly including multimedia objects in your documents. This chapter explores the use of links to indirectly include this type of information in your document.

Many types of information cannot be represented directly in HTML 3. For example, while GIF format images can be included in HTML documents, TIFF and JPEG images cannot be. Nor does HTML directly support the inclusion of audio or animation.

Processed data, such as PostScript or DVI files, cannot be included directly in HTML documents, either. If a converter is available, you can translate this data to

CHAPTER 9
ADDING MULTIMEDIA OBJECTS

HTML. (See How-To 2.5.) However, converters generally create a single HTML document rather than a component suitable for inclusion in an HTML document.

Links provide a means for indirectly including both multimedia information and processed data. When a reader triggers a link to such information, the requested item is retrieved as any other file would be. However, when the browser receives an object that is not HTML or standard text, it uses a helper application to render the object in an appropriate manner. If the user's hardware or software does not support the particular media type retrieved, then the object is not displayed.

This chapter explains the use of links that you allow to include a variety of information objects not directly supported by HTML. The procedures for including these objects, and pointers to helper applications for displaying these objects, are provided. Table 9-1 summarizes the location of the relevant How-To's corresponding to various types of multimedia files and processed data files. How-To 9.1 provides a general approach to as well as a complete example of incorporating external objects into an HTML document.

INFORMATION TYPE	STORAGE FORMAT	HOW-TO'S	FILENAME EXTENSION
application	DVI	9.9	.dvi
application	PostScript	9.8	.ps
audio	AIFF	9.6 and 9.7	.aiff (.aif)
audio	AU	9.6	.au
audio	WAV	9.6 and 9.7	.wav
image	GIF	Chapter 8 and 9.2	.gif
image	JPEG	9.2	.jpeg (.jpg)
image	PNM	9.2	.ppm .pnm .pbm .pgm
image	PICT	9.2	.PICT
image	RGB	9.2	.rgb
image	TIFF	9.2	.tiff (.tif)
video	AVI	9.4 and 9.5	.avi
video	MPEG	9.4 and 9.5	.mpeg (.mpg)
video	QUICKTIME	9.4 and 9.5	.mov

Table 9-1 Multimedia objects covered in this chapter

9.1 Build My Multimedia Home Page

You have a variety of multimedia objects and you want to include these objects in your home page. You want your place on the the World Wide Web to be more dynamic and exciting. In this How-To, you will learn how to build a multimedia home page.

CHAPTER 9
ADDING MULTIMEDIA OBJECTS

9.2 Add an External Image
HTML supports inline images in a limited number of formats. You want to be able to include images in other formats in your HTML documents. In this How-To, you will learn how to incorporate external images in your HTML pages.

9.3 Convert between Image Formats
You want to make your documents with large inline images more efficient. You have added images that can be viewed through an external viewer, but you want to include some of these as inline images. What do you need to do to show the images on your HTML page? In this How-To, you will learn how to convert between image formats.

9.4 Insert a Video
You want to include video clips in your HTML pages. How do you include them in your documents? What kind of support do readers need so they can view this information? In this How-To, you will learn how to add digital video to your pages.

9.5 Convert between Video File Formats
What types of video file formats are there? How do you convert a file from one to another? Readers can view your video clips with a helper application; however, you need the clip in another format so that you can edit it with your current hardware and software. In this How-To, you will learn how to convert between video formats.

9.6 Insert a Sound File
You want to include a voice description of the current document. The text and pictures do not totally convey the point you are trying to make with the current document. How do you include this sound file? And how do you tell your readers how to access this information? In this How-To, you will learn how to place sound files in your HTML pages.

9.7 Convert between Audio File Formats
A variety of audio file formats have been developed on several different platforms. You need to easily convert from one format to another so that you can efficiently edit and tailor the audio that you include in your documents. In this How-To, you will learn how to convert between sound file formats.

9.8 Include a PostScript Document
Much of your documentation is in the PostScript format. You want to build HTML documents that provide Web-based access to these PostScript files. How do you include PostScript documents in your HTML documents? In this How-To, you will learn how to access PostScript files from your HTML pages.

CHAPTER 9
ADDING MULTIMEDIA OBJECTS

9.9   Include a Device Independent (DVI) File

You have written documents using the TeX formatting language. You know you can convert these documents to HTML, but they are more useful to you as either TeX or DVI files. How do you provide access to your DVI files from HTML documents? In this How-To, you will learn how to provide access to DVI files from your HTML pages.

COMPLEXITY
INTERMEDIATE

9.1   How do I... Build my multimedia home page?

COMPATIBILITY: HTML

Problem

I would like to introduce myself to the world. Can I include a voice welcome and introduction on my home page? Better yet, can I include a small video segment of myself stating who I am and what I do? How do I add multimedia elements to my home page?

Technique

You can incorporate multimedia objects into a home page. The use of tailored anchor elements to access helper applications for specified file types is the key to this process. Each multimedia file or processed data file added to the document, with the exception of inline images, is added in this manner.

Steps

The following steps lead you through the creation or modification of a single HTML document titled "Home Page of Me." This document will serve as your business card in the World Wide Web community.

This process assumes that you are using a normal text editor for your document creation. If you use a different kind of editor, some of the steps outlined may not be necessary; be sure to check the documentation for your editor to determine which steps apply.

Step-by-step instructions are provided below to modify a home page, or any page, to include multimedia objects of all sorts.

  1. Change directories to the location where you wish to develop your HTML documents. Open the file containing your HTML home page in your favorite text editor.

9.1
BUILD MY MULTIMEDIA HOME PAGE

edit homepage.htm

2. If you have not created a home page for yourself, review How-To 2.12 to help you create a home page.

3. Follow the procedure identified in Table 9-1 that is appropriate for the media type you want to include. For example, you might want to include a voice introduction to yourself or your Web pages in a home page constructed through the procedure in How-To 2.12.

```
USA<BR>
E-Mail: my_id@mysite.edu
<A HREF="http://www.mysite.edu/~me/audio/intro.au">
<IMG SRC="/icons/sound.xbm" ALT="[Audio Icon]">
Welcome Message</A> (1.2 MB AU Audio)<BR>
```

Or include an image of your project group that can be viewed with a helper application.

```
<TAB INDENT=5>I am currently working on several projects with
<A HREF="http://www.mysite.edu/~me/group.jpg">group gold</A> (1.4 MB JPEG).
These projects include...
```

4. Save the file. Remember to use the .html or .htm filename extension to indicate an HTML document.

5. Attempt to view your home page using as many different browsers as you have access to.

6. If there are problems with the way items display, modify the document as appropriate.

7. When you feel that your home page is ready for the rest of the world, ask your site administrator to install your document on your Web site. Or follow his or her instructions to install the document in your home directory.

How It Works

Multimedia elements other than inline images are added to HTML documents by specifying links that refer to the required files. HTML does not support direct inclusion of such files. So to develop your multimedia home page, you must create or acquire appropriate multimedia or processed data files, install them on your Web server, and provide access to them via links from your home page.

If your software and hardware permit it, you might wish to include a small video or audio segment introducing yourself. Or you might include a reference to a photo of your project team. Your imagination is the limit.

Once you have created or acquired suitable multimedia and processed data files, test them extensively to make sure they work exactly as you wish, then install them on the server. Chapter 11 discusses installation of documents on a server.

CHAPTER 9
ADDING MULTIMEDIA OBJECTS

Use the procedures in this chapter to develop a multimedia home page that will serve as your introduction to the World Wide Web community. You should feel free to experiment with including other elements to create a home page suited to your interests and goals. However, for ease of understanding, the following example extends the home page developed in How-To 2.12.

```
<HTML>
<HEAD>
<TITLE>Home Page of John Q. Public</TITLE>
</HEAD>
<BODY>

<!-- Mark the beginning of this portion with a horizontal rule. -->
<HR>
<!-- Center your name as a level 1 header. -->
<H1 ALIGN="center">John Q. Public</H1>
<!-- Provide any desirable contact information. -->
999 Peachtree St.<BR>
Atlanta, GA 30314<BR>
USA<BR>
E-Mail: my_id@mysite.edu<BR>
<A HREF="http://www.mysite.edu/~me/audio/intro.au">
<IMG SRC="/icons/sound.xbm" ALT="[Audio Icon]">
Welcome Message</A> (1.2 MB AU Audio)

<!-- Mark the beginning of this portion with a horizontal rule. -->
<HR>
<!-- Choose the heading text that you feel appropriate. -->
<H1>About Me</H1>
<!-- The formatting and information should be developed to suit your needs. -->
<TAB INDENT=5>This is the first paragraph in this section about myself.
I have been at MY BUSINESS for the past X years.
<P>
<TAB INDENT=5>I am currently working on several projects with
<A HREF="http://www.mysite.edu/~me/group.jpg">group gold</A> (1.4 MB JPEG).
These projects include...

<!-- Mark the beginning of this portion with a horizontal rule. -->
<HR>
<!-- Substitute the appropriate information in your document. The date should -->
<!-- appear in a long format with the month name written out since the order -->
<!-- conventions for date abbreviations vary. -->
Last modified on CURRENT_DATE by YOUR_NAME (YOUR_E-MAIL)

</BODY>
</HTML>
```

You can now add links to your own multimedia and processed data files. Standard HTML 3 anchor elements can be used to specify these hypermedia links. (See Chapter 7.) The above document contains two such example links. Figure 9-1 shows how this document would appear with one of these links activated.

9.1
BUILD MY MULTIMEDIA HOME PAGE

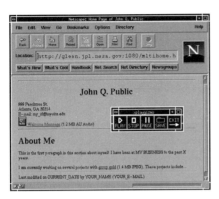

Figure 9-1 Rendering of a multimedia home page

The selection of the link triggers a request for the file specified in the anchor element. If the request is successful, this server generates a response that includes both the type of the requested file and its contents.

Servers maintain a database mapping filename extensions to information types in order to generate type information sent to browsers. Therefore, take care to ensure that the proper filename extensions are used. Chapter 11 and Appendix C provide further information on document installation and document types.

When a browser receives a file from the server, it determines how to present the data based upon the type information provided by the server. Most browsers will only directly render text and HTML documents in their display window. Helper applications display information of other types. This process is illustrated in Figure 9-2.

Comments

When adding elements of your own, remember that the document you are creating may be viewed by thousands, if not millions, of people. You should take into consideration the variety of browsers with differing presentation capabilities during your multimedia document development.

Additional object types and suitable viewers can be added in the same way you would add the file types discussed in this chapter. For example, you can include virtual reality files by configuring the browser to launch an appropriate external viewer when it encounters a virtual reality file, creating links to appropriate objects, and installing a helper application capable of displaying the file. For more information on virtual reality files, try the following URL: http://vrml.wired.com/.

CHAPTER 9
ADDING MULTIMEDIA OBJECTS

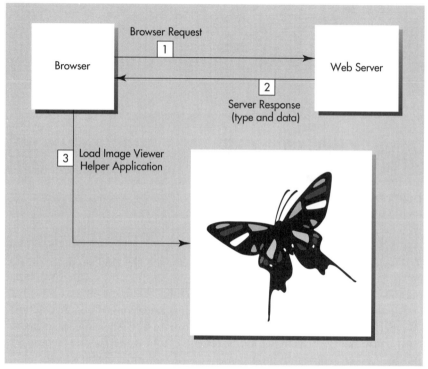

Figure 9-2 Retrieval and rendering process of external objects

COMPLEXITY
EASY

9.2 How do I... Add an external image?

COMPATIBILITY: HTML

Problem

With inline images (Chapter 8), I am limited to GIF format images, X bitmap files, and sometimes JPEG images (Netscape and Mosaic). I would like to include images in other formats. I know that I cannot include them directly because HTML does not support other image formats; however, I need to make these image objects available.

9.2
ADD AN EXTERNAL IMAGE

Technique

You can provide access to images not supported through the inline <IMG> HTML element by establishing a link to the desired image. When a reader selects a link, the browser retrieves the linked file from the server where it is stored and displays it. If the browser does not support direct display of the file, it uses a helper application.

The procedure below shows how to include links to external images in your HTML documents.

Steps

The method for including an external image in your HTML document depends upon the editor used to create the document. In a strictly text-based editor, you manually insert an anchor. With WYSIWIG or macro/menu-based editors, you might add the anchor through macros or menus.

Either way, your HTML document will include the appropriate anchor element, specified by opening and closing anchor tags. The following procedure assumes you create your anchor element in a text editor. If you are not using a text editor, you should consult your editor's documentation to determine if modifications of the procedure are necessary.

1. Open the HTML document you want to edit in your HTML editor. (See How-To 2.3 on HTML editing environments.)

2. Locate the position where you want to include your image. Place the cursor at this location.

3. Insert the text that you want to enclose between the opening and closing anchor tags. If the the image file is large, let the reader know. An example of such a message is included in the text below.

```
owl image (1.2 MB JPEG)
```

4. Place the insertion point where you want the anchor to begin. Insert an opening anchor tag at this location. Minimally, this should include the target of the link, the URL of the image you want to include. You include this URL as the value of an HREF attribute. The following code shows an opening anchor tag.

```
<A HREF="http://www.mysite.edu/images/owl.jpeg">owl image (1.2 MB JPEG)
```

5. Place the insertion point after the enclosed text. Insert a closing anchor tag. The following code shows a complete anchor element for the example image.

```
<A HREF="http://www.mysite.edu/images/owl.jpeg">owl image</A> (1.2 MB JPEG)
```

6. Save your document or continue adding elements by returning to step 2.

How It Works

HTML 3 supports GIF and X bitmap images within a document using the <IMG> element. When this element was added to HTML, GIF was one of the most highly used image formats. Recently, support for direct inclusion of JPEG images has been suggested; however, widespread incorporation of the JPEG format into current browsers has not yet occurred. Netscape Navigator is currently the only browser directly supporting this image format.

Since many images are available in a variety of other file formats, you can use an external image viewer to access images in these formats in HTML documents as shown in Figure 9-3.

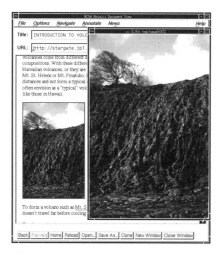

Figure 9-3 Browser and image viewer helper application

Many different image formats exist, and you must have a suitable viewer if you want to view images of a particular type. Generic viewers can recognize and display images in a variety of formats. Consequently, it is easier to use image viewers of this type than to require a separate viewer for each image format.

You access an external image by activating an HTML anchor that links to such an image. This anchor provides no information to the reader about the size and format of the linked image. Therefore, a useful practice is to specify both the format and size of the image in the text of the document. The format information allows the reader to decide whether he or she has an image viewer that can display the linked image. The size information allows the reader to decide whether he or she wants to spend the time required to wait for the image to download.

9.2
ADD AN EXTERNAL IMAGE

A common practice is to provide a smaller inline version of the image as part of the anchor for the linked image. This thumbnail image gives the user a preview of the larger external image. See How-To 8.7 for detailed information on the proper use of thumbnail images.

When a browser receives an image file from a server, it determines how to display the image based upon the format of the image data. Most browsers directly display plain text and HTML documents. Other types of information, such as images, are shown by helper applications.

Comments

The anchor elements in this How-To make use of only the HREF attribute. Chapter 7 provides additional information to HTML 3 anchor elements including information on other available attributes. Appendix A provides a quick reference on HTML 3 anchor elements. See How-To 9.1 for a complete example of incorporating external images into HTML documents.

To properly display external images, both the browser accessing the image and the server providing the image must be configured properly. Your Web site administrator is responsible for properly configurating your server. Instructions for configuring server support for external images are provided in How-To 11.5.

Configuring a browser to support external images requires either the modification of its configuration files or the alteration of a helper program list from the program's menu. You need to examine your browser documentation to determine the procedure to configure support for external images.

The following table lists some suitable image viewers. You need the proper application for your computer system to view non-inline images. This is not a comprehensive list. If a suggested application does not meet your needs, use a Web search engine such as infoseek (http://www.infoseek.com) to find a more suitable application.

PLATFORM	APPLICATION	LOCATION
Mac	JPEGView	ftp://ftp.ncsa.uiuc.edu/Mosaic/Mac/Helpers/
PC	Lview	ftp://akiu.gw.tohoku.ac.jp/pub/network/www/Web/
		Windows/viewers/lview*.zip
UNIX	xv	ftp://ftp.cis.upenn.edu/pub/xv

CHAPTER 9
ADDING MULTIMEDIA OBJECTS

9.3 How do I... Convert between image formats?

COMPLEXITY: INTERMEDIATE

COMPATIBILITY: HTML

Problem

The images I am using are too large. Is there a more compact format I can use?

I would like to make an externally viewable image into an inline image; however, to do this I must have the image object store as a GIF file.

I would like to create a thumbnail version of an image that I can include inline to serve as a link to the larger original.

Ultimately, I need to change my image so that it is in the format that I want.

Technique

Many images are created and stored in a format that is not the best for your desired use. Fortunately, converters exist for a number of popular image formats.

The conversion process requires a familiarity with the use of anonymous FTP or FTP URLs. First, identify an appropriate converter. Next, acquire the converter. Use it to convert your images. Finally, view your converted image using an image viewer to determine whether the image's integrity was maintained through the conversion process.

Steps

The following step-by-step procedure shows how to acquire and use an image converter. The listed converters accept images stored in particular file formats and generate appropriate image files as output.

1. Determine the original image file format as well as the format that you want to use for your converted image.

2. Find the converter you want. Table 9-2 lists some common converter applications. If you cannot find a suitable converter among them, you may wish to use a Web search application to find an applicable converter.

PLATFORM	CONVERTERS	LOCATION
PC, Mac, UNIX	Adobe Photoshop	Adobe Systems, Inc.
		http://www.adobe.com/Apps/Photoshop.html
PC	PaintShop Pro	JASC, Inc., http://www.winternet.com/~jasc/,
		ftp://ftp.winternet.com/users/jasc/psp301.zip

9.3
CONVERT BETWEEN IMAGE FORMATS

PLATFORM	CONVERTERS	LOCATION
UNIX	PBMPLUS	ftp://wuarchive.wustl.edu/graphics/graphics/
		packages/NetPBM/
UNIX (X-Window)	xv	ftp://ftp.cis.upenn.edu/pub/xv/

 Table 9-2 Common image formatting conversion applications

3. Use anonymous FTP or an FTP URL to acquire an appropriate converter. Uncompress, unarchive, and install the converter application as appropriate for your computer platform.

> **HTML** On a UNIX platform, use the uncompress and tar commands to uncompress and unarchive.

> **HTML** On a PC platform, the most common compression/archival program is ZIP. Use the unzip application to uncompress and unarchive.

> **HTML** On a Mac platform, the most common compression/archival program is StuffIt. Use the StuffIt program to uncompress and unarchive.

4. Convert your image file.

5. Examine the results of your image conversion in a suitable viewer. Edit the converted image if necessary.

6. Use the process described in How-To 9.2 to include external images in your HTML document. Use the procedures in Chapter 8 to use inline images.

How It Works

Image objects are created with a variety of applications and stored in many image formats. Many applications save in a single format. This format may not be suitable for use on your World Wide Web pages.

Most image formats provide essentially the same information. Therefore, converting the different formats is only a matter of translating the information from the source format to the target format. Depending on the conversion being performed, however, the converter may perform a more complex transformation where information from the source image must be used to calculate or modify data to generate the target.

You may want images in different formats for several reasons. First, if you wish to include an inline image, the image must be stored in GIF format. Therefore, the first reason you might need an image converter is to generate a GIF image from an image in some other format. Once you have converted the image to GIF, you can include the image inline using the <IMG> element, as described in Chapter 8, or as an external image by including a reference to the image using an anchor as specified in How-To 9.2.

Further, you may wish to use a converter program to generate thumbnail images to provide a preview of images that can be seen with a viewer. To do this, use the editing capabilities of the converter to shrink the entire image or to clip a relevant portion. Save the new image or image portion as a GIF image. Include the new GIF file as an inline image in an anchor element. For example, if you have a 2MB JPEG image of an owl, and you create a 15KB thumbnail version of the same image, you could include the following code as a link to the original image.

```
<A HREF="http://www.mysite.edu/images/owl.jpeg">
<IMG SRC="http://www.mysite.edu/images/owl.gif" ALT="Owl Image"
ALIGN=bottom>
(2 MB JPEG)
</A>
```

Finally, you may wish to remove inline images and provide access to them via an external viewer. The GIF format might not be the most compact of formats for the particular image. You can use a converter to store the image in a variety of formats and determine which will be the most efficient external image. The time it takes to download a particular page has an impact upon the usability of that page by a reader. If your page takes an excessively long time to retrieve, the reader is less likely to wait for the download to complete and is very unlikely to visit the page again.

Comments

Several of the packages mentioned in Table 9-2 allow you to edit and modify the images you convert. You can use these features to fine tune the image and to generate an altered version of the image. You may wish to generate thumbnail images for use as links to other media types such as movie segments or audio.

When you convert an image file, make sure that you provide the correct filename extension on the newly generated image file. The filename extension is used by servers and browsers to determine the type of data being accessed. Table 9-3 lists the common filename extensions for a variety of image types. The final column displays the Multipurpose Internet Mail Extensions (MIME) types that browsers and servers use to send information on image types.

IMAGE FORMAT	FILENAME EXTENSION	MIME TYPE
GIF	.gif	image/gif
JPEG	.jpeg .jpg .jpe	image/jpeg
TIFF	.tiff .tif	image/tiff
Portable Image	.pnm	image/x-portable-anymap
Portable Bitmap	.pbm	image/x-portable-bitmap
Potable Graymap	.pgm	image/x-portable-graymap

IMAGE FORMAT	FILENAME EXTENSION	MIME TYPE
Portable Pixmap	.ppm	image/x-portable-pixmap
RGB	.rgb	image/x-rgb
X Window-Dump	.xwd	image/x-xwindowdump
X Bitmap	.xbm	image/x-xbitmap
X Pixelmap	.xpm	image/x-xpixmap

Table 9-3 Image file formats and common filename extensions

Appendix C provides more complete information about the use of MIME types in the World Wide Web environment.

9.4 How do I... Insert a video?

COMPATIBILITY: HTML

Problem

I want to include movie segments in my HTML 3 documents. However, HTML 3 does not directly support the inclusion of video. Is there a way to provide access to my video object from my HTML 3 documents?

Technique

You cannot insert video segments directly into HTML 3 documents; however, you can include links to video files. The movie object is retrieved and displayed by a helper application.

You can acquire a video object in one of three ways:

- **HTML** Download an existing clip
- **HTML** Copy royalty-free clip-video (much like clip art packages)
- **HTML** Create video clips yourself

The first two approaches are easiest; archives and CD-ROM clip libraries are widespread. The last option requires access to more specialized hardware and software; if you have access to such equipment, familiarize yourself thoroughly with the documentation provided with your hardware and software before you begin. You can view some guidelines for this at URL: http://gnn.digital.com/gnn/special/drivein/projector.html.

Steps

The following procedure lets you create links to video files. Depending upon your editor, you can either insert the appropriate tags manually or use the macro or menu features of your editor. In either case, the HTML document will contain the appropriate anchor element. The directions below assume you are using a text editor to add the element.

1. Open the HTML document you wish to edit.

2. Locate the position where you want to place the link to the desired video object. Move the cursor to this location.

3. Insert the anchor text between the opening and closing anchor tags. An example is shown below.

```
The flight (10MB MPEG Video) of the owl is quite graceful.
```

> Note: You should pay particular attention to including size information for links to video files. Video files tend to be lengthy and may take undesirably long amounts of time to transfer.

4. Place the insertion point where you wish the anchor to begin. Insert an opening anchor tag at this location. Minimally, this should include the URL where the image file is located, using the HREF attribute. The following example shows an opening anchor tag.

```
The <A HREF="http://www.mysite.edu/images/flight.mpeg">flight (10MB MPEG Video) of the owl is quite graceful.
```

5. Move your insertion point to the end of the enclosed text. Insert a closing tag. The following example shows the full anchor element and surrounding text.

```
The <A HREF="http://www.mysite.edu/images/flight.mpeg">flight</A> (10MB MPEG Video) of the owl is quite graceful.
```

6. Save your document or return to step 2 to continue adding elements.

How It Works

HTML 3 does not directly support the inclusion of digital video. The digital video category includes both animations and movie clips. You can include video objects in an HTML document through links to the desired video file. The browser uses an external viewer to display the movie segment. Figure 9-4 shows a browser and the helper application used to display a video object.

9.4
INSERT A VIDEO

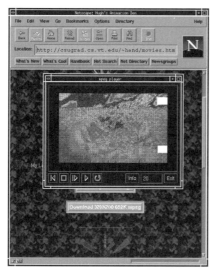

Figure 9-4 Browser and movie viewer helper application

When you create a link to a video clip, include the size and type specifications for the video clip referenced in or near the anchor text. The reader uses this information to determine whether he or she should download and view the referenced video clip.

You may also use a thumbnail image to indicate the content of the video. You could even convert the first frame of the video clip to a GIF image file and reduce it; then you could include it in your document as a link to the video clip. This may not be easy with some MPEG files due to compression. MPEG file compression works by storing the difference between two frames rather than storing the identical portions of the frames twice; therefore, extracting a single frame may require the processing of all preceding frames. For example, if you have a movie clip of an owl in flight, you could use a thumbnail of an owl to provide visual information describing the content of the movie. One example of how this could be done in HTML appears below.

```
<A HREF="http://www.mysite.edu/images/owl.mpeg">
<IMG SRC="http://www.mysite.edu/images/owl.gif" ALT="Owl Image" ALIGN=bottom>
(10 MB MPEG)
</A>
```

When a user activates a link to a video file, the browser requests the specified file. The server responds with both type and data information from the requested movie file. When a browser receives this information, it displays the movie with the helper application appropriate for the movie type.

Therefore, you must install video files on your Web site, or have your Web administrator install them. When properly installed, you can create links to these objects using the standard HTML 3 anchor element. Install video objects in either MPEG or QuickTime format. These formats are the most widely supported by browsers in any computer platform.

Comments

Chapter 7 provides a detailed discussion of the use of the HTML 3 anchor element. Appendix A provides quick reference to this element and a list of valid attributes. You should see How-To 9.1 for a general discussion on including external objects as well as an example in a complete HTML document.

Both the browser accessing the video file and the server providing files must be configured properly. Your Web site administrator is responsible for the proper server configuration. Instructions for configuring server support for video clips are provided in How-To 11.5.

In addition, browsers that are intended to access video files must have a video helper application installed and configured. The way you configure your browser to support helper applications differs from browser to browser. You might need to edit a configuration file used by the browser. Or, you might need to enter the proper information by selecting a Preferences (or similar) option from one of your browser menus. Read your browser's documentation to determine the procedure for configuring your browser to use helper applications for movie files.

The table below lists some video players you can use. You need suitable hardware, a viewer, and a properly configured browser to view video files. This list is not comprehensive. If a suggested application does not meet your needs, you should use a Web search engine to attempt to find a more suitable helper application.

PLATFORM	APPLICATION (FORMATS)	LOCATION
Mac	Sparkle (MPEG)	ftp://sumex-aim.stanford.edu/info-mac/grf/util/sparkle-*.hqx
Mac	SimplePlayer	ftp://ftp.ncsa.uiuc.edu/Mosaic/Mac/Helpers/Simple_Player.hqx
PC	Mpegplay (MPEG)	ftp://alfred.ccs.carleton.ca/pub/cveng/viewers/mpegw*.*
PC	Qtw (QuickTime)	ftp://winftp/cica.indiana.edu/pub/pc/win3/desktop/qtw*.zip
UNIX	xanim (MPEG, QuickTime)	ftp://crl.dec.com/pub/X11/contrib/applications/
UNIX	mpeg_play (MPEG)	ftp://tr-ftp.cs.berkeley.edu/pub/multimedia/mpeg/mpeg-play*.tar.Z

9.5 How do I... Convert between video file formats?

COMPLEXITY: ADVANCED

COMPATIBILITY: HTML

Problem

My video files are not as generically useful across computer platforms as I want them to be. I need to convert my movie files to a more useful format.

Technique

MPEG and QuickTime are the most common video formats on the World Wide Web. If you have Windows AVI format movies or Macintosh-specific QuickTime clips, you must convert them to either MPEG or "flattened" QuickTime. Macintosh-specific QuickTime movies exploit certain features of the Macintosh hardware and software; "flattening" a QuickTime movie removes these dependencies so that the movie supports cross-platform viewing.

Steps

The procedure below outlines the process for acquiring converters and using them to convert video files. These converters accept video files in a particular format and save them in a different video file format.

The process requires a familiarity with the use of anonymous FTP or FTP URLs. Your first task is to identify an appropriate converter. Next, you must acquire the converter and apply it to your existing documents. Finally, you should examine the result of the conversion process prior to installing the converter.

1. Determine the format of your video files and the format to which you want to convert.

2. Find a suitable converter. Table 9-4 lists some software packages and points to their location on the Internet. If you cannot find a converter that meets your needs in the table, use a Web search engine to find a suitable converter.

VIDEO FORMAT	CONVERTERS	LOCATION
MPEG to QuickTime	Sparkle (Mac)	ftp://sumex-aim.stanford.edu/info-mac/grf/util/sparkle-*.hqx
QuickTime to MPEG	Qt2Mpeg (Mac)	http://www.prism.uvsq.fr/public/wos/multimedia/qt2mpeg.sit.hqx
AVI, QuickTime	Mac Video for Windows (MAC)	http://www.prism.uvsq.fr/public/wos/multimedia/vfw11.sit
QuickTime "flattener"	FastPlayer (Mac)	ftp://sumex-aim.stanford.edu/info-mac/grf/util/fast-layer-*.hqx

continued on next page

CHAPTER 9
ADDING MULTIMEDIA OBJECTS

continued from previous page

VIDEO FORMAT	CONVERTERS	LOCATION
AVI to MPEG	XingCD (PC)	Xing Technology
QuickTime, AVI	SoundCap (PC)	ftp://ftp.intel.com/pub/IAL/Indeo_video/smartc.exe
QuickTime "flattener"	QFlat (PC)	ftp://venice.tcp.com/pub/anime-manga/software/viewers/qtfat.zip
QuickTime to MPEG	Qt2Mpeg (UNIX)	http://www.prism.uvsq.fr/public/wos/multimedia/qt2mpeg.zip

 Table 9-4 Common video format conversion applications

3. Acquire an appropriate converter package from an FTP site or software store. Install the converter application as appropriate for your platform.

4. Convert your video files.

5. Use a viewer to examine the video files. The displayed video should be very close to the original. If there are notable flaws, edit or convert the original to create a suitable video file in the correct format.

6. Use the process described in How-To 9.4 to include videos in HTML 3 documents.

How It Works

The video clips that you find or create come in different formats; however, for generic use on the World Wide Web, you want these objects in either QuickTime ("flattened") or MPEG format. Currently, viewers for these formats are available across multiple platforms.

If your clips are in another format, you should acquire an appropriate converter and convert them to a suitable format. Then view these files using a suitable helper application to assure that information was not lost or significantly altered in the conversion process.

If you have access to a video editing application, you may wish to adjust your videos. For MPEG video, you can use the MpegUtil program available for the UNIX platform (http://www.comp.lancs.ac.uk/computing/users/phillip/mpegUtil.html). The Adobe Premiere program serves as an editor for QuickTime movies on both the Macintosh and PC/Windows platforms (http://www.adobe.com/Apps/Premiere.html). Also, a shareware application called QuickEditor for QuickTime editing is available for the Macintosh (ftp://macarchive.umich.edu/powermac or ftp://sumex-aim.stanford.edu/info-mac/grf/util/).

Once you are satisfied with the results of the conversion or editing, you are ready to install the documents on your Web site. You should now be able to make your video files accessible by referencing them in anchor elements as described in How-To 9.4.

Comments

Even if your files are in a suitable format, you must decide whether you want to provide video, and if so, in which format(s). The biggest limitation for MPEG video is that although the MPEG format does support an audio track, most players do not. Until recently, the QuickTime standard was viewed primarily as a Macintosh-specific format, which limited the availability of viewers for other platforms. Further, the requirement that QuickTime movies be "flattened" for cross-platform use adds an additional step in the development process. Weigh these factors when deciding on the format that you ultimately use.

When you convert a video file, make sure you provide the correct filename extension for the newly generated video file. The filename extension is used by servers and browsers to determine the format of the file. Table 9-5 lists the common filename extensions for a variety of video file types. Browsers and servers communicate data type information using Multipurpose Internet Mail Extension (MIME) types; the MIME types for several video file formats appear as well.

IMAGE FORMAT	FILENAME EXTENSION	MIME TYPE
MPEG Format Video	.mpeg .mpg .mpe	video/mpeg
QuickTime Format Video	.qt .mov	video/quicktime
Microsoft Video Format	.avi	video/x-msvideo

Table 9-5 Video file formats and common filename extensions

Appendix C provides more complete information on the use of MIME types in the World Wide Web.

COMPLEXITY
EASY

9.6 How do I... Insert a sound file?

COMPATIBILITY: HTML

Problem

I would like to include sound clips in my home page. How can I provide links to sound files?

Technique

HTML does not allow you to include audio files in your pages; however, you can create a link to an application that will play a specified sound file.

The most commonly used audio file type on the World Wide Web is SUN's AU audio file format. The AU standard supports several types of encoding for sound samples. The most prevalent sample encoding is 8-bit µ-law. The sound quality derived from this encoding is not as high as with other formats; however, use of other formats such as AIFF, IFF, WAV, or MPEG audio yields audio segments that are not as portable. As multiplatform support grows for these other sound formats, the usage of the formats that provide higher quality audio will also increase.

Steps

The following instructions let you create links to sound files in your HTML documents. This procedure assumes that you use a text editor to edit your page. If this is not the case, consult your editor's documentation to determine any necessary changes in the procedure.

1. Open the HTML document you wish to edit in your favorite text editor.
2. Place the insert cursor at the position where you want to create a link to the desired sound file.
3. Insert the text that you want to enclose in the anchor element. When transferring large files, you should specify the file size to warn the reader. An example of such a message appears below.

```
Hoot of an Owl (2 MB AU Audio)
```

4. Position the insertion point where you want the anchor element to begin. Insert an opening anchor tag at this point. Minimally, this tag should include the URL where the sound file is located; use the HREF attribute to specify this value. The following example shows the insertion of an opening anchor tag.

```
<A HREF=http://www.mysite.edu/sounds/owl.au>Hoot of an Owl (2 MB AU Audio)
```

5. Move the insertion point to the end of the enclosed text. Insert a closing anchor tag. The example below shows a complete anchor element linking to a sound file.

```
<A HREF=http://www.mysite.edu/sounds/owl.au>Hoot of an Owl</A> (2 MB AU Audio)
```

6. You can also use a thumbnail image to indicate the nature of the audio file. For example, if you have an audio clip of an owl hooting, you could use a thumbnail image of an owl to provide a visual cue to what the audio file contains, as in the following example.

```
<A HREF="http://www.mysite.edu/sounds/owl.au">
<IMG SRC="http://www.mysite.edu/images/owl.gif" ALT="Owl Image" ALIGN=bottom>
(2 MB AU Audio)
</A>
```

7. Or you can use an icon to indicate the type of object rather than its content. The following code might be used to include an icon for the same audio file.

```
<A HREF=http://www.mysite.edu/sounds/owl.au>
<IMG SRC="http://www.mysite.edu/icons/sound.bmp" ALT="Sound Icon"
ALIGN=bottom>Hoot</A>  of an Owl (2 MB AU Audio)
```

8. Save your document or continue adding elements by returning to step 2.

How It Works

When you create a link to a large file, such as an audio clip, you should include in the text near to the anchor or as part of it the size and type of the file. The reader can use this information to decide whether the file is a suitable size and format to retrieve.

When the reader selects a link, it triggers the retrieval of the object specified in the anchor element. If the request is successful, the server sends a response containing both the type of the requested file (audio/*) and the file itself (audio data).

To perform this task, the server maintains a database that maps filename extensions to information types. If you use audio files on your Web site, make sure you use the proper filename extensions. Chapter 11 provides information on configuring your server to properly transmit sound files.

When a browser receives a file from the server, the browser determines how to display the object based on the type of the file. Most browsers only process pure text and HTML documents in their display window. Other types of information are presented to the reader by prespecified helper applications.

Comments

Chapter 7 provides a detailed discussion of the various attributes that might be used with the anchor element.

To be served and rendered correctly, both the browser accessing the object and the server providing the audio object must be configured properly. Your Web site administrator will be responsible for the proper configuration of your server; instructions for configuring server support for audio are provided in How-To 11.5.

Configuring a browser to support audio usually requires either modifying configuration files or changing a list of helper programs in the browser's menu. Consult your browser's documentation to determine how to configure helper applications for playing audio files.

The Table 9-6 lists some audio players suitable for use as helper applications. You will need suitable hardware such as a sound card and speakers or headphones, a program that plays sound files, and a browser that is configured to support audio.

PLATFORM	APPLICATION	LOCATION
Mac	SoundMachine (AU, AIFF, AIF)	ftp://ftp.ncsa.uiuc.edu/Mosaic/Mac/Helpers/SoundMachine.sit.hqx
PC	WHAM (AU, WAV, AIFF, IFF)	ftp://ftp.ncsa.uiuc.edu/Mosaic/Windows/viewers/wham*.zip
UNIX	showaudio (Metamail) (AU, AIFF, AIF)	ftp://thumper.bellcore.com/pub/nsb/

Table 9-6 Common audio player helper applications

This is not a comprehensive list. Should a suggested application not meet your needs, use a Web search engine such as Lycos (http://lycos.cs.cmu.edu) to find a more suitable helper application.

9.7 How do I... Convert between audio file formats?

COMPLEXITY
ADVANCED

COMPATIBILITY: HTML

Problem

I want to save my homemade audio files in a format that most Web users can access. How do I do this?

Technique

You can acquire audio files in several ways:

- **HTML** You can digitally record voice data through a microphone connected to many multimedia computer systems.

- **HTML** You can use royalty-free audio clips from purchased packages.

- **HTML** You can download audio files from bulletin boards or the Internet.

- **HTML** With appropriate hardware and software, you can digitally record sound directly from a CD-ROM reader.

Audio files come in several formats. The most popular audio format used in the World Wide Web environment is SUN's AU. If you have audio in other formats, you may wish to convert them to AU.

If AU sound quality is sufficient for your task, you should convert your sound file to the AU format. If you require higher quality, the two standards most commonly used other than the AU format are the AIFF and WAV formats. Audio stored in these formats is likely to have better sound quality than AU files.

9.7
CONVERT BETWEEN AUDIO FILE FORMATS

The price of using WAV or AIFF formats rather than AU is reduced portability. If a browser supports audio, it most likely supports the AU format. In addition, the higher quality audio usually requires more storage, resulting in a longer transmission time. This is a particular disadvantage for people with slow Internet connections.

Once you decide on the format you want to use, acquire the appropriate converter and convert your audio files. You should then play these audio files using a suitable helper application to assure that information was not lost or significantly altered in the conversion process.

Once you are satisfied with the results of the conversion, you are ready to install the documents on your Web site. You should now be able to access these audio information objects through appropriately constructed anchor elements as described in How-To 9.4.

The process requires a familiarity with the use of anonymous FTP or FTP URLs. You must first identify an appropriate converter. Next, acquire the converter and apply it to your existing documents. Finally, you should examine the result of the conversion process prior to installing the converter.

Steps

The following shows you how to acquire converters and use them to convert audio files.

1. Determine the source and target file format of your audio information object.

2. Find the converter that you will need to use. Table 9-7 gives examples of some of these environments by software package and pointers to information concerning them. If you cannot find the file formats and/or platforms that you require in Table 9-7, you may wish to use a Web search application to find an applicable converter.

AUDIO FILE FORMAT	CONVERTERS	LOCATION
WAV, SND, AIFF	SoundApp (Mac)	ftp://sumex-aim.stanford.edu/info-mac/snd/util/
SND to AU	μ-law (Mac)	ftp://sumex-aim.stanford.edu/info-mac/snd/util/
AU, WAV, AIFF, SND	SOX (UNIX/PC)	ftp://ftp.cs.ruu.nl/pub/MIDI/PROGRAMS/

Table 9-7 Common audio format conversion applications

3. Use anonymous FTP or an FTP URL to acquire an appropriate converter package. Uncompress, unarchive, and install the converter application as appropriate for your platform.

4. Apply the converter to your source audio files.

5. Use the process described in How-To 9.5 to include audio objects.

How It Works

The file formats available store sound as digital samples of the sound rather than the original analog signal, that is, like a CD rather than a record, and the size of the sample stored in part determines its quality.

Oftentimes audio file conversions are lossy; when converting from a higher quality format to a lower one, loss of information occurs, particularly if the source uses 16-bit encoding and the target uses 8-bit, or the source is stereo and the target is mono. In these cases, you can only convert the file in one direction. Attempting to reverse the process will lead to audio segments in the original file format, but with significantly reduced sound quality.

Sound editors will allow you to modify sound files. Use such tools to tailor sounds or to mask out distortions. The WHAM application specified in Table 9-6 provides extensive sound editing capabilities for the PC platform. Player Pro allows the same kind of audio editing on the Macintosh platform (gopher://sumex-aim.-stanford.edu:70/40/info-mac/_Graphic_%26_Sound_Tool/_Sound/player-pro-442).

Comments

After generating a new audio file, make sure you save the file with the correct filename extension. The filename extension specifies the type of file being accessed. Table 9-8 lists the common filename extensions for a variety of video information object types. Servers and browsers use Multipurpose Internet Mail Extension (MIME) types to pass information concerning transmitted files.

AUDIO FORMAT	FILENAME EXTENSION	MIME TYPE
AU 8-bit, μ-law	.au .snd	audio/basic
AIFF	.aiff .aif	audio/x-aiff
Microsoft Audio	.wav	audio/x-wav

 Table 9-8 Audio file formats and common filename extensions

Appendix C provides more complete information on the use of MIME types in the World Wide Web environment.

9.8 How do I... Include a PostScript document?

INCLUDE A POSTSCRIPT DOCUMENT

COMPLEXITY: INTERMEDIATE

COMPATIBILITY: HTML

Problem

I have a document archive consisting of a set of PostScript files. I need to keep these documents in this format so I can print them when required. Converting all of them to HTML 3 would mean that I would have to maintain the integrity of both sets of documents when changes are made. Can I provide access to my existing archive through HTML 3 documents?

Technique

PostScript is one of the most commonly used printer languages. You can develop and maintain PostScript documents using many different applications. To avoid converting PostScript documents to HTML and maintaining two independent document sets containing the same information, you can use only the original PostScript files.

The disadvantage of this approach is that PostScript documents do not support hypermedia links. The advantages are that the documents are ready to print and that only one set of documents needs to be updated. You will need to decide whether to store your documents as PostScript, HTML, or both.

You can create a link to a PostScript file in an HTML document rather than converting the PostScript file to an HTML document. (See How-To 2.5 for information about document conversion.) When a reader selects the link, the browser retrieves the PostScript file and displays it in a suitable viewer. You need not convert your PostScript documents to HTML to allow World Wide Web access, thus obviating the need to have two sets of the same documents.

When creating a link to a PostScript document, you should indicate in or near the text of the anchor element that the object referenced is a PostScript document. If a reader's browsing environment will not render PostScript documents, then he or she does not need to bother trying to trigger the link. Further, you should specify the approximate length of the document referenced. This allows individuals with a slow network connection to make an informed decision about whether or not to trigger the link.

Steps

The following procedure shows how to link a PostScript file to your HTML documents. If you are creating HTML pages using an editor other than a text editor, consult your documentation to determine the correct procedure for adding an anchor element.

CHAPTER 9
ADDING MULTIMEDIA OBJECTS

1. Open the HTML document you want to edit in your favorite text editor.
2. Move the cursor to the position where you wish to add a link to a PostScript file.
3. Insert the text that you want enclosed between the opening and closing anchor tags.
4. Move your insertion point to where you want the anchor to begin, and then insert an opening anchor tag. The HREF attribute of this tag should specify the URL of the PostScript file. The following example shows an opening tag for such an anchor element.

```
Printer ready version of this document is
<A HREF="http://www.mysite.edu/papers/owl.ps">available. (1.2 MB)
```

5. Insert a closing anchor tag after the enclosed text. The example below shows a complete anchor element of this type.

```
Printer ready version of this document is
<A HREF="http://www.mysite.edu/papers/owl.ps">available</A>. (1.2 MB)
```

6. You can use an icon in the anchor to indicate the type of the linked file. The following code might be used to include an icon for the same PostScript file.

```
Printer ready version of this document is
<A HREF="http://www.mysite.edu/papers/owl.ps">available
<IMG SRC="http://www.mysite.edu/icons/psdoc.gif" ALT="PostScript Icon"
ALIGN=bottom>
</A>. (1.2 MB)
```

7. Save your document or continue adding elements. Add additional links to PostScript files by returning to step 2.

How It Works

Select a link to request the file specified in the anchor element. If the request is successful, the server sends a response containing both the file's Multipurpose Internet Mail Extension (MIME) type (application/PostScript) and the file itself.

To perform this task, the server maintains a database that maps filename extensions to MIME types. Therefore, if you use PostScript files on your Web site, make sure you use the proper filename extensions. Chapter 11 provides more information on configuring servers to support PostScript documents.

When a browser receives a PostScript file from the server, it determines how to display the file based upon the MIME type sent by the server. Most browsers only directly display pure text and HTML documents. Helper applications display other information types, such as PostScript documents. Figure 9-5 shows the results of triggering a link to a PostScript document.

9.8
INCLUDE A POSTSCRIPT DOCUMENT

Figure 9-5 Browser and PostScript viewer helper application

Comments

Chapter 7 provides a detailed discussion of HTML 3 hypertext links. This How-To only uses the HREF attribute of the anchor element; however, you may want to include others as you see fit.

To provide access to PostScript documents on a server, you must properly configure the server to transmit PostScript files. Your Web site administrator is responsible for the proper configuration of your server; instructions for configuring a server to support PostScript documents are provided in How-To 11.5.

In addition, any browser that wishes to access the PostScript documents must also be configured for direct rendering or, more likely, to use a helper application to display the file. Consult your browser's documentation to determine the procedure for configuring helper applications for PostScript files.

The table below lists some PostScript viewers for several platforms. To view PostScript files, you will need suitable hardware, a helper application, and a browser configured to view PostScript documents.

PLATFORM	APPLICATION	LOCATION
Mac	mac-ghost	ftp://sumex-aim.stanford.edu/info-mac/grf/util
PC	gsview	ftp://ftp.ncsa.uiuc.edu/Web/Mosaic/Windows/viewers/gsview
		and gs*exe (both required)

continued on next page

PLATFORM	APPLICATION	LOCATION
UNIX	ghostview	ftp://ftp.cs.wisc.edu/pub/ghost/gnu/ghostview*.gz
	ghostscript	ghostscript*.gz
	ghostscript fonts	ghostscript-fonts*.gz

This is not a comprehensive list. If a suggested application does not meet your needs, you can use a Web search engine to find a more suitable helper application.

9.9 How do I... Include a device independent (DVI) file?

COMPLEXITY: INTERMEDIATE

COMPATIBILITY: HTML

Problem

Most of my previous documents have been developed using the TeX formatting language. DVI files are generated by processing TeX documents. I have an archive of all my DVI files ready to print, and I would like to use HTML documents to provide online access to this archive. I don't want to have to maintain both the HTML and DVI documents. Is there a way I can use the DVI files without converting the entire archive to HTML?

Technique

TeX files can be converted to HTML documents. (See How-To 2.5 for information about converting documents.) However, two separate sets of documents would require twice as much maintenance. You can maintain a single set of TeX documents with their associated DVI files ready. These DVI files can then be accessed from HTML documents.

To accomplish this, create a link that, when selected, causes the browser to retrieve the DVI file and present it to the reader via a suitable viewer.

Steps

The way you include an external object, such as a DVI file, in your HTML page depends on the editing environment used to create the document. These steps assume that you manually insert the anchor element with a text editor. For other editor types, consult your editor's documentation on how to add anchor elements.

The following step-by-step procedure shows how to create a link to a DVI file.

9.9
INCLUDE A DEVICE INDEPENDENT (DVI) FILE

1. Open the HTML document you wish to edit in your text editor.
2. Position the cursor where you want to add the DVI file.
3. Insert the text that you want enclosed in the anchor element.
4. Move the cursor to where you want the anchor element to begin, and insert an opening anchor tag. Set the HREF attribute in this tag to the URL of the DVI file that you want to include. The following example shows such an opening tag.

```
Device Independent (DVI) version of this document is
<A HREF="http://www.mysite.edu/papers/owl.dvi">available. (2 MB)
```

5. Move the insertion point to the end of the anchor text. Insert a closing anchor tag. The following code shows a complete anchor element linking to a DVI file.

```
Device Independent (DVI) version of this document is
<A HREF="http://www.mysite.edu/papers/owl.dvi">available</A>. (2 MB)
```

6. You can use an icon in the anchor to indicate the type of the linked file. The following code might be used to include an icon for the same DVI file.

```
Printer ready version of this document is
<A HREF="http://www.mysite.edu/papers/owl.dvi">available
<IMG SRC="http://www.mysite.edu/icons/dvidoc.gif" ALT="DVI Icon"
ALIGN=bottom>
</A>. (2 MB)
```

7. Save your document or continue adding elements by returning to step 2.

How It Works

Prior to WYSIWYG style editors, formatted documents were developed using tags to mark the various formatted elements in the documents. Various document formatting languages were developed for this purpose: troff, runoff, and TeX. The TeX formatting language provided such features as incorporation of mathematical expressions, tabular formatting, font changes, and a host of additional features.

The TeX application creates DVI files when it processes source files. You can use the DVI files to display or print the formatted document in any number of environments. In most cases, the DVI file needs to be translated to the display device's particular formatting language.

For those who wish to provide access to their TeX documents on the World Wide Web, there are two options.

The first option is to convert the TeX documents to HTML. This approach leads to two sets of documents, each of which requires maintenance when one document is altered. In addition, HTML does not support all the capabilities of TeX, although HTML 3 supports more than previous versions did.

CHAPTER 9
ADDING MULTIMEDIA OBJECTS

The second approach is to maintain the original TeX documents and generate new DVI files as the TeX documents are updated. In this way, the documents are maintained only once and the DVI files are available to be shown on any display capable of processing a DVI file, as well as being accessible via links in HTML documents.

Selecting the link initiates a server request for the DVI file specified in the anchor element. If the request is successful, the server issues a response containing both the data type and the data itself.

To do so, the server maintains a database that maps filename extensions to information types. Therefore, if DVI files are installed on your Web site, be sure you use the proper filename extensions. Chapter 11 provides information on configuring a server to support DVI files.

When a browser receives a DVI file from the server, it determines how to display the file based on the type information provided by the server. Most browsers only directly support pure text and HTML documents in their display windows. Information of other types is displayed by prespecified helper applications. Figure 9-6 shows the result of activating a link to a DVI file.

Comments

HTML 3 anchor elements support a variety of attributes; however, this How-To only makes use of the HREF attribute. For your purposes, you may need to use

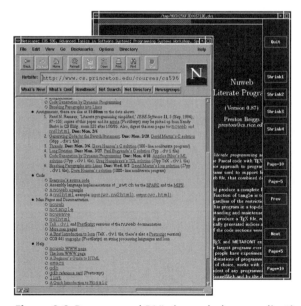

Figure 9-6 Browser and DVI viewer helper application

9.9
INCLUDE A DEVICE INDEPENDENT (DVI) FILE

other attributes. Chapter 7 provides detailed information on HTML 3 anchor elements.

While not as common as the other media types described in this chapter, DVI files require both server and browser configuration. Your Web site administrator is responsible for the proper configuration of your server. How-To 11.5 provides instructions for configuring server support for DVI files.

In addition to your having Web site administrator configure the server, you need to configure browsers to support DVI files. Consult the documentation for your browser to determine the procedure for configuring helper applications such as a DVI viewer.

The table below lists some suitable DVI viewers for use as helper applications. You must have suitable hardware, a DVI viewer, and a browser that is configured properly.

PLATFORM	APPLICATION	LOCATION
Mac	dvi-preview	ftp://ftp.shsu.edu/tex-archive/systems/mac/cmactex/
PC	TrueTeX (Commercial)	ftp://ftp.netcom.com/pub/Tr/TrueTeX/truetex.txt
UNIX	xdvi	ftp://export.lcs.mit.edu/contrib/applications/

This list is not comprehensive. If a suggested application does not meet your needs, use a Web search engine to find a more suitable helper application.

CHAPTER 10
HTML INTERACTIVE FORMS

HTML INTERACTIVE FORMS

How do I...
- **10.1** Create a basic form?
- **10.2** Add a text box to a form?
- **10.3** Add check boxes to a form?
- **10.4** Add radio buttons to a form?
- **10.5** Add password fields to a form?
- **10.6** Add pulldown menus to a form?
- **10.7** Pass information between forms?
- **10.8** Choose a request method to send data to the HTTP server?
- **10.9** Process a form?

You've come this far with HTML and are proceeding along just fine. You know how to create a nice-looking home page that has links to lots of other pages all over the WWW. The thing is, so far the information has been flowing in only one direction. You have been able to show people who read your pages whatever is on your mind, but your readers have had no way of giving you feedback. They can't let you know how they like your page or what they would like you to do differently. That is where forms come into play. You can include forms in your HTML document that allow your readers to send you input in a variety of different ways.

CHAPTER 10
HTML INTERACTIVE FORMS

The form creation process is actually twofold. The first part of the process is to include the HTML tags in your document that create the form. This first part is often referred to as the *front end*. The second part of the process involves creating a script in a language such as Perl or C that processes the information contained in the form. This part of the process is called the *back end*. This chapter deals mainly with the first part, or front end, of the form creation process.

10.1 Create a Basic Form
Before you can let a user interact with your documents, you need to create a basic form. This How-To shows you how to add the tags needed to create a startup form that lets a user enter lines of text.

10.2 Add a Text Box to a Form
There are instances when a user is going to want to enter more than one line of text at a time. This How-To shows you how to add scrollable text boxes of any size to your forms.

10.3 Add Check Boxes to a Form
Sometimes you want to let a user select or check a number of different options or choices. This How-To shows how to add check boxes to a form.

10.4 Add Radio Buttons to a Form
Sometimes you would like to let a user choose only one option from a list. This list works like the buttons on a radio; selecting one item unselects any other item that had been selected. This simple How-To shows how to add radio buttons to your forms.

10.5 Add Password Fields to a Form
There are times when you want a user to enter sensitive information into a field, but you want to disguise this input so a passerby or onlooker cannot read it. This How-To shows the process used to create password fields in which user-supplied information is replaced by asterisks.

10.6 Add Pulldown Menus to a Form
Sometimes you may wish to let a user select from a number of options or choices but only show the currently selected choice on the form. This simple How-To lets you add pulldown menus to your forms.

10.7 Pass Information between Forms
When creating dynamic documents, you may want to pass information from a current form to another form that you will build based partly on information from the current form. This How-To shows how to add hidden fields that can be used to store information to pass from one form to another.

10.8 Choose a Request Method to Send Data to the HTTP Server

Now that you have a complete form, you need a way for a reader to say, "I'm finished," and then to deliver the information contained in the form to the HTTP server. This How-To will show you how to submit a form and how to pick the submission method that is right for you.

10.9 Process a Form

Now that you have a complete form all ready to go, you need a way to bridge the gap between the HTML document that contains the form and the HTTP server that will process the form. This How-To gives you a basic rundown on how to create a Common Gateway Interface (CGI) script that will send and process a form.

COMPLEXITY
INTERMEDIATE

10.1 How do I... Create a basic form?

COMPATIBILITY: HTML 2 OR ABOVE

Problem

I would like to add forms to my documents so I can receive user feedback and create more dynamic documents. How do I do this?

Technique

Creating a form isn't all that difficult. Forms are created as part of an HTML document by including the <FORM> tag, along with its associated tags that create

- **HTML** Text fields
- **HTML** Check boxes
- **HTML** Radio button
- **HTML** Pop-up menus

The form is later submitted to the HTTP server by using either the "get" or "post" method. The form can then be processed by a script.

Steps

The following procedure shows you how to create a form and include it in a document.

CHAPTER 10
HTML INTERACTIVE FORMS

1. Open a new file with any editor or word processor you choose. Make sure that whatever tool you use is able to save documents as text or ASCII, depending on the environment you are in.

2. Create a base HTML document. This document consists of the items needed to make an HTML document. This base document should include:

- **HTML** <HTML> ... </HTML> tags
- **HTML** <HEAD> ... </HEAD> tags
- **HTML** <TITLE> ... </TITLE> tags
- **HTML** <BODY> ... </BODY> tags

Your document should resemble the following:

```
<HTML> <HEAD>
<TITLE>Input Form</TITLE>
</HEAD>
<BODY>
</BODY>
</HTML>
```

3. Put two horizontal rule <HR> tags in the body of your document. Your form will go between these two tags. This step is entirely optional, but it helps the form stand out more. Your document should now look something like this:

```
<HTML> <HEAD>
<TITLE>Input Form</TITLE>
</HEAD>
<BODY>
<HR>
My form will go here!
<HR>
</BODY>
</HTML>
```

4. Add the <FORM> ... </FORM> tags to your document. The basic tag syntax is

```
<FORM METHOD="Get or Post" ACTION="URL" ENCTYPE="type">
Field definitions
</FORM>
```

The <FORM> tag tells a browser that there is a fill-in-the-blank form in this HTML document.

The METHOD attribute states the method to be used when you send the form to the server. The two acceptable methods are "get" and "post". "Get" sends the information in the form to the server at the end of the URL. "Post" sends the information in the form to the server as a data body. "Get"

10.1
CREATE A BASIC FORM

is the default method, but "post" is the method preferred by many HTML designers.

The ACTION attribute gives the address of the script that will process the form. This script may be written in almost any language, but Perl and C are the dominant two choices.

The ENCTYPE attribute specifies how the data is to be encoded. This attribute only applies if you use the "post" method, and even then there is only one possible value, the default value "application/w-www-form-urlencoded". The ENCTYPE attribute is included here only so that you recognize it if you see it.

The METHOD, ACTION, and ENCTYPE attributes are all optional; however, for the sake of clarity, it is best if you always include the METHOD and ACTION attributes.

Now your document and form will look like this:

```
<HTML> <HEAD>
<TITLE>Input Form</TITLE>
</HEAD>
<BODY>
<HR>
<FORM METHOD=POST ACTION="/cgi-bin/MY_SCRIPT">
My form will go here!
</FORM>
<HR>
</BODY>
</HTML>
```

Figure 10-1 shows how this document will look when viewed with a browser. It doesn't look like much yet, but you have built a strong base on which to construct the rest of your form.

Figure 10-1 What you have so far. It doesn't look like much yet...

5. Add an <INPUT> tag so you can accept some input from a reader. The <INPUT> tag is a standalone tag. The syntax for this is

```
<INPUT TYPE="type" NAME="NAME" SIZE="number" VALUE="value">
```

There are many kinds of <INPUT> types available, but you are going to start with the most basic kind, a *text entry* field. To create a text entry field in a document, you include the following between the <FORM> ... </FORM> tags:

```
<INPUT TYPE="text" NAME="NAME" SIZE=30 VALUE="John Smith">
```

6. Put some text around the <INPUT> tag to give readers an idea of what you expect them to enter in the space provided. The document should now look like this:

```
<HTML> <HEAD>
<TITLE>Input Form</TITLE>
</HEAD>
<BODY>
<HR>
<FORM METHOD=POST ACTION="/cgi-bin/MY_SCRIPT">
Enter your name here :
<INPUT TYPE="text" NAME="NAME" SIZE=30 VALUE="John Smith">
</FORM>
<HR>
</BODY>
</HTML>
```

Now you're getting somewhere. You have a form on the screen that a reader can enter information into.

7. Finish off this first form by giving the user a chance to either submit this information or reset the information and enter something else. This is done by using the <INPUT> tag and setting the TYPE to either "submit" or "reset". For example:

```
<INPUT TYPE="SUBMIT" NAME="SUBMIT_BUTTON" VALUE="Submit">
<INPUT TYPE="RESET" NAME="RESET_BUTTON" VALUE="Oops">
```

Here, the TYPE attribute tells the browser what kind of button you are dealing with. The NAME is a variable that you can access later when referring to this information. The value is what is written in the button. Adding these lines to your document, you will have:

```
<HTML> <HEAD>
<TITLE>Input Form</TITLE>
</HEAD>
<BODY>
<HR>
<FORM METHOD=POST ACTION="/cgi-bin/MY_SCRIPT">
Enter your name here:
<INPUT TYPE="TEXT" NAME="NAME" SIZE=30 VALUE="John Smith">
<INPUT TYPE="SUBMIT" NAME="SUBMIT_BUTTON" VALUE="Submit">
<INPUT TYPE="RESET" NAME="RESET_BUTTON" VALUE="OOPS">
</FORM>
<HR>
</BODY>
</HTML>
```

8. Save the document as a text or ASCII file. It is a good idea to give the document a reasonable name such as sampform along with a .htm or an .html

Figure 10-2 An actual form!

extension. By saving the document in this manner you can view it through either the Open Local or Open File commands in your browser. When viewed in this manner, the above document should that look very much like Figure 10-2.

How It Works

The <FORM>...</FORM> tags tell the browser to expect various <INPUT> tags between these two tags. These tags, along with other HTML tags and anything else that's valid in an HTML document, all make up a fill-in-the-blanks form (from now on referred to as simply a form). When the reader presses the Submit button, the contents of the form are sent to the HTTP server in a data stream in the form of:

`action?name=value&name=value`

Comments

What has been created so far is a framework to gather information—the front end of the form. This allows you to interact with a reader, but you still need a script to process this information. The script is dealt with briefly later in this chapter and in greater detail later in the book.

COMPLEXITY
INTERMEDIATE

10.2 How do I... Add a text box to a form?

COMPATIBILITY: HTML 2 OR ABOVE

Problem

Once I have a form in my HTML document, I would like to let readers enter more than one line of text at a time. How do I do this?

Technique

Once you are familiar with setting up a basic form, adding parts to this form is quite easy. To make a text box that creates a scrollable text field on the screen, insert the <TEXTAREA> ... </TEXTAREA> tags somewhere between the <FORM> ...

</FORM> tags. You may have as many <TEXTAREA> tags as needed, and you may include other HTML tags between these tags.

Steps

The following steps show how to add <TEXTAREA> tags to your forms.

1. Decide on the number of text boxes you need (usually one or two is sufficient) and how you are going to lay them out on the form. The number of text boxes used on a form is usually quite easy and straightforward to determine. Add one text box every place you think a reader needs a lot of room to write something. The layout is a matter of personal taste and preference. Don't be surprised if the actual layout you end up with is different from the one you first envisioned.

2. Open the HTML document that contains the form you wish to add the text box to. You may open the document in any text editor or word processor you feel comfortable using. In this case you will expand on the document used in How-To 10.1.

3. Add the <TEXTAREA> ... </TEXTAREA> tags between the <FORM> ... <FORM>tags. The basic syntax is

```
<TEXTAREA NAME="NAME" ROWS="number of rows" COLS="number of columns"> any default text </TEXTAREA>
```

The variable in the NAME attribute is what you will refer to this <TEXTAREA> with when you later reference it in a script. The ROWS attribute is set to an integer for the number of rows the text box has. The COLS attribute is set to an integer for the number of columns the text box will have. The text between the <TEXTAREA> ... </TEXTAREA> tags is the text that initially appears in the text box.

For this example you will create a text box called "comments". It is 5 rows long and 60 columns wide. This should give the reader sufficient area to voice an opinion. If the reader needs more space, the box will scroll. Use this command sequence:

```
<TEXTAREA NAME="COMMENTS" ROWS=5 COLS=60>Your comments go here</TEXTAREA>
```

4. Put some text near the <TEXTAREA> tag to give a reader a better idea of what to enter.

The document should now resemble this:

```
<HTML> <HEAD>
<TITLE>Input Form</TITLE>
</HEAD>
<BODY>
<HR>
<FORM METHOD=POST ACTION="/cgi-bin/MY_SCRIPT">
Enter your name here: <INPUT TYPE="text" NAME="NAME" SIZE=30 VALUE="???">
```

10.2
ADD A TEXT BOX TO A FORM

```
<TEXTAREA NAME="COMMENTS" ROWS=5 COLS=60>Your comments go here</TEXTAREA>
<INPUT TYPE="submit" NAME="SUBMIT_BUTTON" VALUE="SEND ME">
<INPUT TYPE="reset" NAME="RESET_BUTTON" VALUE="OOPS">
</FORM>
<HR>
</BODY>
</HTML>
```

5. Enter any other text or HTML tags to help clarify the document and make it easier to read. For this document, use a level two heading tag <H2> to let people know what to expect and a couple of new paragraph tags <P> to space things out a little more.

```
<HTML> <HEAD>
<TITLE>Input Form</TITLE>
</HEAD>
<BODY>
<H2>INPUT FORM -- Textarea</H2>
<HR>
<FORM METHOD=POST ACTION="/cgi-bin/MY_SCRIPT">
Enter your name here: <INPUT TYPE="text" NAME="NAME" SIZE=30 VALUE="???">
<P>
What do you think:<TEXTAREA NAME="comments" ROWS=5 COLS=60>Your comments go here</TEXTAREA>
<P>
<INPUT TYPE="SUBMIT" NAME="SUBMIT_BUTTON" VALUE="Submit">
<INPUT TYPE="RESET" NAME="RESET_BUTTON" VALUE="OOPS">
</FORM>
<HR>
</BODY>
</HTML>
```

6. Save the document as text. Remember to give it a reasonable, clear name such as sampform.html.

7. Use Open File or Open Local on your browser to make sure your form looks the way you expect it to. If all went well, it will look much like Figure 10-3.

How It Works

The <FORM>...</FORM> tags tell the browser to expect form <INPUT> tags between these two tags. The <TEXTAREA> ... </TEXTAREA> tags create a space for a user to enter data within this form. Once the Submit button is pushed, the information contained in the text area will be sent to the HTTP server. The information can later be accessed by referring to the "name" assigned to the text area with the NAME attribute.

Comments

The appearance of forms is certainly not carved in stone and is largely a matter of personal taste. Some people like to wrap their forms in <PRE> ... </PRE> tags. This gives them more control over where they place items in the form. If you don't like

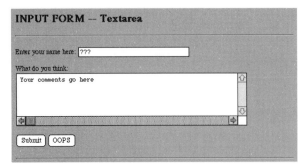

Figure 10-3 The form complete with a text field

how your text box looks, experiment with it. Try changing the values for ROWS and COLS in the <TEXTAREA> tag. You may also want to try moving the text box around the form some. The look of a form is very much a matter of individual taste.

COMPLEXITY
INTERMEDIATE

10.3 How do I...
Add check boxes to a form?

COMPATIBILITY: HTML 2 OR ABOVE

Problem

Now that I have a form in my HTML document, I would like to be able to let users make choices while using it. How do I do this?

Technique

Check boxes allow a user to click on any number of choices from a list. They are added to forms in much the same manner as text boxes. To create a check box, insert an <INPUT> tag between the <FORM> ... </FORM> tags. Inside the INPUT tag, set the TYPE to "checkbox". You may have as many check boxes as needed.

Steps

The following steps show how to add check boxes to forms.

1. Decide how many check boxes you are going to need and how you are going to lay them out on the form. The number of check boxes you need is usually pretty straightforward, since you should have a pretty good idea of how many lists of choices you wish to give a reader. The layout is more of a

10.3
ADD CHECK BOXES TO A FORM

matter of personal taste and preferences. Don't be surprised if the actual layout you end up with is different from the one you first envisioned. In this example, you will have two groups of check boxes: one so readers can select colors they like from a list, and another so readers can pick foods they like. Just for fun, lay out one group horizontally and the other vertically.

2. Open the HTML document that contains the form you wish to add the check box to. You will be expanding on the document used in How-To 10.1.

3. Add the <INPUT> tag for the first check box between the <FORM> ... </FORM>tags. In the <INPUT> tag, set the TYPE to "checkbox". The basic syntax for this is

```
<INPUT TYPE="checkbox" NAME="NAME" VALUE="value" [CHECKED] > "Text"
```

The TYPE attribute declares that this field is a check box. The variable in the NAME attribute is what you will refer to this check box with when you later reference it with a script. The VALUE attribute is what this check box is set to when it is checked. The CHECKED attribute is optional and tells the browser to show this check box as checked when you first view it. "Text" is for whatever text you wish to associate with each particular check box.

The tags for the color check boxes look like this:

```
<INPUT TYPE="checkbox" NAME="COLOR_CHECK1" VALUE=0>Red
<INPUT TYPE="checkbox" NAME="COLOR_CHECK2" VALUE=0>Blue
<INPUT TYPE="checkbox" NAME="COLOR_CHECK3" VALUE=0>Yellow
<INPUT TYPE="checkbox" NAME="COLOR_CHECK4" VALUE=1 CHECKED>Green
```

The tags for food check boxes look like this:

```
<INPUT TYPE="checkbox" NAME="FOOD_CHECK1" VALUE=0>Lobster <P>
<INPUT TYPE="checkbox" NAME="FOOD_CHECK2" VALUE=0>Spam<P>
<INPUT TYPE="checkbox" NAME="FOOD_CHECK3" VALUE=1 CHECKED>Chocolate<P>
```

4. Put some header text near the check boxes so readers have a good idea of what you want them to do.

5. Enter any other text or HTML tags to help clarify the document and make it easier to read. The document should now resemble this:

```
<HTML> <HEAD>
<TITLE>Input Form -- Check Boxes</TITLE>
</HEAD>
<BODY>
<H2>INPUT FORM check boxes</H2>
<HR>
<FORM METHOD=POST ACTION="/cgi-bin/MY_SCRIPT">
Enter your name here: <INPUT TYPE="text" NAME="NAME" SIZE=30 VALUE="???"><p>
What colors do you like:
<INPUT TYPE="checkbox" NAME="COLOR_CHECK1" VALUE="yes">Red
<INPUT TYPE="checkbox" NAME="COLOR_CHECK2" VALUE="yes">Blue
```

continued on next page

continued from previous page
```
<INPUT TYPE="checkbox" NAME="COLOR_CHECK3" VALUE="yes">Yellow
<INPUT TYPE="checkbox" NAME="COLOR_CHECK4" VALUE="yes" CHECKED>Green
<P>
What foods do you like:
<P>
<INPUT TYPE="checkbox" NAME="FOOD_CHECK1" VALUE="yes">Lobster <P>
<INPUT TYPE="checkbox" NAME="FOOD_CHECK2" VALUE="yes">Spam<P>
<INPUT TYPE="checkbox" NAME="FOOD_CHECK3" VALUE="yes" CHECKED>Chocolate<P>

<INPUT TYPE="submit" NAME="SUBMIT_BUTTON" VALUE="Submit">
<INPUT TYPE="reset" NAME="RESET_BUTTON" VALUE="OOPS">
</FORM>
<HR>
</BODY>
</HTML>
```

6. Save the document as text or ASCII.

7. Use Open File or Open Local on your browser to make sure your form looks the way you expect it to. If all goes well, it will look very much like Figure 10-4.

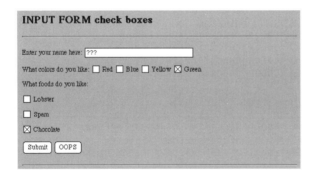

Figure 10-4 The form complete with check boxes

How It Works

The <FORM> ... </FORM> tags tell the browser to expect form <INPUT> tags between these two tags. The <INPUT> tag, when the TYPE is set to "checkbox", creates a check box for the user to click on to select that particular item. The check box toggles between on and off as the user clicks on it. If a particular check box is selected, then the variable name that refers to that check box will be set to *value*. Once the Submit button is pushed, the information contained in the form will be sent to the HTTP server. To see what check boxes were selected and not selected, you can use the names assigned with the NAME attribute and check their values.

10.4 ADD RADIO BUTTONS TO A FORM

Comments

Though check boxes may be physically grouped together on the page or form, it is usually not a good idea to logically group them together under one variable name. It is possible to have more than one check box checked at any given time, so it is a good idea to give each check box its own unique variable name. It is also best to keep the value assigned to the box when it is checked something simple. I usually choose "yes". The example shows one group of check boxes running across the page, and the other group running down the page. This is done purely to illustrate the number of ways you can present check boxes. Experiment to find the presentation you prefer.

COMPLEXITY
INTERMEDIATE

10.4 How do I... Add radio buttons to a form?

COMPATIBILITY: HTML 2 OR ABOVE

Problem

Now that I have a form in my HTML document, I would like to use radio buttons in it so I can let a user pick just one item out of a list. How do I do this?

Technique

Radio buttons are added to forms in much the same manner as check boxes. To create a radio button that allows a user to click on only one of a number of choices from a list, insert an <INPUT> tag between the <FORM> ... </FORM> tags. Inside the <INPUT> tag, set the TYPE to "radio". You may have as many radio buttons as needed, and you may include other HTML tags between these tags.

Steps

The following steps show how to add radio buttons to forms.

1. Decide how many radio buttons you need and how you are going to lay them out on the form. The number is usually quite easy and straightforward to determine. The layout is more of a matter of personal taste and preferences. In this example, you will use one group of radio buttons for a reader to pick a favorite color and another for the reader to pick a favorite food.

2. Open the HTML document that contains the form you wish to add the radio buttons to. For this example, start with the document used in How-To 10.1.

3. Add the <INPUT> tag for the first radio button between the <FORM> ... </FORM>tags. In the <INPUT> tag, set the TYPE to "radio". The basic syntax for this is

```
<INPUT TYPE="radio" NAME="NAME" VALUE=value [CHECKED] > "Text"
```

The TYPE attribute declares this field a radio button. The variable in the NAME attribute is what you will refer to this group of radio buttons as when you later reference them in a script. The VALUE attribute is what this radio button is set to when it is checked. The CHECKED attribute is optional and tells the browser to show this radio button as checked when it is first displayed. "Text" is for whatever text you wish to associate with each particular button.

The tags for the favorite color radio buttons look like this:

```
<INPUT TYPE="radio" NAME="COLOR_RADIO" VALUE=1>Red
<INPUT TYPE="radio" NAME="COLOR_RADIO" VALUE=2>Blue
<INPUT TYPE="radio" NAME="COLOR_RADIO" VALUE=3>Yellow
<INPUT TYPE="radio" NAME="COLOR_RADIO" VALUE=4 CHECKED>Green
```

The tags for the favorite food radio buttons look like this:

```
<INPUT TYPE="radio" NAME="FOOD_RADIO" VALUE=1>Lobster <P>
<INPUT TYPE="radio" NAME="FOOD_RADIO" VALUE=2>Spam<P>
<INPUT TYPE="radio" NAME="FOOD_RADIO" VALUE=3 CHECKED>Chocolate<P>
```

4. Put some heading text near the radio buttons so readers have a good idea of what you want them to do.

5. Enter any other text or HTML tags to help clarify the document and make it easier to read. The document should now resemble the one below.

```
<HTML> <HEAD>
<TITLE>Input Form</TITLE>
</HEAD>
<BODY>
<H2>INPUT FORM radio buttons</H2>
<HR>
<FORM METHOD=POST ACTION="/cgi-bin/MY_SCRIPT">
Enter your name here: <INPUT TYPE="text" NAME="NAME" SIZE=30 VALUE="???"><p>
What is your favorite color:
<P>
<INPUT TYPE="radio" NAME="COLOR_RADIO" VALUE=1>Red
<INPUT TYPE="radio" NAME="COLOR_RADIO" VALUE=2>Blue
<INPUT TYPE="radio" NAME="COLOR_RADIO" VALUE=3>Yellow
<INPUT TYPE="radio" NAME="COLOR_RADIO" VALUE=4 CHECKED>Green
What is your favorite food:
<P>
<INPUT TYPE="radio" NAME="FOOD_RADIO" VALUE=1>Lobster
<INPUT TYPE="radio" NAME="FOOD_RADIO" VALUE=2>Spam
<INPUT TYPE="radio" NAME="FOOD_RADIO" VALUE=3 CHECKED>Chocolate

<INPUT TYPE="submit" NAME="SUBMIT_BUTTON" VALUE="Submit">
<INPUT TYPE="reset" NAME="RESET_BUTTON" VALUE="OOPS">
</FORM>
<HR>
</BODY>
</HTML>
```

10.5 ADD PASSWORD FIELDS TO A FORM

6. Save the document as text or ASCII.
7. Use the Open File command or the Open Local command on your browser to make sure your form looks like Figure 10-5.

Figure 10-5 The form complete with radio buttons

How It Works

The <FORM>...</FORM> tags tell the browser to expect form <INPUT> tags between these two tags. The <INPUT> tag, when the TYPE attribute is set to "radio", creates a radio button for the user to click on to select that choice. You can only select one radio button from any group of buttons associated with the same NAME at any one time. If a particular radio button is clicked on, the variable NAME that refers to that group of radio buttons is set to that button's particular value. Once the Submit button is pushed, the information contained in the form is sent to the HTTP server. To see what radio button was selected, check the NAME variable's value with a CGI script.

Comments

Though radio buttons may resemble check boxes greatly, there is one big difference: Only one radio button from any group of radio buttons may be selected at a time. Therefore, only one name is assigned to the entire group of buttons.

COMPLEXITY
INTERMEDIATE

10.5 How do I...
Add password fields to a form?

COMPATIBILITY: HTML 2 OR ABOVE

Problem

I would like users to enter their password so I can verify that they are who they say they are. How can I let them type their password so a nosy onlooker will not be able to read it?

CHAPTER 10
HTML INTERACTIVE FORMS

Technique

Password fields in forms are displayed as text fields in which the entered text is shown as asterisks. To create a password field, insert an <INPUT> tag between the <FORM> ... </FORM> tags. Inside the <INPUT> tag, set the TYPE to "password". You may have as many password fields as you wish, but you usually only need one.

Steps

The following steps show how to add password fields to forms.

1. Decide how you would like to lay out your form. You will probably want to use only the name and password fields until you can verify that the user is actually who he or she claims to be.

2 Open the HTML document that contains the form you wish to add the password field to. Once again, use the basic document created in How-To 10.1.

3. Add the <INPUT> tag for the password field between the <FORM> ... <FORM> tags. In the <INPUT> tag, set the TYPE to "password". The basic syntax for this is

```
<INPUT TYPE="password" NAME="VARIABLE_NAME" SIZE="number" VALUE="initial value">
```

The TYPE attribute declares this field as a passworded text box. The variable in the NAME attribute is what you will refer to when you later want to check what's been entered here. SIZE is the length of the passworded text field. The VALUE attribute is what this field is initially set to. For example:

```
<INPUT TYPE="password" NAME="PASSWRD" VALUE=secret>
```

4. Put some descriptive text near the field so the reader has a good idea of what you expect him or her to enter.

5. Enter any other text or HTML tags to help clarify the document and make it easier to read. The document should now resemble this:

```
<HTML> <HEAD>
<TITLE>Input Form</TITLE>
</HEAD>
<BODY>
<H2>INPUT FORM passwords</H2>
<HR>
<FORM METHOD=POST ACTION="/cgi-bin/MY_SCRIPT">
Enter your name here: <INPUT TYPE="text" NAME="NAME" SIZE=30 VALUE="???"><p>
What is your password:
<INPUT TYPE="password" NAME="PASSWRD" VALUE=secret>
<P>
<INPUT TYPE="submit" NAME="SUBMIT_BUTTON" VALUE="Submit">
<INPUT TYPE="reset" NAME="RESET_BUTTON" VALUE="OOPS">
</FORM>
```

```
<HR>
</BODY>
</HTML>
```

6. Save the document as text or ASCII.

7. Use the Open File command or Open Local command on your browser to make sure your form looks like Figure 10-6.

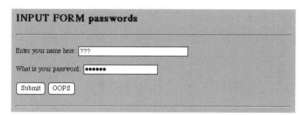

Figure 10-6 The form complete with a password field

How It Works

The <FORM>...</FORM> tags tell the browser to expect form <INPUT> tags between these two tags. The <INPUT> tag, when the TYPE is set to "password", is a text field with text displayed as asterisks. Once the Submit button is pushed, the information contained in the form is sent to the HTTP server. To see what was entered in the field, use the name assigned with the NAME attribute.

Comments

Password fields are, for all intents and purposes, text fields. Instead of displaying what the user typed, the text displays as asterisks. You will still need a CGI script to analyze this password. For information about creating a CGI script, see How-To 10.9.

COMPLEXITY
INTERMEDIATE

10.6 How do I...
Add pulldown menus to a form?

COMPATIBILITY: HTML 2 OR ABOVE

Problem

I would like to allow a reader to select one item from a list of items while showing only the currently selected item on the form. How can I do this?

Technique

Use the <SELECT> ... </SELECT> tags to create a pulldown menu inside a form. To create a pulldown menu, insert the <SELECT> tags between the <FORM> tags. Label each option that can be selected separately with an <OPTION> tag. The form may include other HTML tags and elements.

Steps

The following steps show how to add pulldown menus to forms.

1. Decide which items you wish to place in pulldown menus and how you wish to place these items in your form. Sticking with the food motif, you will create one menu that lets a reader pick a food.

2. Open the HTML document that contains the form you wish to add the pulldown menu to. For now, expand on the document used in How-To 10.1.

3. Add the <SELECT> ... </SELECT> tags between the <FORM> ... <FORM> tags. Between the <SELECT> tags, add each <OPTION> tag:

```
<SELECT NAME="NAME">
<OPTION> An option
.....</SELECT>
```

The variable in the NAME attribute is what you will refer to when you later want to reference this menu. You have one <OPTION> tag for every item in the menu. You may not use any HTML markup tags between these options.

```
<SELECT NAME="MY_PULL_DOWN">
<OPTION>Lobster
<OPTION>Spam
<OPTION>Chocolate
</SELECT>
```

4. Put some descriptive text near the menu so the reader has a good idea of what you want him or her to do.

5. Enter any other text or HTML tags to help clarify the document and make it easier to read. The document should now resemble this:

```
<HTML> <HEAD>
<TITLE>Input Form </TITLE>
</HEAD>
<BODY>
<H2>INPUT FORM pulldown menus</H2>
<HR>
<FORM METHOD=POST ACTION="/cgi-bin/MY_SCRIPT">
Enter your name here: <INPUT TYPE="text" NAME="NAME" SIZE=30 VALUE="???"><p>
Pick a food:
<SELECT NAME="MY_PULL_DOWN">
<OPTION>Lobster
```

10.6
ADD PULLDOWN MENUS TO A FORM

```
<OPTION>Spam
<OPTION>Chocolate
</SELECT>
<P>
<INPUT TYPE="submit" NAME="SUBMIT_BUTTON" VALUE="Submit">
<INPUT TYPE="reset" NAME="RESET_BUTTON" VALUE="OOPS">
</FORM>
<HR>
</BODY>
</HTML>
```

6. Save the document in text or ASCII format.

7. Use the Open File command or Open Local command on your browser to make sure your form looks something like Figure 10-7.

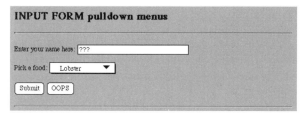

Figure 10-7 The form complete with pulldown menus

How It Works

The <FORM>...</FORM> tags tell the browser to expect associate form tags between these two tags. The <SELECT> ... </SELECT> tags tell the browser to display the text next to each <OPTION> tag as a choice in a pulldown menu. Once the Submit button is clicked, the information contained in the form is sent to the HTTP server. To see what was entered in the field, use the name that was assigned with the NAME attribute. In a pulldown menu, the variable used with the NAME attribute is actually assigned the value in the selected <OPTION> tag.

Comments

Pulldown menus are a kind of cross between check boxes and radio buttons, because they are usually associated with one value. However, it is possible to have more than one option selected at a time. Many people like pulldown menus because they do not use as much space on the screen as check boxes or radio buttons.

CHAPTER 10
HTML INTERACTIVE FORMS

COMPLEXITY
INTERMEDIATE+

10.7 How do I... Pass information between forms?

COMPATIBILITY: HTML 2 OR ABOVE

Problem

I want to build two forms and have the second form contingent on something entered in the first form. Since a form is not accessible again once it is submitted, how can I do this?

Technique

It is possible to pass information between forms with hidden fields. These fields can be accessed by a CGI program or script even after the form has been submitted to determine what course of action to take in building a second form.

Steps

The following steps give a general description of how you can pass information from one form to another. For more complete information on this topic, see Chapter 13.

1. Create an HTML document. For this example, use the one from How-To 10.1.

2. Enter the holder for the hidden field. A hidden field is created with the <INPUT> tag much like a text field.

```
<INPUT TYPE="hidden" NAME="HIDDEN_FIELD"  VALUE="info">
```

Here the TYPE attribute is set to "hidden" so a reader cannot see the field. The NAME attribute is set to whatever name you wish to use to access this field with later. The VALUE attribute is any state information you wish to carry in this field.

```
<HTML> <HEAD>
<TITLE>Input Form</TITLE>
</HEAD>
<BODY>
<HR>
<FORM METHOD=POST ACTION="/cgi-bin/my_script">
Enter your name here: <INPUT TYPE="text" NAME="NAME" SIZE=30 VALUE="John Smith">
<INPUT TYPE="hidden" NAME="HIDDEN_FIELD"  VALUE="info">
<INPUT TYPE="submit" NAME="SUBMIT_BUTTON" VALUE="Submit">
<INPUT TYPE="reset" NAME="RESET_BUTTON" VALUE="OOPS">
```

```
</FORM>
<HR>
</BODY>
</HTML>
```

This form looks identical to the form created in How-To 10.1 when displayed by a browser.

3. After the form is submitted to the server, use a CGI script to refer to the field.

How It Works

When you place a hidden field inside the <FORM> ... </FORM> tags, you create space to hold information. The reader will not see or use this space, but a CGI script can utilize it. You can access this field as you would any other field.

Comments

This is just a very general introduction to this topic, with just enough information to let you recognize it when you see it later. It is very easy to create the hidden field on the form. To utilize this field, though, requires a CGI script written in Perl or C, or some other language. There is an example of this technique and more information on hidden fields in Chapter 13.

10.8 How do I... Choose a request method to send data to the HTTP server?

COMPATIBILITY: HTML 2 OR ABOVE

Problem

Now that my form is all ready to go, what method should I use to send the information to the HTTP server, and how do I tell the form to send this information?

Technique

First decide if you are going to use the "get" or "post" method. This is largely a matter of personal preference, but the consensus seems to be that you should use "post". Use the <INPUT> tag to create a Submit button. When the user selects this button, the information in the form is sent to the HTTP server.

Steps

The following steps give a general overview of the procedure used to decide which method you wish to use when submitting information from a form to a server.

1. Decide what you want to include in your form and how you wish your form to be laid out. For this example, use a simple form that asks a reader for his or her name and comments.

2. Decide which method you wish to use to post your information. You have two choices: "get" or "post". Sometimes this choice is dictated by the type of server your system is using, in which case it is a good idea to call your system administrator and see if he or she recommends one of the two methods. If not, then the choice is a matter of preference. The "post" method seems to be the most common choice.

The "get" method passes the contents of the form as a string in a *query URL*. The server places this string into the environment variable *query_string*.

The "post" method sends the contents as a data block through the standard input stream of the CGI script named in ACTION. The length of this string is stored in the environment variable *content_length*.

No matter which method you choose, the data will still be encoded the same: *field1=content&field2=content&...*

3. Create your HTML document, complete with a form.

```
<HTML><HEAD><TITLE>A Simple Sample Form</TITLE></HEAD>
<BODY>
<HR>
<FORM METHOD=POST ACTION="$ME/post">
Name: <INPUT TYPE="text" NAME="INPUT_NAME" SIZE=30
VALUE="???">
<P>Comment:<TEXTAREA NAME="TEXT_COMMENTS" ROWS=5 COLS=50>
</TEXTAREA>
<P><INPUT TYPE="submit" NAME="SUBMIT_BUTTON" VALUE="SEND">
<HR>
</FORM>
</BODY>
</HTML>
```

4. Save your document in text or ASCII format.

5. Read the next section to see how you can process this and other forms.

How It Works

Selecting the Submit button passes the information in the form to the server. For the above example, if a user entered "John Smith" for "input_name" and "Nice WWW site!" for "text_comments", these would be sent to the server as

```
input_name=John+Smith&text_comments=Nice+WWW+site!
```

It is up to the CGI script processing the form to parse out the data.

Comments

There is much information online that addresses choosing between the "get" and "post" methods. To see what NCSA has to say, access the following URL: http://hoohoo.ncsa.uiuc.edu/docs/setup/admin/NCSAScripts.html

10.9 How do I... Process a form?

COMPLEXITY
INTERMEDIATE+

COMPATIBILITY: HTML 2 OR ABOVE

Problem

Now that I have created this great form, how can I let somebody actually use it over my Web server? Then how can I process the information they send me?

Technique

Information stored in a form is sent to the HTTP server as part of a data stream, either as part of a URL or as a data block. It is possible to use environment variables to extract the user input from this data stream. Processing a form requires a CGI script to act as a sort of go-between among the HTML, the HTTP server, and the information sent in the form. This script may be written in any high-level language your site supports. Favorite choices are Perl and C. The very simple sample script is broken into three parts:

- **HTML** The first part looks at the arguments sent to the server in the URL and determines what actions to take.
- **HTML** The second part displays the form for a user to interact with.
- **HTML** The third part first extracts and decodes the form's information, then processes that information.

Steps

The following procedure uses a form created from techniques used in previous sections of this chapter to show one method to capture and then utilize information from forms.

1. Develop a form that you wish to use. For this example, use a very simple three-item form:

CHAPTER 10
HTML INTERACTIVE FORMS

```
<HTML><HEAD><TITLE>A Simple Sample Form</TITLE></HEAD>
<BODY>
<HR>
<FORM METHOD=POST ACTION="$ME/post">
Name: <INPUT TYPE="text" NAME="INPUT_NAME" SIZE=30
VALUE="???">
<P>Comment:<TEXTAREA NAME="TEXT_COMMENTS" ROWS=5 COLS=50>
</TEXTAREA>
<P><INPUT TYPE="submit" NAME="SUBMIT_BUTTON" VALUE="Submit">
<HR>
</FORM>
</BODY>
</HTML>
```

   2. Create a CGI script in the editor or word processor of your choice. The CGI script in this example is broken up into three parts. The first part, or main program, sets up the routine and decides if the server should send the reader a form to fill out or if the reader has sent the server a form to process. The Perl code for this script appears below.

   The first part of the script is actually broken up into two sections. The first section takes care of the "overhead":

```
#!/usr/bin/perl
$ME = "HTTP://MY_SERVER/cgi-bin/SAMPFORM.CGI";
$PATHINFO = $ENV{PATH_INFO};

print <<EOF;
Content-type: text/HTML

EOF
```

   The first line tells the Perl compiler that this is a Perl script. The next line sets up the address given in the <FORM> tag's ACTION attribute. You should of course replace the "my_server" with your server's URL. The third line grabs the path information from the environment variable *path_info*. This information is used in the next section of the script to determine if the program should send the user a form to fill out, or if the user has sent information from the form. The next four lines initialize the server to expect an HTML document.

```
if ($PATHINFO eq "") {
   &send_form;
} elsif ($PATHINFO =~ m|^/post|){
   &post_form;
}
exit 0;
```

   These lines use the path information to determine what course of action the script is to take. If the path information is blank (""), that means send the user a form to fill out. If the information contains a string that contains

10.9
PROCESS A FORM

the word "post", that means the user has seen the form and pressed the Submit button on the form, and now it is time to process the information in the form.

3. The next part of the script is the *send_form* subroutine. This part outputs to the HTTP server the form you wish the reader to see.

```
sub send_form
{
  print <<EOF ;
<HTML><HEAD><TITLE>A Simple Sample Form</TITLE></HEAD>
<BODY>
<HR>
<FORM METHOD=POST ACTION="$ME/post">
Name: <INPUT TYPE="text" NAME="INPUT_NAME" SIZE=30 VALUE="???">
<P>Comment:<TEXTAREA NAME="TEXT_COMMENTS" ROWS=5 COLS=50> </TEXTAREA>
<P><INPUT TYPE="submit" NAME="SUBMIT_BUTTON" VALUE="Submit">
<HR>
</FORM>
</BODY>
</HTML>
EOF
}
```

This is straightforward. The HTML document prints to the server, allowing a user to interact with the form.

4. The final part of the script is the *post_form* subroutine. This is put into action after the user has submitted the form. This subroutine reads the form's input from the standard input stream, splits the input into appropriate fields and values, then removes any strange characters the server may have added when it encoded the input. You are now free to access the information contained in the form via the names assigned to each field.

```
sub post_form
{
# Get the input.
  read(STDIN, $BUFFER, $ENV{'CONTENT_LENGTH'});
  # Split the name-value pairs.
  @pairs = split(/&/, $buffer);
  foreach $PAIR (@pairs)
  {
    ($NAME, $VALUE) = split(/=/, $pair);
# Un-Webify plus signs and %-encoding
    $VALUE =~ tr/+/ /;
    $VALUE =~ s/%([a-fA-F0-9][a-fA-F0-9])/pack("C", hex($1))/eg;
    $FORM{$NAME} = $VALUE;
  }
```

Without diving too much into Perl (there are other Waite Group Press books on that subject), it is sufficient to say here that this code reads the contents of the standard input into a variable called "$BUFFER". The string in

"$BUFFER" is a *content_length* bytes long string of continuous data sent like this:

```
INPUT_NAME=john+smith&text_comments=nice+web+server
```

The next few lines of code use the split command to separate variables and their values. The lines after that remove those + signs from the value and translate any encoded characters.

```
  print <<EOF ;
<HTML>
<HEAD><TITLE>Here's what was input</TITLE></HEAD>
<BODY>
The name entered was: $FORM{'INPUT_NAME'}. <P>Their comments are
$FORM{'TEXT_COMMENTS'}.
</BODY></HTML>
EOF
```

The final part of this routine outputs another HTML document that utilizes the information sent in the form. To use the person's name in the form, refer to it by "$FORM{'INPUT_NAME'}". This "$FORM{'INPUT_NAME'}" is replaced in the outputted HTML document by "John Smith".

5. The script is now complete. Save it with whatever name you think best describes it. For this example, simply call it sampform.cgi.

```
SAMPFORM.CGI
```

6. If you created your script with a word processor or editor on a system other than the system your server resides on, you will need to transfer the script to the appropriate spot on your server system. Check with your system administrator for information on how to do this for your particular system.

7. Once the script is on the server, change the access rights to the script. Most HTML documents do not need a user to execute them, but CGI scripts do. The mode should be changed to

```
chmod 755 sampform.cgi
```

8. A script that will not run on your server will not work. Compile the script to make sure there are no errors. To compile the script type either

```
SAMPFORM.CGI
```

or

```
perl sampform.cgi
```

If all went well, this should output something that looks like this:

```
Content-type: text/HTML
```

10.9
PROCESS A FORM

```
<HTML><HEAD><TITLE>A Simple Sample Form</TITLE></HEAD>
<BODY>
<HR>
Send me your comments:<BR>
<FORM METHOD=POST ACTION="MY_SERVER/cgi-bin/SAMPFORM.CGI/post">
Name: <INPUT TYPE="text" NAME="INPUT_NAME" SIZE=30 VALUE="???">
<P>Comment:<TEXTAREA NAME="TEXT_COMMENTS" ROWS=5 COLS=50> </TEXTAREA>
<P><INPUT TYPE="submit" NAME="SUBMIT_BUTTON" VALUE="Submit">
<HR>
</FORM>
</BODY>
</HTML>
```

9. Access the CGI script over the Web by using the Open Location command in your browser's menu. Then enter the URL specified by the METHOD action. For example, to use the CGI script used in the sample, type

HTTP://MY_SERVER/cgi-bin/sampform.cgi

replacing "my_server" with your server's actual URL. When first accessed, the form should look much like Figure 10-8.

Once the form is submitted the screen will look like Figure 10-9.

How It Works

The first part of the script sets the table and checks the path_info environment variable to see if the server has sent anything to the script. If nothing was sent, the script sends an HTML document for the browser to display. If the path information contains "post", the server has sent a form that must be processed. The fields are encoded, so they must first be separated, then stripped of all the characters the

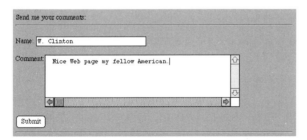

Figure 10-8 The form served by the sample script

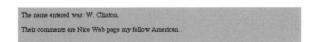

Figure 10-9 The form's information after it is processed

system adds. After this, the information in the fields may be accessed by referring to their variable names. An in-depth analysis of how CGI and forms interact goes beyond the scope of this chapter and will be covered later in Chapter 13. Still, you do not need a total understanding of the form and CGI interaction to successfully use forms.

Comments

Not all system administrators allow users to have their own CGI scripts. It is a good idea to check with your system administrator before starting. Not only will he or she be able to tell you if you can place scripts on your server, the administrator can probably also point you in the right direction. The script given here is a very bare-bones script. It doesn't have any error checking or safety precautions built into it. Plus, the form could have contained other types of form tags. Still, it should give you the basic idea of how CGI and forms interact with each other. Experiment by plugging in your own forms.

For more information on forms and CGI look in the Yahoo directory at http://www.yahoo.com/Computers_and_Internet/Internet/World_Wide_Web/Programming/Forms/.

The final complete CGI script used at the end of this chapter looks like this:

```
#!/usr/bin/perl
#
# This is a CGI script which lets users interact with a form.
# If the CGI PATH_INFO passed to us is empty, then we just
# return a HTML document with a form allowing the user to post
# feedback. If the CGI PATH_INFO is set to post, the user's feedback
# is shown to them
#
#
# URL for this script (without arguments) on this server. Note: this
# server using WN this URL would look slightly different with NCSA
#    "http://address/cgi-bin/name"
#
# Note: the examples use variable names in upper case as per the WPG standard
# only here variable names are in lower case as in the Perl standard
#
# Note: I am using my server's actual URL in this example

$me = "http://zeb.nysaes.cornell.edu/cgi-bin/SAMPFORM.cgi";

# side note: this example is written with NCSA server in mind, but if the WN
# server was used the /cgi-bin/ directory would not be needed as WN can recognize
# that a file is a cgi script by the .cgi suffix.

# Get the argument from the URL.

$pathinfo = $ENV{PATH_INFO};

# Start out by sending a content-type for the document we'll be returning.
```

10.9
PROCESS A FORM

```perl
print <<EOF;
Content-type: text/html

EOF

# See what we're supposed to be doing.

if ($pathinfo eq "") {
  &send_form;
} elsif ($pathinfo =~ m|^/post|){
  &post_form;
}
exit 0;

# &send_form; returns a menu of available options for this gateway
#script.

sub send_form
{
#
# The form for them to interact with -- you can plug your own in
# here...
#
  print <<EOF ;
<HTML><HEAD><TITLE>A Simple Sample Form</TITLE></HEAD>
<BODY>
Send me your comments:<BR>
<HR>
<FORM METHOD=POST ACTION="$me/post">
Name: <INPUT TYPE="text" NAME="input_name" SIZE=30 VALUE="???">
<P>Comment:<TEXTAREA NAME="text_comments" ROWS=5 COLS=50> </TEXTAREA>
<P><INPUT TYPE="submit" NAME="submit_button" VALUE="Submit">
<HR>
</FORM>
</BODY>
</HTML>
EOF

}
# post_form; show them what they entered

sub post_form
{
# Get the input.
  read(STDIN, $buffer, $ENV{'CONTENT_LENGTH'});
  # Split the name-value pairs.
  @pairs = split(/&/, $buffer);
  foreach $pair (@pairs)
  {
    ($name, $value) = split(/=/, $pair);
# Un-Webify plus signs and %-encoding
    $value =~ tr/+/ /;
    $value =~ s/%([a-fA-F0-9][a-fA-F0-9])/pack("C", hex($1))/eg;
    $form{$name} = $value;
  }
```

continued on next page

continued from previous page
```
#
#The form we're outputting based on what the user gave us -- you
#can modify this to meet your requirements
#
   print <<EOF ;
<HTML>
<HEAD><TITLE>Here's what was input</TITLE></HEAD>
<BODY>
The name entered was: $form{'input_name'}. <P>Their comments are
$form{'text_comments'}.
</BODY></HTML>
EOF
}
```

PART 3
SERVING

HOW TO ADMINISTER AND DEVELOP A SERVER SITE FOR HTML DOCUMENTS

CHAPTER 11
SERVER BASICS

SERVER BASICS

How do I...

11.1 Choose server software?
11.2 Install server software?
11.3 Configure the server?
11.4 Register additional MIME types?
11.5 Install documents?
11.6 Start or stop the server?
11.7 Register my server?
11.8 Use Netscape's Client Pull?

A Web server is an application that listens to the Internet, awaiting connections and requests from Web browsers and other user agents, such as search engines. The server examines a request, and, if it is appropriate, supplies the requested services. For most casual users, this abridged description is enough. However, if you are developing your own Web site, you will find the How-To's in this chapter of great benefit.

Browsers use the HyperText Transfer Protocol, or HTTP, to communicate with servers. This is a generic protocol language developed specifically for the transmission of hypertext documents across the Internet. Whenever you specify a URL with the HTTP protocol prefix, you are requesting the use of this protocol to transmit the referenced document. Browsers send an appropriate HTTP request to the specified server.

Servers respond to user agent requests with a two-part response. The first component of the response, the response header, contains a variety of information about the server handling the request and the file or data being sent. For example, the type information is in the response header; this information is used by many browsers to determine whether a helper application is needed to process the object being sent. The second part of the response is the message body. The content of this component is the actual data from the requested file, whether it is an HTML 3 document, an AIFF audio segment, or data of some other type.

This chapter introduces information necessary for establishing and maintaining a Web site. This includes directions for server configuration, document installation, and addition of file types. The examples concentrate on the NCSA HTTPD server package, which serves as the basis for both other UNIX-based servers, such as Netscape's Commerce Server, and servers for other platforms, such as WinHTTPD for Windows 3.1 and Website for Windows NT.

Chapters 12 and 13 discuss server security and gateway application development, respectively.

11.1 Choose Server Software

Once you decide that you are going to establish a server, you need to select and find the appropriate server software. What is appropriate depends upon several factors, such as hardware, operating system, and reliability. This How-To will help you make the right choice.

11.2 Install Server Software

Each server software package will have its own installation guide and requirements. The general installation tasks are similar; however, specific installation details are slightly different from server to server. This How-To examines in detail the installation process for the HTTPD server software developed by NCSA.

11.3 Configure the Server

Each Web site has its own requirements and restrictions. Therefore, simply downloading and installing the software may not be enough to establish a working Web site. This How-To provides information concerning configuring an HTTP server for your site. The specifics of configuring an NCSA HTTPD server are discussed in detail.

11.4 Register Additional MIME Types

Documents of various types can be stored on HTTP servers. Servers specify document types using Multipurpose Internet Mail Extension (MIME) types. The server must know the type of each document so that it can perform its tasks appropriately. If you add a document of a new type to the server, you must register this new type. This How-To describes how you register new types.

11.5 Install Documents

The primary purpose of the server is to respond to requests for documents. To do so, the server must know where documents are stored. This How-To provides directions for installing documents on an NCSA HTTPD server, or on derivative servers such as WinHTTPD.

11.6 Start or Stop the Server

The server must be active to receive requests from clients. Activate the server by starting it, and deactivate it by stopping it. These functions are performed as required for maintenance of the server. This How-To describes how you stop and start a UNIX server.

11.7 Register My Server

When your server site runs properly, you will want to let others know it exists. The instructions in this How-To outline a procedure for introducing your site to the World Wide Web community.

11.8 Use Netscape's Client Pull

The Netscape Client Pull feature provides a means for automatically loading new documents at specified time intervals. This capability provides support for slide shows as well as text-based animation. This How-To explains how to use the Netscape Client Pull feature in your documents.

11.1 How do I... Choose server software?

COMPLEXITY
INTERMEDIATE

COMPATIBILITY: ANY SERVER

Problem

How do I choose server software for my Web site? What are the issues involved? Why is one platform or server more efficient or reliable than another? I need to know what my options are and how I can evaluate these options.

Technique

The purpose of server software is to appropriately respond to client requests. This involves listening for client requests (perhaps simultaneous requests), evaluating them, and generating suitable responses.

To choose the software that best suits your needs, you must first evaluate the capabilities of your hardware and operating system. Use the evaluation in steps 1–3 below to determine whether your platform is adequate for your needs or if you should move to a different one.

CHAPTER 11
SERVER BASICS

Once you have determined your optimal hardware and operating system platform, consider the various server software packages. Select the packages that best meet your needs, according to the criteria that appear in step 4 below.

Finally, acquire your chosen server software, either from the manufacturer or by using FTP.

Steps

This How-To presents step-by-step instructions for evaluating and selecting the appropriate server software package to meet the needs of your Web site. To acquire a particular package, you need to be familiar with the use of anonymous FTP or FTP URLs (unless the chosen package is a commercial product, in which case you will need to contact the appropriate vendor). Appendix F provides a summary of several available server packages.

1. Identify your hardware platform. The list below specifies several hardware platforms suitable to a Web server site.

- **HTML** Apple Macintosh computer and compatibles
- **HTML** IBM PCs, PC compatibles
- **HTML** SUN systems
- **HTML** DEC computer systems

2. Identify the operating system(s) running on your hardware platform. You may need to consult your system's manuals to determine this information. Server software has been developed for the following operating systems.

- **HTML** Mac OS
- **HTML** NEXT operating system
- **HTML** IBM OS/2
- **HTML** UNIX
- **HTML** VMS
- **HTML** MS Windows environment
- **HTML** MS Windows/NT environment

3. Your hardware and operating system greatly affect your choice of server software, since each HTTP server has been engineered for a single platform. If you have a choice of platforms, the following list shows, in decending order, the optimal choices in operating systems for a server site. This order assumes similar processing and memory capabilities on the hardware. The How It Works section below discusses the basis for this order.

- **HTML** UNIX

11.1
CHOOSE SERVER SOFTWARE

- **HTML** VMS
- **HTML** Windows NT, OS/2
- **HTML** Windows, Mac OS

4. Based upon your platform, you are now ready to select a server. You need to think about the features you wish to support on your server. Some of these key issues are described below.

- **HTML** **Hardware and software platform support**
  This criterion places the first restriction upon your choice of server packages. Appendix F provides a brief summary of server software packages by operating system. Each description in this appendix ends with a URL that provides additional information on the specified server.

- **HTML** **Security**
  Different server packages provide different levels and types of security. Levels of security range from restricting access to the entire server to restricting access to individual documents. Access may be restricted by machine address, user name and password, or both.

- **HTML** **Gateway interface compliance**
  Many applications work in conjunction with HTTP server software. These applications serve as gateways between a Web server and resources available at the server site. A common interface specification for such applications is the Common Gateway Interface (CGI), which is explained in Chapter 13. (For current release information, see http://hoohoo.ncsa.uiuc.edu/cgi/overview.html.) However, servers support this interface to varying degrees from full compliance to no gateway application support at all.

- **HTML** **Firewall support**
  Firewalls are another type of security feature. A firewall limits Internet traffic between machines inside and outside the firewall. Running behind a firewall limits your selection of server packages.

- **HTML** **Search capabilities**
  What kind and depth of search capability do you want built into the server software? Additional search capabilities can be built with gateway applications; however, certain server packages directly support searching.

- **HTML** **File inclusion support**
  File inclusion allows your server to incorporate files from your server site into the HTML documents that it distributes. For

instance, this feature could be used to include a standard business letterhead on all the HTML documents at your site.

HTML **Request types supported**
HTTP supports many request types. The most common type is the "get" request, supported by most servers. (Appendix G provides detailed information on additional request types.) Requests for HTML documents are usually the result of "get" requests from browsers.

5. Once you select a list of criteria, you are ready to choose among the various HTTP server software packages available for your platform. Consult Appendix F for a brief description of many commonly used servers.

6. Contact the server software manufacturer or use FTP to acquire your chosen server software. The example below demonstrates how you might use anonymous FTP to acquire the NCSA HTTPD server from a UNIX machine. Open an FTP connection to the ftp.ncsa.uiuc.edu site. Then enter

```
glean dsk 151 >ftp ftp.ncsa.uiuc.edu
Connected to ftp.ncsa.uiuc.edu.
220 curley FTP server (Version wu-2.4(25) Thu Aug 25 13:14:21 CDT 1994) ready.
```

7. When prompted, enter the name "anonymous". For a password, enter your e-mail address.

```
Name (ftp.ncsa.uiuc.edu:dsk): anonymous
331 Guest login ok, send your complete e-mail address as password.
Password:
230 Guest login ok, access restrictions apply.
```

8. Change directories to the location of the current version of HTTPD by entering the following command.

```
ftp> cd Web/httpd/Unix/ncsa_httpd/current
```

9. Change the transfer mode to binary using the binary command.

```
ftp> binary
200 Type set to I.
```

10. Issue the appropriate get command to retrieve the server package appropriate for your UNIX platform.

```
ftp> get httpd_1.4.1_sunos4.1.3.tar.Z
200 PORT command successful.
150 Opening BINARY mode data connection for httpd_1.4.1_sunos4.1.3.tar.Z
(296970 bytes).
226 Transfer complete.
local: httpd_1.4.1_sunos4.1.3.tar.Z remote: httpd_1.4.1_sunos4.1.3.tar.Z
296970 bytes received in 72 seconds (4 Kbytes/s)
```

11.1
CHOOSE SERVER SOFTWARE

How It Works

If you are establishing a Web site for providing information to the World Wide Web community, consider several platform issues. First, your server site must run reliably 24 hours a day. You cannot know at what time or from what location accesses will be made; therefore, your hardware and operating system platform must run reliably on a constant basis (or as constant as possible).

In addition, your server should be efficient. You want to be able to service many incoming requests as quickly as possible. Popular sites service thousands of requests a day. These requests could be spaced over the entire day or could be made within a single hour. In a perfect world, closely spaced or even simultaneous requests would be serviced as quickly as those made at wider intervals. Your hardware and software will have a significant impact upon this performance.

Finally, you should consider the maintenance of a server on your platform. A server should be easily maintained and updated. Keep in mind that, in some cases, ease of maintenance decreases as the number of supported features increases.

With these needs in mind, the available server platforms can be prioritized from most suitable to least as follows: UNIX, VMS, Windows/NT or OS/2, and Windows or Macintosh. The UNIX operating system features true multitasking, the ability to run many processes at the same time. This capability makes it possible for an HTTP server to answer many simultaneous requests. Further, the UNIX operating system provides a clear separation between user processes, such as an HTTP server, and operating system tasks, such as printer manager. This capability improves the reliability of your server significantly. Your server will remain intact under high system loads and will have a reduced likelihood of system crashes. Finally, the UNIX platform was the first to be used for HTTP server development; consequently, many new features and capabilities are added to UNIX servers before they reach servers for other platforms.

Your next best option is a VMS server. Like UNIX, VMS provides significant operating system level support for an HTTP server. Both multitasking and separation of user and operating system tasks are supported.

Windows NT and OS/2 are about equally desirable. They both support servers that, in general, are easier to configure, particularly if you are unfamiliar with UNIX or VMS. They also support both multitasking and task separation, although not as strongly as these features are supported in UNIX or VMS.

Finally, DOS, Windows, and Macintosh are the least favorable for establishing a stable Web site. None of these environments supports true multitasking, nor do they support task separation particularly well. Windows and Macintosh systems simulate a limited form of multitasking, but not to the same degree as either UNIX or VMS. The lack of true multitasking leads to sluggish response time, which increases quickly with the number of requests. The lack of task separation leads to reduced reliability in general; user applications can cause system crashes that place your Web site out of commission until the system is rebooted. System crashes for a single user are annoying, but system crashes for your Web site mean that your site is dead to the world.

For some of the platforms mentioned above, server selection is limited; however, for several, a significant selection with varying capabilities is available. Therefore, consider the features you wish to support when choosing your platform and server.

Comments

Most Web administrators agree that HTML 3.0 documents are best distributed over the Web through the combination of a UNIX-based machine and either the NCSA or CERN HTTP servers. Both of these servers are freely available respectively from URLs http://hoohoo.ncsa.uiuc.edu/docs/Overview.html and http://www.w3.org/hypertext/WWW/Daemon/Status.html.

Finding a UNIX machine is not as difficult a task as it might sound. The Linux operating system is a UNIX clone that has been developed for PC-compatible computers. This operating system is freely available, and information can be found at URL http://sunsite.unc.edu/mdw/linux.html. Seriously consider this option for establishing a reliable, low-cost Web site. Even though Linux runs on a 386 platform, you can greatly increase the reliability and efficiency of your Web site if you have a 486 or Pentium-based system, preferably with more than 16 megabytes of RAM.

11.2 How do I... Install server software?

COMPLEXITY
INTERMEDIATE

COMPATIBILITY: ANY SERVER

Problem

I have selected and acquired my server software. Now I need to install it correctly on my system. NCSA HTTPD server software is one of the most commonly used UNIX-based server packages, and it has been ported to a variety of other platforms. How do I install this package?

Technique

Server software is usually acquired in a compressed archive. This software must then be uncompressed and unarchived to an appropriate location on your hard disk. If a suitable executable copy of the server software has been acquired, the process is complete; otherwise, the server software package needs to be compiled prior to use.

11.2
INSTALL SERVER SOFTWARE

This How-To explains how to install the NCSA HTTPD server. A similar process is required by most server packages; examine your documentation to install your server software.

Steps

The steps below outline the procedure for installing the NCSA HTTPD server on a UNIX system, although many of the instructions given for this server will also apply to other platforms. These instructions are also suitable for updating the server software.

1. If you have a compressed, archive version of this program, you must first uncompress the archive file; if the file is not compressed, you may proceed with step 2. Use the following command to uncompress for the server archive.

```
uncompress httpd_1.4.1_sunos4.1.3.tar.Z
```

2. Unarchive your server software archive. Install the software in an appropriate location on your hard disk. If you have already unarchived and installed your server software in a suitable location, proceed with step 3. This step varies by platform; however, in general, you should place your server software in a location that you can easily access and maintain. The following example shows the installation of the NCSA HTTPD software in the /usr/local directory.

```
glean# ls
adm    include
bin    lib
conf   man
etc    typescript
httpd_1.4.1_sunos4.1.3.tar
glean# tar xf httpd_1.4.1_sunos4.1.3.tar
glean# ls
adm    httpd_1.4.1_sunos4.1.3.tar
bin    include
conf   lib
etc    man
httpd_1.4.1 typescript
```

3. This step is optional, but it is recommended for platforms capable of creating aliases. Create an alias to the location where you installed your server software. This link can be referenced when starting your server rather than the installation directory created in step 2. Thus, when you update the server, your references to your server application need not change. When an update is made, install the new version as specified in steps 1 through 2, and link the update to the old alias. This process is shown in the example below, which demonstrates the creation of an alias for a server installation under UNIX followed by an update to point to a new server installation.

```
glean# ls -l
total 10
lrwxrwxrwx  1 root           10 Jun 15 15:36 httpd -> httpd_1.3R
drwxr-sr-x  2 root          512 Jun 15 15:36 httpd_1.3R
drwxr-sr-x  8 524           512 May 21 23:37 httpd_1.4.1
glean# rm httpd
rm: remove httpd? y
glean# ln -s httpd_1.4.1 httpd
glean# ls -l
total 10
lrwxrwxrwx  1 root           11 Jun 15 15:38 httpd -> httpd_1.4.1
drwxr-sr-x  2 root          512 Jun 15 15:38 httpd_1.3R
drwxr-sr-x  8 524           512 May 21 23:37 httpd_1.4.1
```

4. Finally, create the root directory of your data tree. The root directory is the base of your document hierarchy, the top-level directory where you place most of your Web documents. If you plan to run multiple servers, providing access to multiple hierarchies, select several locations. Choose these locations based upon the goals for the particular data tree. For most situations, you need to choose a hard disk with adequate space for your documents. If your data tree will be relatively static and development has already been completed, you should have a good idea how much disk space is required; however, if the document tree is dynamically changing and growing, you may need to link space from a large drive to your chosen location. The example below demonstrates this task on a UNIX platform.

```
glean# df
Filesystem        kbytes     used    avail  capacity  Mounted on
/dev/sd3a          32791     4102    25410     14%    /
/dev/sd3d         281599   168051    99469     63%    /usr
/dev/sd3e          47185     6347    38479     14%    /var
/dev/sd3g         516811   484585     6386     99%    /export/tools/sparc.sunos.4
/dev/sd3h         807204    40134   726710      5%    /export/home/00
swap              281280       16   281264      0%    /tmp
schemer:/export/home/00/users/dsk
                 1255494   546059   646661     46%    /tmp_mnt/home/dsk
schemer:/export/home/00/users/omonroe
                 1255494   546059   646661     46%    /tmp_mnt/home/omonroe
glean# mkdir /export/home/00/htdocs
glean# ls -F /export/home/00
ht1/       htdocs/          lost+found/   shen@     users/
```

How It Works

Installing server software is usually a straightforward process. Configuring and administering the server is where the complexity increases. You can acquire server

11.2
INSTALL SERVER SOFTWARE

software through either anonymous FTP or via an FTP URL. How-To 11.1 provides an example of using anonymous FTP to acquire server software. Figure 11-1 shows how you could use Netscape and an FTP URL to acquire the same server package.

Software packages are often stored on archive sites in compressed and archived formats. In the UNIX world, compression and archival support often use two separate utilities. For PCs and Macintoshes, these functions are usually supported through the same application. For proper installation, the package needs to be uncompressed and unarchived.

Where you place the server software package is often determined by your convenience; you will need to have access to the configuration files as well as the executable programs. The space required by the server software is fairly fixed; therefore, you won't need large amounts of extra disk space beyond the server software requirements. You may wish, however, to retain enough space to potentially install the next version of the software when it becomes available. Step 3 above shows you how to prepare for such an eventuality. Creating a link to the installation directory and specifying server-related files with respect to this link makes such upgrades easier to manage; all you need to do is replace the link to the old version with a link to the new version.

Finally, choose a location to serve as the root of your data tree. Most servers provide a way to address HTML 3.0 documents and other Web objects outside this hierarchy. However, for security, most documents should reside in this location. The more documents outside this controlled area, the higher the security risk. If

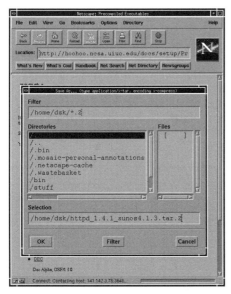

Figure 11-1 Use of FTP URL to acquire NCSA HTTPD server

you plan on running multiple independent servers from your computer, choose several such locations. Figure 11-2 shows a diagram of a UNIX directory hierarchy and displays a potential choice for the root of a data tree.

This choice usually depends on the amount of free disk space in a particular partition. If you expect your Web site to grow, extra space is essential. If your document set is fixed, free disk space may not be as important.

Comments

Many servers—such as OS2HTTPD, WinHTTPD, Website, and others—are based upon the NCSA HTTPD server; consequently, the installation procedures given above for the UNIX HTTPD server apply to them as well. Still, be careful to read the specific installation instructions provided with your server software.

Keep in mind that server software development is an ongoing process; therefore, both software and documentation may change from one day to the next. You should pay attention to the developments and evolution of the server package you choose and make upgrades as new products become stable and available.

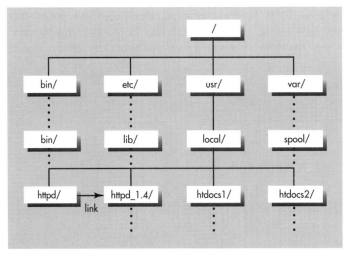

Figure 11-2 UNIX directory hierarchy

11.3 How do I... Configure the server?

COMPLEXITY: ADVANCED

COMPATIBILITY: HTTPD-BASED SERVERS

Problem

I need to tailor the server environment to my needs. What are the various attributes that I need to set? Where are they located, and what values do they take? Can I configure multiple servers to run on the same machine?

Technique

Most servers require three general types of configuration:

- **HTML** Server configuration
- **HTML** Resource configuration
- **HTML** Security configuration

These three configurations tell the server how it should run, what resources it has at its disposal and where they are, and who has access to which resources. The manner in which these configurations are performed may vary among servers; however, most servers require at least the first two to be done prior to startup.

The procedure below provides instructions for performing the first two of the three types of configuration for the NCSA HTTPD server. Initial security configuration is also described for this package. (Configuring and maintaining server security is covered in detail in Chapter 12.) For performing tasks specific to other software, read the documentation for your server software.

Steps

The following procedures provide instructions for configuring an NCSA HTTPD server. The individual steps walk you through tasks in the configuration process. For further information on configuring an NCSA HTTPD server, see NCSA's online documentation at URL http://hoohoo.ncsa.uiuc.edu/docs/setup/Configure.html. Configuration of the WinHTTPD server software is very similar, so hints for configuring this server are included in the steps below as well. The configuration of these server packages entails including the correct commands in the correct configuration file. Configuration file commands are also referred to as directives.

Choosing a Directory

You need to provide a directory for each independent server running on your host machine. This directory contains the configuration files, log files, and possibly unique icons and gateway applications associated with the particular server.

Change directories to the location where you wish to configure the server. If this is your primary server, the configuration directory can be the same as your installation directory. To properly configure a second server, you need to copy the necessary configuration files to another location. The example below demonstrates the creation of a new directory for configuring a second NCSA HTTPD server.

```
glean# cd /usr/local
glean# ls
adm      conf      httpd            include          man
bin      etc       httpd_1.4.1      lib
glean# mkdir httpd2
glean# cp -r httpd/conf httpd2
glean# ls httpd2/conf
access.conf-dist     mime.types
httpd.conf-dist      srm.conf-dist
glean# mkdir httpd2/log
```

Server Configuration

Once you have chosen or created a configuration directory, you must perform any necessary server configuration tasks. For NCSA HTTPD, this process involves editing the httpd.conf file. (For WinHTTPD, this is the httpd.cnf file.)

1. Open httpd.conf in your favorite text editor.

2. Configure (UNIX HTTPD only) the ServerType directive. This directive can take one of two values: "standalone" or "inetd". "Standalone" configures the server to run by itself, while "inetd" specifies that the server be controlled by the inetd process, an application that monitors various network functions. Stand-alone servers tend to run more efficiently than inetd-controlled servers, due to reduced overhead. To establish a stand-alone server, the following line should appear in the configuration file.

```
ServerType standalone
```

Servers using inetd require a slightly different configuration approach than a stand-alone server. Examine URL http://hoohoo.ncsa.uiuc.edu/docs/setup/Configure.html for more information on configuring an inetd server.

3. Assign a port number for the server. The default port for HTTP servers is port 80. To use this port, you must start the server as the privileged user, "root". Port numbers less than 1023 are reserved for the various network services provided by the UNIX operating system. Some common port choices for servers are 1080 and 8080. To configure a server to listen at port 8080, issue the Port command.

```
Port 8080
```

11.3
CONFIGURE THE SERVER

4. UNIX allows you to start several server processes running at startup. Specify the initial number and the maximum number using the StartServers and MaxServers directives. The default values for these directives are, respectively, 5 and 20. You can change these values depending on your hardware capabilities and the volume of traffic you expect. The following lines establish these default values.

```
StartServers 5
MaxServers 20
```

5. Assign (in a UNIX HTTPD configuration) the user and group names for the individual who runs the httpd process. For security, you may not wish the server to run with the privileges of the individual who is executing the httpd process; you probably do not want the server to run as the privileged user, "root"—even if "root" actually starts the server. To configure the server to run as if it were run by username "me" and group "mygroup", issue the following directives in the configuration file.

```
User me
Group mygroup
```

You can specify the values for these directives by user or group names or by user or group numbers. If you use numbers, precede the specific number with the pound sign (#).

6. Next, set the name (e-mail address) of the individual administering this server with the ServerAdmin directive. The following line sets me@www.mysite.edu as the administrator for this server.

```
ServerAdmin me@www.mysite.edu
```

7. Add a line to specify the base address of the directory in the file system you will use to store the various server files. For example, the following line in your configuration file would establish /usr/local/http2 as the base location for your server files.

```
ServerRoot /usr/local/http2
```

8. Specify the location of the various log files used by the server. Specify where the error, transfer, agent, and referer logs are located. If the specified path does not begin with a slash (/), the path is relative based upon the path specified with the ServerRoot directive. Use the following lines to set these locations.

```
ErrorLog logs/error_log
TransferLog logs/access_log
AgentLog logs/agent_log
RefererLog logs/referer_log
```

9. Specify where the process ID for the primary server process will be stored. Use the PidFile directive to specify this information. As with the log files, this specification can be either relative to the server root directory or absolute.

```
PidFile logs/httpd.pid
```

10. Specify how the server refers to itself by using the ServerName directive. Many Web sites use servers with names beginning with "www" as server names. However, simply placing this name in the configuration file will not make this name usable by the outside world. To accomplish this, you must contact your network administrator to use the new name as an alias for your machine. The following line would establish www.mysite.edu as the name of a server.

```
ServerName www.mysite.edu
```

11. Once you have completed the configuration, save this file and configure the server resources.

Resource Configuration

Next, you must configure the resources available to the server. This involves telling the server where it can locate a variety of resources. You can configure this aspect of the NCSA HTTPD server by editing the srm.conf file (WinHTTPD: srm.cnf).

1. Open srm.conf in your favorite text editor.
2. Set the location of your data tree with the DocumentRoot directive. For example, the following line sets the document root to be located in the /export/home/00/htdocs directory.

```
DocumentRoot /export/home/00/htdocs
```

3. Specify the subdirectory of individual user directories visible to this server. This subdirectory is commonly called public_html. (This directive is not supported by WinHTTPD.) If you wish the subdirectory accessible by the server to be referred to as www_docs, you would issue the following directive.

```
UserDir www_docs
```

If someone wished to access a document called doc.htm from the home directory of user through your server, they would use the URL http://www.mysite.edu/~user/doc.htm.

11.3
CONFIGURE THE SERVER

4. The DirectoryIndex directive specifies the name of the default file to open when none is given in a URL addressing the site. If an individual accesses your server without specifying a particular file (for example, http://www.mysite.edu/), the server responds with a predefined default file. The default name used by NCSA HTTPD is index.html (WinHTTPD: index.htm). If a directory does not have a prewritten index, a directory index may be generated dynamically. The following code specifies that the default directory indexes are in files named index.htm.

```
DirectoryIndex index.htm
```

5. The access control information for each directory is stored in a single file. Configure the name of this file with the AccessFileName directive. The default specification appears below.

```
AccessFileName .htaccess
```

See Chapter 12 for information on how to use directory-level access control files.

6. You may register additional document types provided by this server. Several methods for performing this task are described in detail in How-To 11.4.

7. If the server cannot determine the document type of a requested file, it provides a default type in the response to the request. Use the DefaultType directive to designate the default document type that the server uses. In most cases, the Multipurpose Internet Mail Extension (MIME) type "text/plain" is an appropriate value for this attribute. (See Appendix C for additional information on MIME types.) You could use the following line of code to designate this default type:

```
DefaultType text/plain
```

8. You may associate icons with particular document types. For example, a folder icon could be associated with a directory. HTTPD-based servers come with several specified default icons that you may optionally replace or extend with your own. When you issue the AddIcon directive, specify the filename extension with which you desire to associate an icon, as well as the location of the icon on the hard disk. Specify this location using any path aliases that you establish for this server with Alias directives. So, for example, to establish an alias for the icons directory in the /usr/local/http2 directory, and then associate an icon with movie files, issue the following set of directives.

```
Alias /icons/ /usr/local/etc/httpd/icons/
AddIcon /icons/movie.xbm .mpg .qt
```

NCSA HTTPD allows you to establish up to 20 separate directory aliases for your server.

9. HTTPD-based servers provide a special alias for the directory containing CGI applications. (See Chapter 13 for a detailed description of CGI programs.) Specify this location with the ScriptAlias directive. For example, if you want to specify /cgi-bin/ as the alias for this directory, and the actual location of this directory is /usr/local/httpd/cgi-bin, use the following line of code in your configuration file.

```
ScriptAlias /cgi-bin/ /usr/local/httpd/cgi-bin/
```

10. Save this configuration file and proceed with the security configuration.

Security Configuration

Finally, you must configure security. The steps in this section provide a method for configuring an HTTPD-based server with limited security. This represents a bare-bones configuration that allows you to get your server up and running. For advanced security configuration and for security configuration of other servers, see Chapter 12 and the documentation for your server software.

You can configure the security of an NCSA HTTPD server by editing the access.conf file (WinHTTPD: access.cnf).

1. Open access.conf in your favorite text editor.
2. Specify the location of the standard server script directory. The entry contained in the distribution file assumes a default location. The default entry appears in the following code.

```
<Directory /usr/local/etc/httpd/cgi-bin>
Options Indexes FollowSymLinks
</Directory>
```

To modify this entry, change the /usr/local/etc/httpd/ portion of the directory path to wherever you placed the script directory. This is usually in the server root directory (ServerRoot) in a subdirectory called cgi-bin.

3. Modify the second Directory element to point to the root of your data tree. The default entry appears below.

```
<Directory /usr/local/etc/httpd/htdocs>
```

Modify this entry to point to the directory defined as the root of your document hierarchy (DocumentRoot).

4. Save this configuration file.

You have completed the configuration of your server and are now ready to start the server and begin serving HTML 3.0 documents to the World Wide Web community.

How It Works

Server configuration entails establishing values required for the server to run properly. The server needs to know who should own the server process, where various server files are located, who the server administrator is, and a variety of other information. This information forms the constraints under which the server runs.

Resource configuration involves specifying information concerning the data tree. This task includes providing a reference to the root of the document hierarchy. It involves establishing mappings for additional document types. And many times, server-specific as well as general aliases can be established for directories and documents in the data tree. The steps above specify a bare minimum resource configuration. Additional modification and additions can be made to tune the server more extensively. For more detailed information on configuring the server resource map file for HTTPD-based servers, refer to the available online documentation.

If you have chosen a server that, by default, allows access to documents, you need not concern yourself too much with security configuration unless you wish to place restrictions upon some portion of your data tree. Information about security configuration for particular server packages is described in Chapter 12. If you have a server that denies access, such as WN (see Appendix F), you need to configure security prior to starting your server. In this case, examine your server documentation to properly establish your security.

When the server initially runs, it reads the commands from the configuration files. These directives form the constraints under which the server runs. Each server on your system requires a full set of configuration files tailored to specify the constraints and capabilities that you want.

When you alter a configuration file, the server needs to be stopped and restarted for the configuration changes to take effect. Since the configuration files are only read when the server is initially run, the changes are not seen until the server restart causes the configuration files to be read anew.

Comments

The configuration files and formats for servers such as WinHTTPD and OS2HTTPD, which are derived from NCSA HTTPD, are quite similar to those of their parent. Consequently, you can usually use the procedures defined above for configuring these servers.

Certain variations exist between platforms, however. You should examine the documentation for your package, keeping an eye out for these differences. Most server packages have considerable online documentation to help you with the configuration process.

The online documentation provides you with up-to-the-minute information on the current status of your server software. If you have waited a few days to install the package you have downloaded, a better version may have become available in the intervening time.

11.4 How do I... Register additional MIME types?

COMPLEXITY: INTERMEDIATE

COMPATIBILITY: HTTPD-BASED SERVERS

Problem

When I access some documents with a browser, the documents display as a strange mix of control characters because they are a type of file my server won't support. I would like to add documents of this type on my Web site and have them supported by my server. How do I configure the server to support this new document type?

Technique

Multipurpose Internet Mail Extension (MIME) types are used by Web servers and clients to specify the document type of files. This type information is provided to a client through a content type field sent in a server response. The server determines the file type by examining a document's filename extension. This filename extension maps into an internal table that associates filename extensions with document types.

You can modify this table of associations in three ways. This How-To takes you through each method.

Steps

You can use the following three methods to modify or extend the document types that your NCSA HTTPD server can serve properly. These three methods are

- **HTML** Types file modification
- **HTML** Resource map file modification
- **HTML** Access file modification

Types File Modification

The types file is commonly located in the configuration subdirectory. The file supplied with the NCSA HTTPD distribution is called mime.types. The name of this file can be configured in the server configuration file (httpd.conf) using the TypesConfig directive.

1. Open the types configuration file in your favorite text editor. This file will either be named mime.types or whatever you have specified in the server configuration file using the TypesConfig directive.

2. The types configuration file lists the recognized file types, one per line. The MIME type (see Appendix C) is followed by the filename extension that will

11.4 REGISTER ADDITIONAL MIME TYPES

be associated with that type. Comments in this file appear following a pound sign (#) in the line.

3. If you wish to add a new document type, add a new line to this configuration file. For example, if you want to provide support for Excel spreadsheets, add the following line.

```
application/excel    xls
```

4. If you wish to modify an existing entry, move to the type you wish to modify and edit the line. For example, to modify the text/html line to accept both .html and .htm as acceptable extensions, change the following line:

```
text/html    html
```

to this:

```
text/html    html htm
```

5. Once you have made the alterations that you desire, save this configuration file; then, restart the server to realize the changes you have made.

Resource Map File Modification

You can add or modify types using the server resource map file. Issue AddType directives to extend or supersede the default types provided through the types configuration file.

1. Open the server resource map file in your text editor. This file is named srm.conf, or whatever you specified in the server configuration file using the ResourceConfig directive.

2. This file contains a series of directives defining the various resources available to the server. Each line is either a comment or a directive. Comments in this file follow a pound sign (#).

3. To add a new document type or to supersede any default types, add a new line to this file. For example, to provide support for Excel spreadsheets, add the following line to this file.

```
AddType    application/x-excel        .xls
```

4. To add serverwide support for CGI applications outside the specified script directory or server side includes, issue the following AddType directives.

```
# Add support for CGI application through recognition of the cgi extension.
AddType    application/x-httpd-cgi      .cgi
# Add support for server side includes through use of the shtml extension.
AddType    text/x-server-parsed-html    .shtml
```

5. Once you have made the desired changes, save the file. Restart the server to realize the changes you have made.

Access File Modification

You can modify or extend the supported types by changing the access control files, in either the global access control file or at the individual directory level. The types defined in this manner are only available in the designated directories. Such types will supersede those defined in the types configuration file or the server resource map file.

1. Open the access control file in your text editor. The global access control file is named access.conf or whatever you specified in the server configuration file using the AccessConfig directive. The per-directory access control file is in the directory you wish to affect and is called either .htaccess or whatever file name you specified using the AccessFileName directive in the server resource map file.

2. To add a new document type or supersede any default types, add a new line to the file. For example, if you want to provide support for Excel spreadsheets, add the following line:

```
AddType     application/x-excel       .xls
```

If you are modifying the global access configuration file, make sure you are adding the type within the appropriate <DIRECTORY> element(s).

3. If you wish to add directory-level support for CGI applications outside the designated script directory or server side includes, you can issue the following AddType directives.

```
# Add support for CGI application through recognition of the cgi extension.
AddType     application/x-httpd-cgi      .cgi
# Add support for server side includes through use of the shtml extension.
AddType     text/x-server-parsed-html    .shtml
```

4. Save the file and restart the server to realize the changes.

How It Works

The file specified in the server configuration file using the TypesConfig directive indicates the default MIME types (see Appendix C) your server uses. This file defines the base types that will be served. This set of types is usually left unaltered and may be used by several servers to define the supported base types. This approach impacts all servers that look to this file for types definitions.

The types added through the resource configuration file impact only the individual server using that configuration file. These added types extend the allowable types over the entire server. For example, you could use this method to make a

11.5
INSTALL DOCUMENTS

single server capable of serving Excel spreadsheets while other servers running on the same computer do not.

Finally, you can use the access configuration file modification approach for more fine-tuned control than for a particular server. Modifications through this method have an impact only upon the specified directories. If the method is used in a directory level access control file, then the extensions or modification are only available when accessing a document in that directory.

Comments

In general, determine which method you will use to add types based upon how widely you wish to support the new type. Most types can be added at the resource configuration level unless you are particularly worried about security, in which case, global or directory-level access control may be the more suitable option. This is particularly true for types such as CGI applications; you, as the Web site administrator, may wish to limit location of such files to either the script directory or several controlled locations.

In addition, all three methods require you to stop and restart the server for the changes to take effect.

11.5 How do I... Install documents?

COMPLEXITY
EASY

COMPATIBILITY: HTTPD-BASED SERVERS

Problem

I have created Web pages and would like to make them accessible to the World Wide Web community. I already have access to a Web site (see How-To's 11.1–11.3). How do I install my HTML 3.0 documents on this site?

Technique

The approach used to install documents on a server site will vary by hardware and software platform. In general, you install documents by placing copies of these documents in a predefined area of the file system allocated for this purpose. On operating systems that support file-level access control, the access protection of the documents needs to be set properly.

With many servers, documents can also be placed in preconfigured user directories. The following outlines the installation of a document on an NCSA HTTPD server.

Steps

The steps below define two procedures. The first describes the mechanism a Web site administrator could use for installing documents in the main document area of the server. The second instructs users in how to install documents in their home directories that are accessible by the server.

Document Root Installation

If you are a Web site administrator, you can use the following method for installing documents in the data tree. The location of this document hierarchy is specified in the server resource file using the DocumentRoot directive.

1. Examine the documents. Identify the type of each document. If the document type is not supported by your server, either reconfigure the server to support the desired type (see How-To 11.4) or let the author of the document know that the document type is not supported.

2. View each document that is to be placed upon your server in an appropriate viewing environment such as a browser or image viewer. Verify documents of all types before you install them on your server.

3. Once you have checked the documents, move them to an appropriate location in the document hierarchy. If you were to install the file hello.htm in the welcome subdirectory of the DocumentRoot, /export/home/00/htdocs, you could use the following UNIX command.

```
mv hello.htm /export/home/00/htdocs/welcome
```

4. Check the permissions settings for the document. You must set these permissions so that the user running the server has read and execute permission on the document. For example, the following command sets the protection of the hello.htm document to allow all users to read and execute the document.

```
chmod +rx hello.htm
```

For more information on the UNIX chmod command, consult a UNIX reference manual.

5. The document is now accessible through your HTTPD-based server. If you are running a server such as WN, which, by default, denies access to documents, configure the access control to the document to provide the desired access level. This allows your server to service requests for this document.

User Directory Installation

The following process outlines the steps required to install documents in your home directory. Documents installed in this manner are subject to constraints established by your Web site administrator.

11.5
INSTALL DOCUMENTS

1. Contact your Web site administrator to determine if documents in your home directory can be supported through your server. If this option is not supported, you must have the site administrator install the documents that you develop. If documents can be served from your home directory, you need to know which subdirectory to use. Your site administer can provide this information.

2. If you do not already have the designated subdirectory in your home directory, you will need to create it. The default subdirectory specified by the NCSA HTTPD server is the public_html directory. Under UNIX, the following command, issued in your home directory, creates such a directory.

```
mkdir public_html
```

3. Examine the documents. Identify the type of each document. You may have to ask your site administrator which document types are supported by your server. If the document type is not supported, either ask your site administrator to reconfigure the server to support the desired type or attempt to support the document type yourself using a per-directory access control file (see How-To 11.4). The latter option may not be available, depending on the configuration of the global access file. If you cannot support the type on your own, either attempt the former or redevelop the document using a supported type.

4. You should view each document that is to be placed upon your server in an appropriate viewing environment such as a browser or an image viewer. Check that you are not putting incorrect or improper documents on your server.

5. Move the documents to the appropriate subdirectory of your home directory. For example, to install the file hello.htm from your home directory, use the following UNIX command.

```
mv hello.htm public_html
```

6. Check the permissions settings for the documents you install. These permissions must be set so that the user running the server has at least read and execute permission on the documents. For example, the following command sets the protection of the hello.htm document to allow all users to read and execute the document, and also gives the owner write privileges.

```
chmod 755 hello.htm
```

7. The document is now accessible through your NCSA HTTPD server. If your site is running a server that, by default, denies access to documents, configure the proper access control for the document. This step allows your server to service requests for the document.

How It Works

Servers provide the World Wide Web community with access to documents on your machine. For the server to find these documents, they need to be located in a limited number of predefined locations. The two most common locations are a specified document directory and a specific subdirectory of each user's home directory.

The root of the document hierarchy is specified in the server resource map file. The DocumentRoot directive specifies this location. Documents installed in this directory or its subdirectories are visible to the server and may be requested by appropriate clients. The documents in this hierarchy must have protections set so that the server has read and execute permission on the file.

Documents are also commonly installed in users' home directories. The UserDir directive can be used in the NCSA HTTPD server resource map file to designate the particular subdirectory in the home directory where the server looks for documents. Once you place documents in this subdirectory, they will be available for access over the World Wide Web. Set the permissions on these files so that the server can access them and provide them to requesting clients. The documents you place in this directory are subject to the limitations imposed by your Web site administrator.

Use caution when installing documents. Once the document has been made available, anyone with the proper access can request and view the file. You should review each document before installing it on your server. Check for both correctness of the document and suitability of the material. Documents that are improperly formatted or badly designed reflect upon your site as a whole. Further, be wary of publishing materials on the Web that may violate copyright laws.

Comments

If you are a Web site administrator, you should develop rules and procedures for developing and submitting documents for installation on your server. To help prevent future problems, these rules should be cleared through the appropriate publications and legal offices of your business. In addition, you should give your users a clear policy for publishing Web-based materials on your site.

If you are a document developer, you should contact your Web site administrator to provide you with a copy of your site's publication policies. This will give you some guidelines to follow when publishing information over your Web site.

Chapter 12 provides more information about document access control and security configuration.

11.6 How do I... Start or stop the server?

COMPLEXITY: INTERMEDIATE

COMPATIBILITY: UNIX SERVERS

Problem

I have installed my server software and am ready to begin making HTML 3.0 documents available to the World Wide Web community. How do I start my server?

I need to perform some maintenance or reconfiguration of my server. How do I start and stop the server to accomplish my task?

Technique

Maintenance of a server requires you to start, stop, and restart a server. This is true for most servers. How you start the server depends upon the specific parameters that your server accepts and whether the server is run as a stand-alone server or by the Internet services daemon, inetd. Stopping the server entails determining the process ID for the server process and terminating it. To stop and restart the server you can either do a manual stop and start of the server or use a command that will do both.

This How-To describes these three tasks in detail, with specific examples for the NCSA HTTPD server.

Steps

This section provides instructions for starting and stopping UNIX servers. The examples given use the NCSA HTTPD server as a typical UNIX server.

Starting the Stand-Alone Server

You can most often manually start a stand-alone server from a command prompt. If you are running the server through the inetd process, see Starting the inetd Server below.

1. To start the server from a command prompt, run the server program with appropriate parameters for your configuration. Table 11-1 below presents the arguments supported by the HTTPD application.

ARGUMENT	EXPLANATION
-d path	Specifies where the server looks for its configuration files. It should match the location specified using the ServerRoot directive in the server configuration file.
-f file	Tells the server which server configuration file to use.
-v	Prints the version number of the server you are running.

Table 11-1 Command line options for httpd

If you want to run an HTTPD server with the configuration information in the default directory and default files, issue the following command at a UNIX prompt.

```
/usr/local/etc/httpd/httpd
```

If you want to run another server with configuration files in the conf subdirectory of /usr/local/httpd2, issue the following command.

```
/usr/local/etc/httpd/httpd -d /usr/local/httpd2
```

2. If you want the server to run whenever the system reboots, you need to modify the system automated startup files. You must access the system through a privileged user account to perform this task. Once you have logged in to the system as the superuser, open the appropriate startup file in your favorite text editor. This file is called /etc/rc.local on many versions of the UNIX operating system.

3. Add the following lines of code at the end of this file.

```
if [ -f /usr/local/etc/httpd/httpd ]; then
    /usr/local/etc/httpd/httpd -d /usr/local/httpd2
fi
```

Change the second line to reflect the command you would have used from a UNIX prompt.

4. Save this file. The next time the system reboots, the server will start automatically. If you are starting a server with the inetd process, you should proceed to the next set of steps; otherwise, you are done.

Starting the inetd Server

If you are starting an inetd-controlled server, you need to verify or modify several files to make sure they are configured properly.

1. The first file you must examine is the /etc/services file. This file lists many Internet services such as telnet and ftp. Log in as superuser and open the file in your favorite text editor.

2. Add a line for your server. This line should consist of the service name, http, followed by a specification of the port and protocol. The following line adds the http service to port 8080 using TCP.

```
http        8080/tcp
```

3. Save the /etc/services file.

4. Open the /etc/inetd.conf file.

11.6
START OR STOP THE SERVER

5. Add the following line.

```
http stream tcp nowait nobody /usr/local/etc/httpd httpd
```

6. Append to this line any arguments that are suitable for your configuration. For example, if the server root for this server is /usr/local/httpd2, use the following line.

```
http stream tcp nowait nobody /usr/local/etc/httpd httpd -d /usr/local/httpd2
```

See Table 11-1 for applicable command line options.

7. Save the file. You are now ready to start the server.

8. The server is controlled by the inetd process; therefore, to start the server, stop and restart the inetd process. In addition, anytime the system reboots, the server starts automatically when the inetd process starts.

Stopping the Server

The UNIX operating system assigns a process ID to each running process. You use the process ID to terminate a running process.

1. Identify the process ID for the server application. This process ID can be found in one of two ways. If your server provides this information, you can retrieve it from the server log files. For example, an NCSA HTTPD server logs its process ID in the file specified with the PidFile directive in the server configuration file. So if this file were specified as log/httpd.pid in the /usr/local/httpd2 directory, you would issue the following cat command to retrieve the process ID for the server.

```
cat /usr/local/httpd2/log/httpd.pid
```

The other approach is to list the running processes using the ps command and identify the process ID for the server from this list. Use a filtering program such as grep to narrow the list of potential processes. For example, to list all httpd processes, use the following command.

```
ps -aux | grep httpd
```

Then, choose the appropriate process ID from the list.

2. Once you have determined the process ID for the server process, you need to terminate the process using the kill command. For example, if you have determined that the process ID of the server is 4099, issue the following command at the UNIX prompt.

```
kill 4099
```

Stopping and Restarting the Server

Here you have two choices. You can either follow the procedures above for stopping the server and starting the server, or follow the instructions below for stopping and restarting the server in one step.

1. To stop the server and automatically restart it, follow the above directions for stopping the server through step 1.
2. Then instead of using the kill command by itself, add the option -1 to it. For example, if you have determined that the process ID of the server is 4099, issue the following command at the UNIX prompt.

```
kill -1 4099
```

How It Works

Start your server after the initial installation. The server must also be started after your system has rebooted. This may occur for reasons ranging from a software upgrade to a power failure. The server can either be started manually or through an automatic start procedure, depending upon the server type.

Start a stand-alone server manually by executing the appropriate server command at the UNIX prompt. This starts the process. If you are running the server as a user other than yourself, as specified in the server configuration file, run the server as superuser. If the server is run automatically, a suitable command needs to be added to the system startup files. This command tells the system to run the server whenever the system is started. In any case, the first time you run a stand-alone server will be from the command line, unless you wish to reboot your system.

If the server is controlled by the inetd process, you must register the server with this process. This involves modifying several static configuration files that the inetd process uses when starting. These files tell inetd about the processes it will control. Once you have modified these files appropriately, you can stop and restart inetd. This causes the configuration files to be read and your server to be started. You have also configured the server to start whenever the system starts, since inetd is automatically run when the system starts.

You need to shut down the server when you wish to perform extended maintenance on your site or server configuration. You must also bring the server down when you wish to upgrade or change your server software. Shutting down involves identifying the server process ID and having the operating system terminate that process.

Finally, you will stop and restart the server when configuration changes are necessary. Stopping and restarting the server causes the server to initialize itself using the new values stored in the configuration files. Changes made to the configuration files will not take effect until the server has been restarted.

Comments

Configuration alterations in the access.conf, httpd.conf, mime.types, and srm.conf files necessitate a server stop and restart to apply the changes. You can modify these files while the server is running in its previous configuration and use the Stopping and Restarting the Server procedure above to stop and immediately restart the server.

11.7 How do I... Register my server?

COMPLEXITY: EASY

COMPATIBILITY: ANY SERVER

Problem

My server is running, and I have installed several documents. However, I am finding that few people are connecting to my server. How do I let people know that my server is active and what type of information I am providing?

Technique

Once you have created your site, you can register it in appropriate locations to attract the interest of people likely to use your Web site. Do this by registering your site through other Web sites and newsgroups.

This How-To provides step-by-step instructions for publicizing your Web site throughout the world by making use of several available forums.

Steps

Three primary methods are used to announce your server to the world. The following instructions provide a stepwise guide to the registration procedure.

1. Register your server with appropriate Web sites. Registration is often categorized by location of site or subject. The following list provides URL references to selected sites suitable for the registration of your site.

- **HTML** http://web.city.ac.uk/citylive/pages.html
- **HTML** http://web.nexor.co.uk/aliweb/doc/aliweb.html
- **HTML** http://www.ncsa.uiuc.edu/SDG/Software/Mosaic/Docs/whats-new-form.html
- **HTML** http://www.w3.org/hypertext/DataSources/bySubject/Overview.html

CHAPTER 11
SERVER BASICS

HTML http://www.w3.org/hypertext/DataSources/WWW/Geographical
_generation/new_servers.html

HTML http://www.yahoo.com/bin/add

In addition to these Web sites, you should attempt to publicize your Web site through other Web sites at your facility or in your community by contacting the appropriate Web administrator.

2. Submit news of your server site to the Usenet newsgroup comp.infosystems.www.announce. You can access this group through the newsreader program with which you are most familiar. If your server is of particular interest to a particular domain, you may wish to announce its location in other suitable newsgroups. Before taking such an action, consider that you are likely to generate a considerable increase in access volume through such an announcement. Therefore, you should be sure that the information you provide is both interesting and relevant to the newsgroup where you advertise. Usenet News is an extremely large forum, and by selectively choosing the newsgroup(s) to which you announce your Web site, you will attract only those individuals most likely to use and benefit from your site.

3. Finally, you may wish to announce your site through mailing lists. Send announcements to mailing lists related to the information at your site. Since mailing lists distribute to a limited number of subscribed members, this type of an announcement might serve as a test for your decision to announce your site to a general newsgroup. You may wish to announce to a relevant mailing list and wait for feedback from the list membership before placing an item in a newsgroup distributed worldwide. In addition, you will probably wish to send a message to a mailing list such as net-happenings@is.internic.net, which is devoted to listing such announcements.

How It Works

Unless you publicize the existence of your site, very few members of the World Wide Web community will access your server.

The methods described above publicize your site to users who may be interested in the information you are providing. You can announce your site's existence through appropriate newsgroups.

In addition, many existing sites will list new Web sites in a special area of their own site. This provides some free publicity as well as providing users with access points to your server. When you first create your Web site, no other site links to information on your server. This situation will change when people know that your site exists. Registering your site at other locations provides people with initial access to your Web site, and once your site has been found, others will begin to provide links within their own information to relevant documents on your server.

Comments

Keep in mind that you can cross-list with other Web sites in your area or at your facility. Many site administrators will provide a link to your site if they feel it is appropriate. You may in turn provide a link back to their site.

COMPLEXITY
INTERMEDIATE

11.8 How do I... Use Netscape's Client Pull?

COMPATIBILITY: HTTP/1, NETSCAPE NAVIGATOR BROWSER

Problem

I would like to create an interactive slide presentation on the Web. I need to be able to specify a default link to follow after a specified amount of time. How can I create this type of HTML 3.0 document?

Technique

This facility is not supported directly by HTML 3.0. To create a document of this type, however, you can use the Client Pull feature of the Netscape Navigator browser.

The Client Pull feature works by allowing a special use of the <META> element within the head of a document. You can use this element to instruct the Netscape Navigator browser to load a new document in a specified amount of time. Through this mechanism, interactive slide presentations and guided tours can be developed.

Steps

The following procedure shows how to develop documents using the Client Pull feature of the Netscape Navigator browser.

1. Determine the document to which you wish to add the Client Pull feature. This document could be the beginning of a slide show, the first frame of a character-based animation, or a document that gets updated periodically by the server system. In any case, you should open this document in your favorite text editor or HTML editor, although most HTML editors do not support the particular element you are adding.

2. In the <HEAD> element of the document, add a <META> element. Add the following text within the <HEAD> element.

```
<META HTTP-EQUIV="Refresh" CONTENT=
```

3. Continue the previous line as appropriate for the situation. Table 11-2 displays the possible values for the CONTENT attribute.

CONTENT VALUE	USAGE
"number"	Specifies delay for the current document to refresh
"number; URL=URL"	Specifies a URL to load after a delay

Table 11-2 CONTENT attribute values for refresh

For example, if you want to reload the same document after 20 seconds, add the following text in the CONTENT field.

```
20
```

If you want the document http://www.mysite.edu/next.htm to load after a 30-second delay, include the following text in the CONTENT field.

```
"30; URL=http://www.mysite.edu/next.htm"
```

> Note: The URL that you specify in this manner must be a full URL specifying protocol, machine, and desired document.

4. Terminate the <META> element with a greater-than sign (>).
5. Save the altered document. This document is now set to tell a client to pull a new document after the specified delay.

How It Works

The Client Pull feature of the Netscape Navigator browser allows a document to specify that another document be loaded in a defined amount of time. This is supported through the use of a Refresh directive built into the head portion of an HTML document with the use of the <META> element.

The directive includes both the new document to load and the time to wait. Figure 11-3 shows how the HTML document in the code below is displayed using the Netscape Navigator.

```
<HTML>
<HEAD>
<META HTTP-EQUIV="Refresh"
CONTENT="5; URL=http://jasper.cau.auc.edu:8080/dsk/push-pull/doc2.htm">
<TITLE>Sample Client Pull Document 1</TITLE>
<LINK REV="made" HREF="mailto:me@mysite.edu">
</HEAD>
<BODY>
<H1>Sample Looping Document</H1>
```

11.8
USE NETSCAPE'S CLIENT PULL

```
<P>
This is a simple looping example of the Client Pull feature of Netscape.
<P>
This is document 1 of 2.  The other document will be loaded in 5 seconds.
Wait for it...  Follow the bouncing A.
<PRE>
A
</PRE>
Either hit the stop key or go back to the <A HREF="/index.htm">experimental
server</A> to stop looping.
<HR>
<H6>Last Modified: April 12, 1995 by Me</H6>
</BODY>
</HTML>
```

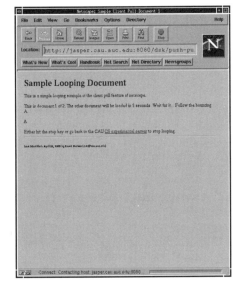

Figure 11-3 First document of pull example

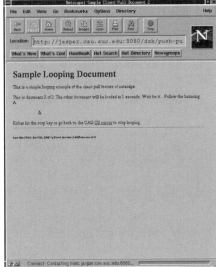

Figure 11-4 Second document of pull example

The document appearing in Figure 11-4 is loaded five seconds after the one that appears in Figure 11-3. These two documents loop back and forth to create the effect of a bouncing letter A. The HTML code for this second document appears below.

```
<HTML>
<HEAD>
<META HTTP-EQUIV="Refresh"
CONTENT="1; URL=http://jasper.cau.auc.edu:8080/dsk/push-pull/doc1.htm">
<TITLE>Sample Client Pull Document 2</TITLE>
<LINK REV="made" HREF="mailto:me@mysite.edu">
</HEAD>
<BODY>
<H1>Sample Looping Document</H1>
```

continued on next page

continued from previous page
```
<P>
This is a simple looping example of the Client Pull feature of Netscape.
<P>
This is document 2 of 2.  The other document will be loaded in 1 second.
Wait for it...  Follow the bouncing A.
<PRE>
     A
</PRE>
Either hit the stop key or go back to the <A
HREF="//www.cis.cau.auc.edu/index.htm">server</A> to stop looping.
<HR>
<H6>Last Modified: April 12, 1995 by Me</H6>
</BODY>
</HTML>
```

The only ways to stop the infinite looping are to press the Stop button on the Netscape Navigator menu bar or to activate a link within one of the two documents.

The Client Pull feature is supported by allowing documents to send a refresh directive in the HTTP response; however, they do not necessarily refresh themselves. They may refresh with some other document. The use of the <META> element with an HTTP-EQUIV attribute tells the server to add the information provided in the response header sent back to the client when this particular document is retrieved. (See Appendix G for more information on HTTP responses.) For example, the document appearing in Figure 11-3 would have the following line in the response header sent with the document.

```
Refresh 5; URL=http://jasper.cau.auc.edu:8080/dsk/push-pull/doc2.htm
```

This line instructs the Netscape Navigator client to refresh the current document with the one specified in the given URL. Similarly, the response header sent along with the document appearing in Figure 11-4 would include a Refresh directive as follows:

```
Refresh 1; URL=http://jasper.cau.auc.edu:8080/dsk/push-pull/doc1.htm
```

This in turn causes the browser to go back to the first document after one second has elapsed. These directives in the response header tell the client when and what to reload.

Comments

This feature is currently only supported by the Netscape Navigator browsers. Whether or not other browser applications will support this feature in the future is unknown. Most other browsers currently ignore the Refresh directive sent in the response header and, consequently, do not refresh after the specified delay.

11.8
USE NETSCAPE'S CLIENT PULL

You can also use the Refresh directive in response headers generated through gateway applications. This allows your CGI program to both generate a response page and load a URL after a suitable delay. (See Chapter 13 for more information on CGI applications.)

CHAPTER 12
HANDLING SERVER SECURITY

HANDLING SERVER SECURITY

How do I...

12.1	Specify allowable features on an HTTPD server?
12.2	Establish domain and address security on an HTTPD server?
12.3	Set up user and password security on an HTTPD server?
12.4	Use HTTPD server side includes?
12.5	Establish directory-level security on a CERN HTTP server?
12.6	Set up file-level security on a CERN HTTP server?
12.7	Install a CERN proxy server?
12.8	Establish domain and address security and password authentication on a MacHTTP server?
12.9	Use public key encryption?

CHAPTER 12
HANDLING SERVER SECURITY

Once you have announced the existence of your Web server, people—many people—will attempt to access your site. You have no control over who will try to view your material, so you will need to decide whether to establish security for your site. If you are distributing sensitive or restricted information, then security constraints are a necessity.

The two most commonly used forms of security provided by server software are domain restrictions and browser authentication. Domain restrictions allow you to specify which machines on the Internet may or may not access your Web site. Browser authentication restricts access by requiring a valid username and password. These two mechanisms can be combined for even stronger security.

The various server software packages provide a variety of security features and hazards. This chapter examines the security capabilities of the following server software.

- **HTML** NCSA HTTPD (UNIX)
- **HTML** WinHTTPD (Windows 3.1)
- **HTML** CERN HTTP (UNIX, VMS)
- **HTML** MacHTTP (Mac)

12.1 Specify Allowable Features on an HTTPD Server

You may not wish to allow certain features to be used in particular portions of your document tree on your HTTPD server. This How-To shows how to specify the features you wish to support in each directory of your document tree.

12.2 Establish Domain and Address Security on an HTTPD Server

HTTPD domain-based security allows you to place restrictions on parts of your document tree based on the domain or machine making a request. This How-To describes how to use this feature on the HTTPD server.

12.3 Set Up User and Password Security on an HTTPD Server

HTTPD supports user authentication security, which requires the user to enter a username and password prior to accessing restricted information. In this How-To, you will learn how to configure password security on an HTTPD server.

12.4 Use HTTPD Server Side Includes

HTTPD supports a feature known as server side includes, which allows inclusion of server-generated, dynamic information in HTML 3 documents. Since server resources are utilized, this feature represents a potential security hazard; however, with careful supervision, this risk can be minimized while still retaining the convenience and usefulness of this feature. In this How-To, you will learn how to use HTTPD server side includes.

CHAPTER 12
HANDLING SERVER SECURITY

12.5 Establish Directory-Level Security on a CERN HTTP Server

You can set access restrictions on a CERN HTTP server to limit actions in specified directories of the document tree through a combination of host filtering and user authentication. These restrictions, unlike those in HTTPD, can only be set to selectively allow access; no means of selectively denying access is supported. This How-To describes how you can set up directory-level security on a CERN HTTP server.

12.6 Set Up File-Level Security on a CERN HTTP Server

In addition to directory-level security as supported in HTTPD, the CERN package provides a way to specify access restrictions at the file level. With the CERN server, individual files within the same directory can be configured with different security constraints. In this How-To, you will learn how to configure file-level security on a CERN server.

12.7 Install a CERN Proxy Server

The CERN HTTP server software can be run as a proxy server allowing communication from behind an Internet firewall. The information in this How-To shows how you can configure your CERN server to act as such a proxy

12.8 Establish Domain and Address Security and Password Authentication on a MacHTTP Server

This How-To describes the basic forms of server-level security available with the MacHTTP server. As the other major Web server packages do, MacHTTP allows domain name and machine name specification as well as user authentication. Methods for securing a server, and the individual documents and directories that it serves, are covered, as is the method for entering usernames and passwords.

12.9 Use Public Key Encryption

Web servers and browsers communicate in the open. Servers transmit Web pages in an unsecured fashion using standard HTTP. In this How-To, you will learn how Web servers and browsers can use public key encryption techniques to provide secure transmission of HTML documents.

CHAPTER 12
HANDLING SERVER SECURITY

COMPLEXITY
INTERMEDIATE

12.1 How do I... Specify allowable features on an HTTPD server?

COMPATIBILITY: NSCA HTTPD, WINHTTPD

Problem

The HTTPD server offers a wide range of features, which is what makes it so versatile. However, some of these features may cause security risks in certain areas. Furthermore, not all features are necessary in all areas of the document tree.

How can I selectively choose which features to allow in which areas of my document tree?

Technique

The HTTPD server software allows you to specify which server features to support in each directory of the document tree. The server finds these specifications in two locations:

- **HTML** The global access configuration file
- **HTML** Per-directory access control files

You can edit the appropriate files to specify the features you wish to support in each directory. If you are not the site administrator, you will likely find it easier to create per-directory access control files in those directories for which you are responsible. The following steps walk you through this process. The available features are described in the How It Works section below.

Steps

These steps show how to specify the features to be supported in a given directory. You may specify this information in either the global access configuration file for the server or in a per-directory access control file located in the directory.

1. To edit a per-directory access control file, begin with step 4 below. Otherwise, change directories to the configuration directory for the server. Usually this is the conf subdirectory of the ServerRoot, for example, /usr/local/etc/httpd/conf.

> Note: You must have write privileges for the global access configuration file to perform this task. If you do not have write privileges for this file, skip to step 4 to edit the per-directory access control file.

12.1
SPECIFY ALLOWABLE FEATURES ON AN HTTPD SERVER

2. Open the global access control file in your favorite text editor. By default, this file is called access.conf (access.cnf in WinHTTPD). If this file is not present, check the server resource map file (srm.conf or srm.cnf) and look for the AccessConfig directive, which should tell you the location and filename of the correct file.

3. At the end of the file, create a directory-sectioning directive to store your feature specifications. A directory-sectioning directive has an opening tag composed of the <Directory> label followed by the path to the directory for which you are creating the sectioning directive. The closing tag is composed of the </Directory> label. For example, to create a directory-sectioning directive for the /usr/local/mydocs directory, insert the following lines in the file.

```
<Directory /usr/local/mydocs>

</Directory>
```

All feature directives for this directory should be contained between the opening and closing tags for this directory-sectioning directive. You should now proceed with step 5.

> Note: If you are using WinHTTPD, use forward slashes (/) in your paths rather than standard PC backslashes (\). A directory-sectioning directive opening tag for the C:\HTDOCS\MYDOCS directory would appear as <Directory C:/HTDOCS/MYDOCS>.

4. Change to the directory where you wish to specify features. In this directory, edit (or create, if necessary) a per-directory access control file. The default name for such a file is .htaccess (#haccess.ctl in WinHTTPD). This name can be changed with the AccessFileName directive in the server resource map file, usually srm.conf or srm.cnf. Open the appropriate file in your text editor. Your insertion point should not be within the boundaries of an existing sectioning directive (unless you are editing the contents of that particular directive). The beginning or the end of the file is a good place to enter a new directive.

5. Insert the directive for the feature you wish to support in this directory. Directives can either be sectioning or single-line directives. For example, to insert a directive that associates the description "My Family Picture" with the file fam1999.gif, insert the following directive.

```
AddDescription 'My Family Picture' fam1999.gif
```

The acceptable feature directives are listed in the How It Works section below.

CHAPTER 12
HANDLING SERVER SECURITY

6. Save the file. If you have made changes to the global configuration files, you must stop and restart the server for your changes to take effect, as described in How-To 11.6.

How It Works

Each feature that you wish to support in a directory is specified with a directive. HTTPD supports two types of directives in access files. The standard directive is specified in a single line. The first string on the line is the directive command; the remainder of the line may contain any necessary data associated with the particular command. The AddDescription directive shown in step 5 above is an example of this type of directive.

The second type of directive is the sectioning directive. A sectioning directive has similar syntax to an HTML 3.0 element: it begins with an opening tag and ends with a closing tag. Directives may be specified within the scope of a sectioning directive. The <Directory> directive used in step 3 above is an example of a sectioning directive. This How-To and the following two cover the current comprehensive set of access file directives. The ones in this How-To determine features allowed in a particular directory or set of directories. The following is a list of these directives and their functions.

> **HTML** **AddDescription**
> Use this directive to associate a description with a particular file. This description is used when an automatic index of the directory is generated. A description is often much more helpful than a filename. This directive can be used in either the global access file or a per-directory access file. For example, to associate the phrase "Hang 10" with the file surf.htm, issue the following directive.

```
AddDescription 'Hang 10' surf.htm
```

> Descriptions may also contain links; therefore, if a brief description is not sufficient, you can link a portion of the description to a Web document.

```
AddDescription 'My <A HREF="http://www.mysite.edu/~me/fam.htm">Family</A>
Picture' fam1999.gif
```

> The above line associates the description "My Family Picture" with the file fam1999.gif; the word "Family" is a hypertext link to the document http://www.mysite.edu/~me/fam.htm.
>
> **HTML** **AddEncoding**
> Use this directive to associate a particular filename extension with an appropriate encoding mechanism. Browsers requesting encoded documents need to have local capability to decode that particular

12.1
SPECIFY ALLOWABLE FEATURES ON AN HTTPD SERVER

type of encoding, as well as support the HTTP encoding header elements. For example, to specify that the .gz filename extension should indicate gzip compression, issue the following directive.

```
AddEncoding x-gzip gz
```

This directive may be used in either type of access file.

> Note: This directive is not supported by WinHTTPD.

(HTML) AddIcon
You may use the AddIcon directive in both the global access configuration file and per-directory access control files. Use this directive to associate a particular icon with a particular file type. If the server performs automatic indexing, this icon is presented with any file meeting the established filename extension criteria. The arguments to this directive are the path to the icon and a list of filenames, wildcards, filename extensions, or one of two special names: ^^DIRECTORY^^ or ^^BLANK_ICON^^.

Several examples of this directive follow.

```
AddIcon /icons/image.gif .gif .jpeg .fif .xbm
```

When the server automatically generates an index for this directory and finds a file with the extension .gif, .jpeg, .fif, or .xbm, it references the /icons/image.gif image to display next to the filename.

```
AddIcon /icons/dir.xbm ^^DIRECTORY^^
```

If a subdirectory is found during automatic indexing, then the /icons/dir.xbm image displays with that index entry.

```
AddIcon (SND,/icons/sound.gif) *.au
```

This example specifies both an icon and an alternative textual message that may be used by browsers that do not support inline images. This directive causes the /icons/sound.gif image to display next to any AU sound file. If the browser does not support inline images, then the text message SND displays instead of the icon.

(HTML) AddType
The AddType directive provides MIME type information for special document types found in a particular directory. This directive contains three parts: the command, the MIME type, and a list of

recognized filename extensions. Use this directive in either the global access file or a per-directory access file.

For example, if you want the server to run CGI executables outside the script directory, issue the following directive.

```
AddType application/x-httpd-cgi .cgi
```

> Note: For this specific type, you must also issue an appropriate Options directive to allow executables. See Options directive below.

AllowOverride

Use of this directive is limited to the global access configuration file. The AllowOverride directive specifies which features may be overridden by a per-directory access control file. The directive is followed by a list of options that may be overridden by the local access control.

Table 12-1 summarizes the available arguments for this directive.

ARGUMENT	FEATURE
All	Local access control may override any features.
AuthConfig	Access security information. (See How-To 12.2–12.3.)
FileInfo	AddType and AddEncoding directives.
Limit	Limit sectioning directive. (See How-To 12.2–12.3.)
None	Local access control may not override any global specified features.
Options	Options directives.

Table 12-1 AllowOverride arguments

DefaultIcon

This directive specifies an icon for the server to use if a specific icon cannot be associated with the desired file. This directive may be used in either the per-directory or the global access control files. If you want to use the icon unknown.xbm when an icon is required but the actual icon is unknown, issue the following directive.

```
DefaultIcon /icon/unknown.xbm
```

A serverwide default icon is usually defined in the server resource map file. The access control directive overrides the server default for a specific directory.

12.1
SPECIFY ALLOWABLE FEATURES ON AN HTTPD SERVER

HTML **DefaultType**
This directive may be used in either the global access file or a per-directory access control file. The data supplied with the directive specifies the default MIME type for files in the directory. If the server is unable to determine the type of a file in the directory based on filename extension, it uses this default type.

A serverwide default type is specified in the server resource map file; however, you can override this default with an access file default type. The most commonly used default type specified in the server resource file is text/plain, which tells the server to treat a data object as a straight ASCII text file if the type of the object cannot be determined.

If you created a directory that contains only GIF files, you might want to issue the following directive.

```
DefaultType image/gif
```

This directive is required if any of the GIF files in the directory do not have the .gif filename extension.

HTML **<Directory>**
Use this directive only in the global access configuration file to specify the directory affected by the enclosed directives. For example, to create a directory-sectioning directive for the /htdocs/private/mydocs directory, use the directive shown below.

```
<Directory /htdocs/private/mydocs>

</Directory>
```

You can use the asterisk as a wildcard character to create a directory directive that affects multiple similarly named document directories. For example, to refer to all the document directories in user home directories (usually in a subdirectory called public_html), use the following directive.

```
<Directory /*/public_html*>

</Directory>
```

HTML **IndexIgnore**
Use this directive in either access file to specify filename patterns that should be ignored by server automatic indexing. Follow the directive command with a list of the filenames (possibly with wildcards) to be ignored by indexing. For example, to ignore all files with the .bak extension, issue the following directive.

```
IndexIgnore *.bak
```

HTML **Options**

Use the Options directive in either the global or a per-directory access file. This directive tells the server which server options are available in a particular directory. Follow the directive with a list of those options that you want to be available. Table 12-2 indicates the options available on the HTTPD server (the final column indicates whether you can use the argument with WinHTTPD).

ARGUMENT	FEATURE	WINHTTPD
All	Makes all options available	Y
ExecCGI	Allows execution of CGI applications	N
FollowSymLinks	Allows following of symbolic links	N
Includes	Allows use of server side includes	N
IncludesNoExec	Allows use of server side includes, except exec	N
Indexes	Generates index file automatically	Y
None	Makes no options available	Y
SymLinksIfOwnerMatch	Allows symbolic links only if owner of link and source is the same	N

Table 12-2 Options arguments

HTML **ReadmeName**

Use this directive in either the global access configuration file or a per-directory access control file. A serverwide readme filename may be established in the server resource map file. The filename specified in this directive is used when automatic indexing occurs. This file is presented to the user at the top of the directory listing.

Comments

If you have modified the global access configuration file, you must stop and restart the server for the changes to take place.

For better security, the site administrator may wish to use the following access practices.

HTML When possible, issue an AllowOverride None directive for directories in the global access configuration file.

HTML Do not allow server side includes. At a minimum, restrict the use of the exec server side command with the Options directive.

HTML Since the site administrator does not have complete control over the content of the directory trees, protect users' home directories.

You can do this by inserting the following directory-sectioning directive in your global access configuration file.

```
<Directory /*/public_html*>
AllowOverride None
Options Indexes SymLinksIfOwnerMatch
</Directory>
```

Modify the argument in the opening tag to reflect the locations of your user document trees.

COMPLEXITY
INTERMEDIATE

12.2 How do I... Establish domain and address security on an HTTPD server?

COMPATIBILITY: NSCA HTTPD, WINHTTPD

Problem

I do not want people outside my business to access some critical documents that I do want to make available to employees within the business. I have some even more sensitive documents that I want to make accessible only to people on a particular computer at my site. How can I attain this kind of security?

Technique

You can restrict access to portions of your server by either allowing or denying access to particular computers or domains on the Internet. This type of security is referred to as domain/address security or host filtering.

You can achieve this level of security by using a <Limit> sectioning directive to modify the access control files of your server either at the global level, the server access configuration file, or the local level in the per-directory access control files.

Steps

The following instructions show you how to establish host filtering security for particular portions of your document tree.

1. To establish host filtering using a per-directory access control file, skip to step 4 below. Otherwise, log in as the Web site administrator and change directories to the configuration directory for the server. Usually this is the conf subdirectory of the ServerRoot.

2. Open the global access control file with your text editor. By default, this file is called access.conf (access.cnf in WinHTTPD). If this file is not present, check the server resource map file and look for the AccessConfig directive, which should tell you the location of the correct file.

3. Locate the directory-sectioning directive associated with the document tree that you wish to protect. If a <Directory> directive does not exist, go to the end of the file and add it. (See How-To 12.1 for more information on creating a directory-sectioning directive.) Your insertion point should be between the opening and closing tags of this directive. Then skip to step 5.

4. Change to the directory where you wish to specify features. In this directory, edit (or create, if necessary) a per-directory access control file. The default name for such a file is .htaccess (#haccess.ctl in WinHTTPD). This name can be changed with the AccessFileName directive in the server resource map file. Open the appropriate file in your text editor. Your insertion point should not be within the boundaries of an existing sectioning directive (unless you are editing the contents of that particular directive); the beginning or the end of the file is a good place to add it.

5. If a <Limit> sectioning directive already exists, modify this directive to suit your new security needs. If not, you can create such a directive by inserting the appropriate opening and closing tags in your access file. The <Limit> opening tag is composed of the command followed by a list of HTTP methods that you wish to restrict. Insert the following lines of code to create a directive to restrict "get" method transactions.

```
<Limit GET>

</Limit>
```

The code within the <Limit> directive establishes the host filtering that occurs when a client requests a transaction of a specified method type in the protected directory.

6. Use a combination of three subdirectives to achieve this protection: order, allow, and deny. The order directive defines the order of evaluation for allow or deny directives. The allow and deny directives respectively permit or restrict access to the machines or domains specified as arguments for the directive. For example, to allow clients running on the machine *mysite.edu* access to the directory, you could use the following <Limit> sectioning directive.

```
<Limit GET>
order deny,allow
deny from all
allow from mysite.edu
</Limit>
```

12.2
ESTABLISH DOMAIN AND ADDRESS SECURITY ON AN HTTPD SERVER

More details on these subdirectives and further examples can be found in the How It Works section at the end of these steps.

7. Save the file. If you have made changes to the global configuration files, you must stop and restart the server for your changes to take effect, as described in How-To 11.6.

How It Works

You can support host filtering by the <Limit> sectioning directive in either a server's global access configuration file or a per directory access control file. This directive begins with an opening tag containing the <Limit> command followed by a list of HTTP methods to which you wish this directive to apply. The methods that are currently understood are: "get", "put", and "post"; however, the "put" method is not currently implemented by HTTPD.

Specify the host restrictions you wish to make, using one of the subdirectives listed below.

> **HTML** order
>> This subdirective specifies the order in which to evaluate allow and deny subdirectives in the <Limit> sectioning directive. The two possible values for the argument of this directive are allow,deny and deny,allow. Depending on which value you select, the server evaluates all allow subdirectives followed by all deny subdirectives, or all deny subdirectives followed by all allow subdirectives. The default order is deny,allow. Thus, the ordering determines whether allows will override denys, or vice-versa.
>
> **HTML** allow from
>> The allow subdirective specifies machines and domains that are allowed to access information in the protected directory. The arguments of this directive are those names, IP addresses, or partial names and addresses for which you wish to allow access. Place a space between each such name or address.
>
> **HTML** deny from
>> The deny subdirective specifies machines and domains that are not allowed to access information in the protected directory. The arguments of this directive are those names, IP addresses, or partial names and addresses for which you wish to deny access. Place a space between each such name or address.

Figure 12-1 shows the results of an attempted access to a document in a directory protected with the following <Limit> directive.

```
<Directory /u/Web/docs/info/ncsaonly>
<Limit GET>
order deny,allow
```

continued on next page

continued from previous page

```
deny from all
allow from .ncsa.uiuc.edu
</Limit>
</Directory>
```

"Get" method access to the documents in this directory is denied to all browsers except those running on machines in the .ncsa.uiuc.edu domain. "Get" requests made from machines within this domain will receive the requested document. Note: the special name all refers to requests from any site.

The <Limit> directive below would deny access to browsers run on the mysite.edu machine, but allow access from anywhere else.

```
<Limit GET>
order allow,deny
allow from all
deny from mysite.edu
</Limit>
```

Thus, host filtering supported by HTTPD allows you to place access restrictions by allowing or denying access to a portion of the document tree by Internet machine name or address or domain name or address.

Comments

<Limit> sectioning directives can be created for each specific HTTP method that may be used to access documents in the protected directory.

The require subdirective of the <Limit> directive is described fully in How-To 12.3, which describes user authentication protection. Further, you can combine host filtering with user authentication to create multiple levels of security.

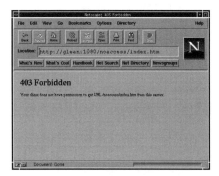

Figure 12-1 Domain-based host filter example

12.3 How do I... Set up user and password security on an HTTPD server?

COMPLEXITY: INTERMEDIATE

COMPATIBILITY: NSCA HTTPD, WINHTTPD

Problem

Host filtering will not suffice for my security needs; the people who need to access the sensitive information are at diverse locations and use a variety of machines in many different domains. Is there a way I can require user authentication with a password before allowing access to a private portion of my document tree?

Technique

The Basic authentication package is supported by a variety of server software packages, including HTTPD. This authentication package requires that a browser submit a username and password to authenticate itself. This information is checked against a list of acceptable users and passwords stored on the server. If the submitted username and password are authorized to access the requested document, the server provides the requested material; if not, access is denied.

HTTPD supports user authentication through the use of password files, group files, and access file directives. The instructions below lead you through the process of setting up user authentication based security for specified portions of your document tree.

Steps

The following steps show how to configure the HTTPD server to provide password-based user authentication for access to portions of your document tree. Using these instructions, you can create password and group files and issue appropriate access file directives. These new access file directives are explained in greater detail in the How It Works section below.

1. Create a password file. HTTPD includes the htpasswd program to aid you in this task (htpasswd.exe in WinHTTPD). Locate this program in the "support" subdirectory of the server. You should change directories to the location where you wish to store a password file. If a password file already exists in this directory, proceed to step 2. Otherwise, create a new password file with this program. For example, to create a new password file called "newpass" in the current directory and add an entry for the user "duke", issue the command below.

```
htpasswd -c newpass duke
```

CHAPTER 12
HANDLING SERVER SECURITY

2. Use the htpasswd application to add password file entries for any users you wish to create. Since the password file already exists, do not use the -c parameter. For example, to add an entry for a user "harpo" in the "newpass" password file, use the following command.

```
htpasswd newpass harpo
```

3. If you wish to establish groups of users who will share similar access privileges, create or edit a group file. If you do not wish to create user groups, skip to step 6. Otherwise, you should change directories to the location where you wish to store the group file.

4. Create a group file or open an existing one in your text editor. Add, delete, or alter entries as appropriate. Each entry is contained on a single line. The line begins with a group name followed by a colon (:). The remainder of the entry is a list of users in the group. For example, the following line designates the *tv* group, composed of users *duke* and *harpo*:

```
tv: duke harpo
```

5. After you make your edits, save this group file.

6. If you wish to establish user authentication protection using a per-directory access control file, proceed with step 9 below. Otherwise, log in to your machine as the Web site administrator and change directories to the configuration directory for the server. Usually this is the conf subdirectory of the ServerRoot.

7. Open the global access control file in your text editor. By default, this file is called access.conf (access.cnf in WinHTTPD). If this file is not present, check the server resource map file and look for the AccessConfig directive, which should tell you the location of the correct file.

8. Locate the directory-sectioning directive associated with the document tree you wish to protect. If a <Directory> directive does not exist, go to the end of the file and add such a directive. (See How-To 12.1 for more information on creating a directory-sectioning directive.) Place your insertion point between the opening and closing tags of this directive, but not within another sectioning directive such as a <Limit> directive. Proceed with step 10.

9. Change directories to where you wish to specify features. In this directory, edit (or create, if necessary) a per-directory access control file. The default name for the file is .htaccess (#haccess.ctl in WinHTTPD). This name can be changed with the AccessFileName directive in the server resource map file. Open the appropriate file in your text editor. Do not place your insertion point within the boundaries of an existing <Limit> directive. The beginning or end of the file is a good location.

12.3
SET UP USER AND PASSWORD SECURITY ON AN HTTPD SERVER

10. Issue an AuthType directive to let the server know the type of authentication scheme to use when access attempts are made. In general, you will use the Basic protection scheme. Insert the following line in the access file.

`AuthType Basic`

11. Give the server a name for the security setup. This information is sent to the browser making an access attempt. The AuthName directive assigns this information. For example, you could use the following directive to assign the name "ProtectionExample" to the setup used to protect the documents in the current directory tree.

`AuthName ProtectionExample`

This name may appear as the title of the pop-up window requesting authentication information.

12. Specify the location of the password file that contains the username and password pairs for users who have access to the documents in this document tree. Use the AuthUserFile directive to designate the location of this file. For example, to specify the /usr/local/httpd/conf/newpass as the password file, issue the following command in your access file.

`AuthUserFile /usr/local/httpd/conf/newpass`

13. Specify the location of a group file with the AuthGroupFile directive. For simple single-user security, specify a dummy file. If you use NCSA HTTPD, insert the following line in your access file.

`AuthGroupFile /dev/null`

If you use WinHTTPD, insert the following line in your access file.

`AuthGroupFile c:/httpd/conf/empty.pwd`

Or to specify an actual group file (such as c:\httpd\conf\group.pwd), use the following directive.

`AuthGroupFile c:/httpd/conf/group.pwd`

14. Finally, create or edit the <Limit> directive for this directory. If a <Limit> directive already exists, modify this directive to suit your new security needs. If not, create the directive by inserting the appropriate opening and closing tags in your access file. The <Limit> opening tag is composed of the command followed by a list of HTTP methods that you wish to restrict. Insert the following lines to create a directive to restrict "get" method transactions.

```
<Limit GET>

</Limit>
```

15. Use the require subdirective to specify the users who have access to the document tree. For example, if you wish to allow users "duke" and "milo" and members of the "tv" group access to the directory, use the following <Limit> sectioning directive.

```
<Limit GET>
require user duke
require user milo
require group tv
</Limit>
```

The specified users and groups must appear as entries in the password and group file, respectively.

16. Save this file. If you have made changes to the global configuration files, you must stop and restart the server for your changes to take effect, as described in How-To 11.6.

How It Works

HTTPD allows the restriction of access to protected material by requiring that a user supply a valid username and password. Three key elements are necessary for this to work with HTTPD.

HTML First, files containing valid username and password pairs must be stored on the server in a read-accessible location.

HTML Next, group files need to be created or modified as necessary.

HTML Finally, access files, either global or local, must be configured to specify which users are eligible to access the protected files in a given manner.

Figure 12-2 shows the result of an attempt to access a document protected with user authentication. Many browsers remember the username and password that you have entered and supply this information the next time authentication is required. If a different username and password pair is required for other restricted documents, the browser prompts you for this new information.

Password Files

The htpasswd program (htpasswd.exe in WinHTTPD) is provided with the HTTPD software and is located in the "support" subdirectory. This application takes either two or three parameters. The format for such a command appears as follows:

```
htpasswd [-c] password_file user_name
```

12.3
SET UP USER AND PASSWORD SECURITY ON AN HTTPD SERVER

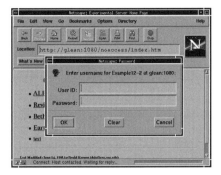

Figure 12-2 User authentication required

You need to use three parameters when you create the first username and password pair in a given password file. The -c parameter specifies that a new password file is being created. The other two parameters, the password filename and the username, are the same whether you are creating a new file or adding an entry to an existing file. For example, the HTTPD procedure to create a new password file called example.pwd with two users, "bill" and "ted", appears below.

```
glean dsk 151 >htpasswd -c example.pwd bill

Adding password for bill.
New password:
Re-type new password:
glean dsk 152 >htpasswd example.pwd ted
Adding user ted
New password:
Re-type new password:
```

The resultant password file might look like this:

```
bill:VCPfU..tx1IjY
ted:KAUrn7rvfOroM
```

Multiple password files may exist on a single server with several stipulations. First, all password files must be stored in a location readable by the server application. Second, each directory may specify only a single password file; therefore, the password file must contain all users who need to access the directory that references that password file.

Group Files

Specifying a list of individual users is often unwieldy. You might choose to create groups of users with similar access privileges. These groups are specified in a group file. The format of a group file is a series of entries with each entry appearing on a single line.

Each line is composed of a group name and a user list. These two elements are separated by a colon (:). For example, the following group file defines two groups: "friends" and "relatives".

```
friends: paul jess steve jeanne
relatives: jenny elliot mom
```

The "friends" group consists of users "paul", "jess", "steve", and "jeanne". The relatives group consists of users "jenny", "elliot", and "mom".

Access Files

The HTTPD user authentication feature also requires the configuration of access files to establish the particular authentication required for designated portions of the document tree. Several access file directives are required to support this security mechanism. These directives may be used in either the global access configuration file or the local per-directory access control files.

> **HTML** **AuthGroupFile**
> The AuthGroupFile directive specifies the location of the group file to be used in the user authentication protection of the current directory. For group-based access restriction, this file must be readable by the HTTPD server. The directive command is immediately followed by the file specification of the group file. For example, the directive below designates the file c:\httpd\conf\group.pwd as the group file for authentication.

```
AuthGroupFile c:/httpd/conf/group.pwd
```

> **HTML** **AuthName**
> This directive indicates the name of the authentication setup being used by the server. This information is passed to a browser making a request so that the end user can determine which username and password he or she needs to use to access the desired material. This name can be arbitrarily chosen by the person configuring the authentication security. The string immediately following the directive command is the name associated with the authentication setup.

> **HTML** **AuthType**
> Currently, the only acceptable authentication type is Basic. However, limited alternatives exist for certain browsers and servers. In general, use the following line in your access file to specify the Basic authentication method.

```
AuthType Basic
```

12.3
SET UP USER AND PASSWORD SECURITY ON AN HTTPD SERVER

HTML **AuthUserFile**

This directive specifies the password file used in the authentication setup. The directive consists of the command followed by the path of the password file to be used. Password files must be readable by the server software for user authentication protection to be handled properly. Further, the specified password file should contain an entry for each user either directly specified in a require subdirective or indirectly included as a group member through a require subdirective. For example, the following directive indicates the use of c:\httpd\conf\password.pwd as the password file for the current authentication setup.

```
AuthUserFile c:/httpd/conf/password.pwd
```

HTML **require (<Limit> subdirective)**

Require subdirectives must occur within a <Limit> sectioning directive. (Other aspects of the <Limit> directive are covered more completely in How-To 12.2.) The require subdirective consists of a directive command, require, followed by a type, either "user" or "group", concluded by a username or group name depending on the stated type. The server restricts transactions of the type specified by the <Limit> directive to only authenticated users specified with require subdirectives. For example, to restrict "get" access of documents in a given directory to valid user "bill" and members of the "relatives" group, include the following <Limit> directive.

```
<Limit GET>
require user bill
require group relatives
</Limit>
```

Comments

<Limit> sectioning directives can be created for each specific HTTP method that may be used to access documents in the protected directory.

The order, allow, and deny subdirectives of the <Limit> directive are described fully in How-To 12.2. Further, user authentication can be combined with the host filtering methods described in How-To 12.2 to create multiple levels of security.

In addition, the usernames and passwords used to support user authentication may or may not have any correlation to the usernames and passwords with which individuals log in to their system.

CHAPTER 12
HANDLING SERVER SECURITY

COMPLEXITY
ADVANCED

12.4 How do I... Use HTTPD server side includes?

COMPATIBILITY: NSCA HTTPD

Problem

I need to include dynamic information in my HTML 3 document, but I don't want to write a small gateway application for each of these tasks. How can I incorporate on-the-fly information in a convenient manner?

Technique

The NCSA HTTPD server provides a mechanism for placing dynamic information within HTML 3 documents. This mechanism is referred to as server side includes.

In an HTTP transaction, a user makes a request and the server responds with the requested item with little regard for the actual content data. When an HTML 3 document containing server side includes is requested, the server reads the document, resolves server side includes, and creates the resultant document.

The procedure below shows you how to use server side includes.

Steps

Enabling server side includes on your Web site involves two primary tasks. You need to make several system configuration modifications, and you need to add the server side include commands to appropriate documents. An explanation of each of these tasks is presented below.

Configuration

This procedure describes the modifications you must make to your server configuration to allow the support of server side includes.

1. If you wish to configure server side includes with a per-directory access control file, skip to step 4. Otherwise, log in to your machine as the Web site administrator and change directories to the configuration directory for the server. Usually this is the conf subdirectory of the ServerRoot.

2. Open the global access control file in your text editor. By default, this file is called access.conf. If this file is not present, check the server resource map file and look for the AccessConfig directive, which should tell you the location of the correct file.

3. Locate the directory-sectioning directive associated with the document tree in which you wish to use server side includes. If a <Directory> directive does not exist, go to the end of the file and add such a directive; see How-To 12.1 for more information on creating a directory-sectioning directive.

12.4 USE HTTPD SERVER SIDE INCLUDES

Your insertion point is between the opening and closing tags of this directive. Skip to step 5.

4. Change directories to the directory where you wish to allow HTML 3 documents with server side includes. In this directory, edit (or create, if necessary) a per-directory access control file. The default name for such a file is .htaccess. This name can be changed with the AccessFileName directive in the server resource map file. Open the appropriate file in your text editor. Your insertion point should not be within the boundaries of an existing sectioning directive; the beginning or the end of the file is a good location.

5. Insert the following AddType directive in this access file. The filename extension may be changed if you wish to associate a different extension with documents that contain server side includes. For example:

```
AddType text/x-server-parsed-html .shtml
```

6. Issue an Options directive to allow server side includes. If no Options directive is present, the default value is All; in this case, you can either continue with step 7 or create an Options directive for this directory. The directive should, at a minimum, include the Includes or IncludesNOEXEC option. For example, the following directive specifies automatic indexing and server side includes with the exception of execs in the configured directory.

```
Options Indexes IncludesNOEXEC
```

7. Save the file. If you have made changes to the global configuration files, you must restart the server for your changes to take effect, as described in How-To 11.6.

Inserting Directives

Once you have configured your server to allow server side includes, you can begin using server side include commands in your documents. The steps below walk you through the process of incorporating server side include commands into your HTML 3 documents.

1. Change directories to the location where the HTML documents in which you wish to use server side includes are stored.

2. Open the document in which you wish to include server side information in your text editor. Move the insertion point to the location in the document where you wish to insert the dynamic information.

3. Issue a server side include command within the context of an HTML 3 comment. The text of the comment should begin with a pound symbol (#). For example:

```
<!--#command tag1="..." tag2="..." ... -->
```

So if you wanted to include the text of the file DocumentRoot/header.htm in your document, you would issue the following directive in your document.

```
<!--#include virtual="/header.htm" -->
```

> Note: A complete list of server side include commands and their valid arguments is presented in the How It Works section below.

4. When your edits are complete, save your document. The filename extension of your document should indicate the presence of server side includes.

5. Check the document in your browser.

How It Works

The NCSA HTTPD server software provides server side includes as a mechanism for incorporating dynamic information into static HTML 3 documents. The server accomplishes this by parsing embedded commands within the text of the document, then evaluating these commands to generate the final document sent to the client.

For the server to properly differentiate documents that have server side includes from those that do not, the server needs to be configured to recognize objects of the text/x-server-parsed-html MIME type, created to support server side includes. Add this type and associate it with an appropriate filename extension. Unless you wish to allow server side includes in documents serverwide, issue the appropriate AddType directives in the access files that control the specific directories in which you wish to permit server side includes. If you do want to globally support server side includes, issue this directive in the server resource map file.

In addition, you must configure the options in the directories where you wish to support server side includes. By default, all options are available in all directories. However, if you need to restrict some options while supporting server side includes, issue an Options directive with either the Includes or the IncludesNOEXEC argument. The Includes option allows use of all server side commands; the IncludesNOEXEC argument allows use of all server side commands except exec. Use of exec may constitute a security risk, hence the need for two separate options.

Below is a list of supported server side include commands, as well as a summary of how they work and the arguments they take. This discussion is followed by Table 12-4, which describes the environment variables that are visible to server side include documents.

HTML config

This command defines several characteristics of file parsing. Table 12-3 shows the tags supported by this command.

12.4
USE HTTPD SERVER SIDE INCLUDES

TAG	VALUE
errmsg	Specifies the error message that is sent to the client if an error occurs during the parsing process.
timefmt	Format to use when a date is requested. The string must comform to the specification of date format strings for the UNIX strftime library function.
sizefmt	Format to use when a file size is displayed. The two acceptable values for this tag are:
	"bytes" Represents the straight byte count of the file.
	"abbrev" Shows an abbreviated file size. (e.g. 1.2MB)

Table 12-3 Tags in a config server side include

For example, the command

```
<!--#config errmsg="Error in parsed HTML" timefmt="%D" sizefmt="abbrev">
```

would set the error message to "Error in parsed HTML", the time format to "%D", so a date might appear as 1/1/99, and the size format to "abbreviated", so a file size of 9,876,543 displays as 9.9MB.

 echo

The echo command can display any of the environment variables specified in Table 12-4. The single valid tag for this command is "var". The value associated with this tag is the variable to be displayed.

For example, to display the current date in your document, use the following server side include.

```
<!--#echo var="DATE_LOCAL">
```

 exec

This include puts the results of executing the command passed as a tag into the resultant document sent to the client. The valid tags for this command are "cmd" and "cgi".

The value of the cmd tag must be a string. This string is passed to /bin/sh for execution. The variables specified in Table 12-4 may be used by this command.

The "cgi" tag is used to refer to a gateway application whose results will be included in the resultant document. The reference to the CGI program should be a standard virtual path to a valid gateway program.

The following include could be used if, for example, you wanted to include a listing of the people currently logged in to the server site within an HTML 3 document.

```
<!--#exec cmd="/usr/ucb/finger">
```

CHAPTER 12
HANDLING SERVER SECURITY

HTML **fsize**

The fsize command has the same valid tags as include: "file" and "virtual". It displays the size of the file referenced in the tag. This data is shown in the format specified with the "sizefmt" tag of the config command.

If you wanted to track the size of a particular file, you might create an HTML 3 document that displays this information whenever you access it. For example, the following include displays the size of the file /export/home/00/ht1/logs/error_log.

```
<!--#fsize virtual="/logs/error_log">
```

HTML **flastmod**

The flastmod command has the same valid tags as include: "file" and "virtual". This command displays the date the target referenced by the tag was last modified. This date is printed in the format specified using the "timefmt" tag in the config command.

Use this command to keep track of when a particular file was last modified. For example, if you wish to always know when the last server error occurred, create an HTML 3 document that dynamically determines when the server error log was last changed. Such a command might look like the following:

```
<!--#flastmod virtual="/logs/error_log">
```

HTML **include**

This command places the text of one document within another. Documents to be included are subject to the standard access control restrictions. This command uses one of two valid tags.

The "file" tag specifies the location of the file to be included relative to the current directory. The target may be another parsed HTML 3 document, but not a CGI application.

The "virtual" tag references a document by way of the virtual path from the DocumentRoot. As with the target of a file tag, this *file* may be another parsed document, but may not be a gateway application. You can find an example of this command in step 3 of Inserting Directives, above.

Several environment variables are set when server side includes are evaluated. These variables appear in Table 12-4.

VARIABLE	VALUE
DOCUMENT_NAME	Current filename
DOCUMENT_URL	Virtual path to the current document
QUERY_STRING_UNESCAPED	Any search query the client sent

VARIABLE	VALUE
DATE_LOCAL	Current date, local time zone
DATE_GMT	Current date, Greenwich mean time
LAST_MODIFIED	Date current document was last modified

Table 12-4 Environment variables set while server side includes are evaluated

Comments

Server side includes provide a means of including dynamic information within HTML 3 documents without resorting to gateway scripts, but there are significant drawbacks: inefficiency and lack of security.

Server side includes decrease server efficiency. The server can no longer act strictly as a dispatcher, since it must not only processes the requests but also read and comprehend the content of the response to generate the appropriate resultant HTML 3 document. This inefficiency can be minimized by only using server side includes in directories that require them. In other words, place the configuration information in either per-directory access control files or within a directory-sectioning directive in the global access configuration file. If potential inefficiency is not an issue, much of the configuration information can be declared serverwide in the server resource map file.

In addition, server side includes represent a security risk. The most flagrant potential risk is the exec command, which allows an HTML 3 document to include the results of the execution of an application. This command could allow unauthorized access to the server machine. You can reduce this risk by using the Options directive to restrict either all server side include commands or only exec commands.

COMPLEXITY
INTERMEDIATE

12.5 How do I... Establish directory-level security on a CERN HTTP server?

COMPATIBILITY: CERN HTTP

Problem

I have sensitive data in certain areas of my document tree that I need to distribute to a select audience via my CERN HTTP server software. How can I make sure that only the people I specify can access the protected documents?

Technique

The CERN server software uses a combination of host filtering and user authentication to provide directory-level server security. Establishing directory-level security entails the following tasks.

- **HTML** Establishing the protection setup
- **HTML** Associating these setups with portions of the document tree
- **HTML** Generating any supporting password and group files

This How-To shows how to accomplish these tasks, letting you establish directory-level security for your CERN server.

Steps

The directory-level security configuration process can be broken down into three broad categories:

- **HTML** Protection setup definition
- **HTML** Directory association
- **HTML** Auxiliary file maintenance

These tasks are handled individually in the procedures below. In each category, several alternative approaches are described.

Examples of several directory-level protection configurations are provided in the How It Works section.

Protection Setup Definition

The CERN server software provides three methods for specifying protection setups. You can

- **HTML** Define named setups in the global configuration file
- **HTML** Define setups as separate external security setup files
- **HTML** Define setups through inline specification

The procedures below cover the first two approaches. Later in this How-To, Association of Directories to Protection Setups describes the third method.

Defining Named Setups

If you wish to define a setup in a separate file, use the procedure under Defining Setup Files. Otherwise, log in to the server machine as the site administrator.

1. Change directories to the location of your global server configuration file. This file is usually located in the config subdirectory of the server software.

2. Open the configuration file in your text editor.

3. Move the insertion point to a new line. You should define your protection setup object before you attempt to associate it with a particular directory. If

12.5
ESTABLISH DIRECTORY-LEVEL SECURITY ON A CERN HTTP SERVER

you are editing an existing setup, move your insertion point to within the setup object and skip to step 7.

4. Insert the following lines of code, substituting whatever you choose for the object name represented by PROTNAME in the code.

```
Protection PROTNAME {
}
```

5. Place your insertion point between the opening curly brace and the closing curly brace.

6. Insert a UserId directive to indicate the user ID that the server must assume to access the protected directory. For example, if the server needs to run as user "me" to access directories owned by this user, issue the following directive.

```
UserId me
```

The default user ID is "nobody".

7. Insert a GroupId directive to indicate the group ID that the server must assume in order to access the protected directory. For example, if the server needs to run as a group called "users" to access the desired directories, use the following directive.

```
GroupId users
```

The default group ID is "nogroup".

8. Insert the following directive to specify the authentication type.

```
AuthType Basic
```

9. Use a ServerId directive to specify a name for the setup. For example, to name the setup "MySetup", use the following directive.

```
ServerId MySetup
```

10. Specify the password file to use with this setup using the PasswordFile directive. To use the password file /home/htpass, include the following line.

```
PasswordFile /home/htpass
```

11. Specify the group file to use with this setup using the GroupFile directive. To use the group file /home/htgroups, include the following line.

```
GroupFile /home/htgroup
```

12. Specify the masks for the setup to indicate the types of transactions and the limitations on them. You can specify this as either a generic mask or a series of transaction-specific masks. The syntax of a mask command is shown below.

```
mask_command group, user user@address, @address, ...
```

Table 12-5 specifies the valid mask commands.

MASK COMMAND	TRANSACTIONS COVERED
delete-mask	Protects "delete" method requests
get-mask	Protects "get" and "head" method requests
mask	Use this mask when method-specific mask unavailable
post-mask	Protects "post" method requests
put-mask	Protects "put" method requests

Table 12-5 Mask directives

The mask command itself is followed by a series of usernames, group names, and machine/domain addresses in any combination. Additional information on the syntax of this list can be found in the How It Works section below. This syntax is referred to as a group definition; it is the same as that used in group files described in the Auxiliary File Maintenance section below. For example, to restrict "put" method requests to user "jenny", use either of the following directives.

```
put-mask jenny
```

or

```
mask jenny
```

The second is more restrictive, in that transactions of all methods are restricted to the user "jenny". If a generic mask is defined, it serves as the default mask if a specific transaction mask is not defined.

13. You have now defined a protection setup. If you have no more protection setups to create at this time, save the current file.

14. Since you have modified the global configuration file, you must stop and restart the server process to put your configuration changes into effect.

Defining Setup Files

You can define security setups as external files. Except for limited exceptions, these files contain the same information as named setups. Files, however, contain neither the UserId nor the GroupId directives. This information is provided at the time the setup file is associated with a document tree.

12.5
ESTABLISH DIRECTORY-LEVEL SECURITY ON A CERN HTTP SERVER

1. Change directories to the location where you wish to store the file that defines a protection setup. Each file defines a single protection setup.
2. Choose a name for your protection setup file and open this file in your text editor.
3. Insert the following directive to specify the authentication type.

`AuthType Basic`

4. Use a ServerId directive to specify a name for the setup. For example, to name the setup "MySetup", use the following directive.

`ServerId MySetup`

5. Specify the password file to use with this setup using the PasswordFile directive. To use the password file /home/htpass, include the following line.

`PasswordFile /home/htpass`

6. Specify the group file to use with this setup using the GroupFile directive. To use the group file /home/htgroups, include the following line.

`GroupFile /home/htgroup`

7. Specify the masks for the setup to indicate the types of transactions and the limitations on them. You can specify this as either a generic mask or a series of transaction-specific masks. The syntax of a mask command is shown below.

`mask_command group, user user@address, @address, ...`

Table 12-5 in the Defining Named Setups section above specifies the valid mask commands. The mask command itself is followed by a series of usernames, group names, and machine/domain addresses in any combination. Additional information on the syntax of this list can be found in the How It Works section below. This syntax is referred to as a group definition; it is the same as that used in group files described in the Auxiliary File Maintenance section below. For example, to restrict "put" method requests to user "jenny", use either of the following directives.

`put-mask jenny`

or

`mask jenny`

The second is more restrictive, in that transactions of all methods are restricted to the user "jenny". If a generic mask is defined, it serves as the default mask if a specific transaction mask is not defined.

8. You have now defined a protection setup. Save the current file.

Association of Directories to Protection Setups

Several methods exist for configuring a particular directory with a specific security setup. The steps outlined below lead you through several variations of the Protect directive in the server configuration file to create these associations. Instructions for using the DefProt directive for this task can be found in the documentation for the CERN server software.

1. Associate a protection setup with a directory in the server configuration file. Change directories to the location of your global server configuration file; this file is usually located in the config subdirectory of the server software.

2. Open the configuration file in your text editor. Move the insertion point to a new line. If you have defined protection setups within your configuration file, this insertion point should be farther down in the file than the protection setup objects you wish to use. If you are editing an existing directory-level protection association, move your insertion point to the desired Protect directive.

3. Insert (or modify) a Protect directive to associate a protection setup with a directory. If you only plan to use a protection setup once, consider associating the directory to an inline specification of a setup, as shown in step 5. If you want to associate a directory with a previously declared setup object in the configuration file, proceed with step 4. Otherwise, associate a directory with an external protection setup file using the directive shown below.

```
Protect template path user.group
```

In this directive, the template is the path to the tree of documents to be protected. The path is an absolute path to the protection setup file that specifies the desired protection for the document tree. Finally, the user.group field specifies the identity the server needs to assume to gain access to the document tree. So, for example, to protect the /horses/mysystem directory using the /WWW/config/prot.setup1 protection setup file with the server running as user "me" in group "users", issue the following directive.

```
Protect /horses/mysystem/* /WWW/config/prot.setup1 me.users
```

You have now protected the specified directory. Proceed with step 6.

4. Using a previously defined protection setup object, insert a Protect directive with the following syntax.

```
Protect template prot_obj
```

12.5
ESTABLISH DIRECTORY-LEVEL SECURITY ON A CERN HTTP SERVER

The template is a wildcard-capable specification of the directory to be protected, and prot_obj is the name used as the second parameter to the Protection directive when creating the object. A wildcard-capable directory specification may include an asterisk (*) to match multiple paths; for example, /horse/* refers to all subdirectories of the /horse directory. Use the following directive to protect the /horses/mysystem directory using the PROTNAME protection setup object.

```
Protect /horses/mysystem PROTNAME
```

You have now protected the specified directory. Proceed with step 6.

5. Associate an inline protection setup with a directory. You should only create an inline protection setup for one-time use. Be careful with the syntax of this usage of the Protect directive. It should appear as follows:

```
Protect template {
     setup
     }
```

Make sure to place a space between the template and the opening brace, as well as to place the closing brace on a line by itself. In addition, comments are not permitted within the scope of an inline setup object. In the syntax above, "template" refers to the directory to be protected while "setup" refers to a series of directives as defined in steps 6–12 of the Defining Named Setups section above. An example of this usage is shown below.

```
Protect /horses/mysystem {
    UserId me
    GroupId users
    AuthType Basic
    ServerId MySetup
    PasswordFile /home/htpass
    GroupFile /home/htgroup
    GetMask jenny elliot mom @(*.*.cau.edu)
}
```

This associates the inline setup provided with the specified directory.

6. When you are done, save the server configuration file. You must now restart the server before your changes can take effect.

Auxiliary File Maintenance

CERN security requires the maintenance of two types of auxiliary files: password files and group files. These files serve the same purpose as they do in the HTTPD server. The formats and maintenance utilities, however, differ. The steps below take you through the creation and maintenance of CERN password and group files.

The CERN server package provides the htadm application to help maintain server password files. The How It Works section below explains how to use this application. However, the first three of the following steps show how to create and add user/password pairs with this program.

1. Change directories to the location where you wish to store a password file.
2. Create a new password file using the following htadm application syntax.

```
htadm -create filename
```

For example, use the following command to create a password file called .htpass in the current directory.

```
htadm -create .htpass
```

3. Add users to the password by calling this application with the syntax appearing below.

```
htadm -adduser filename username password realname
```

For example, the following command creates an entry in the .htpass password file for user "jenny" with password "math" and a real name of Jenny Helen:

```
htadm -adduser .htpass jenny math Jenny Helen
```

You may use this command to create as many users as required. Additional password maintenance functions are described in the How It Works section below.

4. If you do not need to create a group file, you have completed setting up directory-level protections. Otherwise, change directories to the location where you wish to store a group file. Either choose a name for this group file or edit an existing group file. In either case, open your chosen group file in your text editor.
5. A group file is a series of lines, each of which defines a group. The line begins with a group name followed by a colon (:) followed by a list of items. The syntax of an entry is shown below.

```
groupname: item, item, item, item, ...
```

6. An item can be a user, a group, a machine, a domain, or any combination of users or groups with machines or domains. The list defines the group. Create or edit any necessary groups.
7. Save the group file.

How It Works

Like HTTPD, the CERN HTTP server software supports security through host filtering and user authentication. Unlike HTTPD, the syntactic specification of

12.5
ESTABLISH DIRECTORY-LEVEL SECURITY ON A CERN HTTP SERVER

both types of security is remarkably similar in the CERN package. The first component required to establish directory-level protection of a CERN server is the protection setup object or file. Once that is located, you need to know which directives to use. Table 12-6 summarizes the directives used in the specification of a protection setup.

DIRECTIVE	PURPOSE	RESTRICTION
AuthType	Specifies authentication scheme to be used	None
GroupFile	Specifies full path of the group file for this setup	None
GroupId	Designates group server needs to run as	Setup Object
mask commands	See Table 12-5	None
PasswordFile	Specifies full path of the password file for this setup	None
ServerId	Name to differentiate among setups on a server	None
UserId	Designates user server needs to run as	Setup Object

 Table 12-6 Protection directives

The mask command takes a group definition as a parameter. A group definition is a comma-separated list of users, groups, potentially wildcarded Internet address, and combinations of users or groups with an address or addresses. Parentheses are used for logical groupings of users/groups or address templates. For example, the following are all valid group file entries composed of a group name, a colon, and a group definition.

```
us: you, me
```

The group "us" consists of users "you" and "me".

```
them: he, she, it@144.125.*.*
```

The group them consists of users "he" and "she", and also the user "it"; however, "it" must be attempting to access the server from a machine in the auc.edu domain (144.125.*.* is the auc.edu domain). This entry does not restrict users "he" and "she" to a particular machine or domain.

```
us_and_them: us, them, @128.141.*.*
```

The group "us_and_them" consists of all users in the groups "us" and "them" plus users from the CERN domain (128.141.*.* is CERN).

```
some_of_them: them@(*.*.auc.edu, 128.149.*.*)
```

The group "some_of_them" consists of only those members of the group "them" accessing the server from machines in either the auc.edu or the jpl.gov domains (128.149.*.* is the jpl.gov domain).

CHAPTER 12
HANDLING SERVER SECURITY

```
we: (me, myself, i)@144.125.96.233
```

The group "we" consists of the users "me", "myself", and "i" when attempting to access the server from Internet address 144.125.96.233.

Two special predefined groups exist. These groups are "All" and "Anybody". The "All" group consists of all valid users in the designated password file. The "Anybody" group represents protection without user authentication; this is the implied group when an item in a group definition is only an at sign (@) followed by a machine or domain address.

The mask commands specify those individuals who may have a particular type of access to the protected portion of the server. Thus, with the capabilities of the mask directives, you could create protections to support strict host filtering or user authentication. For example, the following setup object performs host filtering that only allows access from machines in the jpl.gov domain (128.149).

```
Protection jplFilter {
    UserId me
    GroupId users
    AuthType Basic
    ServerId HostFilter
    PasswordFile /dev/null
    GroupFile /dev/null
    getmask @128.149.*.*
}
```

Protection setups can also be defined to strictly perform user authentication. For example, the following object defines a protection allowing access for users "jenny" and "david", regardless of what machine they use to access the server.

```
Protection authEx {
    UserId me
    GroupId users
    AuthType Basic
    ServerId UserAuthenticate
    PasswordFile /WWW/.htpass
    GroupFile /dev/null
    getmask jenny, david
}
```

Compared to NCSA HTTPD, the limitation of the protection setups is their inability to deny access to specified users, groups, or machines. However, the tradeoff is the ability to combine specific users and groups with specific machines or domains.

Protection setups are the first stage in establishing directory-level security. The second stage of this process is the association of protection setups with particular portions of the document tree. Use the Protect directive to accomplish this task. Several syntactic forms of this command, along with relevant examples, are provided in steps 3–5 of Association of Directories to Protection Setups in the Steps section above.

12.5
ESTABLISH DIRECTORY-LEVEL SECURITY ON A CERN HTTP SERVER

Finally, the users and groups specified in the protection setup masks need to be defined in the designated password and group files, respectively. CERN password files are maintained using the htadm package distributed with the CERN software. Use this application to create, edit, and check password files. Table 12-7 summarizes the parameters and usage of this application.

PARAMETERS	PURPOSE
-adduser password_file user password real_name	Adds the specified user to the designated file
-check password_file user password	Checks the specified user's password
-create password_file	Creates the designated password file
-deluser password_file user	Deletes the user from the designated file
-password password_file user password	Changes the specified user's password

 Table 12-7 htadm parameters

Group files are maintained with a standard text editor. Groups are specified one per line. Each line is composed of a group name, a colon, and a group definition. The group definition uses the same syntax as described in step 12 of the Defining Named Setups section above.

Once protection setups have been defined and associated with relevant portions of the document tree and necessary auxiliary files have been created, directory-level security is configured for the specified directories. When a client requests a document in a protected directory, the protection setup associated with the directory is examined. If the type of access is restricted and the requester does not fit the appropriate mask criteria, then access is denied.

Comments

Directory-level security can be used in combination with file-level access control (see How-To 12.6) to achieve two levels of security. If both file and directory-level restrictions are imposed, then the conditions defined by both the mask and file-level access control list must be met for access to be granted.

Use of the DefProt directive establishes a default protection setup; however, without an access control list or a Protect directive, no documents are actually protected. If the *setup-file* argument is missing from a Protect rule, this information is inherited from the most recently used DefProt directive. Further information on the DefProt directive can be found in the documentation for the CERN HTTP server at URL http://www.w3.org/hypertext/WWW/Daemon/User/Config/Rules.html.

CHAPTER 12
HANDLING SERVER SECURITY

COMPLEXITY
INTERMEDIATE

12.6 How do I...
Set up file-level security on a CERN HTTP server?

COMPATIBILITY: CERN HTTP

Problem

I need more finely tuned control than directory-level protection. Most of the documents in my protected document tree can be safely viewed by a large group of valid users; however, I want to restrict the access of several particular documents to only a few users out of that large group. Is there a way I can do that?

Technique

The CERN HTTP server lets you set up security on a file-by-file basis using access control list files that reside in directories in which file-level restrictions are desired. In the access control file, each individual file in the directory can be referenced with an allowable transaction method and associated with a group of valid users.

This access control list provides host filtering and user authentication requirements for the file in the protected directory. If directory-level protection is already in force, then the access control list serves as a second level of security.

Thus, the specification of file-level security involves the creation of an access control list file in the directory that is to be protected. The following steps show how to create a CERN access control list file.

Steps

You should be familiar with establishing directory-level security before configuring file-level protection. How-To 12.5 provides this information. You need not include a mask command if you do not wish to require two levels of security.

Once you have established directory-level security for the directory in which you wish to install file-level security, you can proceed with the steps below.

1. To allow the file-level access control list to supersede any masks in the protection setup, insert the following directive in the protection setup associated with the directory protected.

```
ACLOverRide On
```

2. Change to the directory where you wish to install file-level security.
3. Create a file named .www_acl in your text editor. If it already exists, you may edit the previously defined security constraints in the existing file.

12.6
SET UP FILE-LEVEL SECURITY ON A CERN HTTP SERVER

4. Each line of this file represents the security configuration for a particular file or set of files. The general syntax for the access control list file line appears below.

```
file_specification: METHOD_LIST : group_definition
```

To add protection for a file, add a line to the access control list file. The file specification is the name of a file in the current directory, or a wildcard specification matching a number of local files. The METHOD_LIST determines which types of HTTP transactions are permitted. Finally, the group definition is a list of items with the same syntax as either mask parameters or group definitions in group files. The following line allows "get" method access to all files with the .htm file extension by group-list items "dsk" and "them".

```
*.htm: GET : dsk, them
```

5. You may add additional lines to specify file-level security for additional file(s).

6. When you have completed your edits, save the file.

How It Works

CERN server file-level security is configured with access control files. These access control files are located within the directory where the protected files reside. The standard name used by the server package for these files is .www_acl.

This file is composed of entry lines, each of which is examined whenever a request is made for a document within the directory. Actually, unless an ACLOverRide On directive appears in the directory protection setup, the request transaction must meet the restriction specified with the mask directive, if such directives are present. If these directory-level restrictions have been met, the request is then checked against the file-level security in the access control file.

The entries in the access control file are composed of three colon-separated fields. The first field contains the specification of a file to be protected; this specification can potentially contain a wildcard to protect several similarly named files. The second field is a list of HTTP methods that are to be protected for the given file specification. Finally, the last field contains a group definition that has the same syntax as described for mask directives and group file entries, described in How-To 12.5.

Having passed the directory-level security, the file specification and request method are matched against entries in the access control list. Unlike the matching of rules in the configuration file, examination does not stop when a matching file specification and method are found, but continues until no more entries are found or until a valid entry is found.

For example, given the following access control list file:

```
ping*:  GET, POST: jim, alex, @(*.*.auc.edu)
*.htm:  GET, POST, PUT: jenny@(*.*.jpl.gov)
```

a "get" method request by authenticated user "jenny" on a machine in the *.*.jpl.gov domain for the pingpong.htm file would succeed. This is so even though an earlier file specification and method match had been identified, but with a failure for invalid authentication.

For an access control list to be useful, the directory must already be configured in the global configuration file for directory-level security. This is required primarily to establish the password and group files to be used in evaluating group definitions in the access control list file.

Comments

File-level access control requires the definition of directory-level access control within the server's configuration file, either through a Protect or a DefProt directive for the directory in question. This directory-level specification is necessary to specify the password and group files that need to be referenced to verify valid users. If masks are defined in the directory access control, then both the masks as well as the restrictions in the access control list must be met to achieve access.

Inclusion of an ACLOverRide On directive in a protection setup for a directory allow a local access control list file to supersede the restriction specified in the setup. In effect, mask directives in the setup are ignored. Overriding the protection setup is a potential security risk and should be weighed by the site administrator before he or she includes the override directive in a protection setup.

COMPLEXITY
INTERMEDIATE

12.7 How do I... Install a CERN proxy server?

COMPATIBILITY: CERN HTTP

Problem

For security reasons, my site is running behind an Internet firewall, but behind the firewall we still need access to Internet-based information. Can a CERN HTTP server provide proxy service to the machines within the firewall?

Technique

The CERN HTTP server can act as a proxy server. In fact, the server software can function as both a proxy server and a standard HTTP server at the same time.

To provide proxy service, the server's global configuration file needs to be set properly. You can specify various aspects of your proxy: what methods are

12.7
INSTALL A CERN PROXY SERVER

supported, which sites may use your proxy, whether caching occurs, and even whether your proxy server actually uses another proxy server to fulfill requests. Once your proxy is running on the firewall machine, requests from inside the firewall are filtered and serviced through the proxy server accessing information outside the confines of the firewall.

Clients also need to be properly configured to recognize and use the proxy server. Environment variables need to be set to designate a proxy server to use for the various supported Internet protocols. Many popular browsers support proxy access, including Lynx, Mosaic, and Netscape. Tips on configuring particular browsers are provided in the How It Works section below.

The following instructions provide an approach to configuring a CERN server to act as a proxy server.

Steps

Do not start the proxy configuration from scratch. The CERN server software comes with several example configuration files. If you cannot find these files, they are available in the CERN server documentation and can be found at URL http://www.w3.org/hypertext/WWW/Daemon/User/Config/Examples.html. You should select the proxy configuration file that does or does not configure caching, whichever you require.

The following steps show you several ways to modify the available example configurations.

1. Change directories to the location of your global server configuration file; this file is usually located in the config subdirectory of the server software.

2. Open the configuration file in your text editor. Move your insertion point to the first instance of the Pass directive. Modify proxy parameters from this point forward.

3. Oftentimes file and FTP protocols are used interchangeably. For your proxy to support this alias, insert or uncomment the following directive.

```
Map file:* ftp:*
```

4. Selectively comment or uncomment the Pass directives for the protocols you want your proxy to support. Comment lines in the configuration file begin with a pound sign (#). Configure a Pass directive for each protocol you want the proxy to service. For example, the following line supports HTTP protocol proxy support.

```
Pass http:*
```

5. By default, only "get", "post", and "head" HTTP methods are enabled on your proxy server. To support other methods, issue an appropriate Enable directive in your configuration file. For example, to allow "put" method requests, add the following line.

Enable PUT

On the other hand, if you wanted to restrict already enabled methods, issue a suitable Disable directive. For example, the following line disables "post" method requests on the proxy server.

Disable POST

6. Use host restrictions to designate particular domains and machines that may use your CERN server as a proxy. Define a protection to limit access according to the instructions in How-To 12.5. This definition must not contain a reference to any password or group files. Further, use the mask directive to specify a generic mask for this protection. Finally, do not include references to specific users or groups in the mask you set in the protection setup. Once you have created an appropriate protection setup, associate this setup with the particular proxy protocol you wish to protect. Use a standard Protect directive to configure your host restrictions. For example, the following directive associates the PROT1 setup with HTTP protocol proxy service.

Protect http:* PROT1

7. One of the features that a proxy server can provide is the caching of documents retrieved from external sites. This feature provides greater efficiency in situations where particular outside resources are accessed on a regular basis. Selected directives used to configure a caching proxy server are discussed in the How It Works section below. In the configuration of a caching proxy server, start with the caching proxy configuration file provided through either the CERN distribution directories or the URL http://www.w3.org/hypertext/WWW/Daemon/User/Config/Examples.html. If you intend for your server to act as a caching proxy, enable caching by specifying a directory to store cached documents. Use the CacheRoot directive for this task. For example, to enable caching with documents stored in the /usr/local/cache directory, issue the following directive.

CacheRoot /usr/local/cache

8. Skip to step 9 if you are not configuring your server to act as an inner proxy server accessing an outer proxy server that provides access to the Internet. To configure your CERN server as an inner proxy server, issue the following directives indicating the URL of the outer proxy server as the parameter of the directives.

12.7
INSTALL A CERN PROXY SERVER

```
ftp_proxy http://other.proxy.server.edu/
gopher_proxy http://other.proxy.server.edu/
http_proxy http://other.proxy.server.edu/
wais_proxy http://other.proxy.server.edu/
```

Choose only those directives appropriate to the protocols for which you want the outer proxy consulted.

9. Save these changes. Stop and restart the server to realize your changes.

How It Works

For security reasons, many businesses and institutions are placing firewall systems between their own internal networks and the rest of the Internet. This provides greater security against a variety of potential problems. However, the downside is that the firewall not only keeps people out, it also keeps people in.

A proxy server acts as a bridge between those within the firewall and information residing on the Internet that can be accessed through several popular protocols. Figure 12-3 graphically demonstrates the job of a proxy server. Machines within the firewall, in1, in2, and in3, place HTTP requests with the proxy server running on the machine maintaining the firewall. The proxy server acts as the original requester's agent; it retrieves the desired information from sites

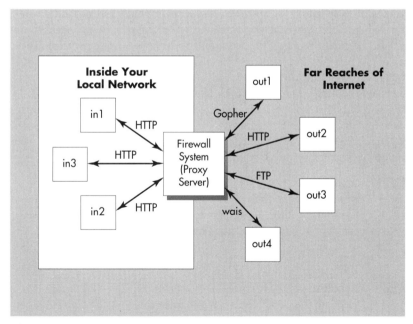

Figure 12-3 Proxy service diagram

423

outside the protected local network, out1, out2, out3, and out4. Then, the proxy passes the retrieved information to the requester.

Many clients support the use of a file proxy, which works the same as an FTP proxy. To support this use of the file proxy, add the line shown in step 3. This line tells the server to treat all file requests as FTP requests.

The CERN server can act as a proxy server for a variety of Internet protocol requests. The CERN proxy server may support the following protocols.

- **HTML** FTP
- **HTML** Gopher
- **HTML** HTTP
- **HTML** news
- **HTML** WAIS

Use a Pass directive, as described in step 4 above, to allow proxy access to any of these services.

You can configure the CERN proxy server to restrict access to particular proxy services. These restrictions are limited to host filtering. To establish this type of protection for a particular type of service, issue a Protect directive to associate a previously defined protection setup with a particular service. Step 6 above includes an example of associating a protection setup with HTTP proxy service.

Caching allows a proxy server to retain documents retrieved beyond a single request. When caching is enabled, a proxy client requests a document from the proxy, and the proxy retrieves the file from the appropriate site as usual. Then, instead of just passing the document back to the requesting client, the proxy server also retains a copy of the document for possible future use.

You enable caching either explicitly by issuing a Caching directive or implicitly by specifying a cache directory using the CacheRoot directive. Since a cache directory is necessary for caching documents, use of this directive serves as sufficient indication to the software that caching is enabled. The list below summarizes some of the directives available for configuring caching.

- **HTML** **Caching**
  Use this directive to explicitly enable caching. The two valid parameters of this directive are On and Off. Add the following line to your configuration file to turn on caching.

```
Caching On
```

- **HTML** **CacheRoot**
  Designate the cache directory using this directive. The single parameter for this directive is the directory where you want cached documents stored. Step 7 provides an example of this directive.

12.7
INSTALL A CERN PROXY SERVER

`HTML` **CacheSize**

Establish the maximum cache size in megabytes with this command. When the size of the cache reaches this limit, the proxy server begins deleting older and larger cached documents. The default size is 5 megabytes. For example, issue the following command to specify a 40-megabyte cache.

```
CacheSize 40 M
```

`HTML` **CacheUnused**

Use this directive to specify how long unused cached files stay in the cache. Multiple instances of this directive specify the time limit for different types of cached documents. If a document matches several of these directives, then the last CacheUnused directive appearing in the configuration file and matching the document applies. For example, if the following set of CacheUnused directives appears in the configuration file, the document ftp://www.mysite.edu/README remains in the cache seven days rather than four and a half days.

```
CacheUnused *                           4 days 12 hours
CacheUnused ftp:*                       5 days
CacheUnused ftp://www.mysite.edu/*      7 days
```

URL http://www.w3.org/hypertext/WWW/Daemon/User/Config provides information on additional directives for more fine-tuned control of proxy server caching.

A CERN proxy server may also act as client with respect to another proxy server. Step 8 above provides information on configuring this feature. This situation arises from a potential need to pass multiple levels of firewalls or to create multiple levels of document caches.

In the first case, security concerns lead to the creation of multiple levels of firewalls to better protect more sensitive areas of the local network. Examine Figure 12-3 again; picture in1 as not a machine, but as a subnet protected by a firewall, with an inner proxy used by the systems inside the subnet to access both the machines in the local network and the outer proxy, which in turn can access the rest of Internet.

In the second case, efficiency concerns lead to the creation of multiple levels of caching proxies. By caching often-used documents, the proxy server obviates the need to retrieve the document at each usage; the proxy sends the previously retrieved copy to service new requests. Multiple levels of caches provide a storage hierarchy supporting the retention of the most frequently used documents at the closest location and provide a means of establishing priority of retained documents. The outer proxy has one set of criteria for retaining documents while the inner proxy has a more specific set of criteria based upon the requirements of those clients serviced by the inner proxy. In this way, the outer proxy caches documents frequently accessed by all of its clients while the inner proxy provides access to documents cached in its own cache as well as those in the outer proxy's cache.

Comments

The steps provided above do not attempt to describe the entire server configuration process. They deal solely with the configuration of the proxy server. You should consult the CERN server documentation for instructions on adding and/or modifying appropriate directives within the configuration file. Online information is available at URL http://www.w3.org/hypertext/WWW/Daemon/User/Config/find_this_URL.

When configuring a proxy server, you must not attempt to establish user authentication on proxy services. The only security that functions properly for proxy service is host filtering.

A CERN server may act as both proxy server and HTTP server at the same time. To configure your server to perform in this way, configure your server as you would for a standard HTTP server, then continue with the procedure defined in this How-To.

Browsers behind a firewall must also be configured for use with proxies. The Netscape Navigator browser provides a dialog box from the Preferences menu that allows you to perform this configuration task. Figure 12-4 displays this dialog.

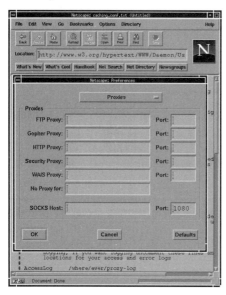

Figure 12-4 Proxy configuration in Netscape

Using this dialog, specify the host names for the machines that serve as proxies for the desired protocol. The No Proxy portion of the dialog allows the specification of Internet domains that are accessible directly without requiring a proxy.

Configuring other browsers to deal with proxies usually involves setting environment variables. Browsers such as Mosaic and Lynx use environment variables to set this information. In UNIX and VMS, the following environment variables configure the protocol-specific proxies.

- **HTML** `ftp_proxy`
- **HTML** `gopher_proxy`
- **HTML** `http_proxy`
- **HTML** `news_proxy`
- **HTML** `wais_proxy`

For example, to configure UNIX Mosaic to access proxy.mysite.edu for HTTP requests, issue the following C shell command before running Mosaic.

```
setenv http_proxy "http://proxy.mysite.edu/"
```

Consult the relevant portions of your browser documentation for other browsers.

12.8 How do I... Establish domain and address security and password authentication on a MacHTTP server?

COMPLEXITY: INTERMEDIATE

COMPATIBILITY: MACHTTP

Problem

I want to allow and deny access to my server MacHTTP based on the machine or network that a user is trying to access from. I would also like to require passwords for certain documents and directories on my server. How can I do this?

Technique

You can restrict access to your server based on the user's machine name, domain name, or IP address by editing the MacHTTP.config file for your server. Two command key words, ALLOW and DENY, enable you to limit the machines and networks that have access to your server.

User authentication handles file-level and directory-level security. User authentication is based on the notion of realms. A realm is a group of files or folders that contain a common substring in their names. A realm is specified in the MacHTTP.config file using the key word REALM. The REALM key word is followed by a name substring and a description. The specified substring is unique to all of the names of the protected files, or of their parent directories. The description is effectively the name of the realm. No blank spaces are allowed in the realm name. (The entire description must be a contiguous string of characters.)

The following procedures show how to add serverwide host filtering and file-level and folder-level user authentication.

Steps

The first procedure below outlines the steps necessary to establish host filtering on your MacHTTP server. These instructions are immediately followed by the process for installing user authentication at the file and folder levels. In both cases, make the necessary modifications to the MacHTTP.config file.

Host Filtering

The following procedure describes the necessary steps for configuring host filtering on your server. Host filtering works across all documents on your server.

1. Open the MacHTTP.config file in your text editor.

2. For each machine or network domain that you want to allow on your server, issue an ALLOW directive. The parameters of the ALLOW command are either names or appropriate IP addresses. For example, to allow access to the server from machine foo.bar.com, add the following directive.

```
ALLOW foo.bar.com.
```

Or to allow access to the server from all machines in the bozo.net network, add the following directive.

```
ALLOW bozo.net.
```

3. For each machine or network domain that you want to prevent from accessing your server, issue a DENY directive. The parameters of the DENY commands are either names or appropriate IP addresses. For example, to deny access to the server from machine foo.bar.com, add the following directive.

```
DENY foo.bar.com.
```

Or to deny access to the server from all machines in the bozo.net network, add the following directive.

```
DENY bozo.net.
```

4. Save this file and restart your server.

> Note: The examples above use entire machine and domain names terminated with a period (.). MacHTTP also allows the specification of a substring, indicated by the absence of the terminating period. The server allows or denies access to all machines or domains that contain this substring in their name or IP address.

User Authentication and Password Creation

User authentication provides file-level and directory-level security on MacHTTP servers. The process below describes the two components necessary to configure user authentication. The first component of configuration is the specification of files to be protected. The second is the specification of usernames and passwords that allow access to protected files.

1. Open the MacHTTP.config file in your text editor.
2. For each set of files or folders you want to protect, issue a REALM directive. The REALM command requires two parameters: a string that defines which files are in the realm and a description that serves as the name of the realm. For example, to create the realm "round" protecting files containing the string "cam" in their path, issue the following REALM directive.

```
REALM cam round
```

> Note: The name of the realm may not contain any blank spaces. Therefore, a name such as "round realm" is invalid, but "round_realm" is not.

3. Save this file and restart your server.
4. Add users by selecting the Passwords interface found at the bottom of the Edit pull-down menu.
5. Select the realm you want this user to have access to in the pull-down menu found at the bottom of the Passwords interface. (All realms that have been declared in the config file should show up here.)
6. Enter a username and a password with which this user will access protected files in this realm.
7. If you want this user to have access to multiple realms, repeat steps 5 and 6 for every realm that you want to allow this user to access.
8. Exit this dialog.

CHAPTER 12
HANDLING SERVER SECURITY

How It Works

MacHTTP provides both host filtering and user authentication security. The host filtering facilities let machines and domains, specified by name or IP address, be allowed or denied access to the server as a whole. User authentication provides finer-tuned security by requiring a username and password to access any files or folders containing a specified string in their path.

Host filtering uses the ALLOW and DENY commands to specify access restrictions. The ALLOW and DENY key words are followed by an explicit machine name followed by a period, or a substring of the machine or domain name without a period, specifying that every access from a machine or network that contains the substring should be either allowed or denied access. You specify machines and domains by either name or IP address.

For example, to allow access to all machines whose IP addresses start with 128.122.1, and to deny access to all machines in the bar.com domain, enter the following statements.

```
ALLOW 128.122.1
DENY bar.com.
```

Notice that the bar.com entry is followed by a period. All domain names are case-sensitive and must be followed by a period. Also notice that the IP address is not followed by a period. This allows machines with IP addresses starting with 128.122.1 to access the server; this specification includes machines such as 128.122.12.7, 128.122.1.1, and 128.122.193.74. If you want to be specific, append a period to the end of the IP address. For example, to allow access from only the machine with IP address 128.122.1.1, issue the following directive.

```
ALLOW 128.122.1.1.
```

MacHTTP assumes that you will specifically deny and allow all machines if you use the DENY or ALLOW statements. That is, there is an implicit DENY for all machines if you use the ALLOW command. This means that if you want to allow access from all machines with the exception of a machine called, say whoopy.fun.gov, you would need to expressly allow all machines before denying this last one with the following statements.

```
ALLOW 1
ALLOW 2
ALLOW 3
ALLOW 4
ALLOW 5
ALLOW 6
ALLOW 7
ALLOW 8
ALLOW 9

DENY whoopy.fun.gov.
```

12.8
MACHTTP SECURITY ISSUES

Notice that there are no periods following the numbers. This means that any machines whose IP addresses start with the numbers 1–9 will be allowed access, with the exception of whoopy.fun.gov, which is specifically denied access.

In a similar fashion, if you wanted to deny access from all machines except machines in the spew.org domain, but you also wanted to deny access from one machine within this domain called "pooky", you could take advantage of the explicit DENY and use the following statements.

```
ALLOW spew.org.
DENY pooky.spew.org.
```

MacHTTP's user authentication facility supports security at the file and folder levels. Use the REALM directive to specify the protected files and folders. This command takes two parameters: a name substring and a description. The name substring determines which files are protected. The description serves as the name of the protected realm. (The description must not contain blank spaces.)

For example, to create a realm called My_Friends that controls all files and directories whose names contain the string "friend", enter the following statement in your config file.

```
REALM friend My_Friends
```

Now you could create a folder on your server called "friend", "friends", "my_friend23", or any other legal filename that contains the string "friend". Only users associated with the "My_Friends" realm can access the files in this folder. Likewise, if you had a file on your server called cool_friends.html, this file would also be governed by the My_Friends realm.

Similarly, if you wanted to create realms for Trusted_Users, Officers, Presidents, and Riff_Raff, you could declare the following realms.

```
REALM trust     Trusted_Users
REALM office    Officers
REALM pres      Presidents
REALM rifraf    Riff_Raff
```

Any files that contained "trust" somewhere in their URL would be governed by the Trusted_Users realm; likewise, any URL on this server containing "office" would fall under Officers, "pres" under Presidents, and so on.

Once you have set up your realms, you need to create usernames and passwords for people who will be able to access these documents. This is a relatively easy task that can be done using the Passwords interface found at the bottom of the Edit pull-down menu when your MacHTTP server is running. Figure 12-5 displays the dialog you see when selecting this option.

A user can be removed from a realm using this same interface. The interface lists the entries as Username•Realm, so delete the entry for the realm(s) that you no longer want this user to access.

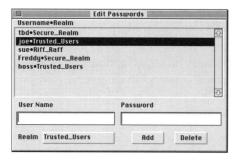

Figure 12-5 MacHTTP Passwords interface

Comments

MacHTTP's security features are similar to the features found in NCSA's HTTPD and the CERN server, if somewhat crude in comparison. MacHTTP doesn't let you allow and deny machines and networks on a per-directory level as the NCSA server does. But user authentication is easy to set up and administer, and it provides an adequate level of security for most installations.

12.9 How do I... Use public key encryption?

COMPLEXITY: INTERMEDIATE

COMPATIBILITY: PUBLIC KEY ENCRYPTION CAPABLE SERVER AND BROWSER

Problem

I have confidential documents that I want to provide to select users in a secure fashion. The Basic authentication scheme will not suffice because under this scheme, servers transmit documents and browsers send requests in the open. Consequently, unauthorized individuals monitoring the network traffic may view my confidential pages.

Technique

Servers and browsers use encryption on documents and requests prior to transmission over an open connection. The recipient decrypts the transmission prior to presenting the document or servicing the request. Thus, diverting or examining transmissions only yields an encrypted transmission.

12.9 USE PUBLIC KEY ENCRYPTION

Steps

For a browser or server that has built-in encryption capabilities, the actual encryption process should be transparent and not require any additional work on your part. The only exception to this may be a requirement to acquire a certification of authenticity transported by a secure means. (See http://www.verisign.com/netscape/index.html for additional information on receiving a digital ID for use with a Netscape Commerce Server.)

For browsers and servers requiring plug-in components, installation and configuration will vary. The steps below provide a generic approach for finding the appropriate encryption software.

1. Determine the type of public key encryption software necessary for you to communicate. Table 12-8 specifies the common public key encryption software.

ENCRYPTION SOFTWARE	LOCATION
PGP	http://www.efh.org/pgp/pgpwork.html
RIPEM	http://www.cs.indiana.edu/ripem/dir.html

Table 12-8 Common public key encryption software

2. Download a software package suitable for your hardware and software platform. Source and executable code for these packages may be accessed through the references provided in Table 12-8.

3. Examine the manual for the software package to determine how to generate, maintain, and publish public keys.

4. Configure your browser and server to call the plug-in package when receiving an encrypted transmission.

Configuring an NCSA HTTPD Server with PGP/PEM Hooks

The following procedure provides a stepwise approach for configuring an HTTPD server to serve encrypted HTML pages and respond to encrypted requests.

1. If you did not compile your server with the -DPEM_AUTH flag set, you need to acquire such a server or recompile with this flag set. (This must be an export-controlled version of 1.5.)

2. Retrieve scripts that will call the encryption software to either decrypt requests or encrypt documents. (These scripts are available in distributions of HTTPD 1.3, and will likely be available through the export-controlled version of 1.5.)

3. Edit and install the scripts as necessary and described within the scripts.

4. Edit the server configuration file httpd.conf. Add the following directives to add pointers to the PGP and PEM scripts, respectively.

```
PGPEncryptCmd /usr/local/somewhere/pgp-enc
PGPDecryptCmd /usr/local/somewhere/pgp-dec
PEMEncryptCmd /usr/local/somewhere/ripem-enc
PEMDecryptCmd /usr/local/somewhere/ripem-dec
```

The paths should specify where these scripts are located on your server site.

5. Add the following two lines to indicate the name of the server entity used to identify the server's public key.

```
PGPServerEntity webmaster@mysite.edu
PEMServerEntity webmaster@mysite.edu
```

This entity should be the same one you place on the public/private keys that you generate for your server.

6. To protect desired HTML pages with encryption, open the local or global access file in an editor.

7. Within the file or within the proper <DIRECTORY> element in the global file, change or add an AuthType directive with a value of PEM or PGP as desired.

```
AuthType PEM
```

The remainder of the access file can be modified as described in How-To's 12.1–12.3.

8. Close the file or edit another <DIRECTORY> element.

Configuring an NCSA X-Mosaic Browser with PGP/PEM Hooks

The steps below guide you through configuring NCSA's X-Mosaic browser to use a plug-in PGP- or PEM-based package to encrypt/decrypt HTTP requests and responses.

1. If you did not compile your Mosaic browser with the -DPEM_AUTH flag set, you need to acquire such a browser or recompile with this flag set.

2. Open your X resources file and add the following resources. Modify the data values to correspond to appropriate information for your system.

```
Mosaic*pemEncrypt: /usr/local/somewhere/ripem-enc
Mosaic*pemDecrypt: /usr/local/somewhere/ripem-dec
Mosaic*pemEntity: me@mysite.edu
Mosaic*pgpEncrypt: /usr/local/somewhere/pgp-enc
Mosaic*pgpDecrypt: /usr/local/somewhere/pgp-dec
Mosaic*pgpEntity: me@mysite.edu
```

12.9
USE PUBLIC KEY ENCRYPTION

The entity value should correspond to the key name that you previously sent to the server administrator.

3. Save the resource file and restart your X environment.

How It Works

Transferring encrypted transmissions over the Web requires the use of several HTTP header elements and compatible encryption/decryption software supported by both the browser and server. The actual encryption/decryption software may be supplied as part of the browser or server, as it is with Netscape's Navigator and Commerce Server, or as external plug-in components, as it is with NCSA's HTTPD and Mosaic. Once you add the plug-in components, or acquire a package with included software, the actual encryption/decryption process is transparent.

The benefit of plug-in encryption is that you are not limited to those encryption technologies supplied with your browser or server. The primary disadvantage is that you are required to acquire, install, and configure the plug-in encryption modules to meet your needs. On the other hand, the benefit of built-in encryption is that your use of it is transparent from the start. The disadvantage is that you are limited to the encryption technologies supplied with your browser or server.

The proposed public key protection differs slightly from the prototype scheme implemented by NCSA. The following discussion examines the proposed scheme. (See the Comments below for an examination of NCSA's prototype implementation.) If you are unfamiliar with HTTP, consult Appendix G as a reference.

First, the browser requests a file protected by encryption.

```
GET /protected/mydoc.htm HTTP/1.0
UserAgeny: MyBrowser/1.0
```

The server denies this initial request for the document unless the request includes required authentication information. This denial includes a copy of the server's public key in the WWW-Authenticate HTTP response header field. For example, such a response might look like the following:

```
HTTP/1.0 401 Unauthorized -- authentication failed
WWW-Authenticate: Pubkey realm="RealmName", key="EncodedServerPublicKey"
```

When the browser determines that the server denied an unauthorized request, the browser prompts the user for an authorized username and password. The browser concatenates this username and password with the IP address of your machine, a time stamp, and the browser's public key. A colon separates each of these fields. The browser encrypts this string using the server's public key and generates a new request.

```
GET /protected/mydoc.htm HTTP/1.0
UserAgeny: MyBrowser/1.0
Authorization: Pubkey EncodedEncryptedString
```

The server unencodes and decrypts the authorization data. The server checks the structure of the data to confirm that it contains five colon-separated fields. Next, the IP address contained in the string is matched against the IP address of the machine actually making the request. The server, then, compares the time stamp to the current server time. If any of these checks fail, authorization is denied. Once these checks succeed, a process similar to the Basic authentication scheme is used to check the validity of the specified username and password for the requested document.

Once the server completes these checks, it generates a response. This response uses the browser's public key to securely transfer the information necessary for the browser to decrypt the requested document. The server encrypts the document itself using a single-key encryption method such as DES or IDEA; for large documents, public key encryption methods require significantly more time than single-key encryption systems. The response body contains this encrypted document. The response header includes fields that, in conjunction with the browser private key, allow decryption of the response body. These fields include DEK-Info, Key-Info, and MIC-Info. Such a response might appear as follows:

```
HTTP/1.0 200 OK
DEK-Info: DES-CBD,...
Key-Info: DES_ECB,...
MIC-Info: MD5,...
Content-Length: ...

Encrypted Document
```

The browser uses its private key and the information in the header to decrypt the transmitted document, which it presents to the user. (For more information on these additional header fields, see Request for Comments number 1421, available at URL http://www.w3.org/hypertext/WWW/AccessAuthorization/rfc1421.html.)

Comments

NCSA implemented a prototype of this scheme using either PGP or RIPEM for HTTPD 1.3 and Mosaic (X-Window version); however, because of legal restrictions, they removed the hooks for this scheme. Current documentation indicates that encryption mechanisms may be added back to HTTPD in an export-controlled version of 1.5.

Netscape's Navigator and Commerce Server make use of RSA encryption technology. This encryption software is built-in. Therefore, these packages will use this encryption software as necessary in a transparent manner.

The NCSA prototype implementation supports calls to external encryption software to encrypt/decrypt transmissions. An example transcript of the HTTP request process under this prototype appears as follows:

First, the browser requests a document.

12.9
USE PUBLIC KEY ENCRYPTION

```
GET /protected/mydoc.htm HTTP/1.0
UserAgent: Mosaic/X 2.2
```

The server denies access.

```
HTTP/1.0 401 Unauthorized
WWW-Authenticate: PEM entity="webmaster@mysite.edu"
Server: NCSA/1.3
```

The browser retrieves the public key for the specified entity using the finger command and sends an encrypted request as the body of an HTTP request using a proprietary content type. Table 12-9 shows the proprietary MIME types created to support this prototype.

MIME TYPE	PURPOSE
application/x-www-pem-request	Body contains a PEM-encrypted request.
application/x-www-pgp-request	Body contains a PGP-encrypted request.
application/x-www-pem-reply	Body contains a PEM-encrypted response.
application/x-www-pgp-reply	Body contains a PGP-encrypted response.

Table 12-9 Proprietary MIME types to support encryption system prototype

The browser generates an encrypted request by using the retrieved public key to encrypt the actual request. The browser places this encrypted request as the HTTP request body. The request header specifies both the browser's PEM or PGP entity and the content type from those mentioned in Table 12-9.

```
GET / HTTP/1.0
Authorization: PEM entity="me@mysite.edu"
Content-type: application/x-www-pem-request

--- BEGIN PRIVACY-ENHANCE MESSAGE ---
Encrypted request...
--- END PRIVACY-ENHANCE MESSAGE ---
```

The server generates a response in a similar fashion. The server retrieves the public key for the specified entity from a local key file and generates an encrypted response. This encrypted response becomes the body of the HTTP response sent. The header of the response uses one of the reply MIME types listed in Table 12-9.

```
HTTP/1.0 200 OK
Content-type: application/x-www-pem-reply

--- BEGIN PRIVACY-ENHANCE MESSAGE ---
Encrypted response...
--- END PRIVACY-ENHANCE MESSAGE ---
```

CHAPTER 13
THE COMMON GATEWAY INTERFACE (CGI)

THE COMMON GATEWAY INTERFACE (CGI)

How do I...

- **13.1** Pass data to a CGI application?
- **13.2** Send information to a browser from CGI applications?
- **13.3** Create a simple CGI application?
- **13.4** Install a CGI application?
- **13.5** Create a query document using the <ISINDEX> element?
- **13.6** Access client data in sh CGI scripts?
- **13.7** Parse client data in CGI programs and scripts?
- **13.8** Specify Netscape Server Push?
- **13.9** Write a CGI application to send me e-mail?

Common Gateway Interface (CGI) applications are the source of dynamic, interactive HTML documents. They can present snapshots of current server information. They can accept user-specified data, process it, and respond with ad hoc HTML 3 pages generated from the processed information.

CHAPTER 13
THE COMMON GATEWAY INTERFACE (CGI)

CGI applications present changing data, such as up-to-the-minute stock quotes. They can interpret and process input, such as sending an e-mail message. And they can provide a dynamic response to input data, such as presenting the results of a database query. This chapter discusses common gateway interface issues, from the interaction between the server, browser, and CGI program to interpreting data passed to CGI programs. Finally, this chapter describes the development of CGI programs by presenting and explaining how to allow people to send you e-mail.

CGI applications are often referred to as gateway applications, programs, or scripts. The name may vary, but the purpose of these programs remains the same, to generate dynamic World Wide Web documents.

The server executes gateway programs locally; therefore, these applications may access system resources beyond those commonly available through the server. Consequently, CGI applications represent a potential security risk for the server site, and the server administrator may restrict the development, installation, and maintenance of applications.

13.1 Pass Data to a CGI Application

When a user activates a link or a button triggering a CGI application, the server launches that program. First, the CGI application needs to acquire information. In this How-To, you will learn how the server receives information from an HTML page and sends it to CGI applications.

13.2 Send Information to a Browser from CGI Applications

Once a CGI program has performed its appointed task, it sends the result to the server, which passes it on to a browser. In this How-To, you will learn how to use the two most common methods for transmitting information to a browser from a gateway application.

13.3 Create a Simple CGI Application

You want people to access up-to-date data through an HTML document, but you don't want to make an employee modify the document every ten minutes. In this How-To, you will learn how to develop a CGI application to generate an HTML page from raw data whenever the page is accessed.

13.4 Install a CGI Application

You have created a CGI application to generate dynamic HTML documents. Now you want people to link and send data to your program. In this How-To, you will learn how to make your gateway program accessable from your servers.

13.5 Create a Query Document Using the <ISINDEX> Element

The HTML <ISINDEX> element allows users to input a single piece of data. In this How-To, you will learn how to use this element to provide data to gateway programs.

13.6 Access Client Data in sh CGI Scripts

If you are running a UNIX-based server, your first CGI application is likely to be developed in this Bourne shell script language. In this How-To, you will learn how to access input data in a CGI Bourne shell script.

13.7 Parse Client Data in CGI Programs and Scripts

You develop gateway programs in many different languages. Acquiring user data from HTML forms is a common task, independent of the CGI programming language chosen. In this How-To, you will learn how to acquire data from HTML forms.

13.8 Specify Netscape Server Push

With the Netscape viewer, you can develop gateway applications that provide automatically updating HTML pages. In this How-To, you will learn how to create CGI applications to generate server pushed HTML pages.

13.9 Write a CGI Application to Send Me E-mail

In this How-To, you will learn how to combine all the necessary elements of CGI application development to build a CGI e-mail support package.

COMPLEXITY
ADVANCED

13.1 How do I... Pass data to a CGI application?

COMPATIBILITY: HTML, HTTP, CGI/1.1

Problem

When I create dynamic documents, I need to send input data from my HTML page to the server. This data passes through many hands before my CGI application can process it and generate an HTML document. The HTML document that calls the CGI application directly affects how information is passed to my gateway program. What is this process? And how will the data eventually reach my application? How is the passing mechanism determined?

Technique

Your CGI application receives data from three sources: the server, a user, and the author of the HTML page triggering the application. Ultimately, all data passed to your gateway program is sent by the server. The data supplied by the server is available via special environment variables. This type of data is commonly available to gateway programs of all types. Details on these environment variables are documented in the Comments section below.

CHAPTER 13
THE COMMON GATEWAY INTERFACE (CGI)

Browsers transform user and author data, and then send it to the server. The server, in turn, sends it to your CGI application in a manner prescribed by the common gateway interface protocol. Both of these data types are sent in the form of attribute/value pairs. (For example, a pair might associate the value "red" with the attribute "color.") User data is supplied by the reader, and author data is supplied by you, or whoever is authoring the HTML page accessing your gateway program.

CGI provides several mechanisms for passing data to your applications. The way data is sent depends on the input and the HTTP request method used. There are three common methods:

- **HTML** Command line arguments: The server starts your application and passes the data on the command line.

- **HTML** Environment variables: The gateway program accesses data placed in specified environment variables. The server places this information in these locations before starting your application.

- **HTML** Standard input data block: The server launches the gateway program and places a data block in an area accessible to your program. The gateway application then reads and interprets this data.

Steps

The way the server passes data to your application is based on the way you gather your input data and how you send it. In addition to user input, the server places specific information in the execution environment of your CGI application, independent of how user data is passed.

This How-To demonstrates how to pass user and author data to gateway programs from your HTML documents.

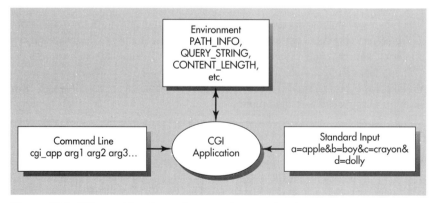

Figure 13-1 CGI provides three data passing mechanisms

13.1
PASS DATA TO A CGI APPLICATION

Sending Command Line Argument Input Data

<ISINDEX> user data generates command line arguments. This is the only way a server passes command line arguments to a gateway application. To generate CGI application input data as command line arguments, use an <ISINDEX> element to request user data.

1. Open the searchable document in a text editor.

2. Include an <ISINDEX> element in the <HEAD> element of the document.

3. Save this document.

> Note: <ISINDEX> elements may only be used in searchable documents. If your server does not support all HTML documents as searchable documents, this element may only be used in dynamically searchable documents generated by gateway applications.

Sending Input Data Through the Environment

Two types of data can be made available through environment variables. Server-specified data is available when any gateway application is started. This commonly available data is described in the Comments section below.

This section describes how to send user-entered and author-entered data via the QUERY_STRING environment variables. This data is entered via an HTML interactive form. The procedure below describes how to create this embedded form.

1. Open the document from which data will be sent to your gateway application.

2. Move your insertion point to the location in the document where you want to request and specify data.

3. Insert a <FORM> element. This element should use the "get" method. Enclose in the <FORM> element any elements necessary to request the desired data. For example, the following element transmits the user data via environment variable to the *cgi_app* CGI application.

```
<!-- Appropriate HTML elements for document -->
<FORM METHOD="GET" ACTION="http://www.mysite.edu/cgi-bin/cgi_app"
ENCTYPE="application/x-www-form-urlencoded">
...
<INPUT TYPE="submit" VALUE="Mail">
</FORM>
<!-- More HTML elements to conclude document -->
```

Chapter 10 provides more information on the creation of HTML forms.

4. Save this document.

Sending Additional Author Input Data Through the Environment

This section describes how you can specify author data to be passed to a gateway application via the PATH_INFO environment variables. This data is included as additional path information in a URL referring to the target gateway application. Thus, you can send this type of information via either an ACTION attribute of a form when user input is also required, or via a standard link anchor when user input is not required. The procedure below describes how to send this type of author data.

1. Open the document from which additional author data will be sent to your gateway application.

2. Move your insertion point to the location in the document where you specify the URL of the gateway application.

3. If this is in a <FORM> element, include on the tail end of the form's ACTION URL the desired author data. Enclose in the <FORM> element any elements necessary to request the desired user input. (Chapter 10 provides more information on the creation of HTML forms.) For example, the following element transmits the user data via environment variable to the *cgi_app* CGI application. The PATH_INFO environment variable stores the author data "author_data".

```
<!-- Appropriate HTML elements for document -->
<!-- The form's method may be either GET or POST -->
<FORM METHOD="GET" ACTION="http://www.mysite.edu/cgi-bin/cgi_app/author_data"
ENCTYPE="application/x-www-form-urlencoded">
...
<INPUT TYPE="submit" VALUE="Mail">
</FORM>
<!-- More HTML elements to conclude document -->
```

Or, if in an anchor, include on the tail end of the anchor's HREF URL the desired author data. For example, the following element transmits the author data via the PATH_INFO environment variable to the *cgi_app* CGI application.

```
<!-- Appropriate HTML elements for document -->
A standard link can be used to pass
<A HREF="http://www.mysite.edu/cgi-bin/cgi-app/author_data">author data</A>
to a gateway application.
<!-- More HTML elements to conclude document -->
```

4. Save this document.

13.1
PASS DATA TO A CGI APPLICATION

Sending Input Data Through Standard Input

This is the most common method of passing input data. Unlike the other methods, this approach is not hindered by the size restriction of a command line or environment variables.

This section describes how you can send data to your CGI application as a data block on the standard input stream. This data is entered through an HTML document with a form specifying the "post" method. The procedure below describes how to pass data to CGI applications through the application's standard input.

1. Open the document from which data will be sent to your gateway application.

2. Move your insertion point to the location in the document where you want to request and specify data.

3. Insert a <FORM> element. This element should use the "post" method. Enclose in the <FORM> element any elements necessary to request the desired data. For example, the following element transmits data by the standard input to the *cgi_app* CGI application.

```
<!-- Appropriate HTML elements for document -->
<FORM METHOD="POST" ACTION="http://www.mysite.edu/cgi-bin/cgi_app"
ENCTYPE="application/x-www-form-urlencoded">
...
<INPUT TYPE="submit" VALUE="Mail">
</FORM>
<!-- More HTML elements to conclude document -->
```

How It Works

Your CGI application receives information by three means:

- **HTML** Command line arguments
- **HTML** Environment variables
- **HTML** Standard input

Sending Command Line Argument Input Data

The server generates command line inputs by interpreting the data entered into an <ISINDEX> element. For example, Figure 13-2 displays a sample document containing an <ISINDEX> element. The input field generated by the <ISINDEX> element prompts the user for information from an HTML document.

The reader enters data in the input field. Once the data is entered, the browser generates a "get" method HTTP request. The browser submits a query URL with the "get" request. This URL is composed of the current URL with the input data appended as a query string. Each word in the input field is separated by a plus sign in the query URL:

Figure 13-2 <ISINDEX> tag causes user to be prompted for search terms from an HTML document

URL?arg1+arg2+arg3+arg4...

This query URL is passed to the server, which starts the gateway program in the URL with the arguments on the command line:

cgi_app arg1 arg2 arg3 arg4...

> Note: You can also pass author data by simulating the results of an <ISINDEX> input request. The query URL in the above form would take the place of a standard URL when specifying a link anchor. Generally, an appended query string that does not contain an equal sign (=) is considered an <ISINDEX> type request. For example:
>
> <A HREF="/cgi-bin/app?data">...</A>.

Sending Input Data Through the Environment

"Get" method HTML forms generate user data sent via environment variables. For example, the following elements transmit one piece of user data and two pieces of author data via environment variable to the specified CGI program. (Chapter 10 provides more information on the creation of HTML forms.)

```
<!-- Appropriate HTML elements for document -->
<FORM METHOD="GET" ACTION="http://www.mysite.edu/cgi-bin/cgi_app"
ENCTYPE="application/x-www-form-urlencoded">
Enter the Text of your message below:<BR>
<TEXTAREA NAME="arg1" ROWS=10 COLS=40></TEXTAREA>
<INPUT TYPE="hidden" NAME="arg2" VALUE="dsk@cau.auc.edu">
<INPUT TYPE="hidden" NAME="arg3" VALUE="Miscellaneous">
<INPUT TYPE="submit" VALUE="Mail">
</FORM>
<!-- More HTML elements to conclude document -->
```

13.1
PASS DATA TO A CGI APPLICATION

The text area element in the above form represents information entered by the reader that the gateway application accesses. The two hidden input elements contain information specified by the author of the HTML page calling the gateway application.

When the reader enters data in the input fields of the form and presses the Submit button, the browser generates a "get" method HTTP request. The "get" request includes a query URL composed of the gateway URL specified by the form's ACTION attribute, with the input data appended. Data is transformed to encode special characters and spaces prior to submission to the server. The appended query string contains attributes and values separated by equal (=) signs, with each attribute/value pair separated by the ampersand (&):

URL?arg1=val1&arg2=val2&arg3=val

This query URL is sent to the server, which runs the gateway program represented by the URL in the following environment.

QUERY_STRING="arg1=val1&arg2=val2&arg3=val3"

> Note: A query URL in the format above can replace a standard URL as the target of a link anchor in an HTML document. Use this method as well as hidden form input fields to send author data as attribute/value pair data to a gateway application.

Sending Additional Author Input Data Through the Environment

The PATH_INFO environment variable stores data that is appended to a URL. Whether the URL is the target of a link, the action of a "get" method form, or the action of a "post" method form, you can send author data through this variable. For example, the ACTION URL and the link target URL below both specify author data sent to the *cgi-app* gateway application.

```
<!-- Appropriate HTML elements for document -->
<FORM METHOD="GET" ACTION="http://www.mysite.edu/cgi-bin/cgi-app/author_data"
ENCTYPE="application/x-www-form-urlencoded">
Enter the Text of your message below:<BR>
<TEXTAREA NAME="arg1" ROWS=10 COLS=40></TEXTAREA>
<INPUT TYPE="submit" VALUE="Mail">
</FORM>
<!-- More HTML elements to conclude document -->
A standard link can be used to pass
<A HREF="http://www.mysite.edu/cgi-bin/cgi-app/author_data">author data</A>
to a gateway application.
<!-- More HTML elements to conclude document -->
```

When a link or button is pressed, the reader triggers an appropriate HTTP request. The METHOD attribute of the form specifies the method to use if the results of a form are submitted. A standard "get" method request is performed if a link is activated. The browser generates a URL to submit with the request. This URL is composed of the gateway application's URL, with the author-specified data appended. Table 13-1 displays the possible browser-generated URLs depending on the access method.

ACCESS TYPE	URL GENERATED
Link	URL/author_data
"get" method form	URL/author_data?user_data
"post" method form	URL/author_data

 Table 13-1 URLs generated to send author data

This URL is passed to the server that runs the gateway program represented by the URL. The server places the author data in the PATH_INFO environment variable:

PATH_INFO="/author_data"

Sending Input Data Through Standard Input

Standard input passed data is generated through an HTML form with the "post" method specified. For example, the following <FORM> element sends data to the *cgi_app* application's standard input.

```
<!-- Appropriate HTML elements for document -->
<FORM METHOD="POST" ACTION="http://www.mysite.edu/cgi-bin/cgi_app"
ENCTYPE="application/x-www-form-urlencoded">
Enter the Text of your message below:<BR>
<TEXTAREA NAME="arg1" ROWS=10 COLS=40></TEXTAREA>
<INPUT TYPE="hidden" NAME="arg2" VALUE="dsk@cau.auc.edu">
<INPUT TYPE="hidden" NAME="arg3" VALUE="Miscellaneous">
<INPUT TYPE="submit" VALUE="Mail">
</FORM>
<!-- More HTML elements to conclude document -->
```

When this form is submitted, one piece of user data, "arg1", and two pieces of author data, "arg2" and "arg3", are sent to the standard input of the *cgi_app* application.

The reader enters data in the form's input fields. Once the Submit button is pressed, the browser generates a "post" method HTTP request containing a gateway URL specified by the form's ACTION attribute. The input data from the form is transformed and sent to the server in the request body. (See Appendix G for information on the format of an HTTP request.)

13.1
PASS DATA TO A CGI APPLICATION

The server runs the gateway application specified by the URL in the request. The server sends the input data to this program's standard input. The environment variable CONTENT_LENGTH stores the number of characters sent by the server.

The data sent on the standard input is formatted as a series of attribute/value pairs. The attributes and values are separated by equal signs (=), and each pair is separated by an ampersand (&):

arg1=val1&arg2=val2&arg3=val3

General Information on Data Passing

The data passing approach chosen is based upon the request type ("get" or "post") and nature (<ISINDEX>, form, or link) of the input being sent. Table 13-2 summarizes these options. The Input Provider column specifies where the input to the gateway application originates. Readers generate "user" data when they input information into the HTML document calling the gateway application. Authors specify "author" information when they append information to a target URL or when they include hidden input fields in a form. The URL column shows the format of the URL generated by the browser and sent to the server as part of the HTTP request. The final column specifies the way the gateway application receives the input data.

ACCESS TYPE	INPUT PROVIDER	URL	PASSING METHOD
<ISINDEX>	User	URL?arg1+arg2...	Command line
Link	Author	URL?arg1+arg2...	Command line
"get" form	User	URL?arg1=val1&arg2=val2...	Environment
Link	Author	URL?arg1=val1&arg2=val2...	Environment
"get" form	User and author	URL/author_data?arg1=val1...	Environment
"post" form	User and author	URL/author_data	Env./std. input
Link	Author	URL/author_data	Environment
"post" form	User	URL	Standard input

Table 13-2 Data passing methods for various interaction types

> Note: When author data is passed through a query URL ("get" method form style or <ISINDEX> style), the HTML document author is responsible for encoding the special characters in the query string. (See below.)

When a client sends information from an HTML form, special characters in the data are transformed prior to transmission to the server. This is done so that the meanings of special characters are not misinterpreted. Table 13-3 shows the special characters and how they are transformed in a data block or a query string.

451

CHARACTER NAME	CHARACTER	INPUT VALUE
Tab	\t	%09
Carriage return	\n	%0A
Exclamation point	!	%21
Double quote	"	%22
Pound	#	%23
Dollar sign	$	%24
Percent sign	%	%25
Single quote	'	%27
Open parenthesis	(	%28
Close parenthesis	)	%29
Plus sign	+	%2B
Comma	,	%2C
Slash	/	%2F
Colon	:	%3A
Semicolon	;	%3B
Less than	<	%3C
Greater than	>	%3E
Question mark	?	%3F
Open bracket	[	%5B
Back slash	\	%5C
Close bracket	]	%5D
Caret	^	%5E
Back quote	`	%60
Open brace	{	%7B
Pipe	|	%7C
Close brace	}	%7D
Tilde	~	%7E

Table 13-3 Permuted characters and escaped values

How-Tos 13.6 and 13.7 discuss procedures for accessing the input data and transforming it into a usable format.

13.1 PASS DATA TO A CGI APPLICATION

Comments

Information is placed in the environment by the server and is made available when a gateway application is launched. Table 13-4 explains commonly accessed environment variables and the values they hold. This information will help you develop your own CGI applications.

ENVIRONMENT VARIABLE	VALUE
CONTENT_LENGTH	Length of data block on standard input for "post" or "put" method requests.
CONTENT_TYPE	MIME type of the information being sent via the "post" or "put" method.
PATH_INFO	String containing the additional information appended to the application path.
QUERY_STRING	Contains the information appended to the URL passed to the server.
	This information follows the question mark. <ISINDEX> data is available both through command line arguments and through this variable.
REMOTE_ADDR	IP address of the remote machine accessing the server.
REMOTE_HOST	Name corresponding to the remote machine accessing the server.
	If this information is unavailable, this entry is left blank.
REMOTE_IDENT	Contains the unauthenticated ID of the user requesting the CGI application.
REQUEST_METHOD	Specifies the HTTP method sent to the server by the client ("get", "post", etc.)
SCRIPT_NAME	Contains the name of the script being called as it would appear in a URL.
SERVER_NAME	Specifies the name of the server being accessed.
SERVER_SOFTWARE	String contains the name and version of the server software being run.

Table 13-4 Commonly accessed environment variables

A full specification of environment variables available to CGI applications can be found via the CGI specification at http://hoohoo.ncsa.uiuc.edu/cgi/overview.html. Further, additional environment variable information is usually available. These variables have the HTTP_ prefix. The information contained in these variables is directly incorporated from the client's HTTP request header (as described in Appendix G). So for example, HTTP_USER_AGENT would contain the data passed to the server in the User-Agent field of the HTTP request header.

Warning: User input data passed through "get" method requests (command line and environment variable) is subject to size limitation due to command line and environment size limits.

CHAPTER 13
THE COMMON GATEWAY INTERFACE (CGI)

13.2 How do I... Send information to a browser from CGI applications?

COMPLEXITY: ADVANCED

COMPATIBILITY: HTML, HTTP, CGI/1.1

Problem

I want to send my results from a gateway application to the server and then to a browser. How does the server get the information, and what does it do with it? I need to know the details of this process to properly build my CGI programs.

Technique

The browser receives gateway-generated information via the server in two ways:

- **HTML** Parsed header: Gateway application results are placed on its standard output. The server takes this information, manipulates it, and sends it to the client.

- **HTML** Nonparsed header: A gateway program beginning with the "nph-" prefix indicates that the CGI application is a nonparsed header (nph) program. This means that results sent to the standard output by this type of application are not processed by the server, but passed directly to client through the server.

Through these two methods, information is passed to the server. Figure 13-3 shows the relationship between these two methods in relation to the browser, the server, and your CGI application. The upper arrow represents the path of the parsed header method. The lower arrow represents the pass through using a nonparsed header program. In either case, the end result is an HTTP response sent to the browser. (See Appendix G for information on HTTP responses.)

Steps

The following step-by-step procedures show how to pass information to the browser via parsed and nonparsed header methods.

> *Warning: It is imperative that server directives from parsed header applications and response headers from nonparsed header applications terminate with a blank line. This blank line indicates the end of the header and the beginning of any attached object.*

13.2
SEND INFORMATION TO A BROWSER FROM CGI APPLICATIONS

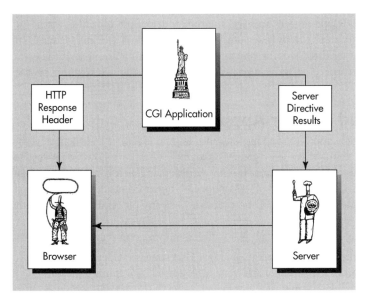

Figure 13-3 Passing of information from a gateway application to the browser

Parsed Header

If the results generated by a CGI application are relatively simple in nature, you don't need to fine tune the response header that will be eventually passed to the browser. Use the following procedure to pass CGI information to the browser via the server.

1. Issue a server directive as the first line of your gateway application output. Servers currently support three allowable server directives:

- **HTML** Content-type: type/subtype
- **HTML** Location: URL
- **HTML** Status: code message

For example, the following line might be used in a Bourne shell script. Substitute corresponding statements used in other development languages.

```
echo Content-type:   text/html
```

The How It Works section describes these three server directives.

2. Follow the server directive with a blank line. For example, in a Bourne shell script, issue the following command. In other development languages, use corresponding commands.

```
echo
```

3. In a Content-type server directive, the remainder of the output is the object returned to the browser (an HTML document, a GIF image, etc.). In a Status server directive, the remainder of the output is the text of the error message returned to the browser; simple text is the safest format for such a message.

Nonparsed Header Applications

With an nph application, the full response header that is sent to the client must be generated and returned by your gateway program. Use the following process to generate a minimal HTTP response header. Additional response header fields that could be included are discussed in Appendix G. Nonparsed header programs tend to be slightly faster since the server need not perform any processing nor make any additions.

Many, but not all, browsers can deal with less information than this minimum.

1. Issue a status line. The first line of an HTTP response header contains a specification of the protocol and version, followed by a status code, and ending with a status message. For example, *HTTP/1.0 200 OK* would be an appropriate first line. This should be the first line placed on standard output by your application. In a Bourne shell script, you could enter

```
echo "$SERVER_PROTOCOL 200 OK"
```

2. In the next line, specify the date that the current document was put together. Your gateway application should calculate this information and place it on the standard output. For example, *Date: Sat, 25-Dec-99 14:24:32 GMT*. Since all servers work according to Greenwich Mean Time (GMT), make sure that the times you generate are for this time zone. The following code segment is appropriate for generating this information in a Bourne shell script.

```
echo -n "Date: "
/usr/bin/date -u -'+%a, %d-%h-%y %T GMT'
```

3. Specify the server software and version being used. This information is found in the SERVER_SOFTWARE environment variable. For example, if you're using NCSA version 1.3 server software, send the line *Server: NCSA/1.3* to the standard output next. You could use the following code in a Bourne shell script.

```
echo "Server: $SERVER_SOFTWARE"
```

4. Include a MIME version field. The current version is 1.0. So, a line like *MIME-version: 1.0* should appear next. You could use the following code in a Bourne shell script.

```
echo "MIME-version: 1.0"
```

13.2
SEND INFORMATION TO A BROWSER FROM CGI APPLICATIONS

5. Add other header fields as required by the status code and the resultant data being transmitted back to the browser. (See the Comments section below and Appendix G.)

6. Terminate the HTTP response header with a blank line. For example, use the following code in a Bourne shell script.

echo

7. If a Content-type field appears in the response header, the remainder of the output after the blank line is the object returned to the browser (an HTML document, a GIF image, etc.).

How It Works

Your application sends its results to the standard output. If the name of your gateway program does not begin with the "nph-" prefix, the server parses and interprets the results your application places on the standard output. If your application name starts with the "nph-" prefix, the server assumes that the program is a nonparsed header program and retransmits the results from the gateway application without modification.

In the case of a parsed header application, the server reads and interprets the server directive. The remaining results placed on the standard output are interpreted based upon the server directive. Unless the Content-type directive is used, additional results passed to the standard output may cause problems. The server then generates an appropriate HTTP response header and attaches any associated data to it. Figure 13-4 displays this process for the three accepted server directives, which are

- **HTML** Content-type: type/subtype: Indicates that the object in the HTTP response body is of the specified MIME type.
- **HTML** Location: URL comment: Indicates that the requested file is in a different location. The URL specifies where the desired information is located.
- **HTML** Status: code message: Allows you to specify an exit status for your CGI application.

With respect to nph gateway applications, the data placed on the standard output by your application is passed directly back to the client. Therefore, your application generates a complete HTTP response header with associated data.

In either case, the browser receives an HTTP response header and any relevant data objects.

Comments

Both methods rely on passing information to the server via the standard output. The difference is that nonparsed header gateway applications are responsible for

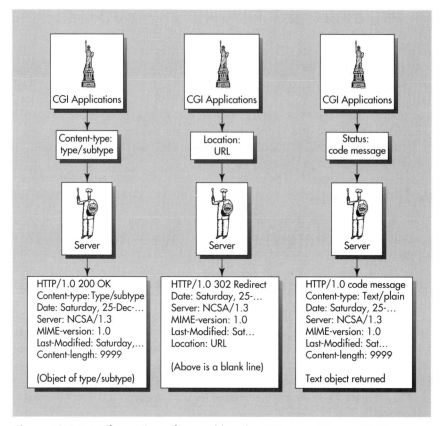

Figure 13-4 Transformation of parsed header CGI output to an HTTP response message

generating an entire HTTP response header plus any generated results from execution. CGI programs with parsed headers just provide a server directive and allow the server to construct an appropriate HTTP response header. Appendix G provides information on HTTP response header fields you can use in your nonparsed header CGI applications.

Status codes and status messages tell the browser the status of its request. Status codes range from 200 to 599. A code within the 200 to 299 range indicates a successful transaction.

A code from 300 to 399 specifies some manner of redirection. This usually implies that a Location field will appear later in the response header defining the URL to use in lieu of the requested one.

Status codes between 400 and 599 indicate errors. The nature of the error is often explained in a small HTML or text document in the HTTP response body.

When using a nonparsed header application, you are responsible for generating the complete response header and any attached object. Using particular status codes suggests the inclusion of specific header fields and attached objects. Table 13-5 maps status codes to suggested header fields beyond the minimum suggested in the nonparsed header procedure given in the Steps section above.

STATUS CODE	SUGGESTED RESPONSE INFORMATION	ATTACHED OBJECT?
200 - 299	Content-type, Content-length (if known)	Yes
300 - 399	Location	No
400 - 599	Content-type, Content-length	Yes (error message)

Table 13-5 Suggested header fields for response status catagories

Aside from error codes and complete success, the status code you are most likely to use is code 204. This code indicates no response and successful completion. An HTTP response using this code results in no change to the document currently seen in the browser. This code is handy for specifying the default action to be taken in an imagemap, or to demonstrate how a particular browser displays a link. In either case, you can specify the following gateway application as the target URL.

```
#!/bin/sh

# Indicate status followed by a blank line
echo Status:   204 No response, but successful
echo
```

13.3 How do I... Create a simple CGI application?

COMPLEXITY: INTERMEDIATE

COMPATIBILITY: HTML, HTTP, CGI

Problem

I want to create a simple gateway application. I don't require user input data, but I do want to generate a document on the fly from information available on the server host machine. How can I do this?

Technique

This How-To shows how to write an application to generate an HTML document from data existing at the server site. The sample application uses the Bourne shell scripting language for demonstrative purposes. This language is both easy to use and reasonably portable. The technique presented should be easy to transfer to other development languages.

Steps

The procedure below documents the development and incorporation of a Bourne shell CGI script to execute a command and return the results of that command as a dynamically created HTML document. The actual commands depend on whether you are authoring in sh, Perl, TCL, or another scripting language.

1. In a text editor, create a file called first.cgi.

2. The script must begin with the following line specifying the execution environment.

```
#!/bin/sh
```

3. Issue a server directive to the standard output. In the case of a script written to process a command and report the output, the most likely directive you will use is Content-type. The actual type you specify should correspond to whatever type of file your application will send back to the browser.

```
echo Content-type: text/html
```

The above code segment indicates that the attached file is an HTML document.

> Note: How-To 13.2 goes into detail on the use of the three valid server directives.

4. Terminate the server directive with a blank line indicating that the attached object follows. Use a single *echo* statement to generate this blank line.

```
echo
```

5. Set the PROG variable to the program you wish to run. For example, if you wish the script to generate the local date and time on the server, use the following line.

```
PROG=/usr/bin/date
```

6. Since the server directive you used indicates that an HTML document is attached, generate the HTML-formatted output of your specified command. The following segment of code generates the beginning of an HTML document to be returned to the browser.

```
cat << EOF
<HTML>
<HEAD>
```

13.3
CREATE A SIMPLE CGI APPLICATION

```
<TITLE>
EOF

echo "$PROG Response Page"

cat << EOF
</TITLE>
</HEAD>
<BODY>
<H1>
EOF

echo "$PROG Response Page"

cat << EOF
</H1>
<HR>
EOF
```

The cat << EOF commands cause the script to output the proceeding text until an EOF is reached.

7. Run the specified program on the server. You need to format the results for presentation by the browser. The following code executes the program and formats the results as the content of a <PRE> element.

```
echo \<PRE\>
$PROG
echo \</PRE\>
```

8. End the document by closing the <BODY> and <HTML> elements.

```
cat << EOF
</BODY></HTML>
EOF
```

9. Save this script file, and exit the editor.

10. Change permissions on the script file if necessary to make it executable.

11. Test the application. The results seen should start with a server directive followed by a blank line. The blank line is followed by an attached document. The results that should appear from the execution of the script developed in this How-To should look like this:

```
Content-type: text/html

<HTML>
<HEAD>
<TITLE>
/usr/bin/date Response Page
</TITLE>
</HEAD>
```

continued on next page

continued from previous page

```
<BODY>
<H1>
/usr/bin/date Response Page
</H1>
<HR>
<PRE>
Sat Dec 25 14:24:32 EDT 1999
</PRE>
</BODY></HTML>
```

12. Make the script available for use through your HTML documents. First, install the script and register it with your server. For servers like NCSA or CERN, gateway applications should be placed in a cgi-bin directory by default.

13. Determine the URL of your installed CGI application.

14. Refer to your gateway script as the destination for HTML links.

How It Works

Gateway applications of this type process data and generate results that are sent back to the client in some specified format. Figure 13-5 diagrams the execution of such a CGI application. The application generates an appropriate server directive, separated from the body of the message by a blank line. The object returned to the browser follows the blank line.

The script using the program */usr/bin/date* developed in this example is on the CD, with the filename first.cgi.

When a link specifies this gateway script as its destination, the application generates a parsed header and a message body, which are passed to the server. The server processes this information and generates a full HTTP response header to return to the client.

Figure 13-6 shows the page resulting from the activation of a link to the *first.cgi* script.

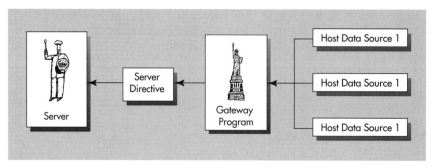

Figure 13-5 Execution of a CGI application requiring no client-based input

13.4 INSTALL A CGI APPLICATION

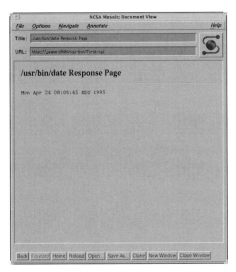

Figure 13-6 The result of activating a link to *first.cgi*.

Comments

More complex methods are necessary for dealing with CGI applications that require some level of user input. These methods are investigated more deeply in later How-To's in this chapter.

For detailed information on HTTP response header information and parsed versus nonparsed headers, see How-To 13.2.

COMPLEXITY
EASY

13.4 How do I...
Install a CGI application?

COMPATIBILITY: NCSA HTTPD, CERN HTTP

Problem

Once I've written my gateway application, I need to make it available. Where do I need to place the application so I can access it from an HTML document, and how do I create a reference to it?

Technique

This How-To describes standard procedures for installing CGI applications on NCSA or CERN servers. Other servers provide different means for registering allowable gateway applications. The Comments section provides useful references to information on installing gateway applications on several other servers.

NCSA and CERN servers use two installation methods: script directories and file types. NCSA allows for both types, while the CERN server allows only script directories.

> Note: You may need to discuss script installation policy with your Web site administrator before installing any CGI application. CGI applications are run on the host machine, and therefore represent a potential security risk.

Steps

The following sections provide detailed instructions for installing CGI applications on NCSA and CERN servers.

Script Directory, NCSA

You make script directory specifications in the server resource map file. The steps below describe how to install your CGI application using this method.

1. If you are installing your application to an existing script directory, skip to step 5 below. Otherwise, change to the directory containing the server resource map file and load the srm.conf file into your text editor.

> Note: To specify new script directories, you must have server administrator privileges.

2. Append a ScriptAlias directive to the srm.conf file. The format for this command is as follows:

ScriptAlias virtual_directory physical_directory

The virtual directory refers to the path you should put in a URL to reference this script directory. The physical directory represents the actual directory located on the machine running the server; if a relative path is specified, the ServerRoot is assumed to be the base path.

The following lines designate the /usr/local/httpd/bin/ and ServerRoot/my-cgi-bin/ directories as script directories. In URLs, refer to them as /local/bin/ and /mybin/, respectively.

```
ScriptAlias /local/bin/ /usr/local/httpd/bin/
ScriptAlias /mybin/ my-cgi-bin/
```

Any URL specified for a link anchor or HTML form action as http://www.mysite.edu/mybin/myscript causes the server to execute *ServerRoot/my-cgi-bin/myscript*. You can have as many ScriptAlias directives in your configuration as you wish.

13.4
INSTALL A CGI APPLICATION

3. Save the configuration file.
4. Stop the server and restart it. This causes the server to read the altered configuration file and treat your script directories properly.
5. Move or copy your executable CGI application to a script directory. In UNIX, use the mv or cp command. For instance, to move the gateway program *first.cgi* to /usr/local/httpd/bin, issue the following command.

```
mv first.cgi /usr/local/httpd/bin
```

> Note: To install applications in existing directories, you need write access to the script directory.

6. Make sure that the application is executable by all users, since the user associated with the server needs execution access to your code. Use the following UNIX command to give read and execute privileges to all users.

```
chmod ugo+rx first.cgi
```

Script Directory, CERN

The CERN Web server provides a script directory mechanism for installing gateway programs. The steps below describe how to install your programs using this method.

1. If you are installing your application to an existing script directory, skip to step 5. Otherwise, change to the directory containing the server configuration file and load the httpd.conf file into your text editor.

> Note: To specify new script directories, you must have server administrator privileges.

2. Add exec rules to this file. The format for this command is Exec /virtual_directory/*/physical_directory/*. You may add as many script directories as you want with Exec rules. The physical directory represents the location to which the server should map the virtual directory when seen in a URL. The following line designates the /usr/local/httpd/bin/ directory as a script directory. In URLs, refer to this directory as /local/bin/.

```
Exec /local/bin/*    /usr/local/httpd/bin/*
```

> Any URL specified as a link anchor or HTML form action referencing http://www.mysite.edu/local/bin/myscript causes the server to execute /usr/local/httpd/bin/myscript.

3. Save the configuration file.

4. Stop the server and restart it. This causes the server to read the altered configuration file and treat your script directories properly.

5. Move or copy your executable CGI application to a script directory. In UNIX, use the mv or cp command. For instance, to move the gateway program *first.cgi* to /usr/local/httpd/bin, issue the following command.

```
mv first.cgi /usr/local/httpd/bin
```

> Note: To install applications in existing directories, you need write access to the script directory.

6. Make sure that the application is executable by all users, since the user associated with the server needs execution access to your code. Use the following UNIX command to give read and execute privileges to all users.

```
chmod ugo+rx first.cgi
```

File Type, NCSA

With this method, gateway programs can be placed anywhere. The server recognizes an application by an extension type. This type can be established across all documents on a particular server, or on an individual directory basis.

1. If you are installing your application to a directory with an access file set for CGI applications, or your server has been configured to allow CGI applications anywhere, skip to step 4 below. If you are configuring the server to allow gateway applications anywhere, change to the directory containing the server resource map file, load the srm.conf file into your text editor, and skip to step 3. If you are configuring a single directory for gateway applications, change to the directory you are configuring and load the access control file (the default name is .htaccess) into your text editor. If an access file does not exist, create one using the filename specified in the server resource map file. The directive you are looking for is AccessFileName.

2. Insert the following line in the access control file. This line allows execution of gateway applications in this directory.

```
Options ExecCGI
```

> Note: To specify execution of CGI applications in a particular directory, you need to have read and write access to the directory level access control file.

13.4
INSTALL A CGI APPLICATION

3. Insert an AddType directive. This directive tells the server how to interpret files with a given extension. For example, if you want all files with the extension .cgi to be treated as gateway programs, insert the following line into the access control file.

```
AddType application/x-httpd-cgi    .cgi
```

> Note: To specify the file type across a server, you must have server administrator privileges. For individual directories, you need to have read and write access to the directory level access control file.

4. Move or copy your executable CGI application to the desired directory. If you have set the server so that gateway programs can reside anywhere, then the only restriction is that the chosen directory be visible to the server. In UNIX, use the mv or cp command. For instance, to move the gateway program *first.cgi* to /usr/local/httpd/bin, issue the command

```
mv first.cgi /usr/local/httpd/bin/first.cgi
```

> Note: You need to have read and write access to the directory where you wish to place your application.

5. Make sure that the application is executable by all users, since the user associated with the server needs execution access to your code. Use the following UNIX command to give read and execute privileges to all users.

```
chmod ugo+rx first.cgi
```

How It Works

Both NCSA and CERN servers allow you to configure directories so that the server treats your files in these directories as gateway programs. Once you have configured directories as script directories, whenever the server sees a URL addressing the logical name for such a directory, it launches the filename attached to the URL as a CGI application. To install an application, move the executable code or script to the directory and make sure that it can be executed by the server. The procedures in this How-To show the steps required to establish script directories and install applications in them.

The other means provided by the NCSA server for installing gateway programs is by file type and modification of access control files. Access control files may appear anywhere visible to your server. They control how files in the current directory and its subdirectories are accessed. In the access control file, specify that the server treat all files ending with a particular file extension as CGI applications.

Gateway applications can then be installed anyplace that is controlled by the modified access file. If the server resource map file is modified, then applications may appear wherever they are visible to the server as long as they have the correct filename extension.

Comments

Documentation for CGI application installation for various servers can be found at the URLs in Table 13-6.

SERVER	CGI INFORMATION URL
NCSA	http://hoohoo.ncsa.uiuc.edu/docs/tutorials/cgi.html
CERN	http://www.w3.org/hypertext/WWW/Daemon/User_3.0/CGI/Overview.html
WN	http://hopf.math.nwu.edu/
MacHTTP	http://www.biap.com/tutorials/Extending_MacHTTP/ExtendingMacHTTP.html
WinHTTPD	http://www.city.net/win-httpd/

Table 13-6 Common Gateway Interface documentation for various servers

13.5 How do I...
Create a query document using the <ISINDEX> element?

COMPLEXITY: INTERMEDIATE

COMPATIBILITY: CGI

Problem

I am interested in creating a searchable document. The search criterion is a simple list of terms. How do I place a query for the search terms and information on how to access this data from my CGI application into my document?

Technique

This How-To describes the process for developing a gateway program to manage an <ISINDEX> query document. Since <ISINDEX> documents generate query URLs by appending a query string to the current URL, CGI applications that generate and handle <ISINDEX> query documents must have two components: one to generate the query page and one to generate the response page.

13.5 CREATE A QUERY DOCUMENT USING THE <ISINDEX> ELEMENT

When the URL is triggered, the application checks the number of command line arguments to determine whether to generate the query page or the response page. <ISINDEX> query terms are sent to the application as command line arguments. (See How-To 13.1 for more information on how information is passed to gateway applications.) Figure 13-7 displays the approach taken with this technique.

Steps

The following procedure delineates the steps you should follow to develop your <ISINDEX> gateway applications. The example provided has been developed using the Bourne shell script language to run the finger utility with any arguments specified in the <ISINDEX> field. When developing your applications, use the appropriate constructs in your development language to accomplish the tasks demonstrated in the steps. When you have completed the procedure, you can use the URL for your <ISINDEX> application as you would any other URL (for the target of a link, an open location, etc.).

1. Open a text editor and begin writing the source for your <ISINDEX> application. Place any necessary header information in your application (script to use, header files, helper functions, etc.). In the example *finger* script, this step includes specification of the Bourne shell as well as defining a variable pointing to the *finger* program.

```
#!/bin/sh
#Finger <ISINDEX> application
FINGER=/usr/ucb/finger
```

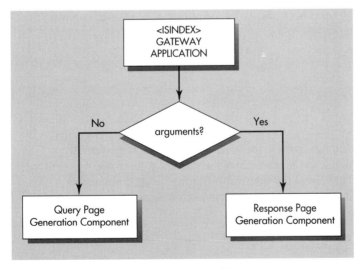

Figure 13-7 <ISINDEX> application architecture

2. Determine if any command line arguments have been passed to your application program. If no arguments are present, call the query generation component. If arguments are present, process them and call the response generation component. In the sample application, use an *if* statement to determine whether arguments are present. The *then* portion leads to the query generator, while the *else* (step 6) leads to the response generator.

```
# Determine if command line arguments are present.
if [ $# = 0 ]; then
```

3. Develop the query generation component. The first part of the query generation sends the Content-type server directive, followed by a blank line. Since you are using an <ISINDEX> element, specify text/html as the type. In the example, the echo command places this information on the standard output.

```
echo Content-type: text/html
echo
```

> Note: If this <ISINDEX> application is a nonparsed header application ("nph-" prefix on the application filename), generate the full response header as described in How-To 13.2.

4. Attached to this response header, include an HTML document that has the <ISINDEX> element in the <HEAD> component. The <HEAD> component should also contain an appropriate title for the generated document. In the sample application, use the cat command to place this information on the standard output. (This particular cat command also places the body on the standard output in step 5.)

```
cat << EOF
<HTML>
<HEAD>
<TITLE>Finger Query</TITLE>
<<ISINDEX>>
</HEAD>
```

5. Add information relevant to the application and the proper format for submitting input text in the body of the document. In the Bourne shell file, a cat command places this information on the standard output (continued from the listing in step 4). The EOF command signals the end of the information.

```
<BODY>
<H1>Finger Query</H1>
<HR>
This is a "finger" query page. Enter a series of user@host entries in the
available search dialog.
```

13.5
CREATE A QUERY DOCUMENT USING THE <ISINDEX> ELEMENT

```
<HR>
</BODY>
</HTML>
EOF
```

6. Develop a response to the query. The response to the query is like any other gateway application response. A server directive (or response header for nph applications) is sent, terminated with a blank line. The blank line is followed by an attached file, if required. The sample application signifies the response generation component with the *else* command from the *if* statement entered in step 2.

```
else
```

7. The response document is begun by sending the appropriate server directive on the standard output. As with the query component, the sample application uses the echo command to perform this task.

```
# Generate Response Document

echo Content-type: text/html
echo
```

8. Generate the attached file by processing and sending back an appropriately generated document. In the sh script example, this is done using a cat command. The processing of the arguments is embedded in the document generation process.

```
cat << EOF
<HTML>
<HEAD>
<TITLE>Finger Response</TITLE>
</HEAD>
<BODY>
<H1>Finger Response</H1>
<HR>
Input Terms Were: $*
<PRE>
EOF

$FINGER $*

cat << EOF
</PRE>
<HR>
</BODY>
</HTML>
EOF
```

9. Add any necessary closing information. In the example application developed in this procedure, the closing information is simply the termination of the *if* statement that checked the argument count.

```
fi
```

10. Save the application and compile it, if necessary.

11. If feasible, test your application. First, run it with no arguments to see that it generates a proper HTML document with <ISINDEX> in the <HEAD>. Then, if the response component generates a readable output (for example, text or HTML), run your application with command line arguments.

12. Install your <ISINDEX> application as described for CGI application installation in How-To 13.4.

How It Works

When a browser first accesses the URL of your application through a link or an open location, your application launches without command line arguments (unless the author or opener has appended a query string to the URL). Your application detects that no command line arguments are present and executes the query generation component. When the user enters the desired input in the query page, the server launches the same application; however, the browser appends a query string composed of the user response to the URL. Therefore, the server converts the query string into command line arguments and launches your application. This execution of your application receives command line arguments and runs the response component of the application.

The sample application developed through the above procedure can be found in file second.cgi on the CD.

When a link to a URL without a query string attached associated with an <ISINDEX> gateway application is triggered, the server launches the application without command line arguments; therefore, the query generation component executes. For the sample application, running the query generator component results in the HTML document seen in Figure 13-8.

If you enter data in the provided query field and submit the request, the browser generates a request with the inputs attached to the URL as a query string. This URL is submitted to the server, which launches the gateway application with the items in the query string passed as command line arguments. If you launch the sample application with the query text seen in Figure 13-8, the result is a document like the one shown in Figure 13-9.

Comments

Even though the sample application was developed using the Bourne shell language, the components represented in the code can be used for <ISINDEX>

13.5
CREATE A QUERY DOCUMENT USING THE <ISINDEX> ELEMENT

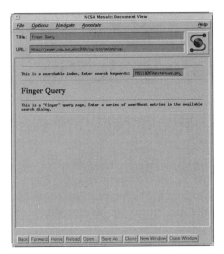

Figure 13-8 Execution of *second.cgi* without command line arguments

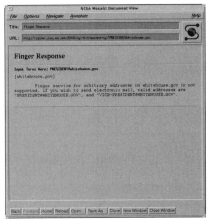

Figure 13-9 Execution of *second.cgi* with command line arguments

applications written in any development language. You need to map your language's constructs into the three primary tasks specified:

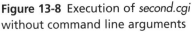 Decision

 Query generation

 Response generation

Steps 7 and 8 of the procedure can be modified if a different type of response is required, based upon the processing of the data. In the example script, the response from finger was presented, whether it generated a valid response or an error. In your application, you may wish to send a different response message based upon the results of processing the data. For example, if the input is processed correctly, you might send a TIFF file with a Content-type: image/tiff, a redirection command with a Location:URL, or a particular error with a Status directive. If an error is generated, you might want to respond with an HTML document describing the error that occurred.

The finger program is a UNIX utility that provides information concerning valid users on specified machines. The formats for acceptable command line arguments are provided in Table 13-7. Multiple command line arguments are acceptable.

COMMAND LINE ARGUMENT	INFORMATION REQUEST
user	Information for user on current machine
user@host	Information for user on host machine
@host	List users currently on host machine

Table 13-7 Information request arguments of finger

473

CHAPTER 13
THE COMMON GATEWAY INTERFACE (CGI)

COMPLEXITY
INTERMEDIATE

13.6 How do I... Access client data in sh CGI scripts?

COMPATIBILITY: CGI, BOURNE SHELL

Problem

For reasons of portability, I've decided to write gateway applications using Bourne shell scripts. I need to retrieve user-specified form data. The information is encoded and sent by several means; is there an efficient mechanism for accessing the data that was originally entered?

Technique

Your first step in developing a Bourne shell application that requires user input data is the retrieval of the input data. This common task is performed by all CGI applications that require input data. This information can be in several forms:

- **HTML** Query string from a "get" method form
- **HTML** Standard input from a "post" method form
- **HTML** Command line arguments from an <ISINDEX> query

This How-To provides step-by-step instructions for retrieving and accessing input data from both "get" and "post" method forms. How-To 13.5 presents a way to retrieve <ISINDEX> data.

Steps

To access user input data from a Bourne shell script, you develop and install a helper application that parses the input data and places it in environment variables that can be accessed by your shell script.

The helper application called *shparse* has been developed in the C language, and the first three steps involve the creation and installation of this program.

The remainder of the steps provide instruction on incorporating the helper function in your gateway scripts and offer a simple example script. If the *shparse* program has already been compiled and installed in a location visible to your sh application, you should skip ahead to step 4 below.

1. Copy the following files from the CD to a local directory where you will build the *shparse* program.

parse.h : This file contains necessary header information.

parse.c : This file holds the helper function and declarations for reconstructing "post" method form data.

13.6
ACCESS CLIENT DATA IN sh CGI SCRIPTS

parseget.c : This file holds the helper function and declarations for reconstructing "get" method form data.

shparse.c : This file holds the main *shparse* application.

2. Using your C compiler, compile the three C files that you have just copied in the previous step, and rename the output *shparse*. For example:

```
gcc -o shparse parse.c parseget.c shparse.c
```

3. Move the *shparse* application to a location visible to your shell gateway programs. Make sure that the file security for the *shparse* application is set for execution by all individuals who need access to it.

4. Open your Bourne shell application in your text editor.

5. Insert the following lines to specify a Bourne shell script and to read the user input data into environment variables.

```
#!/bin/sh

eval `shparse`
```

6. Develop the rest of your application. All input data appears in environment variables with the INPUT_ prefix. The remainder of each variable name is the attribute associated with the attribute/value pair. If multiple inputs have the same attribute, they are placed in the environment individually as INPUT_SUF, INPUT_SUF_D1, INPUT_SUF_D2, and so forth.

> Note: If you wish to change the default prefix from INPUT_ to something else, modify the shparse.c file prior to compilation.

7. Test your application by running it with suitable environment variables set and providing data on the standard input, if necessary. If the application works as you expect, proceed to the next step; otherwise, debug your sh script as necessary.

8. Install your application in a suitable location. See How-To 13.4 for information on application installation.

How It Works

The first step in your CGI application is to call the *shparse* application in the manner prescribed above. Figure 13-10 shows how your Bourne shell script and the *shparse* application interact with each other and with the server.

Once the input data has been parsed, your script can access and process this data as necessary to generate the proper response. The response is passed back to the server, and from the server to the browser. The output of your gateway application should conform to the standard specifications as described in How-To 13.2.

CHAPTER 13
THE COMMON GATEWAY INTERFACE (CGI)

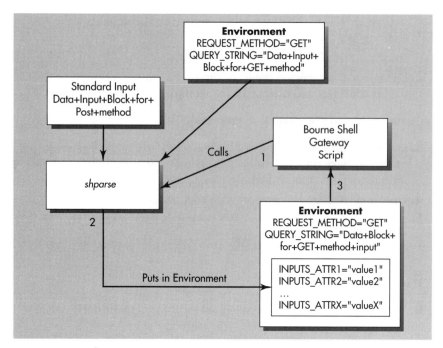

Figure 13-10 *shparse* and your Bourne shell gateway program

Below is a sample application written using the *shparse* application developed in this How-To.

```
#!/bin/sh

eval `shparse`

echo Content-type: text/plain
echo

echo argc is $#. argv is "$*".
echo

echo Environment Variables
echo SERVER_SOFTWARE = $SERVER_SOFTWARE
echo SERVER_NAME = $SERVER_NAME
echo REQUEST_METHOD = $REQUEST_METHOD
echo HTTP_ACCEPT = "$HTTP_ACCEPT"
echo PATH_INFO = "$PATH_INFO"
echo PATH_TRANSLATED = "$PATH_TRANSLATED"
echo SCRIPT_NAME = "$SCRIPT_NAME"
echo QUERY_STRING = "$QUERY_STRING"
echo REMOTE_HOST = $REMOTE_HOST
echo REMOTE_ADDR = $REMOTE_ADDR
echo REMOTE_USER = $REMOTE_USER
```

```
echo AUTH_TYPE = $AUTH_TYPE
echo CONTENT_TYPE = $CONTENT_TYPE
echo CONTENT_LENGTH = $CONTENT_LENGTH

echo Form Inputs
echo INPUT_T1 = $INPUT_T1
echo INPUT_T2 = $INPUT_T2
echo INPUT_T3 = $INPUT_T3
```

This application displays generic environment variables plus the environment variables INPUT_T1, INPUT_T2, INPUT_T3. These three environment variables are assumed to have been generated by the evaluation of the results of *shparse*. The values associated with form input fields T1, T2, and T3 are stored respectively in the previously mentioned environment variables.

Comments

The above programs and scripts were developed and tested on a UNIX platform machine. Modification may be necessary depending on the target platform.

Further, complications will arise if an attribute name ends in the suffix _DX or more than ten values are associated with a particular attribute.

COMPLEXITY
ADVANCED

13.7 How do I... Parse client data in CGI programs and scripts?

COMPATIBILITY: CGI

Problem

The browser transforms HTML form data prior to submitting it to the appropriate server, and ultimately to my gateway application. How do I process this data to regenerate the original data submitted by the user?

Technique

You have created a form to query the reader for information necessary for the generation of a dynamic document. Each entry the user makes is associated with an attribute, or name, defined in your form. The form data is passed to your application through the server. However, this information is modified in the process. Since most CGI applications need to transform and parse this data, a systematic approach to regenerating the input data is desirable.

This How-To presents a generic method suitable to break the data block passed to your gateway application into its original form. Figure 13-11 gives an overview of this processing technique.

The browser receives the data entered into HTML forms. For safety and security reasons, the browser transforms the special characters in this form data. The browser transmits this data to the server through either a "get" or a "post" method transaction. Depending on the method, your gateway application retrieves the data from the environment or standard input, respectively. You must then transform the data to restore the special characters. Your application can now proceed to processing the data and generating an HTML results page.

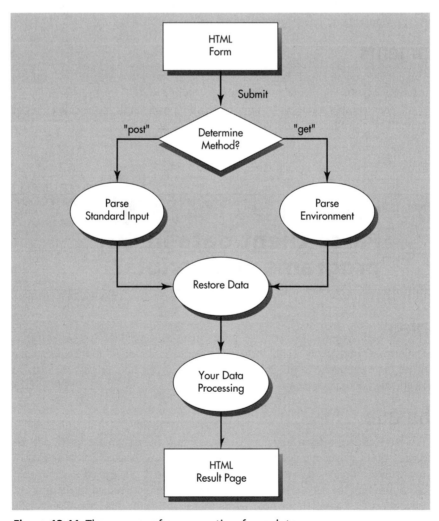

Figure 13-11 The process of regenerating form data

13.7
PARSE CLIENT DATA IN CGI PROGRAMS AND SCRIPTS

Steps

The steps below allow you to parse and transform the modified data passed to your program. The original data will be placed in a specified location with each of the attributes specified in your HTML form associated with the data the user entered.

The Comments section below describes the use of this procedure with several common gateway application development languages.

1. Open the source code of your gateway application.

2. Determine the request method used to pass data to your application. This information is stored in the REQUEST_METHOD environment variable. In C, you retrieve this information using the *getenv* function; for example, the following line stores the method type in the *app_check* variable.

```
/* Check to determine what method was used to call this application.   */
app_check=getenv("REQUEST_METHOD");
```

3. Parse the data from the appropriate source depending upon the request method. If the request method is "get", parse the data from the QUERY_STRING environment variable. If the request method is "post", retrieve the data from the standard input. For example, in Perl, the following lines retrieve the data sent by a "get" request.

```
#Read the form data from the environment
$data = $ENV{ QUERY_STRING };
```

For a "post" request, the following lines retrieve the data.

```
#Determine the length of the POST'd data.
$len = $ENV{ CONTENT_LENGTH };
#Read the form data from the standard input
read(STDIN, $data, $len);
```

4. Separate the attribute/value pairs.

5. Break the pairs into attributes and values.

6. Restore the special characters. This process depends significantly upon your implementation language. The How It Works section below describes this process.

> Note: You can combine steps 4 through 6 if this combination yields a more suitable implementation.

7. Implement the data processing and result generation components of your gateway application. (See How-To 13.6 for an example using Bourne shell.)

8. Save your gateway application.

9. Compile your program, if necessary.
10. Test your application. You may need to set environment variables manually and supply standard input data to perform this task. Correct any errors.
11. Install your application in a suitable location. See How-To 13.4 for information on application installation.

How It Works

Your CGI application must retrieve and restore form data prior to use. When a reader triggers the Submit button for your form, the browser packages and transmits the entered data. The HTTP request type specified in the form's METHOD attribute determines how the browser sends this data.

"Post" is the preferred transmission method because a "post" data block does not have as many size constraints. The maximum size of the command line and maximum length of an environment variable both constrain a "get" method data block. With the "get" method, the browser transforms the form data and appends it to the URL submitted to the server. With the "post" method, the browser composes the information entered in a form into a data block that it passes to the server as the attached object in the HTTP request.

The server passes the data to the CGI application either as an environment variable or as standard input, for "get" and "post" requests respectively. You must transform this data back into standard ASCII, then resolve it back into attribute/value pairs. These attribute/value pairs can then be accessed by the CGI application.

The browser transforms the input data by stringing together attribute/value pairs. The browser places an equal sign (=) between each attribute and its value and places an ampersand (&) between each pair. It converts the spaces in any attribute or value to plus signs (+) and converts any special characters into an escaped value (as seen in Table 13-3 in How-To 13.1.)

Therefore, breaking the data passed to the gateway program at ampersands reconstitutes the pairs, and breaking the pairs at equal signs separates the components of the pair. The restoration of each attribute or value to its original format is accomplished by examining each character and modifying it appropriately. Plus signs in the input are changed back to spaces. Escaped characters when encountered are converted back to their original ASCII form.

For example, the form shown below has three data fields named "message", "teacher", and "topic" that will be composed and sent to the CGI application t2. The "post" method will be used to pass the data to the application.

```
<HTML>
<!-- Sample Data Entry Form - Calls CGI application t2 -->
<HEAD>
<TITLE>Sample Form</TITLE>
</HEAD>
<BODY>
```

13.7
PARSE CLIENT DATA IN CGI PROGRAMS AND SCRIPTS

```
<H1>Sample Form</H1>
<HR>
<FORM METHOD="POST" ACTION="http:// www.mysite.edu/cgi-bin/t2"
ENCTYPE="application/x-www-form-urlencoded">
Enter the Text of your message below:<BR>
<TEXTAREA NAME="message" ROWS=10 COLS=40></TEXTAREA>
<INPUT TYPE="hidden" NAME="teacher" VALUE="dsk@cau.auc.edu">
<INPUT TYPE="hidden" NAME="topic" VALUE="Miscellaneous">
<INPUT TYPE="submit" VALUE="Mail">
</FORM>
<HR>
<H6>Last Modified: March 9, 1995 by dsk@cau.auc.edu</h6>
</BODY>
</HTML>
```

Figure 13-12 shows how Prodigy's Web Browser presents this form. It has a single visible input field and a Submit-type button labeled Mail. Two hidden input fields are also present.

When the button is pressed, the browser composes an input block and passes the information to the specified CGI application via the server. The data block generated for this sample form looks like this:

```
message=This+is+a+sample+of+text+input.++This+might+have%0Abeen+entered+into
+the+sample+form+whose%0Asource+appears+in+figure+5%2D8%2D1.++How+will+it%0A
be+processed%3F&teacher=dsk@cau.auc.edu&topic=Miscellaneous
```

Comments

The CD contains source code in several programming languages that accomplishes the tasks specified in the steps above. Following are specific instructions for each of these languages.

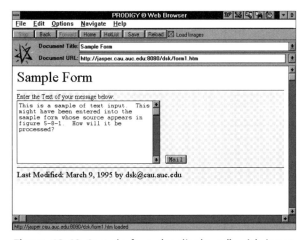

Figure 13-12 Sample form (as displayed) with input

CHAPTER 13
THE COMMON GATEWAY INTERFACE (CGI)

C

The C implementation of this process requires the files parse.h, parse.c, and parseget.c. The file main.c provides you with a template to use for your C gateway program development.

To use these files, copy the file main.c to the filename that you wish to use to store your main function. This file contains the C statements necessary to parse and restore HTML form data.

Edit this file to add any includes necessary to your application, to add any variables that need to be declared, and to add the statements necessary to accomplish the remainder of your program. You access the forms data through the inputs array.

Compile the main.c, parse.c, and parseget.c together with any other required C files to generate your executable application. You can test your application by simulating "get" or "post" requests by placing suitable information in the environment and on the standard input.

For the example form shown in Figure 13-12, the inputs array after executing the supplied code contains the data (input_count = 3) shown in Table 13-8.

ENTRY	DATA
inputs[0].attribute	"message"
inputs[0].value	"This is a sample of text input. This might have\nbeen entered into the sample form whose\nsource appears in figure 5-8-1. How will it\nbe processed?"
inputs[1].attribute	"teacher"
inputs[1].value	"dsk@cau.auc.edu"
inputs[2].attribute	"topic"
inputs[2].value	"Miscellaneous"

Table 13-8 Contents of input array for Figure 13-12

Multiple entries in the inputs array support multiple values for the same attribute. If the query string sent to your application were as follows:

`t1=a1&t2=a2&t1=a3`

the inputs array would store multiple entries for the same attributes. The values in the relevant variables for the query string above are shown in Table 13-9. The attribute "t1" would have values of "a1" and "a3."

VARIABLE	VALUE
input_count	3
inputs[0].attribute	"t1"
inputs[0].value	"a1"

13.7
PARSE CLIENT DATA IN CGI PROGRAMS AND SCRIPTS

VARIABLE	VALUE
inputs[1].attribute	"t2"
inputs[1].value	"a2"
inputs[2].attribute	"t1"
inputs[2].value	"a3"

 Table 13-9 Duplicate values example under C

C++

The C++ implementation uses the following files from the CD: Inputs.h, parse.h, parse.c, parseget.c, and Inputs.cpp. When creating a C++ CGI program, add these files to the compile line. These files declare and define the Inputs class you will use to retrieve and restore form data.

The Inputs class is responsible for the parsing and converting of the form data. The public interface to the class provides the necessary access mechanism for the use of HTML form input. This class provides two methods: count and the indexing operator [ ]. The count method returns the number of attribute/value pairs that the browser sent. The indexing operator receives an attribute in the form of a string and returns a value associated with that attribute. In instances of multiple values, repeated use of the indexing operator with the same attribute index cycles through all values associated with the attribute. The return of a null pointer indicates the end of the cycle.

> Note: To guarantee finding all values, do not attempt to access the value of a second attribute until you have cycled through all values of the first.

When you declare an object of this class in your application, all the data management is performed for you. Plus signs in the input are changed back to spaces. Escaped characters (see Table 13-3 in How-To 13.1) when encountered are converted back to their original ASCII form. The inputs object will provide you with access to the pass data through the indexing operator.

In your application program, you must add the following line to include the declaration of the Inputs class.

```
#include "Inputs.h"
```

You perform the retrieve and restore functions by declaring an object of class Input. If you pass no parameters, the default values are assumed for maximum number of pairs, length of attribute fields, and length of value fields. Specification of parameters will substitute the value given for the default. The following several lines of code provide a few example declarations of objects.

```
Inputs inputs;              // Take defaults
Inputs inputs(10);          // Only 10 input pairs maximum
Inputs inputs(10,64);       // Only 10 inputs and max attrib length of 64
Inputs inputs(10,64,128);   // Only 10 inputs, 64 max on attrib, 128 max on val
```

Access is provided to this data through the use of the indexing operator. The index used is the attribute for which you want to find the value. In the example shown in Figure 13-12, indexing the inputs object would yield the results in Table 13-10.

VARIABLE	VALUE
inputs["message"]	"This is a sample of text input. This might have\nbeen entered into the sample form whose\nsource appears in figure 5-8-1. How will it\nbe processed?"
inputs["teacher"]	"dsk@cau.auc.edu"
inputs["topic"]	"Miscellaneous"

Table 13-10 Data access under C++ from form in Figure 13-12

The Inputs class provides a cycling method for accessing multiple values associated with an attribute. For example, the input string below would indicate that the attribute "t1" has values of "a1" and "a3".

`t1=a1&t2=a2&t1=a3`

The resultant inputs object would return the first value in the first access, the second value in the second access, and a null pointer on the third access attempt. The values in the relevant variables derived from the query string above are shown in Table 13-11.

VARIABLE	VALUE
inputs["t1"]	"a1"
inputs["t2"]	"a2"
inputs["t1"]	"a1"
inputs["t1"]	"a3"
inputs["t1"]	(char *)NULL

Table 13-11 C++ handling of duplicate values

The order in which the accesses occur is significant. The cycle for the "t1" attribute resets at the access of the value of attribute "t2". The null pointer returned in the last line indicates a full cycle through the values of attribute "t1".

13.8 SPECIFY NETSCAPE SERVER PUSH

Perl

The Perl implementation of the data retrieval and restoration process uses the file main.pl from the CD. You can use this file as a template for your gateway scripts. Copy this file to whatever name you wish for your Perl CGI application, and add the commands necessary to implement the processing and result generation portions of your script.

The Perl commands in main.pl provide you with the necessary retrieval and restoration of the form data. The script first checks the HTTP method used in the request. Based upon this information, the script determines the location of the input data block. The transformation of the data occurs in the following order.

1. All spaces restored
2. Attribute/value pairs separated
3. All ampersands (&) restored
4. Pairs separated into attributes and values
5. Special characters restored for all attributes and values
6. Array inputs defined

Your commands access the form data submitted through the inputs array. Use the attribute name as the index to access the value. For example, the form shown in Figure 13-12 fills the inputs array as shown in Table 13-12.

VARIABLE	VALUE
inputs{message}	"This is a sample of text input. This might have\nbeen entered into the sample form whose\nsource appears in figure 5-8-1. How will it\nbe processed?"
inputs{teacher}	"dsk@cau.auc.edu"
inputs{topic}	"Miscellaneous"

Table 13-12 Figure 13-12 data access from Perl

COMPLEXITY
ADVANCED

13.8 How do I... Specify Netscape Server Push?

COMPATIBILITY: CGI, NETSCAPE NAVIGATOR

Problem

The information in my document changes very frequently. I would like update my HTML document as new information arrives. How can I create such a document?

Technique

The Netscape Navigator supports a mechanism called Server Push to provide this capability. Instead of a standard HTTP access as described in Appendix G, a Server Push keeps the connection between client and server open. When a request from the client is serviced, an initial response is made. The client/server connection is not closed until the server drops the connection. While connected, the server sends updated documents, which the browser displays as they arrive.

The Server Push capability is supported through the use of CGI applications that repeatedly generate and send new documents to the browser at intervals specified by the application. The initial response generated by the gateway program indicates that the response is composed of multiple documents, each of which replaces the previous one. A step-by-step process for developing such an application is given below.

Steps

Change directories to a location where you wish to build your Server Push gateway program and begin the development process. The method below deals with the response generation portion of your application. The tasks performed should be accomplished using the commands in your chosen programming language.

1. Start your application by retrieving any data that the user has submitted to your gateway application. You will find a procedure for accomplishing this task in How-To's 13.6 and 13.7.

2. Decide whether the input data, if any, will be processed before, during, or after the generation of your response document. If your response depends upon the results of processing, then processing, or at least partial processing, must occur prior to response generation. If the results are directly embedded in the response, then the processing must occur during response generation. Finally, if the response is independent of the processed data, processing may occur after the response is generated. The decision on when and how processing is performed needs to be decided on an application-by-application basis. Based on this decision, intersperse the processing as appropriate among the steps below.

3. Generate the response header indicating that the document will be updated. This response uses the standard Content-type server directive. However, the type specified should be multipart/x-mixed-replace;boundary=boundary_string where the boundary_string is replaced by some boundary string indicator of your choice. For example, in Perl you could use the print command as shown below.

```
print "Content-type: multipart/x-mixed-replace;boundary=WhyNot\n\n";
```

4. Send the boundary string, preceeded by two dashes to signal the beginning of a response document. To begin a response document place – –*boundary_string* on the standard output. In C, you might use the printf command.

```
printf("--WhyNot\n");
```

5. Place the Content-type server directive appropriate for the document type you will be attaching on the standard output, followed by a blank line. In Perl, you could use the puts command to accomplish this task.

```
print "Content-type: text/plain\n";
```

6. Output your attached document in the format specified in step 5.
7. Perform whatever processing tasks are required (waiting for new data from an outside source, waiting a specified amount of time, processing the next data set). When you have performed this task and are ready to generate an update to the current document, return to step 4; the new document will replace the currently viewed one. If you are not going to generate any more updates, continue with step 8.
8. Send the boundary string surrounded by pairs, – –*boundary_string*– –, of dashes to the standard output. In Perl, you would use the print command for this task.

```
print "--WhyNot--\n";
```

9. Once your application has been developed, and compiled if required, you can install this gateway application using the procedure described in How-To 13.4.
10. Reference the URL for this gateway application as you would any other CGI program.

How It Works

The use of this procedure is shown through the development of an example Server Push gateway application. This sample application is written in the Perl scripting language. Further, this sample Server Push application requires no input from the user. The purpose of this program is to provide a snapshot of the individuals logged in to the server when the document is first retrieved (see Figure 13-13), and then again 30 seconds later through the use of the finger network utility. The source for this application appears on the CD in file nph-push.cgi.

When this script is initially accessed, the document provides information about who is currently logged in to the server system as shown in Figure 13-13. Figure 13-14 shows what is displayed 30 seconds later.

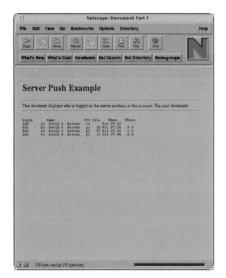 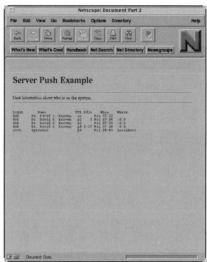

Figure 13-13 Results of running the finger utility

Figure 13-14 Updated finger results 30 seconds later

Between the generation of the first and second documents, an additional user logged in to the system. If you wanted to perform a more systematic monitoring, you could have placed the finger document generation phase in a loop.

This application follows the procedure described above. There is no input to be dealt with and processing occurs during response generation. The initial response header is sent, signaling that the following response messages will successively replace the previous message. The boundary string is sent to signal the first document. The first message is the immediate result of the finger command, with some HTML formatting around it. To make sure the output buffer is flushed, the signal for the second document is sent. Once this document is complete, some internal processing occurs; namely, the application sleeps for 30 seconds. Finally, the second document, another HTML formatted finger result, is sent. The overall message concludes with the boundary string, surrounded by dashes, being sent to the standard output.

Comments

When using the Server Push capability and buffered output, you must make sure to flush your output buffer when a particular component message is complete. If you do not, your component objects may simply appear one after the other after several have been generated. In the Perl script example described in this How-To, the line *selection(STDOUT); $|=1;* flushes the standard output after the completion of the first HTML document.

If you do not provide a termination for the multipart document response by including a final boundary string (– –*boundary_string*– –), the only way to stop updating the document is to activate a link in the document or use a stop facility provided by your browser.

Finally, implementation of a Server Push gateway application should be done in a language that terminates the application when the user interrupts the request, with the stop facility for example. Applications written in the Bourne shell scripting language may not terminate when an interrupt occurs, which means that server resources continue to be used even though the browser no longer requests them.

13.9 How do I... Write a CGI application to send me e-mail?

COMPLEXITY: ADVANCED

COMPATIBILITY: CGI, C, HTML 2

Problem

Some browsers support mailto resources, but not all. I want to allow people to send me e-mail through a Web page whether their browser supports this or not. How can I generate an HTML form and gateway application to accomplish this task? What must I do to extend this capability to allow e-mail to be sent to other users?

Technique

Establishing e-mail Web pages for a specified group of users requires two gateway applications. The first generates an HTML form to gather the e-mail message to be sent. The second CGI program receives the input from this form, determines whether the target of the e-mail is in a defined set of allowed targets, sends the e-mail if appropriate, and generates a resultant HTML document. Figure 13-15 displays the interactions among the components of the developed package.

This How-To shows a step-by-step process for developing, installing, and maintaining a CGI e-mail handling package on your server.

Steps

The C source code for the e-mail package is available on the CD in files mailgen.c and mailsend.c; you also need helper files parse.h and parse.c.

1. Change directories to the location where you wish to perform your development tasks.

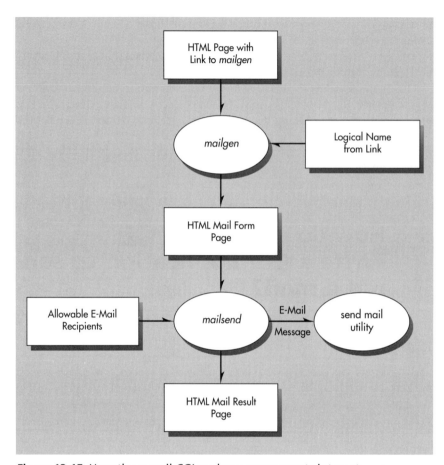

Figure 13-15 How the e-mail CGI package components interact

2. Copy the mailgen.c file from the CD. This file contains the source code for the application that will generate an e-mail form for any target.
3. Choose a name for the mailsend component of this package.
4. Open the mailgen.c file in your text editor.
5. Identify the following line and modify it to specify the URL for the mailsend CGI application.

```
/* This should point to the URL of the application that will send the *
 * mail to the designated recipient.                                  */
#define MAILSEND http://www.mysite.edu:8080/cgi-bin/mailsend
```

This URL reflects the name chosen in step 3.

13.9
WRITE A CGI APPLICATION TO SEND ME E-MAIL

6. Compile mailgen.c, and install the executable as you would any other gateway program. The default name for this executable is *mailgen*. See How-To 13.4 for details on CGI application installation. Access this gateway application through a standard link with the logical name of the destination passed as additional path information.

7. Copy files parse.h, parse.c, and mailsend.c from the CD.

8. Open the mailsend.c file in your text editor. This file contains the source code for the application that sends the results of a form generated by *mailgen* to the appropriate recipient.

9. Identify and modify the line defining the location of your server system's mailsend utility. On UNIX systems, this utility is usually either "sendmail" or "smail".

```
/* You should specify your mail program in this define.           */
#define SENDMAIL "/usr/lib/sendmail"
```

10. Identify and modify the line specifying the location of the file containing the list of allowable e-mail destinations.

```
/* The ALLOW define specifies the location of the allowable users file.*/
#define ALLOW "/usr/local/some_directory/.allow"
```

11. Compile these three files to create the *mailsend* application. If you do not call this application *mailsend*, be sure you specified the URL of this application in step 5. You can now install *mailsend* as you would any other CGI program. See How-To 13.4 for more information on installing gateway applications. Access this gateway application through the specified action in the form generated by *mailgen*, or whatever you choose to call the application installed in step 6.

12. Begin allowing the generation of e-mail pages for selected users. Your first task at this stage is to define a group of users you wish to provide with this service. Either you or they need to establish a logical name used to refer to them within the context of this e-mail package. This logical name helps generate the mail form, as well as verifying that the user is allowed to receive mail via this application.

13. Change directories to the location where you wish to store the file of allowable e-mail recipients. This is the directory you specified in the ALLOW define from step 10.

14. Open the file specified in the ALLOW define.

15. Add a line for each e-mail recipient. A line is composed of the logical name, followed by white space, followed by the e-mail address.

16. After entering all valid recipients, add a line containing the word "end".

17. Generate e-mail forms for submitting mail to users specified in the ALLOW file by referencing the URL of the *mailgen* CGI application. Appended to this URL should be the logical name of the mail recipient in the form of path information. For example, if the *mailgen* program were located in the /cgi-bin directory, and if you wished to create a link to a mail page for registered logical name "paul", the requested URL would be http://www.mysite.edu/cgi-bin/mailgen/paul.

How It Works

The two programs, *mailgen* and *mailsend*, interact with each other and with the ALLOW file to provide a mechanism to support e-mail for a set of registered users. The e-mail package is launched when a link referencing the URL of the *mailgen* application is triggered. For example, http://www.mysite.edu/cgi-bin/mailgen/abner specifies the e-mail entry page associated with the logical name "abner".

> Note: You can also enter the package by sending the proper data fields to the *mailsend* application via the "post" HTTP method; however, in general, most users enter the package through *mailgen*.

When the link is triggered, a mail entry form is dynamically tailored to the specific logical name passed via additional path information. For example, the form displayed in Figure 13-16 was generated by a link designating logical name "dsk" as the target.

The user fills the data fields with his or her name, return address, and the body of the message. When the Submit button is pressed, the input data is sent by "post" method to the *mailsend* CGI application.

The *mailsend* application is responsible for processing and storing the data, as well as providing the user with a response concerning the data items in question. The input data is passed to the application through an input data block on the standard input. *mailsend* calls the C *build* function to parse and convert the attribute/value pairs.

The *mailsend* application goes through the following steps in the process of delivering mail messages.

1. Retrieves the user input data from the form. This task is performed by the procedure in How-To 13.7 for parsing HTML "post" method form data.
2. Opens the file of allowable mail recipients and checks for the specified logical name among those listed. If not present, *mailsend* returns an error document.
3. Opens a pipe to the mailsend utility.
4. Writes the mail message to this pipe.

13.9
WRITE A CGI APPLICATION TO SEND ME E-MAIL

5. Closes the pipe to the mailsend utility. This action, in effect, causes the e-mail to be sent to the specified recipient.

6. Begins generation of a response page.

7. Formats and presents the page to the user.

8. Closes the generated document.

If the data present in Figure 13-16 were submitted, then the resultant document would look like the one shown in Figure 13-17. The mail application on the server site would be responsible for handling the delivery of the mail to the destination.

Comments

The package developed in this How-To has been compiled and tested in the UNIX environment. Porting the application to other environments requires some modification.

Figure 13-16 Mail entry form

Figure 13-17 E-mail response page

CHAPTER 14
BEYOND HTML

14. BEYOND HTML

How do I...

- 14.1 Add sound tracks to my Web page?
- 14.2 Add marquees of scrolling text?
- 14.3 Include an AVI video in my Web page?
- 14.4 Change the font size and color?
- 14.5 Include frames in my Web page?
- 14.6 Include client side imagemaps?
- 14.7 Create new windows for linked documents?
- 14.8 Create an HTML style sheet?
- 14.9 Cascade HTML style sheets?
- 14.10 Write a basic Java applet?
- 14.11 Include a Java applet in an HTML document?
- 14.12 Include a JavaScript script in an HTML document?
- 14.13 Write a basic JavaScript script?
- 14.14 Find a VRML browser?
- 14.15 Create a VRML document?

The World Wide Web is changing at a remarkable rate. New browsers, such as Microsoft Internet Explorer 2.0 and Netscape 2.0, with new HTML extensions, are unveiled. New technologies, such as Java and VRML, are introduced to the World Wide Web. The range of capabilities available to Web page authors is growing every

CHAPTER 14
BEYOND HTML

day. This chapter examines some of the new HTML extensions and new technologies. Because some of the content of this chapter is based on beta versions of software and rapidly evolving languages and protocols, some of this information may be out of date by the time you read this.

14.1 Add Sound Tracks to My Web Page

A sound track can add to the multimedia experience of viewing a page. However, there is no standard way to have a sound play in the background while reading a Web page. This How-To shows how you can use an HTML extension in Microsoft Internet Explorer 2.0 to play sound tracks in the background.

14.2 Add Marquees of Scrolling Text

Text scrolling across a page is a unique way to grab the attention of a reader. This How-To shows how to use an HTML extension in Microsoft Internet Explorer 2.0 to create marquees of text that can scroll across the screen in a variety of styles.

14.3 Include an AVI Video in My Web Page

Animations can make a Web page more entertaining or useful. However, they require the use of an external application that will display animations, which not all Web users may have. This How-To shows how to use an HTML extension in Microsoft Internet Explorer 2.0 to add an inline video in AVI format to your Web page.

14.4 Change the Font Size and Color

Changing the font size and color can help make your page more aesthetically appealing, and help draw attention to important information. This How-To explains how to use HTML extensions in Netscape to change the font size and color.

14.5 Include Frames in My Web Page

Frames are a way in Netscape to divide the browser window into a number of independent sections, each displaying a separate document. A link in a document in one frame can load a document in another frame. This How-To discusses how to create frames in a Web page and link documents to different frames.

14.6 Include Client Side Imagemaps

Imagemaps offer useful, creative ways to provide links to other documents. Creating imagemaps, however, can be difficult and often requires knowledge of CGI applications. This How-To shows how to create a client side imagemap in Netscape 2.0, in which all the information about the imagemap is located within the HTML document.

CHAPTER 14
BEYOND HTML

14.7 Create New Windows for Linked Documents

Often it's useful to have a document that's referenced in a link in a Web page appear in a separate window, so the reader can easily compare the two documents. This How-To shows how to use an HTML extension supported by Netscape 2.0 to automatically open a separate window and place the linked document there.

14.8 Create an HTML Style Sheet

Style sheets provide a mechanism for supporting consistent style across multiple Web pages. Style sheets allow you to extend and enhance HTML elements in significant ways. This How-To shows how to build style sheets as proposed in the HTML 3 standard.

14.9 Cascade HTML Style Sheets

You can combine style sheets with other style sheets as well as with HTML <STYLE> elements. This combination leads to aggregate style sheets and alternative style sheets. This How-To explains how to attach styles and style sheets to Web pages to provide alternative and aggregate presentation styles for the page.

14.10 Write a Basic Java Applet

Java is a new object-oriented programming language that allows designers of Web pages to create new, highly interactive pages. This How-To shows how to write a basic Java applet, or application, for use in a Web page.

14.11 Include a Java Applet in an HTML Document

Once a Java applet is written, code must be included in the Web page so that the page can access the applet. This How-To shows how to include tags so that the page can access and run the appropriate Java applet.

14.12 Include a JavaScript Script in an HTML Document

JavaScript is a new scripting language developed by Netscape that allows users to create scripts without delving into complex languages like Perl or Java. The scripts can be included in the same document as the rest of the Web page. This How-To shows how to use the <SCRIPT> tag in Netscape to run JavaScript scripts.

14.13 Write a Basic JavaScript Script

JavaScript can be used to create detailed, highly interactive pages. While JavaScript is a topic suitable for an entire book, this How-To will show the basics of writing a JavaScript script.

CHAPTER 14
BEYOND HTML

14.14 Find a VRML Browser
The Virtual Reality Modeling Language (VRML), like HTML, serves as a basis for network-based documents. As with HTML Web pages, you need a suitable browser to view these documents. This How-To shows how to locate a browser suitable for use on your hardware platform.

14.15 Create a VRML Document
The intricacies of VRML are beyond the scope of this book. However, an introduction to the recognition and creation of such documents will provide you with a glimpse into this growing area of Web documents. This How-To explains how to create a basic VRML document and how to recognize such a document if you retrieve one.

14.1 How do I... Add sound tracks to my Web page?

COMPLEXITY: INTERMEDIATE

COMPATIBILITY: INTERNET EXPLORER 2.0

Problem
I would like to include some music that will play on the user's computer when he or she reads my page. How can I include a sound track on my Web page?

Technique
Microsoft's Internet Explorer 2.0 supports the HTML extension <BGSOUND>, which allows users to add sounds that will play in the background for those who are using that browser. Other browsers may treat this as any other unsupported HTML element. The browser supports a number of different sound formats and allows you to control the number of times the sound is played.

Steps
Identify the appropriate sound for your page and open the document that contains the HTML code for the page.

1. Insert the <BGSOUND> tag in the body of the page. The location of the tag within the body is not important; the sound will be played as soon as the page is loaded, regardless of the location of the tag. No closing tag is required.

14.1
ADD SOUND TRACKS TO MY WEB PAGE

```
<BODY>
<!-- text and HTML markup tags -->
<BGSOUND>
<!-- more text and HTML markup tags -->
</BODY>
```

2. To identify the name of the sound file, include the attribute SRC and set it equal to the name of the file. For example, to include a file named bam.wav, use

```
<BODY>
<!-- text and HTML markup tags -->
<BGSOUND SRC="bam.wav">
<!-- more text and HTML markup tags -->
</BODY>
```

3. Like many other HTML tags, you can specify the full pathname of the file or include a URL that goes to a sound file on another computer. For example, if the sound file is located in the directory sounds/loud, use

```
<BODY>
<!-- text and HTML markup tags -->
<BGSOUND SRC="sounds/loud/bam.wav">
<!-- more text and HTML markup tags -->
</BODY>
```

If the file is accessible by HTTP from the computer www.widgets.com in the same directory as the example above, you would enter

```
<BODY>
<!-- text and HTML markup tags -->
<BGSOUND SRC="http://www.widgets.com/sounds/loud/bam.wav">
<!-- more text and HTML markup tags -->
</BODY>
```

4. To play the sound more than once, you can use the LOOP attribute. Set the attribute equal to the number of times you want the sound played. To play the sound from the last step three times, enter

```
<BODY>
<!-- text and HTML markup tags -->
<BGSOUND SRC="sounds/loud/bam.wav" LOOP=3>
<!-- more text and HTML markup tags -->
</BODY>
```

5. To continuously play a sound in the background, set the LOOP attribute equal to "infinite". Setting LOOP equal to "-1" has the same effect. To make the sound in the last example play continuously, enter

```
<BODY>
<!-- text and HTML markup tags -->
<BGSOUND SRC="sounds/loud/bam.wav" LOOP=INFINITE>
<!-- more text and HTML markup tags -->
</BODY>
```

CHAPTER 14
BEYOND HTML

How It Works

When Internet Explorer loads a page that contains the <BGSOUND> tag, it loads the sound file specified by the SRC attribute. The browser then plays the sound the number of times indicated by the LOOP attribute. The browser will play the sound once if the LOOP attribute is missing.

Comments

As of this writing, Internet Explorer supports three sound formats: WAV, AU, and MID (MIDI). Sound files in other formats will not be played by Internet Explorer. Note that <BGSOUND> is an HTML extension supported only by Internet Explorer. Other browsers, such as Netscape and Mosaic, will skip over the tag and not load or play the specified sound. You can find updated information about <BGSOUND> on the Web at the URL http://www.microsoft.com/windows/ie/IE20HTML.htm.

COMPLEXITY
INTERMEDIATE

14.2 How do I... Add marquees of scrolling text?

COMPATIBILITY: INTERNET EXPLORER 2.0

Problem

I would like to bring attention to some text on my Web page by scrolling it across the page. How can I easily create a marquee of scrolling text for my page?

Technique

Microsoft's Internet Explorer 2.0 supports the HTML extension <MARQUEE>, which allows people using that browser to see marquees of text that scroll across the screen. A number of attributes for the tag allow you to control the size, scrolling behavior, and color of the marquee.

Steps

Open your document and identify the text you want to use as the marquee and the location in the page for the marquee.

1. Place the <MARQUEE> tag at the beginning and the </MARQUEE> tag at the end of the text that will be in the marquee. This creates a default marquee that scrolls across the screen once. For example:

```
<MARQUEE>This is an example of a marquee</MARQUEE>
```

14.2
ADD MARQUEES OF SCROLLING TEXT

2. You can control the type of scrolling used with the BEHAVIOR attribute. The BEHAVIOR attribute supports three values, which are described in Table 14-1.

VALUE	DESCRIPTION
"alternate"	Bounces the text back and forth between the two sides of the screen
"scroll"	Starts the text all the way off the screen and moves it across the marquee all the way off the screen on the other side
"slide"	Starts the text all the way off the screen and moves it across the marquee until the text touches the margin on the other side of the screen

 Table 14-1 Values for the BEHAVIOR attribute in <MARQUEE>

The default value for BEHAVIOR is "scroll". To create a sliding marquee, use

`<MARQUEE BEHAVIOR=SLIDE>This is an example of a sliding marquee</MARQUEE>`

To create a bouncing marquee, use

`<MARQUEE BEHAVIOR=ALTERNATE>This is an example of a bouncing marquee</MARQUEE>`

3. The DIRECTION attribute controls the direction the text moves across the marquee. DIRECTION can have two values: "left" (for text scrolling from left to right) and "right" (for text scrolling from right to left). The default value is "left". To create a scrolling marquee that goes from right to left, use

`<MARQUEE DIRECTION=RIGHT>This is an example of a marquee moving right to left</MARQUEE>`

4. You can control the speed of the marquee with two attributes, SCROLLAMOUNT and SCROLLDELAY. SCROLLAMOUNT sets the number of pixels between each redraw of the marquee. That is, the next time the marquee is drawn, the contents of the marquee will be moved down by the number of pixels set by the SCROLLAMOUNT attribute. The SCROLLDELAY attribute sets the delay, in milliseconds, between redraws. A marquee can be speeded up by increasing the value of the SCROLLAMOUNT attribute (moving the text a greater distance between redraws), decreasing the value of the SCROLLDELAY attribute (shortening the time between redraws), or both. For example, to create a scrolling marquee that moves the text 25 pixels between redraws, you would use

`<MARQUEE SCROLLAMOUNT=25>This is an example of a marquee</MARQUEE>`

To create a marquee that waits 10 milliseconds between redraws, use

`<MARQUEE SCROLLDELAY=10>This is an example of a marquee</MARQUEE>`

To combine the two attributes in the same marquee, use

```
<MARQUEE SCROLLAMOUNT=25 SCROLLDELAY=10>This is an example of a marquee</MARQUEE>
```

5. You can set the number of times the marquee scrolls across the page with the LOOP attribute. To create a continuously scrolling marquee, set LOOP equal to "-1" or "infinite". To create a marquee that will scroll across the screen five times, use

```
<MARQUEE LOOP=5>This is an example of a marquee that scrolls 5 times</MARQUEE>
```

To create a marquee that scrolls continuously, use

```
<MARQUEE LOOP=INFINITE>This is an example of a continuously scrolling marquee</MARQUEE>
```

6. The BGCOLOR attribute sets the background color of the marquee. The attribute can be set to a hexadecimal set of red, green, and blue intensities (known as an RGB triplet), or to one of a set of special color names supported by Internet Explorer. For example, the following two lines each create a marquee with a red background.

```
<MARQUEE BGCOLOR="#FF0000">This is an example of a marquee with a red background</MARQUEE>
<MARQUEE BGCOLOR="Red">This is an example of a marquee with a red background</MARQUEE>
```

7. The HEIGHT and WIDTH attributes adjust the height and the width of the marquee. They can either be set equal to a specific distance in pixels, or a percentage of the width or height of the screen. To create a marquee that is 300 pixels wide and 50 pixels high, use

```
<MARQUEE WIDTH=300 HEIGHT=50>This is an example of a marquee</MARQUEE>
```

To create a marquee that is 20 percent of the height of the screen and 75 percent of the width of the screen, use

```
<MARQUEE WIDTH=75% HEIGHT=20%>This is an example of a marquee</MARQUEE>
```

8. The ALIGN attribute sets the vertical alignment of the text around the marquee. ALIGN can have three values: "top" (for text aligned with the top of the marquee), "middle" (for text aligned with the middle of the marquee), and "bottom" (for text aligned with the bottom of the marquee). The ALIGN attribute does not control the alignment of text within the marquee. For example, to align text that follows the marquee with the top of the marquee, use

```
<MARQUEE ALIGN=TOP>The text that follows this marquee will be aligned with the top of the marquee</MARQUEE> Some text that follows the marquee.
```

14.2
ADD MARQUEES OF SCROLLING TEXT

9. The HSPACE and VSPACE attributes adjust the horizontal and vertical margins, respectively, of the marquee. These attributes are set equal to the size, in pixels, of the margin. For example, to create a marquee with a 10-pixel margin on the top and bottom and a 15-pixel margin on the left and right, use

```
<MARQUEE VSPACE=10 HSPACE=15>This is an example of a marquee with horizontal and vertical margins</MARQUEE>
```

An example of the <MARQUEE> tag is shown in Figure 14-1. The HTML code used to create the figure can be found on the CD-ROM as file 14-1.html.

How It Works

When Internet Explorer recognizes the <MARQUEE> tag in a file, it creates a marquee on the page, using values from any attributes in the <MARQUEE> tag. The text moves across the marquee in the style defined by the attributes, or by using the default values if no attribute values are specified.

Comments

The <MARQUEE> tag is currently supported only by Internet Explorer. Users with other browsers, such as Netscape and Mosaic, will be unable to see the marquee; the text will appear normally on the page. The use of long text strings in marquees

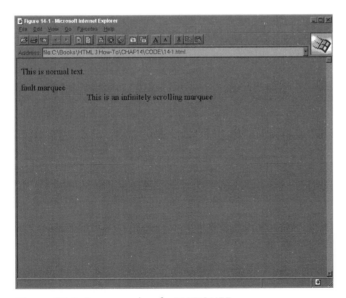

Figure 14-1 An example of <MARQUEE>

and short values for the SCROLLDELAY attribute may slow down the user's computer, particularly a slower machine or one running other applications at the same time. You can find updated information about <MARQUEE> on the Web at the URL http://www.microsoft.com/windows/ie/IE20HTML.htm.

14.3 How do I... Include an AVI video in my Web page?

COMPLEXITY
INTERMEDIATE

COMPATIBILITY: INTERNET EXPLORER 2.0

Problem

I have a video clip in AVI format that I would like to include in my Web page, so that the video displays on the screen as the user reads the page. Is there a way to play an AVI video on my Web page?

Technique

Microsoft's Internet Explorer supports inline AVI videos, which can be played on the page instead of by an external application. The browser supports attributes that allow you to control the size of the video display, the number of times it plays, and when to start the video.

Steps

Find the video clip you want to include in the page. Open your document and find the location where you want to add the video clip.

1. Use the <IMG> tag (see Chapter 8) to insert the video. Set the attribute DYNSRC equal to the name of the video. DYNSRC can be a filename, a full path, or a URL to the video file. For example, to include a video with the filename mars.avi, enter

```
<IMG DYNSRC="mars.avi">
```

If the video is accessible by HTTP from www.widgets.com in the directory videos/mars.avi, enter

```
<IMG DYNSRC="http://www.widgets.com/videos/mars.avi">
```

2. For those browsers that don't support AVI videos, you can specify an image to be shown in its place. To do this, set the SRC attribute equal to the filename of the image. In the example from the last step, to add a reference to an image called mars.gif, you would enter

```
<IMG DYNSRC="mars.avi" SRC="mars.gif">
```

3. Use the START attribute to tell the browser when to start playing the video. START can have two values, "fileopen" and "mouseover". If START is set equal to "fileopen", the video starts playing as soon as the file has finished loading. If START is set equal to "mouseover", the video will not start playing until the user moves the mouse cursor over the animation. The default value is "fileopen". To insert a video that doesn't start playing until the user moves the cursor over the video, use

```
<IMG DYNSRC="mars.avi" SRC="mars.gif" START=MOUSEOVER>
```

It's possible to use both "fileopen" and "mouseover" for the START attribute. In this case, the video will play as soon as the file loads, and again each time the cursor passes over the video. To do this, enter

```
<IMG DYNSRC="mars.avi" SRC="mars.gif" START=FILEOPEN,MOUSEOVER>
```

4. You can add a set of video controls beneath the video clip with the CONTROLS attribute. For example, to add a set of video controls to a clip, use

```
<IMG DYNSRC="mars.avi" SRC="mars.gif" CONTROLS>
```

5. The number of times the video displays can be set with the LOOP attribute. The LOOP attribute can be set to the number of times the video is played. Setting LOOP equal to "infinite" or "-1" plays the video continuously. To play a video clip five times, use

```
<IMG DYNSRC="mars.avi" SRC="mars.gif" LOOP=5>
```

Or, to play the video continuously, use

```
<IMG DYNSRC="mars.avi" SRC="mars.gif" LOOP=INFINITE>
```

6. The LOOPDELAY attribute controls the amount of time the browser waits before replaying a video. Set the LOOPDELAY attribute to the number of milliseconds the browser waits after the end of the video before replaying it. For example, to wait two seconds between replays of a continuously looping video, use

```
<IMG DYNSRC="mars.avi" SRC="mars.gif" LOOP=INFINITE LOOPDELAY=2000>
```

How It Works

When Internet Explorer identifies the DYNSRC attribute in the <IMG> tag, it loads the video file specified by that attribute. The browser then displays the video, using the values provided by any attributes or the default values.

Comments

Besides the attributes mentioned above, you can use other <IMG> attributes. See Chapter 8 for a full discussion of the attributes supported by <IMG>. Currently, only Internet Explorer 2.0 supports inline AVI video, so users using other browsers will be able to see only the image. You can provide a link to the animation (in AVI or another format) that people with other browsers can see with an external application. For example, to include a link to an MPEG version of an animation, enter

```
<A HREF="mars.mpg"><IMG DYNSRC="mars.avi" SRC="mars.gif"></A>
```

You can find updated information about including AVI videos on the Web at the URL http://www.microsoft.com/windows/ie/IE20HTML.htm.

14.4 How do I... Change the font size and color?

COMPLEXITY EASY

COMPATIBILITY: NETSCAPE 2.0

Problem

I would like to be able to change the font size and color for some, but not all, of the text in my document. How can I use HTML tags to change font size and color?

Technique

Older versions of Netscape support the <FONT> tag, and specifically the SIZE attribute, which allows you to increase or decrease the size of the font. Netscape 2.0 now supports the COLOR attribute for <FONT>, which allows you to change the color of the font.

Steps

Open your document and identify the text whose font size and/or color you want to change.

1. Place <FONT> at the beginning and </FONT> at the end of the selected text.

```
<FONT>This text will be altered from the rest of the page</FONT>
```

2. The SIZE attribute changes the size of the font contained within the <FONT> element. Set SIZE to a number between 1 and 7, with 1 the smallest font. The default value is 3. For example, to place text in a very large font, use

`<FONT SIZE=7>This text is very large</FONT>`

3. You can change the font size of the entire document with the <BASEFONT> element at the beginning of the document. Use the SIZE attribute to change the default font size. For example, to create a document whose default font size is 2, use

`<BASEFONT SIZE=2>`

4. You can also use the SIZE attribute to change the font size relative to the default font size by using a + or - sign to indicate the change from the default size. For example, to place text in a font two sizes larger than the default size, use

`<FONT SIZE=+2>This text is two sizes larger than the default</FONT>`

5. The COLOR attribute changes the color of the text contained within the <FONT> element. Set the attribute to a set of hexadecimal numbers that control the red, green and blue intensities (known as an RGB triplet). "FF" is used for full intensity, and "00" for no intensity. For example, to make a section of text appear blue, use

`<FONT COLOR="#0000FF">This text appears blue</FONT>`

An example of using the <FONT> tag to control font size and color is shown in Figure 14-2. The HTML code used to create this page can be found on the CD-ROM as file 14-2.html.

How It Works

When Netscape identifies the <FONT> tag, it reads the attributes and makes the required changes in the size or color of the font. When the browser reads the <BASEFONT> element, it adjusts all the text on the page to the font size specified by the SIZE attribute.

Comments

The <FONT> and <BASEFONT> tags are not widely supported, so people using browsers other than Netscape may not be able to see the different font sizes or colors. If you are trying to emphasize text, it would be better to use one of the standard markup tags, like <EM> and <STRONG>, that are supported by all browsers. See Chapter 3 for a detailed description of character markup tags. You can find updated information about Netscape extensions at the URL http://www.netscape.com/assist/net_sites/index.html.

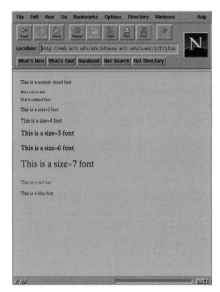

Figure 14-2 An example of different font sizes and colors

14.5 How do I... Include frames in my Web page?

COMPLEXITY
ADVANCED

COMPATIBILITY: NETSCAPE 2.0

Problem

I see some pages around the Web where the screen is broken into separate windows or frames. How can I add frames to my documents?

Technique

Frames are created through the use of frame documents, which in turn are created by using <FRAMESET> tags and <FRAME> tags.

Frame documents are not all that different from regular HTML documents. In frame documents, the <FRAMESET> container is used in place of a <BODY> container. The <FRAMESET> container describes the different HTML "sub" documents that will make up the frames on the page.

The basic structure of a frame document is

14.5
INCLUDE FRAMES IN MY WEB PAGE

```
<HTML>
<HEAD>
</HEAD>
<FRAMESET>
other FRAMESETS or FRAME tags or NOFRAME tags
</FRAMESET>
</HTML>
```

The <FRAMESET> ... </FRAMESET> tags are used as the container of the frame document and also to define the size of the frames. The tag has two attributes, ROWS and COLS. ROWS describes the numbers of rows of the screen to be allocated to each frame. COLS describes the number of columns of the screen that each frame in the document will be allocated. These numbers may be given as an absolute number or a percentage value, or an * may be used to indicate that the corresponding frame should receive all the remaining space. For example,

```
<FRAMESET ROWS="50%, 25%,25%>
```

creates three frames. The first frame is twice as long as the other two frames.

```
<FRAMESET COLS=150,*>
```

creates two frames. The first has a fixed column width of 150 pixels; the second receives the remaining part of the screen.

It is possible to nest <FRAMESET> ... </FRAMESET> tags inside of other <FRAMESET> ... </FRAMESET> tags in order to create all sorts of effects.

The second tag used to create frames is the <FRAME> tag. It defines a frame within a frameset and has six possible attributes. The <FRAME> tag syntax is

```
<FRAME SRC="url" NAME="window_name" MARGINWIDTH="value"
MARGINHEIGHT="value" SCROLLING="yes|no|auto" {NORESIZE}>
```

SRC is the URL of the source document to be displayed in this frame.

NAME is an optional attribute that assigns a name to a frame so that the frame may be used by links in other documents. All names must begin with an alphanumeric character. The following names are reserved, though, as they have special meanings.

- **HTML** _blank-->: Always load this link into a new, unnamed window.
- **HTML** _self-->: Always load this link over itself.
- **HTML** _parent-->: Always load this link of its parent or itself if it has no parent.
- **HTML** _top-->: Always load this link at the top level or itself if it is at the top level.

MARGINWIDTH: An optional attribute used to set the width of the margins of the frame. If used, the value is in pixels.

MARGINHEIGHT: The same as MARGINWIDTH, except it controls the upper and lower margins of the frame.

SCROLLING: Used to describe whether the frame should have a scroll bar. Setting this attribute to "yes" means the frame always has a scroll bar. Setting the attribute to "no" means the frame never has a scroll bar. Use of the "auto" setting displays a scroll bar when needed. This is an optional attribute, with "auto" being the default.

NORESIZE: An optional attribute. If a NORESIZE appears in the tag, the user will not be able to change the size of the frame. By default, all frames can be resized.

For example,

```
<FRAME SRC="http://www.myserver.com/title.html" NORESIZE>
```

loads the document retrieved at www.myserver.com/title.html into the defined frame. Because of the NORESIZE attribute, the user cannot change the size of this frame.

Finally, the <NOFRAME> ... </NOFRAME> tag may be used in conjunction with the other frame tags. Use the <NOFRAME> tag to provide alternative information to browsers that are non-frame-capable clients. A frame-capable client ignores all items found inside the <NOFRAME> tag.

For example:

```
<NOFRAME>
The information on the page makes use of frame technology. For best
results, use the latest version of Netscape.
</NOFRAME>
```

The above code causes the message between the tags to be displayed by any browser that cannot render frames.

Steps

The following steps show one way that you can add frames to your documents.

1. Think about the number of frames you want to use in your document and the screen layout. It may help to design the initial screen layout on paper. This example contains three documents in three frames: a header in a top frame, and two equally sized frames underneath on left and right parts of the screen. These frames contain a graphic and a description, respectively.

14.5
INCLUDE FRAMES IN MY WEB PAGE

A quick sketch of the layout:

```
|------------------------------------------|
|                  Header                  |
|------------------------------------------|
|     Graphic       |    Description       |
|     frame         |    frame             |
|                   |                      |
|                   |                      |
|-------------------|----------------------|
```

2. Compose the individual documents that will make up the individual frames. This example has three frames, therefore three separate documents. Each document is as follows:

A very simple header document, header.html:

```
<HTML>
<!-- header.html -->
<!-- This document is used as the header frame for the frameset -->
<HEAD><TITLE>Cartoons</TITLE></HEAD>
<BODY>
<center>
<H1>A Cartoon</H1>
Enhanced with Netscape 2.0 Frames
</center>
</BODY>
</HTML>
```

The document picture.html contains the graphic you want to show in the second (left side) frame:

```
<HTML>
<HEAD><TITLE>A toon</TITLE></HEAD>
<!-- picture.html -->
<!-- this document simply loads a picture -->
<BODY>
<IMG ALIGN=CENTER SRC="slow.GIF">
<P><small>My favorite cartoon<Sup>1
<P>
1</SUP>By Jz</small>
</BODY>
</HTML>
```

Finally, facts.html contains the information you want to show in the third (right side) frame:

```
<HTML>
<!-- facts.html -->
<!-- simple document that contains information to be shown in a frame -->
<HEAD><TITLE>Facts</TITLE></HEAD>
<BODY>
```

continued on next page

CHAPTER 14
BEYOND HTML

continued from previous page
```
<H2>Some notes about cartoons</H2>
Cartoons have been around for a long time.  Almost as soon as papers
first came into existence, cartoons started popping up in them.  Today
comics can be found in almost any language known to man.
<P>
Cartoons serve many functions:
<UL><LI>To entertain
<LI>To enlighten
<LI>To inform
</UL>
Or some combination of all three.
<P>
A good source of cartoons on the web is
<A HREF="http://www.phlab.missouri.edu/~c617145/comix.html">
Comics 'n Stuff</A>
<P>
<P>
</BODY>
</HTML>
```

These three documents are all quite simple, but when combined into frames on a screen, they can be quite effective.

3. Create the document that will hold the three frames. This can be done with any text editor. This document will begin and end like any other HTML document, with the <HTML> tags.

4. Define the first frameset. This is done with the <FRAMESET> tag:

```
<FRAMESET ROWS="70,*">
```

This tag, in effect, splits the screen into two horizontal sections. The first section is 70 rows long. The remaining section occupies the rest of the screen.

5. Add the first frame with the <FRAME> tag:

```
<FRAME SRC="header.html" NORESIZE>
```

This tag causes the document header.html to display in the first frame, the one designated to be 70 rows long. The user cannot resize this frame.

6. Add a second frameset that will be nested into the first frameset. This is done with

```
<FRAMESET COLS="50%,*">
```

This tag creates another frameset in the area of the screen not occupied by the header.html frame. This new frameset consists of two frames of equal size.

7. Add the second and third documents to their respective frames.

14.5
INCLUDE FRAMES IN MY WEB PAGE

```
<FRAME SRC="picture.html" MARGINHEIGHT=0 MARGINWIDTH=4 SCROLLING=no
NAME="toon">
<FRAME SRC="facts.html" NAME="story" NORESIZE>
```

This works just as the <FRAME> tag did in step 5, only these frames are included in the second frameset.

8. Close the two framesets.

```
</FRAMESET>
</FRAMESET>
```

9. Include some information for browsers that do not support frames. This is done by inserting information between <NOFRAME> ... </NOFRAME> tags. The information included here can be anything from a simple message to a nonframe version of your document. For a sample of this, you may view the entire document shown at the end of this section.

10. Save and name the document. For this example, use toon_dem.html. The entire document:

```
<HTML>
<TITLE>About Cartoons</TITLE>

<!-- Create the first frameset and load the first frame -->

<FRAMESET ROWS="70,*">
<FRAME SRC="header.html" MARGINHEIGHT=0 MARGINWIDTH=0 SCROLLING="no" NORESIZE>

<!-- Create the second frameset and load the second and third frames -->

<FRAMESET COLS="50%,*">
<FRAME SRC="picture.html" MARGINHEIGHT=0 MARGINWIDTH=4 SCROLLING=no
NAME="toon">
<FRAME SRC="facts.html" NAME="story" NORESIZE>

</FRAMESET>
</FRAMESET>
<NOFRAME>

<!-- The following is used by non-frame-aware browsers -->

<H2>Cartoons</H2>
<IMG ALIGN=LEFT SRC="slow.GIF">
Cartoons have been around for a long time.  Almost as soon as papers
first came into existence cartoons started popping up in them.  Today
comics can be found in almost any language known to man.
<P>
Cartoons serve many functions:
<UL><LI>To entertain
<LI>To enlighten
<LI>To inform
```

continued on next page

continued from previous page

```
</UL>
Or some combination of all three.
<P>
A good source of cartoons on the web is
<A HREF="http://www.phlab.missouri.edu/~c617145/comix.html">
Comics 'n Stuff</A>
<HR>
Note:this is one of my favorite cartoons<P>
</NOFRAME>

</HTML>
```

11. View the document to make sure it looks the way you think it should. Figure 14-3 shows how the sample document looks when viewed by a browser that supports forms.

12. Just to be cautious, view your document with a browser that does not support frames to see if it looks okay. Figure 14-4 shows what the sample document looks like when seen through an older version of Netscape.

13. Experiment some with different frame settings.

How It Works

The first <FRAMESET> tag splits the screen into two parts: a top section with a length of 70 pixels and a bottom section that occupies the remaining portion of the screen. The first <FRAME SRC> tag loads the header.html document into the top frame. The next <FRAMESET> tag splits the remaining section of the screen into two equal frames. The next two <FRAME SRC> tags load the picture.html and the facts.html documents into these frames. When a frames-aware browser encounters these tags, it renders the documents in three separate frames.

The <NOFRAME> tags render information on browsers that do not support frames.

Figure 14-3 A frames demonstration

Figure 14-4 The sample document when viewed by Netscape 1.1

Comments

Frames are a new, dynamic, and powerful addition to HTML. This example gives a general overview of frames. It only covers the basics. If you are interested in exploring frames further, check the latest online documentation at the Netscape home page: http://home.netscape.com/.

It should also be noted here that frames, while being powerful tools, are, as of this writing, not part of the HTML standard. They are in fact only supported by the latest version of the Netscape browser. If you want to create HTML documents that look relatively the same from one browser to the next, you probably do not want to use frames.

COMPLEXITY
INTERMEDIATE

14.6 How do I... Include client side imagemaps?

COMPATIBILITY: NETSCAPE 2.0

Problem

I want to develop an imagemap, but I don't have the time or the know-how to write a CGI application that will read an imagemap and return the appropriate page. How can I include a simple imagemap on my page?

Technique

Netscape 2.0 supports client side imagemaps, where the different regions of the image are specified within the document or in another HTML document. The syntax is similar to that for the proposed SHAPE attribute in HTML 3. (See How-To 7-17.) No CGI applications are required to read client side imagemaps. They therefore even work while not connected to the Internet; handy for examining local Web pages.

Steps

Open your document. Then, load an image with a viewer, such as Photoshop, that allows you to get the pixel locations on the image so you can specify image locations in the links.

1. First, identify areas on the image that you want to have serve as links. As of this writing, the only shape supported is a rectangle. Note the pixel locations of the upper left and lower right corners of the rectangle.

CHAPTER 14
BEYOND HTML

2. In the HTML document, insert the <MAP> and </MAP> tags. Use the NAME attribute for <MAP> to give a unique name for the imagemap. For example, to create an imagemap named mymap, you would enter

```
<MAP NAME="mymap">
</MAP>
```

3. Between the <MAP> and </MAP> tags, insert an <AREA> tag. There should be one <AREA> tag for each link on the map. If your imagemap has three areas, enter

```
<MAP NAME="mymap">
<AREA>
<AREA>
<AREA>
</MAP>
```

4. The SHAPE attribute of <AREA> identifies the shape of the area in the imagemap. Since rectangles are the only currently supported shape, SHAPE can have only one value, "rect".

```
<MAP NAME="mymap">
<AREA SHAPE="RECT">
<AREA SHAPE="RECT">
<AREA SHAPE="RECT">
</MAP>
```

5. The COORD attribute identifies the boundaries of the area on the imagemap. For "rect", COORD has four values, separated by commas: the x coordinate of the upper-left corner, the y coordinate of the upper-left corner, the x coordinate of the lower-right corner, and the y coordinate of the lower-right corner. For example, for three rectangles in different areas of the image:

```
<MAP NAME="mymap">
<AREA SHAPE="RECT" COORD="10,10,30,50">
<AREA SHAPE="RECT" COORD="50,50,70,70">
<AREA SHAPE="RECT" COORD="90,90,120,95">
</MAP>
```

6. For each area, the HREF attribute identifies the URL of the document that should be loaded if that area is selected by the user. The document can be a local file or a document on another server. Adding HREF attributes to the above example:

```
<MAP NAME="mymap">
<AREA SHAPE="RECT" COORD="10,10,30,50" HREF="info.html">
<AREA SHAPE="RECT" COORD="50,50,70,70" HREF="projects/info/data.html">
<AREA SHAPE="RECT" COORD="90,90,120,95" HREF="http://www.widgets.com/">
</MAP>
```

7. The imagemap information can be referenced to an image on the page by adding the USEMAP attribute to the <IMG> element. USEMAP is set equal to the name of map information from the NAME attribute of <MAP>. For example, if the file "imagemap.gif" serves as the imagemap, using the information from the last step, you would enter

```
<IMG SRC="imagemap.gif" ALT="An imagemap" USEMAP="#mymap">
```

The map description does not have to be in the same document as the imagemap itself. If the map description is stored in the file maps.html in the same directory as the file with the imagemap, you can use

```
<IMG SRC="imagemap.gif" ALT="An imagemap" USEMAP="maps.html#mymap">
```

How It Works

When a user clicks on an image that includes the USEMAP attribute, Netscape reads the corresponding imagemap description contained within the <MAP> element. If the user selects an area described by one of the <AREA> tags, the browser loads the document identified by the HREF attribute.

Comments

Netscape 2.0 is the only browser that supports client side imagemaps, so people using other browsers cannot access those imagemaps. Since the USEMAP attribute takes precedence over ordinary links, there are two ways to work around this. One way is to enclose the image in a link that references a standard imagemap routine:

```
<A HREF="/cgi-bin/imagemap.cgi"><IMG SRC="imagemap.gif" ALT="An imagemap"
USEMAP="#mymap"></A>
```

This method requires that you have configured an imagemap CGI application and set up the appropriate description files for that application. Another way is to include a link to a document that gives an error message and informs the user that the imagemap can only be accessed by those browsers that support client side imagemaps:

```
<A HREF="error.html"><IMG SRC="imagemap.gif" ALT="An imagemap"
USEMAP="#mymap"></A>
```

You can find updated information about client side imagemaps in Netscape at the URL http://www.netscape.com/assist/net_sites/html_extensions_3.html. Microsoft Internet Explorer may soon support imagemaps as well. For updated information, check out http://www.microsoft.com/windows/ie/IE20HTML.htm.

14.7 How do I... Create new windows for linked documents?

COMPLEXITY
EASY

COMPATIBILITY: NETSCAPE 2.0

Problem

I would like to include a link to a document in my Web page, but instead of loading that document in the same browser window, replacing the previous page, I would like the new document to go into a separate window. Is there a way of creating new windows for linked documents?

Technique

Netscape 2.0 supports the TARGET attribute of the anchor tag <A>, which identifies the name of a new window that opens, containing the new document. The TARGET attribute can also be used with the <BASE> tag to identify a default target window name for all links in a document that do not include the TARGET attribute.

Steps

Open your document. Identify the links that you want to have go to separate windows.

1. To send the document referenced in a link to another window, add the TARGET attribute and set it equal to the name of the window. For example, to send the document referenced by a link to a window named The Widgets Page, you would enter

```
<A HREF="http://www.widgets.com/" TARGET="The Widgets Page">Go to the
Widgets Page</A>
```

2. The TARGET attribute can also be used in the <AREA> element (see How-To 14.6) in client side imagemaps. This allows the link for a specific area of an imagemap to appear in a separate window. For example, to send the document referenced by a link in an imagemap to another window named The Widgets Page, enter

```
<AREA SHAPE="RECT" COORD="90,90,120,95" HREF="http://www.widgets.com/"
TARGET="The Widgets Page">
```

3. The TARGET attribute can also be used in the <FORM> element. This sends the output of a form submission to a separate page. For example, to send the results of a form to a page thanking the user for filling out the form, enter

14.7 CREATE NEW WINDOWS FOR LINKED DOCUMENTS

```
<FORM ACTION="results.cgi" TARGET="Thanks!">
```

4. Netscape reserves certain "magic" target names for specific purposes. The magic names and their uses are described in Table 14-2.

NAME	DESCRIPTION
"_blank"	Loads the referenced document into a blank window
"_self"	Loads the referenced document into the same window where the anchor was selected
"_parent"	Loads the referenced document into the parent frameset of the current document (see How-To 14.5)
"_top"	Loads the referenced document into the full body of the window if frames are being used (see How-To 14.5)

Table 14-2 "Magic" values for TARGET

For example, to load a document to a new, blank window, use

```
<A HREF="http://www.widgets.com/" TARGET="_blank">Go to the Widgets Page</A>
```

5. To send all the links on a page without the TARGET attribute to a specific window, add the <BASE> element to the header of the page (that is, within the <HEAD> and </HEAD> tags) and set the TARGET attribute of it equal to the name of the window. For example, to send all links without a TARGET attribute to a window named Default Window, enter

```
<BASE TARGET="Default Window">
```

How It Works

When Netscape encounters a URL, imagemap listing, or form with the TARGET attribute, it creates a new window with the title of the window set to the value of the TARGET attribute. However, if the TARGET attribute is set to one of the reserved "magic" names, the browser executes the specific task defined by that name.

Comments

A new window is created only if a window does not already exist with a particular name. If a named window does exist, the document displayed in that window is replaced with the one currently being referenced. Names for TARGET must begin with a letter or number, with the exception of the "magic" names listed in Table 14-2. Also, the TARGET attribute is currently supported only by Netscape. Other browsers ignore the attribute and load the documents normally. For updated information about targeted windows in Netscape, check the URL http://www.netscape.com/assist/net_sites/new_html3_prop.html#Target.

CHAPTER 14
BEYOND HTML

COMPLEXITY
INTERMEDIATE

14.8 How do I... Create an HTML style sheet?

COMPATIBILITY: HTML 3, CASCADING STYLE SHEETS 1 (AS OF 11/95 DRAFT)

Problem

I want to establish standard styles for use in many of my Web pages. I want to enhance Web pages that I retrieve to maximize the capabilities of my browser. For legal reasons, a section of all my Web pages needs to appear the same. How can I create a style sheet for my documents?

Technique

Style sheets serve a variety of purposes. You can attach them to a variety of Web pages to create a consistent look for a group of documents. As a Web surfer, you can create a style sheet that your browser will apply to all incoming documents. The style sheet mechanism provides a versatile means of extending, enhancing, and modifying the way browsers present Web pages.

You create style sheets through a standard text editor. You specify a set of parameters and values that you want to associate with HTML elements of a particular type, such as <P> elements, or a particular class within an element, such as <P CLASS="red">. Each style sheet may define properties for any number of elements. Each entry in a style sheet is composed of a selector indicating the HTML 3 element that is modified and one or more declarations indicating properties to set or modify.

Style-sheet-capable browsers read the style sheets associated with a Web page and those designated by the reader and attempt to apply the styles to the page. A cascading mechanism helps to resolve conflict among multiple applicable styles. (See How-To 14.9 for information on how to cascade style information.)

Steps

The following procedure steps you through the style sheet creation process. You should select the elements and properties that you want to include. A full list of properties that may modify HTML 3 elements is provided in the How It Works section below.

1. Open the style sheet in a text editor.

> Note: Comments in style sheets are indicated by two dashes at either end of the comment.

14.8
CREATE AN HTML STYLE SHEET

2. Use the @import command to import and combine existing style sheets with the current style sheet. Conflicts in declarations are resolved in favor of the declarations of the importer. Thus, to include the entries from sheet1.css, issue the following command.

```
@import sheet1.css -- Use entries from sheet1, but override as follows --
```

3. If you are modifying or adding a property to an existing entry, move to that entry in the sheet and proceed with step 4. Otherwise, specify the selector for the HTML 3 element that you want to modify. The following examples represent possible selectors.

The following selector indicates the modification of <H1> elements.

```
H1
```

The following selector indicates the modification of <H1> and <H2> elements.

```
H1,H2
```

The following selector indicates the modification of "red" class, <P> elements.

```
P.red
```

The following selector indicates the modification of "red" class elements.

```
red
```

The following selector indicates the modification of <H2> elements that follow <P> elements.

```
(P) H2
```

4. Include the declaration(s) for the selector within opening and closing curly braces ({ and }). For example, the following declaration indicates that the browser should draw the selected element using the color red.

```
{ color: red }
```

> Note: If warranted, a declaration may conclude with either an !important or !legal statement, indicating a stronger reason to use a particular declaration. For example, { color: red !important }

5. Return to step 2 to continue editing; otherwise, save your style sheet.

How It Works

Style sheets are composed of standard text. A style sheet consists of a series of entries, each composed of a selector and a declaration. The selector indicates the HTML 3 element(s) affected by the properties in the declaration. A declaration may end with either a !legal or !important designation, indicating an imperative for using the particular declaration.

You may specify a selector in several forms. Selectors may specify a very narrow or very broad portion of a Web page, ranging from a particular class of an HTML element preceded by some other element to the entire page. In addition, the declarations for a selected element are inherited by those elements contained within the selected elements. For example, using HTML as the selector indicates that the declaration applies to all elements contained within the <HTML> element, namely the entire document. Generally, the selector falls into the following categories (brackets indicate optional user additions):

> **HTML** **element**
> You can select a single HTML element for which the declaration applies. For example, you might use the following selector to indicate application to <H1> elements.
>
> `H1`
>
> **HTML** **element1,element2[,element3,...]**
> Use this form to apply the same declaration to a number of HTML elements. The following selector indicates application of the declaration to <H1> and <H2> elements.
>
> `H1,H2`
>
> **HTML** **element.class**
> Use this form to specify a declaration that applies to only a particular class of a particular HTML element. Thus, the following selector specifies the application of the selector to <P> elements with "red" class designation.
>
> `P.red`
>
> **HTML** **class**
> Use this form to apply the same declaration to all HTML elements with the specified class. The following selector indicates that the declarations apply to all HTML elements of the "red" class.
>
> `red`
>
> **HTML** **(preceding_element1) [(preceding_element2) ...] element**
> Use this form to indicate that a declaration only applies when the

last HTML element is contained within the specified preceding HTML elements. The following selector applies to all <STRONG> elements within <P CLASS="red"> elements.

```
(P.red) STRONG
```

Declarations specify the properties of the selector that are set by the style sheet entry. Style sheets allow modification of a large variety of properties. The current HTML 3 style sheet working draft specifies level 1 and level 2 properties. Level 2 properties are still subject to frequent change. (See http://www.w3.org/pub/WWW/TR/WD-style for a current status of level 2.)

Each declaration is composed of a property and a value. The property indicates what to modify, and the value indicates the value of the modification. The following level 1 properties are, for the most part, stable. (For additional level 1 properties and information, see URL http://www.w3.org/pub/WWW/TR/WD-style.) In the following discussion, refer to Table 14-3 for acceptable units of length.

ABBREVIATION	UNIT TYPE	DESCRIPTION
cm	centimeters	
em	ems	Width of the character *m*
en	ens	Half the width of an *m*
in	inches	
mm	millimeters	
pc	picas	
pt	points	
px	pixels	Single cell on display

Table 14-3 Style sheet length units

Font-Related Properties

font-size
Value: *length* | *percent* | # | xx-small | x-small | small | medium | large | x-large | xx-large

The browser usually determines the default font size. You can specify a size, a percentage of the font size in the parent element, or a relative size using either a number or one of the descriptive literals above (e.g., small, medium). For example, use the following to set the font sizes of <H5> and <H6> elements, respectively.

```
H5 { font-size: 12pt }
H6 { font-size: small }
```

> **HTML** **font-family**
> Value: *family-name1|generic-family1* [*family-name2|generic-family2* ...]

The browser generally determines the default font family used to present Web pages. This property allows the specification of a prioritized list of font families to use. Replace spaces in font family names with dashes (e.g., new century schoolbook becomes new-century-schoolbook). CSS level 1 defines the following generic family names: cursive, fantasy, serif, and sans-serif. You should generally include a generic font family at the end of your font family list. For example, use the following to establish a font list for paragraphs (<P> elements).

```
P { font-family: helvetica new-century-schoolbook cursive }
```

> **HTML** **font-weight**
> Value: # | extra-light | light | demi-light | medium | demi-bold | bold | extra-bold

The default font weight is medium. You set the weight with either a number or one of the designated string literals (e.g., bold). The number should range from -3 to 3 corresponding to the literals, beginning with extra-light. For example, use the following to present an entire Web page as light.

```
HTML { font-weight: light }
```

> **HTML** **font-style**
> Value: italic | oblique | normal | small-caps

This property determines the style of font that a browser uses to display the elements specified by the selector. The default value is normal. You can use this property to alter the style. For example, use the following to designate that browsers should display <H4> elements as small caps.

```
H4 { font-style: small-caps }
```

> **HTML** **font**
> Value: *size [/line-height] family [weight] [style]*

Use this property as a shorthand for setting various font attributes at once. Setting a font property by itself overrides the shorthand value. For example, use the following to set the font of <STRONG> elements that follow <P CLASS="script"> paragraphs.

```
(P.script) STRONG { font: 16pt/20pt cursive bold normal }
```

Color- and Background-Related Properties

> **HTML** **color**
> Value: *color-value*

14.8
CREATE AN HTML STYLE SHEET

Use this property to set the color for the selector. You may specify the color value in several ways. These methods include by name, by 3-tuple (three numbers corresponding to the red, green, and blue components of the desired color), or by hexadecimal value. The list of supported color names has yet to be determined. The proposal calls for the acceptance of RGB values as either 3-tuples or hexadecimal. For example, use one of the following to set a red color for <H1 CLASS="red">.

```
H1.red { color: red }
H1.red { color: 1.0 0.0 0.0 } -- Floating point 3-tuple --
H1.red { color: 255 0 0 }     -- One byte value 3-tuple --
H1.red { color: #F00 }        -- Single digit hexadecimal --
H1.red { color: #FF0000 }     -- Double digit hexadecimal --
```

HTML background
Value: transparent | *color_value* | URL

Set the background of an element as either a particular color, a background pattern, or transparent. The default value is transparent. You indicate a color as described for the color property above. Use a URL to indicate a background pattern. For example, use the following to set the background of unordered lists (<UL>) and list elements (<LI>), respectively.

```
UL { background: #F00 }
LI { background: "http://www.mysite.edu/pix/checker.gif" }
```

The background property is not inherited by contained elements per se; however, since the default background is transparent, the designated background may still apply.

Text-Related Properties

HTML text-decoration
Value: underline | overline | line-through | box | shadowbox | box3d | cartouche | blink | none

Use this property to associate a decoration with a particular selector. For example, to create a boxed <H2 CLASS="boxed"> element, use the following:

```
H2.boxed { text-decoration: box }
```

HTML text-position
Value: # | sub | super

This property sets the level of the enclosed text. The sub and super literals represent subscript and superscript respectively. A number value indicates the relative position of the text with respect to the baseline. For example, use the following entry to designate that all "up" class elements use superscript.

```
up { text-position: super }
```

Layout

HTML margin-left, margin-right
Value: *length* | *percent* | auto

Use these two properties to set the left and right margins of the selector. The value can either be a length, a percentage of the parent element's width, or an automatic setting. Horizontal margin values may be negative. For example, to set the left margin of a list element (<LI>) to be 20 percent of its parent's width and the right margin to 5 percent, use the following:

```
LI { margin-left: 20%, margin-right: 5% }
```

HTML margin-top, margin-bottom
Value: *length*

These properties establish the top and bottom margin for an element. Vertical margins must be positive. For example, to provide a two-point margin above and below each paragraph (<P>) element, use the following entry.

```
P { margin-top: 2pt, margin-bottom: 2pt }
```

Web pages appear differently depending on the style sheets associated with them. In Figures 14-5 and 14-6, a different style sheet is attached to the same Web page. The source code for this page appears below.

```
<HTML>
<HEAD>
<TITLE>Style is Everything</TITLE>
<LINK TITLE="Style Sheet 1" REL=stylesheet HREF="style1.css">
</HEAD>
<BODY>
<H1>Going in Style</H1>
<P>
Putting on the Ritz
</BODY>
</HTML>
```

Figure 14-5 shows how this page appears with the following style sheet.

```
H1 { color: #F00 }
P { font-size: 16pt, color: #00F }
```

Changing the <LINK> element to attach the style sheet below results in the Web page seen in Figure 14-6.

```
H1 { color: #00F, background: #FFF }
P { font-size: 8pt, color: #0F0 }
```

Figure 14-5 Web page with Style Sheet 1

Figure 14-6 Web page with Style Sheet 2

Comments

The cascading style sheet standard is currently still in draft stages. The elements described in this How-To are fairly stable; however, they may be subject to change. For up-to-the-minute information on style sheet development, you may want to consult the evolving draft of the style sheet standard at URL http://www.w3.org/pub/WWW/TR/WD-style.

The only browser currently supporting cascading style sheets is Arena for the X-Window environment. This experimental browser implements many of the features of HTML 3 and is available from URL http://www.w3.org/pub/WWW/Arena/.

COMPLEXITY
INTERMEDIATE

14.9 How do I... Cascade HTML style sheets?

COMPATIBILITY: HTML 3, CASCADING STYLE SHEETS 1 (AS OF 11/95 DRAFT)

Problem

I need to associate style sheets with my Web pages. How can I do that, and how do the attached style sheets interact among themselves to resolve conflicting property specifications?

Technique

You can associate style information with your Web page in several manners:

- **HTML** You can embed the style information directly through a <STYLE> header element.

HTML You can import separate style sheets through the <STYLE> element.

HTML You can attach style sheets directly through <LINK> elements.

Browsers combine and integrate style information determined from these sources as well as any local style sheets. The browser follows strict rules on which style information to combine and which style information has precedence. It then uses this combined style information to present the Web page to the viewer.

Steps

As an author, you add style information in two ways:

HTML You can incorporate the information in a <STYLE> element.

HTML You can attach independent style sheets using the <LINK> element.

The following procedures walk you through these processes.

<STYLE> Element Process

You can use the <STYLE> element to mix and match existing style sheets with local overrides to develop a combined set of stylistic information for use with a particular Web page.

1. Open your HTML page in a text editor.

2. Locate the <HEAD> portion of the document.

3. If a <STYLE> element does not exist, create one using the following lines.

```
<STYLE NOTATION="application/css">
</STYLE>
```

You will add style information between the opening and closing tags of this element.

4. Use the @import command to import any stand-alone style sheets. For example, to include the sheet1.css and sheet2.css style sheets, insert the following two lines in the <STYLE> element.

```
@import sheet1.css
@import sheet2.css
```

5. Add declarations that you want to have override the declarations in the imported style sheets.

6. Save the Web page.

<LINK> Element Process

You can use the <LINK> element to attach style sheets to a Web page. This process is semantically equivalent to importing a style sheet from within a <STYLE> element.

14.9
CASCADE HTML STYLE SHEETS

1. Create a style sheet as described in How-To 14.8.
2. In a text editor, open the Web page to which you want to add a style sheet.
3. Find the <HEAD> element of your Web page.
4. Add a <LINK> element with the HREF attribute set to the URL of the style sheet you want to attach. The TITLE attribute serves as the combination mechanism; all style sheets attached by <LINK> with the same title are combined. Therefore, set the TITLE attribute to indicate the group of style sheets with which the one you want to add should combine. For example, to attach sheet1.css to the "Company" group of style sheets, you would add the following <LINK> element.

```
<LINK REL=stylesheet TITLE="Company" HREF="sheet1.css">
```

The REL attribute should be set to "stylesheet".

5. Perform step 4 for each style sheet you want to attach.
6. Save your Web page.

How It Works

The cascading style sheet model allows you to associate stylistic information with presented Web pages. A browser generally may receive stylistic information from three sources:

- **HTML** Reader style information: A particular reader has created a style sheet (as described in How-To 14.8), or the browser has built-in style constraints. In either case, the browser combines this information with incoming style information.

- **HTML** External style sheets: External style sheets are linked to a Web page via <LINK> elements. Each such style sheet is separately requested by the browser.

- **HTML** Internal style information: Web pages contain internal style information in <STYLE> elements.

The browser accumulates style information from these three sources to derive a single set of style constraints. The first possible conflict that may arise in this process is the potential multiplicity of grouped external style sheets. This situation arises when <LINK> elements with different TITLE attributes occur in the same Web page. All external style sheets with the same TITLE are combined; however, the choice of which combined style sheet to use rests with the reader. The model suggests that the reader should be able to choose among the TITLEs for the desired combined style.

The model suggests the following steps in resolving conflicts whenever stylistic information is combined and applied to a particular element.

1. Remove declarations for the same property for the same selector by removing the more imported, least local declaration. Thus, if a color declaration for the <H1> element appears in both the <STYLE> element for a page and an imported style sheet, then the declaration from the <STYLE> element remains.
2. If rules for the same selector and property still exist, remove all but the declaration specified last.
3. Determine all declarations applicable to a particular element.
4. Applicable declarations are sorted by weight with !important or !legal declarations being heavier than normal declarations.
5. Sort the applicable declarations by information origin with incoming style information overriding reader style information.
6. Sort the applicable declarations by the detail of the selector specification. For example, a <STRONG> element appearing within an <LI> element is more specific than a <STRONG> element alone.
7. Allow specific property declarations to override a generic property. For example, specification of a font-size property would override the value from a font property.
8. If a conflict still remains, resolve the conflict in favor of the declaration declared last.

After proceeding through this resolution scheme, the browser applies the remaining declarations to the element in question.

Comments

Style sheets are currently supported only by the experimental Arena browser for the X-Window environment (URL http://www.w3.org/pub/WWW/Arena/). Even this browser does not support the selection among titled combined style sheets. Adding style sheet capability to existing browsers may lead to some discrepancies between the proposed model and the implemented solution.

The proposed style sheet model is subject to rapid change; therefore, you should examine URL http://www.w3.org/pub/WWW/TR/WD-style for the latest status information on style sheets.

14.10 How do I... Write a basic Java applet?

COMPLEXITY: INTERMEDIATE

COMPATIBILITY: HOTJAVA 1.0A3/NETSCAPE 2.0

Problem

I'm interested in making my page more interactive by adding Java applets: programs that can be run from my page. However, I don't know anything about the language and don't know where to begin. How do I write a simple Java applet?

Technique

A full understanding of Java is beyond the scope of this book. Those who have written programs in C++ will find Java familiar, but others may have difficulty trying to learn the language. However, most applets have a similar structure that can be briefly described and then duplicated for other applets. This How-To shows how to create a basic but useful applet that displays the current time. How-To 14.11 shows how to incorporate the applet into an HTML document.

Steps

Because Java is evolving, this How-To shows how to write an applet using two versions of Java: the older alpha version and the newer beta version. Some browsers require the applets be written in the older format, while others require the newer format. There are small but notable differences between the two versions.

These examples show how to write a simple but useful applet that displays the current time on the page. The alpha version is called CurrentDateAlpha, and the beta version CurrentDateBeta.

Alpha Version

Open a file in a text editor. The name of the file should be whatever you want to name the applet, appended with the suffix .java, such as MyApplet.java.

1. First specify any libraries of routines that need to be included for the applet to run correctly. Applets in general require a library named browser.Applet. For this applet, you will need two other libraries: java.util.Date (which will provide a command to obtain the current time) and awt.Graphics (which includes graphics routines for displaying the results of the date on the page). Libraries are added with the import command:

```
import java.util.Date;
import browser.Applet;
import awt.Graphics;
```

CHAPTER 14
BEYOND HTML

Be sure to add a semicolon (;) after each line, as this is the method Java uses to indicate the end of a line.

2. Java is based on creating program classes that are based on previous classes. This allows a program to call on a number of higher-level classes without explicitly referencing them in the code. The class to extend upon here is called Applet (which you have included by importing the browser.Applet library). Use the class command and the name of the current applet to define a new class based on the Applet:

```
class CurrentDateAlpha extends Applet {
```

Note the open brace at the end of the line in lieu of a semicolon. This indicates that the lines that follow it all belong to the class CurrentDateAlpha.

3. Define the current date by creating a new variable, *d*, of the class Date and setting it equal to the current date, as follows:

```
Date d = new Date();
```

4. The applet now needs an initialization routine that defines an area on the page to display the date. This is done with a routine called init(), which is public and returns no data (void). In the routine, a resize command defines the area, in pixels, of the area of the page reserved for displaying the date.

```
public void init() {
    resize(300,25);
}
```

5. You now need a routine to display the date on the page. Create a graphics routine called paint that contains the necessary commands:

```
public void paint(Graphics g) {
```

6. To display the date, the applet must convert the information stored in the date variable into a string that can be drawn on the page. Run a function called toString(), which converts the date variable *d* into a string, and set it equal to a new variable *s* of class String:

```
String s = d.toString();
```

7. The final part of the applet is the command that prints the string containing the current date on the page. Use the routine g.drawString(), part of the awt.Graphics package imported at the beginning of the applet, to do this. The command needs three values: the string, the x pixel location of the beginning of the string, and the y pixel location for the bottom of the string. For example, to print the time and append the string "Current time: " to the beginning of it, and place it near the beginning of the window, use

14.10
WRITE A BASIC JAVA APPLET

```
    g.drawString("Current time: "+s, 5, 25);
    }
}
```

Note that since this is the last command of the applet, you need to include the closing braces for the paint routine and the overall class.

8. You can now run the applet through the Java compiler. If the compiler doesn't find any errors, it produces another file with the name of the applet and the file suffix .class, which contains the executable code for the applet. In this case, it creates a file named CurrentDateAlpha.class. The exact method of submitting the applet to the compiler varies from system to system. For example, if you use a UNIX system, enter at the prompt the command:

```
javac CurrentDateAlpha.java
```

The full code of the document is included on the CD-ROM as file CurrentDateAlpha.java.

Beta Version

Open a file in a text editor. Name the file whatever you want to name the applet, appended with the suffix .java, such as MyApplet.java.

1. First, specify any libraries of routines that need to be included for the applet to run correctly. Applets in general require a library named java.applet.Applet. For this applet, you will need two other libraries: java.util.Date (which will provide a command to obtain the current time) and java.awt.Graphics (which includes graphics routines for displaying the results of the date on the page). Add libraries using the import command:

```
import java.util.Date;
import java.applet.Applet;
import java.awt.Graphics;
```

Be sure to add a semicolon (;) after each line, as this is the method Java uses to indicate the end of a line.

2. Java is based on creating program classes that are based on previous classes. This allows a program to call on a number of higher-level classes without explicitly referencing them in the code. The class to extend upon here is called Applet (which you have included by importing the browser.Applet library). Use the public class command and the name of the current applet to define a new class based on the Applet class:

```
public class CurrentDateBeta extends Applet {
```

Note the open brace used at the end of the line instead of a semicolon. This indicates that the lines that follow it all belong to the class CurrentDateBeta.

3. Define the current date by creating a new variable, *d*, of the class Date and setting it equal to the current date, as follows:

```
Date d = new Date();
```

4. The applet now needs an initialization routine that defines an area on the page where the date is displayed. This is done with a routine called init(), which is public and returns no data (void). In the routine, a resize command defines the area, in pixels, of the page section reserved for displaying the date. For example:

```
public void init() {
    resize(300,25);
}
```

5. Next, include a routine to display the date on the page. Create a graphics routine called paint that contains the necessary commands:

```
public void paint(Graphics g) {
```

6. To display the date, the applet must convert the information stored in the date variable into a string that can be drawn on the page. Run a function called toString() that converts the date variable *d* into a string, and set it equal to a new variable *s* of class String:

```
String s = d.toString();
```

7. The final part of the applet is the command that prints the string containing the current date on the page. The routine g.drawString(), part of the java.awt.Graphics package imported at the beginning of the applet, does this. The command needs three values: the string, the x pixel location of the beginning of the string, and the y pixel location for the bottom of the string. For example, to print the time after the string "Current time: ", and place it near the top of the window, use

```
    g.drawString("Current time: "+s, 5, 25);
    }
}
```

Note that since this is the last command of the applet, you need to include the closing braces for the paint routine and the overall class.

8. Finally, run the applet through the Java compiler. If the compiler doesn't find any errors, it produces another file that contains the executable code for the applet. The filename is the name of the applet and the file suffix .class. In this case, it creates a file named CurrentDateAlpha.class. The exact method of submitting the applet to the compiler varies from system to system. For example, if you use a UNIX system, enter at the prompt the command:

```
javac CurrentDateBeta.java
```

The full code of the document is included on the CD-ROM as file CurrentDateBeta.java.

How It Works

First, the browser loads any libraries of routines that might be necessary for the browser to work. A new applet is created by extending an existing Applet class, thereby calling upon all the parent routines to the applet. This particular applet uses a command to find the current date on the machine, converts it to a string, then invokes a display routine to print it on the screen.

Comments

The Java language is still under development, as the alpha and beta versions of the sample applet above attest. The language will likely change more before a final, stable version is released. To keep up with the current status of the language, check the Java home page at Sun Microsystems, http://java.sun.com.

The newer releases of Netscape directly support Java (beta) applets.

COMPLEXITY: INTERMEDIATE

14.11 How do I... Include a Java applet in an HTML document?

COMPATIBILITY: HOTJAVA 1.0A3/NETSCAPE 2.0

Problem

I have written a Java applet and I'd like to include that applet in my Web page. How can I add a Java applet to an HTML document?

Technique

There are two slightly different ways to add a Java applet to an HTML document. The alpha version, used by HotJava 1.0a3, uses the <APP> tag to insert a link to the applet. The newer beta version, used by Netscape 2.0 and which may be incorporated into a later version of HotJava, uses the <APPLET> and <PARAM> tags to incorporate a Java applet into a page. This How-To looks at both ways to add an applet.

Steps

For either method, open your HTML document and locate the section of document where you want to add the applet.

Alpha Version (HotJava 1.0a3)

1. Insert the <APP> tag where you want to include the applet in your document. There is no closing tag. Set the CLASS attribute equal to the name of the applet. For example, if you want to include an applet named CurrentDateAlpha.class in your page, enter

```
<APP CLASS="CurrentDateAlpha">
```

2. If the applet is located in a directory other than the directory with the HTML document, you need to include the full pathname or URL for the applet. You can do this by including the <APP> tag's SRC attribute and setting it equal to the pathname or class. If the applet was located in the directory applets/new, you would use

```
<APP CLASS="CurrentDateAlpha" SRC="applets/new/">
```

Note that the trailing slash is required for the browser to correctly locate and load the applet.

3. The ALIGN attribute sets the alignment of the text that follows the applet. ALIGN can have three values:

- **HTML** "top" (text is aligned with the top of the applet)
- **HTML** "middle" (text is aligned with the middle of the applet)
- **HTML** "bottom" (text is aligned with the bottom of the applet)

The default value is "bottom". To include an applet that aligns the following text with the middle of the applet display, enter

```
<APP CLASS="CurrentDateAlpha" ALIGN=MIDDLE>
```

4. The HEIGHT and WIDTH attributes control the height and width of the applet display. Set each attribute to the desired size of the display in pixels. For example, to set the size of the applet display to 50 pixels wide and 75 pixels high, use

```
<APP CLASS="CurrentDateAlpha" HEIGHT=75 WIDTH=50>
```

5. If an applet requires values for certain variables in order to correctly run, the values can be supplied as additional attributes within the <APP> tag. The variable name is given as an attribute and is set equal to the value to be passed to the applet. For example, if the applet needs the value "Eastern" for the variable *TIMEZONE*, enter

```
<APP CLASS="CurrentDateAlpha" TIMEZONE="Eastern">
```

14.11
INCLUDE A JAVA APPLET IN AN HTML DOCUMENT

Figure 14-7 The result of an alpha Java applet as seen in HotJava

A sample output of the CurrentDateAlpha applet (described in How-To 14.10) as seen in HotJava is shown in Figure 14-7. The HTML code used to create the output is on the CD-ROM as file 14-7.html.

Beta Version (Netscape)

1. Place the <APPLET> and </APPLET> tags where you want the applet to be in your document. Set the CODE attribute equal to the name of the applet. For example, to insert the applet CurrentDateBeta.class into a Web page, enter

```
<APPLET CODE="CurrentDateBeta"></APPLET>
```

2. If the applet is not located in the same directory as the HTML document, use the CODEBASE attribute to provide the location of the applet. CODEBASE can be a pathname or a URL. If the applet in the last step is located in the directory applets/new, use

```
<APPLET CODE="CurrentDateBeta" CODEBASE="applets/new"></APPLET>
```

3. The WIDTH and HEIGHT attributes are required for the <APPLET> element. Just as for the <APP> element, they give the width and height of the applet display area in pixels. To create a display area 50 pixels wide and 75 pixels high for the applet, use

```
<APPLET CODE="CurrentDateBeta" WIDTH=50 HEIGHT=75></APPLET>
```

4. Similar to WIDTH and HEIGHT, VSPACE and HSPACE set the vertical and horizontal margins, respectively. Set the attributes equal to the size of the margin in pixels. To insert an applet with a vertical margin of 20 pixels and a horizontal margin of 10 pixels, enter

```
<APPLET CODE="CurrentDateBeta" WIDTH=50 HEIGHT=75 VSPACE=20 HSPACE=10></APPLET>
```

5. The ALIGN attribute controls the alignment of the applet. ALIGN can be set to more values than the <APP> tag's ALIGN attribute. The <APPLET> tag's ALIGN supports many of the values used by the <IMG> element (see Chapter 8). The valid values for ALIGN include

- **HTML** "left" (left side of the screen)
- **HTML** "right" (right side of the screen)
- **HTML** "top" (aligns with the top of the tallest item on the line)
- **HTML** "texttop" (aligns with the top of text on that line)
- **HTML** "middle" (aligns the baseline of the line with the middle of the applet display)
- **HTML** "absmiddle" (aligns the middle of the line with the middle of the applet display)
- **HTML** "baseline" (aligns the baseline of the line with the bottom of the applet display)
- **HTML** "bottom" (same as "baseline")
- **HTML** "absbottom" (aligns the bottom of the line with the bottom of the image)

For example, to align the line that follows the applet with the top of the applet display, enter

```
<APPLET CODE="CurrentDateBeta" WIDTH=50 HEIGHT=75 ALIGN=TOP></APPLET>
```

6. The NAME attribute gives the applet instance a specific name for potential future reference. This is a more advanced feature, which allows applets on the same page to communicate with each other. For example, to give an applet instance the name "current", enter

```
<APPLET CODE="CurrentDateBeta" WIDTH=50 HEIGHT=75 NAME="current"></APPLET>
```

7. There are two ways you can insert text that those browsers that don't support Java applets can display. One way is to use the ALT attribute and set it equal to a text string that explains what the applet is. For example, to include the ALT attribute in the applet above, enter

14.11
INCLUDE A JAVA APPLET IN AN HTML DOCUMENT

```
<APPLET CODE="CurrentDateBeta" WIDTH=50 HEIGHT=75 ALT="This is a Java
applet that displays the current time."></APPLET>
```

Another way to do this is to place the text between the <APPLET> and </APPLET> tags. This text displays in browsers that don't support Java applets, but is ignored by those that do run applets. To revise the above example using this method, enter

```
<APPLET CODE="CurrentDateBeta" WIDTH=50 HEIGHT=75>This is a Java applet
that displays the current time.</APPLET>
```

8. Use the <PARAM> element to pass values for variables to the applet. Place the <PARAM> tag between the <APPLET> and </APPLET> tags. Set the NAME attribute equal to the name of the applet variable and the VALUE attribute equal to the value assigned to that variable. Place each variable and value to be passed to the applet in a separate <PARAM> tag. For example, to pass the value "Eastern" for the variable *TIMEZONE* to the applet, use

```
<APPLET CODE="CurrentDateBeta" WIDTH=50 HEIGHT=75 NAME="current">
<PARAM NAME="TIMEZONE" VALUE="Eastern">
</APPLET>
```

A sample output of the CurrentDateBeta applet (described in How-To 14.10) as seen in Netscape 2.0 is shown in Figure 14-8. The HTML code used to create the output is on the CD-ROM as file 14-8.html.

Figure 14-8 The result of a beta Java applet as seen in Netscape 2.0

How It Works

For both the <APP> and <APPLET> elements, the tag instructs the browser to load and run the Java applet named in the tag. The browser creates a display area for the applet on the page based on the size of the display area and the alignment of the display as specified by attributes in the tag. The browser also passes values for any applet-specific variables that the applet requires so it runs correctly.

Comments

Currently, the only browsers that support Java applets are HotJava 1.0a3 (which supports the alpha method for including applets, using the <APP> element) and Netscape 2.0 (which supports the beta method, using the <APPLET> and <PARAM> elements). Other browsers do not run the applets and instead (in the beta method) display any alternate text.

If you have both alpha and beta versions of an applet available, you can include both in your page to accommodate people using different browsers. Simply include the <APP> tag within the <APPLET>...</APPLET> tag. Browsers that support the beta version of Java ignore anything contained within the <APPLET> tag. Browsers that support the alpha version ignore the <APPLET> tag and use the <APP> tag contained within the <APPLET> tag instead. For example:

```
<APPLET CODE="CurrentDateBeta" WIDTH=50 HEIGHT=75>
<APP CLASS="CurrentDateAlpha"></APPLET>
```

COMPLEXITY
ADVANCED

14.12 How do I... Include a JavaScript script in an HTML document?

COMPATIBILITY: NETSCAPE 2.0

Problem

I want to be able to do more with my pages than simple HTML allows me to do. I have heard about JavaScript, and it sounds easier to use than other scripting languages. How do I go about adding a JavaScript script in my HTML documents?

Technique

JavaScript is a powerful, fairly easy-to-use addition to the Netscape browser. According to the Netscape release, it "allows cross-platform scripting of events,

14.12
INCLUDE A JAVASCRIPT SCRIPT IN AN HTML DOCUMENT

objects and actions." You can use JavaScript to accomplish many tasks that you would have previously needed Java or Perl to perform. JavaScript is an object-based scripting language like the Java language, only JavaScript is less extendable and simpler to use.

To include a JavaScript script in an HTML document, use the <SCRIPT> tag. The <SCRIPT> tag's format is

```
<SCRIPT LANGUAGE="language.name" [SRC="a URL for the script"]>
a JavaScript script
</SCRIPT>
```

In this format, language is the language the script is written in, and SRC is an optional attribute that gives the URL of the script to be loaded. LANGUAGE is mandatory unless the SRC attribute gives the scripting language.

> Note: As of this writing you must still call a JavaScript script "LiveScript" in the LANGUAGE attribute. This note should also act as a disclaimer. JavaScript is very new. It is changing as this is written and probably will be changing as you read this.

Steps

The following steps give a rudimentary introduction to how you can add JavaScript scripts (see How-To 14.13) to your Web pages.

1. Create a basic HTML document using any text editor. For this example, use the very basic document that follows.

```
<HTML>
<HEAD>
<TITLE>JavaScript Demo</TITLE>
</HEAD>
<BODY>
The above line was written from a JavaScript script. And so is the
following line.
<P>
</BODY>
</HTML>
```

2. Enter the <SCRIPT> tags.

3. Enter the JavaScript script between the two tags. This example uses two very simple scripts that write to the screen. The script lines are

```
<SCRIPT LANGUAGE="LiveScript">
document.write("Simple demo...")
document.write("<P>")
</SCRIPT>
```

and

```
<!-- Second Script -->
<SCRIPT LANGUAGE="LiveScript">
document.write("<P>THE END...")
</SCRIPT>
```

Notice the HTML tags embedded in the writes. These function just as they would normally in HTML.

4. Save and name the document.

5. View the document to make sure it works the way you think it should. For example, look at the following:

```
<HTML>
<HEAD>
<TITLE>JavaScript Demo</TITLE>
<!-- Note: as of this writing: JavaScript scripts still need to be set to -->
<!-- Their original name of LiveScript... -->
<!-- I assume this will change someday.   -->
<!-- Will LiveScript still be valid?  Your guess is as good as mine... -->
</HEAD>
<BODY>
<!-- First Script -->
<SCRIPT LANGUAGE="LiveScript">
document.write("Simple demo...")
document.write("<P>")
</SCRIPT>
The above line was written from a JavaScript script. And so is the following line.
<P>

<!-- Second Script -->
<SCRIPT LANGUAGE="LiveScript">
document.write("<P>THE END...")
</SCRIPT>

<!-- It may not seem like much now, as you do this without using JavaScript, -->
<!-- but in the next section you will see some of the power of JavaScript. -->

</BODY>
</HTML>
```

When viewed by a browser that supports JavaScript, the example looks like Figure 14-9. A browser that does not support JavaScript only displays "The above line was written from a JavaScript script. And so is the following line."

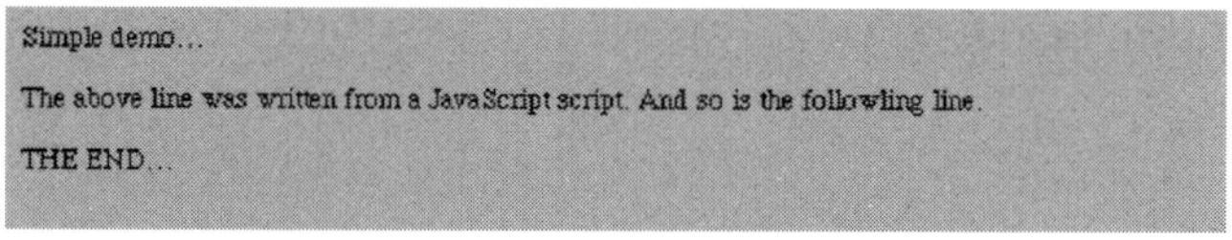

> Simple demo...
>
> The above line was written from a JavaScript script. And so is the followling line.
>
> THE END...

Figure 14-9 A simple document partially generated with JavaScript

How It Works

A browser that supports JavaScript reads and evaluates the scripts that are embedded between the <SCRIPT> tags. JavaScript functions are stored but not evaluated until they are executed by events in the page.

Comments

It is possible to do a lot with JavaScript. JavaScript can be a very helpful tool when it comes to event handling tasks such as reading and validating information from forms and responding to other types of user actions, such as clicks. JavaScript, while not as powerful as Java or Perl, is less cumbersome and therefore easier to learn and use than the other two. How-To 14.13 delves a little deeper into JavaScript.

COMPLEXITY: ADVANCED

14.13 How do I...
Write a basic JavaScript script?

COMPATIBILITY: NETSCAPE 2.0

Problem

I want to do more things with my pages than simple HTML allows me to. I know I could use Java or Perl, but I am looking for something a bit simpler to learn. I have heard about JavaScript, and it sounds like it will meet most of my needs. How do I go about writing a basic JavaScript script?

Technique

JavaScript is a property-based scripting language that makes use of objects. It is a small but complete, fully functional language. JavaScript does not allow you to create new objects as you can with Java. Instead, you use a group of predefined objects to accomplish your tasks.

CHAPTER 14
BEYOND HTML

The object hierarchy is as follows:

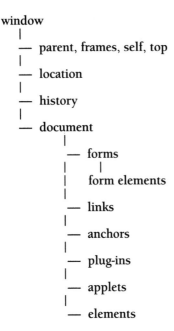

The document object and all objects above the document are always available. All the objects below the document object are created on the fly, depending on the HTML code in the document.

For example, the sample script below has a form that contains a text field called "name".

```
<INPUT TYPE="text" NAME="name" SIZE=20>
```

To refer to that text field, you must use the object name complete with all its ancestors:

```
document.forms[0].name
```

To use the value of that text field, use

```
document.forms[0].name.value
```

As of this writing, all forms in a document are stored in a forms array. To refer to the first form, you use "forms[0]" for the first form, "forms[1]" for the second form, and so on.

Now that you have objects to use, you need to know when to use them. This is where *event handlers* come into play. Event handlers are the result of certain user actions, such as clicking on a button or check box, or selecting certain text.

14.13
WRITE A BASIC JAVASCRIPT SCRIPT

For example, the following code causes the JavaScript function doform() to execute when the button defined by this tag is clicked on.

```
<INPUT TYPE="button" VALUE="Go for it" ONCLICK="doform(this.form)">
```

The function uses the items created by <INPUT TYPE> tags in the current form as parameters.

The types of event handlers currently supported are

- **HTML** onFocus: Script to run when the form element is the focus of input
- **HTML** onBlur: Script to run on loss of input focus
- **HTML** onChange: Script to run when a field's value is changed
- **HTML** onSelect: Script to run when a text field is selected
- **HTML** onSubmit: Script to run when a form is submitted
- **HTML** onClick: Script to run when a button is clicked

Outside of objects and event handlers, JavaScript greatly resembles other programming languages you are probably already familiar with.

JavaScript has variables. To create a variable, name the variable with the var statement or simply use it. For example:

```
var score
score = 0
```

Both of the above statements create a variable named *score*.

JavaScript has a set of built-in functions. It also allows the declaration of user-defined functions (brackets indicate optional user additions):

```
function name ([parameter] [, parameter] [, ..., parameter] ) {
    statements }
return
```

JavaScript has complete sets of assignment (=), arithmetic (+, -, *, /), logical (&&, ||, !), and comparison (==, >, >=, <, <=, !=) operators.

JavaScript also supports many types of control structures, such as

```
if (condition) {
    statements
} [else {
    else statements} ]
```

and

```
while (condition) {
    statements}
```

547

and

```
for ([initial expression;] [condition;] [update expression]) {
    statements
}
initial expression = statement | variable declaration
```

As you can see, JavaScript is a complete language. You can use different combinations of objects and event handlers along with all or some of the other features of JavaScript to create JavaScript scripts.

The key words currently used and reserved by JavaScript are

break	continue	else	false
for	function	if	in
null	return	this	true
var	while	with	

For the latest list of all the items and features, refer to the Netscape home page at http://home.netscape.com/.

Steps

The following steps show one way you can create and use a JavaScript script. This is a basic script, yet it takes advantage of many of the nicer features of JavaScript. There are, of course, many other ways to create JavaScript scripts.

1. Decide what you want to do and then decide if JavaScript really is the best way to do it. This example uses forms to make a simple test for a user to take, and you'll need an application to test the answers sent by a form and grade the results. This is a fine application for JavaScript.

2. Create a base HTML document for your JavaScript script. For this example, use

```
<HTML>
<HEAD>
<TITLE>JavaScript Example</TITLE>
</HEAD>
<BODY>
<H2>Knowledge Tester</H2>
<HR>
<HR>
</BODY>
</HTML>
```

There's not much here yet, but it's a good start.

3. Add the form that contains the questions for the user to answer and for JavaScript to process.

14.13
WRITE A BASIC JAVASCRIPT SCRIPT

```
<FORM>
Enter your name please:
<INPUT TYPE="text" NAME="name" SIZE=20><P>
Who's buried in Washington's grave?
<INPUT TYPE="text" NAME="question1" SIZE=15 ><P>
Roosters lay eggs (true or false)?
<INPUT TYPE="text" NAME="question2" SIZE=5 ><P>
<INPUT TYPE="button" VALUE="Go for it" ONCLICK="doform(this.form)">
<HR>
<BR>
Result:
<INPUT TYPE="text" NAME="score" SIZE=15 >
<BR>
</FORM>
```

When viewed through a browser, this form looks like Figure 14-10.

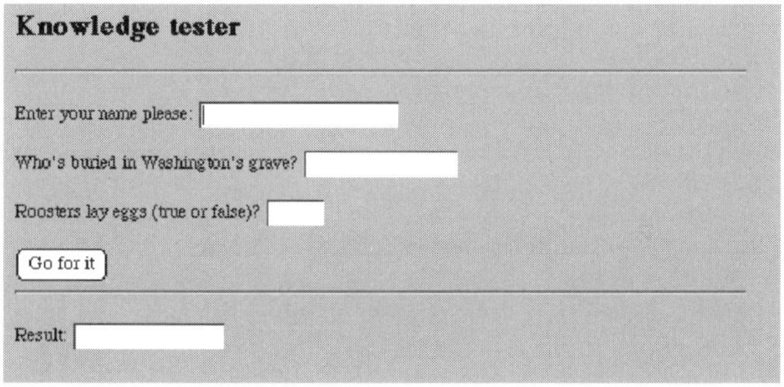

Figure 14-10 A form to be processed by a JavaScript script

This is a pretty typical form, except for the ONCLICK event handler, which is the JavaScript extension. This causes the JavaScript doform() to execute when the user clicks on the button.

4. Now that you have the form to interact with, you need the JavaScript to process this form. To start the script, place the <SCRIPT> ... </SCRIPT> tags in the header of your document.

```
<SCRIPT LANGUAGE="LiveScript">
</SCRIPT>
```

Once again, it is worth noting that as of this writing, JavaScript scripts must be called "LiveScript" in the LANGUAGE attribute. LiveScript was the original name for JavaScript. You are placing this script in the header. Also, you want the script to contain a function that executes when the user clicks on the form's button.

5. Define and insert the JavaScript function. Make sure that the function name is the same used when the function is called in the <INPUT TYPE="button" ...> tag. The function used in this example is

```
function doform(form) {
   if (confirm("Are you sure "+document.forms[0].name.value+"?")){
      score=0
      if (document.forms[0].question1.value=="Washington"){
            score=score+1; }
         if (document.forms[0].question2.value=="false"){
            score=score+1; }
      form.score.value = (score / 2)*100
   }
  else
      alert("Please come back again.")
}
```

6. Save and name the HTML document with the JavaScript script in it. The entire document and script will look like this:

```
<HTML>
<HEAD>
<TITLE>JavaScript Demo</TITLE>
<SCRIPT LANGUAGE="LiveScript">
function doform(form) {
   if (confirm("Are you sure "+document.forms[0].name.value+"?")){
      score=0
      if (document.forms[0].question1.value=="Washington"){
            score=score+1; }
         if (document.forms[0].question2.value=="false"){
            score=score+1; }
      form.score.value = (score / 2)*100
   }
  else
      alert("Please come back again.")
}
</SCRIPT>
</HEAD>

<BODY>
<H2>Knowledge tester</H2>
<HR>
<FORM>
Enter your name please:
<INPUT TYPE="text" NAME="name" SIZE=20><P>
Who's buried in Washington's grave?
<INPUT TYPE="text" NAME="question1" SIZE=15 ><P>
Roosters lay eggs (true or false)?
<INPUT TYPE="text" NAME="question2" SIZE=5 ><P>
<INPUT TYPE="button" VALUE="Go for it" ONCLICK="doform(this.form)">
<HR>
<BR>
Result:
<INPUT TYPE="text" NAME="score" SIZE=15 >
```

14.13
WRITE A BASIC JAVASCRIPT SCRIPT

```
<BR>
</FORM>
</BODY>
</HTML>
```

7. View the document with the latest version of Netscape to make sure everything is working properly. When first executed, the screen should look like Figure 14-10. After the user answers the questions and clicks the Go for it button, the screen should resemble Figure 14-11.

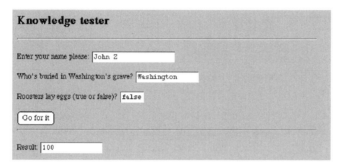

Figure 14-11 The screen with the processed information

8. Experiment! The best way to learn JavaScript is to change this example and see what effects your changes have. Once you are comfortable with this script, start writing your own scripts.

How It Works

When the user clicks on the Go for it button, the information in the form is sent to the doform() function named in the <INPUT TYPE> tags and defined in the header of the document.

Four fields of information are sent to the function:

HTML name: Named by the first <INPUT TYPE> tag and referenced by document.forms[0].name

HTML question1: Named by the second <INPUT TYPE> tag and referenced by document.forms[0].question1

HTML question2: Named by the third <INPUT TYPE> tag and referenced by document.forms[0].question2

HTML score: Named by the fifth <INPUT TYPE> tag and referenced by document.forms[0].score

The value of any of the above fields can be found by appending .value to the reference for that field, such as

```
document.forms[0].name.value
```

The first statement in the function:

```
if (confirm("Are you sure "+document.forms[0].name.value+"?")){
```

sets up a control structure and gives the user a chance to back out. It uses the confirm method to display a dialog box, such as the one shown in Figure 14-12, in the user's window.

Figure 14-12 A dialog box created by JavaScript

The results from the dialog box are then processed by the if statement. If the user responds negatively (clicks no), the function executes the else block. In this case, that puts up a "Please come back again." message in an alert box. The function then exits, returning control to the form.

If the user responds positively, the function executes the statements under the if statement. These statements work as follows:

```
score=0
```

creates a variable to calculate the user's score.

The following statements:

```
if (document.forms[0].question.1.value=="Washington"){
    score = score + 1; }
if (document.forms[0].question.2.value=="false"){
    score=score+1;}
```

compare the value of the information entered in the form with the correct answer. If the value equals the correct answer, then the user's score is incremented.

Finally, the user's final score is calculated by

```
document.forms[0].score.value= (score /2)*100
```

This value is placed into the score field created with the form. When the function exits, the updated score value is shown in the field.

Comments

In the old days (last year), you would have used Perl to do something like the above example. Though this example is very rudimentary, as it contains no error checking and is case-sensitive, you can still see how easy JavaScript makes certain tasks, such as validating forms input.

Please note: JavaScript is a vast enough topic that it could easily be the subject of a book. This section did not even go into such matters as methods or object properties. For more information on these, consult the latest Netscape documentation.

COMPLEXITY
EASY

14.14 How do I... Find a VRML browser?

COMPATIBILITY: VRML

Problem

While surfing the Web, I have found sites providing 3D information. I need a viewer to explore and examine these 3D models and virtual worlds. How can I find a VRML browser?

Technique

The Virtual Reality Modeling Language (VRML, pronounced "vermel") provides a platform-independent means of specifying three-dimensional models and constructs. Servers can easily distribute such models across the World Wide Web. In fact, specific constructs in the language provide the ability to create links to other worlds or Web pages.

VRML documents are becoming increasingly more abundant on the World Wide Web. Consequently, a need for VRML viewers has developed, driving the creation of numerous products running on a variety of hardware and software platforms.

Figure 14-13 shows a world rendered using the WebFX VRML viewer integrated into the Netscape Navigator browser. Figure 14-14 displays a world using a stand-alone VRML viewer.

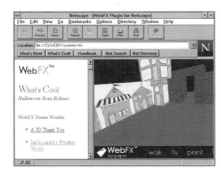

Figure 14-13 VRML world using WebFX Navigator plug-in

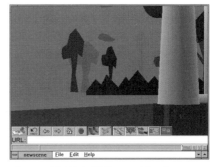

Figure 14-14 VRML world using Fountain viewer

Steps

The following procedure shows how to acquire a VRML browser and configure your Web browser to recognize VRML worlds.

1. Examine Table 14-4 to find a VRML viewer to meet your hardware and software requirements.

2. Download or purchase the VRML viewer you have selected.

3. Follow the applicable installation instruction for your VRML viewer.

4. If the VRML viewer's installation process does not automatically configure your Web browser, configure your browser to launch this viewer when it receives a document with the MIME type x-world/x-vrml. (For more information on MIME types, see Appendix C.) This configuration process is browser specific.

How It Works

Web servers transmit VRML worlds in the same way that they transmit any other objects, such as audio files. The server signals the browser that it is sending a VRML world. The browser recognizes this signal and runs an appropriate VRML viewer.

A large variety of VRML browsers have been developed recently. Table 14-4 lists several available VRML viewers by software and hardware type.

PLATFORM	VRML BROWSER	URL
cross-platform	VRweb	http://www.iicm.tu-graz.ac.at/Cvrweb
cross-platform	WebSpace	http://www.sgi.com/Products/WebFORCE/WebSpace/
Mac/PowerMac	Virtus Voyager	http://www.virtus.com/voyager.html
Mac/PowerMac	VRML Equinox	http://www.ipsystems.com/nps/EquiInfo.html
Mac/QD3D	Whurlwind 3D Browser	http://www.info.apple.com/qd3d/Viewer.HTML
PC/Windows 3.1, 95	Fountain	http://www.caligari.com/ws/fount.html
PC/Windows 3.1, NT, 95	NAVFlyer 2.2b	ftp://yoda.fdt.net/pub/users/m/micgreen
PC/Windows 3.1, NT, 95	VR Scout	http://www.chaco.com/vrscout/
PC/Windows 3.1, NT, 95	WebFX	http://www.paperinc.com/webfx.html
PC/Windows 3.1, NT, 95	WorldView	http://www.webmaster.com/vrml
PC/Windows NT	AmberGL	http://www.divelabs.com/vrml.htm
PC/Windows NT, 95	GLView	http://www.snafu.de/~hg/
PC/Windows NT, 95	VRealm	http://www.ids-net.com/ids/vrealm.html
SGI/IRIX 5.2	i3D	http://www.crs4.it/~3diadm/i3d-announce.html
SGI/X-Window	WebView	http://www.sdsc.edu/EnablingTech/Visualization/vrml/webview.html
SGI,SUN/X-Window	WebOOGL	http://www.geom.umn.edu/software/weboogl/

Table 14-4 VRML browsers

Comments

VRML worlds and associated image files may be large; therefore, do not be too surprised at experiencing delays if you are accessing the Web over a 14.4K modem. For additional information on viewers and VRML software, see URL http://rosebud.sdsc.edu/vrml.

14.15 How do I... Create a VRML document?

COMPLEXITY INTERMEDIATE

COMPATIBILITY: VRML

Problem

I want to create three-dimensional spaces for the World Wide Web community to visit. How does the virtual reality modeling language (VRML) provide this capability? How do I author VRML documents?

Technique

You author VRML documents using either a text editor or a three-dimensional modeling application. The VRML language allows you to specify three-dimensional objects in an ASCII text file. Using a text editor, you can create a VRML document by stringing together appropriate VRML constructs. Alternatively, you can graphically create three-dimensional spaces using suitable software that saves in VRML format.

Steps

You can create VRML documents in one of two ways. You can use a VRML editing environment to graphically create three-dimensional spaces, or you can directly create a VRML document by inserting VRML constructs in a text file.

Three-Dimensional Editing Environment

Recently, a large number of three-dimensional modeling packages have been developed for the creation of VRML documents. The procedure below outlines the steps for acquiring and installing a modeler suitable for your hardware and software platform.

1. Find a modeler suitable for your software and hardware platform. Table 14-5 summarizes several available modeler packages.

PLATFORM	MODELER	URL
Mac	STRATA StudioPro Blitz	http://www.strata3d.com:80/tools/studiopro/index.html
Mac/PC	Virtus WalkThrough Pro	http://www.virtus.com/vwtpro.html
PC	ClayWorks	http://cent1.lancs.ac.uk/tim/clay.html
PC	Fountain/Caligari	http://www.caligari.com/ws/fount.html
PC	Spinner	http://www.3dweb.com/
PC	TriSpectives	http://www.eye.com/cgi-bin/htimage/homepage.map?139,99
PC	World Builder	http://ruok.caligari.com:80/lvltwo/2product.html
PC	Home Space Builder	http://www.us.paragraph.com/whatsnew/homespce.htm
PC/SGI/SUN	G Web	http://www.demon.co.uk/presence/gweb.html
SGI	Ez3d Modeler	http://www.webcom.com/~radiance/
SGI	Medit	ftp://sgigate.sgi.com/pub/Performer/RealityCentre/Medit_dist
SGI	WebSpace Author	http://webspace.sgi.com/WebSpaceAuthor/index.html

Table 14-5 VRML modelers

2. Download or purchase the selected software.

3. Follow the instructions provided to install your modeler software.

4. Configure your Web browser to launch this application, if your modeler will also serve as your default VRML viewer.

5. Open your modeler application and create your three-dimensional model.

6. Save your model to a file with the .wrl filename extension. If your modeler supports a variety of formats, select VRML.

Text Editor Creation

VRML documents contain standard ASCII text. This text represents the various constructs available through VRML. The following steps lead you through the VRML document creation process using a text editor.

1. Open a new document in your text editor.

2. Insert the following line. This line indicates that the file contains ASCII-based VRML constructs.

```
#VRML V1.0 ascii
```

3. Add desired VRML elements until you have created your desired scene. A variety of commonly used elements appears in the How It Works section below.

4. Save the document. Use the .wrl filename extension when you save to indicate that the file is a VRML document.

14.15
CREATE A VRML DOCUMENT

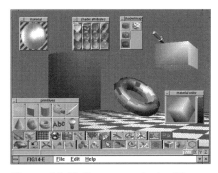

Figure 14-15 Scene created with a 3D modeler

How It Works

Using a modeler is the easier of the two construction methods. A modeler allows you to visually create your three-dimensional information space. You can see on the screen what your model will look like when rendered. For example, Figure 14-15 shows a scene composed of three visible objects: a cylinder, a torus, and a cube; this scene was built using the Fountain modeler. (See reference in Table 14-5.) The VRML file for this scene is available on the accompanying CD.

The challenge you face when creating a VRML document with a 3D modeling package is learning how to draw in a three-dimensional space. If you are familiar with CAD packages or other 3D environments, the transition is fairly easy. The user interfaces of these VRML environments vary significantly. The primary source of information on these products is documentation provided online either with the package or via the Web, and your own experience with the product. As you become more comfortable with the package, your productivity and accuracy will improve.

Ultimately, when you finish building your 3D scene, you save it to a VRML file. Many modelers support a variety of output formats. For access over the World Wide Web, you should save your scene in VRML. The standard filename extension used to indicate a VRML scene is .wrl. Use this extension when saving each of your scenes.

You can create or modify a VRML document using a text editor. The VRML format saves 3D information in standard ASCII text[57] and stores 3D scenes in a hierarchy of nodes referred to as a scene graph. The scene graph specifies both the objects in the scene and the order in which those objects are evaluated. Nodes earlier in the scene graph can affect nodes later in the scene.

Each VRML node has several general characteristics:

HTML Name: Each node can have a unique name associated with it.

HTML Type: Each node has a particular type, such as Cube or Translation.

CHAPTER 14
BEYOND HTML

HTML Parameters: Each node has a set of parameters specifying the specific characteristics of the individual node. For example, a sphere node would have a *radius* parameter.

HTML Child nodes: Nodes may contain other nodes, thereby creating the hierarchical structure of a scene graph.

The standard format for specifying a node in a VRML scene graph is *ObjectName ObjectType { Parameters Children)*. For example, the following nodes specify a scene containing a pinkish cone, a purple cube, and a perspective camera. Figure 14-16 displays this scene in a VRML browser. A pound sign (#) indicates that the remainder of a line is a comment.

```
#VRML V1.0 ascii

Separator { # 1st Grouping
    PerspectiveCamera { # Establish Perspective
        position    160 -200 430
    }

    Separator { # position, color, and place cube
       Transform { # set position
          translation 160 -200 -2
       }
       Material { # set color
          diffuseColor .3 .1 .3
       }
       Cube { # create a cube using established color at specified position
          width 100
          height 100
          depth 100
       }
    }

    Separator { # position, color, and place cone
       Transform { # set position
          translation 120 -80 50
       }
       Material { # set color
          diffuseColor 1 .5 .5
       }
       Cone { # create a cone using established color at specified position
          bottomRadius 50
          height 80
       }
    }
}
```

A Separator node represents the root of the hierarchy. This node has a PerspectiveCamera child and two Separator children. The camera object indicates to the VRML browser the initial perspective of the scene. Each of the two Separator children contains three children: a Transform, specifying the base location objects,

14.15
CREATE A VRML DOCUMENT

Figure 14-16 Small scene created by a text editor

a Material, specifying the material used to draw objects (purple and pink, respectively), and a visible object (e.g., Cube and Cone).

VRML nodes fall into four broad categories: shapes, properties, groups, and WWW. The list below details several of the more widely used node types; for a complete description of VRML version 1, see URL http://rosebud.sdsc.edu/vrml, or check out *VRML Construction Kit* (Waite Group Press). Lengths and distances in VRML are measured in scaled meters.

Shapes

HTML AsciiText

This object type defines a string of characters. The commonly used parameters of this type are *string* and *justification*. The justification property has three possible values: LEFT, CENTER, or RIGHT. For example, to create a centered string object displaying "I love VRML", you could use the following object.

```
AsciiText { string "I love VRML" justification CENTER }
```

HTML Cone

This creates a cone object in the scene graph. The *height* and *bottomRadius* properties set the cone's parameters. For example, the following node describes a cone that is 20 meters high and has a base with a radius of 10 meters.

```
Cone { height 20 bottomRadius 10 }
```

HTML Cube

Use this node type to create a cubic object. The *height*, *width*, and *depth* properties of this node need not have the same value. For example, the specification of a 40x20x20 box in VRML would appear as

```
Cube { height 40 width 20 depth 20 }
```

CHAPTER 14
BEYOND HTML

HTML Cylinder

A node of this type creates a cylinder in the scene graph. This shape has a *height* and a *radius* property. The following line creates a cylinder with a base radius of 5 and a height of 25.

```
Cylinder { radius 5 height 25 }
```

HTML Sphere

You can create a sphere object with this node type. The only required property of this node type is a *radius*. For example, use the following line to create a sphere of radius 75.

```
Sphere { radius 75 }
```

Properties

HTML FontStyle

The FontStyle node type takes three parameters: *size*, *style*, and *family*. A FontStyle node affects all text in objects appearing after and below it in the scene graph hierarchy until another FontStyle node supersedes it. The possible values of the *style* property are NONE, BOLD, and ITALICS. The values of *family* are SERIF, SANS, and TYPEWRITER. The following node sets the font to serif, bold, 10 point.

```
FontStyle { size 10 style BOLD family SERIF }
```

HTML Material

This node describes the material used to render all shapes after and below it in the scene graph. The most commonly used property is *diffuseColor*, which, specified as an RGB triplet, sets the color used to draw shapes. Each value in the color triplet ranges from 0 to 1, indicating the intensity of the color component. For example, to color shapes red, use the following Material node.

```
Material { diffuseColor 1 0 0 }
```

HTML Transform

This node establishes the relative location used to place shapes appearing below or after the Transform node in the scene graph. Two useful properties of this node type are *translation* and *scaleFactor*. The following node sets the translation to four meters in the positive x direction and scaling of two in the y direction only. (In scaling, x and z values are set to one to indicate no scaling.)

```
Transform { translation 4 0 0 scaleFactor 1 2 1 }
```

14.15
CREATE A VRML DOCUMENT

HTML PerspectiveCamera
A perspective camera node establishes a viewpoint for the scene. If only one such camera is specified, browsers often take this as the initial view of the scene. The most commonly set property of this node type is *position*, specifying the location of the camera. The following camera is positioned at x, y, z coordinates 25, 72, -200.

```
PerspectiveCamera { position 25 72 -200 }
```

Group

HTML Group
This node contains an ordered list of other VRML nodes. The property nodes accumulate as they are traversed in the order. This accumulated information is passed back to the parent of the group node in the scene graph.

```
Group {
    ...         # object 1
    ...         # object 2
}
```

HTML Separator
A separator node is like a group node. It contains an ordered list of child nodes. The difference between a separator and a group is that the accumulated property information in a separator is discarded at the end of the separator. The parent node continues with the accumulated transformations, in effect, prior to the separator.

```
Separator {
    ...         # object 1
    ...         # object 2
}
```

WWW

HTML WWWAnchor
This node type works exactly like a separator object, except that it supports several additional properties. These properties are: *name*, *description*, and *map*. The value of the *name* property indicates the URL to load when a child of this grouping node is selected. The value of the *description* property may be used by a VRML browser to display a description of the URL linked through the *name* property. The *map* property can have one of two values: NONE or POINT. A POINT value indicates that the coordinate selected in the scene should be appended to the URL specified by the *name* property. This capability gives rise to the possibility of a 3D "image" map.

```
WWWAnchor {
    name "http://rosebud.sdsc.edu/vrml"
    description "Link to VRML Repository"
    ...         # object 1
    ...         # object 2
}
```

> **HTML** **WWWInline**
> This node allows a VRML document to incorporate another VRML document located at a specified URL. Use the *name* property to assign this URL value. For example, to include the world located at http://www.mysite.edu/myworld.wrl, you would use the following node in the scene graph.

```
WWWInline { name "http://www.mysite.edu/myworld.wrl" }
```

Using these nodes, you can successfully create and edit VRML worlds. This list serves as a brief introduction to the nodes and node properties available in VRML. For a complete specification of VRML 1.0, examine URL http://rosebud.sdsc.edu/vrml.

Comments

VRML 1.0 is still experimental in nature. Consequently, many browsers and modelers speak slightly different dialects of VRML. Several also provide additional proprietary constructs.

When authoring, keep in mind that VRML documents can rapidly become very large. The larger the file, the longer a Web browser takes to download and present it. Consequently, users with a low bandwidth network connection, such as a 14.4K modem, will experience significant delays in viewing your VRML documents.

In addition, the complexity of your VRML document and the processing power of the viewer's machine impact the speed of rendering. A VRML document that renders and updates quickly on an SGI Reality Engine might take considerably longer to display and update on a 486 machine.

CHAPTER 15
SOME OF THE BEST SITES ON THE WEB

SOME OF THE BEST SITES ON THE WEB

A book on HTML isn't complete without some reference to pages on the Web that are cool. The following, while by no means all-encompassing, is a list of some of the best and coolest spots on the Web. The criteria for inclusion were two:

- **HTML** Visual interface
- **HTML** Behind-the-scenes HTML

The description of each Web page listed below includes a discussion of why its visual interface deserves mention and what HTML was used to make the page truly outstanding. Hopefully, perusing the pages in this chapter will give you inspiration for your own Web pages.

The Spot

URL: http://www.thespot.com/
Owner: Fattal & Collins
Webmaster: Troy Bolotnick
Purpose: Entertainment

The Spot centers around the "adventures" in the lives of a bunch of young, good-looking people. Love it or loathe it, The Spot is one of the most active sites on the World Wide Web. The Spot is also one of the slickest spots on Web; it is a fine example of what a little imagination and lots of expert coding can do. Figure 15-1 shows a clip from The Spot.

The look and feel of The Spot is great. It is easy for anybody to navigate to wherever they wish to go.

The Spot makes great use of tables in a monthly calendar that lets you read the daily diary entries of the inhabitants of The Spot. You name a technique and The Spot uses it.

CHAPTER 15
SOME OF THE BEST SITES ON THE WEB

The Spot came under a lot of fire when it first arrived on the spot (sorry) for pretending to be a real place. The creators have now come clean—so to speak—with Spot Tech, which explains how The Spot works. Like it or not, The Spot is one of the most popular and well-executed sites on the Web.

> Note: Check out The Spot FAQ for views from the authors.

The Heart: A Virtual Exploration
URL: http://sln.fi.edu/biosci/heart.html
Owner: The Franklin Institute
Webmaster: webteam@sln.fi.edu
Purpose: Education

The Heart: A Virtual Exploration is a fine example of education on the Web. It takes a topic that could be quite daunting, such as the human heart, and breaks it down into easy-to-understand pieces. It is a great example of things to come. Figure 15-2 shows The Heart's top page.

The amount and level of information here is very impressive. There are definitions, graphics, explanatory text, and activities. It makes learning about the heart painless and fun.

There really is nothing cool going on behind the scenes here. The one downside of this page is that it doesn't use any advanced techniques to deliver information. For example, the activities, a series of tests, would be a lot more fun to do if they were done with a form and made interactive.

The Heart is a great site for information and learning, but it could be given a little pizzazz by incorporating some forms and imagemaps.

Figure 15-1 The Spot's main menu

Figure 15-2 The top page of The Heart

CHAPTER 15
SOME OF THE BEST SITES ON THE WEB

WebZine

URL: http://www.peli.com/
Owner: Pelican Publishing
Webmaster: Orley Amos
Purpose: Information and entertainment

WebZine is an electronic magazine that represents a collection of writing talents and topics. It is informative and fun to read. Figure 15-3 shows the WebZine cover page.

The color choices and the layout of WebZine are great. Each section is easy to find and easy to read. It is also easy to advance from section to section or within parts of the same section.

WebZine makes nice use of tables to break up the different sections and the different parts of each section. WebZine also changes the background and text color, which is simple to do. It doesn't slow down the system as much as a background image, yet it still gives the magazine a distinctive look and feel.

WebZine's well-planned layout makes it easy and fun to read.

The Uncanny X-Page

URL: http://www.students.uiuc.edu/~m-blase/x-page.html
Owner: Marty Blase
Webmaster: Marty Blase
Purpose: Information and entertainment

The Uncanny X-Page is devoted totally to the world's most popular mutants: Marvel Comic's X-men. The page, which is not sanctioned by Marvel, is a nice example of what a lot of dedication and work can produce. It is the definitive

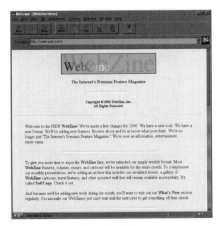

Figure 15-3 The WebZine cover page, making nice use of forms

source of X-information. Figure 15-4 shows the X-Page title page when viewed with Netscape 2.0.

The pages are loaded with graphics and choices. Each separate topic has its own menu bar. The background image is also good.

This was one of the first non-Netscape-owned pages to make use of frames; the table of contents always stays in a window while another window shows whatever information you have chosen.

This page is not put together by a professional Web team, but from its look and feel you could never tell. It certainly is as nice to look at and fun to read (if you're a fan) as anything on the Web.

People On-Line

URL: http://pathfinder.com/people/toc.html
Owner: People Magazine (Time Life)
Webmaster: 74774.1513@compuserve.com
Purpose: Infotainment

The online version of the very popular *People* magazine. All the glitz and glamour of the magazine translate well to the Web. Figure 15-5 shows a sample "cover."

This page has a very nice look and feel. Many of the same images from the paper magazine make their way to the electronic version, and for some reason the look and feel of the electronic version is better. There is even a part of the site that is updated daily with all the latest celeb news and entertainment news.

This page makes great use of graphics and imagemaps. The screens are well laid out and condensed. There is also a nice built-in key word search that lets you find related articles.

Figure 15-4 The Uncanny X-Page—notice the use of frames

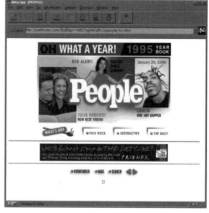

Figure 15-5 The cover of People On-Line

CHAPTER 15
SOME OF THE BEST SITES ON THE WEB

A great mix of information, slick presentation, and smooth layout makes this one of the best conversions from paper to electronics on the Web.

The Heather Locklear Internet Fan Club

URL: http://www.riv.be/garyfs/index.html
Owner: Gary F. Spradling
Webmaster: Gary F. Spradling
Purpose: A tribute from the president of the fan club

There are hundreds of pages on the Web devoted to actors and actresses. The Heather Locklear page, which is maintained by Gary F. Spradling, is certainly one of the best. If you want information on or photos of this very popular actress, this is the place to come. Figure 15-6 shows the Heather Locklear Internet Fan Club.

The graphics look smooth and the layout is clean and easy to look at. This is also one of few sites on the Web that allow you to register so you may be informed when the site is updated. The site contains everything you probably need to know about Heather Locklear.

Notice the excellent background image and choice of colors. It is one of the first sites to take advantage of Microsoft's Internet Explorer.

This is an amazing, well-executed job by a devoted fan. It looks as good and professional as anything you'll find on the Web.

The Point

URL: http://www.pointcom.com/
Owner: Point Communications
Questions: editor@pointcom.com
Purpose: Index of leading sites on the Web

Figure 15-6 The Heather Locklear Internet Fan Club (index2.html)

The Point is one of the premier index sites on the Web. While other index sites tend to list many sites, The Point only lists reviews of sites it considers to be in the top 5 percent of all Web sites. It is a well-executed and valuable reference. Figure 15-7 shows The Point's reviews menu.

The Point is one of the best-looking and easiest-to-navigate index sites. The writing makes many of the listings more fun to read than your average index.

In addition to the visual interface, it's also obvious that lots of thought went into the layout and design of this. The authors made good use of graphical imagemaps.

ESPNET SportsZone

URL: http://espnet.sportszone.com/
Owner: ESPN
Webmaster: Starware
Purpose: Complete sports updates and information

If you want to know anything about sports, this is the place to check first. All major sports are covered, with standings, scores, and articles. There is even a section devoted to some of the less major sports. This is a fine sports reference. Figure 15-8 shows the ESPNET SportsZone's home page.

ESPNET has a nice design and layout, easy to look at and easy to navigate. Even the ads look cool.

Notice the great use of tables and imagemaps in the various table of contents and menu bars. The scripting is also impressive: the "up-to-the-minute" scores really are pretty much up to the minute.

One of the finest sites on the Web. A great blend of information and presentation and what all sites should strive for.

Figure 15-7 The Point's reviews menu

Figure 15-8 The ESPNET SportsZone home page

CHAPTER 15
SOME OF THE BEST SITES ON THE WEB

Webaholics Top 50 Links List

URL: http://www.ohiou.edu/~rbarrett/webaholics/favlinks/entries.html
Owner: Rich Barrette
Webmaster: Rich Barrette
Purpose: A fun place to promote a site

Do you have a site that you think is cool and that you would like to share with the world? That's the purpose of the Webaholics Top 50 Links List. It is a list that simply consists of 50 links added interactively by readers. Once added, a link starts at number one, then gets bumped down as other links are added. Figure 15-9 shows a standard Top 50 list.

The visual interface just consists of a list of links. Since that is the purpose of this site, listing the links is all that is necessary.

The code behind the scenes is very impressive. This page makes good use of forms and CGI scripting. You enter your URL with a form, and then it is instantaneously added to the top of the list while it bumps off the 50th item.

This page shows how simple design and a little programming can make for a fun and informative stop.

WebComics Daily

URL: http://www.cyberzine.com/webcomics/comics.html
Owner: David de Vitry
Webmaster: David de Vitry
Purpose: Entertainment for comic lovers

If you are interested in seeing the actual comics that appear on the Web, WebComics Daily is a good, graphics-intensive alternative to those lists of links.

Figure 15-9 The Top 50 list

WebComics inlines the various daily comics from all over the Web into five easy-to-read pages. Figure 15-10 shows a typical page from WebComics Daily.

This page has a great design with a simple yet effective graphical tool bar. The choice of comics is nicely laid out on the top of each page. Each toon is labeled clearly.

This is no easy task, collecting the URLs of all the daily strips on the Web and then inlining them all in one well-organized, easy-to-read "magazine." This site also makes fine use of backgrounds to give it a real cool feel.

It has got to be a labor of love on Mr. de Vitry's part to create such a fine Web resource. Be forewarned, though; this is not a stop for someone with a slow connection.

SEDS Internet Space Warehouse

URL: http://www.seds.org/
Owner: Students for the Exploration and Development of Space, University of Arizona Chapter
Webmaster: Chris Lewicki <webmaster@seds.org>
Purpose: Information about and images of astronomy, space exploration

If you are interested in learning about astronomy and seeing some intergalactic images, check out SEDS. Figure 15-11 shows the SEDS home page.

Visitors to the SEDS home page are greeted with a view of the planet Earth taken from a hypothetical camera on the surface of the moon. Above it, a list of links allows users to learn more about the organization, study the planets, or look up images of planets, stars, and spacecraft.

The page uses an ingenious combination of normal links and imagemaps. A list of links is grouped together in the center of the page. Above and below the links

Figure 15-10 A typical page from WebComics Daily

Figure 15-11 The SEDS home page

CHAPTER 15
SOME OF THE BEST SITES ON THE WEB

are imagemaps that provide access to some of the same resources listed in the text links, as well as to new links. The designers also spent a great deal of time organizing the comprehensive archive of space images and providing a graphical interface that allows users to see thumbnails of the full images as well as a search index for finding a particular image.

If you're accessing the Web through a slow connection, the use of lots of images may make accessing the site frustrating. However, if you have any interest in space, or an interest in a well-designed, graphics-rich Web page, the SEDS Internet Space Warehouse is a must-see.

boston.com

URL: http://www.boston.com/
Owner: The Boston Globe
Webmaster: Dave Margulius <margulius@globe.com>
Purpose: Information about Boston

Planning a trip to Boston? If so, make sure you visit boston.com before you leave. Figure 15-12 shows the boston.com home page.

A very basic page greets visitors to boston.com, with a handful of links to different resources. The information on the other side of those links, though, is enough to answer anyone's questions about Boston. Visitors can read the current issue of the *Boston Globe*, check out restaurant reviews, search classified ads, and take part in online discussions.

Load the boston.com page. Now reload it. If everything's working, the featured links you saw the first time should have been replaced with a different set. The site uses a CGI script to generate the HTML code for the home page on the fly, randomly selecting the featured links from a list. The site has power: redundant

Figure 15-12 The boston.com home page

Sun SPARCstation 20 servers run the Netsite commerce server from Netscape and access 40-gigabyte RAID disks. The site has a T3 connection to the Internet so that they can handle heavy traffic with ease.

The boston.com site provides one-stop shopping for information about the Boston area. The site emphasizes information, and keeps graphics and imagemaps down to a minimum, so that those using text-based browsers or who have turned off image loading can still make good use of the pages.

Amazon.com Books

URL: http://www.amazon.com
Owner: Amazon.com Books
Webmaster: webmaster@amazon.com
Purpose: Selling books

Looking for a book to buy? Try Amazon.com books. Figure 15-13 shows the Amazon.com home page.

Amazon.com, which modestly bills itself as "Earth's biggest bookstore," offers a catalog of one million titles. A search engine allows users to search the catalog by title, author, subject, or key word. You can add (and remove) books from a "shopping basket," and arrange for payment when you're ready to buy them.

CGI scripts generate dynamic HTML documents, so that when you return to the home page, a different book may be advertised than on your original visit. The search engine for the book catalog is very efficient; it can scan through the contents of the catalog and return an HTML document with the results of the search in only a few seconds.

Amazon.com shows how to combine a large catalog of information with a Web page and search engine to allow visitors to quickly find the information they need.

Figure 15-13 The Amazon.com home page

CHAPTER 15
SOME OF THE BEST SITES ON THE WEB

Red Dirt Shirt

URL: https://hoohana.aloha.net/~reddirt/
Owner: Red Dirt Shirts
Webmaster: reddirt@aloha.net
Purpose: T-shirt catalog

Looking for a T-shirt? Red Dirt Shirts has their catalog online. Figure 15-14 shows the Red Dirt Shirt home page.

The home page itself is not remarkable, but the list of "cool shirts" offered for sale shows a good way to create a catalog page on the Web. Small graphical images of the shirts are combined in a form so that people can see the variety of shirts available and immediately select those they want to buy.

The site uses a secure server from Netscape to provide safer transaction of credit card information for those using the Netscape browser (note the different protocol in the URL for the secure site: https instead of http).

The Red Dirt Shirts page shows how a catalog of merchandise can be simply and effectively created on the Web.

Figure 15-14 The Red Dirt Shirt home page

HTML QUICK REFERENCE

This appendix lists the tags used in various versions of HTML, divided by subject, for quick reference when you're working on a page. References to the How-To's that describe the tags in greater detail are included. Tags that are available only in HTML 3 and/or Netscape are noted in the definition; otherwise, the tag is from HTML 2.0. If a tag has an attribute that can be included in the tag, it is shown in an indented list below the tag. An ellipsis (…) is used to indicate where text can be placed between tags. Text in italics indicates a variable that should be replaced with the appropriate filename, key word, or number.

Document Basics

These tags provide the basic structure for an HTML document.

ELEMENT	HOW-TO	DEFINITION
<BODY>…</BODY>	2.8	Marks the beginning and end of the body of an HTML document
<HEAD>…</HEAD>	2.2	Marks the beginning and end of the header of an HTML document
<HTML>…</HTML>	2.2	Marks the beginning and end of an HTML document
<TITLE>…</TITLE>	2.2	Identifies the title of an HTML document (used in the heading)
<!-- …-->	2.7	Makes a comment in an HTML document

Physical Text Styles

These tags allow you to change the physical style of text in your document, that is, change how the text is displayed for the user.

APPENDIX A
HTML QUICK REFERENCE

ELEMENT	HOW-TO	DEFINITION
<B>...</B>	3.2	Makes text bold
<BASEFONT SIZE=*n*>	2.11	Puts text in a large-print font (HTML 3)
<BLINK>...</BLINK>		Makes blinking text (Netscape)
<FONT SIZE=*n*>...</FONT>	2.11	Changes the font size by a value *n* (Netscape) (*n* can be any number from 1 to 7, or a positive or negative number to indicate an offset from the base font size)
<I>...</I>	3.3	Italicizes text
<S>...</S>	3.7	Puts text in a strikethrough font (HTML 3) (also <STRIKE>...</STRIKE>(Netscape))
<SMALL>...</SMALL>	2.11	Puts text in a small-print font (HTML 3)
_{...}	3.6	Puts text in a subscript (HTML 3)
^{...}	3.6	Puts text in a superscript (HTML 3)
<TT>...</TT>	3.5	Puts text in a teletype (fixed-width) font
<U>...</U>	3.4	Underlines text

Content Text Styles

These tags allow you to change the content style of the text in your document, that is, change the implied meaning of the text.

ELEMENT	HOW-TO	DEFINITION
<ABBREV>...</ABBREV>	3.15	Identifies an abbreviation (HTML 3)
<ADDRESS>...</ADDRESS>		Specifies the author, contact information, etc., of the page
<ACRONYM>...</ACRONYM>	3.15	Identifies an acronym (HTML 3)
<AU>...</AU>	3.16	Identifies an author (HTML 3)
<CITE>...</CITE>	3.9	Specifies a citation
<CODE>...</CODE>	3.11	Includes code (from a computer program)
<CREDIT>...</CREDIT>		Names the source of a quotation block or figure
<DEL>...</DEL>	3.17	Marks text deleted from an earlier version of the document (HTML 3)
<DFN>...</DFN>	3.12	Specifies a definition
<EM>	3.8	Emphasizes text
<H*n*>...</H*n*>	3.1	Identifies heading for a document (*n* a whole number from 1 (largest heading) to 6 (smallest heading))
ALIGN *alignment*		Sets the alignment of the heading (*alignment* can be "left", "center", "right", or "justify") (HTML 3/Netscape)
SRC = *graphic filename*		Includes a graphic as a bullet for the header (HTML 3)

APPENDIX A
HTML QUICK REFERENCE

ELEMENT	HOW-TO	DEFINITION
<INS>...</INS>	3.17	Marks text inserted from an earlier version of the document (HTML 3)
<KBD>...</KBD>	3.14	Identifies input or output from a computer
<Q>...</Q>	3.10	Identifies a quotation (HTML 3)
<PERSON>...</PERSON>	3.16	Identifies a person
<SAMP>...</SAMP>	3.13	Specifies a sample of literal characters
<STRONG>...</STRONG>	3.8	Strongly emphasizes text
<VAR>...</VAR>	3.11	Specifies a variable

Document Spacing

These tags control the spacing in your document.

ELEMENT	HOW-TO	DEFINITION
<BLOCKQUOTE>...</BLOCKQUOTE>		Creates a quotation block
<BQ>...</BQ>		Creates a quotation block (HTML 3)
 	4.3	Inserts a line break
CLEAR = *alignment*		Clear textwrap (*alignment* can be "left", "right", or "all")
<FN>...</FN>	4.6	Includes a footnote (HTML 3)
ID = *footnote name*		Specifies the name of the footnote for reference in a link
<HR>	4.1	Adds a horizontal line
ALIGN = *alignment*		Alignment of the line (Netscape) (*alignment* can be "left", "right", or "center")
SIZE = *n*		Specifies the thickness of the line (Netscape)
NOSHADE		Makes the line black (Netscape)
SRC = *graphic filename*		Specifies a custom image for the line (HTML 3)
WIDTH = *n%*		Specifies the width of the line (Netscape) (*n* can be any number from 0 to 100)
<NOTE>...</NOTE>	4.5	Includes an exclamatory note
CLASS = *class type*		Type of exclamatory note (*class type* can be "note", "caution", or "warning")
<P>...</P>	4.3	Creates a paragraph
ALIGN = *alignment*		Alignment of the paragraph (*alignment* can be "left", "center", "right", or "justify")
ID = "*name*"		Name of the paragraph for reference in links (HTML 3)
<PRE>...</PRE>	4.4	Identifies preformatted text

continued on next page

continued from previous page

ELEMENT	HOW-TO	DEFINITION
WIDTH = *n*		Width of text in characters
<TAB>		Inserts a horizontal tab
ALIGN = *alignment*		Alignment of the tab (*alignment* can be "left", "center", "right", or "justify")
ID = *tab name*		Location of a tab stop in a line
TO = *tab name*		Goes to horizontal location of the named tab stop

Mathematical Formatting

These tags allow you to format mathematical formulas in the text of your document without resorting to displaying the formulas as images. Note that all of the tags in this section are supported only by HTML 3.

ELEMENT	HOW-TO	DEFINITION
$...$	5.1	Identifies a mathematical equation
<OVER>	5.1	Separates the numerator from the denominator in an equation
<LEFT>	5.1	Marks the left bracket of an equation, use with (, [, |, || or &ltbrace; ({)
<RIGHT>	5.1	Marks the right bracket of an equation, use with),], |, || or &rtbrace; (})
<TEXT>...</TEXT>	5.1	Includes text in a mathematical expression
<ABOVE>...</ABOVE>	5.1	Draws an arrow above the included characters
<BELOW>...</BELOW>	5.1	Draws an arrow below the included characters
<BAR>...</BAR>	5.1	Draws a bar over the included characters
<DOT>...</DOT>	5.1	Draws a dot over the included characters
<DDOT>...</DDOT>	5.1	Draws a double dot over the included characters
<HAT>...</HAT>	5.1	Draws a hat over the included characters
<TILDE>...</TILDE>	5.1	Draws a tilde over the included characters
<VEC>...</VEC>	5.1	Draws a vector symbol over the included characters
<SQRT>...</SQRT>	5.1	Puts the included text inside a square root symbol
<ROOT>...<OF>...</ROOT>	5.1	Places the text to the right of the <OF> element inside a root symbol, using the number to the left of the <OF> element to specify the power of the root
<ARRAY>...</ARRAY>	5.1	Specifies an array
ALIGN = *alignment*		The alignment of the array (*alignment* can be "left", "center", "right", or "justify")

APPENDIX A
HTML QUICK REFERENCE

ELEMENT	HOW-TO	DEFINITION
COLDEF = "x"		The alignment of columns within the array (x can be any combination of L for left, C for center, or R for right)
<ROW>	5.1	Starts a new row of the array
<ITEM>	5.1	Identifies an item in the array

Tables

These tags allow you to create tables in HTML 3 or Netscape.

ELEMENT	HOW-TO	DEFINITION
<CAPTION>...</CAPTION>	5.3	Identifies the table caption
ALIGN = alignment		Alignment of the caption (alignment can be "top" or "bottom")
<TABLE>...</TABLE>	5.2	Defines a table
BORDER		Shows the lines of the table (HTML 3)
BORDER=n		Shows the lines of the table to the specified thickness (Netscape)
ALIGN = alignment		The alignment of the table (alignment can be "bleedleft", "left", "center", "right", "bleedright", or "justify")
UNITS = units		Units to be used for alignment (units can be "en", "relative", or "pixels")
COLSPEC = "xn"		Alignment of columns of the table (x can be L for left, C for center, or R for right, n is any number)
WIDTH = n		A fixed width of the entire table (n is any number)
<TH>, <TD>	5.4, 5.5	Defines a table heading <TH> or a data table entry <TD>
ALIGN = alignment		The alignment of entries in the row (alignment can be "left", "center", "right", "justify" or "decimal")
VALIGN = alignment		The vertical alignment of table row entries (alignment can be "top", "middle", "bottom", or "baseline")
ROWSPAN = n		Number of table rows the cell should cover
COLSPAN = n		Number of table columns the cell should cover
NOWRAP		Turns off word wrapping in the table cell (Netscape)
WIDTH = n		Width of the cell, in pixels (Netscape)
WIDTH = n%		Width of the cell, in percentage of the table (Netscape)
<TR>	5.6	Starts a new row in the table
ALIGN = alignment		The alignment of entries in the row (alignment can be "left", "center", "right", "justify", or "decimal")
VALIGN = alignment		The vertical alignment of table row entries (alignment can be "top", "middle", "bottom", or "baseline")

Lists

These tags allow you to create a number of different types of lists in your document.

ELEMENT	HOW-TO	DEFINITION
<OL>...</OL>	6.1	Creates an ordered (numbered) list
COMPACT		Displays a compacted version of the list
CONTINUE		Continues the numbering from the last numbered list (HTML 3)
SEQNUM = n		Specifies the starting number of the list (HTML 3)
TYPE = type		Specifies the type of numbering used (Netscape) (type can be A, a, I, i, or 1)
START = n		The starting number of the list (Netscape)
<UL>...</UL>	6.2	Creates an unordered (bulleted) list
BLANK		Supresses the display of the bullets (HTML 3)
COMPACT		Displays a compacted version of the list
SRC = graphic filename		Replaces the bullets with the specified graphic (HTML 3)
TYPE = type		Specify the type of bullet to use (Netscape) (type can be "circle", "disc", or "square")
WRAP = alignment	6.4	Wraps the contents of the list horizontally across or vertically down the screen (alignment can be "horiz" or "vert") (HTML 3)
<DL>...</DL>	6.7	Creates a glossary list
COMPACT		Displays a compacted version of the list
<MENU>...</MENU>	6.5	Creates a menu list
<DIRECTORY>...</DIRECTORY>	6.6	Creates a directory list
<DT>	6.7	Identifies a defined term in a glossary list
<DD>	6.7	Identifies a definition in a glossary list
<LI>	6.1, 6.2, 6.5, 6.6	Identifies a list item in <OL>, <UL>, <MENU>, or <DIRECTORY>
TYPE = bullet type		Specifies the type of bullet to use for this and subsequent list entries in a bulleted list (Netscape) (bullet type can be "circle", "disc", or "square")
TYPE = number type		Specifies the type of numbering used for this and subsequent list entries in an ordered list (Netscape) (number type can be "A", "a", "I", "i", or "1")
VALUE = n		The starting number of this and later entries in a numbered list (Netscape)

APPENDIX A
HTML QUICK REFERENCE

Links

These tags allow you to create links to Web pages, FTP and Gopher sites, and other Internet resources.

ELEMENT	HOW-TO	DEFINITION
<A>...</A>	7.5-7.14	Defines an anchor for a link
HREF = *URL*		Specifies the destination of the link, using its URL
NAME = *name*		Specifies the name of a section of a document for later use in links
SHAPE = *shape*	7.16	The shape of a link embedded in a figure (HTML 3) (*shape* can be "circle x,y,r"; "rect x,y,r,h"; "polygon x1,y1,x2,y2,...,xn,yn"; or "default")
<BASE *URL*>	7.3	Defines the base URL of the relative links in a document (located in the header of the document)
<LINK>	7.4	Defines the relationship between the current document and other documents
REL		The type of relationship between the current document and other documents
REV		The reverse relationship between other documents and the current one

Images

These tags allow you to incorporate images into your pages.

ELEMENT	HOW-TO	DEFINITION
<BODY BGCOLOR="#*nnn*"> ...</BODY>		Changes the color of the background (Netscape) (*nnn* are hexidecimal values for the colors red, green, and blue (RGB))
<BODY BACKGROUND="*URL*"> ...</BODY>		Sets the brackground to display the specified graphic (HTML 3/Netscape)
<BODY TEXT="#*nnn*"> ...</BODY>		Changes the color of the text to the specified hexidecimal RGB value (Netscape)
<BODY LINK="#*nnn*"> ...</BODY>		Changes the color of links to the specified hexidecimal RGB value (Netscape)
<BODY VLINK="#*nnn*"> ...</BODY>		Changes the color of visited links to the specified hexidecimal RGB value (Netscape)
<BODY ALINK="#*nnn*"> ...</BODY>		Changes the color of an active link to the specified hexidecimal RGB value (Netscape)

continued on next page

continued from previous page

ELEMENT	HOW-TO	DEFINITION
<FIG>...</FIG>		Includes a figure (HTML 3)
SRC = *graphic filename*		The filename of the figure
ALIGN = *alignment*		The alignment of the figure (*alignment* can be "bleedleft", "left", "center", "right", "bleedright", or "justify")
WIDTH = *n*		Fixed width of the figure
HEIGHT = *n*		Fixed height of the figure
UNITS = *units*		Units of the WIDTH and HEIGHT measurements (*units* can be "en" or "pixels")
IMAGEMAP = *URL*		Declares the image to be an imagemap using the given URL
<IMG>	8.2	Includes an inline image
ALIGN = *alignment*	8.3	The alignment of the image (*alignment* can be "top", "middle", "bottom", "left", or "right")
ALIGN = *alignment*	8.3	The alignment of the image (Netscape) (*alignment* can be "left", "right", "texttop", "absmiddle", "baseline", or "bottom")
ALT = "*text*"	8.4	A text decription of the image
BORDER = *n*		Size of the picture border, in pixels (Netscape)
HEIGHT = *n*	8.5	Fixed height of the image (HTML 3)
WIDTH = *n*	8.5	Fixed width of the image (HTML 3)
UNITS = *units*	8.5	Units of the WIDTH and HEIGHT measurements (*units* can be "en" or "pixels")
HSPACE = *n*		The horizontal runaround space, in pixels (Netscape)
VSPACE = *n*		The vertical runaround space, in pixels (Netscape)
ISMAP	8.9	Declares the image to be an imagemap
SRC = *graphic filename*		The filename of the image
LOWSRC = *graphic filename*		The filename of a low-resolution version of the image (Netscape)

Forms

These tags allow you to create forms that include different types of inputs; they also specify what to do with the results of the form when submitted.

ELEMENT	HOW-TO	DEFINITION
<FORM>...</FORM>	10.1	Defines a form
ACTION = *URL*		The location (URL) of the script that will process the form results
METHOD = *method*		Method of sending the form input (*method* can be GET or POST)

APPENDIX A
HTML QUICK REFERENCE

ELEMENT	HOW-TO	DEFINITION
<INPUT>		Creates an input area of the form
TYPE =		Type of form input
CHECKBOX	10.4	A checkbox
FILE	10.9	Allows user to attach a file (HTML 3)
ACCEPT = "text"		Limits the range of acceptable files
HIDDEN		An invisible input
IMAGE	10.9	Returns information on where the user clicked on the image (HTML 3)
RADIO	10.5	A radio button
RANGE	10.9	A number field with inputs limited to a specific range (HTML 3)
MIN = n		Miniumum value of the range
MAX = n		Maximum value of the range
PASSWORD	10.6	A password
SCRIBBLE	10.9	Lets user write (scribble) on top of an image (HTML 3)
TEXT	10.3	A single-line text input
SUBMIT	10.1	A button to submit the form input
RESET	10.1	A button to reset the form input
NAME = *name*		The name of this input variable, as seen by the script (but not displayed in the form)
SIZE = n		Defines the size of the text display for a TEXT form
MAXLENGTH = n		The maxiumum length of a TEXT input item
VALUE = "*text*"		Value used to initialize HIDDEN, RANGE, and TEXT fields
DISABLED		Disables the field to prevent text from being entered
CHECKED		Initializes a field in a CHECKBOX or RADIO to be selected
SRC = *graphic filename*		Specifies the image filename for IMAGE, SCRIBBLE, SUBMIT, and RESET
<ISINDEX>		Defines a searchable index
<OPTION>	10.7	Specifies an option in a <SELECT> menu form
DISABLED		Disables the entry to prevent its selection
SELECTED		Initializes the entry to be selected
<SELECT>...</SELECT>	10.7	Creates a menu of selections
NAME = *name*		The name of the input variable, as seen by the script (but not displayed in the form)
MULTIPLE		Permits multiple selections to be made from the menu
DISABLED		Disables the menu to prevent selections
WIDTH = n		Fixed width of the menu
HEIGHT = n		Fixed height of the menu

continued on next page

continued from previous page

ELEMENT	HOW-TO	DEFINITION
UNITS = *units*		Width units for WIDTH and HEIGHT (*units* can be "en" or "pixel")
<TEXTAREA>...</TEXTAREA>	10.3	Creates a multiline text input area for a form: any text located between the tags becomes the initial value for the form
NAME = *name*		The name of the input variable, as seen by the script (but not displayed in the form)
ROWS = *n*		Number of rows down the text area should be
COLS = *n*		Number of columns across the text area should be
DISABLED		Disables the menu to prevent input

WWW RESOURCES

This book can't go into full detail on every WWW and HTML topic, nor can it provide information on every WWW browser, server, or related application. This appendix is a brief list of information available on the Web and elsewhere on the Internet that will allow you to study in greater detail some of the topics addressed in the book, and also allow you to find Web-related software for your use.

> Note: The URLs provided below were accurate when this appendix was written. However, URLs often change and Web sites sometimes disappear, so some of the sites listed below may no longer be valid.

Basic Information on WWW and HTML

The World Wide Web (W3) Consortium

`http://www.w3.org/`

Home to general information on the World Wide Web and links to all areas of WWW and HTML.

The WWW Section of Yahoo

`http://www.yahoo.com/Computers/World_Wide_Web`

Links to hundreds of pages regarding WWW and HTML.

APPENDIX B
WWW RESOURCES

The World Wide Web FAQ

http://sunsite.unc.edu/boutell/faq/index.html

The compilation of Frequently Asked Questions (FAQs) from Usenet.

Indexes

ALIWEB

http://web.nexor.co.uk/public/aliweb/aliweb.html

A searchable database of Web pages based on descriptions of sites by their creators.

HARVEST

http://harvest.cs.colorado.edu/

An indexing tool used to create a Web page index searchable by content.

JumpStation II

http://js.stir.ac.uk/jsbin/jsii

A searchable database of Web sites obtained by a robot.

Lycos

http://www.lycos.com/

An extensive database of Web pages with sophisticated search tools.

TradeWave Galaxy

http://www.einet.net/

A subject-based guide to Web pages (formerly EINet Galaxy).

W3 Search Engines

http://cuiwww.unige.ch/meta-index.html

A page with links to a number of WWW search engines.

WebCrawler

http://webcrawler.com/

A search engine that uses its own index or checks the Web in real time to answer queries.

World Wide Web Worm (WWWW)

http://www.cs.colorado.edu/home/mcbryan/WWWW.html

A searchable database that can find Web pages by title or URL.

Yahoo

http://www.yahoo.com/

A popular, extensive database of Web pages.

Browsers

Text-Based Servers

Agora

http://www.w3.org/hypertext/WWW/Agora/Overview.html

A browser that uses e-mail to transfer pages, for those without full Internet access.

Emacs W3

http://www.cs.indiana.edu/elisp/w3/docs.html

An Emacs subsystem that can run WWW documents.

Line Mode Browser

http://www.w3.org/hypertext/WWW/LineMode/Status.html

A line-based (as opposed to screen-based) browser for dumb terminals.

Lynx

http://www.cc.ukans.edu/about_lynx/about_lynx.html

A screen-based text browser for UNIX, VMS, and DOS systems.

Macintosh

Enhanced Mosaic (Spyglass)

http://www.spyglass.com/three/index.html

An enhanced version of NCSA's Mosaic, marketed solely to other companies.

MacWeb

http://galaxy.einet.net/EINet/MacWeb/MacWebHome.html

A full-featured Web browser created by TradeWave.

APPENDIX B
WWW RESOURCES

Mosaic for Macintosh

`http://www.ncsa.uiuc.edu/SDG/Software/MacMosaic/MacMosaicHome.html`

The Macintosh version of the Mosaic browser.

Netscape Navigator

`http://home.netscape.com/`

The Macintosh version of the very popular Netscape Navigator browser.

Samba

`http://www.w3.org/hypertext/WWW/Macintosh/Overview.html`

A historical Macintosh browser.

NeXTSTEP

NeXT Browser-Editor

`http://www.w3.org/hypertext/WWW/NextStep/Status.html`

A combined Web browser and editor written by Tim Berners-Lee.

OmniWeb

`http://www.omnigroup.com/Software/OmniWeb/`

A Web browser marketed by Lighthouse Design.

UNIX (X Windows)

Arena

`http://www.w3.org/hypertext/WWW/Arena/`

A prototype HTML 3 Web browser developed by the World Wide Web Consortium.

Chimera

`http://www.unlv.edu/chimera/`

A small Web browser whose capabilities can be extended by users.

Enhanced Mosaic (Spyglass)

`http://www.spyglass.com/mos_home.htm`

An enhanced version of NCSA's Mosaic, marketed solely to other companies.

APPENDIX B
WWW RESOURCES

Mosaic for X Windows
http://www.ncsa.uiuc.edu/SDG/Software/XMosaic/

The X Windows version of the Mosaic browser.

Netscape
http://home.netscape.com/

The X Windows version of the very popular Netscape Navigator browser.

tkWWW
http://www.w3.org/hypertext/WWW/TkWWW/Status.html

A combined Web browser and editor using the tcl/tk programming toolkit.

Viola
http://xcf.berkeley.edu/ht/projects/viola/docs/viola/about.html

A Web browser created using the Viola hypermedia language.

Windows

Cello
http://www.law.cornell.edu/cello/cellotop.html

A popular full-featured Web browser.

Enhanced Mosaic (Spyglass)
http://www.spyglass.com/mos_home.htm

An enhanced version of NCSA's Mosaic, marketed solely to other companies.

Galahad
http://www.mcs.com/~jvwater/main.html

A graphical user interface for the BIX online service, with built-in Web browser.

Mosaic for Windows
http://www.ncsa.uiuc.edu/SDG/Software/WinMosaic/HomePage.html
The Windows version of the Mosaic browser.

Mosaic in a Box (Spry)
http://www.spry.com/mbox/index.html

An enhanced version of NCSA Mosaic, included in Spry's Internet in a Box.

Netscape

http://home.netscape.com/

The Windows version of the very popular Netscape Navigator browser.

Quarterdeck Mosaic

http://www.qdeck.com/beta/qmosaic.htm

An enhanced version of NCSA Mosaic.

SlipKnot

http://www.interport.net/slipknot/slipknot.html

A graphical Web browser that does not require a SLIP or PPP connection or TCP/IP.

WinWeb

http://galaxy.einet.net/EINet/WinWeb/WinWebHome.html

A full-featured Web browser created by TradeWave.

Servers

Macintosh

MacHTTP

http://www.biap.com/

A Web server program now superseded by WebSTAR.

WebSTAR

http://www.starnine.com/webstar/webstar.html

An enhanced, commerical version of MacHTTP.

OS/2

GoServe

http://www2.hursley.ibm.com/goserve/

A server program that supports the Web and Gopher protocols.

APPENDIX B
WWW RESOURCES

UNIX

CERN httpd
http://www.w3.org/hypertext/WWW/Daemon/Status.html

A server program developed at CERN and available for most versions of UNIX.

Jungle
http://catless.ncl.ac.uk/Programs/Jungle/

A server written using the tcl/tk programming toolkit.

NCSA httpd
http://hoohoo.ncsa.uiuc.edu/docs/Overview.html

A server program written at NCSA.

Netsite
http://home.netscape.com/MCOM/products_docs/server.html

A server program written by Netscape noted for its speed, efficiency, and ease of use. The Commerce version has encryption capabilities for the safe transfer of credit card numbers and other information.

PHTTPD
http://www.signum.se/phttpd/

A free, fast Web server program for computers running the Solaris (SunOS) operating system.

Plexus
http://www.bsdi.com/server/doc/plexus.html

A public-domain Web server written in Perl.

WN
http://hopf.math.nwu.edu/docs/overview.html

A Web server that incorporates navigation features and conditionally served files.

VAX/VMS

VAX/VMS server
http://kcgl1.eng.ohio-state.edu/www/doc/serverinfo.html

A Web server program created at Ohio State.

Windows

HTTPS (Windows NT)
http://www.w3.org/hypertext/WWW/HTTPS/Status.html

A Web server program available for Intel-based systems and the DEC/Alpha.

WebSite (NT and Windows 95)
http://clubweb.ora.com/

A Web server, with included Enhanced Mosaic browser, that runs on 386 and higher machines.

Windows httpd
http://www.city.net/win-httpd/

A small and very fast Web server based on NCSA httpd.

HTML Editors

Macintosh

Arachnid
http://sec-look.uiowa.edu/about/projects/arachnid-page.html

An HTML editor that won a 1995 Apple Enterprise Award.

HoTMetaL PRO
http://www.sq.com/products/hotmetal/hmp-org.htm

A commerical HTML editor, with a less powerful but free version also available.

HTML Editor
http://dragon.acadiau.ca/~giles/HTML_Editor/Documentation.html

A semi-WYSIWYG HTML editor.

HTML Grinder
http://www.matterform.com/mf/grinder/htmlgrinder.html

An HTML editor that uses special plug-in modules to handle sophisticated tasks.

HTML-HyperEditor
http://balder.syo.lu.se/Editor/HTML-HyperEditor.html

APPENDIX B
WWW RESOURCES

An HTML editor written as a HyperCard stack that supports special characters used in other languages.

HTML Pro

http://www.ts.umu.se/~r2d2/shareware/htmlpro_help.html

An HTML editor that supports the creation of macros to allow users to include new HTML tags.

World Wide Web Weaver

http://www.student.potsdam.edu/web.weaver/about.html

An HTML editor that features extended support for CGI scripts.

UNIX

A Simple HTML Editor (ASHE)

ftp://ftp.cs.rpi.edu/pub/puninj/ASHE/README.html

An HTML editor written in C using Motif and the NCSA HTML Widget.

City University HTML Editor

http://web.cs.city.ac.uk/homes/njw/htmltext/htmltext.html

A free, easily configurable HTML editor written using the Andrew toolkit.

HoTMetaL PRO

http://www.sq.com/products/hotmetal/hmp-org.htm

A commerical HTML editor, with a less powerful but free version also available.

tkHTML

http://www.ssc.com/~roland/tkHTML/tkHTML.html

An HTML editor written using the tcl/tk toolkit.

Windows

HoTMetaL PRO

http://www.sq.com/products/hotmetal/hmp-org.htm

A commerical HTML editor, with a less powerful but free version also available.

APPENDIX B
WWW RESOURCES

HotDog
http://www.sausage.com/

An HTML editor with a Windows 95-style interface that supports HTML 3 tags and Netscape extensions.

HTML Assistant Pro
http://fox.nstn.ca/~harawitz/index.html

A commerical HTML editor based on a popular shareware editor.

HTMLed Pro
http://www.ist.ca/htmledpro/

A commerical HTML editor with many advanced features.

HTML Writer
http://lal.cs.byu.edu/people/nosack/index.html

An HTML editor that allows you to edit more than one document at a time.

InContext Spider
http://www.incontext.ca/articles/webware/control1.html

A commercial browser, bundled with Spyglass Enhanced Mosaic, that supports advanced HTML features.

Webber
http://www.csdcorp.com/webber.htm

An HTML editor that includes a validator program to look for invalid HTML markup.

WebEdit
http://wwwnt.thegroup.net/webedit/webedit.htm

An HTML editor that supports HTML 3 tags.

Web Wizard
http://www.halcyon.com/webwizard/index.html

An HTML editor available in 16-bit and 32-bit versions.

APPENDIX B
WWW RESOURCES

HTML Document Development

HTML 2.0 Specification
http://www.w3.org/hypertext/WWW/MarkUp/html-spec/index.html

A full description of the final draft of HTML 2.0.

HTML 3.0 Draft Specification
http://www.hpl.hp.co.uk/people/dsr/html/CoverPage.html

A full description of the current draft of HTML 3.

HTML Style Guide
http://www.w3.org/hypertext/WWW/Provider/Style/Overview.html

Tim Berners-Lee's excellent guide to designing WWW documents.

NetSpace Guide for HTML Developers
http://netspace.org/netspace/wwwdoc.html

Lots of links to documents on creating effective HTML documents.

Subjective Electronic Information Repository
http://cbl.leeds.ac.uk/nikos/doc/repository.html

Links to hundreds of WWW development documents.

URL Descriptions
http://www.w3.org/hypertext/WWW/Addressing/Addressing.html

Definitions of the various types of URLs, as well as discussion of URNs and URIs.

WWW Development Page (Virtual Library)
http://www.charm.net/~web/Vlib/

Links to a wide range of HTML development documents.

Common Gateway Interface (CGI)

CGI Documentation
http://hoohoo.ncsa.uiuc.edu/cgi/

Information on the Common Gateway Interface and including CGI scripts in programs.

APPENDIX B
WWW RESOURCES

CGI Programs (C)

`http://wsk.eit.com/wsk/dist/doc/libcgi/libcgi.html`

A library of commonly used CGI routines, written in C.

CGI Programs (Perl)

`http://www.seas.upenn.edu/~mengwong/perlhtml.html`

A library of commonly used CGI routines, written in Perl.

Forms and Imagemaps

NCSA Forms Documentation

`http://hoohoo.ncsa.uiuc.edu/cgi/forms.html`

Information on using forms in conjunction with CGI scripts.

Image Maps: CERN httpd

`http://www.w3.org/hypertext/WWW/Daemon/User/CGI/HTImageDoc.html`

A tutorial for creating imagemaps for the CERN httpd server program.

Image Maps: NCSA httpd

`http://wintermute.ncsa.uiuc.edu:8080/map-tutorial/image-maps.html`

A tutorial for creating imagemaps for the NCSA httpd server program.

WWW Usenet Newsgroups

Browsers

`comp.infosystems.www.browsers.mac`

Discussion about Macintosh browsers.

`comp.infosystems.www.browsers.ms-windows`

Discussion about Microsoft Windows browsers.

`comp.infosystems.www.browsers.x`

Discussion about X Windows browsers.

`comp.infosystems.www.browsers.misc`

Discussion about other classes of browsers.

APPENDIX B
WWW RESOURCES

Document Authoring Groups

`comp.infosystems.www.authoring.cgi`

Discussion of CGI applications.

`comp.infosystems.www.authoring.html`

Discussion of HTML markup.

`comp.infosystems.www.authoring.images`

Discussion of the use of images in WWW documents.

`comp.infosystems.www.authoring.misc`

Discussion of other questions about document creation not covered in the above groups.

Servers

`comp.infosystems.www.servers.mac`

Discussion about Macintosh servers.

`comp.infosystems.www.servers.ms-windows`

Discussion about Microsoft Windows servers.

`comp.infosystems.www.servers.unix`

Discussion about UNIX servers.

`comp.infosystems.www.servers.misc`

Discussion about other classes of servers.

Other Discussion and Announcement Groups

`comp.infosystems.www.advocacy`

Discussion (and arguments) about various WWW applications and products.

`comp.infosystems.www.announce`

Announcement (no discussion permitted) of new and improved WWW sites.

APPENDIX B
WWW RESOURCES

```
comp.infosystems.www.misc
```

Discussion about WWW topics not covered by any of the above newsgroups.

WWW Mailing Lists

```
www-talk@info.cern.ch
```

Discussion about WWW among experts. To subscribe, e-mail listserv@info.cern.ch with the line

```
subscribe www-talk Your Name
```

in the body of the message. Subscription requests can also be sent to www-talk-request@info.cern.ch to be processed by a human.

```
www-announce@info.cern.ch
```

Used for "low-volume" announcements of products and services. Use the listserv address above to subscribe (replace www-talk in the body with www-announce), or e-mail www-announce-request@info.cern.ch.

MULTIPURPOSE INTERNET MAIL EXTENSIONS (MIME)

World Wide Web clients, such as browsers and servers, use MIME protocol to communicate information about the type of data requested and sent via HTTP. The sections of this appendix describe MIME and explain how it is used in the World Wide Web environment.

What Is MIME?

The Multipurpose Internet Mail Extensions (MIME) were developed as an extension to the Internet mail protocol to provide for incorporation of multimedia objects. The original definition for Internet mail dealt primarily with the transmission and reception of plain text messages. This mail protocol, as defined in RFC 822 (for more information, see http://info.cern.ch/hypertext/WWW/Protocols/rfc822/Overview.html), specified several message header elements that provided direction for routing of the mail messages. The development of this protocol provided a standard that all Internet mail programs could use.

The Internet mail protocol, however, left message content largely unmentioned, since the assumption was that the message would be simple text. In today's world of Internet mail, complex multipart, multimedia messages are becoming commonplace. MIME was developed to support this type of complex mail message. It does so by adding suitable header fields to describe message content and delimit multimedia objects. A standard, such as MIME, is necessary to provide for interoperability among Internet mail programs that support complex mail messages. For example, the following message represents a multipart message containing text, audio, and PostScript components.

APPENDIX C
MULTIPURPOSE INTERNET MAIL EXTENSIONS (MIME)

```
MIME-Version: 1.0
Content-type: multipart/mixed; boundary=SomeString

--SomeString
Content-type: text/plain
Text message body

--SomeString
Content-type: audio/basic
An audio object

--SomeString
Content-type: application/postscript
A postscript object

--SomeString--
```

(For an official list of registered media types, see URL ftp://ftp.isi.edu/in-notes/iana/assignments/media-types.)

The headers define the MIME version and the kind of message being sent. In this case the message is specified as multipart/mixed, and indicates the string that will be used to delimit the subcomponents. Each subcomponent has individual type/subtype specifications to describe the content of the particular subcomponent. The delimiter string marks the beginning and end of a subcomponent as well as marking the termination of the message. For more details on MIME, the specification is contained in RFC 1521 available at http://www.ncsa.uiuc.edu/SDG/Software/Mosaic/Docs/rfc1521.txt.

MIME Content-type Header and the Web

The portion of MIME protocol that is of central interest to HTML document developers is the Content-type header field. The World Wide Web environment uses MIME content type information in several ways. Table C-1 specifies a set of the more commonly used MIME types that may be encountered in that environment.

> Note: Types or subtypes with the "x-" prefix are nonstandard, private, or experimental types or subtypes. Any type or subtype not officially registered should have this prefix attached.

MIME TYPE/SUBTYPE	DESCRIPTION	COMMON FILE EXTENSIONS
application/mac-binhex40	Binhex archive format	hqx
application/msword	Microsoft Word	doc
application/octet-stream	Binary data	bin
application/oda	Office Document Architecture	oda
application/pdf	Adobe Acrobat PDF format	pdf

APPENDIX C
MULTIPURPOSE INTERNET MAIL EXTENSIONS (MIME)

MIME TYPE/SUBTYPE	DESCRIPTION	COMMON FILE EXTENSIONS
application/postscript	PostScript document	ps eps
application/rtf	MS Rich Text format	rtf
application/x-csh	C shell script	csh
application/x-cpio	POSIX CPIO format	cpio
application/x-dvi	Device-Independent format	dvi
application/x-gtar	GNU tar format	gtar
application/x-hdf	NCSA HDF data	hdf
application/x-latex	LaTeX document	latex
application/x-netcdf	Net Common Data Format	cdf nc
application/x-pl	Perl script	perl pl
application/x-sh	Sh shell script	sh
application/x-shar	Shell archive	shar
application/x-stuffit	Macintosh Stuffit archive	sit sea
application/x-tcl	Tcl script	tcl
application/x-tex	TeX document	tex
application/x-texinfo	TexInfo format	texinfo texi
application/x-troff	troff document	t tr troff
application/x-troff-man	troff with man macros	man
application/x-troff-me	troff with me macros	me
application/x-troff-ms	troff with ms macros	ms
application/x-wais-source	WAIS source	src
application/zip	Zip compressed document	zip
audio/basic	Basic audio file (8-bit PCM)	au snd
audio/x-aiff	AIFF audio file	aiff aif
audio/x-wav	Microsoft audio format	wav
image/gif	GIF image	gif
image/jpeg	JPEG image	jpeg jpg jpe
image/tiff	TIFF image	tiff tif
image/x-portable-anymap	Portable image format	pnm
image/x-portable-bitmap	Portable Bitmap format	pbm
image/x-portable-graymap	Portable Grayscale image format	pgm
image/x-portable-pixmap	Portable Pixmap format	ppm
image/x-rgb	RGB image	rgb
image/x-xwindowdump	X-Window dump	xwd
image/x-xbitmap	X bitmap	xbm
image/x-xpixmap	X pixelmap	xpm

continued on next page

APPENDIX C
MULTIPURPOSE INTERNET MAIL EXTENSIONS (MIME)

continued from previous page

MIME TYPE/SUBTYPE	DESCRIPTION	COMMON FILE EXTENSIONS
message/rfc822	MIME message	mime
multipart/mixed	Multipart messages	
text/plain	Normal text (ASCII)	txt
text/richtext	Microsoft Rich Text format	rtx
text/html	HTML text	html htm
video/mpeg	MPEG format video	mpeg mpg mpe
video/quicktime	Quicktime format video	qt mov
video/x-msvideo	Microsoft video format	avi
video/x-sgi-movie	SGI format movie	movie
x-world/x-vrml	VRML virtual environment	vrml vrm

Table C-1 MIME types commonly or specifically used with the World Wide Web

In addition, the World Wide Web environment defines several additional experimental and nonstandard MIME content types. Table C-2 lists some of them, along with references to the How-To's within this book that describe these particular MIME content types.

MIME TYPE/SUBTYPE	DESCRIPTION	HOW-TO REFERENCE
application/x-www-form-urlencode	Encoding for form data	10.1, 13.1
application/x-httpd-cgi	CGI applications (cgi filename extension)	13.4
multipart/x-mixed-replace	Netscape Server Push	13.8

Table C-2 World Wide Web specific MIME types

The categories specified in these tables are not a complete list of MIME content types; however, they do cover a large percentage of common types. The WWW-specific types described are all nonstandard MIME content types and may not be suitable for all clients, servers, and client/server combinations.

The HTTP protocol specifies the content types of HTTP requests and responses using MIME type/subtype designations. (See Appendix G on HTTP.) When a client issues a "get" request of an HTTP server, the server sends a Content-type field in the header of its response indicating the type of information enclosed in the response body. When a client issues a "post" request, it includes a Content-type field in the request header specifying the format of the data being sent to the server:

Content-type: application/x-www-form-urlencoded

Content-type fields for both MIME and HTTP are composed of the header name, Content-type, and at least two fields specifying a type and a subtype:

Content-type: type/subtype

APPENDIX C
MULTIPURPOSE INTERNET MAIL EXTENSIONS (MIME)

The type specification can be chosen from the following list:

- **application:** The file needs to be processed or manipulated in some manner by the recipient. For example, a PostScript object should be sent to an appropriate PostScript viewer.
- **audio:** The file is an audio object. This object should be rendered using the appropriate software and hardware, if available. If a suitable rendering environment is unavailable, many browsers allow the reader to save the object to a file.
- **extension-token:** This refers to a type beginning with the "x-" prefix. Use this prefix for all experimental, nonstandard, or private types. For example, the x-world type specifies a virtual environment.
- **image:** The file is an image of some type and should be treated appropriately.
- **message:** The file conforms to a different message standard, such as rfc822.
- **multipart:** The file is composed of multiple objects, each having its own respective type and subtype. The multipart type requires another header element specifying a boundary string to delimit the various component objects.
- **text:** The message body is composed of text. This text may be in a variety of formats. For example, the text could be an HTML document or a plain text document.
- **video:** The message body contains a video component. The object should be displayed using appropriate hardware and software.

The second portion of the Content-type header field is the subtype. The subtype is used to provide a more detailed specification of the content. For example, the content type text/plain represents a plain text file. The content type text/html designates an HTML page. The variety of subtypes precludes the delineation of all possible subtypes; however, Tables C-1 and C-2 provide a good subset of World Wide Web related content types, both type and subtype.

MIME and the Web Client

Web clients use MIME content types to determine which external viewer to launch when a server sends it a given document. When a client sends a request to an HTTP server, the server's response includes a response header, and possibly a message body, depending on the results of the request. One of the fields in the response header is Content-type, which specifies the content type of the response's message body.

APPENDIX C
MULTIPURPOSE INTERNET MAIL EXTENSIONS (MIME)

Similarly, Gopher servers provide information concerning message content FILL (message data type in a Gopher framework). However, when local files are accessed or an FTP transaction occurs, no information concerning the type of information being accessed is available. Therefore, the client must determine type and present the information in an appropriate manner. The mechanism used by most browsing software is to determine the type based upon the filename extension of the object accessed. Table C-1 provides a list of the most commonly used MIME types with respect to World Wide Web transactions. With respect to the types specified in Table C-2, specific configuration instructions for browsers to support these types are provided in the referenced How-To's. For example, the multipart/x-mixed-replace type is currently only supported by the Netscape browser and requires no additional configuration, whereas the x-httpd-cgi type requires a modification of the server's configuration files.

Browsers usually maintain a database of file extensions and their associated MIME types. This database is accessed by the client whenever a file needs to be resolved into a type prior to being displayed to the user. This information can usually be modified and extended by the user through configuration control. For example, to modify the MIME database in MacWeb, you modify part of the program resource fork accessible via a pull-down menu in the application. On the other hand, modification of the database for X-Windows Mosaic involves editing the mime.types file.

MIME and the Web Server

Servers also base content type determination on file type extensions. When a client makes a request, the server determines the Content-type field to use in the response header based on the filename extension of the file. Thus, files on the server with a .tif extension generate a Content-type:image/tiff field in the response header. Similarly, files with the .htm extension are sent with a Content-type: text/html in the server's response header.

Additional extensions can be identified to map to the same content type. For example, both the .htm and .html extensions may signify an HTML document; this is particularly true of PC servers that are limited to three-character file extensions. Whenever additional extensions or new types need to be added to the server, the MIME types database for the server needs to be updated. For the NCSA HTTPD server, this database is contained in the mime.types file in the conf subdirectory.

If the server cannot resolve a filename extension to a type, or if the requested file does not have a filename extension, the server sends a default type in the response header. Many servers use text/plain as a default type; however, depending on the server, this default type might be configurable. For example, the DefaultType directive in the server resource map file will set this default type for an NCSA HTTPD server.

UNIX QUICK REFERENCE

Even though you may be creating your documents on a Windows or Macintosh system, you will find that many apsects of HTML, such as directory paths in URLs, are borrowed directly from UNIX. Despite its reputation as a user-unfriendly operating system, basic UNIX commands can be easily learned and used. In fact, if you have used DOS on a PC before, you will find UNIX very similar (but with some differences). Here's a brief list of UNIX commands that may be of use to you.

Changing Directories

To change from the current directory to a subdirectory, type

`cd directoryname`

To change from the current directory to a subdirectory several levels down, type

`cd directoryname1/directoryname2/directoryname3`

(Note that UNIX uses forward slashes to separate directory names, unlike DOS, which uses backslashes.)

To change from the current directory to the parent directory (one level up), type

`cd ..`

To change from the current directory to a directory several levels up, type

`cd ../../..`

To change to a directory that branches off from a common parent directory, type

`cd ../directoryname`

APPENDIX D
UNIX QUICK REFERENCE

To go to your home directory, regardless of your current location, type

`cd`

Listing the Contents of a Directory

To list the contents of a directory, simply type

`ls`

To display a long listing, including the filename, size, date created or modified, and owner, type

`ls -l`

To list all files, including hidden files (whose filenames begin with a period), type

`ls -a`

To place symbols beside specific names (a / after directory names, * after executable files), type

`ls -F`

Moving and Deleting Files and Changing Filenames

To change the name of a file from file1 to file2, type

`mv file1 file2`

To move file1 to a subdirectory, type

`mv file1 directoryname/file1`

To move file1 to a parent directory, type

`mv file1 ../file1`

To move a group of files that begin with the name file to a subdirectory, type

`mv file* directoryname/.`

To delete a file named file1, type

`rm file1`

To delete the entire contents of a directory, type

`rm *`

(Use this command with care. Once you delete a file, it's gone for good.)

Creating and Removing Directories

To create a subdirectory in the current directory, type

```
mkdir directoryname
```

To remove an empty subdirectory from the current directory, type

```
rmdir directoryname
```

To remove a subdirectory and all the files and directories contained within it, type

```
rm -r directoryname
```

Setting File and Directory Permissions

To change the permissions on a file to allow or prevent others from accessing it, type

```
chmod nnn filename
```

To change the permissions on all files in a directory to allow or prevent others from accessing them, type

```
chmod nnn directoryname
```

where *nnn* are three digits that define how a file or directory can be accessed by various users; the first digit represents the user, the second digit the user's group (a subset of users on the computer system), and the third digit all users on a system. The various number values the digits usually take are

- 0 No access
- 4 Read-only access
- 5 Read and executable access
- 6 Read and write access
- 7 Read, write, and executable access

For example, to make a file readable, writable, and executable for yourself, but only readable and executable for other users, type

```
chmod 755 file1
```

Or to allow all users to read and write to a document, type

```
chmod 666 file2
```

HTML STYLE GUIDE

Suggestions for Do's and Don'ts

The Web is a wide open, freewheeling place. There are no set rules that govern what a person should or shouldn't do with his or her pages. Much of what appears on a page is left to a combination of the creator's individual style and the browser's predetermined set of standards. The following Do's and Don'ts are meant only as guidelines and suggestions for creating readable, nonfrustrating home pages.

Do's

The following Do's, while certainly not carved in stone, will help make your pages more readable. They are general enough to apply to almost any page.

- **HTML** Label your pages. With search utilities and Web crawlers, readers can find your pages in any number of ways. Help them locate your pages by using a label to identify each page.

- **HTML** List an author somewhere (preferably on the top or bottom) on your pages. Take credit for the work you put into your pages.

- **HTML** Use informative titles in <TITLE> tags. This allows users to easily jump to where they want to go in their "history list." This also makes it easy for users to add your pages to their hotlists.

- **HTML** Give readers an idea of how complete your pages are. It sometimes seems as if 90 percent of the Web is always under construction and the other 10 percent isn't working. It's a good idea to let readers know the current state of your pages. However, "under construction" should not be synonymous with "lots of stuff here doesn't work."

APPENDIX E
HTML STYLE GUIDE

- **HTML** Give an e-mail address where users may contact you if they have comments or problems.

- **HTML** Give warnings with any links that lead to explicit documents or images. Not everybody on the Web is as open-minded as you are.

- **HTML** Give warnings with any links that lead to large images or documents. It's a considerate touch to label links with the size of documents or images. This way, users have a general idea of how long it may take for the document to load.

- **HTML** A last-modified date is always good to have. It lets readers know how current your information is.

- **HTML** A creation date on your page, while not essential, is certainly a nice feature. It lets readers know how long you've been around.

- **HTML** If you include browser-specific tags (such as the Netscape enhancements) in your documents, add a statement to the document so that people who don't use the browser in question know why things look so strange.

- **HTML** Use the ALT attribute with the <IMG> tag so that people with nongraphical browsers can get an idea of what they could be seeing.

- **HTML** When possible, make image backgrounds transparent. They look cleaner and more professional that way.

- **HTML** Remember you are writing an electronic document, not a paper document. Things that look fine on paper, such as multiple columns, may not work so well on a scrollable document. The medium is different. It is up to you to figure out how you want to make the most out of that difference.

- **HTML** If you think your document is something people might be interested in printing and referring to later, make a nonhypertext copy available for people to print.

- **HTML** Try to use proper (or at least understandable) grammar and syntax. It will make your pages smoother to read. Try to have several people proofread your pages.

- **HTML** Before you do any actual encoding of your documents into HTML, outline your page's structure. Remember, learning HTML is easy. The hard part is designing your pages so that people can easily access the information you are providing.

APPENDIX E
HTML STYLE GUIDE

Don'ts (General)

The following is a list of suggestions of what to avoid on your Web pages. These are very general suggestions meant to work with any pages.

- **HTML** Don't use links to documents that don't exist. There is nothing more frustrating than the message

```
Error Code XXX file not found.
```

- **HTML** Don't insult your readers unless they have a pretty good idea when they come to your page that they could get insulted.

- **HTML** Don't copy images from somebody else's page unless you get their permission first.

- **HTML** Avoid anchoring links to words that are device dependent and don't really describe what the link leads to. For instance:

```
You may <A HREF="MANUAL.HTML">Click here</A> for users manual.
```

Instead try to use

```
A <A HREF="MANUAL.HTML">User's manual</A> is available.
```

- **HTML** Don't include trailing blanks or punctuation marks in tags. It doesn't look nice. For example:

```
Here is <A HREF="MYDOC.HTML">my document!</A>
```

Instead, this could be:

```
Here is <A HREF="MYDOC.HTML">my document</A>!
```

It is a simple change, but it looks much cleaner.

Don'ts (Conservative)

The following is a list of conservative don'ts. The authors don't usually follow these don'ts, but other more purist types do. They are presented so that you may decide if you wish to follow them or not.

- **HTML** Don't use browser-specific tags and elements. Using too many browser-specific tags makes a document nonreadable to somebody not using that browser. There are people out there who don't like the way Netscape incorporates tags into their browser that are either not supported by HTML 3 or are supported in a different manner.

- **HTML** Don't use more than one or two horizontal rules per page.

- **HTML** Don't use graphic lines (colored or horizontal lines with pictures in them); they needlessly slow down the server.

APPENDIX E
HTML STYLE GUIDE

HTML Don't use heading levels out of order. In other words, don't do something like the following:

```
<HTML>
<HEAD><TITLE>Bad example?</TITLE></HEAD>
<BODY>
<H4>Going!</H4>
<H2>Going!!</H4>
<H1>Gone!</H1>
</BODY>
</HTML>
```

HTML Don't use a lot of bold or italics or exclamation marks. Italics seem to be especially hard to read with some browsers.

HTML Don't put a lot of WORDS IN CAPITALS. Usually there is no need to shout on the Web.

HTML Don't change the default colors of the text and links.

Making Your Page Shine

Follow these suggestions if you wish to make your pages more memorable.

HTML Use a distinct background.

HTML Start your page with a nice graphic logo.

HTML Center titles.

HTML Don't be afraid to use icons or images to make your page more readable and more pleasing to the eye. Even if you are not an artist, there are plenty of sites around that offer icons to be downloaded. Since these sites change often, it's best to search for icons or consult a big index such as Yahoo or the Whole Internet Catalog.

HTML Take time to plan the navigational aids you use in your pages. It's a good idea to include a navigational marker at the top or bottom of each page. The marker can contain the basic Next, Previous, Top of Server, and Home Page links.

HTML Plan and structure your links. Ideally, you want to set up your documents so that readers have numerous ways of finding information, but you want to avoid cluttering your pages with excess or redundant links. It takes practice, common sense, and experimentation to work out the optimal blend of information and links to that information.

SUMMARY OF SELECTED SERVER SOFTWARE

Provided below are brief descriptions of some of the HTTP servers available. Each of these descriptions concludes with a reference to a URL where additional and up-to-date information can be found.

The servers listed below are those most commonly used; however, if none of these is suitable, examine URL http://www.w3.org/hypertext/WWW/Servers.html for an up-to-date list of available server software.

UNIX

This platform has the greatest variety of servers available. Since the original HTTP servers were developed on this platform, most new developments and enhancements appear first on UNIX servers. Several popular UNIX servers are described below.

CERN HTTP Server

One of the best features of this server is its ability to act as a proxy server, allowing you to run a server and access outside servers through an Internet firewall. Further, this software is fully CGI/1.1 compliant and comes packaged with a variety of gateway applications, including active image support. This server supports "head", "get", "post", and "put" client requests. For information as well as the software itself, use this URL

http://www.w3.org/hypertext/WWW/Daemon/Status.html

APPENDIX F
SUMMARY OF SELECTED SERVER SOFTWARE

GN
This freeware server software provides both HTTP and Gopher service. Use is restricted per the standard GNU license (http://hopf.math.nwu.edu/docs/Gnu_License). Security is handled through domain or IP address restrictions on a per-directory basis, or over the entire server. However, user authentication is not supported. Unlike most other servers, the default is to deny access to information unless explicit permission is given. Installation and configuration of this server is similar in many ways to creating a standard Gopher server; therefore, those familiar with Gopher should have an easier time installing this package. The server supports "get", "head", and "post" requests. Further information on this server is available at URL

http://hopf.math.nwu.edu:70/

NCSA HTTPD
This application, available freely from the National Center for Supercomputing Applications, supports "get", "head", and "post" HTTP requests. Security is provided for host filtering through specification of domains or IP addresses; in addition, password security is supported. These measures provide access protection at the directory level. Server side includes and directives are supported via a parsed HTML type that is processed by the server prior to transmission to a browser. (See How-To 12.4 for additional information on server side includes and directives.) This software and relevant information can be found at URL

http://hoohoo.ncsa.uiuc.edu/docs/Overview.html

Netscape Servers
The Netscape Communications Corporation markets two server packages: the Communications Server and the Commerce Server. The primary difference between these two applications is the level of security capabilities provided by the Commerce Server. Both servers support the basic authentication and directory level domain and address restrictions, but the Commerce Server supports more extensive security measures. These servers are fully CGI/1.1 compliant, and they support a variety of package-specific components. Both applications support "get", "head", and "post" requests. Information is available at URL

http://home.netscape.com/

WN
This is another freeware HTTP server application distributed under the GNU license (http://hopf.math.nwu.edu/docs/Gnu_License). It provides a variety of cutting-edge features that are both useful and experimental. WN provides security features that include IP address and domain restrictions, user authentication

APPENDIX F
SUMMARY OF SELECTED SERVER SOFTWARE

support by password, and an experimental digest authentication process. Like GN, the default access to documents is to deny access. This package is fully CGI/1.1 compliant and also includes a full suite of built-in search capabilities. Server side includes are supported, as well as conditional server includes. "Get", "head", and "post" requests are currently supported. Further information can be found at URL

http://hopf.math.nwu.edu

VMS

Currently, only two servers have been developed for the VMS platform. The first of these is a port of the CERN HTTP server. The second was developed for the VMS platform; thus, this server is reputedly better adapted to the VMS environment.

CERN HTTP Server

This is a port of the popular UNIX server. The features are identical to the original package. This server software can be found at the URL

http://delonline.cern.ch/delphi$www/public/vms/distribution.html

DECthread HTTP Server

As a native VMS server, this software is reputed to better exploit the features of the VMS operating system than the CERN server. The DECthread server was developed using the DECthreads model, which should lead to significantly faster access than the CERN server, particularly when multiple simultaneous requests are made. This server is CGI compliant and comes equipped with a variety of useful gateway applications. Finally, the server supports "get" and "head" requests. Information and software can be found at the URL

http://kcgl1.eng.ohio-state.edu/www/doc/serverinfo.html

Windows NT

Several server software options are available for this platform. They support a large variety of standard features while being in an environment comfortable for Windows NT users. Two of these servers are described below.

HTTPS

This server supports "get", "head", and "post" client requests. It is CGI compliant; however, it does not support either access control or user authentication security. Additional information about this product is available at URL

http://emwac.ed.ac.uk/html/internet_toolchest/https/CONTENTS.HTM

APPENDIX F
SUMMARY OF SELECTED SERVER SOFTWARE

Website

The Website server is a commercial package developed by the O'Reilly and Associates publishing firm. The package runs on both the Windows NT and Windows 95 platforms. The basis for this application is the WinHTTP server developed for the Windows 3.1 platform. Website is CGI compliant and supports "get", "head", and "post" requests. Beyond standard CGI, it has some additional capabilities to run Windows applications such as Excel and Visual Basic within HTML documents. For security, both basic authentication, and IP address and domain restrictions are supported. The following specifies the minimum running requirements for this application.

- **HTML** 80386 or higher processor
- **HTML** VGA or better display
- **HTML** 3.5" disk drive
- **HTML** 12+ MB RAM (16 MB suggested)
- **HTML** at least 5MB of free hard disk space
- **HTML** Windows NT 3.5 with TCP/IP connectivity

Additional information and ordering information is available through the URL

http://clubweb.ora.com/

OS/2

Several server packages have been developed for OS/2. This section describes two of them, GoServe and HTTPD. URLs specifying up-to-date information are provided at the end of each description. For more information on OS/2 server options, use URL

http://w3.ag.uiuc.edu/DLM/HTTPDforOS2.html

GoServe

The GoServe package supports both HTTP and Gopher protocols. This product is distributed freely under the IBM OS/2 Employee Written Software program and subject to the IBM license (http://ww2.hursley.ibm.com/goserve/license.txt) agreement for OS/2 Tools. The server supports HTTP/1.0, including "get", "head", and "post" requests. Further, CGI standards for gateway applications are included. Security is provided by the Basic authentication package. Directory access security is provided by domain and address restrictions. Additional information concerning this package can be found at URL

http://www2.hursley.ibm.com/goserve

APPENDIX F
SUMMARY OF SELECTED SERVER SOFTWARE

OS2HTTPD

This port of the NCSA HTTPD server to the OS/2 platform supports many of the original's features with the exception of access control and user authentication. For further information on this product, see URL

ftp://ftp.netcom.com/pub/kf/kfan/overview.html

Macintosh

Currently, the only HTTP server available for Macintosh users is the MacHTTP server, also now known as WebSTAR. A description of this server appears below.

MacHTTP (WebSTAR)

This server will run on a Macintosh running the System 7 operating system. MacTCP is also required. MacHTTP will service "get", "head", and "post" requests. It also supports a number of built-in search capabilities; however, use of these features require that AppleScript be installed. This server is CGI compliant and loads AppleScript, MacPerl, HyperCard, or custom applications developed with its own set of AppleEvents.

MacHTTP supports several security features. Access control can be limited on a domain or machine basis by restricting access to particular IP addresses or domain specifications. In addition, folder and document level security can be established through username and password access control.

This server is available as shareware. You can find registration information and download an evaluation copy from the following URL.

http://www.biap.com/machttp/machttp_software.html

Windows 3.1

Several server packages have been developed for the Windows and Windows for Workgroups environments. These servers are fairly full featured; however, they suffer from a lack of true multitasking and task separation. The WinHTTPD server package is briefly described below.

WinHTTPD

This port of the NCSA HTTPD UNIX server to the Windows environment retains many of the features supported by its UNIX parent. The server supports "get", "head", and "post" method requests, CGI 1.1 compliance, directory level access control via domain restriction and the Basic authentication package, and automatic directory indexing. For commercial use, this package requires a registration fee. Further information, restrictions, and the software itself are available at URL

http://www.city.net/win-httpd

THE HYPERTEXT TRANSFER PROTOCOL (HTTP)

The HyperText Transfer Protocol (HTTP) was developed as the standard exchange protocol for use with the World Wide Web. This is the language that is spoken between Web clients and Web servers.

Client/server communication can be viewed as a telephone conversation between two individuals. However, the vocabulary and grammar of the conversation are restricted to the HTTP language. The conversation is started by a client (a Web browser) dialing the exchange of the desired server. When the server picks up the connection, the client starts the conversation by making a request, stating its requirements and a description of itself. The server responds with an answer to the request, followed by a description of itself and of the results of the request. At this point, the conversation ends, and the phone receiver is placed back on the hook.

These conversations are very structured. Each party only speaks once in a particular conversation involving a single request and a single response. What this means in a Web sense is that if you attempt to load an HTML 3.0 document with four inline images, your client will have to hold five discrete conversations to load the entire document; one to request the base document followed by four more to retrieve the images.

Further, clients and servers have exceedingly limited memories of previous conversations. Thus, if you have entered information in an HTML 3.0 form, this data is passed to the appropriate gateway application (see Chapter 13); however, the server simply acts as a translator passing on the information. It does not keep a copy of this information. Therefore, many gateway applications encode this

APPENDIX G
THE HYPERTEXT TRANSFER PROTOCOL (HTTP)

information back into the documents that they generate as hidden input fields. If they did not, the same information would need to be requested at several levels of nested HTML 3.0 forms.

Each conversation between a client and a server is composed of four parts:

- **HTML** Open connection
- **HTML** Request
- **HTML** Response
- **HTML** Close connection

This HTTP communications process is shown in Figure G-1 and explained in detail below.

Open Connection

The first stage of HTTP communications involves the client requesting a connection to a particular server. If a port number is given, the client will attempt to

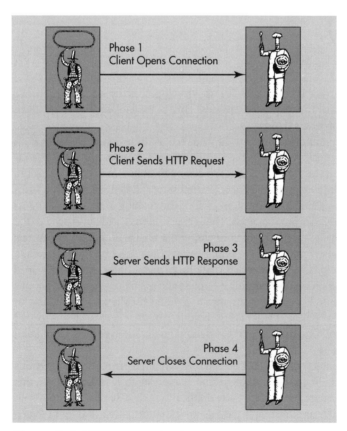

Figure G-1 HTTP communication process

APPENDIX G
THE HYPERTEXT TRANSFER PROTOCOL (HTTP)

connect to that port; otherwise, the default port number 80 is used for the connection. For example, if you requested that a server open the URL list in the code below, the client attempts to establish a connection with the www.mysite.edu machine at port 8080.

```
http://www.mysite.edu:8080/new/index.htm
```

HTTP Request

Once a connection has been established, the client sends an HTTP request. An HTTP request is a composed of two parts: the request header and the request body.

The request header also contains two components. The first line of the header contains the method field. In the case of the example in this appendix, a simple "get" method request would be generated. The method field that might be associated with this request appears as follows:

```
GET /new/index.htm HTTP/1.0
```

The remainder of the header is a series of attributes describing the client and its capabilities to the server. For example, the following might be the remainder of the request header sent for retrieving the document in this appendix.

```
Accept: text/plain
Accept: text/html
...
Accept: */*
User Agent: Mozilla/1.1N (X11; I; SunOS 4.1.3_U1 sun4m)
```

The request header ends with a blank line. The remainder of the request is the request body.

The body of a request is often empty; when it is not, it is most frequently used to send an encrypted actual request, send input data via a "post" method request, or to provide the information entity for a "put" method request. The header and body are separated by a blank line. This blank line must be included even if a request body is empty. The blank line is a signal to the server that the request header component is ended.

The first line of the request header is the method line. This line follows the format specified below:

```
Method      Identifier      Version
```

The method is the HTTP method that the client wishes to use; Table G-1 presents several commonly used methods. (For a comprehensive list of methods, you may wish to examine http://www.w3.org/hypertext/WWW/Protocols/HTTP1.0/HTTP1.0-ID_22.html#HEADING27 or a speculative listing of methods in http://www.w3.org/hypertex/WWW/Protocols/HTTP/Methods.html.) The identifier is the path to the information to use with the specified method. The

623

version field states the protocol and version of the protocol being used, most often HTTP/1.0.

METHOD	EXPLANATION
"get"	Retrieves the information entitiy specified by the identifier
"head"	Retrieves the header information concerning the information entity specified by the identifier
"put"	Places the information contained in the request body at the location specified by the identifier
"post"	Passes the information contained in the request body to the entity specified by the identifier and returns the results

Table G-1 Commonly used HTTP/1.0 requests

The method line is followed by a series of attributes supplied by the client that the server may use as desired. Table G-2 presents a description of several commonly used HTTP/1.0 attributes. (For more information about additional attributes you may wish to reference URL http://www.w3.org/hypertext/WWW/Protocols/HTTP1.0/HTTP1.0-ID_24.html#HEADING36 or http://www.w3.org/hypertext/WWW/Protocols/HTTP/HTRQ_Headers.html.)

ATTRIBUTE	EXPLANATION
Accept: type/subtype	Describes the MIME types of the documents supported by the client making the request.
	Each such MIME type should be declared in an Accept element.
	The asterisk (*) may be used as a wildcard.
Content-length: number	The number of bytes contained in the request body.
Content-type: MIME	Specifies the MIME type of file contained in the request body.
UserAgent: string	Tells the server the specific type of client making the request.

Table G-2 Commonly used HTTP/1.0 request header directives

HTTP Response

The server follows up a request with a suitable response. The response also contains two parts: a header and a body.

As in a request, the response header has two components. The first line of the response header is the status line. The status line includes the HTTP version, a status code, and a status message.

The status line has the following format:

```
Version      StatusCode      StatusMessage
```

The version represents the version of HTTP used for the communication (usually HTTP/1.0). The status code and status message inform the client of the results of a request. A complete listing of standard status codes and messages is

APPENDIX G
THE HYPERTEXT TRANSFER PROTOCOL (HTTP)

provided at URL http://www.w3.org/Protocols/HTTP1.0/HTTP1.0-ID_27.HTML#HEADING49; however, some of the more commonly used status codes and messages are presented in Table G-3. The status codes are three-digit numbers that can be categorized in terms of the first digit of the code.

- **HTML** If the first digit is a 1, the result is informational.
- **HTML** If the first digit is a 2, the request was understood and successfully completed.
- **HTML** If the first digit is a 3, additional actions are required to complete the request.
- **HTML** If the first digit is a 4, an error was found in the client's request.
- **HTML** If the first digit is a 5, the client sent a valid request; however, the server was unable to fulfill the request.

CODE	MESSAGE
200	Completed successfully.
201	Created. Server side resource created through either "put" or "post" request.
202	Request has been queued, but results unknown.
203	Completed, but all information was not returned.
204	No Content. No new information available. Client should not alter current document.
301	Moved Permanently. Requested information moved to another location.
302	Request completed, but desired data is at another location.
304	Not Modified. Document that was requested conditionally based upon modification date has not been modified. Client should not alter current document.
400	Syntax error in request.
403	Forbidden. Authorization to access requested information not allowed.
404	Not Found. Information requested was not found at the location specified.
500	Internal Server Error. The server encountered a problem and was unable to service the request.
501	Server does not support requested method.

Table G-3 Commonly used HTTP/1.0 status codes and messages

So for the retrieval started in the example, the following status line might be generated.

```
HTTP/1.0 200 OK
```

The status line is followed by a series of attributes describing both the document being retrieved as well as the server providing the document.

Table G-4 displays many of the commonly used response header attributes. A complete specification of the HTTP response headers for HTTP/1.0 can be found at

APPENDIX G
THE HYPERTEXT TRANSFER PROTOCOL (HTTP)

URL http://www.w3.org/Protocols/HTTP1.0/HTTP1.0-ID_28.html#HEADING80; other potential headers are described in URL http://www.w3.org/Protocols/HTTP/Object_Headers.html.

ATTRIBUTE	EXPLANATION
Public: methods	Describes the nonstandard methods that this server supports
Content-length: number	The number of bytes contained in the response body
Content-type: MIME	Specifies the MIME type of the information entity contained in the response body
Date: date	The date and time the request was serviced
Title: string	The title of the document that was requested
Server: string	Tells the client the specific type of server responding
WWW-Link: links	Provides the client with information from the <LINK> element of the HTML 3.0 document retrieved

 Table G-4 Commonly used HTTP/1.0 response header directives

A sample set of attributes appears below.

```
Date: Sunday, 17-Dec-1995 11:30:00 GMT
Server: NCSA/1.4.1
MIME-version: 1.0
Content-type: text/html
Last-modified: 16-Jun-1995 10:35:39 GMT
Content-length: 247
```

The response header ends with a blank line.

The remainder of the response is the body. This contains the actual data being transferred. This could be an HTML 3.0 document, a GIF image, or any other document type supported by the server.

Close Connection

The conversation is complete, and the connection between the server and the client is closed.

The HTTP standard, like the HTML standard, is continuing to develop. The HTTP-NG standard is currently under consideration. The proposed new standard would support many additional features and request types. If you are interested in the progress of HTTP-NG, you should examine the information at URL http://www.w3.org/hypertext/WWW/Protocols/Overview.html.

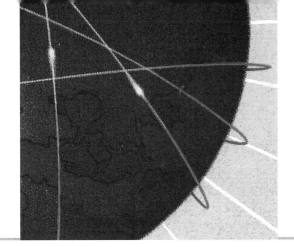

INDEX

" symbol, 68, 71
symbol, 68, 73
    comment prefix, 361, 403
    number prefix, 355
    in URLs, 215-216
%20 in URLs, 219
& prefix, 67-73
../ in URL, 204, 210
/ and HTML tags, 30, 33
// in URL, 201
3D modeling (VRML), 553-562
; semicolon terminator, 68, 73
< > HTML tags. *See* tags
< > symbols, 71
    for HTML tags, 30, 33, 54
    printing, 173
? in URLs, 214, 222
@ in URLs, 221
^ for math superscript, 137
_ for math subscript, 137
{ } for math fractions, 137-138
~ tilde in URLs, 225-226

A

abbreviation, 113-114, 578
access control, 357, 362-365, 466-468
    See also security
access file directives. *See* security directives

acronym, 113-114, 578
ACTION attribute, 310-311, 328, 330, 446, 449-450
address, 200-202. *See also* URLs
AIFF audio format, 291-292, 294-295
alias, server directory, 349-350, 357-359
ALIGN attribute
    array, 139
    headings, 97
    image, 246-249, 265-266
    paragraph, 125, 267
    tab, 74-76
    table, 141, 146, 149, 151, 154
alignment
    decimal, 146, 149, 151
    image and text, 246-249, 265-267
    images, 125
    text, 125
    vertical, 147, 149, 151
ALT attribute, 249-251, 540
America Online, 7-8
ampersand prefix, 67-73
anchors, 16, 50
    data sending, 213
    e-mail, 224
    Gopher, 219
    hypermedia, 276-277, 279, 286, 288, 292, 298, 301
    image, 258-259

627

anchors *(continued)*
   imagemap, 260-262
   newsgroup, 223
   pages, 209, 211, 215-216, 225, 231-232
   Telnet, 220
   WAIS, 222
animation. *See* video
archived software, 44-45, 49, 52, 283, 295, 348-349, 351
Arena browser, 12, 529, 532, 590
arguments style, 112-113
array, 139
asterisks, for password, 322-323
attribute/value pairs, 54, 63-64, 444, 449, 451, 475, 479-485
attributes
   ACTION, 310-311, 328, 330, 446, 449-450
   ALIGN
      applet, 540
      array, 139
      headings, 97
      image, 246-249, 265-266, 506
      marquee, 504
      paragraph, 125, 267
      tab, 74-76
      table, 141, 146, 149, 151, 154
   ALT, 249-251, 540
   BACKGROUND, 65, 263-264
   BEHAVIOR, 503
   BGCOLOR, 504
   BLANK, 174-176, 190
   BORDER, 141, 143, 153
   CHECKED, 317, 320
   CLASS, 65
   CLEAR, 265-267
   CODE, 539
   CODEBASE, 539
   COLDEF, 139
   COLOR, 508-509
   COLS, 314, 316, 511
   COLSPAN, 146-147, 149-150, 154, 156-157
   COLSPEC, 142-143, 151-152, 154
   COMPACT, 166, 169, 171-172, 182
   CONTENT, 373-374
   CONTINUE, 166, 169
   CONTROLS, 507
   COORD, 518
   DIRECTION, 503
   DP, 75-76, 146, 149
   DYNSRC, 506-507

attributes *(continued)*
   ENCTYPE, 310-311
   HEIGHT, 504, 539
   HREF
      anchor, 209, 211-213, 215, 217, 219-220, 222-224, 226
      links, 207, 258-262
      URLs, 205, 518
   HSPACE, 505, 540
   HTTP-EQUIV, 373-374, 376
   ID, 64, 74-76
   INDENT, 74-76
   ISMAP, 260, 262
   LANG, 64, 108-109
   LANGUAGE, 543, 549
   LOOP, 501-502, 504, 507
   LOOPDELAY, 507
   MARGINHEIGHT, 512
   MARGINWIDTH, 512
   METHOD, 310-311, 327-328, 450
   NAME
      anchor, 215
      applet, 540-541
      frame, 511
      input, 311-312, 317-318, 320-323, 326
      map, 518
      select, 324-325
      textarea, 314-315
   NORESIZE, 512
   NOWRAP, 98-99
   REL, 207
   REV, 207
   ROWS, 314, 316, 511
   ROWSPAN, 146-147, 149-150, 154, 157
   SCROLLAMOUNT, 503-504
   SCROLLDELAY, 503-504, 506
   SCROLLING, 512
   SEQNUM, 167, 169
   SHAPE, 229-230, 517-518
   SIZE, 79-80, 311-312, 322, 508-509
   SRC
      frame, 511-516
      image, 97, 244-248, 250-251, 258, 260-262, 265-267
      list, 169, 171-172
      script, 543
      sound, 501-502
   START, 167, 169, 507
   TARGET, 520-521
   TITLE, 531

attributes *(continued)*
    TO, 74-76
    TYPE, 168, 311-312, 316-319, 321-323, 326
    UNITS, 142-143
    USEMAP, 519
    VALIGN, 147, 149, 151
    VALUE, 167, 169, 311-312, 317, 320, 322, 326, 541
    VSPACE, 505, 540
    WIDTH, 142-143, 504, 539
    WRAP, 176-177
    See also tags
audio
    converters, 295
    editing, 296
    formats, 291-293
        AIFF, 291-292, 294-295
        AU, 291, 294-295, 502
        conversion, 294-296
        IFF, 291-292
        MID (MIDI), 502
        MPEG, 291-292
        WAV, 291-292, 294-295, 502
    players, 293-294
    Web page sound, 500-502
authentication. *See* user authentication
author, 207-208
author names, 114-115, 578
authoring tool, 17-19
AVI video, 289-290, 506-508

B

back end, 308
BACKGROUND attribute, 65, 263-264
background pattern, 263-264
background style, 527
background, transparent, 251-254
biographical data, 82, 84-85
BLANK attribute, 174-176, 190
body content, 132
bold text, 56-57, 99-100, 117, 578
BORDER attribute, 141, 143, 153
Bourne shell script, 455-457, 459-462, 469-472, 474-477
braces for fractions, 137-138
breaks, line, 75, 98, 124-126, 132, 173, 188, 265-267, 579
breaks, paragraph, 76-77, 124-126, 132, 267, 315, 579

browser authentication, 382
    See user authentication
browsers, 11-15, 589-592, 598
    and comments, 62
    HTML document recognition, 33-36
    HTML document testing, 41, 48, 50, 85-90
    and proxy server, 426-427
    text, <ALT> for image, 249-251
bullets, 97, 99, 170-172, 174-175, 179-180, 186, 190

C

caching, proxy server, 421-422, 424-426
caption, list, 166, 171, 183
carriage returns, 64-65, 127-128
cells
    alignment, 146, 149, 151-152, 154
    data, 148-150
    heading, 145-147
    row, 150-154
CGI (Common Gateway Interface), 260, 262, 345, 441-442, 597-598
CGI applications, 361-363
    creating, 459-463
    data access, 474-477
    data parse/restore, 477-485
    data passing from, 454-459, 621-622
    data passing to, 443-453, 621-622
    e-mail package, 489-493
    and forms, 309, 311, 313, 321, 326-336
    installing, 463-468
    query document, 468-473
    Server Push, 485-489
character references, 67-73
character sample, 111-112, 117
character set, 67-73
character styles
    content, 94, 105-118
    physical, 94, 99-105, 116-118
characters, special, 451-452, 478-480, 483, 485
check box, 316-319
CHECKED attribute, 317, 320
citation style, 107-108, 578
CLASS attribute, 65
CLEAR attribute, 265-267
click here syndrome, 232
Client Pull, 373-377
client/server communication, 621-626
code, 204, 459, 625

INDEX

code style, 109-110, 117, 578
COLDEF attribute, 139
color, background, 263-264
color style, 526-527
colors, number of, 242, 252, 264
colors, transparent, 252
COLS attribute, 314, 316, 511
COLSPAN attribute, 146-147, 149-150, 154, 156-157
COLSPEC attribute, 142-143, 151-152, 154
column alignment, 139, 146, 149, 151-152, 154
column headings, 145-147, 153
column size, 142
columns, list, 175-177
columns, textarea, 314
command line arguments, 444-445, 447-448, 474
command line interface, 88-89
commands style, 112-113
comments, # prefix, 361, 403
comments, HTML tag, 58-62
COMPACT attribute, 166, 169, 171-172, 182
compressed software, 44-45, 49, 52, 283, 295, 348-349, 351
configuration, server, 353-359, 370-371
contact information, 82-85
CONTENT attribute, 373-374
Content-length, 624, 626
CONTENT_LENGTH, 451, 453, 477
Content-type field, 360, 455-457, 460, 470, 473, 486-487, 602-606, 624, 626
CONTENT_TYPE variable, 453, 477
CONTINUE attribute, 166, 169
conversion
 audio formats, 294-296
 image formats, 282-285
 video formats, 289-291
converters, 18, 45, 48-54
copyright laws, 366
creation date, 85, 612

D

data access, CGI, 474-477
data cells, 148-150, 154
data parse/restore, CGI, 477-485
data passing from CGI, 454-459
data passing to CGI, 443-453
data tree, 350-352, 356, 358, 364, 366

database search, 222
date conventions, 84
decimal alignment, 146, 149, 151
default page, 212-213
defined term style, 110-111, 578
deletions, 115-116, 578
device independent files, 300-303
directives
 Accept-type, 624
 AccessConfig, 385, 392, 396, 402
 AccessFileName, 385, 392, 396, 403, 466
 ACLOverRide On, 418-419
 AddDescription, 386
 AddEncoding, 386-387
 AddIcon, 387
 AddType, 387-388, 403-404, 467
 allow, 392-393
 ALLOW, 428, 430-431
 AllowOverride, 388
 AuthGroupFile, 397, 400
 AuthName, 397, 400
 AuthType, 397, 400, 409, 411, 415
 AuthUserFile, 397, 401
 CacheRoot, 422, 424
 CacheSize, 425
 CacheUnused, 425
 Caching, 424
 configuration, 353-359
 Content-length, 624, 626
 Content-type, 455-457, 460, 470, 473, 486, 602-606, 624, 626
 DefaultIcon, 388
 DefaultType, 389
 DefProt, 412, 417, 420
 deny, 392-394
 DENY, 428, 430-431
 <Directory>, 385-386, 389, 392, 396, 402
 Disable, 422
 Enable, 421-422
 GroupFile, 409, 411, 415
 GroupId, 409, 415
 IndexIgnore, 389-390
 <Limit>, 391-394, 397-398, 401
 Location, 455, 457-458, 473
 Map, 421
 mask commands, 409-412, 415-416, 422
 Options, 390, 403-404, 407, 466
 order, 393
 Pass, 421, 424

INDEX

directives (*continued*)
    PasswordFile, 409, 411, 415
    Protect, 412-413, 416, 420, 422, 424
    ReadmeName, 390
    REALM, 428-429, 431
    request header, 624
    require, 394, 398, 401
    response header, 626
    ScriptAlias, 464
    ServerId, 409, 411, 415
    Status, 455-458, 473
    UserAgent, 624
    UserId, 409, 415
directory list, 179-181, 188
document
    installing, 363-366
    looping, 373-377
    Refresh, 373-377
    style, 611-614
    types, 357, 360-363
domain restrictions, 382. *See* host filtering
DP attribute, 75-76, 146, 149
DVI files, 300-303

E

e-mail, 201, 224-225, 489-493
echo command, 405
editing environments, 42-48, 57-58
electronic mail, 201, 224-225, 489-493
elements
    described, 30, 33, 38, 54
    inserting, 54-58
    See also tags
emphasis, 99-101, 105-107, 117, 509, 578-579
en units, 142-143
encoding, 386-387
encryption, 432-437
ENCTYPE attribute, 310-311
entity references, 67-73
environment variables, 443-446, 448-451, 453, 475-477
EOF command, 461, 470-471
equation symbols, 136-140
escaped characters, 451-452, 478-480, 483, 485
event handlers, JavaScript, 545-547
exec command, 390, 404-405, 407, 465

F

file size
    audio, 292-293
    images, 279-282
    PostScript, 297
    video, 286-287
finger utility, 469, 473, 487-488
firewall system, 420-427
font
    color, 508-509
    fixed-width, 102-103, 117, 127-128, 578
    size, 78-82, 508-509
    style, 525-526, 560, 578
footer content, 132
footer, and line, 122, 131
footnote, 579
formatting languages, 51-53
forms
    check box, 316-319
    creating, 309-313
    data exchange, 326-327
    hidden fields, 326-327
    password field, 321-323
    post_form, 331, 335
    processing, 329-336
    pulldown menus, 323-325
    radio buttons, 319-321
    request method, 309-311, 327-329
    resources, 598
    send_form, 331, 335
    send to HTTP server, 327-329
    tags, 584-586
    text box, 313-316
fractions, 137-138
frames, 510-517
front end, 308, 313
FTP (File Transfer Protocol), 201, 216-218
FTP, anonymous, 216-218, 282-283, 289, 295, 346

G

gateway applications. *See* CGI
get method, 309-311, 327-329, 445, 447-451, 453, 474, 479-480, 604, 623
GIF (Graphic Interchange Format), 241-243, 248, 251, 267

GIF *(continued)*
  converters, 243, 254-255
  GIF format, 280, 283-284
  GIF89a format, 251-252
  imagemap, 260-262
  interlaced, 254-255
  transparent, 251-254
GIFCONVERTER, 243, 254-255
GIFTOOL, 242-243, 252, 254-255
glossary list, 181-184, 190, 234
GMT (Greenwich Mean Time), 456
Gopher, 201, 218-220
GraphicConverter, 242, 252, 254, 257
graphics
  and page design, 23
  See also images

H

hardware, and servers, 344-345
header
  nonparsed, 454, 456-459, 470
  parsed, 454-458
  request, 623-624
  response. *See* response header
headings
  column, 145-147, 153
  list, 166, 171, 183
  styles, 97-99, 578
  table, 145-147, 153
  use of, 132
home directory, 364-366
home page. *See* page
horizontal rule, 122-124, 130-132, 253-254, 310
host filtering, 391-394, 408, 414-416, 418, 422-425, 428-429
hot spots, 260-263
HotJava, 537-539, 542
HREF attribute
  anchor, 209, 211-213, 215, 217, 219-220, 222-224, 226
  links, 207, 258-262
  URLs, 205, 518
.htm/.html extension, 33, 35-38, 83-84, 88-90, 606
HTML (HyperText Markup Language), 20-21, 29
HTML document
  body text, 62-66
  comments, 58-62

HTML document *(continued)*
  creating, 36-48
  file conversion to, 48-54
  fine tuning, 50, 53
  font size, 78-82
  home page, 82-90
  opening, 88-90
  recognizing, 32-36
  resources, 594-597
  special characters, 67-73
  tabs, 73-78
  tag insertion, 54-58
  text alignment, 73-78
  viewing, 87-90
HTML editors, 18, 594-596
HTML elements. *See* elements *and* tags
HTML extensions
  Internet Explorer
    <BGSOUND>, 500-502
    <IMG> video, 506-508
    <MARQUEE>, 502-506
  Netscape, 11, 14, 18, 21
    alignment, 73, 77, 265-267
    backgrounds, 263-264
    font, 78-80, 508-509
    frames, 510-516
    imagemaps, 517-520
    Java applet, 533-542
    JavaScript, 542-553
    lists, 167-169
    windows, 520-521
HTML style guide, 611-614
HTML style sheets, 522-532
HTML tags. *See* tags
HTTP (HyperText Transfer Protocol), 201, 211-213, 341, 621-626
HTTP communications, 621-626
HTTP-EQUIV attribute, 373-374, 376
HTTP-NG standard, 626
HTTP_ prefix, 453
HTTP request methods, 346-347, 623-624
  get, 309-311, 327-329, 445, 447-451, 453, 474, 479-480, 604, 624
  head, 624
  post, 309-311, 327-329, 446-447, 449-451, 474, 479-480, 604, 624
  put, 623-624
HTTP responses, 341-342, 624-626
  and CGI, 454-459, 462, 470, 486, 488

INDEX

HTTP responses *(continued)*
   and Content-type, 604-606
   document recognition, 36
   and <META>, 39, 376
HTTP servers, 615-619
   security, 345, 351, 355, 363
      CERN HTTP, 407-427
      HTTPD, 384-407
      MacHTTP, 420-427

I

icons, 292-293, 298, 301, 387-388
   creating, 241-244
   document type, 357
   thumbnail images, 256-257
ID attribute, 64, 74-76
IFF audio format, 291-292
imagemaps
   clickable, 260-263
   client side, 517-520
   links, 229-231
   resources, 598
images
   alignment, 246-249, 265-267
   background, 263-264
   clickable, 257, 260-263
   converters, 282-284
   external, 278-281
   formats, 242-243, 278, 280, 282-285
   in headings, 97
   hot spots, 260-263
   icons, 241-244
   inline, 244-246, 283-284
   interlaced, 254-255
   as links, 258-259
   size, 256-257, 279-282
   tags, 583-584
   thumbnail, 256-257, 281-282, 284, 287, 292
   transparent, 251-254
   viewers, 277, 281
   See also graphics
include command, 406
INDENT attribute, 74-76
indentation, 174, 183, 189
index resources, 588-589
indexing, and style tags, 112, 114-115, 117-118
indexing operator [], 483-484
INPUT_ prefix, 475
input, tags, 584-586

Inputs class, 483-484
insertions, 115-116, 579
interlacing, 254-255
Internet access, 8-11
Internet Explorer HTML extensions, 500-508
Internet service providers, 9-11
ISDN (Integrated Services Digital Network) line, 9-10
ISMAP attribute, 260, 262
ISPs. *See* Internet service providers
italics, 100-101, 117, 578

J

Java applet, 533-542
JavaScript, 542-553
JPEG format, 243, 280, 284

K

key word search, 213-214, 222
keyboard style, 112-113, 117, 579

L

LANG attribute, 64, 108-109
languages, 64
   quote marks, 108-109
layout style, 528
line break, 75, 98, 124-126, 132, 173, 188, 265-267, 579
line rule, 56, 122-124, 131-132, 253-254, 310, 579
line through text, 103-104, 117, 578
links, 15-17, 50, 53
   adding to page, 231-235
   to binary files, 210, 218
   click here, 232
   data sending, 213-214
   to DVI files, 300-303
   to e-mail, 224-225
   to external images, 278-281
   to FTP site, 216-218
   to Gopher site, 218-220
   to graphics, 210-212
   imagemap, 229-231
   to images, 210-212, 258-259
   to lists, 227-228
   to local page, 209-211
   to multimedia objects, 271-272, 274-278

links *(continued)*
    to other directories, 225-226
    to other pages, 211-213
    to page section, 214-216
    to PostScript files, 297-300
    problems with, 231-235
    to processed data, 272
    between resources, 206-208
    shape of, 229-231
    to sound files, 210-211, 291-294
    to tables, 227-228
    tags, 583
    to Telnet site, 220-221
    to text files, 210-212
    time delay, 373-377
    to Usenet newsgroup, 223-224
    to video files, 285-288
    to WAIS site, 221-223
    vague, 232-234
lists
    bulleted, 170-172, 174-176, 180, 186, 190
    directory, 179-181, 188
    glossary, 181-184, 190, 234
    headings, 166, 171, 183
    indenting, 174, 183, 189
    and links, 227-228, 234
    menu, 178-179, 187
    multicolumn, 175-177
    nested, 172, 184-193
    numbered, 165-169, 184-185, 190
    ordered, 165-169, 184-185, 190
    sublists, 184-192
    tags, 582
    unmarked, 173-175, 188-190
    unordered, 170-172, 174-175, 179-180, 186, 190
LiveScript (JavaScript), 542-553
Location directive, 455, 457-458, 473
LOOP attribute, 501-502, 504, 507
looping document, 373-377
Lynx browser, 12, 427, 589

M

Macintosh system, 345, 347
MacWeb, 12
mail, electronic, 201, 224-225, 489-493
mailing lists, 372
mailto URL, 201, 208, 224-225
MapEdit, 261

marquee (scrolling text), 502-506
math format tags, 580-581
math symbols, 136-140, 580-581
menu, links, 227-228
menu list, 178-179, 187
menu, pulldown, 323-325
metainformation, 38-39, 56-57
METHOD attribute, 310-311, 327-328, 450
MIME (Multipurpose Internet Mail
    Extensions) types, 601-606
        AddType, 387
        audio types, 296
        default type, 357, 389
        encryption, 437
        and HTTP, 624, 626
        image types, 284-285
        PostScript, 298
        registering, 360-363
        video types, 291
mnemonics, 67-73
modems, 8, 10
modification date, 82, 84-85
Mosaic browser, 11-12, 427, 589-592
movie files, 285-288
MPEG audio format, 291-292
MPEG video format, 287, 289-291
multimedia objects, 271-272, 274-278
multitasking, 347
music. *See* sound

N

NAME attribute
    anchor, 215
    applet, 540-541
    frame, 511
    input, 311-312, 317-318, 320-323, 326
    map, 518
    select, 324-325
    textarea, 314-315
names style, 114-115
navigation, 14-15
Netscape HTML extensions, 11, 14, 18, 21
    alignment, 73, 77, 265-267
    backgrounds, 263-264
    font, 78-80, 508-509
    frames, 510-516
    imagemaps, 517-520
    Java applet, 533-542
    JavaScript, 542-553

INDEX

Netscape HTML extensions (continued)
    lists, 167-169
    windows, 520-521
Netscape Navigator, 11, 14, 21, 80-81
    Client Pull, 373-377
    proxy server, 426-427
    Server Push, 485-489
news, 201, 223-224
newsgroups, 372, 598-600
NOWRAP attribute, 98-99
nph applications, 454, 456-459, 470
nph- prefix, 454, 457, 470
numbering, list, 165-169, 184-185, 190

O

Open File interface, 88-89
Open URL interface, 89
operating system, and servers, 344-345
OS/2 system, 345, 347
outline format, 184-192

P

page author, 207-208
page, default, 212-213
page design, 22-23, 116-118, 191-193
page, external image, 278-281
page, home page, 14
    adding links, 231-235
    creating, 82-87
    and lists, 192-193
    multimedia objects, 274-278
    style, 116-118, 611-614
    viewing, 87-90
page, inline image, 244-246, 254-255
page location, 16-17, 19-20
page reviews, 565-575
page style, 116-118, 611-614
page testing, 275
pages
    Amazon.com Books, 574
    boston.com, 573-574
    ESPNET SportsZone, 570
    Heart, The, 566
    Heather Locklear Internet Fan Club, 569
    People On-Line, 568-569
    Point, The, 569-570
    Red Dirt Shirt, 575
    SEDS Internet Space Warehouse, 572-573

pages (continued)
    Spot, The, 565-566
    Uncanny X-Page, The, 567-568
    Webaholics Top 50 Links List, 571
    WebComics Daily, 571-572
    WebZine, 567
paragraph, 76-77, 124-126, 132, 267, 315, 579
password files, 395, 397-399, 408-409, 411, 413-414, 417
password, in forms, 321-323
password, FTP, 218
password, Telnet, 220-221
passwords, 395-401, 429-431
    htpasswd program, 395, 398
path information, 330
    in URLs, 200-204
    PATH_INFO, 446, 449-450, 453, 476
PBMPLUS library, 243, 254-255
permissions setting, 364-365
persons, names, 114-115, 579
PICT format, 242
pixel coordinates, 229-230
pixel size, 242, 252
pixels, as units, 142-143
POP (Point of Presence), 10
port number, 220-222, 354, 368, 622-623
post method, 309-311, 327-329, 446-447, 449-451, 474, 479-480, 604, 623
PostScript files, 297-300
pound sign (#), 68, 73
PPP (Point to Point Protocol), 9-10
preformatted text, 54, 127-129, 315, 579-580
protocols, URL, 200-202, 205-206
public key encryption, 432-437
publication policies, 366
pulldown menus, 323-325

Q

query/response, 468-473
QUERY_STRING, 445, 449, 453, 476, 479
query URL, 328, 447-449, 451, 468, 472
QuickTime video format, 288-291
quotes, 68, 71, 108-109, 579

R

radio buttons, 319-321
realms, 428-429, 431
Refresh directive, 373-377

REL attribute, 207
relative units, 142-143
Reload command, 15
REMOTE_ADDR variable, 453, 476
REMOTE_HOST variable, 453, 476
REMOTE_IDENT variable, 453
REQUEST_METHOD variable, 453, 476, 479
request methods, 346-347, 623-624
    get, 309-311, 327-329, 445, 447-451, 453, 474, 479-480, 604
    post, 309-311, 327-329, 446-447, 449-451, 474, 479-480, 604
Reset button, 312
resizing images, 256-257
resource configuration, 353, 356-359
resource map file modification, 360-362
resources, Web, 587-600
response header, 341-342, 624-626
    and CGI, 454-459, 462, 470, 486, 488
    and Content-type, 604-606
    document recognition, 36
    and <META>, 39, 376
response/query, 468-473
REV attribute, 207
RGB format, 285
row headings, 145-147
ROWS attribute, 314, 316, 511
ROWSPAN attribute, 146-147, 149-150, 154, 157
rule, horizontal, 56, 122-124, 131-132, 253-254, 310, 579

S

sample characters, 111-112, 117
scaling images, 256-257
scene graph, 557-562
script, CGI. *See* CGI
script, forms, 309, 311, 313, 321, 326-336
SCRIPT_NAME, 453, 476
ScriptAlias directive, 464
scroll attributes
    SCROLLAMOUNT, 503-504
    SCROLLDELAY, 503-504, 506
    SCROLLING, 512
scrolling marquee, 502-506
security
    access control files, 357, 362-365, 418-420, 466-468

security *(continued)*
    CERN HTTP server
        directory-level, 407-417
        file-level, 418-420
        proxy server, 420-427
    configuration, 353, 358-359
    directives. *See* security directives
    directory-level, 407-417
    encryption, 432-437
    file-level, 418-420
    group definition, 410-411, 415, 417, 419-420
    group files, 395-396, 399-400, 408-409, 411, 413-414, 417
    host filtering, 391-394, 408, 414-416, 418, 422-425, 428-429
    htadm program, 413-414, 417
    htpasswd program, 395, 398
    HTTPD server
        features, 384-391
        host filtering, 391-394
        server side includes, 390, 402-407
        user authentication, 395-401
    MacHTTP server, 427-432
    mask commands, 409-412, 415-416, 422
    password files, 395, 397-399, 408-409, 411, 413-414, 417
    passwords, 221, 395-401, 429-431
    protection setup, 408-413, 416-417, 422, 424
    server, 345, 351, 355, 363
        CERN HTTP, 407-427
        HTTPD, 384-407
        MacHTTP, 420-427
        proxy, 420-427
    server side includes, 390, 402-407
    user authentication, 395-401, 408, 414, 416, 418, 428-432
security directives
    AccessConfig, 385, 392, 396, 402
    AccessFileName, 385, 392, 396, 403, 466
    ACLOverRide On, 418-419
    AddDescription, 386
    AddEncoding, 386-387
    AddIcon, 387
    AddType, 387-388, 403-404, 467
    allow, 392-393
    ALLOW, 428, 430-431
    AllowOverride, 388
    AuthGroupFile, 397, 400
    AuthName, 397, 400

INDEX

security directives *(continued)*
    AuthType, 397, 400, 409, 411, 415
    AuthUserFile, 397, 401
    CacheRoot, 422, 424
    CacheSize, 425
    CacheUnused, 425
    Caching, 424
    DefaultIcon, 388
    DefaultType, 389
    DefProt, 412, 417, 420
    deny, 392-394
    DENY, 428, 430-431
    <Directory>, 385-386, 389, 392, 396, 402
    Disable, 422
    Enable, 421-422
    GroupFile, 409, 411, 415
    GroupId, 409, 415
    IndexIgnore, 389-390
    <Limit>, 391-394, 397-398, 401
    Map, 421
    mask commands, 409-412, 415-416, 422
    Options, 390, 403-404, 407, 466
    order, 393
    Pass, 421, 424
    PasswordFile, 409, 411, 415
    Protect, 412-413, 416, 420, 422, 424
    ReadmeName, 390
    REALM, 428-429, 431
    require, 394, 398, 401
    ServerId, 409, 411, 415
    UserId, 409, 415
semicolon terminator, 68, 73
SEQNUM attribute, 167, 169
server configuration, 353-359, 370-371
server directives, 455-458, 460, 462, 473
    See also directives
server document installation, 363-366
server, inetd, 354, 367-371
server maintenance, 347, 351, 367-371
SERVER_NAME, 453, 476
server, proxy, 420-427
server publicity, 371-373
Server Push, 485-489
server registration, 371-373
server resources, 592-594, 599, 615-619
server responses, 341-342, 624-626
    and CGI, 454-459, 462, 470, 486, 488
    and Content-type, 604-606
    document recognition, 36
    and <META>, 39, 376

server root directory, 350-352, 356, 358, 364, 366
server security. *See* security
server side includes, 390, 402-407
server software
    choosing, 343-348
    installing, 348-352
    listed, 615-619
    updating, 349-352, 367-371
SERVER_SOFTWARE, 453, 456, 476
server, standalone, 354, 367-371
server start/stop, 367-371
server updates, 349-352, 367-371
SHAPE attribute, 229-230, 517-518
shell account, 9-10
shell script, 455-457, 459-462, 469-472, 474-477
shparse application, 474-477
SIZE attribute, 79-80, 311-312, 322, 508-509
slide shows, 373
SLIP (Serial Line Interface Protocol), 9-10
sound
    converters, 295
    editing, 296
    formats, 291-293
        AIFF, 291-292, 294-295
        AU, 291, 294-295, 502
        conversion, 294-296
        IFF, 291-292
        MID (MIDI), 502
        MPEG, 291-292
        WAV, 291-292, 294-295, 502
    players, 293-294
    Web page, 500-502
spaces, 64-65, 71, 127-128
spacing, 121-132, 579-580
SRC attribute
    frame, 511-516
    image, 97, 244-248, 250-251, 258, 260-262, 265-267
    list, 169, 171-172
    script, 543
    sound, 501-502
standard input blocks, 444, 447, 450-451, 474
START attribute, 167, 169, 507
status codes, 458-459, 624-625
Status directive, 455-458, 473
strikethrough, 103-104, 117, 578
style guide, 611-614
style sheets, 522-532
styles
    content, 94, 105-118

637

styles *(continued)*
    heading, 97-99, 578
    physical, 94, 99-105, 116-118
    titles, 97-99, 577
    use of, 116-118, 522-532, 577-579
Submit button, 312, 327-328
subscript, 104-105, 137, 578
superscript, 104-105, 137, 578
system crash, 347-348

T

table alignment, 141
table caption, 143-145, 153, 155
table column alignment, 146, 149, 151-152, 154
table of contents, 227-228
table definition, 140-143
table elements (data cells), 148-150, 154
table examples, 152-160
table headings, 145-147, 153
table layout, 140-160
table and links, 227-228
table with <PRE> tag, 127-129
table rows, 150-154
table tags, 581
table title, 143-145, 153, 155
tabs, 73-78, 127-128, 580
    in list, 174, 183, 189
tags, 30, 33-34, 38, 42-48, 54-58
    <!-- --> comments, 58-62, 577
    <A> anchor, 50, 583
        data sending, 213
        e-mail, 224
        Gopher, 219
        hypermedia, 276-277, 279, 286, 288, 292, 298, 301
        image, 258-259
        imagemap, 260-262
        newsgroup, 223
        pages, 209, 211, 215-216, 225, 231-232
        TARGET, 520-521
        Telnet, 220
        WAIS, 222
    <ABBREV>, 113-114, 578
    <ABOVE>, 580
    <ACRONYM>, 113-114, 578
    <ADDRESS>, 578
    <ALT>, 249-251
    <APP>, 537-538, 542

tags *(continued)*
    <APPLET>, 537, 539-542
    <AREA>, 518-520
    <ARRAY>, 139, 580-581
    <AU> author, 115, 578
    <B> bold, 56-57, 99-100, 117, 578
    <BAR> horizontal bar, 138, 580
    <BASE>, 39, 204-206, 211, 520-521, 583
    <BASEFONT>, 79, 509, 578
    <BELOW>, 580
    <BGSOUND>, 500-502
    <BIG> font, 79
    <BLINK>, 578
    <BLOCKQUOTE>, 579
    <BODY>, 34, 38, 62-66, 83-85, 263-264, 310, 577, 583
    <BOX>, 137-138
    <BQ> blockquote, 579

 line break, 75, 98, 124-126, 132, 173, 188, 265-267, 579
    <CAPTION>, 143-145, 153, 155, 581
    <CENTER>, 73-74, 77
    <CITE>, 107-108, 578
    <CODE>, 109-110, 117, 578
    <CREDIT>, 578
    <DD>, 174-175, 181-184, 188-191, 582
    <DDOT> double dot, 138, 580
    <DEL> deletion, 116, 578
    <DFN> definition, 110-111, 578
    <DIRECTORY>, 180, 188, 582
    <DL> descriptive list, 173-175, 181-184, 188, 582
    <DOT>, 138, 580
    <DT>, 173-175, 181-184, 188-191, 582
    <EM> emphasis, 101, 105-107, 117, 509, 578
    <FIG> figure, 584
    <FIGURE>, 229-230
    <FN> footnote, 579
    <FONT>, 80, 508-509, 578
    <FORM>, 309-310, 313, 445-450, 520, 584
    <FRAME>, 510-512, 514-516
    <FRAMESET>, 510-511, 514-516
    <HAT> hat (^), 138, 580
    <HEAD>, 34, 37-40, 65, 83-85, 205, 310, 373, 577
    <H*n*> heading, 84, 97-99, 315, 578
    <HR> horizontal rule, 56, 122-124, 131-132, 253-254, 310, 579
    <HTML>, 34, 37-38, 83-85, 310, 577

638

tags *(continued)*
    <I> italics, 100-101, 117, 578
    <IMG>, 244-248, 250-251, 258, 260-262, 265-267, 506-508, 519, 584
    <INPUT>, 311-313, 316-317, 319, 322, 326, 585
    <INPUT TYPE>, 547, 550-551, 585
    <INS> insertion, 116, 579
    <ISINDEX>, 39, 214, 445, 447-448, 451, 453, 468-474, 585
    <ITEM>, 139, 581
    <KBD> keyboard, 112-113, 117, 579
    <LEFT>, 138, 580
    <LH> list heading, 166, 171, 183
    <LI> list item, 165-168, 170-172, 176, 178-180, 185, 582
    <LINK>, 39, 206-208, 530-532, 583
    <MAP>, 518-519
    <MARQUEE>, 502-506
    <MATH>, 137-140, 580
    <MENU>, 178-179, 187, 582
    <META>, 39, 56-57, 373-376
    <NEXTID>, 39
    <NOFRAME>, 512, 515-516
    <NOTE>, 579
    <OF> and square root, 138, 580
    <OL> ordered list, 165-169, 185, 190, 582
    <OPTION>, 324-325, 585
    <OVER>, 137, 580
    <P> paragraph, 76-77, 124-126, 132, 267, 315, 579
    <PARAM>, 537, 541-542
    <PERSON>, 115, 579
    <PRE> preformatted text, 54, 127-129, 315, 579-580
    <Q> quotes, 108-109, 579
    <RANGE>, 39
    <RIGHT>, 138, 580
    <ROOT> square root, 138, 580
    <ROW>, 139, 581
    <S> strikethrough, 103-104, 578
    <SAMP> sample, 111-112, 117, 579
    <SCRIPT>, 543-545, 549
    <SELECT>, 324-325, 585-586
    <SMALL> font, 79, 578
    <SQRT> square root, 138, 580
    <STRIKE> strikethrough, 104, 578
    <STRONG> emphasis, 99-100, 105-107, 117, 509, 579
    <STYLE>, 40, 529-532

tags *(continued)*
    <SUB> subscript, 104-105, 137, 578
    <SUP> superscript, 104-105, 137, 578
    <TAB>, 74-76, 580
    <TABLE>, 129, 140-143, 153, 155, 581
    <TD> table data, 148-150, 154, 158, 581
    <TEXT> math, 580
    <TEXTAREA>, 313-316, 586
    <TH> table heading, 145-147, 153, 581
    <TILDE>, 138, 580
    <TITLE>, 37, 40, 83, 310, 577
    <TR> table row, 150-154, 581
    <TT> teletype font, 102-103, 117, 578
    <U> underline, 101-102, 578
    <UL> unordered list, 170-172, 174-176, 186, 190, 582
    <VAR> variable, 109-110, 579
    <VEC> vector, 138, 580
    See also attributes *and* elements
TARGET attribute, 520-521
task separation, 347
Telnet, 201, 220-221
TeX documents, 300-302
text alignment, 73-78
    with image, 246-249, 265-267
text box, 313-316
text, deleted, 115-116, 578
text editors, 42-48, 57-58
text entry field, 311
text, icons, 243
text, inserted, 115-116, 579
text, preformatted, 54, 127-129, 315, 579-580
text, scrolling (marquee), 502-506
text styles, 527
    content, 94, 105-118, 578-579
    physical, 94, 99-105, 116-118, 577-578
text, wrap around image, 249, 265-267
three-dimensional modeling, 553-562
thumbnail images, 256-257
TIFF format, 242, 284
tilde tag, 138, 580
tilde in URLs, 225-226
time standard (GMT), 456
TITLE, 132
    attribute, 531
    styles, 97-99, 577
    tag, 37, 40, 83, 310, 577
TO attribute, 74-76
traffic, 20
Transparency program, 254

transparent GIF, 251-254
TYPE attribute, 168, 311-312, 316-319, 321-323, 326
types file modification, 360-361

U

underline, 101-102, 578
UNITS attribute, 142-143
UNIX platform, 344, 347-349
 commands, 607-609
 and links, 225-226
 servers, 615-617
URLs (Universal Resource Locators), 16-17, 21
 and data inclusion, 213-214
 and FTP, 216-218
 and Gopher, 219
 image source, 245-247, 258, 260-261
 interpreting, 200-202
 in links, 212
 mailto, 224
 to open file, 89
 query, 328, 447-449, 451, 468, 472
 relative, 202-204
 and Telnet, 220
 and Usenet news, 223
 and WAIS, 222
Usenet news, 201, 223-224
Usenet newsgroups, 372, 598-600
user authentication, 395-401, 408, 414, 416, 418, 428-432
user directory, 364-366
username, 217-218, 220-221, 225

V

VALIGN attribute, 147, 149, 151
VALUE attribute, 167, 169, 311-312, 317, 320, 322, 326, 541
variable style, 109-110, 579
video clips, 506-508
video converters, 289-290
video editing, 290
video files, 285-288
 conversion, 289-291

video players, 288
virtual reality. *See* VRML
virtual reality files, 277
VMS platform, 345, 347, 617
voice welcome, 274-275
VRML (Virtual Reality Modeling Language), 553
 browsers, 553-555
 documents, 555-562
 modelers, 555-557
 nodes, 557-562
 .wrl extension, 556-557
VSPACE attribute, 505, 540

W

WAIS (Wide Area Information Servers), 201, 221-223
WAV audio format, 291-292, 294-295
Web access, America Online, 7-8
Web authoring tool, 17-19
Web browsers. *See* browsers
Web Consortium, 18, 20, 587
Web pages. *See* pages
Web resources, 587-600
Web site
 development, 341, 343-348
 publicizing, 371-373
 reviews, 565-575
 See also server
Web space, 19-20
WebMap, 261
WIDTH attribute, 142-143, 504, 539
windows, linked document, 520-521
Windows, 345, 347, 617-619
WinWeb, 12
World Wide Web Consortium, 18, 20, 587
World Wide Web. *See* Web
WRAP attribute, 176-177
.wrl extension (VRML), 556-557
WYSIWYG editors, 42-48, 57-58

X

X bitmap format, 280, 285
x- prefix, 602, 605

ENVIRONMENTAL AWARENESS

Books have a substantial influence on the destruction of the forests of the Earth. For example, it takes 17 trees to produce one ton of paper. A first printing of 30,000 copies of a typical 480-page book consumes 108,000 pounds of paper, which will require 918 trees!

Waite Group Press™ is against the clear-cutting of forests and supports reforestation of the Pacific Northwest of the United States and Canada, where most of this paper comes from. As a publisher with several hundred thousand books sold each year, we feel an obligation to give back to the planet. We will therefore support organizations which seek to preserve the forests of planet Earth.

WAITE GROUP PRESS™

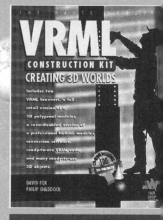

PERL 5 INTERACTIVE COURSE
John Orwant

This customized course in Perl includes an unique Web-based component with an online "mentor" to answer your specific Perl questions, a special Internet mailing list just for readers of this book that allows students to ask questions or "meet" other students, and online quizzes and exams for immediate feedback on your progress. After successfully completing the exams, you can download a personalized Certificate of Achievement.

Available July 1996
850 pages
ISBN: 1-57169-064-6
U.S. $49.99 Can. $67.99
1–CD-ROM

HTML 3 INTERACTIVE COURSE
Richard J. Simon, Brian C. Baines, Michael Gouker

This personalized, Web-based course gets you started writing HTML-based Web pages from the very first chapter. You'll create a Web page that grows more sophisticated lesson-by-lesson. An online component offers online testing for immediate feedback, an online mentor to answer your specific HTML questions, an Internet mailing list for interaction with other students, and a Certificate of Achievement that can be downloaded after successful completion of the tests—suitable for framing or attaching to a resume.

Available July 1996
600 pages
ISBN: 1-57169-066-2
U.S. $39.99 Can. $53.99
1–CD-ROM

VRML CONSTRUCTION KIT
David Fox and Philip Shaddock

Clear instructions on every aspect of VRML (Virtual Reality Modeling Language), including polygons, lines, points, cones, cylinders, spheres, text, manipulating 3D graphics, translation, transformation, light sources, materials, texture mapping, and camera angles. The CD includes 2 VRML browsers, a full-retail version of a 3D polygonal modeler, a save-disabled version of a professional NURBS modeler, conversion software, ready-to-use VRML code, and many ready-to-use 3D objects and textures.

Available May 1996
600 pages
1-57169-068-9
$36.99 USA Can. $50.99
1–CD-ROM

Send for our unique catalog to get more information about these books, as well as our outstanding and award-winning titles.

WAITE GROUP PRESS™

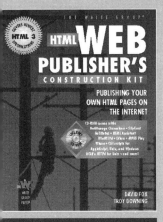

HTML WEB PUBLISHER'S CONSTRUCTION KIT
David Fox, Troy Downing

This resource provides clear instructions on how to build your own home page on the Web, using sample Web pages for illustration. The CD includes all the software needed, including easy-to-use tools, such as an HTML Editor for page creation, browsers, and viewers for manipulating graphics, sound, and movies.

Available now
700 pages
ISBN: 1-57169-018-2
U.S. $36.95 Can. $53.95
1–CD-ROM

PERL 5 HOW-TO
Aidan Humphreys, Mike Glover, Ed Weiss

Perl 5 How-To shows you how to use Perl to manipulate text, mark up pages for the Web, convert text pages to hypertext, parse files and process the resultant data, write scripts that locate and replace strings, or just write a quick and portable program. The CD includes all the examples and a copy of Perl.

Available June 1996
900 pages
ISBN: 1-57169-058-1
U.S. $44.99 Can. $59.99
1–CD-ROM

JAVA PRIMER PLUS
Paul M. Tyma, Gabriel Torok, Troy Downing

Java Primer Plus is a complete, step-by-step guide to Java, the hot new Internet programming language, including practical code examples and a complete reference to *all* of Java's standard APIs. The included CD contains Java Developer's Kit from Sun, Java binaries, a Java compiler, bonus third-party applets, and all the source code from the book.

Available March 1996
600 pages
ISBN:1-57169-062-X
U.S. $39.99 Can. $53.99
1–CD-ROM

TO ORDER TOLL FREE, CALL 1-800-368-9369
TELEPHONE 415-924-2575 • FAX 415-924-2576
OR SEND ORDER FORM TO: WAITE GROUP PRESS, 200 TAMAL PLAZA, CORTE MADERA, CA 94925

Qty	Book	US/Can Price	Total
___	HTML 3 Interactive Course	$39.99/$53.99	___
___	HTML Web Publisher's Construction Kit	$36.95/$53.95	___
___	Java Primer Plus	$39.99/$53.99	___
___	Perl 5 How-To	$44.99/$59.99	___
___	Perl 5 Interactive Course	$49.99/$67.99	___
___	VRML Construction Kit	$36.99/$50.99	___

Calif. residents add 7.25% Sales Tax ___

Shipping
USPS ($5 first book/$1 each add'l) ___
UPS Two Day ($10/$2) ___
Canada ($10/$4) ___
TOTAL

Ship to:
Name _____
Company _____
Address _____
City, State, Zip _____
Phone _____

Payment Method
☐ Check Enclosed   ☐ VISA   ☐ MasterCard

Card#_____ Exp. Date _____

Signature _____

SATISFACTION GUARANTEED OR YOUR MONEY BACK.

This is a legal agreement between you, the end user and purchaser, and The Waite Group®, Inc., and the authors of the programs contained in the disk. By opening the sealed disk package, you are agreeing to be bound by the terms of this Agreement. If you do not agree with the terms of this Agreement, promptly return the unopened disk package and the accompanying items (including the related book and other written material) to the place you obtained them for a refund.

SOFTWARE LICENSE

1. The Waite Group, Inc. grants you the right to use one copy of the enclosed software programs (the programs) on a single computer system (whether a single CPU, part of a licensed network, or a terminal connected to a single CPU). Each concurrent user of the program must have exclusive use of the related Waite Group, Inc. written materials.

2. The program, including the copyrights in each program, is owned by the respective author and the copyright in the entire work is owned by The Waite Group, Inc. and they are therefore protected under the copyright laws of the United States and other nations, under international treaties. You may make only one copy of the disk containing the programs exclusively for backup or archival purposes, or you may transfer the programs to one hard disk drive, using the original for backup or archival purposes. You may make no other copies of the programs, and you may make no copies of all or any part of the related Waite Group, Inc. written materials.

3. You may not rent or lease the programs, but you may transfer ownership of the programs and related written materials (including any and all updates and earlier versions) if you keep no copies of either, and if you make sure the transferee agrees to the terms of this license.

4. You may not decompile, reverse engineer, disassemble, copy, create a derivative work, or otherwise use the programs except as stated in this Agreement.

GOVERNING LAW

This Agreement is governed by the laws of the State of California.

SOFTWARE LICENSE AGREEMENT

LIMITED WARRANTY

The following warranties shall be effective for 90 days from the date of purchase: (i) The Waite Group, Inc. warrants the enclosed disk to be free of defects in materials and workmanship under normal use; and (ii) The Waite Group, Inc. warrants that the programs, unless modified by the purchaser, will substantially perform the functions described in the documentation provided by The Waite Group, Inc. when operated on the designated hardware and operating system. The Waite Group, Inc. does not warrant that the programs will meet purchaser's requirements or that operation of a program will be uninterrupted or error-free. The program warranty does not cover any program that has been altered or changed in any way by anyone other than The Waite Group, Inc. The Waite Group, Inc. is not responsible for problems caused by changes in the operating characteristics of computer hardware or computer operating systems that are made after the release of the programs, nor for problems in the interaction of the programs with each other or other software.

THESE WARRANTIES ARE EXCLUSIVE AND IN LIEU OF ALL OTHER WARRANTIES OF MERCHANTABILITY OR FITNESS FOR A PARTICULAR PURPOSE OR OF ANY OTHER WARRANTY, WHETHER EXPRESS OR IMPLIED.

EXCLUSIVE REMEDY

The Waite Group, Inc. will replace any defective disk without charge if the defective disk is returned to The Waite Group, Inc. within 90 days from date of purchase.

This is Purchaser's sole and exclusive remedy for any breach of warranty or claim for contract, tort, or damages.

LIMITATION OF LIABILITY

THE WAITE GROUP, INC. AND THE AUTHORS OF THE PROGRAMS SHALL NOT IN ANY CASE BE LIABLE FOR SPECIAL, INCIDENTAL, CONSEQUENTIAL, INDIRECT, OR OTHER SIMILAR DAMAGES ARISING FROM ANY BREACH OF THESE WARRANTIES EVEN IF THE WAITE GROUP, INC. OR ITS AGENT HAS BEEN ADVISED OF THE POSSIBILITY OF SUCH DAMAGES.

THE LIABILITY FOR DAMAGES OF THE WAITE GROUP, INC. AND THE AUTHORS OF THE PROGRAMS UNDER THIS AGREEMENT SHALL IN NO EVENT EXCEED THE PURCHASE PRICE PAID.

COMPLETE AGREEMENT

This Agreement constitutes the complete agreement between The Waite Group, Inc. and the authors of the programs, and you, the purchaser.

Some states do not allow the exclusion or limitation of implied warranties or liability for incidental or consequential damages, so the above exclusions or limitations may not apply to you. This limited warranty gives you specific legal rights; you may have others, which vary from state to state.

SATISFACTION REPORT CARD

Please fill out this card if you wish to know of future updates to
HTML 3 How-To, or to receive our catalog.

Name: _____ **Last Name:** _____

ess: _____

t: _____

_____ **State:** _____ **Zip:** _____

me Telephone: (_____) _____

il Address: _____

product was acquired: Month _____ Day _____ Year _____ **Your Occupation:** _____

all, how would you rate *HTML 3 How-To*?

- ☐ cellent   ☐ Very Good   ☐ Good
- ☐ ir   ☐ Below Average   ☐ Poor

did you like MOST about this book? _____
_____

did you like LEAST about this book? _____
_____

e describe any problems you may have encountered with ling or using the disk: _____
_____

did you use this book (problem-solver, tutorial, reference…)?
_____

is your level of computer expertise?

- ☐ ew   ☐ Dabbler   ☐ Hacker
- ☐ wer User   ☐ Programmer   ☐ Experienced Professional

computer languages are you familiar with? _____
_____

e describe your computer hardware:

- uter _____ Hard disk _____
- Disk drives _____ 3.5" Disk drives _____
- card _____ Monitor _____
- r _____ Peripherals _____
- d board _____ CD-ROM _____

Where did you buy this book?

- ☐ Bookstore (name): _____
- ☐ Discount store (name): _____
- ☐ Computer store (name): _____
- ☐ Catalog (name): _____
- ☐ Direct from WGP   ☐ Other _____

What price did you pay for this book? _____

What influenced your purchase of this book?

- ☐ Recommendation   ☐ Advertisement
- ☐ Magazine review   ☐ Store display
- ☐ Mailing   ☐ Book's format
- ☐ Reputation of Waite Group Press ☐ Other

How many computer books do you buy each year? _____

How many other Waite Group books do you own? _____

What is your favorite Waite Group book? _____
_____

Is there any program or subject you would like to see Waite Group Press cover in a similar approach? _____
_____

Additional comments? _____
_____
_____

Please send to: Waite Group Press
                     200 Tamal Plaza
                     Corte Madera, CA 94925

☐ Check here for a free Waite Group catalog

SATISFACTION CARD

BEFORE YOU OPEN THE DISK OR CD-ROM PACKAGE ON THE FACING PAGE, CAREFULLY READ THE LICENSE AGREEMENT.

Opening this package indicates that you agree to abide by the license agreement found in the back of this book. If you do not agree with it, promptly return the unopened disk package (including the related book) to the place you obtained them for a refund.